WALKER PERCY:

A LIFE

WALKER PERCY:

A LIFE

PATRICK H. SAMWAY, S. J.

Farrar, Straus and Giroux

NEW YORK

Farrar, Straus and Giroux
19 Union Square West, New York 10003

Copyright © 1997 by Patrick H. Samway, S.J.
All rights reserved
Published simultaneously in Canada by HarperCollinsCanadaLtd
Printed in the United States of America

Library of Congress catalog card number: 97-060385

To the Younger Generation ("You Guys")

John, Maureen, Liz, Matt, Patrick, Brian-Martin, Tom,

Michael-Ali, Christopher, Jaleh, Lee, Lyn, Stephen,

Caitlin, Kevin Patrick, Stephen Patrick, David,

Sarah, Luke Augustine, Stephen Bernard,

Peter Anthony . . .

CONTENTS

FOREWORD

I first met Walker Percy in 1978 as the result of a letter I wrote after I had finished graduate school and started teaching English literature at a Jesuit college in upstate New York. When the head of the English Department at Loyola University in New Orleans invited me to give a series of talks on William Faulkner and Flannery O'Connor, I learned that Dr. Percy had taught at Loyola and that he lived in the area. I hoped he might be available for lunch at the Jesuit residence—and so I wrote to him. He answered that he would be glad to meet me and asked if I could get the use of a car and wend my way across the Lake Ponchartrain Causeway to Covington for lunch at his house.

He met me on a wonderfully clear October day at the Kumquat, the bookstore run by his daughter Ann Percy Moores, and I followed his pickup to his handsome English château on the Bogue Falaya. His wife, Mary Bernice ("Bunt"), and Ann joined us at lunch. As we talked, I thought of some of Percy's philosophical essays on language theory but became conscious of Ann's deafness only when I saw that her father turned directly to her whenever they spoke. I knew then that the Helen Keller story lived in their house. Neither parent used sign language, which initially surprised me. A lunch was served—iced tea, thick gumbo with extra shrimp, and an avocado salad—followed by the taking of a few photos. I drove back to Ann's bookstore to browse a bit and from there I returned to New Orleans.

I next saw Dr. Percy in early February 1986 at a ceremony at Loyola, when I presented him with the Edmund Campion Award, given by the Catholic Book Club, among whose previous recipients were T. S. Eliot,

Paul Horgan, John La Farge, S.J., and Jacques Maritain. Later that year, while having dinner with one of my former professors and his wife, Joseph and Yvonne Blotner, the question came up: "What research project would you like to do in the best of all possible worlds?" "A biography," I replied. "Of whom?" Yvonne asked. "Walker Percy," I said spontaneously, since it had been in the back of my mind. "Well, go ahead," my companions retorted enthusiastically. All I could utter was "He is too private and I don't want to hear his big NO." But after thinking about it for a few weeks, I sent off a second letter.

Dr. Percy wrote me a rather formal letter on January 8, 1987, that contained the best compliment I have ever received; he said he was very gratified that I would want to undertake such an enterprise: "There is no one I'd rather entrust such a project to." He added there was one slight hitch, which proved to be a typical feigning motion: he himself preferred not to undergo hours of being interviewed, though I would be free to talk with anyone I chose and collect any information I thought necessary. He added, "So what can I tell you? I can tell you this: since I am seventy, long past the life expectancy of men in my family, and since you are a good deal younger, I am happy to approve in advance your post-mortem project." Moreover, he would make copies of his letter and give them to his two daughters and his wife as a way of indicating they had his consent to say whatever they wanted. "I know," he concluded, "this is hardly a satisfactory answer to your letter." It was clear that we had different notions of "satisfactory." Though I was literary editor of *America*, a weekly publication, I managed to free up some time and travel to Covington. We had another lunch, and in talking about our future relationship, Dr. Percy politely reiterated the main points in his letter. I was relieved that in no way did he have second thoughts or change his mind. When I returned to New York City, I started my research by networking the classmates from his medical school days at Columbia University.

In the spring of 1988, Loyola was kind enough to offer me a visiting professorship in its City College, which meant that I would teach one course at night and have my days free to visit the Percys and talk with their friends in Covington. On occasion, Walker (who introduced me now as his friend) and I would lunch at his house or at the Winner's Circle restaurant and have our talks afterward. He would stretch out his lanky frame on his living-room sofa and look up as I asked my questions. There was never any strain; my only concern was that his memory might occasionally be faulty. I soon learned, as Eudora Welty explained in one of her essays, that "place" is important in the life of a Southern writer. As Walker talked about particular places, I could piece together fragments and snippets of his life. He taught me to triangulate all sorts of situations, as his character Father Simon Smith does in his fire tower in *The Thanatos Syndrome*, and get a fix on events from as many angles as possible.

These were always pleasant moments together, whether at an award ceremony in Jackson, Mississippi, or when we sipped Jack Daniel's in the quiet of his living room. Bunt would frequently be present, correcting a memory lapse or sharing a recollection of her own, often in the kitchen of the Cajun cottage they now occupied and had helped design. (This was next door to the château, which they had vacated and turned over to Ann and John Moores and their two children.) From the interaction of Bunt and Walker, and particularly from their frankness, I realized how honestly they communicated with each other: words were placed right out there to be handled and dealt with. I had had no idea when I began this project, nor did Walker, that he would soon become ill and need more and more privacy and medical care. Even after the onset of his prostate cancer, we continued to see each other, though less often.

Gradually my admiration for Walker was tempered by a degree of "objectivity," if such a word is appropriate for a writer like Percy, who was deeply devoted to language theory and semiotics. I saw him in enough different situations to learn where his center was. It came out in his hesitation to lead a discussion, or in his dry humor, or in his affection for their Pembroke corgi, Sweet Thing. I felt it when he spoke publicly from a prepared text that stressed life's principal sticking points, or when he picked up his grandsons, David and Jack, from school to take them home, or when he responded to the rather dry task of signing books for friends of friends: "Sure, be glad to. Let me do it now. It won't take but a minute." And he always seemed available to me, and never really minded being interviewed. He would say, "Do I have to say 'Testing, testing'?" as I attached the pin microphone to his sweater. He always spoke so that I could hear him, if sometimes with a slight stammer when he got stuck on an idea or an expression.

As an on-again, off-again part of his life, I knew that I needed to avoid the temptation of arriving at a set thesis that would provide a too easy matrix for what I saw and knew. Walker was a living, breathing person, making decisions and writing books that absorbed him. I continually had to adjust the focus on my binoculars, so to speak, and even look at his life through the opposite end. We were both in the process of discovering. I had to keep myself poised for what would appear; I often had that Bakhtinian sense not only that the constellations in the sky were made up of stars that emanated light years ago but that their positions in space only gave the appearance that they were a flat surface.

Actually, I knew that each star was on a different plane that only expert measurements could calculate. And what was worse—or better—the constellations seemed to shift as both they and I traveled through time and space.

After Walker's death on May 10, 1990, Robert Giroux, Walker's editor as well as mine, asked me whether I thought we should have a memorial service for Walker in New York. I suggested the Church of St. Ignatius on Park Avenue at 84th Street, and we called the pastor, Walter Modrys, S.J., who generously granted permission. After contacting several of Walker's friends to speak at the service, I reached Eudora Welty, who said at once, "I can come in two days, if that would be O.K. Or should I come tomorrow?" I told her to wait until fall, since nothing could easily be scheduled for the summer.

In the later afternoon of October 24 I joined Eudora Welty, Shelby Foote, Wilfrid Sheed, Mary Lee Settle, Stanley Kauffmann, and Robert Giroux for the memorial in the presence of Bunt and Walker's other daughter, Mary Pratt Lobdell. Since the public had been invited, we wondered how many of the approximately 1,200 seats would be filled. It was impressive to see scores of standees.

Those talks by seven people who knew Walker give some interesting insights into his character. In sketching Walker's life, for example, Bob Giroux talked about the role of "literary clinician" that Walker performed brilliantly in all his writings, but most especially in his Jefferson Lecture in Washington, D.C., entitled "The Fateful Rift: The San Andreas Fault in the Modern Mind." Giroux rightly pointed to this seminal lecture, a résumé of Walker's grappling with scientific questions and his preoccupations with the "semiotic" of Charles Sanders Peirce. He cited Walker's belief that the view of the world we are consciously or unconsciously obtaining from modern science is radically incoherent. A corollary to Walker's proposition is that modern science is itself incoherent when it tries to evaluate man as a total human being. The solution is not to be found in something extra-scientific, like New Age religion, but within science itself. At this forum in the capital, Walker reminded scientists of the intellectual validity of the artistic enterprise. He stressed, from an epistemological point of view, literature's thought-fulness not as an aberration but as something normal.

Miss Welty picked up on the image of the doctor and the dual tensions that existed within Walker: "Let us for a moment imagine a scene wherein the two Walker Percys confront each other for the first time: the doctor who now intends to desist from practice and the writer who now intends to begin," she said. "When the writer presents himself in the doctor's office, the doctor says, 'You propose to write, as Walker Percy?

Let me advise you, you've had no experience. As a writer you're in your infancy. You think you are ready to take over what I have to say? Let's see you prove it.' So the infant climbs up into the doctor's chair, gives it a spin, and writes *The Moviegoer*."

Miss Welty stated that he did not start out naïvely as a "wide-eyed young dreamer," but as someone who already had a firm grasp on the world from his medical training and natural bent of mind. Walker Percy was a writer pursuing truth, which yields itself obligingly to art—the indirect, allusive, suggestive, and ever-changing route, guided by the imagination. For Welty, his characters are ordinary people often jolted by metaphysics or comic situations. And as a diagnostician, Walker becomes our Hermes, reading the signs and portents of despair and leading us home. "The physician's ear and the writer's ear are pressed alike to the human chest," Welty continued, "listening for the same signs of life, and with the same hope and with a like involvement in the outcome. Each listens for the heartbeat with his own heart, scans the brain of his fellow man with his own brain, to find out whether mankind is living or dying at the moment." Walker transforms truth into the believable.

Wilfrid Sheed, novelist, biographer, and literary critic, highlighted the Catholic apocalyptic dimension of the truth that Walker wrote about. Above all, he had to stay cool and dry in confronting the end of time, "because the Gospels indicate that it will turn up in strange places and take strange forms." Yet his death and resurrection, for Sheed, provided an occasion for celebration; Walker's voice lives in and through his writing.

For Mary Lee Settle, he acted as a tutor, as he was for numerous people, especially for young adults who would come to him with their tearful stories and wait for his consoling words. After Settle converted to Roman Catholicism and was received into the Church one evening in Charlottesville, Walker wrote her: "Well, welcome. It is a very untidy outfit you're hooking up with." During Settle's talk I thought of how Walker himself underwent a tremendous conversion pretty much by himself.

Though he was a writer who treasured his privacy, Walker had to rely on editorial colleagues to assist him in seeing his books through the press, usually an arduous task because he made corrections in his manuscripts down to the last minute. As his editor at Knopf for *The Moviegoer* he was blessed to have Stanley Kauffmann, who was also noted as a film critic. In his tribute, Kauffmann outlined the discovery and editorial genesis of a first novel that won the prestigious National Book Award. Walker was drawn to the novel form, as was Shelby Foote, his closest friend for sixty years, who served as both coach and cheerleader (especially from the 1950s). With his wife, Gwyn, Shelby traveled with Walker and Bunt over the years; Walker told me that only the best of friends can repeatedly do that. "One secret of the longevity of our friendship," Foote noted, "was that each of us knew what would make the other angry, and we were careful not to venture into such areas—except on purpose, which would open the matter to drumfire argument and laughter, time and time again, all down the years." Unfortunately, Walker had not lived long enough to see his friend's involvement in the highly successful Civil War television series on the PBS network, which he would have greatly enjoyed.

Since I had concelebrated at Walker's funeral and read the Gospel, I recounted this moving ceremony at the Benedictine abbey outside Covington, where he was buried. Arriving in advance of the Mass, I first spotted a group of Puerto Ricans from Kenner having a picnic and then several young dancers exercising in the open air in preparation for a recital. It struck me that the juxtaposition of this funeral and such expressive human and creative activities resembled a scene in a Percy novel, one that Walker had almost composed himself in the spirit of Wallace Stevens's famous line: "Let be be finale of seem."

Although it is important to gather personal recollections in writing a biography, they do not sustain the narrative or tell the whole story. One must likewise avoid the temptation to interpret the fiction of a creative writer as implied or suppressed biography. Such an approach is fortified by the widely held belief that works of fiction emerge from the deep recesses of ongoing lives, transformed by the imagination. In his forewords to the novels, Walker offers helpful warnings and enigmatic signposts that should be considered carefully. A balance must be maintained that does justice to both the life of a fiction writer and his works; yet distinctions must be made that neither inhibit nor prohibit speculation. In writing this biography, I have looked at both the man and the author-creator. Walker Percy's life formed and informed his fiction and nonfiction, which in turn formed and informed his life. And while I aim to shed light on Walker's writings, my intention is not to write a book of literary criticism based on biography. Others have done that in various ways with skill and insight. My aim is to trace Walker Percy's life and explain the dynamism that gave this life depth, charm, and coherence.

As Deirdre Bair notes about herself in the introduction to her life of Simone de Beauvoir, she also tried to write a biography without holding prior theory or thesis. I too allow Walker's life to unfold as he lived it, with all its seeming contradictions and confusions in thought and expression—in particular, the violent deaths of his father and mother, so different in manner and so close in time; his subsequent adoption by his cousin, William Alexander Percy, whom he called "Uncle Will"; his excellent education throughout his formative years; his extended bout with tuberculosis that occurred during his days as an intern at Bellevue Hospital in New York; his marriage to Mary Bernice Townsend and their conversion to Catholicism; and his dogged determination to become a successful novelist and semiotician.

Both the man and the author intrigue me, and I find in my own life that he is still teaching me. Walker's life, from his earliest days in Birmingham until his final moments in his bedroom in Covington, revealed a man who had much courage and wisdom. He often maintained that one of the hardest moments in life was to get through those ordinary Wednesday afternoons. He knew that an interior creative life, which sometimes ceases to function for long stretches, can turn into loneliness and bouts of depression. Part of his battle was to keep himself in the mainstream and cope with the intrusive challenges he wanted so much to resist. Lewis P. Simpson, in the 1991 Flora Levy Lecture in the Humanities at the University of Southwestern Louisiana in Lafayette, said of his friend Walker Percy that he spent the larger part of his life preoccupied with creating—and with searching out, and not less acting out—the implications of a highly self-conscious visionary quest, eminently ironic, bitingly satirical, and darkly comic, for the meaning of our essentially visionless condition:

Visionless, that is, save in the sense that it seems to have had a capacity to engender in us a disastrous penchant for dreaming abstract, demonic dreams of scientific and political power, which fundamentally may represent not the desire for control over history but deep, nihilistic longings for its destruction. As incarnated in his essays and novels, the story of Percy's quest records the drama not of an endeavor to restore a transcendent redemptive vision of meaning, nor even of an effort to restore the capacity for such a vision, but essentially a more basic, and more desperate, effort, consisting simply in the struggle to restore in us the *need* for recovering the capacity for vision.

Walker offered me, in turn, an irresistible challenge to discover the roots of his vision. While writing this biography, I also edited two books that illuminate his six novels and two works of nonfiction—first, *Signposts in a Strange Land* (1991), his significant uncollected or difficult to locate essays, speeches, and letters; and second, *A Thief of Peirce: The Letters of Kenneth Laine Ketner and Walker Percy* (1995), the record of an epistolary friendship of two men passionately interested in the "semiotic" of the American philosopher Charles Sanders Peirce (1839–1914). During the later years of Walker's life, Professor Ketner of Texas Tech University served as Walker's mentor in analyzing Peirce's theory of signs.

In the preparation of this biography, I have had the assistance and cooperation of many people who deserve my deep gratitude, especially Mrs. Mary Bernice Percy and her two daughters, Mary Pratt Lobdell and Ann Boyd Moores. I am also indebted to Zoltán Abádi-Nagy, Louise H. Abbot, Martin Adamo, Ralph Adamo, Virginia Alexander, Mr. and Mrs. Ross G. Allen, William Rodney Allen, Donie Drane DeBardeleben Allison, Nicholai Anastasyev, Judith B. Andry, Fr. Anthony, O.C.S.O., Dolores Elizabeth Artau, Helene Atwan, Ron Austin, L. Fred Ayvazian, M.D., Paul Badde, Clinton Bagley, Elizabeth Dubus Baldridge, John T.M. Baldwin, Mr. and Mrs. Lawrence Baldwin, Jr., Rev. William Barnwell, Raphael Barousse, O.S.B., Garic Kenneth Barranger, Milly Barranger, Marion Knox Barthelme, Andrew Becnel, O.S.B., Charles Greenleaf Bell, Madison Smartt Bell, Gerard Belliveau, Morris C. Benners, Mr. and Mrs. Robert Berlin, Jason Berry, Doris Betts, Professor and Mrs. Charles Bigger III, Farris Block, Professor and Mrs. Joseph L. Blotner, William E. Borah, Sheila Bosworth, Judi Bottoni, Lawrence Bouchea, O.S.B., James C. Boulware, Lee C. Bradley, Jr., John Branton, Dominic Braud, O.S.B., Cleanth Brooks, Ashley Brown, Melvin D. Brown, S. Curtland C. Brown, Jr., M.D., Simonne Baldwin Brown, Philip A. Bryant, Ruth Bryant, Raymond Bulliard, F.S.C., Dr. and Mrs. Peter Douglas Bunting and family, Robert W. Burch, Rebecca R. Butler, Vincent P. Butler, Jr., M.D., Crispin Butz, O.F.M., and the Franciscan community in Santa Fe, New Mexico, John Martin Byrnes, Mr. and Mrs. Vincent Malcolm Byrnes, William Byron, S.J., Martha Dyer Campbell, Rev. Will D. Campbell, Arthur Carpenter, Mr. and Mrs. James D. Carr, L. M. Kit Carson, Betty Carter, James C. Carter, S.J., Peggy Castex, John E. Cay, Jr., Elise Kalb Chapin, Daniel Charbonnier, Fannie Cheney, Lynne V. Cheney, Beach Chenoweth, M.D., Bénédicte Chorier, Gary M. Ciuba, Thomas H. Clancy, S.J., Henry Toole Clark, M.D., Mr. and Mrs. Verne Clark, Edward Clement, Maurice Edgar Coindreau, Vincent M. Colapietro, Hunter M. Cole, Robert Coles, M.D., Scott J. Collier, Yvonne Collins, Jesse Core, Dennis Corrado, C.O., Joyce H. Corrington, Raymond T. Cothern, Mr. and Mrs. Thomas Cowan, Eleanor Spalding Craft, Nancy Crampton, Joan St. C. Crane, Howard Crockett, Dennis W. Cross, Mr. and Mrs. George Cross, Professor and Mrs. J. Donald Crowley, Robert E. Daggy, Robert Dana, Mr. and Mrs. David C. Davenport, Mark David, Alan Davis, Mr. and Mrs. Tony Davis, Edward Deano, Janet Decker, John N. Deely, Stephanie Coyne DeGhett,

Nicholas Dellis, John F. Desmond, Paula Devlin, Emily Diamond, Helen Dietrich, Stephanie Dinkins, Sheena Dooley, William Dowie, Hugh Downs, Suzanne Ballard Dowouis, Brian Doyle, Charles ("Pie") Dufour, Robert Dunne, Marcelle Dunning, M.D., Professor and Mrs. Edward J. Dupuy, Maurice duQuesnay, David Duty, Robert Eckert, Edna Bea Sprague Edwards, R.N., Thomas W. Eldringhoff, Judge and Mrs. Frederick S. Ellis, Gerald Fagin, S.J., Chester Fairlie, Jr., M.D., Rev. Patrick Farrell and the community of St. Joseph's Catholic Church in Greenville, Mississippi, Rhoda K. Faust, Dr. and Mrs. Richard Faust, Francis L. Fennell, Hill Ferguson, Marie Irène Ferrer, M.D., Joseph H. Fichter, S.J., Larry E. Fink, Mary Kathryn Finlay, Georgia Fisher, Pamela Reid Fischer, Charles Fister, Agnes Fleck, O.S.B., Thomas Fleming, Charles A. Flood, M.D., Mark Flynn, Mr. and Mrs. Shelby Foote, Professor and Mrs. Ben Forkner, Jean Todd Freeman, Mr. and Mrs. Leroy Frick, Mr. and Mrs. Joseph Friend, Catherine Fry, Ikuko Fujihira, Ernest Gaines, Michael Paul Gallagher, S.J., Louis Gallo, Joan E. Gaulene, Tim Gautreaux, H. Michael Gelfand, Ellen Gilchrist, Robert Giroux, Diana Gonzalez, Elena Graf-Gonzalez, Larry Gray, Michel Gresset, Jan Nordby Gretlund, Emilie Griffin, Benedict Groeschel, C.F.R., Helen McDonald Grossman, Huey S. Guagliardo, Jo Marie Gulledge, John R. Hadd, Martha Lacy Hall, C. Martin Hames and the staff of the Altamont School in Birmingham, Alabama, Barry Hannah, Archbishop Philip M. Hannan, Dr. and Mrs. Frank J. Hardart, Jr., George Hardart, M.D., Marie Thérèse Hardart, John Edward Hardy, Michael Hargraves, Nancy Hargrove, F. Gentry Harris, M.D., Eileen Lane Hasel, George L. Hawkins, Jr., M.D., Jean Brock Hawley, Josephine Haxton (Ellen Douglas), Kenneth Haxton, Jr., Charlotte Hayes, Lyn Hayward, Alexander Heard, George Herget, Olga Hess, Linda Whitney Hobson, Rev. Timothy Hodapp, Raymond Hogan, M.D., W. Kenneth Holditch, Paul Horgan, Mary B. Hotaling, Barbara Howes, Mary Deems Howland, George W. Hunt, S.J., Fara Impastato, O.P., Walter Isaacson, Brenda Jackson, Shelley Jackson, Germaine Jacquette, M.D., Susanne M. Jensen, Elizabeth Dale Johnson, Nell Bolling Johnson, Wendell Jones, Jr., Michael Jung, O.S.B., Stephen Kanaga, David Kappes, Sadamichi Kato, Stanley Kauffmann, Aelred Kavanagh, O.S.B., Lucille Owens Keady, Mary Keady, Mr. and Mrs. Bern Keating, Edwin L. Kendig, Jr., M.D., J. Gerald Kennedy, Jeanne D'Arc Kernion, O.S.B., Caroline Kerrigan, Professor and Mrs. Kenneth Laine Ketner, Thomas Key, Mr. and Mrs. Henry Kisor, Philip Knapp, M.D., Leon K. Koury, Wilson Krebs, Jill Krementz, Larry K. Kvols, M.D., Judith LaCour, Ruth H. Laney, Michelle Lapautre, Marian Larmann, O.S.B., Joseph A. Larose, Rev. Stephen W. Lawler, Mr. and Mrs. John Lawrence, Seymour Lawrence, Lewis A. Lawson, Mr. and Mrs. Michael Leahy, Milton Leathers IV, Nancy Lemann, Nicholas Lemann, Alfred E. Lemmon, Elmore Leonard, Earl Lewis, Henry W. Lewis, Pamela Lewis, Stanley W. Lindberg, Carol Livaudais, Margaret Gresham Livingston, John Walker Lobdell, Robert Lobdell, Richard Lucore, George F. Lundy, S.J., Raymond Luomanen, M.D., Louis Luzbetak, S.V.D., Farris Gambrill Lynn, Fanny Genden Lyons, William Mac-Candless, O.S.B., Jean MacDonald, Joseph McAuley, John J. McCarthy, S.J., Gerard McCollam, James McConkey, Hugh McCormick, James Hart McCown, S.J., Marjorie McDonough, James P. McFadden, John McGrath, Val Ambrose McInnes, O.P., Clement J. McNaspy, S.J., Rev. George Madathiparampil, David Madden, Nancy Malone, O.S.U., Charles Mann, Leo Luke Marcello, Mattie L. Marshall, Valerie Martin, Frank C. Maxon, Jr., M.D., Professor and Mrs. John R. May, Fr. Methodius, O.C.S.O., Park Jeong-Mi, R.S.C.J., Mr. and Mrs. Salvatore Milazzo, Hugh Miller, Mae Miller, Peggy Miller, Shirley Miller, R.S.C.J., William M. Miller, Robert Milling III, Henry Pipes Mills III, William Mills, David Miss, Mr. and Mrs. Robert E. Miss, Stephen Patrick Miss, Mr. and Mrs. Rex Mixon, David Moltke-Hansen, Vincent Montalbine, Henry R. Montecino, S.J., Professor and Mrs. Marion Montgomery, Joseph Moons, C.P, and the community of Passionist Fathers at Holy Name Church in Birmingham, Alabama, David Lawson Moores, John David Moores, John Percy Moores, Nancy Morgan, Dr. and Mrs. Gilbert H. Mudge, Thomas F. Mulcrone, S.J., Kent Mullikin, the National Endowment for the Humanities for a Summer Stipend and a Travel Grant, John P. Nelson, Bishop Martin J. Neylon, S.J., Anke L. Nolting, Elizabeth O'Brien, Elzbieta H. Oleksy, Dr. and Mrs. Ernest Oliver, James Olney, Walter J. Ong, S.J., Joseph P. Parkes, S.J., Lucy Parlange, Noel E. Parmentel, Barbara Parnass, Henry Frazier Parry, M.D., Gertrude Patch, R.S.C.J., Gary P. Pate, John R. Payne, S.J., Cary Peebles, Mr. and Mrs. Billups Phinizy Percy, Mr. and Mrs. LeRoy Percy, William Alexander Percy II, William Alexander Percy III, Les A. Phillabaum, Clay Clement Pitlick, Noel Polk, Patricia Lewis Poteat, Jonathan Potter, Dannye Romine Powell, Peggy Whitman Prenshaw, Bernadette Prochaska, F.S.P.A, Lucy Provosty, Wyatt Prunty, Irène A. Rathe, Abbot Patrick Regan, O.S.B., William J. Rewak, S.J., Joan Ridley, O.P., George M. Riser, Jr., M.D., James Robertshaw, Sally Robertson, James E. Rocks, Dr. and Mrs. Richard J. Rodeheffer, Edward J. Romagosa, S.J., Monsignor Elmo R. Romagosa, Sandra Brenner Rosenthal, Martha R. Roy, Eunice Royal, Louis D. Rubin, Jr., Kyle J. Scafide, Gilbert Schricke, Raymond A. Schroth, S.J., Richard R. Schulze, Jr., M.D., Joseph Schwartz, Kathleen Scullin, Thomas A. Sebeok, Laura Ann Phinizy Segrest, William A. Sessions, Mary Lee Settle, Charles M. Shaffer, Louis Shaffner, Bernice Shepherd, Edward A. Sheridan, S.J., Paschal G. Shook, Brent Short, Richard A. Shrader, Lewis P. Simpson, Barbara Sims, Ralph

B. Sipper, Marcus Smith, Robert McDavid Smith, William Jay Smith, William Sorum, M.D., Leon Southerland, Mr. and Mrs. Bolling P. Spalding, Mr. and Mrs. Daniel Hughes Spalding, Jr., Mr. and Mrs. Jack Spalding, Professor and Mrs. Billups Phinizy Spalding, Mr. and Mrs. Richard Spangenberg, Elizabeth Spencer, Mr. and Mrs. James L. Sprunt, Jr., Roger Straus, Mark Stricherz, Sheila Stroup, Dabney Stuart, Walter Sturdivant, Anne E. Sullivan, Thomas J. Sullivan, Walter Sullivan, Mary Lee Sweat, Kathryn Talalay, Helen Tate, Rev. and Mrs. L. Jerome Taylor, Jr., William Tazewell, Joseph Tetlow, S.J., Ben C. Toledano, Roulhac Toledano, Joan G. Tolhurst, Jay Tolson, David S. Toolan, S.J., Ann Trousdale, Francis B. Trudeau, Jr., M.D., Jean Umiker-Sebeok, Thomas A. Underwood, Gene Usdin, M.D., Simone Vauthier, Margaret Kirk Virden, Daniel T. Wackerman, Ann Waldron, Elinor Ann Walker, Carolyn Wallace, John Henry Walker, Nell Pape Waring, M.D., William W. Waring, M.D., Rebecca Warren, Sam Waterston, Ambrose Wathen, O.S.B., Eudora Welty, David Hugh Werning, Walter West, Karl-Heinz Westarp, Dr. and Mrs. Donald G. Wetherbee, Otis B. Wheeler, Earl White, M.D., John White, Marvin Yeomans Whiting, Sondra Wilk, Mary Wasson Wilkinson, Miller Williams, Jeffrey D. Wilson, Mercedes Arzù Wilson, Eugene H. Winick, Earl G. Witenberg, M.D., Nancy Tate Wood, Edward Worthington, Jonathan Yardley, and Dennis Yeager.

WALKER PERCY:

A LIFE

1

The Birmingham Years
1916–29

It is said that anyone who grows up in the Mississippi Delta knows the anecdotal histories of 1,200 people, and indeed many Southerners pride themselves on their ability to trace quickly some fairly complicated family trees. Although Walker Percy rarely spoke about his family history (see the Appendix), he knew that it was both long and complicated.[1] His sense of it was deeply embedded in his consciousness, because certain prominent last names were often repeated as first or middle names in subsequent generations of Percys—a common feature of Southern nomenclature.[2]

Such naming guaranteed that the ghostly presence of an ancestor would haunt the person carrying it. For example, his grandfather was named Walker Percy, his great-grandfather's brother was John Walker Percy, and his great-great-grandfather's wife's brother-in-law, John Williams Walker, had a son, LeRoy Pope Walker, who was Secretary of War under Confederate President Jefferson Davis and a brigadier general in the Confederate Army. (Walker Percy once wrote his friend Shelby Foote that he took the name of John when he converted to Catholicism because he had "two Southern surnames for a name, even if one of them was that of a distinguished Confederate Sec'y of State." Foote corrected him about Secretary Walker—"he wasn't distinguished" and he was Secretary of War.[3]) In reverse irony, LeRoy Walker's brother was Percy Walker—a name fans often misused for Walker Percy (if they were not miscalling him Perry Walters).[4] In addition, family names seem to be constantly recycled, sometimes in a curiously asexual manner. Walker Percy's brother, Billups Phinizy ("Phin") Percy, for example, has a daughter, Melissa Phinizy Percy, who is married to a second cousin, Bolling Phinizy Spalding, and their son is named Phinizy Percy Spalding. Indicative of Walker's own awareness of his ancestry, one of his daughters, Mary Pratt Percy Lobdell, is named after her great-grandmother Mary Pratt DeBardeleben Percy, a key figure in the Percy family history. (In one draft of the novel *The Thanatos Syndrome*, Percy has a character named Alice Pratt, in this case a young woman from Montgomery, Alabama.[5]) Since he spent his formative years in Birmingham (Alabama), Athens (Georgia), and Greenville (Mississippi), he willy-nilly learned his family history from Percy, Debardeleben, and Phinizy relatives.

Walker Percy's family roots on his father's side go back to the British Isles and Mississippi and Louisiana, and more immediately to Alabama. One way to appreciate the Percy family history is to relate it to the topology and rapid growth of Birmingham as an important center for coal, iron, and steel. The Percys rose to national prominence at the precise time that Birmingham began to explore and capitalize on its valuable mineral resources. From one perspective, the suicides of both Walker Percy's grandfather and father caused much headshaking for Walker's peers still living in Birmingham and continue to pose questions difficult to answer. Yet it is fair to say that as each generation of Percys settled down, the decisions made by his ancestors—whether to enhance their earthly existences and enjoy the fruits of their labors or to abandon even life itself—profoundly affected him. It should also be noted that the death of his mother—a victim of suicide, as Walker characterized it to at least two friends—proved to be the most unresolved experience of his life. Whatever considerations of alienation he used in his fiction were ultimately rooted in the very fabric of his being.

Although suicide is often motivated by deeply felt feelings of loss and abandonment, real or metaphorical—as an author of a major work on suicide, George Howe Colt, explains—it can represent for many some form of psychic gain.[6] What is important to remember is that Walker Percy, like his two brothers, constantly integrated new experiences into his life. Bertram Wyatt-Brown, who has studied the relationship between artistic creativity, honor, psychological depression, melancholy, and suicide in the Percy family, notes that while Walker Percy perceived the "flawed and dissonant" honor of his ancestors, which can lead to moral and physical death, there is nevertheless "a largely redemptive note" in Percy's fiction, based on his deep Christian faith "that serves as a final statement."[7] In discussing the relationship of his work to that of Faulkner's *The Sound and the Fury*, Percy once told Lewis A. Lawson, "I would like to think of starting where Faulkner left off, of starting with a Quentin

Compson who *didn't* commit suicide. Suicide is easy. Keeping Quentin
Compson alive is something else."[8]

Literary critic John F. Desmond notes that "all of Percy's novels
reveal how much Kierkegaard's idea of despair as spiritual suicide dom-
inates his vision, far beyond but not unrelated to the concern with literal
suicide. Despair permeates every novel, exemplified by the self 'refusing
to be itself'—by role-playing, by bestialism, by deference to experts, by
objectification, and by suicide itself. So pervasive is despair in his work
that one can speak of a condition of cultural suicide or general thanatos;
yet his protagonists also struggle against it, struggle to become ex-
suicides."[9] According to Desmond, Percy did not lapse into self-defeating
silence in his fiction, but through language and portrayals of sexuality
he affirms the selfhood of the creative artist. In short, Percy saw himself
as a wayfarer with an unusual and unique family background. During
his life, particularly after he contracted tuberculosis as a young doctor,
he journeyed into uncharted territory for which existing maps gave an
indication of which general direction to take, but not necessarily which
specific roads to follow.

Walker Percy's father, LeRoy Pratt Percy, son of Walker and Mary
Pratt DeBardeleben Percy, was born on June 23, 1889, and grew up conscious of the great expectations attached to the only male in a leading
Birmingham family. The manner of his life and death had an inevitable
impact on the way his son, the subject of this biography, saw the world
and made choices for his own future. Educated for two years (1904–6)
at Lawrenceville School in New Jersey, LeRoy was one of the three associate editors of *Olla Podrida*, the school's yearbook, where it was noted
in his last year that "Perc"—as LeRoy was called—had won two first
testimonials in his junior year but none in his senior. "His friends say
he could head the class 'if he wished to.' Anyhow, he has the dark eyes
and hair of that type of genius." In his junior and senior years, Perc was
a member of the Gun Club and in his junior year was on the gun team;
he made the class baseball team and became a member of the Calliopean
Society. Like most of his classmates, LeRoy entered Princeton after leaving Lawrenceville. *The Nassau Herald of the Class of 1910* records this brief
sketch of him at Princeton: "5'10" in height, Episcopalian, a Democrat,
his favorite sport tennis, and English literature his favorite academic subject." He belonged to the Whig Society and the Tiger Inn, named the
legal profession as his vocation in life, and kept a low profile while at
college. In the "Class Prophecy"—not without the type of jejune humor
his classmates would enjoy—LeRoy ("Puss") Percy is depicted as a devoted missionary in Africa.

After Woodrow Wilson, then president of Princeton, presented him with his bachelor of literature degree in 1910, LeRoy went to Harvard to study law, and while there he served on the editorial board of *The Harvard Law Review* (January 1912–June 1913). In the fall of 1913, he started advanced studies at the University of Heidelberg as a young Werther, a sojourn that later influenced his son to make a similar trip. LeRoy returned to Birmingham and began practicing law in 1914 as a member of the firm of Percy, Benners & Burr, where he remained until his death in 1929.

In Greenville, Mississippi, LeRoy's first cousin William Alexander Percy—later known as "Uncle Will"—returned home in September 1914 from a trip to Sicily and France—"a tourist in a tourist's world, with no premonitions," as he writes in *Lanterns on the Levee*. Will was working on his book of poetry, *Sappho in Levkas*. He and his father, U.S. Senator LeRoy Percy, planned to head for Alaska for some bear hunting. While away, they were wholly unaware of another family returning from a different type of vacation. Mr. and Mrs. Billups Phinizy of Athens, Georgia, and three of their five daughters, among whom was Martha Susan ("Mattie Sue," born May 3, 1890), were returning from Europe.[10] To receive the news of the European trip, Mattie Sue's older sister, Bolling (pronounced "Bo-leen") Phinizy Spalding and her young son, Jack, traveled from Atlanta to Athens.[11]

Clearly an attractive person with an openness and sociability typical of young women of her day, Mattie Sue, a graduate of the Lucy Cobb Institute in Athens and Miss Finch's School in New York, had a full social calendar. The drives between Athens and Birmingham—or Atlanta, or Augusta, for that matter—would be endured by her and many others of her age to foster all-important social contacts.[12] Yet Mattie Sue's days as a single woman were numbered. In mid-November she and her friends from Atlanta and Augusta were among those entertained by LeRoy Pratt Percy at his home in Birmingham; the group had come together to renew friendships made at the Greenbrier, a 6,500-acre resort surrounded by the panoramic beauty of the Allegheny Mountains in White Sulphur Springs, West Virginia.[13] It had been the custom for Mrs. Phinizy to spend August with her daughters at this grand hotel.[14]

Mattie Sue's father, Billups, a wealthy cotton factor (born in Augusta in 1861), became president of the Southern Mutual Insurance Company in 1904 and was one of the most prominent men in Athens. He also served as president of the Bank of the University for many years, director of the Georgia Railroad & Banking Company of Augusta, trustee of the Atlanta Trust Company, president of the Commercial Club of Athens, chairman of the board of directors of the Southern Manufacturing Company, and vice president of the Athens Railway & Electric Company.[15] Billups took great pride in his accomplishments and gave his family the leisure and resources to live very comfortably.[16] His wife, Nellie Stovall Phinizy, three years younger than her husband, was known as a gracious hostess in Athens.

By May 1915, Mattie Sue had set her eyes on LeRoy Pratt Percy.[17] She mentioned as much to her older sister, Anne Barrett ("Annie B.") Johnson. The courtship of Mattie Sue by LeRoy intensified during the summer months and both families made plans for a wedding. On the first of September, Martha Susan Phinizy married LeRoy Percy in Athens at a noon ceremony, presided over by the Rev. Eugene Lott Hill, in the Phinizy residence with members of the family and friends from Birmingham, Charleston, Atlanta, Greenville, and Norfolk in attendance, including Senator and Mrs. LeRoy Percy and their son, Will.[18] It was one of the most brilliant marriages of the year in Athens. After a wedding breakfast for 175 guests, the newlyweds left on an afternoon train for a trip West.[19] *The Birmingham Age-Herald* noted that this "marriage united two of the most prominent old families of the South. For three years the bride has been one of the most popular of the younger college set in Athens, the old and aristocratic university town . . . Mr. Percy is one of the most popular young men in society and a brilliant and prominent attorney in this city." One Athenian said to Senator Percy, "You have stolen a rose from our garden," to which he replied, "Yes Madam, and we are very proud of the theft."[20]

Yet, as the newlyweds made their way to the East Coast, all was not well with Mattie Sue's health. In mid-October, her mother left quickly for New York, where she was joined by her husband; her daughter was lying ill in Roosevelt Hospital during the early stages of pregnancy. Initially the doctors held out very little hope for recovery, but her condition improved. By early November, Mattie Sue was recuperating at her family home and LeRoy traveled to Birmingham to resume work.[21] During the second weekend of December, Mattie Sue felt well enough to join her husband there. They took up residence in January in their new home at 1024 South 24th Street (also known as Caldwell Terrace).[22] From this house set on a hill, Mattie Sue and LeRoy could look out and have a panoramic view of the city. Yet Mattie Sue always considered Athens her hometown.

The eruption of the world war that had started in Europe almost two years earlier was a shock and worry for all Americans. Even though Birmingham could profit a good deal from the sale of war materials, the community was caught up in an intense debate about the morality of engaging the United States in "foreign" warfare. LeRoy's father expressed his opinions publicly: a banner headline in *The Birmingham Age-Herald* (April 25, 1916) proclaimed: PERCY MAINTAINS NO JUSTIFICATION IN GOING TO WAR. After consulting with Senator John H. Bankhead, the father of Tallulah, he made public a letter he had written to him the previous week concerning the war. He was well aware that German submarines had sunk English freight vessels on which Americans were working and that English sailors had taken a number of Austrian and German passengers from an American steamship. He conceded in his letter that the rights of Americans had been violated by both Great Britain and Germany but contended that in neither case was there sufficient cause to justify the United States going to war.

On May 28, 1916, Walker Percy was born in St. Vincent's Hospital in Birmingham. During the difficult fourteen-hour delivery, Dr. Norman Paige Cocke used forceps.[23] The following day, as President Wilson's speech before the League to Enforce Peace maintained that the United States was ready to join in any feasible association of nations to preserve worldwide peace, *The Birmingham Ledger* announced that the Percys were receiving congratulations on the birth of a son. Grandmother Nellie Phinizy and Annie B. wasted no time in traveling to Birmingham to assist Mattie Sue and see baby Walker. Friends and family were pleased not only that the mother and child were in good health but also that the distinguished Percy line would continue to exist. Yet as Mattie Sue breast-fed her infant, young Walker "was 'poisoned' by his mother's milk, could not take food, lost weight, developed 'rashes' and remained in a state of malnutrition."[24] These are his own words, written as an adult, and make one wonder whether Walker Percy from his earliest days had latent feelings of being rejected by his mother. In addition, Mattie Sue was worried about her baby contracting typhoid or tuberculosis, both of which raged that summer throughout the Birmingham area. Almost daily the newspapers published horrifying statistics; by the end of July, 346 cases of typhoid had been reported locally. And if that was not bad enough, Dr. George Eaves revealed that in May and June 67 people had died from tuberculosis.[25]

In early October, Mattie Sue was in Athens visiting her parents.[26] Though the Phinizys were traditionally Presbyterian and the Percys Episcopalian, an ongoing religious debate was being waged in Birmingham. This debate would play a critical role in determining whether or not LeRoy's religious beliefs were significant as he contemplated suicide in 1929. By 1916 the Independent Presbyterian Church had experienced considerable growth, with candidates waiting to enter, due in large measure to the ministry of the Rev. Henry Edmonds. (In a preliminary draft of *The Moviegoer*, one character is called "Dr. Edmunds," the Episcopal minister who lives in Binx Bolling's hometown.[27]) After two years of ministering to a congregation that followed the Calvinistic tradition and held fast against Darwin's and Spencer's theories, Dr. Edmonds found himself more and more in disagreement with a number of church elders. He could not accept a belief that man is totally depraved. Contrary to the traditional Presbyterianism of the time, he denied the value of the Virgin Birth and the Resurrection as proofs of Jesus's divinity.[28] Tilting in the direction of the social gospel of Walter Rauschenbusch and its concomitant liberalism, Dr. Edmonds tended to accept the tenets of new scientific theories. Though not all members of South Highland Presbyterian Church were concerned about the intricacies of theological debates, a sufficient number began to take sides and discuss the issues in public.[29] Finally, the congregation had to decide whether or not to resolve the case within the walls of the church or in the denominational courts, and eventually Dr. Edmonds appeared before the Presbytery of North Alabama to be examined. He would not change his view that the death of Jesus had no consequence for salvation. Though the Presbytery charitably asked him to reconsider his views and refrain from speaking or writing publicly about them, he refused to do so. Dr. Edmonds decided he would start the Independent Presbyterian Church, and many prominent families followed him, including Mr. and Mrs. LeRoy Pratt Percy. Their commitment to this new church would be made evident in succeeding years, especially when LeRoy became an active deacon.[30]

During the final days of President Wilson's second campaign in 1916, many Americans were disturbed to learn that the German submarine *Deutschland* was harbored in New London, Connecticut. William Alexander Percy was the first Percy to commit himself seriously to the war effort; he would soon know firsthand what others were merely reading about. He sailed for Europe on November 18 as a representative of the Belgian Relief Association of America.[31] While staying en route in Aldwych, a section of London, he wrote back to a former teacher that he had been waiting impatiently for a ship to arrive to take him to Holland, under the protection of an escort ship. His words catch the grim and anxious poetry of war:

This London! A huge military place under gray skies by day and jungle blackmen at night and housing the youth of the world. Everywhere the soldier lads from Australia, New Zealand and Canada. Those who were not conscripted, but came. Here they are allowed to spend their days of leave before being sent to France . . . or God knows where. They roam the streets with no money and no friends and seek the cheapest vices for diversion.[32]

In Birmingham the city fathers planned for the inevitable war effort—specifically by entering into negotiations for a $15 million expansion program to erect a new steel plant, several blast furnaces, and batteries of by-product coke ovens and benzol plants.

President Wilson announced in February 1917 that the United States could not remain on friendly terms with any imperial government whose submarines attacked neutral ships, and this signaled America's intention to join the Allies. Wilson said he was anxious to avoid war; at the same time, he refused to be intimidated by the Germans. When Grandmother Phinizy visited Mattie Sue and LeRoy, they wondered whether this stressful situation was affecting Grandfather Walker, who had been suffering from depression and sought treatment in Baltimore; he had returned home before his treatment was completed.[33] They had every reason to be anxious.

On February 8, Grandfather Walker shot himself. The next day, *The Birmingham Age-Herald* printed a long report that featured his photo, showing him fashionably dressed and wearing a bowler. It stated that shortly after 3 p.m., as he was cleaning his shotgun in preparation for a hunting trip in Mississippi, it accidentally discharged a shot that pierced his heart. He died immediately. His son had talked to him that afternoon and the two had made arrangements to go hunting in Greenville. An hour or so afterward, the father went up to his bedroom, adjacent to which was a narrow room that served as a storage place for hunting equipment and golf bags. The position of his body and the 12-gauge shotgun, with its one exploded shell, seemed to indicate that he had stooped over to pick up the weapon and its trigger had become entangled in the straps of the hunting case. After the shot he fell facedown on the floor. At the time of death both his wife and his son were in the house. His son was the first to reach him and Pratt was prostrated with grief.

Gradually a steady stream of friends and relatives ("hundreds," according to the paper) made their way to the Percy residence on Arlington Avenue. LeRoy gave his account to the paper's reporter:

Father had been at home all day, and we had talked after lunch about going to Greenville for a short hunt on the estate of my uncle. The suggestion seemed to please him, and so he agreed to leave Thursday night. He left me and went upstairs to his room. Shortly after 3 o'clock I heard a muffled noise, but did not pay any attention to it. A few minutes later I went upstairs to talk with father concerning our plans, and it was then that I discovered his body, face down upon the floor in the room where he kept his guns, his golf sticks and hunting togs. From the position of his body and the gun, it seems that he picked up a gun with its muzzle pointing toward him, and that it was accidentally discharged. I immediately called for the physician and the coroner and they came.

Senator Percy came for the funeral from Greenville. Was this an accidental death or a suicide? Later generations of Percys indicated that suicide was not improbable; they seemed to accept it as a fact. A clue that the rector of St. Mary's-on-the-Highlands, the Rev. W. N. Claybrook, considered it a suicide is that, uncharacteristically, he did not list a cause of death in the church's burial registry. Young Walker would think of it as an "accident," a word that doubtless suppressed his true feelings.[34]

On April 2, 1917, President Wilson, desirous of vindicating the principles of peace and justice against a "selfish and autocratic power," urged Congress to declare a state of war with Germany. The Senate voted 82–6 in favor of war. Will was enjoying the sunshine of Paris when he heard that le Président Veelson had finally acted. He and some friends were invited to be the guests of the French Senate to hear Premier Alexandre Ribot welcome the United States as an ally.[35] Immediately young men started pouring into recruiting offices in Birmingham and around the country. By the end of April, Congress had passed a bill to raise an army by selective draft. A Liberty Day parade with 15,000 participants was held in Birmingham. A recruiting station was opened to accept volunteers, many of whom had never handled a gun. On registration day, between 25,000 and 30,000 men and women marched in Birmingham's streets; nearly 20,000 locals registered, including many blacks. The city was resplendent in flags and bunting, and the official parade culminated with a banquet at the Tutwiler Hotel. In the wake of this excitement, U.S. Steel announced that it would expand its operations in the Birmingham area and spend $11 million to improve its facilities. The Tennessee Coal & Iron Company (TCI) was expected to join in the effort to build 600 houses for workers, as well as a new blooming mill and a new plate mill.

For LeRoy such an investment of capital would also mean a great increase in his work schedule. His personal worries were not inconsiderable: he had recently lost his father, his wife was pregnant with their second child (LeRoy Pratt was born on August 23), and he had to console and care for his widowed mother. Above all, he had to decide soon whether to wait and be conscripted or to volunteer.

Having returned home, Will Percy entered the Officers' Training Camp at Camp Stanley in Texas that August. For LeRoy, the moment of decision had come; he entered the war effort as a private in the aviation section of the Signal Corps on March 9, 1918, and was detailed to the School of Military Aeronautics at the University of Texas in Austin. He qualified as a reserve military aviator and was commissioned as a second lieutenant in the Air Service in late September. He was then sent to Brooks Field in Texas as an instructor (after some time at Kelly Field, according to his son LeRoy) and then to Eberts Field near Lonoke, Arkansas.[36] Family folklore maintains that he cracked up one or two of the smaller planes.

After LeRoy's departure, Mattie Sue wasted no time in taking the boys back to Athens.[37] After the death of Grandfather Walker, they apparently decided to sell their house. Years later, Walker said he retained only a dim image of this house. LeRoy and his family now moved into Grandmother Pratt's house at 2217 Arlington Avenue, an impressive structure on the corner of Arlington and Highland.[38]

Will was attached to General William Hay's 92nd Division in August 1918 as a brigadier instructor to train black troops, many of whom outranked him. He wrote to his father from the headquarters of the 74th Brigade, asking to be informed when and if LeRoy was assigned overseas.[39] Less than a month later, Will expressed great enthusiasm over the news of the American offensive. He had recently received a letter from his father, which contained a rhapsody on flying from LeRoy—a "really exhilarating and fine piece of literature. He's a splendid fellow and I certainly wish him luck."[40] When the armistice was signed, Will felt that the United States had capitulated to the Germans: "LeRoy must be disgusted at never having his chance at a Boche," he wrote home, "though I'm sure he'll never regret the time lost in training. I've seen very little of our flyers—particularly over our line. Our mastery of the air may have been complete but it was certainly never apparent to the infantry. We were bombed day and night by every kind of varmint that could fly and our serene squadrons could only heave into the empyrean after the party was over."[41] In December, LeRoy was discharged from the Air Service; his formal service had lasted exactly nine months. He could now return home, reunite with his family, and resume his legal career.

Returning home was especially exciting for those who had been overseas. Will expressed great pride in seeing General Pershing review the troops on a snow-covered field in February 1919: "It was superb, a veritable 'army with banners.' " The clothes and equipment may not have been the best, he wrote, "but when our boys get their shoes shined, clean their wrapped leggings, cock their overseas cap over one ear and press their overcoats, which strikes them just above the knees and manages to convey a go-to-hell, O-damn-you effect, they are the most capable looking and endearing bunch in the world. Anyone who hasn't lived with them during this war has missed all the fun of it—that's the main reason why I always wanted to be in the line."[42] Will, discharged in

April, was promoted to captain of the Infantry Officers Reserve Corps. In a snappy uniform and sporting a Sam Browne belt and Croix de Guerre, he was greeted by his parents in New York. Stopping in Tennessee on the way back to Greenville, he discussed the possibility of teaching at the University of the South in Sewanee.

By early spring, LeRoy had definitely settled into the house on Arlington and had become an active member of the Independent Presbyterian Church.[43] Records in the Jefferson County Courthouse show that Grandmother Pratt conveyed for one dollar her house and property to LeRoy on June 10, 1920. One of the few souvenirs of the Arlington days is a picture of LeRoy in his military uniform, holding a chubby young LeRoy dressed in a smock, while Walker, in a sailor suit, stands on a stool next to his father. Father LeRoy's arms envelop both his sons. LeRoy told them how the German flying ace Max Immelmann invented a combat tactic of going into a loop and then descending into a barrel roll to escape.[44] (In *Love in the Ruins*, the German pilot is transformed into Art Immelmann.) As legal work increased after the war, LeRoy and his partners decided to expand their law firm, welcoming James Rice to Percy, Benners & Burr. LeRoy proved to be a versatile lawyer, and when he thought a jury wanted to hear colloquial language, he knew how to use it.[45]

Young Walker recorded some of the events in his early life. His first memories were of living in the house on Arlington, an easy streetcar ride to Five Points; the first movie he saw was a Krazy Kat cartoon at the Five Points Theatre, though he recalled Happy Hooligan with equal affection.[46] He also remembered a spectacular fire at the Packard Automobile Company and catching the streetcar at Highland with his black nurse and riding the "Loop" for a nickel—her way of babysitting.[47] On occasion, he was also driven in the family's 1920 Ford to see his father play golf, walking the course with him and meeting his father's friends.

In June 1920, Yale University Press published Will's second book, *In April Once, and Other Poems*, which included a poignant section entitled "From a Soldier's Notebook." The volume took its title from Will's forty-page play in blank verse depicting the life of Guido, a thirteenth-century Florentine who sacrifices himself for a leper and a jailer. William Faulkner reviewed the book in the Ole Miss student newspaper, *The Mississippian*, chiding Will for having an old-fashioned muse. Faulkner wrote that the poet suffered the misfortune of having been born out of his time: "He should have lived in Victorian England and gone to Italy with Swinburne."[48] Faulkner said that Will was "like a little boy closing his eyes against the dark of modernity, which threatens the bright simplicity and the colorful romantic pageantry of the middle ages with which his eyes are full." Yet he ended with a compliment—taken as a whole, "the gold outweighs the dross." (The title of one poem, "Sanctuary," perhaps anticipated the title of Faulkner's novel.) Will's plea in "An Epistle from Corinth," which Faulkner liked, reveals a not so hidden cri de coeur on the part of the author, who was known by a few in the Greenville community to be homosexual: "I know the loveliness/Of flesh and its sweet snare, and I am hurt/At finding nothing where I sought for much."[49] If Will was offended by Faulkner's review, he never acknowledged it publicly.

In Greenville, as elsewhere in the South, the Ku Klux Klan grew more active after the war. Senator Percy delivered an extemporaneous address in March 1922 to the citizens of Washington County, entitled "Ku Klux Klan Unnecessary," in response to the address of a member of the Klan, "Colonel" Joseph G. Camp.[50] Will said he never heard a speech that was so exciting or so much fun.[51] Born in Washington County, the Senator said he felt proud to be among his own people and speak as one of them. He looked back on the aftermath of the Civil War, when the KKK emerged as "a desperate remedy for a helpless, scourged and torn people," but the KKK was no longer needed since the "white man is in control of every department of government, of the courts, judges and juries." Blacks are told they will not be harmed, "but little does he know the Negro if he feels that reassurance will do aught to lessen their alarm. This is a real thing and a real menace." Walker later remembered his father talking about Hugo Black and the Klan, saying that had his father lived, he would never have believed that Justice Black would become one of the most liberal members of the Supreme Court.[52] The Senator's speech also provoked an editorial in *The Memphis Commercial Appeal*, which prompted a letter from LeRoy in Birmingham to his uncle in Greenville: "I believe that your speech is going to stand as one of the great speeches of the time. I hope that some one will have it printed in pamphlet form and distribute it through the country."[53] The Senator had become a father substitute for LeRoy, and they even planned to go on a hunting trip together, though Will preferred not to engage in blood sports.[54]

Senator Percy wrote ten months later to Caroline Yarborough Percy in Los Angeles, inquiring about her eldest son's education and adding news about their relatives in Birmingham: "Tell the boys I had a great duck hunt in Louisiana last week. LeRoy Pratt and myself hunted ducks and snipes together and had a fine time of it. I am rather counting on going to Alabama to take a bird hunt with LeRoy Pratt next week while Cam [Camille, the Senator's wife] stays with Mattie Sue. We have not seen any of them [LeRoy's sons] for a couple of years."[55] LeRoy kept his uncle informed about his hunting plans on office stationery that now listed seven partners in the law firm.[56] He had begun to suffer periods of depression as a result of the tensions that sometimes arose in his law office. As Walker remembered, his father would not leave his problems in the office but would bring them home.

Senator Percy, Cam, and Will went to Florida as the crape myrtle began to bud.[57] The Senator had been concerned both about Will, who was not well at that time, and J. Gervys Lusk, a young man from Greenville in need of employment.[58] The Greenville Percys were noted for their genuine concern for the welfare of the younger members of the community. From the Palm Beach Hotel, Will left on a United Fruit steamer to Panama, while the Senator spent the 1923 Easter weekend fishing near New Orleans.[59] Still preoccupied by the KKK, he felt that they had destroyed the feeling of community harmony in Greenville. On one occasion, a stranger entered the Percy home in mid-May with an obviously concocted story about a car accident. Will decided the man was actually there for sinister purposes, perhaps to assassinate his father.[60]

One memory of bird hunting with his father that stayed with Walker all his life had to do with an unusual bird he had spotted. He had never seen such a beautiful bird before; it flew fast, suddenly folded its wings, and fell like a stone into the woods. When Walker asked what it was called, the black boy with them said, "That's a *blue dollar* hawk." Walker was also told, "Well, it's the way he balls himself up and rolls when he falls." When he asked his father if the boy was right, his father said, "No, he got it all wrong. It is a *blue darter* hawk." But Walker always preferred the boy guide's metaphor.[61]

In a curious move, Mattie Sue in late July bought from her husband the house and property on Arlington Avenue for one dollar.[62] It clearly put Mattie Sue in an advantageous legal position should anything happen to her husband. LeRoy knew that the Senator and his wife had health problems, and perhaps he was providing for eventualities should his own health decline. Indeed, Cam's health took a turn for the worse. In October 1924, she had an attack of appendicitis, which, because it had turned gangrenous, meant an immediate operation.[63] She withstood the operation and stayed in the hospital for three weeks. The Senator was exhausted by his wife's emergency, and in late November asked LeRoy to consider joining him on another hunting trip, this time to Lake Arthur, Louisiana.[64]

For the Percy family in Birmingham, however, 1925 seemed to be a year that had all the outward signs of health and prosperity: first, their cousins the Henry Ticknor DeBardelebens moved to Shades Mountain; second, the Percys moved to Mountain Brook; third, LeRoy served as president of the Birmingham Country Club.[65] Young Walker would learn about Percy family history not only from his grandmother and parents in Birmingham but also from the ongoing conversations with two childhood cousins, Donie Drane DeBardeleben and her brother Newton Hanson DeBardeleben. Like Walker, LeRoy, and Phin (Billups Phinizy, Walker's youngest brother, born January 3, 1922), Donie and Newt were caught up as children in the *Sturm und Drang* of the DeBardeleben enterprises. The Percys went to the DeBardelebens' rustic house for Sunday dinners, and the cousins played in the nearby woods. Their lives and families overlapped. Walker's response in later years was to interiorize his family history and rarely mention it, even to his daughters. Perhaps he did not want to deal explicitly with the family history of whatever branch, preferring to lock it within himself, knowing that it would pour out of him in some creative way.[66]

Mattie Sue and LeRoy and their three boys moved over Red Mountain to a new house across from the country club, though they continued to pay taxes on the house on Arlington Avenue. Borden Burr, the president of the Rock House Land Company, sold a lot to LeRoy Percy, again for one dollar, at the intersection of unpaved Ridge Drive and Country Club Road.[67] As president of the country club, LeRoy was immersed in its activities, and he was building a modern ranch-style brick house across the road from the sixth green and seventh tee.[68] The large windows gave the house a welcoming and airy character. The front entrance, the upper part of which was a scalloped façade, was built deliberately to set it off from the nearby Gresham house. Standing in the front doorway, one looked down a long, sweeping lawn leading to Country Club Road. Outside the master bedroom was a patio onto which LeRoy could wheel out his bed and sleep under the stars. Some of the relatives thought that his desire to do this might have been due to a sleep disorder. (In *The Moviegoer*, Binx Bolling talks about his father's insomnia: "One of my few recollections of him is his nighttime prowling. In those days it was thought that sleeping porches were healthful, so my father stuck one onto the house, a screen box with canvas blinds that pulled up from below . . . My father had trouble sleeping and moved out with us." Sometimes Binx's father would take his Abercrombie & Fitch sleeping bag and spend the night in the rose garden next to the house.)

It was no secret that land surrounding the new country club would soon rank among the most desirable property in Birmingham. A newspaper ad alerted readers to the advantages of living in the area, and a fair number of the well-to-do families were quick to relocate.[69] It was not uncommon for Walker and his friends Meredith Hazzard and Wells Stanley to hike up nearby Red Mountain to the old mines served by a railroad spur and try to locate hidden stills.[70] One of the area's distinctive features was the Rock House, also known as Indian Palace and Devil Drop, and the wooded section developed by the Rock House Land Company. Eventually a little train ran up to this area, a few miles from the Percy house; it stopped at Carlyle and would bring day-trippers to see the Rock House, an outcropping about fifty feet high and fifty yards long filled with tunnels where the limestone had dissolved. It was a favorite place to picnic because of its hilltop position surrounded by wildflowers. Walker and LeRoy and Donie and other playmates would look for arrowheads left long ago by the Indians. One schoolmate a year younger than Walker who lived on Ridge Drive was William M. ("Jig") Miller; he often played with the Percy boys. Jig would encourage the studious Walker to join in the mud-ball fights they so enjoyed in the lot next to the Greshams'. The remnants of a tennis court between the Percy house and the former Robert Munger property in Mountain Brook still exist. The Percys were considered a happy family; Mrs. Percy was a quiet and not particularly outgoing person who loved to play tennis and Mr. Percy would take his boys to Keith's Vaudeville Theatre and to the weekend baseball games at Rickwood Field.

The Percys visited Vestavia, the home of George B. Ward on Shades Mountain, which resembled the Roman temple of Vesta. Walker refers to it obliquely in *The Last Gentleman*: "Directly opposite the castle [belonging to the Vaughts], atop the next ridge to the south, there stood a round, rosy temple. It was the dwelling of a millionaire who had admired a Roman structure erected by the Emperor Vespasian in honor of Juno and so had reproduced it in good Alabama red bricks and Georgia marble. At night a battery of colored floodlights made it look redder still." After its completion in 1925, Ward gave lavish parties on the grounds of his estate.[71]

Walker always enjoyed looking at his father's books, "mysterious things with pages full of marks without pictures."[72] He looked at the words and realized that the word "the" was repeated in several places. "There was a pattern here, something going on! Amazing!" Later Walker delighted in reading the Sunday comics, particularly the Gumps, Gasoline Alley, Little Orphan Annie, Moon Mullins, and Winnie Winkle the Breadwinner. (Walker and Eudora Welty would later entertain each other by recalling the comic strips they had read as children. Jiggs would make it into *The Last Gentleman*.) Sitting in a red-leather brass-studded chair, LeRoy read aloud to his sons from Kipling's *Jungle Book* and Robert Louis Stevenson's *Treasure Island*. Walker was captivated by the scene where Jim Hawkins tumbles into an apple barrel, falls asleep, and wakes up to hear Long John Silver's plans for a mutiny.[73] His father also gave him a copy of *The Swiss Family Robinson*, and Walker would ask him to reread the passage about their going back to the shipwreck to retrieve the goats, cows, and pigs.[74] Another favorite of father and son was Conrad's *Lord Jim*. This was an age, too, of "sending off for something," and like other boys his age, Walker sent off for free samples of Postum and a gold-filled Elgin railroader's pocket watch with an elk engraved on the back.[75]

Walker himself had difficulty trying to recall with certitude his early education. He attended Miss Lyda H. Stillwell's kindergarten.[76] Miss Stillwell was remembered for her thick glasses and especially by young LeRoy as someone who would spit through her front teeth when she talked. Probably Walker started attending Miss Stillwell's when he was four or five. Since the kindergarten was just down the street from the Percy house, Walker walked back and forth to school, passing the Barrett residence, a family name that was later preserved in Walker Percy's fiction.[77]

From Miss Stillwell's, Walker went to the Margaret Allen School, located at 2124 Highland, run by three sisters, Ruth, Willy, and Margaret (Beth) Allen. These sisters conducted their classes for the younger students on the first floor, while Birmingham University School (BUS), founded in 1922, occupied the upper floor. Walker would have stayed in the Margaret Allen School until he entered, most likely, the fifth form at BUS.[78] By the fall of 1925, BUS was ready to begin classes in a new wooden-framed building on Waucoma Street, up Highland Avenue just across the street from the impressive, white-marbled Enslen house.[79] Captain Basil Manly Parks, the school's founder and headmaster, and his wife lived in the Peters house adjacent to the school property on Waucoma. Mrs. Parks, a regular chatterbox by all accounts, prepared lunch for those who wished to buy sandwiches and apples from her; a boy was considered a genius if he could carry on a conversation with her and finish lunch at the same time.

When Walker, age nine, and LeRoy, age eight, began attending BUS, there were sixty-nine boys who could look forward to thirty-six weeks of schooling. BUS had an impressive group of male teachers. Captain Parks had a military background, including service in the Field Artillery Corps of the U.S. Army. This portly, balding man, who frequently shouted as he tried to get his students to solve math problems, was both feared and revered by the students, many of whom considered him "mean as a yard dog."[80] They long remembered his military orders: "Fifth form, rise. About face! March!" Parks kept a red rubber whip with a wooden handle in his closet and used it. Once when a student fired a pistol in school, Captain Parks punished him with the whip and dismissed him without hesitation. Another faculty member, Dr. Robert A. Mickle (the name "Mickle" occurs in *The Last Gentleman*), taught Latin, which began in the fifth form. He often called those who found it difficult to learn their declensions and conjugations "infernal scoundrels." Still another was Paul J. Benrimo, who had studied Latin and Spanish at Vanderbilt, the University of Chicago, and Harvard. It was normal for students to take at least four years of Latin at BUS. Newell C. Griffin taught English, history, and French; his harelip provoked wry reactions among his students, who realized they were speaking French with a funny accent. Graduation classes at BUS were sometimes small. When Paschal Shook, three years older than Walker, graduated in 1929, there were four in his class but only two graduated; in Paschal's mind, the school had a good reputation, but it was not top-flight. In those days before the Depression, well-to-do families sent their children to private schools; this changed with the Depression. Walker and his classmates tended to meet girls not at private schools but at dancing classes.

The Percy boys would either be driven to school in the family La Salle by Elijah ("Lige") Collier, who lived in a house behind the main house on Ridge Drive, or ride their bikes up the back side of Red Mountain and then coast downhill to school. Phin, often isolated from his two brothers, felt he grew to know Lige more than he did his parents.[81] His two older brothers were surprised once to see the short, studious Dr. Mickle drive up in his Studebaker, enter the house, take out his pipe, place it in his mouth under his stained mustache, and drink hard liquor with their father. Young LeRoy felt embarrassed to have someone from outside the house see his father drink. Disdaining bathtub gin and white lightning, the senior LeRoy aged his own bourbon in a charcoal keg, even getting down on his hands and knees to start the siphoning process in order to fill up his decanter.[82] In those days of Prohibition, bootleg liquor was delivered surreptitiously either by the dry-cleaning man or by Eddie Patillo, who would make his appointed rounds sporting his leather puttees as he rode up and down Red Mountain on his motorcycle.

Mattie Sue would sometimes take the three boys for part of the summer to Brinkwood, a house that Will Percy and his friend Huger Jervey owned jointly near Sewanee, Tennessee. Walker and Robert Daniel (a relative of Thomas Frank Gailor, the Episcopal Bishop of Tennessee) became fast friends. Such vacations in the mountains were considered healthful for young Walker, who had his share of medical problems as a boy—measles, chicken pox, and scarlet fever as a child— though, as he was careful to record clinically later on, no diphtheria, chorea, or mumps.[83] He had some type of nonrecurring allergic skin reaction as a child and his tonsils came out when he was seven. At times he had been subject to attacks of anorexia with some nausea and vomiting.

In the fall of 1925 Walker's father suffered a bout of ill health. When he recovered, he took young Walker and his brother LeRoy hunting ducks in the swampy White River, which empties into the Arkansas side of the Mississippi about seventy miles north of Greenville; they used a houseboat as their base of operations.[84] (In *The Gramercy Winner*, Laverne Sutter's father took Laverne hunting in southern Alabama and on the White River in Arkansas.) Senator Percy paid $55 to cover LeRoy's dues at the Swan Lake Club in the Greenville area: "I didn't know he was still a member of the Club. His failure to make remittance is unquestionably due to his sickness."[85] The Senator's cotton crop at Panther Burn, a plantation in which he had part interest, had turned out well, with each acre of cotton producing a full bale that year; it was the best crop the Delta had ever produced.[86] In much the same way, the Percys in Birmingham were thriving. On March 15, 1926, Mattie Sue and LeRoy entered into an arrangement with the Rock House Land Company concerning the obligations of properly maintaining their property.[87] Mountain Brook echoed with the sounds of hammers and saws as new houses were constructed, and those in charge of development made sure that property owners maintained driveways and access roads. Two months later, Robert and Virginia Jemison, working through the New South Land Company, conveyed property to LeRoy Percy for one hundred dollars, for which LeRoy assumed one half of the $18,000 debt.[88] The house and grounds on Ridge Drive clearly indicated that LeRoy Percy was a successful lawyer whose family enjoyed the fruits of prosperity.[89]

By early April the sanctuary of Independent Presbyterian was completed, thanks in good measure to the work of Deacon Percy and the other church officials.[90] The church building, constructed of Shades Mountain sandstone, reflected the English perpendicular style of Gothic architecture. The Percys would now drive over the mountain to church; moreover, such weekly trips allowed them to keep in contact with old friends. Yet in later years Walker would be at a loss to say whether Presbyterianism had any impact on his life.

The Senator made plans to go on a duck and prairie chicken hunt near Edmonton in Saskatchewan that fall with LeRoy.[91] It might have been sometime during one of these trips in the West that LeRoy took Walker to California, since Walker later referred to it: "The closest I ever got [to filmmakers] was when my father once took me to Hollywood as a boy, and I remember seeing Chester Morris driving down the street."[92]

In one photo from this period, young Walker, then ten years old and dressed in knickers and high-button shoes and wearing a striped tie and jacket, posed with his classmates and teachers at the entrance to Rhodes Park across from BUS.[93] The somewhat serious Walker seems to blend in comfortably with the other students and faculty looking intently into the camera. One can get a sense that the younger boys had many role models to look up to. The impression given by the photo is that Walker is among the youngest students at BUS.

In Greenville, disaster struck during the morning hours of April 21, 1927, as sirens warned that the levee had broken. The next day the flood-waters reached Greenville. Upriver from town, the 1,500 men and women who had piled up sacks against a raging current knew their efforts were futile. As Greenvillian Noel Workman explains: "The break spilled nearly 470,000 cubic feet of water per second into the Delta. Plantations became inland lakes."[94] Greenville became a city of makeshift boardwalks as the creeping waters hid the streets five feet down. People maneuvered lethargically in skiffs, and small boats and trains leaving Greenville were soon engulfed in the swirling waters. As chairman of the local committee of the Red Cross and as Mayor John Cannon's appointee to deal with the relief effort in Greenville, Will was in charge of rescuing 60,000 people and trying to save 30,000 head of livestock—and what was most disheartening, of trying to stop the looting that occurred. The whites were evacuated on boats and barges commandeered from the Standard Oil Company. Cam, the Senator, and their close friends Adah and Charlie Williams stayed to help as best they could. The problem centered on what to do with the 7,500 blacks, homeless and in need of funds and shelter and food. The Red Cross prepared a camp for them at Vicksburg, and plans were made for their exodus. Yet some announced that they did not want to leave, and they were supported by a group of planters. The Senator felt that if the Delta were depopulated of its blacks, there might be dire consequences. Not willing to be bullied by some blockhead planters, Will argued the opposite case with his father, but Will was overruled and the blacks stayed on. In June, the Senator served as chairman of the Resolutions Committee of the National Flood Control Convention in Chicago.

That summer was most likely Walker's first trip to Camp Winnepe in Eagle River, Wisconsin. Started in 1911, Winnepe normally had a regular session that went from the end of June to the end of August.[95] Coach Homer Thomas of Birmingham, along with four associates, was the director and manager. Bear Bryant, later the famous football coach at the University of Alabama, was one of the counselors. When the campers arrived at Eagle River, just south of Michigan's Upper Peninsula, after a

350-mile trip from Chicago, they hiked the three miles to the camp, which spread out over seventy acres. An older Walker reminisced about his summer trips to Winnepe and Chicago—and having his pocket picked:

I first used to stop here as a boy on my way to summer camp in Eagle River, Wisconsin—for three summers I think, ages 10, 11 and 12. A bunch of boys, twenty or thirty I guess, herded by the camp director, would board the Pullman in Birmingham, Alabama, in the afternoon, join another bunch from New Orleans in St. Louis and arrive the next morning in Chicago. The train for Wisconsin didn't leave until late in the afternoon. What to do with 50 or 60 boys? Well, it was always the same thing. Visit the stockyards in the morning and the Field Museum in the afternoon. The Field Museum I could see some reason for, though it was not exactly exciting and all I can remember is a tableau of a cave man crouched around an artificial fire. But I still wonder why it was thought educational to watch cattle and pigs get knocked in the head, strung up by their hind legs, their throats cut until the floor was running in blood.

Anyhow that was the invariable routine until some of us cut out and made excursions on our own. I remember, for instance, playing hooky and spending hours in Marshall Field's, which had the best model airplane department in the world. There were lovely flying scale models of World War I Spads, Sopwith Camels, Curtiss-Wrights suspended by thread, and you could buy kits, supplies of balsa wood, Japanese rice paper, airplane cement with its powerful banana oil fragrance. For me, unlike Proust, the past is recaptured not by tasting the piece of madeleine and tea but by smelling Marshall Field's airplane cement.[96]

In this same recollection, he said, "I recall being taken by my father for a swim in some vast cavernous place in downtown Chicago, perhaps the YMCA, perhaps an athletic club, and wearing a chain and disc around my neck. There is the recollection either that Johnny Weissmuller was there or at least that it was the pool where he trained for the Olympics before he became Tarzan." (In *The Moviegoer*, Binx Bolling recalls going through the Field Museum with his father.) It is not surprising Walker Percy would use Chicago as a place with a "genie-soul."

On October 5, much to the delight of all Birminghamians, *The Spirit of St. Louis* landed at Roberts Field in Birmingham, after Lindbergh's successful solo flight to Paris. More than 1,500 people gathered in the Municipal Auditorium, including Governor Bibb Graves, and Walker was one of the lucky persons to greet the hero; it was a thrilling experience for any boy that age. Looking back on his life, Walker Percy recalled this encounter and his own dream of achievement in the air: "At twelve, I wanted to fly the Pacific because Lindbergh had flown the Atlantic."[97] ("Lucky Lindy" made his way into *The Last Gentleman*.) Walker enjoyed building model airplanes, as he once said when asked by William Stage to identify his favorite toy. "That's easy. It was a model airplane that I made when I was twelve, a World War I Sopwith Camel. It was a flying model, too, made of Japanese rice paper and balsa wood with a wind-up propeller."[98] Though Walker loved model airplanes, he had a fear of real airplanes as an adult, sometimes traveling separately from other members of his immediate family.

When her mother became a widow in October, Mattie Sue made sure that she saw her grandchildren more often. Now there were signs that her husband had deep-seated problems of his own. About this time, young Robert McDavid Smith was out riding with his parents one Sunday afternoon and they stopped at the Percy house, where they saw LeRoy pruning roses. Robert noticed that the sleeves of Mr. Percy's white shirt almost concealed two bandages, one around each wrist. Mr. Smith inquired, "Roy, what happened to your wrists?" "I cut them picking up some glass," was the reply. Later Robert's father was told what had happened: "Mr. Percy tried to commit suicide." Robert also learned of another incident involving Mr. Percy that he believed to be true. Will Denson, who had a reputation as a mean-spirited lawyer, easily intimidated people inside and outside court. Once after a heated argument with LeRoy, the two decided to take their pistols to a secluded spot and, in an honorable Southern tradition, engage in a duel. When LeRoy warmed up by destroying pinecones that he had set up, his marksmanship made Denson realize he had better back off. LeRoy's Lawrenceville training had paid off in an unexpected way.[99] While away at Camp Winnepe, Walker was spared his father's attacks of anxiety, which seemed to become more frequent.

One day during the following June, as Cam Percy's health further declined, the Senator received a phone call from Mattie Sue. Her husband was showing signs of deteriorating mental stability, and she needed his advice. She thought LeRoy's bouts of depression dated at least from 1925, when he spent a few weeks at the Phipps Psychiatric Clinic at Johns Hopkins Hospital.[100] Given the Senator's and his wife's own bouts of ill health, his trip to Birmingham showed great love and compassion for LeRoy and his family. After his visit, a distraught Mattie Sue sat down and wrote a heartfelt letter of thanks on her husband's stationery:

Dear Uncle LeRoy—I wish I could half-way thank you enough for coming over. It helped us all *so much*. Today is the best day Roy has had. He has had no tenseness at all, in spite of "The Crouching Beast." I do feel so much better about him, every way. I will try so hard to get him to do what we agreed was the best. I hope Aunt Cam did not miss or need you very much while you were away. Please tell her how very much it meant to us to see you. Best love to you both. Yours with a lighter heart, Mattie Sue.[101]

The suicide of their forty-year-old father occurred while Walker and LeRoy were on vacation at Camp Winnepe. It took place on Tuesday, July 9, 1929, shortly after 11 a.m. He was shot by a charge from a 20-gauge double-barreled shotgun. Clothed only in his underwear, he had climbed the stairs to the attic, a small area above the central section of the house used mostly for storage. He had recently returned from a trip to French Lick, Indiana, a favorite resort of the Percy clan. The maid reported that Mr. Percy had been in bed that morning. As a matter of fact, she was searching for him when she heard the gun go off in the attic. Only she and little Phin, age seven, were in the house. They rushed upstairs and stood in amazement before the sprawled body of the father (Phin said he never retained a recollection of the event).[102] Mattie Sue was downtown shopping at the time of the shooting and did not reach home until 1 p.m.

When a call was made to Camp Winnepe, the two boys sadly packed up and the Rev. Randolph, a friend of the Percys, accompanied the boys back home. They undoubtedly arrived in Chicago on the Chicago & North Western train Number 12 on Wednesday, barely in time to take the 10:45 p.m. Illinois Central's overnighter *The Seminole*, arriving in Birmingham late Thursday afternoon. Even if they had taken Number 104 on Tuesday evening, they missed the Thursday morning funeral services at the Percy house on Ridge Drive.[103] When Robert McDavid Smith peered out the window of his house that day, he said he had never before seen so many elegant cars lining the neighborhood streets. Walker and his mother and brothers were now on their own and the pain of loss would never go away. For years, it was rumored that LeRoy's ghost inhabited the attic, and word had it that Dr. J. B. Rhine, the noted parapsychologist from Duke University, visited the Percy house years later to gather information.[104]

For Walker Percy the novelist, the death of the father figure in his novels is linked to Kierkegaard's notion of suicide. In actuality, Walker never saw his father in death. His father was alive when Walker went to Camp Winnepe and he never saw him again. In short, his father simply disappeared from sight forever. One book that Walker Percy treasured, and kept in his library, was the Gospel of St. John in the New-Century Bible edition given to him by his father.

If one accepts the premise that Binx reflects to some extent the life and thoughts of Walker Percy, then Binx's search for his father perhaps represents something deep within Walker Percy. In a draft of *The Moviegoer*, Percy portrays Binx's father in a most curious way.[105] Dr. Jack Bolling is described as a depressed "prophet," "the first postmodern man," a brilliant and sensitive man who also happens to be a drug addict; he came to New Orleans once and entered into some unspecified "interior pilgrimage" in what is described as a quest for death. Dr. Bolling finally dies of yellow jaundice during a hepatitis epidemic after being AWOL from the army and spending time in the Ozanam Inn on Camp Street in New Orleans. Binx's grandmother tells Binx that his father took instructions in Catholicism from Father Dansereau, who likewise shares some information about Dr. Bolling: "Yet he was one of the finest, most impressive men I ever knew. And we got along splendidly. He used to say that he took care of the body and Dr. Edmunds, the Episcopal minister, and I took care of the soul—even though I suspect he was somewhat ironical the way he said it." Binx, in turn, shares what he remembers about his father: "The time between the wars was a time when people knew that the old life was slipping away. They knew well enough that something was wrong but they thought it was a question of trying things to set it right again. My father's doctor told him to take up a hobby, so he bought a telescope and some German star maps and one night he triumphantly called the family outside to show us the great nebula in Andromeda. My grandmother read Alexis Carrel and Dr. Rhine and talked of the fascinating insights into the new psychology." Binx accepts his father's death with a good deal of equanimity. Of course, Walker Percy decided not to publish this material.

In the typescript of *The Last Gentleman*, Will Barrett reflects on his father; here, curiously, the portrait seems to be more William Alexander Percy than LeRoy Percy: "He, too, was a lawyer, a soldier, a brave and honorable man. But he was a very sad man. Yet he took some satisfaction in his sadness. He loved Brahms and the Gilbert Murray translations better than the law. He grew old very quickly. At forty-two, he had the arteries of an old man. I think he was glad to die."[106]

In a letter to Dr. Robert Coles, Walker Percy, after reading the typescript of Coles's extended profile of him, discusses the deaths of his paternal grandfather and father: "One thing I'm sorry about. I'm afraid I put an unwarranted crimp in your freedom to deal with my father's (and his father's) suicides, and the suicide scene in *The Last Gentleman*. I didn't mean to. Both events are matters of public record and I don't in the least mind you dealing with them as you wish . . . It's just that I do not myself advertise it ('Author chats about suicides in family, etc.').''[107] Walker told Coles that both his grandfather and father were manic-depressives.

The narrator in *The Second Coming* dramatizes an event in Will Barrett's life that seems to reflect more authentically Walker Percy's own search for his deceased father. The golf course only adds to this sense of authenticity: "As he searched for the ball deep in the woods, another off thing happened to him. He heard something and the sound reminded him of an event that had happened a long time ago. It was the most important event in his life, yet he had managed until that moment to forget it." The shooting by the father is put in the most dramatic context possible: "Only one event had ever happened to him in his life. Everything else that had happened afterwards was a non-event." In the crucial scene of recall, while father and son are out hunting, the father scolds the son for not placing the shotgun he had received for Christmas on the other side of the fence before going through it. Clearly the young Will is searching for affection from his father: "He couldn't remember being hugged before except at funerals and weddings, and then the hugs were perfunctory and the kisses quick cheek kisses and that was all right with him, he didn't want to be hugged or kissed then or now." In a moment of recognition, the father says that he and his son are "the same," dramatically implying that what happens to the father will also happen to the son—their fates are identical. When the boy hears a shot and realizes his father has been wounded, he rushes to his side and feels for his father's heart, which continues to beat strongly.

One version of this episode in the novel is that the father fell and accidentally discharged his gun.[108] Yet thirty years later, Will has an imaginary dialogue with his dead father about this event: there were actually four shells in his father's Winchester Super-X Greener: one that shot the quail, one supposedly meant for another quail that wounded young Will, one that wounded the father, and a fourth unspent one meant for Will. Because of this realization, Will is free because he knows the truth, and it is this knowledge that leads him to pass a judgment about his father's later suicide: "It dawned on him that his father's suicide was *wasted*. It availed nothing, proved nothing, solved nothing, posed no questions let alone answered questions, did nobody good. It was no more than an exit, a getting up and going out, a closing of the door." Will Barrett becomes determined, at this point, not to waste his life.

Walker Percy once wrote to me: "Will and I are somewhat alike though, in background and family and suicidal fathers—though mine didn't try to kill me."[109] Later in *The Second Coming*, Will finds release when he discovers the ecstasy of love with Allie: "And what samurai self-love of death, let alone the little death of everyday fuck-you love, can match the double Winchester come of taking oneself into oneself, the cold-steel extension of oneself into mouth, yes, for you, for me, for this, the logical and ultimate act of fuck-you love fuck-off world, the penetration and union of perfect cold gunmetal into warm quailing mortal flesh, the coming to end all coming, brain cells which together faltered and fell short, now flowered and flew apart, flung like stars around the whole dark world." [Question: "Do you ever feel that way?"] "No, I don't think so. In a way, I am Will Barrett, and in a way, I am also Allie. I think any novelist is in all of his characters; they are Jungian projections of himself."[110]

Bertram Wyatt-Brown believes that neither marital stress nor financial difficulties played a role in the father's desperate act; it should be noted that LeRoy committed suicide *before* the stock crash of "Black Tuesday," October 29, 1929.[111] Mattie Sue asked D. K. McKamy to be the administrator of her husband's estate and to rent out the house until she could make decisions about where to live. In early August she sold her husband's law books and in October their La Salle automobile. One can get some estimate of the size of the Percy estate from the probate records filed after Mattie Sue's death. She received as executrix of her husband's estate $44,757.46, from rent on the house and stock dividends and sale of stocks. In turn, she dispensed from the estate for taxes and bills a total of $73,862.17. The estate, for which no exact sum is listed but which must have been considerable, reimbursed her for $29,104.71. The estate of LeRoy Percy made the financial lives of Mattie Sue and her boys quite comfortable.[112] There was now little left to do; Mattie Sue sought temporary refuge in the only place she really knew as home. She moved with her three sons to Athens.

2

Athens and Greenville
1929–33

After her husband's death in the summer of 1929, Mattie Sue sought emotional and physical refuge with her three boys at the Phinizy home in Athens, a modest city trying to live up to its classical namesake. The county seat of Clarke County on the banks of the Oconee River, it had a population of roughly 21,000 and was considered a well-balanced community, due in large part to the efforts of Mayor A. G. ("Lon") Dudley. As the sixth-largest city in the state, Athens had a modest downtown facing the University of Georgia quad. One could enjoy four years of academic studies and then walk across Broad Street and become part of the business community and live on East Hancock Avenue or one of the other streets that skirted the campus.

When the four Percys arrived at 324 Milledge Avenue South, they were greeted affectionately by family and friends. In order to provide the boys with a routine and allow them to meet new friends, the two oldest were sent off to camp that summer. Senator Percy wrote from Greenville in mid-August with great concern to "My Precious Mattie Sue," apologizing for having the letter typed since his handwriting was so bad. He informed her of the latest news of the Greenville Percys: his son, Will, had left for a vacation at the north rim of the Grand Canyon, his wife, Camille, was a little bit stronger, and so on. He went on to counsel Mattie Sue about the agonizing decision she was facing:

You may have decided what you are going to do in regard to living in Athens or Birmingham and if you have come to a decision, don't let what I say in any way influence you to change it . . . Will is decidedly of the opinion that if you are happier in the surroundings at Athens that the difference so far as the boys are concerned is not enough to warrant you living in Birmingham. I go with him to this extent. If living in Birmingham is more difficult for you, if it means a greater burden of unhappiness, then remain in Athens. On the other hand, if you, having already been brave beyond words, can go back there and find your life's inspiration in planning for these boys and can carry on there, then I have the feeling that Birmingham will offer them more in the future than Athens. I am not fixed on this conviction because I am not familiar with Athens and what it might offer. Don't feel that you have to make an immediate decision and don't be governed absolutely by the feeling that it is necessary for you to sacrifice your own life for the boys.

I hope very much that within the next month or two I can get to see you. I want you to feel that it will always be a pleasure for me to hear from you and to advise with you about anything in the world, if you think my advice can be of any assistance. Write me about the boys when they get back from the camp and be sure and give them Will's and my love and try to get them in the habit of thinking about us.[1]

Will was back in Greenville in early September and discussed with his father Mattie Sue's situation, especially one point the Senator had not brought up: whether they should invite her and her boys to live in Greenville. To a certain extent, inviting them might not be in the best interests of the Senator's wife, since Camille needed rest and quiet about the house.

The daily lives of Walker and his brothers did not radically change after the move to Athens to be with their grandmother. The surroundings certainly were different, but not the social customs. The Phinizys were aristocratic Southerners whose lineage matched the Percys'. The name, originally Finicci or Finissi, traces its roots back to Ferdinand Victor François Phinizy, born in Parma, Italy, in 1760. He had traveled to France and in 1777 enlisted in the Regiment Gatanais as part of Lafayette's expeditionary forces.[2] The descendants of Ferdinand Phinizy established themselves firmly in Georgia society. Jacob Phinizy, for example, the fifth child of Ferdinand and Harriet Hays Bowdre Phinizy, became a prominent banker, farmer, businessman, and a leading citizen of Augusta, serving as mayor from 1901 to 1903 and becoming the seventh president of the Georgia Railroad & Banking Company.[3] When Walker arrived in Athens, Jacob had become a legend, and very much a part of the memory of Walker's cousin Laura Ann Phinizy. Before Jacob died in 1924, he sent his private railroad car to pick up Laura Ann and her parents, Martha and Barrett Phinizy, and talked to them from his big bed, as five bulldogs lounged about. Jacob's brother, Billups, Walker Percy's maternal grandfather, had married in 1886 Nellie Gretter Stovall, a native of Augusta.[4]

Nellie Phinizy, Walker's grandmother, was not in the best of health to greet Mattie Sue and the boys. She suffered from tic douloureux, which at one point prompted her to go to Boston, where Dr. Harvey Cushing operated on her. Walker often saw Grandmother Phinizy in her bedroom with something warm on her face, trying to cope with the pain, or sitting at her large rolltop desk writing letters, paying bills, and attempting to fulfill her husband's expectations. A stern Presbyterian who had a mind of her own, she would pray on her knees every night before going to bed, not read (or even use scissors) on Sunday, and would say "ain't" defiantly because she and others of her social class did so. Her attitude remained with Walker all his life: "There's something to be said for the Protestant ethic," he remarked. "You're supposed to be working at what you're fit to work at. Nothing wrong with that."[5] (Walker would later draw on his mother's family, and especially their Georgia Presbyterianism, as the inspiration for Tom More's wife, Ellen Oglethorpe.[6]) Grandmother Phinizy's relationship with her husband had been formal; in the old fashion, she called him "Mr. Phinizy" to his face as well as in polite company.

Grandfather Phinizy had his own mannerisms too. After breakfast, he would invariably pull out his watch, look at the time, and announce to those at table, "Make haste."[7] Once during a July Fourth weekend, Nell and Billups Phinizy Johnson, the daughter and son of Aunt Annie B. and her first husband, visited their grandfather and informed him they were competing in a swimming meet at the Cloverhurst Country Club. "O.K., do your best," he told Billups, and then called Nell aside and told her that he did not approve of girls appearing in public in the skimpy swimming suits they used at the meets. Nell reluctantly did not swim that day.

As a widow, Grandmother Phinizy relied heavily on her servants for assistance in managing the large house, occasionally delegating authority to Carlton, a black, whose drinking problem and gruffness sometimes made him unpopular with the three boys, though he was devoted to Grandmother Phinizy. In addition, Moina and another black woman, Mattie L. Marshall, worked as maids. A charming black woman just over five feet tall, Mattie started working for the Phinizys in the early 1920s, just after she had married and moved into her new house on Hancock Street.[8] She had a particular affection for young Phin because he was the smallest of the three Percy boys and clearly needed the most attention. Since Grandmother Phinizy did not like to drive the Packard herself, she relied mostly on a white chauffeur named Haynes (Haines is the chauffeur for the Grey family in *The Gramercy Winner*). Another servant, John

Houghton, described as an "ancient little Negro with dim muddy eyes and a face screwed up like a prune" in *The Last Gentleman*, and the son of a slave, worked as a gardener; he had been hired as the coachman but never learned to drive a car.[9] Once, when Grandmother Phinizy wanted to board her matched pair of horses at a particular stable, John Houghton cited a price she considered extravagant, so off he went again to negotiate with the stable owner, who finally agreed on five dollars a month. Later when Grandmother Phinizy wanted some manure for her garden, John Houghton was again dispatched to the stable. Grandmother Phinizy did not appreciate the stable owner's message: "Horses what is boarded for five dollars a month don't give no manure."[10] Much earlier, when his daughter Bolling was sick, Grandfather Phinizy found her sitting on John Houghton's lap in the kitchen; they were quietly eating corn bread and sipping "pot likker." "You're killing my daughter," Grandfather Phinizy said. "No," came the reply, "you're starving her to death—I'm *curing* her." In many ways, after Grandfather Phinizy's death, John Houghton ran the house as the primary male figure on the premises. Grandmother Phinizy occupied herself a good deal of the time by cultivating her flower beds, especially her lilies of the valley, and one of the first things Mattie Sue did when she arrived was to start a small flower garden on the south side of the house.

Sitting for hours on the front porch reading the fat Random House edition of *The Brothers Karamazov*, Walker watched his mother carefully tend her roses.[11] Now quieter and sadder than before among the people she had known all her life, Mattie Sue continued to grieve. Gradually, she put away her widow's black and would wear bright colors on occasion.[12] "Poor Mattie Sue" was the phrase that inevitably came to people's lips. Since Bolling Spalding avoided the beaches in summertime, she would take her children, Jack, Hughes, and Eleanor, for visits to Athens. On occasion, when he did not go to the Presbyterian Sunday school with Nell Johnson, Walker would accompany his Spalding cousins to Mass.[13]

As a newcomer in town, Walker made friends easily, one of whom was Edwin Southerland, who lived near the Phinizys.[14] Nearby lived the Barrett Phinizy family, and next to them, Will Erwin, son of Judge Alexander Erwin, a Stovall kinsman, who with his two brothers maintained a tennis court that was popular with everyone, young and old. It was here that Mattie Sue had learned to play tennis before she was married. Both Walker and Roy enjoyed the game, and so many players turned up on weekends that only foursomes were allowed to play. Laura Ann Phinizy, an outgoing, articulate girl related to Walker through Ferdinand Phinizy's second marriage, often dropped by Grandmother Phinizy's house to see her three cousins, sitting with them after dinner under the bright streetlight near the small wall that bordered Grandmother Phinizy's property. Laura Ann and Walker were the same age. She would sometimes join Walker and Roy and their friends to go to the movies at the Palace to see Rudy Vallee, John Barrymore, Constance Bennett, Joan Crawford, and Mary Astor on Saturday afternoons. They eagerly awaited the construction of the Strand, the new theater in town and the first to have piano playing between features.

Walker's other female cousin, Nell Johnson, was also part of the moviegoing group. A year and a half older than Walker, she had moved to Athens from Norfolk, Virginia, with her older brother Billups and their parents after Grandfather Phinizy had talked her father, Edward Hammond Johnson, formerly a baseball coach at the University of Georgia, into coming back to Athens to manage the Athens Manufacturing Company.[15] Among the Phinizy clan, Nell was always considered an endearing, outspoken person, with an acute memory and a total devotion to the University of Georgia and its football team. In commenting on Grandmother Phinizy, whom she called "Nana," and her five daughters, Nell said, "In Athens, the young ladies were trained to live in society. The Phinizy daughters all lived in a social whirl." Billups and Walker were friendly but never close (Billups was voted "most noisy" and "most mischievous" by his 1930 senior class[16]). After her husband's death, Annie B. remarried, this time to Josiah ("Uncle Joe") Billing. Walker knew her as a withdrawn, tubercular woman who spent most of her time resting in bed, cared for by Henny Lee Hattie.[17]

Walker started at Athens High School in September 1929, and it is clear he had an affection for the place. Though he could catch a streetcar in front of his house, he preferred to ride his bike to Athens High School, an imposing two-story stucco building with a large tower in the middle. Dolores Elizabeth Artau, a popular teacher at Athens High School when Walker and his brothers arrived, taught English, Spanish, and French.[18] She knew the Percy boys and also understood their special situation, as did the other teachers. Walker enrolled that year in five courses.[19] Roy also proved himself a good student, though his mark in science indicated that he might not follow exactly in Walker's footsteps. As his two brothers went in one direction, Phin left every morning to go in the opposite direction—to Miss Fowler's third-grade class at Barrow Elementary School. It was a long year for Phin, being in a separate school for 161 days (as noted on his report card) without his brothers, yet he weathered it well—A's in scholarship, conduct, and health.

Walker had little trouble adjusting to life in a new house. In many ways Walker's Aunt Louise, his mother's youngest sister, was like an older sister to him, Billups, Nell, Roy, and Phin. She was, after all, only ten years older than Walker, and because she was the youngest she had a governess, Miss Lawrence, who lived with the Phinizys. Wednesday nights were special, because all the family, whenever possible, would gather at Grandmother Phinizy's for dinner. Gradually, the rhythm of daily life became more constant, and a good deal of it centered on maintaining family contacts and fostering friendships.

Walker and LeRoy were avid fans of both the high school and university football teams. One of Walker's fondest memories of Athens was one day in the stadium when he had been flying a model airplane and it flew into the middle of a football scrimmage. Catfish Smith, the All-American end, brought it over to Walker and shook his hand.[20]

Just as the boys were adjusting to their new environment, Will's mother, Camille Percy, began a noticeable decline, having been stricken with paralysis, and died on October 7.[21] After the funeral, Will left with his father for the Springs Hotel in French Lick, Indiana, where he could find distraction from his mourning by correcting the proofs of his *Selected Poems*.[22] On the way home, the Senator suffered an attack of appendicitis in Memphis and was taken to Baptist Hospital, where he was operated on in early November.[23] Will planned to stay in Memphis until his father regained his strength, and hoped to be in Greenville for Christmas.[24] Yet this was not to be; after eight long weeks of decline, the Senator died in the hospital the day before Christmas.

The entry in the Ball Diary—kept by Henry ("Harry") Waring Ball of Greenville—for Christmas discusses the Senator's death and funeral: "He was unquestionably the leading man in this state, and one of the first in the South. There is no one to fill his place. The cemetery was a bog of half-melted snow, and the procession a mile long." Unable emotionally to stay in town after the funeral, Will sought solace with close friends in New York.

After the Senator's death, Mattie Sue retreated more and more into herself. She always remembered the thoughtful help the Senator had given her when her own husband died. The Phinizys and Percys were strong and their families had weathered difficult times before. Particularly in the months after the New York stock market crash at the end of October, it was painfully clear that these times were a prelude to a worldwide crisis. Though the Percys and Phinizys were economically well off, they knew that there could be a sudden and irrevocable change in their fortunes.

As the school year drew to a conclusion, Laura Ann, Nell, and their friends looked forward to the "proms" that were so popular. Wealthy families would entertain the younger set on Saturday evenings; records

were played as the boys in suits and girls in their prettiest dresses prom-
enaded back and forth on the sidewalks. Some would tease Walker and
his "sweetheart"—Martha Lee Allan. Other, more adventurous couples
might wander for an all too brief moment into the bushes. On Saturday,
May 17, Grandmother Phinizy, with the assistance of Mattie Sue and
Louise, gave a prom party expressly in Walker's honor at her house.[25]

At the explicit invitation of Will Percy, who visited Athens briefly,
Mattie decided to take her three sons to Greenville in early June.[26] Walker
never forgot Uncle Will's short visit. He would always consider Will's
generous invitation a key turning point in his life: "We had heard of
him, of course. He was the fabled relative, the one you liked to speculate
about. His father was a United States senator and he had been a decorated infantry officer in World War I. Besides that, he was a poet. The
fact that he was also a lawyer and a planter didn't cut much ice—after
all, the South was full of lawyer-planters. But how many people did you
know who were war heroes and wrote books of poetry? One had heard
of Rupert Brooke and Joyce Kilmer, but they were dead."[27] Walker's
recollected image of Will in the introduction for the new edition of *Lanterns on the Levee* was written over thirty years after Will's death. Is it an
accurate portrait of the real person Walker knew for twelve years? Will's
charming presence radiated through his "beautiful and terrible eyes"
that had a sad cast about them. Forty-five and gray-haired at the time
thirteen-year-old Walker first met him, he seemed both youthful and
terribly worldly. Recently Will had traveled to far-off Bora Bora. Will's
selfless offer to invite Mattie Sue and her boys to live with him in Greenville seemed normal to Walker. Only in retrospect did he realize that
Will had given up his bachelorhood and taken on the burdens of parenthood without the assistance of a spouse. "Will Percy not only did not
chuck anything; he shouldered somebody else's burden. Fortunately for
us, he did not subscribe to Faulkner's precept," Walker wrote, "that a
good poem is worth any number of old ladies—for if grandmothers are
dispensable, why not second cousins? I don't say we did him in (he
would laugh at that), but he didn't write much poetry afterwards and
he died young." Whatever Will lost or gained in the transaction, Walker
knew what he gained—"a vocation and in a real sense a second self,
that is, the work and the self which, for better or worse, would not
otherwise have been open to me." For her part, Mattie Sue considered
Will's gracious invitation a temporary one; she needed to know firsthand
whether or not she and the boys could adjust satisfactorily in a small
Delta city with relatives she trusted but did not really know.

The car carrying Mattie Sue and her boys arrived in Greenville on
a Sunday in early June.[28] Will had alerted Shelby Foote, then living on

Washington Avenue, that Walker would be visiting. The two boys soon became close friends.[29] Mattie Sue and the boys returned to Athens after spending June in Greenville. Once he said goodbye to his relatives, Will headed to New York, where he embarked on a trip to Morocco, Spain, and Portugal.[30] He wanted to be psychologically and physically refreshed when his new family joined him on a permanent basis. Walker and LeRoy joined Nell at the YMCA camp, which began in early July.[31] LeRoy loved to fish for bream and proudly displayed his catch for all to see. Mattie Sue took Phin to Dillard, Alabama, to stay with Annie B. in what proved to be a long, hot, and dry summer with the temperature climbing to 108 degrees in mid-July.[32] Phin also spent some time at a nearby camp; his main preoccupation was learning to swim. With the house empty, Grandmother Phinizy went to see the Spaldings in Atlanta.[33] Once summer camp let out, Mattie Sue took the boys and Nell in her coupe (they loved sitting in the rumble seat) to Brinkwood. She had to make a decision at this point, whether or not to move permanently to Greenville.

Walker slowly absorbed an entirely new environment when Mattie Sue and her boys moved to Greenville at the end of the summer of 1930—including the Mississippi River, the cutoff body of water later known as Lake Ferguson, and the expansive and fertile Mississippi Delta. Will Percy described it in *Lanterns on the Levee* as "our soil, very dark brown, creamy and sweet-smelling, without substrata of rock or shale . . . built up slowly, century after century, by the sediment gathered by the river in its solemn task of cleansing the continent and deposited in annual layers of silt on what must once have been the vast depression between itself and the hills."[34] The land does not drain into the river but tilts away from it. The Delta, Will noted, measures 196 miles from north to south and 50 miles across at its widest point. Other rivers and creeks—Rattlesnake Bayou, Quiver River, the Tallahatchie, and the Sunflower—meander about the countryside and eventually empty into the Yazoo. For Will, the big river had a haunting attraction, not only because of its savage nature and austere beauty but because it was remote and unaffected. Greenville, a thriving commercial center in the Delta, bustled with activity. It was far different from the rustic hill country of the state described in Faulkner's short stories. Aunt Bolling Spalding, on the other hand, had a different opinion of Greenville; she thought it was the ugliest city she had ever seen.[35]

A native scholar and writer, Charles G. Bell, once described Greenville, the Mississippi River, and the local Indian mounds as having a shared symbolic landscape.[36] The most sustained poetic view of the city in the 1930s, written by Bell in his masterly *Delta Autumn*, records an autobiographical journey back to the carefree days of adolescence in

Greenville, where he and Walker were friends and high school class-mates. Bell caricatures Walker as someone captivated by the apocalypse:

> *Walker has gone fanatic; he always reads*
> *The Book of Revelations; in the beasts*
> *He finds the symbols of atomic blast,*
> *He goes to all revivals, gets up to stand*
> *Crying: "Beware, our judgment is at hand."*

As a teenager, Walker wrote a poem about Greenville, entitled "Main Street on Saturday," that rivals Shelby Foote's "Beale Street" about Memphis.[37] His images and rhythms, characteristic of Jean Toomer and other writers influenced by jazz, capture the diversity of the town on the busiest day of the week.

When *The Married Land*, Bell's first novel in a projected trilogy, appeared in 1962, Walker wrote in his review: "Charles Bell is a good poet and the English language is his. At his command the words hop and spin like so many tops. No tentative constructions here, no first-novel spavins and jerks, no stretched and straining paragraphs; rather does the language do his bidding."[38] While Percy recognized more than he let on, he did indicate that the contrasting landscapes are "allegorical places, symbols for alternative dwelling places of the spirit." Yet the literary genius of this place that inspired Bell's work might not have been as benign as Percy infers. When the second volume, entitled *The Half Gods*, appeared in 1968, he chose not to review it. And for good reason: Charles Bell, partially appropriating the persona of Walker Percy himself, had integrated a good bit of the Percy family history and folklore into his novel. Percy felt his privacy had been breached, in a way that could not be recouped, by someone he admired. When Robert Coles mentioned to Percy that he had interviewed Bell, Percy exploded at the mention of the name, no doubt still harboring some residual anger about this novel.[39] After Percy read the galleys, he specifically requested that his name not be mentioned in the acknowledgments. It was quite clear that he did not want to be associated with the novel in any way.[40] Its most poignant and upsetting sections deal with death and suicide, particularly the slightly disguised passage depicting the suicide of LeRoy Percy in Birmingham:

That day I walked up to the screen porch, just there, I heard a shot that rang through the walls. There was a scream and the sound of a body threshing. The world of vision opened. I saw into the house like a stage. It was the attic. The body of a man was lying with one shoe off, far back under the eaves . . . Until then I didn't know how your father died, only what was in the papers—though they called it suicide.[41]

When Bell's own father, Judge Percy Bell, an important figure in Greenville society, was dying of emphysema and an enlarged heart, and did not want to spend his final days and weeks in a vegetative state, he committed suicide with a gun that Charles had brought him as he lay wan and exhausted in the King's Daughters Hospital in Greenville.[42] Thus Walker Percy had a kindred spirit in the person of Charles Bell, and from different perspectives, both men dramatized in their fiction how suicidal fathers dramatically alter the lives of their sons.

But for Walker, William Alexander Percy *was* Greenville, and that made all the difference. What Uncle Will offered Walker, his two brothers, and his mother—and their friends who came to the imposing house on 601 Percy Street—was his writing and speaking out about what he considered important topics. "It was to encounter," as Walker wrote, "a complete, articulated view of the world as tragic as it was noble. It was to be introduced to Shakespeare, to Keats, to Brahms, to Beethoven— and unsuccessfully, it turned out, to Wagner whom I never liked, though I was dragged every year to hear Flagstad sing Isolde—as one seldom if ever meets them in school." Will gave Walker a totally new perspective on life through the tales of Marcus Aurelius and the poetry of Browning and Gluck's *Orfeo* and Viola's speech about frustrated love in *Twelfth Night*: "Make me a willow cabin at your gate,/And call upon my soul within the house . . ." Walker would listen intently and catch the spirit and beauty of what he heard and root it in his memory. Will felt imaginatively exhausted, however, by the deaths of his parents and remarked in a 1930 newspaper interview, "I can see no more poetry."[43] Because Walker listened intently to what was said to him, it is no wonder that he developed a keen interest in the origins and structure of language; above all, Walker's interest in language led him to explore the relationship between the written and spoken word and the worlds that words embody.

Though he would come to hold divergent views from Will, especially concerning politics, religion, and certain aspects of relations between blacks and whites, Walker defended in general Will's opinions because of the convincingly informed and philosophic stances that Will took. Will idolized President Franklin Delano Roosevelt.[44] Even if Will "was regarded in the Mississippi of his day as a flaming liberal and 'nigger-lover' and reviled by the sheriff's office for his charges of police

brutality," Walker would brush that aside. He believed, as he once explained to a Japanese scholar, that his uncle had a "class obligation" to
help the blacks.[45] Will, with all his mannerisms—"the quirk of the
mouth, the shadowed look, the quick Gallic shrug, the inspired flight of
eyebrows at an absurdity, the cold Anglo-Saxon gaze"—gave Walker, as
a boy, the enormous freedom to develop and grow.

Yet Walker had no intention of being Will's clone or entering into
the shady groves of a long-lost Stoa. Once when Will read aloud the
section of the fight between Richard and Saladin in *Ivanhoe*, for example,
Walker instinctively identified with Saladin because he knew Will favored Richard. Will was considered by his peers as someone who integrated a love of poetry with an ability to assume difficult tasks and bring
them to completion.

In his 1941 book Will gives his own unadorned account of the advent of his cousins: "My favorite cousin, LeRoy Percy, died two months
before Mother's death, and his brave and beautiful wife, Mattie Sue Phinizy, two years after Father's. Their three boys, Walker, LeRoy, and Phinizy, came to live with me and I adopted them as my sons. Walker was
fourteen, LeRoy thirteen, and little Phin nine. Suddenly my household
was filled with youth, and suddenly I found myself, unprepared, with
the responsibility of directing young lives in a world that was changing
and that seemed to me on the threshold of chaos." Having survived one
war, Will during the 1930s reflected the pre-World War II mentality that
assessed Western civilization with great gloom, sometimes crudely: "For-
nicating like white trash is one thing, but leave it to this age to call it
the New Morality."

As Hodding Carter, Jr., wrote of Will: "Ever since the poor whites
began swarming into the Delta, Will Percy was unsure of the future."[46]
Walker would wonder about Will's views and sometimes quiz him.
(Walker's quiet and endearing habit of questioning people about their
views remained with him throughout his life.) Yet, no matter the response Will gave, Walker was reluctant to criticize Will because he
admired him so. It did not take long for Walker to begin to realize
under Will's tutelage that the South had been victorious in many ways
and had coped with shifts of power that few Northern liberals understood.

No matter how kind Will was toward the newly arrived Percys, their
presence was bound to upset his world and tether him to particulars he
would have preferred to avoid. It was the acceptance of this limitation
on his freedom that Walker most admired about Will. Given all the sociological arabesques and scenarios that one might create, however,
Walker always felt that Will "was the most extraordinary man" he had

ever met, and though he did not use the word "love" in this context, Walker always felt he owed Will an unpayable debt.

The boys did not take long to settle in. Walker described Will's house as a type of "the bastard Greek Revival popular in the late 1880s, a tall, frame, gabled pile with a portico and two-story Ionic columns."[47] The house he saw had been altered by Camille Percy; it was now "stuccoed" with a balcony over the main entrance, plus two additions—a large porte cochère on the Broadway side and a sun parlor on the opposite. Will's friend David Cohn once described the house as one in which Moroccan rugs, Mexican wood screens, Japanese paintings, Victorian bric-a-brac, old-fashioned mahogany furniture, and brass beds all somehow achieved a harmony that defied analysis.[48] Walker delighted in riding the elevator and roaming the vast dusty attic filled with spiked German helmets, binoculars, Springfield rifles, cartridge belts, puttees, and bayonets. Phin was mystified by an aluminum leg he found in the attic. On the roof there was a widow's walk from which one could see for miles in any direction. Since the house had no round towers or turrets, as did others of the same period, it seemed from the outside like an enormous box. There was a saving grace in the tall windows that provided the natural light that brightened the somber building.

On the first floor, the living room boasted an expensive gold silk couch, an imposing Capehart (a huge phonograph that played—and automatically *turned over*—"78 rpm records"), an extensive record collection, statues of Lorenzo de' Medici in bronze and Venus in marble, a bust of Dave Cohn done by Epstein, and in the back an exceptionally well-stocked library. Will had a fondness for Wagner and Beethoven, though he also liked Ravel and Debussy; his record collection ran the gamut from Bach, Haydn, and Mozart to Prokofiev, Shostakovich, and Bloch.[49] The formal dining room faced Broadway, the kitchen was on the back side, and upstairs were three suites with bathrooms in between. There was also a single bedroom, in addition to a large glassed-in area that served as a perfect sleeping porch on hot summer nights. The boys lived, dormitory style, in one of the two bedrooms on the back side of the house; Mrs. Percy, sometimes joined by Phin, lived in the other half of the suite. These were the quarters that Will's mother once used. Will originally had one of the suites upstairs, but eventually moved to the first floor.[50]

Uncle Will, in a gesture of goodwill that conflicted with strongly negative feelings, hired Lige Collier to work in his prized formal garden. Lige, who had come over from Birmingham and lived above the garage, provided continuity in the boys' lives. They liked Lige's uninhibited qualities and his frankness; this small, wiry, gray-haired man with good humor kept a careful eye on his charges. Will knew that he could continue to count on Holt, an ex-slave who had accompanied the Senator on hunts. The Percys also relied on two huge women, Arciel ("Ar-seal") Ross, a cook and maid, and Louisa ("Lou-eye-ser") Atkins, the mother of Ford ("Fode") and the presiding genius of the kitchen, whom Will called the "Queenly Woman." When she became overbearing and, in Dave Cohn's mind, slovenly in her role as cook, Will laid down the law, but to no avail. Will eventually fired her and replaced her with Theresa, who remained as long as Will lived. At different times, there was a series of chauffeurs: Milton, Ernest Jones, and Fode, whom Walker considered a rapscallion, but charming enough.

Outside the big house on Percy Street, Will kept up as best he could an aging tennis court and a small formal garden with irises, azaleas, blue Spanish scilla, bleeding hearts, and prize roses. A wrought-iron gate prevented the neighborhood children from trampling the flower beds, and Will welcomed the garden club ladies who came to share their horticultural secrets.

It did not take long for Walker to make friends. Shelby Foote, though slightly younger than Walker, became a regular visitor to the Percy household. Will liked Shelby and thought he would make a good companion for Walker, even though he was a year behind Walker in school. Before the Percy boys arrived, Will said to him, "Shelby, I have three kinsmen coming. And I would appreciate your helping entertain them. I hope you'll come over and see them as often as possible." To which Shelby replied, "Mr. Will, I'll be glad to." This short reply would change Shelby Foote's life. During his high school days, Shelby lived with his widowed mother, aunt, and uncle in a stucco house not far from Greenville High.

Walker showed up for school on the first day of class wearing knickers, high-laced shoes, and no socks, definitely a gauche thing to do, according to Sarah Farish, who entered that day as a freshman. Walker began taking the usual courses for sophomores planning to go to college—English with Miss Julia Sheldon, math and science with Mr. Edward Lueckenbach, history with Miss Kathleen McBrayer, Latin with Miss Mary Moss, and physical education with Coach Murphy. Yet one teacher stood out above the rest. Though not a great scholar, Miss Louise E. Hawkins gave her students a love for literature, especially for Shakespeare. Like Shelby, Walker enjoyed memorizing Shakespearean sonnets in Miss Hawkins's class: "It might sound like a bad thing to do, but it worked out rather well. She had a real love for it."[51] When Shelby, who once declared that he was a genius and could do anything he wanted, made a B in her class for some assignment, she changed it to C because he should have made an A.[52] Another time, Shelby went to her room in the boardinghouse where she lived and was amazed to see the meagerness of her living quarters. Walker sang Miss Hawkins's praises in a dramatic high school essay entitled "Grammar at the Crossroads."

LeRoy, a year behind Walker, would accompany his brother to school, and their school lives often intersected. Though close, the boys were very different temperamentally; sometimes friction would occur, much to the annoyance of their mother. Feeling initially detached from his older brothers, Phin entered fourth grade at Central School on Broadway; he went there until he changed to E. E. Bass Junior High for his seventh and eighth grades.

As the academic year started, students read that "Waker" Percy was among the five new freshmen (sic), and that LeRoy and his brother had already started playing tennis, often with their friends on the court adjacent to the Percy house.[53] At this time, Walker took an interest in writing, and even claimed credit for starting Shelby's career as a writer: "I remember we started out in the same study hall at Greenville High School. At the time, I was writing poetry, verse, for a high school class. I got very proficient. The teacher would assign sonnets, and I would crank out a sonnet and sell it for fifty cents. Everybody had to write a sonnet, so . . . Shelby saw me writing poetry, so I really take credit for launching Shelby on his literary career."[54] Walker did not actually sell any of his poetry to Shelby, who was emerging as an accomplished writer in his own right. He did write several poems for Margaret Kirk, who received high marks for them in English class. Unlike Shelby, it never occurred to Walker during his first days in high school that he might become a professional writer.[55]

If Walker had any doubts as the school year began about the standing of the Percy family in Greenville, his fears would be allayed in October. Since Will was anxious that his father be remembered in a fitting way, he commissioned sculptress Malvina Hoffman, author of *Sculpture Inside and Out* (1939), to design a medieval knight in armor, called *The Patriot*, to be placed over the grave of Senator Percy.[56] This statue stands upright with his arms crossed in front of him, resting on a long sword. A sunburst etched into the stone behind him gives the impression that the knight is standing in front of a theater curtain. The back of the stone bears these words from Matthew Arnold's "The Last Word":

> *They out-talked thee, hissed thee, tore thee?*
> *Better men fared thus before thee;*

> Fired their ringing shot and passed,
> Hotly charged—and sank at last.
>
> Charge once more, then, and be dumb!
> Let the victors, when they come,
> When the forts of folly fall,
> Find thy body by the wall!

It was a flamboyant tribute on Will's part. He encouraged artists whenever he could, including Leon K. Koury, born in Greenville, a son of Syrian immigrants. He started sculpting when Will made him a gift of fifty pounds of clay.[57] Koury, later a student of Hoffman in New York, was noted for his impressive statues and busts, including those of Will Percy, William Faulkner, and Hodding Carter, Jr. Knowledgeable about the small homosexual community in Greenville, Koury considered Uncle Will a closet homosexual, and others who held the same opinion about Will did not talk about it in public. It is highly unlikely the three boys ever knew of this.

When Mattie Sue returned from Athens in late November from the wedding of her sister Louise and Thomas Tillman, she brought Grandmother Pratt Percy to Greenville.[58] The Phinizys were delighted that Bolling's new son, Billups Phinizy, was in good health. Will's widowed aunts, Nana Pearce and Lelia Warren, also returned to Greenville to become reacquainted with the Percy boys.[59] Walker was surprised to find out that Aunt Nana, a cute and peppy woman, seemed to speak better French than she did English. On occasion she would tutor Phin, thus creating the only Francophile among the Percy boys. Once she read to Shelby the section of Thomas Mann's *The Magic Mountain* that is written in French. The boys delighted in hearing her speak to her cat in French and at Brinkwood asking for her *petit déjeuner*. Aunt Lelia would often resort to mannered expressions, for example, describing people she did not like as being "common as a pig's something or other." (The fourth aunt, Rita, would join the gathering on occasion with her husband, Thomas E. Mount.) "The Aunts," as they were called, came most Sundays for dinner (though Aunt Nana was a good cook in her own right) and were always part of the extended Percy family.

It was customary on these Sundays for Will, often with Walker, to retire at two o'clock to listen to classical music. Will had little affection for twentieth-century music, like Stravinsky's *Le Sacre du Printemps*. Once while sitting on the Percy porch listening to the radio with Uncle Will and Walker, Mozart's *Eine Kleine Nachtmusik* came on; Shelby was overwhelmed by the beauty of it. Walker and Shelby would listen on their own to jazz or the music of Bing Crosby and Kay Starr. "Now, Mr. Will," Shelby once said, "you have to listen to this—a song called 'If I Could Be with You'." Will listened and was asked, "Did you like it?" "She sounds like a whore," Will replied.[60]

Because of the presence of Mattie Sue and the aunts, it might seem that the senior members of the Percy household were women, and to a great extent this was true. Yet there were always male friends who would come to stay, sometimes for extended periods. Robert Horton, a door-to-door salesman for Staff of Life Feed and esteemed as a former football player for the University of Tennessee, lived with the Percys. He impressed Walker with his agility, especially when he put on his socks while standing straight up. After he married an Olympic broad jumper, he and his bride would often join the Percys for Sunday dinner. That fall, too, Will's friend Dave Cohn came to town to visit.[61] Cohn, who lived in an upstairs bedroom for two years, became symbolic in Walker's mind of the openness of the Percy household. Phin, on the other hand, often thought the house resembled a hotel.

Dave Cohn, a graduate of Greenville High School, the University of Virginia, and Yale, moved to New Orleans, where he managed the Feibleman department store. In 1930, when the firm merged with Sears, Roebuck, Cohn felt drawn to make some changes in his life, perhaps due in part to the influence his literary friends—Lyle Saxon, William Faulkner, Oliver La Farge, Sinclair Lewis, Ben Wasson, Hodding Carter, Jr., Roark Bradford, and of course Will Percy. After he retired, Cohn moved back to Greenville. "Oh, Dave, Greenville is the most peaceful place on the earth," Mattie Sue had once exclaimed, just as two gunshots were heard outside the window. "Oh, Dave, I take that back."[62] Cohn, like Uncle Will, demonstrated to Walker that it is possible to have a career, gather information, and yet write over an extended period of time and see the results published as a book. The Percy boys remembered Cohn walking up and down the hall, smoking a cigar, and scratching his head as he pondered material for his first book, published in 1935 as *God Shakes Creation*. (It was later reissued in expanded form as *Where I Was Born and Raised*.[63]) One of the people Cohn consulted while writing this book was Hortense Powdermaker, the sociologist then doing research in Indianola for her book *After Freedom: A Cultural Study in the Deep South*. Cohn sometimes took Phin rabbit hunting down in the "burrow pits" by the Mississippi. His two-year presence in the house clearly made a lasting impression on all three Percy boys. In retrospect Cohn regarded his friend Will, whom he describes as "a lawyer, soldier, planter, poet, traveler, Roman Catholic worker, Rotarian, gardener, and bachelor parent to three adopted sons," as someone who derived his earthly nourishment from "an insubstantial world of light and air."[64] Yet Cohn also portrayed him as an eighteenth-century gentleman and as "the loneliest man I ever knew." Cohn eventually prompted Will to write his memoirs and trace the inner and outer struggles that had made his life so remarkable. Though Cohn's *God Shakes Creation* and Will's *Lanterns on the Levee* cannot be considered mirror images of each other, they nevertheless have much in common.

Walker quickly sensed that the commercial, intellectual, and social life in Greenville was different from what he had known in Birmingham and Athens. For one thing, it was all compactly located in one small area, making it easy to explore. The regular layout of the town as it fanned out on the east bank of the Mississippi—that is, on the east bank of Lake Ferguson—meant that Walker could go anywhere he wanted by either walking, cycling, or taking the streetcar for five cents. Lake Ferguson had been created when the waters of the Mississippi were diverted away from town. Running parallel to the lakeshore and the imposing levee were Broadway and Theobald Street. Washington Avenue and Main Street, the two principal streets, began at the levee and ran perpendicularly away from it as they moved eastward and then southward until they eventually converged. South of Main Street and running parallel with it were Central and Percy Streets. Intersecting Main Street at right angles leading away from the levee and going toward Broadway were Walnut, Poplar, Shelby, and Hinds Streets. And clustered in the central part of this grid were the important banks, stores, and other buildings. The centrally located city library, presided over by Miss Amanda Worthington, was close to the Presbyterian and Catholic churches.

The large and medium-sized houses of the whites were located along both Washington Avenue and Main Street and tended to be in the southern and eastern parts of town. As in most small towns in the South in the 1930s, the blacks lived in their own community, and except for gatherings at funerals, whites dealt with them mostly in kitchens. In all sections of Greenville, black and white, it was common knowledge that Will Percy, in good weather and bad weather, would receive whoever came to see him. Given the mores of the time and the social standing of the Percy family, Walker did not have either black playmates or black classmates while living in Greenville, but this does not mean that he would not ask a key question at the very heart of a segregated society —how could a small Southern community, with the aristocracy going to seed, the poor whites on the rise, and the blacks eking out an existence survive together by relying on the soil as the only means of livelihood?

Greenvillians of all ages and races knew very well what was going on beyond the boundaries of their neighborhoods.

In addition to a Chinese-American population (the second-largest concentration in the South, according to Hodding Carter, Jr.) greater Greenville had a considerable number of Italians who had been imported earlier to work the large plantations, particularly across the Mississippi.[65] The Jewish community, in this backwater of Protestantism, was both well integrated and influential. As one Mississippi writer who lived in Greenville expressed it: "These are people who are deeply interested in the humanities, the arts, political freedom, and surviving."[66] Jews had arrived in Greenville shortly after the Civil War from Russia, Poland, Germany, and a few from Alsace. They worked hard in lowly jobs like peddling until over the years some became plantation owners, bankers, lawyers, and merchants. In 1864 Morris Weiss from Prussia opened up his store at "Blantonia," and by the following year Greenville was created out of this property, thanks in large part to Harriet Blanton Theobold, Blanton's widow. Gradually men with names like Gunsberger, Witkowski, Morris, Landau, Pohl, Moyse, Goldstein, and Alexander came into prominence. Another well-known Jew, Joseph Weinberg, owned the Weinberg Building, where Nelms & Blum was located and where Senator Percy and Will had their law office on the fourth floor.[67] Though many of the Jews gradually assimilated into their neighbors' lifestyles, their corporate presence in Greenville made a lasting impression on young Walker and planted the seeds of his abiding interest in the relationship between Judaism and Christianity. It would be one of the problems that Percy would try to deal with all his life, as he wrote in *Lost in the Cosmos*: God "is somehow inextricably and permanently, even hopelessly, involved with the two, the Jews and the Catholic Church, until the end of the earth."

Out of the Jewish milieu in the Delta emerged one of the city's most important teachers, Caroline Stern, born in 1868 in Arcola, Mississippi. After her family moved into a house on Union Street, Miss Carrie began teaching the fifth grade; she was only sixteen. Encouraged by Eli Everett Bass, the superintendent of schools, she studied art in New York, and on her return to Greenville, she helped organize the first public school art course in Mississippi. She became an Episcopalian for a while and took to consulting the Ouija board for spiritual guidance. In 1916 Miss Carrie published a book of poems, *At the Edge of the World*. All soul and heart, fragile as glass, Miss Carrie encouraged the intellectually inquisitive, like Dave Cohn, who brought along lawyer Will Percy, to ponder the secrets of English and Italian poetry. Miss Carrie became Will's "favorite friend." Her death in 1920 left a void for those who knew and loved her, though her memory is still alive in the Greenville community.[68] Love of writing, poetry, and fiction, Miss Carrie's heritage, could easily be discerned in *The Pica*, a school newspaper named after the magpie (not the typographic measure), published during the 1930–31 school year under the editorship of Billy Keady, a star pupil in his fourth consecutive year as class president.[69]

Though he tried unsuccessfully to publish a short story in *Liberty* magazine when he was ten, Walker made his writing debut in 1930 in *The Pica*, with an unsigned humorous article on the life of Percy Castereign-Percy.[70] His second piece, "The Passing of Arthur," which appeared in October and was reprinted a year later, concerned King Arthur and the sword Excalibur; it would indirectly provide the title for his fourth novel. Walker had made a beginning as a writer, but being a new student, he would have to wait for more of his work to be accepted. In these years, he loved to build model airplanes, such as the open-cockpit Spad or the Sopwith Camel, which he constructed out of Japanese rice paper and balsa wood and flew by means of a windup propeller, and once gave Shelby a model of a Sopwith Camel he had built.[71] One of his masterpieces was the Lockheed Winnie Mae flown by the ill-fated Wiley Post. (Percy once reminisced to Foote, "I used to make ghostly spiritual but flyable Lockheed Vegas and you used to make solid, structurable, admirable, perfect, unflyable P-51's."[72]) Walker delighted in reading the comics, especially Scorchy Smith, Gloria, Homer Hoopee, and Rollo Rollingstone, whose first name later would be one of Walker's nicknames.[73] He also enjoyed studying Wilson's three-volume *American Ornithology*, which gave him an abiding interest in watching birds and imitating their songs.

The younger set amused themselves in the early weeks of the fall by going to the Paramount Publix at the corner of Washington Avenue and Broadway and to the Grand on Main Street. In the beginning of December the Paramount featured *Tom Sawyer*, Will Rogers in *Lightnin'*, and Marlene Dietrich in *Morocco*. Walker started attending the movies almost every week; years later he thought that he had seen just about every film that passed through Greenville, sometimes more than two movies a week. The logistics were relatively simple; of the fifty cents one took to school, only ten cents was spent on soup for lunch; and then if one skipped out on the last-period study hall, one could see a matinee for thirty-three cents and have enough left over for a candy bar. As the main character in Walker Percy's unpublished story "Confessions of a Movie-goer" says, "I cannot say whether I am as I am because I have been going to the movies all my life and have become like the movies, or whether it is that the movies are like me. It doesn't matter. There is a deep kinship between us."[74] Like his peers, Walker would have received numerous invitations for Christmas teen dances at the Elks Club (known for its great poker games), the Legion Home, and the Elysian Club, which had a ballroom upstairs. Despite a sense of normalcy that was beginning to establish itself in Walker's life, his grades at the end of the semester—B in plane geometry, C in English, C in physics, and C in Latin—were lackluster.

In a small, tight-knit community, relationships between girls and boys, rarely overtly sexual in nature, were taken for granted. Walker's male friends tended to date Elizabeth and Sarah Farish, Maria Hilliard, Caledonia Jackson, Martha Dyer, Margaret England, Joyce Neal, and Margaret Kirk. And it was not uncommon for young men and women of different ages to socialize with one another. A favorite routine for this group was to go to the Neals' on Friday night and the Farishes' on Saturday night.[75] Walker sometimes dated Ruth Wasson of the class of 1935, much against Uncle Will's advice; Will felt that Ben Wasson, Ruth's formidable brother, who was a friend of Faulkner, might not approve.[76] Walker also liked Mary Jane Carney and Camille Sarason, one of the more popular girls, who was a year ahead of him in school and perhaps a model for Ethel Rosenblum in *The Last Gentleman*.

Walker's steady girlfriend, however, was Margaret Kirk (with whom, he once mentioned in a letter to Charles Bell, he never "made any time" at all). Her family had a plantation north of Greenville and had moved to Main Street after her grandfather died. Margaret, a stunning young woman according to her contemporaries, with a good deal of self-possession, visited the Percy house with Walker, something that was a bit of a rarity for young women in those days. She even referred to Will Percy, a friend of her mother, as "Uncle Will."[77] She and Walker would go to the Fountain Terrace for Cokes, and on an occasional Sunday to St. James Episcopal Church. They made a fine couple and were well matched, though they always remained a bit formal. Walker said, "Margaret was my real girlfriend, who was almost not approachable. I was lucky just to take her to the movies."[78] He once wrote to Shelby about Margaret: "You have to admit she was a looker. I can afford to tell you now that I was never allowed a single kiss, not even a little peck on the cheek—even after a $25 corsage."[79] During the fall and winter vacations, Walker and Margaret would be among those driving to dances (sometimes without chaperones) at Rosedale, Indianola, Cleveland, Clarksdale, and Greenwood, among other towns in Mississippi.

For Will, the return of the students to school in January meant that he could resume his usual round of legal business, a boring task for him and one he willingly relinquished to his partners, D. S. Strauss and Ernest Kellner, Jr. He would rather engage in something that gave him more pleasure, like reading the works of Robert Frost, Conrad Aiken, T. S. Eliot, Edna St. Vincent Millay, and Emily Dickinson with a local study group.[80]

By this time, the Percys were becoming accustomed to constant visitors and guests in the house. Mattie Sue and the boys had a chance to meet poet and biographer Carl Sandburg when he came to lecture and stay at the Percy home. He delighted the family, including Shelby, by playing a guitar and singing ballads for hours.[81] Stark Young, Stephen Vincent Benét, Roark Bradford (who wrote the foreword to Will Percy's *Collected Poems*), and Vachel Lindsay also stayed with Will Percy. Will had a close literary correspondence with DuBose Heyward after Heyward's poem "Fragments" received an award in the 1923 Poetry Society of South Carolina contest.[82] On the other hand, he recoiled against H. L. Mencken's contempt for the South. Dave Cohn once accompanied Dorothy Thompson and Raymond Gram Swing to visit Trail Lake, the Percy plantation south of Greenville, as part of their research on sharecropping.[83] Miss Thompson even stayed with the Percys for a few days, sipping old-fashioneds with Will, talking about gardening, and enjoying each other's company. Langston Hughes gave a reading at St. Matthew's AME Church in February 1932; Will introduced the invited guest to an audience of both blacks and whites.[84] When Jonathan Daniels visited Greenville, he spent a wonderful few days visiting Will, Roark Bradford, and Dave Cohn.[85] Will was also good friends with Gerstle Mack, a handsome man who had written biographies of Toulouse-Lautrec, Cézanne, and Courbet, as well as chronicling the 1906 San Francisco earthquake and fire. Walker, according to Shelby, once had a strong but passing interest in the works of El Greco and Velázquez.[86]

By this time Mattie Sue felt comfortable in her new environment and made a small circle of friends. One indication, however, of how quietly Mattie Sue behaved in those days is that Margaret Kirk never retained any memory of her, though she could recall the aunts. Sarah Farish has a lingering memory of Mattie Sue and thought her beautiful, but sad and haunting. "She wasn't really active in any social life," Sarah said. "She was still grieving." Mattie Sue grew close to Adah Williams, a Catholic and the vivacious wife of Charles Williams, and would sometimes join Mitchell Finch, Will's competent secretary and a top-flight golfer, and others for an evening of bridge.[87] The Ball Diary recorded her presence, along with Nana Pierce and Rita Mount, at an afternoon tea: "We all like young Mrs. LeRoy Percy very much."[88]

Though Walker's mother would sometimes encourage the boys to go to the Presbyterian Sunday school, they stopped going once there was no pressure to do so. Walker simply found these classes boring. "Walker knew from the start that neither Presbyterianism nor the Episcopal Church had the answers for him."[89] In fact, he considered himself are-ligious. Will, who once professed Roman Catholicism, maintained a certain affection for it; after his mother's death, he commissioned a bas-relief of a child touching a mother's medal for St. Joseph's Church.

Walker looked forward to the completion of the new Greenville Country Club that was moving farther out of town. As he had in Birmingham, he played golf in Greenville; it was the one sport he would play until the end of his days. He could also spend hours at the movies; toward the end of February, the Paramount featured Al Jolson in *Big Boy*, Greta Garbo in *Inspiration*, Gary Cooper in *Fighting Caravans*, and Edward G. Robinson in *Little Caesar*, followed by Bela Lugosi in *Dracula*.

Whereas Walker was studious and seemed to prefer his privacy, LeRoy, never shy and more robust than Walker, ventured out of himself more, due to his developing friendship with the spunky and attractive Sarah Farish. The two were so drawn to each other that Uncle Will worried the relationship might hinder LeRoy's schoolwork. Walker and Sarah both delighted in LeRoy's good nature and sense of fun and largesse. When the English classes of Misses Sheldon and Lillian McLaughlin joined forces to act out a rendition of Brutus attacking the State of Rome, Shelby, in the role of an attorney, played opposite LeRoy's Brutus. The latter was eventually acquitted, much to the delight of the other classes who attended the performance.[90] Will could be fairly direct when it came to planting seeds about the education of his charges after high school. In an interview with Will printed in an April issue of *The Pica*, Billy Francis wrote: "Mr. Percy thinks the University of North Carolina is one of the liveliest universities he knows, with a very strong English department that is accomplishing something."[91] Will apparently was thinking this early about directing the three boys toward different but honorable professions in the South—medicine, plantation farming, and the military—and he was dropping hints in ways that were not so subtle. At the end of the school year, *The Pica* was judged to be the best high school paper in the state. For Walker the year ended exactly as the first semester had, except that he received a B in physics; he had not yet hit his stride.

According to Shelby, Walker and Margaret Kirk, LeRoy and Sarah, and Shelby and Mary Elizabeth Yates drove that summer to Brinkwood for a two-week vacation. Mrs. Farish came along as a chaperone. Brinkwood, an imposing two-story, six-bedroom house with a tremendous screen porch, was located not far from the University of the South in

Sewanee. It sat on a gentle grassy lawn that gave some breathing space to the house. Except for the caretakers' house (Mr. and Mrs. Harrison and their children were close to various generations of Percys) and a barn made of split logs, the property was quite secluded. A tremendous tree provided shade over the porch and one could look for miles out to the bluish green of the countryside. The three couples hiked in the rolling mountains, played games, teased one another, sat around and talked, listened to the radio, and even sneaked a drink or two. One could hike to Fullerton's Bluffs or visit Lost Cove, known for its famous cave, described with great nostalgia in *Lost in the Cosmos*: "It's a tiny valley of the Cumberland plateau sealed off by a ridge. No roads, no phones, no TV. Only three farms and a cave. Good water, sweet white corn, quail, squirrel, deer, fish, and wild pig." Yet it turned out to have been a less than successful vacation; only LeRoy and Sarah were on speaking terms at the end.

Will often saw another side of Walker at Brinkwood. He once wrote to Gerstle Mack: "Walker and Shelby are at Brinkwood living a monastic life."[92] Walker derived a great sense of beauty from Brinkwood and its surroundings; it was the source of one of his less successful high school poems, "On a Natural Bridge."[93] Brinkwood was their home away from home, and the Percy boys spent part of each summer there, often with Shelby and other companions. One book that Walker read and remembered years later was *The Purple Heights*—"about an artist who has a very hard time but who in the end wins out both in love and art."[94] Will encouraged Walker and Shelby to read Romain Rolland's novel series *Jean-Christophe*—a book that Binx Bolling mentions in *The Moviegoer* as being "a larger-scale, better-written but equally romantic version of the artist's struggle against all odds, with the same sort of 'Ode to Joy' finale."[95]

The rather secluded University of the South, the nearby Monteagle Assembly Grounds (founded in 1882 as a type of Southern Chautauqua), and a small band of writers who lived in the area were associated in Walker's mind with Brinkwood. In 1930 a socioliterary group known as the Agrarians, including Robert Penn Warren, Andrew Lytle, and Allen Tate, published their immensely popular manifesto, *I'll Take My Stand: The South and the Agrarian Tradition*. The twelve essays mirrored much of the thinking about Southern society, culture, religion, industry, and the arts up to 1930, just as in a more sustained way Matthew Arnold, Thomas Carlyle, and others did in Victorian England. The book lit up the prospects for the rest of the century and gave direction, as the essayists fervently intended, to future decision makers in the South. Poet Allen Tate married novelist Caroline Gordon in 1925, and by 1930 they had bought a house named Benfolly outside Clarksville, Tennessee.[96] Though the Tates lived in Europe on a Guggenheim grant for seven months in late 1932, they spent a considerable amount of time at Benfolly during the early 1930s. Andrew Lytle, a native of Murfreesboro, Tennessee, whose mother had a summer home at Monteagle in the late 1920s, wrote most of his biography of General Nathan Bedford Forrest at Benfolly. Robert Penn Warren, who had been associated with Allen Tate at Vanderbilt University, taught at Southwestern in Memphis during the academic year 1930–31, as did the Tates for two years in the mid-1930s. Though Uncle Will knew many creative writers connected with Vanderbilt and the University of the South, he did not have "a great deal of use for any of the Fugitive poets," as Walker wrote. Will had written to Tate and the editors of *The Double Dealer* in New Orleans. Apparently Walker had very little direct contact with these writers since he had little interest in picking up or reading poetry books, much less in seeking out their authors.[97] Walker knew neither John Crowe Ransom nor Donald Davidson, and Uncle Will could only summon up a "certain wryness" at the mention of their names. At Brinkwood, Shelby showed Uncle Will the John Crowe Ransom poem "Bells for John Whiteside's Daughter," with its famous third stanza: "The lazy geese, like a snow cloud/Dripping their snow on the green grass,/Tricking and stopping, sleepy and proud,/Who cried in goose, Alas." Uncle Will's only response, according to Shelby: "That's not the way geese act."

Though a classmate of Walker and only five months younger, Charles Bell was perhaps too precocious for this group and tended not to be invited to these gatherings at Brinkwood.[98] Yet Walker and Charles were friends, due in great part to the way Charles structured his life to pursue those activities that genuinely interested him; Walker saw this as an appealing freedom of spirit. Charles had hit on an idea that gave him a good deal of leisure time in grade school and high school; he told his father that the notes he had taken in class on any specific day were actually the assignments for the following day. He chose to while away his time swinging in trees like a Delta Tarzan or writing poetry or reading *The Book of Knowledge*. Charles rarely prepared even for Miss Leila May Shell's geometry class, because he felt that geometric figures and equations were stored somewhere in his brain and he could locate them and call them up whenever he wanted. Walker, on the other hand, dutifully prepared himself for this class, especially as he began to sense the precision and balance offered by mathematical models. Once Charles and a friend, Earl Sansing, climbed into an old military academy nearby and manufactured some nitroglycerin; they were so afraid it might blow up the building that they rushed to the riverbank and poured it into the

Mississippi. Charles also delighted in looking at the night sky through a telescope, often with Walker. Sometimes Walker would go to Charles's home in the evenings and they would take out Charles's two-and-a-half-inch refractor telescope, or Charles would bicycle over to the Percy house and look through the three-inch telescope that had belonged to Walker's father. In fact, stargazing became such a hobby for Charles that he later chose to go to the University of Virginia partly because it had a renowned observatory. (Walker Percy used this hobby in one of his novels: in *The Last Gentleman*, Will Barrett becomes a seer after buying a new German Tetzlar telescope, "a canister jam-packed with the finest optical glasses and quartzes, ground, annealed, rubbed and rouged, tinted and corrected to a ten-thousandth millimeter. It was heavy and chunky, a pleasant thing.")

Charles gradually grew to admire Will Percy as a gentle man and a man of refinement—like a member of the Russian aristocracy, not without a slightly effete side to his nature. On the occasions when Charles would go the Percy house, he would spend a good deal of time looking at Will's record collection, handling each of the jackets of the records—Brahms, Beethoven, Tchaikovsky. From there he advanced in his late teens and early twenties to the "cleaner forms" of Gregorian chant. Once when Walker put on a record of some late Romantic piece, Charles immediately insisted, "Take it off. I refuse to listen to anything since Bach." In art, he felt drawn to Fra Angelico and Giotto, but not Titian; it was a process of eventually discovering what he called the "Homeric calm." Walker did not share Charles's penchant to explore medieval forms, perhaps because, unlike Charles, he was not striving to synthesize a "generative religion of an early cycle culture"—Egyptian, Homeric, medieval—in music, art, and literature. As he observed the two teenagers, Judge Bell sensed something about Walker while he was in high school that no one else had. Once after Walker had visited the Bells, the judge said to his son, "Walker looks like a Byronic hero. He also looks like someone who is going to be consumptive."

When not at Brinkwood, summer vacations were times when Walker rode out with Will to check on the crops at Trail Lake. Will had hired Walter Beard to manage Trail Lake and Walter Boland to manage Klondike, a plantation that became part of Trail Lake even though it maintained its own corporate identity.[99] Located in turkey and panther country, it looked ragged and unkempt in an area full of fallen logs and charred stumps. Will went infrequently to Trail Lake (he had lost $100,000 and the plantation was mortgaged to the hilt), since he had little or no interest in farming. Over the years the plantation grew as new sections were acquired; at its peak at the end of the decade, 150 families, ranging in size from two to thirteen in one family (about 600 people), farmed the land with the aid of approximately 350 mules.[100] Though one might get the impression that Trail Lake was not all that far from the image of "our own dear Land of Cotton," portrayed by Irwin Russell in his famous "Christmas Night in the Quarters," Will nevertheless made Trail Lake as progressive a plantation as he could.

Uncle Will's spontaneous bursts of outrage eventually instilled in the boys a certain apprehension: they were aware of his shifts of temperament. Shelby once put a couple of Phin's tennis balls in a glass chandelier that hung in the library. When Phin came in, he spotted the tennis balls, grabbed a chair, and as he reached for the balls, the entire chandelier came crashing down. Shelby and LeRoy went down to the Weinberg Building to report the accident to Will.

"What's the matter?" he demanded as he came out of his office.

"Uncle Will, that chandelier in the library. It got broke. We put Phin's tennis balls in it, and when we tried to get them down, it fell."

"Goddamn it," Will snorted, "people who do not know how to take care of property decently shouldn't be around it."[101]

School opened in mid-September 1931. *The Pica* resumed publication, featuring editorials written by Don Wetherbee on a variety of topics, ranging from fires to swimming. Margaret Kirk wrote a predictable essay about the difficulty of adjusting to school after summer vacation. Fortunately, she did not mention the stay at Brinkwood.[102] Walker began the school year by becoming involved more in writing and to a lesser extent in the theater. In mid-November, the Little Theatre of Greenville presented the first performance of the season. Louise Eskrigge Smith, Lillian McLaughlin, Harper Richards, and Helen Williams Spiars held a series of meetings at the Percy house to discuss the three one-act plays they were presenting. (The name Christine Eskrigge occurs in a draft of *The Moviegoer*.[103]) With eight other students, Walker traveled to see the Ben Greet Players perform.[104] The gossip column "Luna" marked the debut of Walker's stint as its author, the Man in the Moon. Writing for *The Pica* was to give Walker needed confidence to publish poetry and other writings. His first published poem, entitled "The Rainbow," appeared in December. Buoyed by his poetic effort (and improved grades), Walker tried again—a portrayal of the goddess of love, as a statue, speaking out.[105] Though one can only speculate as to the real person speaking out, Walker or his mother, this poem is not unlike Faulkner's 1924 poem "The Marble Faun," in which the faun "cannot break/My marble bonds." His other poem in the same issue, "The New Year," signals a new day. Though he was a contributor to *The Pica* and a winner of the annual poetry contest in February, Walker's name did not appear on the masthead.[106] He published two contributions, a poem ("To the Father of Our Country") and a book review of Paul Leicester Ford's *The True George Washington*. Walker's own voice was beginning to emerge, a sign that he was more at ease and more comfortable in expressing ideas in writing.

In March, the first of Walker's three poems in *The Pica* reveals a winter scene typical of what one would find at Trail Lake. The underlying style of A. E. Housman is quite noticeable in this poem, entitled "In a Cotton Field," as the narrator describes black workers plowing under a cotton field. The other two, "Carpe Diem" and "Easter Lilies," assume a definite shift in tone; the first is a song of joy to a young woman and the second a reflective description of flowers in a church sanctuary.[107]

$\mathbf{J}$ust as Walker had begun to demonstrate that he could write and that life was opening up before him on many levels, disaster struck. His mother died suddenly. The full story of her death can never be known, partially because the doctor who signed the death certificate never ordered an autopsy, which made it impossible to establish for certain whether she died of a heart attack or from drowning. In addition, the records of the Wells Funeral Home, which handled her funeral, no longer exist. On the Saturday following Easter, a distraught Mattie Sue, accompanied by ten-year-old Phin, drove her Buick coupe a short distance northeast of town. She was looking for LeRoy, who was with Buddy Branton. They were out cycling and not expecting to see Mrs. Percy.[108] Mattie Sue turned off onto a dirt road heading toward the Metcalfe plantation. As she drove onto the small wooden Black Bayou bridge, the car suddenly plunged into Deer Creek. It was twelve-thirty in the afternoon. Panic-stricken, Phin grabbed for his mother, who had reached out to hold him. His adrenaline pumped as he looked at his trapped mother; her foot seemed to have been lodged between the brake and the accelerator pedals. With very little air left in his lungs, he scrambled out through a window. Phin was delirious as he realized that his efforts to help his mother had been futile.

When he reached the bank, Phin ran to the nearby farm of Eddie LaFoe, whose son Eddie was his classmate.[109] When LaFoe and others arrived at the bridge, they found that the Wells ambulance had already been summoned. They tried for over an hour to revive Mattie Sue, but to no avail. When Will arrived, he had Phin driven back to Percy Street. LeRoy and Buddy arrived at the scene on their bicycles after the ambulance had passed them and were absolutely stunned. LeRoy could not control his grief. Walker was riding in a car not far away when he learned of the accident. When he reached Deer Creek a guard recognized him and would not let him approach very close.[110]

The Ball Diary provides one account of Mattie Sue's death:

Yesterday, Mrs. LeRoy P. Percy, driving herself and accompanied only by her ten-year-old son, plunged through a bridge into Deer Creek and was killed. When taken from the car she was dead, but unwounded. It is conjectured she may have died of heart-failure. The boy escaped by swimming after trying to save his mother. She was a very sweet young woman, and we were fond of her. We had hoped that she and Will might marry. Tragedy pursues the Percy family like nemesis.[111]

There had been rumors in Greenville that Mattie Sue had fallen in love with Will, and wanted to marry him, but he refused. "There was some talk that Mr. Will and Mattie Sue would get married. But it was just talk," Shelby said. Had Mattie Sue gone for a drive to see her friend Mrs. Sally Metcalfe? Had she decided to turn around on the Metcalfe Road because she had lost her way? LeRoy thought the most probable explanation of his mother's death was that she was out searching for Walker rather than him and had a heart attack (she had asthma and was not a very strong woman after her husband's death). Cousin Nell Johnson represented her side of the family at the funeral on Sunday afternoon, at which the Rev. John W. Young, pastor of the First Presbyterian Church, presided.[112]

Phin was traumatized by the event. His mother, according to Shelby, had held on to him as he tried to extricate himself from the car. After Mattie Sue's funeral, her mother, who happened to be visiting the Percys at the time of her daughter's death, subsequently revisited Greenville in spite of her painful memories.[113] Explanations of Mrs. Percy's death are not satisfactory. It presented a most disturbing dilemma: would a mother want to commit suicide with a young boy in the car? Had Mattie Sue "stumbled into" suicide, as psychiatrists might say? Had she wanted to commit suicide since her husband's death and waited until her sons had been accepted by Will? Did she choose the precise moment her mother was also in town? Shelby, who was not a witness to the event, believed that she was simply driving out to locate LeRoy and Buddy Branton. Don Wetherbee found it "totally unbelievable" that Mrs. Percy would commit suicide that way. For Donie DeBardeleben, the answer was also clearly in the negative: a mother's instinct is to preserve the life of her children. Bolling Spalding told her son Jack that Walker's mother died of a heart attack; she was dead before she hit the water.[114]

Like his brothers, Walker was stunned by his mother's death, and in one of his accounts of it he reduced it to its simplest terms: "She veered off the road, lost control of the car, and went into a small river, a creek."[115] He once wrote on an official form that his mother died by accident.[116] During the rest of his life, however, he held in his true feelings: his father had committed suicide and he would always believe that his mother had done the same, a secret he kept hidden even from members of his family and his closest friends.[117] To deal with this second parental suicide was undoubtedly one of the greatest burdens of Walker Percy's life. Her departure was the most definitive form of rejection, the rationale of which could never be fathomed. Unlike at the death of his father, Walker was a partial witness to what he perceived as his mother's self-nullification, which made it all the more tragic. (When Percy created his first major heroine, Kate Cutrer, she was someone "there in the shadows" who had suicidal tendencies.)

Shelby had talked to Walker about his father's suicide in Birmingham and about the right of an adult to make a decision to terminate one's life. Walker said it was something that could never be resolved, yet Shelby believed that Walker did resolve it: "I think Walker really understood his father."[118] The question remains: how well did he understand his mother? Walker once said cryptically—and perhaps in a code that a fellow physician would understand—to Robert Coles, "To lose a mother is not the same as losing a father."[119] The loss of his mother was the greatest unresolved event in Walker Percy's life, and would manifest itself later in his fiction in ways that Walker himself might not even have suspected. Even in the mid-1970s, artist Lyn Hill sensed that the death of Walker's mother was the "ultimate abandonment" that left Walker with a good deal of unresolved anger.[120]

For Walker and his brothers, there was need for quiet and consoling words. They looked now to Uncle Will for their total support, which he gave without reserve. Aunt Ellen Murphy, apparently having marital problems and needing to get away from Birmingham, spent considerable time in Greenville after Mattie Sue's death; she provided a motherly figure the boys desperately needed and presided as the woman of the household. For a while, Phin and Uncle Will shared Will's suite, since the boy had begun having nightmares. In the evenings, Will would read Greek mythology to him. Will took Phin to Johns Hopkins Hospital in Baltimore; in between counseling sessions, they had a marvelous time together touring Washington. Clearly Phin was in need of psychological counseling and special attention at home, something not always understood by the others. Once, after Mattie Sue's death, when the Percy boys and Shelby were in the apple orchard at Brinkwood, they scooped out a cavelike recess to play in, and Phin became overwrought by the experience, which conjured up the sense of drowning. LeRoy severely scolded Shelby for not thinking of Phin sufficiently. To ensure that Phin had companionship, Will asked a friend to be with him at times at Brinkwood. Their housekeeper also insisted that Walker gain weight and heaped food on his plate. After she left, he put it in his napkin and threw it away. Walker never felt comfortable about having formal meals in his teenage years.

Gradually, however, the boys picked up their lives and resumed the routine of school. During a conference in April in Jackson, *The Pica* was awarded the Sweepstake Cup for the best high school publication, an award for the best athletic page, and another for editorial excellence. It tied for the best special edition, tied for the award for feature writing, and was cited for the best business record and notable achievement in circulation. Perhaps because this event took place during the tragic moment in Walker's life, he is not pictured or listed among the honorees.[121] In selecting topics to report on, Walker chose a theme that one would not expect him to write about: "Soup Kitchen Open to All," which describes a walk down Main Street in the direction of the levee, where one may see "an ill-sorted array of our darker citizens in a straggling sort of line receiving food."[122] Some sat at a rough-hewn table in the kitchen and devoured the food, while others took their provisions home. "The aged and white-haired old man receives the same share as the wide-eyed picaninny. Anything from a scrub-bucket to a dipper that will hold water is used. Indeed, this strange company presents a very novel and interesting sight." Walker is quick to note that one or two whites frequent the kitchen, though they sit quietly in another compartment. "None seem downcast or woebegone, but rather cheerfully optimistic as though their sole aim is to provide for the present day." The Red Cross, using prison labor and income provided by the Paramount and the Grand, and with free milk from the Darnell Dairy, ran the operation and helped to find employment "for these victims, and gradually the number of receivers is reduced . . . Sergeant Prewitt is very successful in obtaining many foods wholesale from the dealer and in generally reducing costs until the average meal given the individual is purchased at a cost of only two cents." In this report, Walker reveals a developing social consciousness arrived at by a specific scene; his treatment of it suggested that he was moving away from Will Percy's views with an objectivity that replaces the sentimentality of a previous generation of writers.

That summer, Will organized a vacation designed to help the boys deal with their grief; most of all, he wanted them to get away from Greenville, see some new sights, and have new adventures. It was decided that Mitchell Finch would drive Billy Francis, Walker, and LeRoy in her old Chevrolet through the Raton Pass in southeastern Colorado to Arizona and eventually to California. They stayed at the Bright Angel Lodge overlooking the Grand Canyon, built in 1896. They also took a trip through the ocher terrain of the South Rim, as Walker Percy discussed in an impersonal way in his essay "The Loss of the Creature." In an October issue of *The Pica*, Walker wrote an article entitled "Red Butte" about part of his trip through Arizona, and one can see Will's classical influence at work: "At dusk, when the sun hung low in the distant hills to the west, shadows cast from projecting cliffs and ledges remind one of a magnificent frieze carved on the side of an ancient Roman building by some skilled sculptor." Their destination was Los Angeles, where the Olympics were being staged. Athletes from thirty-seven nations had assembled at an Olympic Village, a new concept then. Though it was still the Depression and it was difficult to raise money to train athletes, the United States proved victorious, thanks to such gifted athletes as Babe Didrikson; the United States won a total of forty-one gold medals, the most of any country. Driving up the coastal road on the way to San Francisco, they visited a family at Huntington Beach for two weeks. Next door to the house where they were staying was an open-air movie theater, and Walker spent "the whole time" sitting in a rocking chair watching the movies for free.[123] When Walker returned home, he wrote a report on San Francisco for *The Pica* entitled "Chinatown—The Orient and the Occident Meet."

From San Francisco, they drove through Nevada to the northwestern part of Wyoming to a dude ranch in the area of Jackson Hole, located in the Teton Range. (In *The Gramercy Winner*, the Grey family went to a dude ranch in Wyoming where "everyone lived in separate cottages and only met for meals.") The mountain peaks and deep valleys offered untold vistas, and the large uninhabited spaces gave him a different taste of the vastness of the world. Walker felt a freedom in the West, particularly in passing through New Mexico, which beckoned to some spiritual need within him. Someday he would seriously consider moving to a land of open plateaus and unspoiled fields. He would have fit in with the tall, lanky cowboys, though one has difficulty imagining Walker summoning up the physical energy to keep a ranch going. Will had taken the train to Jackson Hole with Phin and was glad when Mitchell's car pulled in safe and sound.[124] For about two weeks, the group enjoyed horseback riding, softball games (Phin would sometimes be the umpire), talking to the ranchers and cowboys, and trips to Yellowstone National Park. Phin spent hours collecting mountain flowers and pasting them into a scrapbook. Mitchell and Billy drove back to Greenville; Will and the three boys came back by train. The rest of the summer was spent at Brink-wood.[125] These times together were of great importance to the boys, who always remained close to one another, especially after they married.

There was one urgent matter that now needed attention: whether or not to return to Athens. That prospect was quickly turned down: "It came down to a choice, he [Will] gave us a choice as to whether we wanted to stay with him in Greenville or return to Athens to our grand-mother, Mrs. Billups Phinizy. We kind of took a vote and chose to stay in Greenville."[126] In May, Will filed a petition for adoption; he had con-sulted with the three boys as well as some relatives. The boys were will-ing and even anxious to stay with Will. On October 5 the adoption process was completed: the Percy boys were "hereby declared heirs at law of the petitioner, W. A. Percy, to the same extent as if they were his own sons." With Will in charge, certain decisions were made without a family vote. In order to improve LeRoy's grades so he could go to col-lege, Uncle Will was threatening to send him to Episcopal High in Alexandria, Virginia; he had received a D in physics that semester.

Now a senior, Walker could savor his last year in high school, in-cluding the ten football games scheduled for the season. Walker cele-brated their victory over Carr Central of Vicksburg in a poem in *The Pica* entitled "When the Green Met the Gold," which reveals, above all, a sense of security in his life, a communal rallying cry signaling victory and hope, and only incidentally an ode honoring Tom Payne, the Hor-nets' fullback.[127] He also read and reviewed favorably J. B. Priestley's novel *Faraway*.[128] On a deeper level, what might have attracted him to read and review this particular book was Uncle Will's love of the South Seas. If imitation is a good way to begin a writing career, then the poems that Charles Bell and Walker wrote for the October 28 issue of *The Pica* show that both had done their homework. Walker seemed to catch Poe's eeriness through his use of meter and rhyme. The poem deals with Walk-er's descent into the depths of sleep—and death. It is worth noticing that, though Walker describes a Dantesque vision of the underworld, he is not horrified by it to the extent that he flees it. Rather, he sees that the living and the dead are "wed" here:

SOMNIUM

(In the manner of Poe)

In the dreariest days of December
When the living and dying are wed.
On a night that I long shall remember
I slept by the river of dead.

By the dull-watered tarn of the dying
I wearily rested my head,
Where the ghosts of the cypress were sighing,
Where the phantoms uncannily tread.

And the hordes of bats were crawling
With shrieks to the caverns below.
And the owl of death was calling
With a wail that dead men know.
And they parted the sod and the willows
And whispered so sadly and low,
And they leaned on the mold of the pillows
That were granite three ages ago. . . .

No dream ever haunted my vision
Like the ghoul-haunted woods of the dead;
No region was ever Elysian
So close to these rivers of red;
No soul-anguished bard in his pages
Ever noted the fear-haunted tread
In the dreariest night of the ages
When the living and dying were wed.

Walker, feeling more confident in his creative abilities, talked often with
Shelby about the power and mystery of language: "We used to wonder
why a thing would sound so good and not be good. I remember we
talked—and here we were about 17 or 18—about this. Like with
Longfellow—'shall fold their tents, like the Arabs,/And as silently steal
away.' Why does that sound so good and why is it so bad? So we tried
to figure out just what the hell was going on. We did a good deal of
that. And we read voraciously. We were each other's college, even back
in high school."[129] Sometimes Shelby would balk at the routine at Greenville High and sprawl out on the sofa and read away from the others.[130]

In what was perhaps his best high school poem (reprinted as a tribute to E. E. Bass), Walker showed control and maturity as he reflected
on life and death:

TWILIGHT OF THE LIVES

Before the azure arch of day is crowned
By diadems of stars, and the outlet bends
His nighted way on leafy paths and sends

His hollow note down dismal halls, a sound
Of funeral knells of birds, yet day is gowned
In solemn gray, a church-like peace descends
On earth and men in gentle tones; it lends
A pause to time till shades of night surround
The firmament. So in the aftermath
When furrowed brows ease thoughts of life and death,
And contemplation sings in gold repose,
The wearied bodies trace no more this path
Of life, but draw once more an even breath,
Before the sombre curtains gently close.[131]

In a late November issue, Walker wrote an article entitled "Africa—Land of Race Problems," which focused on Professor Holloway (Walker did not provide a first name), a visitor from South Africa who had come to Greenville to study the racial situation. Walker interviewed him about the racial makeup of his country and, during the course of their discussion, learned about Gandhi, who had first achieved prominence in South Africa.

In the annual Christmas play, *Why the Chimes Rang*, Alice Finlay played an angel and Walker a rich young man. Though a very amateur thespian, Walker was recognized for his poetic talent, no doubt for the only time in his life. When the Mississippi High School Press Association presented its awards, Walker won double honors—first and fourth places in poetry. At Christmas *The Pica* published his poem describing Greenville after an ice storm and a second, entitled "Einstein," which explored Walker's interest in scientific issues. This poem, probably inspired by William Blake, points to a fundamental need within Walker to find symmetry in a chaotic world. "My favorite writer in my teens," he wrote, "was H. G. Wells, who believed that all events in the cosmos, even human history, can be explained by natural science and a rather crude science at that."[132] In this poem he acknowledges an agenda for his life, not rooted in historical sources but in what the world reveals as immutable. He needed to find some way to integrate what he saw and felt about his everyday life with what he was learning about the mysteries of biological growth on earth and astronomical explosions in the farthest sky. Walker had not found an answer to the questions he was posing to himself, but he had found the right words and phrases to express his inquiring mind. Walker, who sometimes made light of his high school poetry, formulated the direction he wished to take in another poem, "After the Storm." Walker possessed great powers of concentration all his life; he could block out background noises, whether in the library at Percy Street or at Brinkwood. He found solace in the written word and could imaginatively explore the unknown worlds that books offer. In particular, Walker seems to have understood that poetry and fiction give us the second chance that life seems to deny us.

As January 1933 began, and in spite of his academic and literary successes, Walker's romantic life seemed to be in the doldrums. "The Man in the Moon" portrays a rather downcast Walker: "Margaret Kirk caters to college boys, too. First she was 'that way' about Old Miss, but now it's Simpleton Simpson of Alabama. Poor old Charlie Hall is still plugging away for headman. Too, Walker looks rather downcast. What happened at the Greenville–Shaw basketball game? Did Margaret E. soothe your wounded feelings, huh?" LeRoy's spirits were equally downcast; he was sent to Episcopal for the remainder of his high school years.

In March, Franklin Delano Roosevelt took the oath of office as President. There were a few bonds between the Percys and the Roosevelts: Will's father had hunted bear with FDR's fifth cousin, Teddy Roosevelt; both Will and FDR were Harvard men; at the 1924 and 1928 Democratic conventions, FDR nominated Governor Alfred E. Smith, a Catholic, for the presidency and was supported by Will's father, who actively campaigned on his behalf in Greenville.[133] FDR had succeeded Al Smith as governor of New York and in 1929–30 faced the problems of the national Depression. When FDR passed through Atlanta during the 1932 campaign, he attracted the largest crowd the South had ever seen up to that point. He ultimately received 22,822,000 popular votes to Hoover's 15,762,000. Uncle Will initially admired FDR, but he later changed his mind when "one day I read that the President of the United States had excoriated bitterly and sorrowfully 'the infamous sharecropper system.' "[134] When he inquired of a friend in Washington what locality the President was referring to, he was told—and the reply knocked the breath out of him—Uncle Will's Trail Lake. What seemed to irritate Will most was the upward mobility of the "poor whites" who would profit a good deal from Roosevelt's programs.[135]

Walker had a different assessment of FDR: "During the depression of the 1930s and afterward there were stirrings of liberal currents not only in the enthusiasm for the economic legislation of the Roosevelt Administration but also in a new awareness of the plight of the Negro. Mississippi desperately needed the New Deal and profited enormously from it. Indeed the Roosevelt farm program succeeded too well. Planters who were going broke on ten-cent cotton voted for Roosevelt, took federal money, got rich, lived to hate Kennedy and Johnson and voted for Goldwater—while still taking federal money."[136] At sixteen Walker was too young to vote in the election, but he had an uncanny ability to size up people and he enjoyed repeating the banter of Uncle Will and his friends sitting in Will's parlor on a Sunday afternoon in 1933: "Roosevelt is doing a good job; no, the son of a bitch is betraying his class."[137] Walker was always well aware of the social and political changes that took place in the South; it constituted a central part of his philosophical orientation to the world.

Toward the end of his senior year, Walker continued to write for *The Pica*. On Saturday, April 8, he went to Jackson with Howard Dyer, Joe Neff, Shelby, and Phin to see the exhibition tennis match between Hans Nusslein and Big Bill Tilden; his report shows an ability to transform action into narration. Not surprisingly, Walker had the honor that spring of being the highest individual scorer in the Mississippi High School Press Association. He had scored thirty-two points and his nearest rival, T. C. Shields, had twenty-three. When questioned about the method he pursued in producing successful writings, Walker was uncommunicative: a mere "Just luck" and "Accidents will happen" were all the interviewer was able to glean from him.

When Walker thought about his future education, he favored St. John's in Annapolis, Maryland, and Rollins College in Florida. It did not take long, however, for Uncle Will to convince him that the University of North Carolina would be the suitable place to pursue a degree. Walker offered little opposition, mainly because he was not absolutely convinced what academic direction he should take. He had never seen Chapel Hill, but the choice seemed sound and he was ready. Admittance to such a university was not difficult.

With LeRoy away at Episcopal, Walker had more time to be with Phin, who still exhibited feelings of anxiety about his mother's death. It would not be until January 1939 that Phin would have a chance to talk with Harry Stack Sullivan. Walker, knowing that he was about to leave the family nest and feeling a certain fatherliness toward his young brother, once approached Phin. "Let's walk around the block," Walker suggested, and started touching his nose, a habit that showed he was nervous. "Phin, you know about the facts of life, about the birds and bees?" "Walker, I think so." "Good." And that was all the fatherly advice Phin got.

Judging by the high quality of her poetry and essays in *The Pica*, the most articulate and intelligent girl in Walker's class was Alice Archer Finlay. Though Alice is rarely mentioned by Walker's peers as one of the girls he would see and date, Phin spontaneously remembered her as someone who visited the Percy house. Although related to the Wetherbees, Alice was not part of the "crowd" that Walker hung around with.

Shelby considered her flamboyant, outgoing, and smart—but not someone you saw at a lot of dances. Walker, too, was known as someone who
did not like to attend dances. ("Dances bored Walker," Shelby said.)
Alice's sister, Mary Kathryn, remembered Walker coming to their house
to fetch Alice for a date. Though four years younger than Alice, Mary
Kathryn thought of Alice and Walker as sweethearts.[138] (When he was
in his sixties, Walker told a group of friends, who were talking one evening about "puppy love," that he was once infatuated with a girl in
Greenville whose father owned a store.[139]) After Alice's mother died, her
father, a drugstore owner, remarried and moved into an apartment with
his new wife. He died when Alice was sixteen, and in *The Pica* Alice
wrote about visiting her father's grave. Perhaps it was this bond of lost
parents that held them together.

One clue to Walker's lingering affection for Alice appeared years
later when, in the process of writing *The Last Gentleman*, he depicted a
scene in which Will Barrett returns to a city much like Greenville, where
he encounters two women—Alice and Mary—the names of the Finlay
girls. Apparently Will Barrett and Mary had graduated together from
high school; he was the valedictorian and she the salutatorian. She had
sat behind him in Latin class as they memorized *Forsan et haec olim mem-
inisse juvabit* ("In the future we will recall all of this with joy"): "We
were the smartest ones in class, weren't we, Will?" "Yes." "I wonder
why it was we never spoke to each other. I don't guess we ever spoke
ten words in the whole four years." "I don't know why that was."[140]

The Latin they had memorized, especially the word *juvabit*, implies
an untold story. Walker once said, "Alice was very attractive. I have
often thought about her and wondered what she did. She was a good
writer."[141] The paths of Alice and Walker would cross each other in the
future, though they never really stayed in touch. (Years later Walker
wrote to Shelby: "Please note in *The Pica* who won the poetry prize and
how catty Alice Finlay was toward Margaret Kirk. Why was I chasing
Margaret who was a nut instead of Alice who was something, I can't
say. I hadn't realized how Don Wetherbee dominated everything."[142]) As
Walker was about to leave for college, he would not leave behind a high
school sweetheart, even though he had liked and dated the most articulate girl in his class.

Years later at a formal occasion Walker reflected fondly on the
Greenville years:

But surely what counted were the people, the people who took the trouble to
communicate their love of books to young people who—at least in my case—
would never have discovered it for themselves. And the other writers to whom

one is finally and forever indebted. Frankly, it didn't matter at the beginning whether the book was *Tom Swift* or *Huckleberry Finn* or *War and Peace*. What was important was that somebody took the trouble to hand you a book and to communicate his own excitement, so that you had the curiosity to take a look and see what was going on, and then came the breakthrough—through other people. In turn, through them you were introduced to a world you had never known and yet always seemed to have known.[143]

Uncle Will joined other parents in sponsoring a dance at the Legion Home in honor of their sons and daughters.[144] From hindsight, Shelby put these high school years in a minimalist perspective: "Our only distraction, aside from a smattering of verses, which had better go unmentioned, was that you went to the Field Meet (in Latin?) and I wound up editor of *The Pica*."[145] For Walker, they were formative years in his development as a fledgling writer.

During summer vacation, Walker and LeRoy went to the Chicago World's Fair (also called "The Century of Progress," whose motto was "Science Finds, Industry Applies, Man Conforms").[146] Walker remembered this fair, situated on land reclaimed from Lake Michigan, as being spotlessly clean, with huge high-rise apartments and futuristic highways: "Obviously the main vision of the future had to do with locomotion, how to get from one place to another as fast as possible. What was even odder was that this vision of the future seemed perfectly natural at the time."[147] Ironically, the new technological wonders were accompanied by Hitler's ascendancy to power. "As well as any other date, it marked the beginning in earnest of the terrors, convulsions, holocausts, and tyrannies which have best characterized this century of progress—a convulsion which had in fact begun earlier, though nobody knew it, in 1914." Walker considered the fair to be emblematic of his life:

My discovery was that the technological vision of the future happiness of Chicago in 1933 did not work for the world any more than my own allegiance to scientism worked for me . . . A good deal of grief had to come to pass before it finally began to dawn on us that there is a great leftover in this technological vision of the future and that this leftover is nothing less than man himself. It is no derogation of the beauty and truth of science and the benefits of technology to suggest that man can be encompassed by science or technology, and that if he does not transcend it, he will fall victim to it. And so in my case, it has been precisely that leftover, that most peculiar phenomenon in the Cosmos, man, man *qua* man, man *qua* woman, which has engaged me ever since, toward the end of a modest taking account of man by [the] proper science of man, which in my view even includes novel-writing.

Once Walker was back in Greenville after a brief excursion to Mexico with LeRoy, he and Don Wetherbee (who had decided to go to Chapel Hill because he respected Uncle Will's judgment) packed their bags for college. Will had communicated to Walker in not so subtle ways his distaste for the profession of law, and in Walker's mind running a plantation was simply not in the cards. Though Will had risen to the occasion and defended his country during World War I, Walker could not see himself entering the military. As he wrote to a future classmate at Chapel Hill: "No, Uncle Will never came to Chapel Hill. But it was his choice, my going there—though he was a graduate of Sewanee and Harvard. I think he chose well."[148]

What inspired Walker to choose science? Years later, when he filed an application form for medical school and had to cite a book that had influenced him in this direction, he listed Sinclair Lewis's novel *Arrowsmith*: (Question: "How did you get interested in the idea of studying medicine?" Answer: "I have always been interested in science, particularly chemistry and zoology. The idea of making new discoveries to combat disease has always fascinated me. I think I first became seriously interested when I read Sinclair Lewis's *Arrowsmith* in high school."[149]) In this novel, Dr. Arrowsmith's mentor is Dr. Max Gottlieb, whose name figures prominently but sadly in *Love in the Ruins* and *The Thanatos Syndrome*. Sinclair Lewis's hero is Arrowsmith, a young man who chooses the hard path of science and medicine. He fights sham and compromise, rejects alluring temptations for honest values, and opts for pure research over commercialized idealism. Yet Dr. Gottlieb speaks words (with his Germanic accent) that would appeal to a young scientist: "To be a scientist—it is not just a different job, so that a man should choose between being a scientist and an explorer or a bond-salesman or a physician or a king or a farmer. It is a tangle of very obscure emotions, like mysticism, or wanting to write poetry . . . But the scientist is intensely religious—he is so religious that he will not accept quarter-truths, because they are an insult to his faith." Walker went to Chapel Hill eager to read and learn as much as he could, having spent most of that summer reading Faulkner.[150]

3

The College Years
1933–37

Chapel Hill has been called "the Southern part of heaven" by thousands of alumni, a lovely place where town and gown compatibly mingle. If anybody is responsible for having shaped the university during Walker's four years there, it was Frank Porter Graham, "Dr. Frank," a native of Fayetteville, North Carolina. He entered the university in 1905 and subsequently studied at Columbia University, the University of Chicago, and the London School of Economics before assuming his post at Chapel Hill. A slightly graying man, with a firm jaw and warm eyes, Graham instilled a fresh spirit into the university community—a new openness of discussion and inquiry that was not always appreciated by the politicians who drew up the university's budget or by alumni who wanted the university to remain exactly as they remembered it. At one of the Founder's Day convocations while Walker was a student, Graham expressed his vision of education. He urged the men and the relatively few women at Chapel Hill to develop integrated personalities, achieve a spiritual radiance in their work, and undertake those adventures that would make the world freer and fairer.[1] To assist this process, he encouraged a faculty that included Frederick Henry Koch, Kenan Professor of Dramatic Literature; Howard Washington Odum, Kenan Professor of Sociology; Urban Tigner Holmes, professor of French, and George Coffin Taylor, professor of English. None of these distinguished men, however, was without his critics; to Donald Davidson, one of the Agrarians, sociologists like Howard Odum represented a threat. The South was conservative, religious, segregationist, and had a deep sense of history, whereas sociologists, in Davidson's opinion, dealt with a discipline that was progressive, scientific, and ahistorical.[2] Davidson asked a probing question: would a Southern sociologist use the South as his laboratory and try to transform society, one that had been negatively portrayed by liberal journals of opinion? H. L. Mencken had led the attack against the South and many felt his indictment in *The American Mercury* needed a profound and articulate response. Ironically, Davidson and Odum were made from a similar mold, one far removed from the South of Thomas Nelson Page; that is perhaps why they understood each other so well.

Odum's *An American Epoch: Southern Portraiture in the National Picture* (1930) and *Southern Regions of the United States* (1936), as well as his probing essays in *The Journal of Social Forces* (which he founded in 1922) and the data gathered by his Institute for Research in Social Science, helped in the process of diagnosing Southern ills and prescribing a remedy. In *Southern Regions of the United States*, Odum suggested a go-slow approach to the race question. (On one football trip to Athens, Walker told Grandmother Phinizy he had heard that Professor Odum had talked disparagingly about the Phinizys, how they had changed their name from Finicci to Phinizy to Americanize it. When Grandmother Phinizy heard about this, she had her chauffeur drive her to Chapel Hill so that she could instruct the good professor in person about the distinguished history of the Phinizy family![3]) The student body had been entirely white when Walker arrived, but overtures were being made to open up the professional schools to blacks. That fall, Thomas R. Hocutt, a black student from Durham, sought entrance into the School of Pharmacy, yet the judge who heard the case refused admittance on the grounds that the applicant did not have proper qualifications. In those years, this type of controversy would have been little noticed by the typical student at Chapel Hill.

Freshman orientation began on September 19. Walker drove up to Chapel Hill with Don Wetherbee and his parents, registered for classes with 610 other freshmen, and reported to Robert Lawson, M.D., for his physical examination. In late September, 250 students tested positive for tuberculosis and had X rays taken. Those who had active TB, however, were very few. Walker wrote on one of the forms he filled out that he was a Presbyterian.[4] He also listed a possible family contact—Roland Shine, one of his father's friends, who worked in Birmingham. At that time, the total student body at Chapel Hill numbered 2,610. It was duly noted that Walker was considered deficient for not having studied a modern foreign language in high school.

Since the College of Liberal Arts was on a quarter system (fall, winter, spring, summer), Walker paid $25 for the first quarter's tuition.

Walker roomed with Don in 308 Manly for the first quarter. They were regionally outnumbered; thirteen out of twenty-eight men on this floor were North Carolinians and ten others came from New York. But Walker took it all in stride; he was not in the least perturbed by any disturbances that either Don or the other students would make: "He would turn in at nine o'clock and that was that. No matter how much noise I made, I couldn't wake him up for the world."[5] Don and Walker got on well, though they had different temperaments; Walker would begin college with a science major leading to further studies in medicine and ultimately wind up a literary figure, whereas Don started with a strong interest in literature and government, worked as a reporter and editor, and ultimately became a practicing physician. "It was the elegance and order and, yes, beauty of science which attracted me," Walker once wrote. "It is not merely the truth of science that makes it beautiful, but its simplicity. That is to say, its constant movement is in the direction of ordering the endless variety and the seeming haphazardness of ordinary life by discovering underlying principles which as science progresses become ever fewer and more rigorously and exactly formulated—at least in the physical sciences."[6]

Walker looked forward to reading literature, as a liberal arts major for two years, and then to taking courses in science and math in his last two years. In addition to "Foundations of Modern History," introductory math, and Botany 41, he had Ernst Christian Metzenthin, an associate professor, for thirty-six weeks of beginning German, in a course that met five times a week. Apparently at this time he read Thomas Mann's *Buddenbrooks*.[7] He traveled to Germany with Professor Metzenthin less than a year after entering Chapel Hill, and did so precisely because he had taken a course with him; a reference to this trip, and particularly of the narrator's father encountering a young boy singing a Brahms lied, is alluded to in an early version of *The Moviegoer*. A prominent figure on campus, Professor Metzenthin gave a public lecture that fall in Gerrard Hall in honor of the 450th anniversary of the birth of Martin Luther. Walker and his friends talked of taking two or three years off to go to Paris and hitchhike around the European countryside, but Uncle Will—and the work ethic in general—discouraged such a trip.

Walker took a placement test in English on September 25. His freshman class was subsequently divided into three sections, which Walker called "advanced, average and retarded English."[8] For this test, Walker imitated Faulkner's style in the Benjy section of *The Sound and the Fury* by using no capitalization and no punctuation, and thus found himself placed in one of the lower sections taught by George Frank Sensabaugh.

"They put me in the retarded English class and the professor really thought I was hot stuff," Walker once said. "Compared to the rest of the dummies, I guess I was."[9]

Walker had heard a story about Faulkner from Uncle Will. Approximately a decade before the Percy boys arrived there, Faulkner had visited his friend Ben Wasson in Greenville. As a freshman at Ole Miss in 1916, Wasson had met Faulkner on campus, became friends with him (they were Sigma Alpha Epsilon [SAE] fraternity brothers), and served for a time as Faulkner's agent and editor. Will Percy invited them both to play tennis on his court. Faulkner, as Wasson recalled, was in a bohemian mood and wandered about Greenville barefoot. He had been drinking. Before they left, Mrs. Wasson said, "Well, Bill, aren't you and Ben going to play tennis?"

"Yessum," Faulkner replied.

"You've forgotten your shoes, haven't you?"

"No'm, I just like to play tennis barefooted."

A rather anxious Will Percy was waiting at the curb to greet Faulkner. Beyond the Lombardy poplars lining one side of the house were several young men and women Will had invited as his guests. After Ben introduced the two poets to each other, Will said, "You're in time, Mr. Faulkner, to try a twosome with me, if you don't object too much to an inferior partner." Faulkner mumbled his reply, and they walked to the tennis court together. As playing began, Faulkner lumbered about the court, lunging and losing his balance. He finally fell down. Will turned to Ben. "I don't believe your friend feels very well. Maybe you'd better take him for a drive." As Faulkner was assisted from the court by Ben, he was heard complaining about his bad leg, the result of a flying injury he claimed he received while on an RAF training mission in 1918 near Toronto. The next day Will dismissed the entire incident: "Lucky he didn't break a leg. It's probably true that the Lord does look after drunks." Walker repeated this story a number of times; his version was that Faulkner arrived totally intoxicated and proceeded to embarrass everyone.[10] (Walker later blurbed Ben Wasson's memoir, *Count No 'Count: Flashbacks to Faulkner*, which recounted this episode, calling the book a "touching, unique and revealing memoir of William Faulkner.") Faulkner was never invited to the Percys' again. Walker would always admire Faulkner's writings and at an advanced age maintained that *The Sound and the Fury* was one of the most important novels in Western literature.[11]

Walker was soon admitted to a more advanced English section called the "Flying Squadron," to which Don had also been assigned. In his freshman year, Don studied English with Professor Harry Russell, and most likely encouraged Walker to join that section. Later both LeRoy and Shelby took his course, and probably did so at Walker's urging. Walker remembered Harry Russell, as he once told me, as "the most distinguished professor in the English Department," though he could not remember whether he knew him as a teacher or just knew him outside of class.

The Sunday following the first day of class, rushing began and lasted for a period of twelve days. Bids were tendered to freshmen in early October through the faculty advisors on fraternities.[12] Don was pledged to Delta Psi, a fraternity his father had belonged to at Ole Miss. Walker was pleased by the bid from SAE; his cousin Newt De-Bardeleben, who was pledge captain, had put in an especially good word. (Binx Bolling in *The Moviegoer* likewise looks up to his cousin Walter: "For a year after I joined the fraternity I lived in the hope of pleasing him by hitting upon just the right sour-senseless rejoinder, and so gaining admission to his circle, the fraternity within the fraternity.") Known as a forthright person, good bridge player, partygoer, and a smart, self-confident politician and raconteur, Newt DeBardeleben (Walker once referred to him as Newt DeBoodledepoot) told Ross Allen a bit about Walker's background, including the circumstances surrounding the death of Walker's father.[13] Hazing for the SAE pledges was not particularly dangerous or exciting; it consisted of blindfolding pledges on a dark night, driving them out of town on back roads, and abandoning them to find their way back to campus. While being hazed, Walker, Ross, and John ("Moose") Cay, Jr., accidentally stumbled onto a bed of mint, and they concocted a passable mint julep with some corn liquor. By this time, too, Walker had started smoking.

As always, Walker enjoyed going to the movies. In a biographical form Walker Percy filled out for his fiftieth class reunion, he listed a few memories of campus life, the last of which was "Prof. Smith's 2:00 p.m. class at the Carolina Theatre." The Carolina Theatre (it cost thirty cents) began its seventh year of service in 1933 with an incredible array of films during the first week of classes: *Moonlight and Pretzels, Goodbye Again, India Speaks, Tugboat Annie, Hold Your Man, Another Language,* and *Three-Cornered Moon.* Manager E. Carrington Smith announced the cancellation of the nudist colony film, *Back to Nature,* which would be shown later in the fall.[14] When the theater became a bit stuffy in the Carolina heat, students would shout out with great abandon, "Air! Air! You're killing us." More than the influence of specific films, it was the genre itself—and the need to observe carefully what was happening on the big screen—that provided Walker a counterpoint to the lab work done in Davie and Venable Halls.

As classes commenced, Paul Green, the noted playwright on campus, gave an interview in *The Daily Tar Heel*, the campus newspaper, in which he prophesied that the motion picture would be the most important form of drama in the future. With the advent of sound into the motion picture, Green argued, the movie world has been able to celebrate its coming of age: "The motion picture, and by that I include the sound, can express anything the human mind can imagine. There is no picture which the mind is able to visualize that defies reproduction on the screen. Through the combination of the eye and the ear with almost unlimitable resources for their expression, the motion picture has possibilities yet undreamed of."[15] In early October, the Carolina Theatre featured George Arliss in *Voltaire*; the screenplay was by Paul Green, his fourth work for the movies. Green was also adapting for the screen his play *The House of Connelly*, first performed in New York in October 1931.

Each quarter an assortment of politicians, creative writers, and artists came to campus. While Walker was at Chapel Hill, Thomas Wolfe, Reinhold Niebuhr, James A. Farley, and Gertrude Stein spoke, and Gladys Swarthout of the Metropolitan Opera sang. (Shelby once saw Wolfe on campus—and claimed he looked as big "as a giant Californian sequoia." Walker saw him, too, descending the steps of the library.[16]) Walker thought that it was in the nature of things for a young Southerner in the 1930s to write a Thomas Wolfe novel about growing up in the South and coming to terms with school and life.[17]

As Walker began his college career, he became acquainted one way or another with the opinions of those personalities on campus who made a difference. Coach Chuck Collins spoke at a pep rally for the freshmen (who were expected to form the nucleus of the cheering section). Kay Kyser, a former Carolina cheerleader who became a famous orchestra leader, first formed his musical organization at the university and announced that he wanted the college boys to have a new college pep song. An editorial writer in the campus newspaper alerted his fellow students to the dangers of Hitler's agenda: "Hitler intends to bring Great Britain, Italy, and Germany together as allies, none of whom wish to see France the greatest military power in Europe. As is the case in most German territory, militarism is made the prime factor in the growth of the German Republic."[18] When Upton Close, a former editor of *The Peking Daily*, spoke to the student body, he warned them not only about the Nazis but about the growing threat of the Japanese in the Pacific. Walker had entered a large, diversified new world and felt charged by what he was experiencing; in Greenville, on the other hand, Shelby felt the absence of his friend, to judge by some poems he wrote during this time.

Of the football games that Chapel Hill played that year, perhaps the most disappointing was the victory of the Georgia Bulldogs (30–0) before a crowd of 10,000 at Kenan Stadium. The losing game with Georgia Tech on October 28 before a crowd of 9,000 coincided with homecoming weekend, replete with parades, fireworks, and pep rallies. On this occasion Walker invited Margaret Kirk, a student at Sweet Briar in Virginia, to Chapel Hill—which may have inspired his unpublished short story "Homecoming." Emerson Gill and his orchestra played for the annual Thanksgiving set of dances known as the Fall Germans. Newt De-Bardeleben was one of twenty-six students who received all A's at the end of the quarter. Among those who made the fall honor roll for receiving a grade of B or higher were Don Wetherbee, Louis Shaffner, and Walker (A's in English and math, B's in German and history).[19] SAE proudly boasted the highest fraternity scholarship average for the fall quarter.[20]

When classes resumed in January 1934, Walker and Don moved to the ground floor of the middle section of Old East that faces Old West, primarily to avoid walking constantly up and down stairs. Once relocated, Walker became acquainted with two North Carolinians: Samuel E. Elmore, an SAE sophomore from Spindale and editor of the yearbook, *The Yackety Yack*, and David M. Warren. The latter, a native of Edenton and a history major, would take long walks and go to the movies with Walker. David was an observant student with a well-developed aesthetic sense. Two of Walker's closest friends hailed from Wilmington. James Carr, whose father, a UNC alumnus, was the U.S. District Attorney for the Eastern District of North Carolina, joined the staff of *The Yackety Yack* in his freshman year, as did Walker, who had intentions of being a staff photographer. Walker was once given a roll of film and told to take whatever pictures he wished, and once they were developed and printed, he would be judged on the quality of his work. One picture, entitled "South Building from the Old Well, Summer 1934–35," is a bit decentered, perhaps revealing a sense of perspective that was in advance of his classmates'. Whatever the case, Walker was not asked to continue on the staff of the yearbook.[21] One weekend, Jimmy took Walker home to meet his parents and spend a weekend. The other Wilmingtonian, James L. Sprunt, Jr., an SAE sophomore majoring in history—his father and Walker's father were classmates at Princeton—might have been the one that gave Walker the unfortunate nickname of "Pussy," a variant on his father's nickname of "Puss" at Princeton. When Walker moved to Old East, Sprunt roomed in the same dorm in the middle section on the second floor with David H. Scott, Jr., another SAE from Wilmington.[22] Jimmy Sprunt and Walker enjoyed going to the movies together and it was not long before they became good buddies—their wit bonded them together—and they stayed close throughout their lives. One of Walker's best recollections of his freshman year was sitting with Ansley Cope, a senior, and William Minor, another classmate, in an eating place run by Will Sadler near West House; he particularly enjoyed the camaraderie between Ansley and Bill.[23] One of Walker's unhappiest moments in Old East occurred when a Delta Kappa Epsilon (DKE) swiped a painting Uncle Will had given him. It was never returned.[24]

During the Christmas vacation, Walker dreamed up a hoax that made him a campus hero. Was this another attempt at fiction? With connections on *The Daily Tar Heel*, it was not difficult to arrange with reporters to slip in a phony story under a sensational banner headline in the January 10 edition: CAROLINA STUDENT IS STAR-WITNESS IN DARING $300,000 BANK ROBBERY. The subhead gave the gist of the story: "Walker Percy of Greenville, Miss., Gives Chief Testimony in Prosecuting Louis the Lip, Former Henchman of Al Capone, For Brazen Attempt to Rob Home-town Bank." The story gave Walker a notoriety on campus he had not expected. According to the published report, the sum of $300,000 was delivered to the Trader's Depository Bank at Greenville, Mississippi, from the Federal Reserve Bank. When additional money was sent to Greenville, it was placed in a cage near the cashier's window, guarded by two plainclothes policemen, who soon left to get something to eat. When Walker entered the bank to cash a check, he was brushed aside by a strongly built individual who grabbed the money and walked calmly out of the bank, tipping his hat to Walker and driving off in his car. Walker said he had just witnessed a $300,000 heist by Louis the Lip, a Chicago beer baron. A version of this story that appeared in *The Pica* thirteen days later (Shelby was a staff writer then) featured the headline WALKER PERCY SHOWS METTLE IN TRIAL OF CAPONE'S HENCHMAN. The story, borrowed from *The Daily Tar Heel*, noted that Greenville's "noble graduate" was the sole witness to this robbery. "Percy always showed great promise as a newspaperman, and the manner in which he told *The Tar Heel* reporter this episode indeed does him justice." But the Greenville High reporter had more savvy than his Chapel Hill counterpart: "This school is indeed proud to claim such a hero as its graduate. But there are a couple of things that we are not quite clear on: how did Percy get in the bank at six in the morning, and when was the robbery; we never heard about it. The story is under quite large headlines, but this town never heard it mentioned. Last, but not least, we know that Walker Percy was confined to bed at the time that he tells of the robbery."

In March, Professor Meno H. Spann lectured on German politics, about the Nazi desire to create a purely Aryan race. Hitlerites, he said, were pledged to cultivate Nordic instincts and turn away from rationalism, which they consider the cause of the degeneration in Western civilization.[25] A group of German students met for the last time during the winter quarter at the home of Professor Metzenthin to discuss a fifty-day summer trip to Bonn, Tübingen, the University of Württemberg, Berlin, the medieval cloister at St. Gallen in Switzerland; for an additional sum, they could attend the Passion Play at Oberammergau and see a Wagnerian opera.[26] They would leave by freight steamer from Norfolk in mid-June. At this gathering Walker committed himself to this trip, which would make a profound difference in his life.

Walker clearly enjoyed his life as a student. He made friends easily, though he had a tendency to remain apart at times. With Don Wetherbee and Lou Shaffner, he was one of thirty-seven students who made straight A's for the second quarter.[27] As summer approached, his brother Roy graduated from Episcopal. His affection for Sarah Farish, about to head off for Sophie Newcomb College in New Orleans, had not diminished at all. For Walker, a rising sophomore at Chapel Hill, the summer would be spent not at Brinkwood but in Germany. With Professor Metzenthin, whom Walker grew to characterize as a curmudgeon, and a small band of fellow students, he sailed on a Black Diamond freighter to Antwerp. During the journey across the Atlantic, Walker realized he did not look forward to spending much time with these particular students. From Antwerp they took a train to Bonn, the first real European city that Walker would have a chance to explore. Kätharina Metzenthin, a teacher, and the only Metzenthin living in Bonn in 1934, lived at 56 Schumannstrasse in a fashionable section of the city.[28] Whether Frau Metzenthin is the "friend" that Walker talked about in his interview with Jan Gretlund is not altogether clear. What is certain is that the father of the family Walker lodged with was a member of the SA, the Sturmabteilung, and his son (or nephew) was a member of the Hitlerjugend about to enter the SS, the Schutzstaffel, who instructed Walker about the history of the Teutonic Knights and the taking of the oath at Marienburg.[29] Walker traveled to nearby Cologne and headed straight for the ancient cathedral, one of the most impressive in Europe. Cavalierly approaching the main portal, he was told by an attendant to discard his cigar and be more respectful when entering a holy building.[30]

Walker decided after two weeks in Germany not to stay with his fellow Chapel Hillians, and so took a *Rheinfahrt* on his own, down past the Drachenburg Castle above Königswinter, under the bridge at Remagen, admiring, as he went along, all the marvelous castles and forts that dot the Rhine. He wandered as a solitary traveler through the Black Forest. In Munich he saw the Karlplatz, the Odeonplatz with the Feldherrenhalle and Theatinerkirche, the carillon on the tower of the New Town Hall with the two-tiered movable figures and the marvelous spry Brunnenbuberi fountain near the Karlstor.

Walker was not far from Dachau, a short bicycle ride across the sodden moors northwest of Munich, yet he had no idea of the horrors that were already being committed there, nor, like most Americans, had he heard of Bergen-Belsen, Ravensbrück, Sachsenhausen, Flossenburg, Theresienstadt, Mauthausen, Auschwitz-Birkenau, or Treblinka. Before he arrived in Munich, posters proclaimed a long life both to President Hindenburg and to the Führer, Adolf Hitler. Munich's *Neueste Nachrichten* ran an announcement authorized by Heinrich Himmler, the police commissioner of Munich, stating that Dachau would soon be the site of a prison camp mostly for Jews, Gypsies, anti-Nazi clergy, and political prisoners. While Walker was in Munich, Adolf Eichmann was an *Unterscharführer* and Rudolf Hess was a *Blockführer* at Dachau. Walker tried to cross over into Austria sometime after July 25, but was stopped at the border, which had been closed because of the assassination of Chancellor Engelbert Dollfuss, whose Vaterlandische Front had suffered a devastating setback as a result of Hitler's psychotic determinism. Soon Walker returned to Bonn, rejoined the college group, and sailed back to the States. He had observed the tremendous excitement everywhere at the "rejuvenation" of Germany in a Nietzschean sense—the death of old values and the creation of horrible new ones.

When Walker returned to the United States, he had many stories to tell. One of his most receptive listeners was Shelby, who had recently been told that he would remain at Greenville High another year. Shelby himself had read the news carefully, listened attentively to the reports on Germany, and written a poem entitled "Five Images," which contains allusions to the growing conflict.[31] He was also responsible for the headline that appeared in *The Pica*: WALKER PERCY, G.H.S. ALUMNUS, TELLS OF HITLERITES: STATES THAT ANOTHER DISASTROUS WAR IS IMMINENT.[32] The incident in Bonn, told from Walker's youthful perspective, is revealing:

The man in the Nazi uniform struck me deliberately across the head twice before I could ask him why he was doing so. Hitler was just passing by, and I was watching with interest the adoration shining from the faces of the on-lookers. I turned to my attacker with a puzzled expression and saw that his face was reddened with anger. When he raised his arm to strike a third time I threw up my guard; he backed off a bit and, raising his arm with the palm extended toward the small man with the Chaplin mustache and dishevelled hair, said thickly:

"Heil, Hitler!"

You may be sure I wasted no time in doing likewise when I found that this was his reason for striking me. He was angry because I had not saluted his god with all due respect.

Shelby also describes Walker's non-trip to Austria, maintaining that Hitler was probably the greatest student of mob psychology the world had ever seen. His effectiveness could be measured by the theatrical manner in which he delivered his speeches to massed troops. In Shelby's account, young Walker had seen and initially refused to salute the person most responsible for the Holocaust.

That this trip to Bonn made a lasting impression on Walker can be found in his use of it in his novel *The Thanatos Syndrome*. In a passage in the first draft, Father Simon Smith, whose original last name was Schmidt, says he once visited relatives in Bonn with his father, a music professor from Loyola University in New Orleans.[33] In revising the text, Percy drew this startling parallel: just as the Nazi doctors used cruel experiments with prisoners of war in order to make scientific advances and purify the German race, so too a certain group of scientists in Louisiana (called the Louisiana Weimar psychiatrists in the novel) were adding heavy sodium to the water supply in order to manipulate human behavior, particularly that of children—thus the thanatos syndrome continued even to our day. Father Smith's confession and footnote add dramatic weight to the episode and provide the connective link. (Though Percy had written about priests before writing this novel—briefly about Father Smith in *Love in the Ruins*, Father Boomer in *The Last Gentleman*, Father Weatherbee in *The Second Coming*, and more at length about Father John in *Lancelot*—the only other Smith character in his fiction who shares the same mystical bent as does Father Smith is Lonnie Smith in *The Moviegoer*. It could well be argued that Father Smith is a Lonnie redivivus.) There is another dimension in the novel that arises directly from Walker's 1934 trip to Germany. The Holocaust appears as a divine contradiction: how could a loving God allow the destruction of millions of people? Are Roman Catholics spiritual Semites? This belief was enunciated in modern times by Pius XI in his encyclical *Mit Brennender Sorge* (1937), which lashes out against Nazism. It is also expressed by the Jäger boy in *The Thanatos Syndrome*, who maintains that Catholics are part of the "Judaic conspiracy." If Father Smith and his ilk are spiritual Semites, then Roman Catholics are also part of the Chosen Race and through them God continues to speak to this world. Percy was aware of this encyclical, which became part of a later moment of reflection on the significance of his college trip to Germany.[34] Even as a college student abroad, Walker was struggling with issues that provided the threads out of which his art of fiction would be woven.

After his trip to Germany, Walker was not expected to return to Greenville until the following Christmas.[35] He stopped off at Brinkwood for a short respite, as captured in a photograph of Walker, Newt and Donie DeBardeleben, Hughes Spalding, Roy, and Phin taken about this time.[36] Donie had a friend who owned a private plane, a biplane with an open cockpit, to the delight of Roy and Hughes, who once sat up front, elbow to elbow, doing loops.

Walker's final freshman grades (A in English, B's in German and history, and C in botany) prompted him to study harder as a sophomore. He registered in the "Tin Can," a temporary dance hall and sports arena, on September 20, and started classes the next day. He signed up for the final course in introductory German, English 21, a survey course of English literature; and Math 13, a course in analytic geometry—a comparatively light schedule considering his growing proficiency in German. Since Walker had separated himself from Professor Metzenthin's group abroad, it is likely that he signed up for the German section taught by Professor Spann, whom he also remembered as very rigid. This year Walker and Jimmy Carr decided to room together on the second floor of Old East in the section that faces Cameron Avenue, thus beginning a friendship that both cherished. Harry W. Stovall, Jr., a freshman who lived next door, caught Walker's attention because, during a period when students often drifted away from religious practices, he took his Catholic faith seriously.[37] Walker told Jimmy Sprunt about his summer trip, and without elaborating on it mentioned that the Germans were involved in some questionable type of medical experiments on human beings. Walker had brought back a bottle of Polish vodka. One of his friends, who had been taking occasional nips, picked up the bottle to examine the label more closely and shouted, "My God, I've been drinking furniture polish!"[38]

For those students who wanted distraction, Professor Smith began his "movie class" with *The Girl from Missouri* and *Crime Without Passion*. Walker made sure that his brother LeRoy (whom he tended to call Roy now) was welcome on campus. Roy decided to major in economics, and never felt that Walker was a rival, perhaps because they never took classes together. Roy pledged SAE, served as one of the fraternity editors for *The Yackety Yack*, and was destined to have an important role in governing the fraternity.[39] Two of those who pledged with him, Harry Stovall and George Alexander Heard, became Walker's friends.

James Stephens, the Sinn Feiner critic and novelist, lectured in mid-November on the Irish renaissance, stressing that American writers would achieve true greatness only when they got out of their own back yard and chose more universal subjects. He listed Faulkner and Caldwell among the leading writers of prose in the United States and said that some Americans with talent had become the victims of sectional writing and did not speak to all mankind. Walker read and enjoyed Stephens's novel *The Crock of Gold*.[40]

It was a busy time socially for Walker. The annual Fall Germans commenced with a tea dance in the late afternoon on Friday, November 16, followed in the evening by the formal Sophomore Ball in the Tin Can. The two dance leaders were Henry Clark and Walker, whose date was Margaret Yates from Birmingham.[41] The next day Walker took Margaret to the Carolina-Duke game. For the formal dance in the Tin Can, Walker suited himself up in white tie and tails and escorted Jean Brock, a Virginia native who was a sophomore at Sweet Briar College. Jean later married Hayden Clement, a DKE and a friend of Walker who was two years behind him.[42] Walker would also date Barbara Fulton and former Greenville classmate Maria Hilliard; when Maria and Sarah Farish were together, Walker would call them the "two partridges."[43] For her second year in college, Sarah switched to Arlington Hall near Washington, in order to be closer to Roy.

At the end of the fall quarter Walker received all A's in his courses; academically it was his best quarter at Chapel Hill.[44] While Roy spent Christmas vacation with Moose Cay, Walker went back to Greenville to be with Uncle Will and young Phin, who, more than his two brothers, felt the lack of a mother and a father.[45] Walker learned about a disturbing moment in Shelby's life. Apparently one of the female teachers at Greenville High accused Shelby of misconduct, and he was summarily expelled from school. When Uncle Will heard about it, he went to see Mrs. Foote at the ferry company where she worked: "Lillian, Shelby has gotten in great trouble. Why don't you have him come over to the house? There is no one there but Phin and me, and he would be no trouble." When his mother agreed, Shelby moved into 601 Percy Street for a week or so, spending long hours in Will's library reading to his heart's content, especially C. M. Doughty's *Travels in Arabia Deserta* and Burton's edition of *The Arabian Nights*.[46] At a faculty meeting, Miss Hawkins, who knew both parties, protested that the accusation was unfair and ridiculous, and Shelby was readmitted to school. The accusing schoolteacher proved to be mentally unsound and was sent to an asylum.[47]

When classes resumed in January 1935, Walker took German 21 (emphasizing Lessing, Goethe, and Schiller), English 22, a continuation of the English literature survey, and introductory chemistry. When the January issue of *The Carolina Magazine* appeared, friends of Walker were able to read his essay entitled "The Willard Huntington Wright Murder Case," in which he discussed the identity of S. S. Van Dine, the mystery writer whose highly successful books were published by Scribner's. Even after Wright wrote a caricature of himself, the public never caught on. Walker felt that among Wright's major works, in addition to his book on the philosophy of Nietzsche, was his novel entitled *The Man of Promise* (1916), which Walker considered almost a biography of Wright himself. The February issue included a rather mixed review by Walker of Claude Houghton's *This Was Ivor Trent*. In March appeared the most important essay Walker wrote in college: "The Movie Magazine: A Low 'Slick.' " Walker maintained that there were two types of popular magazines— "pulps" and "slicks." The pulps were hardly distinguishable one from another, and mostly concerned the activities of adventurers; slicks, on the other hand, included movie magazines, *Popular Mechanics*, *The Saturday Evening Post*, *Contract Bridge*, and *Liberty*. "Careful research has unearthed as possible steady movie magazine readers, lovelorn old maids, high school boys and girls, romantic working girls, and fanatical movie scrapbook keepers. College students may be included as a possible type, but their motives in reading are entirely healthy and transient." The mention of high school boys would seem to indicate that his own interest went back a few years. The comment by a real or imaginary college-student letter writer prefigures the attitude of Binx in *The Moviegoer*: "I used to feel tired and blue whenever I had a test facing me the next day at college, until I finally went to a movie the night before one. The next day I made the highest mark I have ever made. No more do I dread test days." Walker predicted these slicks would "go down in history as an eloquent manifestation of a particularly crude Americanism." He concluded by advocating better movie magazines that would do justice to the superior movies then being made. At the Carolina, Robert Flaherty's documentary *Man of Aran* was showing, a movie that deserved analysis in one of the better movie magazines Walker envisioned.

During the spring quarter, Walker took German 22 (taught by Professor Kent J. Brown), economics, chemistry, and English 50 (a twelve-week course on Shakespeare taught by Professor George Coffin Taylor, for which Walker received a grade of B). Professor Taylor, a popular though demanding teacher according to Jimmy Sprunt, had his students memorize a good bit of Shakespeare; the last question on his exam reflected this tendency: "During the remaining time, quote all the Shakespeare that you can."[48]

Walker spent part of the summer at Brinkwood and invited Margaret Yates to visit with him and Shelby. Walker also read George Santayana's *The Last Puritan: A Memoir in the Form of a Novel*, which is set in New England and concerns Peter Alden, the dark sheep of the Alden family, and his son Oliver, the last Puritan. Walker wrote that this novel "meant a great deal to me when I read it."[49] Before Oliver leaves England at one point in the novel, his father commits suicide since he wants his son to depend less on him and more on his mother. The death scene is presented in only a few sentences: "All was ready. Papers, bank account, even clothes would be found in perfect order. There was nothing more to do but quietly to go to sleep and never to wake up again." When Oliver again returns to the States, he joins the army and is sent back overseas to France. He is killed after the war in a motorcycle accident in Dijon, leaving a portion of his money to his mother. Though Oliver had sought commitment, he actually lived a life withdrawn from others. Life provided no guidelines as to what career choices he should make. Oliver's loyalties sapped his strength, gave him no genuine vision, and made the world commonplace for him. Walker doubtless found a partial image of himself in Oliver, and would have been haunted by the similarity of the fates of their fathers. This novel could well have substituted for the philosophy courses Walker never took.

The fall quarter resumed on September 20, 1935. Walker moved into a third-floor room with Harry Stovall, Jimmy Sprunt, and Jimmy Carr in the SAE house.[50] Total enrollment reached 2,765 (only 281 women) that year and a new core curriculum was instituted. The famous freshman history course was replaced by a social science course—a combination of government, sociology, history, and economics. A comprehensive biology course was also integrated into the curriculum. Such changes would affect Shelby Foote, who drove up to Chapel Hill that fall with Don Wetherbee.[51] It was Shelby's first time at Chapel Hill. Naturally Shelby was interested in pledging SAE, but the fraternity's Eminent Archon announced that Shelby would not be tendered a bid because some of his ancestors were Jewish—a decision extremely difficult for Walker to accept. Roy was commissioned to tell Shelby the bad news. After living two months in Steele, Shelby joined another fraternity, Alpha Tau Omega, located at 303 East Franklin. In his second and last year, Shelby lived in a boardinghouse. Fortunately, he was put in the "Flying Squadron" right away. Since they were two years apart, Walker and Shelby never had any classes together.

Though Walker never went to church in Chapel Hill, he nevertheless admired those who were faithful to their religious commitments, like Harry Stovall. Each Sunday morning and on some weekdays, the janitor in the fraternity house would wake up Harry at dawn for early Mass celebrated by the Catholic chaplain to the university. William Carmichael, one of the more visible Catholics in those days, was wont to say that there weren't enough Catholics in Chapel Hill in the 1930s to fill a phone booth. After one particularly rambunctious Saturday evening, the janitor left a note for Harry notifying him that he would not be around to wake him up the following morning. Unfortunately Harry never saw the note and blamed Jimmy Sprunt for mislaying it. "It is bad enough monkeying around with your own soul," Harry exploded, "but when you do it with someone else's, that's even worse."[52] Harry Stovall would have no idea how impressed Walker was by his faithful dedication, precisely because it was such a countercultural thing to do. The influence of European theologians and learned philosophers was all very good, but Walker pointed to Harry's faithful participation in the Catholic liturgy as one of the moments in his life that led to his conversion.[53]

Shelby and Walker saw a good deal of each other; they went to movies and football games together and delighted in Chapel Hill's 8–1 record that year. They read each other's papers (while at Chapel Hill, Shelby published in *The Carolina Magazine* nine stories, one poem, and four book reviews, including two on works by Faulkner and Caroline Gordon). Shelby enjoyed prowling around the nine stories of the library posing as a precocious graduate student. Walker and Shelby had only one disagreeable moment together. On a train ride they started arguing about racial problems. Shelby maintained that both blacks and whites would have a lot to gain if integration were instituted all down the line. Walker was furious: "Shelby, you call yourself a Southerner!" He got up and went away until he could cool off.[54]

With countless others from Chapel Hill and Duke and North Carolina State University, these two friends would on occasion seek out illicit pleasures. Once a small group of students from Chapel Hill rode out to a dive called Pappa Rogge's on the road to Durham. After a beer or two, they unwisely began flirting with two women whose male partners objected. One of the men jumped Shelby, and Shelby knocked him down, soiling his stylish trousers. In a split second one of the women grabbed Walker, mistaking him for Shelby, and punched him in the mouth. Walker could only cry out, "But you're a woman! You're a woman!" The ensuing scuffle ended in a standoff. A third college student, nicknamed "Embryo," hid while all this was taking place, and Walker later told Shelby, "You know, Embryo was the only one who had any sense." Sometimes four or five of them would take a room in Raleigh and spend a weekend there, and pick up girls. Walker and his fellow students were familiar with a bawdy house in Raleigh, as well as one on the edge of Chapel Hill called either Katy May's or Katy Mae's. (When I asked one of Walker's classmates to spell the name of this establishment, he said, "Well, I don't think I ever saw it in print.") At one such place, they happened to run into a prominent public person, much to their embarrassment. In hindsight, Walker felt that those of his generation from Greenville "got crossed up," as they moved in two generations "from a genteel repressed Southern Presbyterian sexuality—with barely enough room for an awkward piece maybe twice or three times" to a later spirit that was at ease in expressing its sexuality amid "the blue-grey rooftops and chimney pots."[55]

In the fall Walker signed up for courses in economics, chemistry, and zoology (taught by Professor Robert E. Coker in Davie Hall). Coker, who taught two of Walker's classes, enjoyed entertaining his students by spreading out his arms and legs to show the comparative anatomy of various vertebrates. He was deemed to be a genuine scientist by his students.[56] In one class, Professor Coker dissected a dogfish, something Walker would later associate, in an address to high school teachers, with poetry. (Chapel Hill was known for its behaviorist orientation in psychology, and Walker noted that students studied the similarities between men and animals, rather than the differences.[57]) For his part, Professor Coker thought Walker "very agreeable" and a "good worker" and wrote that he would be a "desirable" prospective medical student.[58] At the beginning of the next quarter, Walker signed up for Chemistry 61 and 24, one or both taught in Venable Hall by Professor Ralph W. Bost (Walker called him "Boss"), and Physics 24, taught in Phillips Hall by Professor Otto Stuhlman, Jr. Professor Bost, who was one of Walker's favorite teachers, taught in a large amphitheater. He noted in a letter of reference for Walker that he only had contact with Walker in the lecture hall and in the lab, but nevertheless considered him "much better than average." Professor Bost echoed Professor Stuhlman's opinion that Walker would make a "very desirable" prospective medical student. Professor Stuhlman thought he knew Walker "comparatively well" and considered him a "hard worker."[59]

During spring break of 1936, which occurred in mid-March, Walker and Shelby took a bus to New York City, sitting long hours on uncomfortable wooden seats.[60] Each had $200 in his pocket, more than enough to pay for six nights at Sloane House on West 34th Street, which then cost $1.50 per night. Exhausted when they arrived, they slept soundly through the first night. Shelby sensed that Walker had been to New York before, because he knew the layout of the city and the subways. Walker went alone to see Osgood Perkins in S. N. Behrman's comedy *End of Summer* at the Guild Theatre. Together they went to movies, heard Arturo Toscanini conduct the New York Philharmonic on Sunday afternoon, enjoyed jazz in the Ubangi Club on Seventh Avenue in Harlem, and saw exotic dancing at the Copacabana.

Because of his academic success and his congenial personality, Walker was sought out by various clubs and organizations on campus. He was inducted, along with Ross Allen and Moose Cay, into the Order of Gimghouls at Gimghoul Castle in Glandon Forest, just off the edge of campus. Mostly a social club that would sponsor two big parties a year, Gimghoul encouraged its members to congregate in the castle whenever they wished to enjoy one another's company. Roy would also be inducted into Gimghoul and be chosen Rex. In addition, Walker was invited to join, along with Don Wetherbee and Jimmy Carr, Amphoterothen, a society whose Greek name is derived from the phrase "from both sides" or "on both sides," as well as the 13 Club, in which the initiates were required to wear a ridiculous costume with a twelve-link chain necklace and wander the campus for thirteen days, counting off to the number 13 in a loud voice. On the thirteenth day, all the initiates would gather and point to each other as the thirteenth or "missing" link in the chain.[61] On March 25, Carolina's chapter of Alpha Epsilon Delta (AED), the national honorary premedical fraternity, initiated its charter members at a formal banquet. Walker was one of the charter members along with Henry Toole Clark, Jr., the president of the Interfraternity Council. Two months later, Joseph Patterson succeeded Louis Skinner as president of AED, and Walker was selected to be vice president and Lou Shaffner treasurer.[62] At the end of the winter quarter, Walker made the honor roll; he received two A's (Chemistry 61 and Physics 24) and one B (Chemistry 42). On May 14, he was inducted into Phi Beta Kappa.[63] Unfortunately, a number of Walker's classmates and friends never realized that he received this honor, for both his graduating yearbook and his graduation program omitted his name from the list of members.

During the warm spring days, Walker would often take the recently published four volumes of Douglas Southall Freeman's *R. E. Lee: A Biography* to the upper porch at SAE, put up his feet, and follow carefully the battles of the Civil War (the book is mentioned repeatedly in *The Last Gentleman*).[64] For his classmates, this is their quintessential image of Walker. He was so taken by the events of the Civil War and so identified with Robert E. Lee that he visited some of the battlefields, stopping off at Washington and Lee University in Lexington, Virginia.[65] At the end of his junior year, Walker received B's in chemistry and zoology (taught by Professor Henry Wilson) and took an "Incomplete" in physics.

That summer, Jimmy Sprunt drove to Greenville by way of Memphis with his cousin Albert Cox and Jimmy Carr. Their intention was to drive to the Texas Centennial Exposition in Dallas. The visitors stayed a couple of nights at 601 Percy Street and took a trip out to Trail Lake.

Because Walker was also working part-time at Gamble Brothers & Archer Clinic in Greenville, he agreed to go as far as Dallas.[66] Shelby did not join him; he was working for the U.S. Gypsum Company in Greenville. They did find time, however, to hear *Madame Butterfly* in Memphis. Walker had a keen eye for young ladies, and it was clear that he had no interest in society types. But when he spotted "someone easy on the eyes" at the opera, he said to Shelby, "Life is a strange thing. That is the most beautiful, desirable girl I have ever seen in my life. I would give anything to know her."[67] Walker's shyness prevented him from going over and introducing himself, even though Shelby was giving him a gentle nudge. After the opera, Walker and Shelby drove to the Memphis Country Club for a dinner Dave Cohn had arranged for them to attend, and sitting there at the table was the beautiful young woman. Apparently Walker lost any budding romantic interest when he learned that she had gone to Vassar.[68]

Uncle Will sailed from Los Angeles on the SS *Monterey* on June 24 for Samoa, where he lived among the villagers of Laulii and wrote an unpublished essay, "The White Plague." While in the South Pacific, he had little contact with his adopted sons. "They are strongly opposed to a summer trip so I will put Roy to work on Trail Lake, Phin in camp in North Carolina and Walker will drift. Perhaps they will spend August or part of it in Sewanee," Will wrote Charlotte Gailor, the daughter of Bishop Thomas Frank Gailor.[69] It is probable that, as Walker drifted, he spent some time at Brinkwood. If so, this could well have been the time he first met novelist Caroline Gordon (author of *Penhally* and *Aleck Maury, Sportsman*), who with her husband, the poet Allen Tate, was living that August in the cabin belonging to Andrew Lytle's family at nearby Monteagle.[70] The Tates stayed on at least through the following spring. Walker's first recollection of Tate was of him playing tennis, perhaps with Uncle Will.[71] Walker saw Tate only a few times and did not develop a correspondence with him.[72] Out of Gordon's stay came her short story "The Brilliant Leaves," which takes place in the Monteagle-Sewanee area (Peter Taylor's "Heads of Houses" occurs in the same locale). Will, in his role as guardian of the Percy boys, paid the taxes on the house on Arlington in Birmingham, even though Grandmother Pratt had moved to another location.[73] That December, Shelby gave his personal copy of *The Brothers Karamazov* to Walker as a Christmas present.

In the first quarter of his senior year, Walker opted not to take any classes. Because he had a surplus of credits, he wanted to take time off to visit medical schools. He moved into Mrs. Patterson's boardinghouse with Jimmy Carr near the President's House on East Franklin. Walker attended the Carolina–NYU football game at Yankee Stadium that fall.[74]

While in New York, Walker went to see Cab Calloway at the Cotton Club, which had relocated to 48th Street after the 1935 riots in Harlem.[75] Most likely, he was back in Chapel Hill to take the medical aptitude test on December 4. For the winter quarter, Walker took History 134 (taught by Professor Mitchell B. Garrett), a course on the Napoleonic period. He had read *War and Peace* by that time and was most interested in this period.[76] In addition to courses in zoology and mathematics, he took English 82 (taught by Professor Raymond A. Adams), a course in nineteenth-century American literature that focused on the works of Poe, Emerson, Thoreau, Lowell, Hawthorne, and Melville. For his grades, Walker received three B's and one C (zoology). Walker had a copy of his transcript forwarded to Harvard Medical School, where he was eventually rejected. He was crushed—so much so that later one of his closest medical friends, who taught at Harvard, believed this was the reason Walker would never visit Boston or accept a visiting professorship at Harvard when it was offered to him.[77]

On his application to Columbia University's College of Physicians and Surgeons (P & S) Walker enclosed a photo of himself looking out at the camera, eyes direct, studious, and intelligent. Walker noted that six years previously he had made up his mind to study medicine, most likely working in the field of ductless glands. Fortunately, Walker had enough money to cover the tuition and would not have to work at all while in medical school. His health was good; during his four years in college, he spent only three days in the infirmary. He listed no physical defects, nor had he ever been treated by a physician for a disorder of the nervous system.

Charles Flood, M.D., the assistant dean at P & S, wrote to Dean Allan W. Hobbs at Chapel Hill stating that he had received an application from Walker, and because distance prohibited a personal interview with their admissions committee he asked the dean to write a letter of recommendation. Dean Hobbs replied on February 22: "In answer to your inquiry about Walker Percy I can say that I consider him an ideal prospect for a physician. He has a fine personality, background, manners, ability, character; everything which I should imagine would be in his favor. His record is good in this institution and we can recommend him without any qualifications." Dr. Flood noted that Dean Hobbs had written a "good" recommendation in place of a personal interview, and that Walker's overall recommendations were "good and v. good." Flood then notified Walker that he was admitted into P & S, provided he could pay for his expenses during the first year; Walker had received an excellent general index rating.

On being accepted, Walker submitted an application for a medical-student qualifying certificate for New York State, which he received in midsummer. In their letters, Professors Stuhlman, Bost, and Coker indicated that Walker was the type of future physician they would select to visit their sickrooms. Stuhlman and Coker thought that Walker was better than average mentally, while Bost thought he was much better than average. In answering a question about Walker's personal attractiveness and the impression he made on others, Stuhlman wrote "very nice," Bost left the answer blank, and Coker wrote that he was "very agreeable—unusual good address." All three agreed that Walker was intellectually adept; they had nothing unfavorable to say about his moral character.

In mid-March, Walker sent Dr. Flood the registration fee; he also indicated he would forward the qualifying certificate to study medicine in New York State.[78] In his last quarter at Chapel Hill, he assumed a grueling course load, including three hours a week of mathematics with the tall, personable Professor Ernest Mackie; two classes in advanced chemistry, one of which was a six-hour theoretical and analytic chemistry session with Professor James T. Dobbins; a physics lab that completed eight hours of general physics; and English 44, a course in public speaking that met five times a week with Professor William A. Olsen. Professor Dobbins, a mild man with a sense of metaphor and country wit, would encourage his students with images that made them smile: "Don't be a June bug on a spring chicken."[79] Not surprisingly, it was Walker's worst quarter for grades, including a D in public speaking. In looking back on his speech course, Walker would raise his shoulders in apparent pain: "That was horrifying. I hated it. It was so traumatic."[80] He was often seen carrying around John Punnett Peter's 405-page tome entitled *Body Water: The Exchange of Fluids in Man* (1935), no doubt preparing himself for his medical classes in New York City.

President Graham presided at the 142nd annual commencement on June 8. After an invocation, the prizes and fellowships were announced. Shelby stepped forward to receive the Student Library Award; he finished his career at Chapel Hill the same day as Walker. When Walker stepped forward to receive his B.A. degree, he was also presented with a Bible as a gift. Once the ceremony was over, many of the guests adjourned to the Carolina Inn. Nell Johnson had traveled to be with her cousin; she felt it important that her side of the family be represented on this occasion. Phin and Uncle Will also attended. Walker's final grades were sent to P & S on June 22, thus completing his application form. A notation on his transcript suggests that his grades were also sent

to the Medical College of the State University of New York for a certificate to study medicine in New York State. Though Walker had himself
clearly chosen to go to medical school, he always felt a certain pressure
to do so from Uncle Will. Having rejected further studies for a career as
a lawyer, soldier, or cleric, he opted to become a physician: "Medicine
was left as the obvious last resort."[81]

4

The Medical School Years

1937–41

During the summer of 1937 Walker made plans to begin his medical education, and bought a Ford for $2,170 (a present from Uncle Will).[1] The dean and registrar of UNC sent Walker's spring grades to P & S (the College of Physicians and Surgeons at Columbia University). His qualifying certificate was likewise sent from the New York State Department of Education to P & S. Late that summer he said goodbye to family and friends in Greenville and started northward in his car to New York, driven by David Scott, the young black man who worked for Uncle Will.

Once in New York, Walker did not go directly to Washington Heights but stayed for several weeks at the YMCA on West 63rd Street, north of Columbus Circle. Its location provided a perfect place to explore New York. It was only a short stroll to Central Park West, a street noted for luxurious apartments with panoramic views of the New York skyline. In Central Park, Walker could wander about at his leisure, visiting the expansive Sheep Meadow, the Ramble, the Reservoir, and the Great Lawn north of Belvedere Castle—places that provided inspiration for the first sentence of *The Last Gentleman*: "One fine day in early summer a young man lay thinking in Central Park." Since the novel is Walker's most autobiographical work of fiction, this sentence indicates that a turning point was taking place both in Walker's life and in the life of his protagonist.

Before moving uptown to West 168th Street, Walker had time to explore the city, visit the museums and parks, go to the movies, and learn the subway routes. Uprooted, without family or friends his own age, Walker intuitively felt the need to explore his new environment. The narrator of "Confessions of a Movie-goer"—an early version of *The Moviegoer*—gives a highly personal account of how one medical student spent his days in New York:

I descend into the earth at Columbus Circle and perhaps an hour later pop up in some district I have never seen before—that very few New Yorkers have seen before—New Lots Avenue, City Island, Forest Hills, Washington Heights, Fordham Road. By then it is usually early evening. The lights are just coming on in the dusk. Children are beginning to leave the streets and go home for supper. It is especially satisfying to emerge in a neighborhood which is undergoing a change despite itself, either falling upon hard times or being newly developed. I don't know which is more delightful, coming upon some vulnerable old Loew's being engulfed by an industrial growth but still carrying on, showing movies under twinkling stars and between terra cotta urns and cherubim—or a brand new Tudor, a spic-and-span cube of concrete in some raw suburb. Or best of all, to come up in a district where something has gone wrong, where the development has failed or been passed over, a backwater, an old-new development of weedy lots and ancient real estate signs and buckling sidewalks and abandoned foundations.

To crisscross the city, to master its boundaries, to feel its vitality was a way of dominating an environment so that it would become his to use. These first few weeks of wandering aimlessly around the big city planted a seed for Walker's first published novel.

When Walker finally moved to Washington Heights, the hospital and medical school complex was already in full bloom.[2] Located immediately south of the George Washington Bridge, it stretches from 163rd to 168th Street and from Broadway almost to the Hudson River, on a site that many years earlier was the home of the Highlanders baseball club. In 1921, under the leadership of Edward S. Harkness, the final phase of P & S's New York odyssey to upper Manhattan began, when Presbyterian Hospital and Columbia University established a legal bond. P & S and the twenty-two-story Presbyterian Hospital formally merged in 1928 and the new complex set a standard for medical education. Directly across from the National Guard Armory on 168th Street stands the College of Physicians and Surgeons, which had moved uptown from West 59th Street.

When Walker arrived this environment still had a luster of newness. Any arriving student would have been impressed by the clean lines of these buildings, with their functional interiors and the latest in modern equipment. The impressive medical library was directly above the main

entrance, a constant reminder to all who entered of what would be expected of them. Farther south and directly behind the college stood the
West, Center, and East Wings of Presbyterian Hospital. On three floors
of all three wings was located the Sloane Hospital for Women. On the
Broadway side of West 168th Street, east of P & S, stood Vanderbilt
Clinic, which, while retaining its name, merged with the outpatient de-
partment of Presbyterian Hospital. Babies Hospital, an independent institution until 1932, when it first affiliated and then merged with
Presbyterian Hospital, likewise faced onto Broadway. The Neurological
Institute, which had moved from East 67th Street and Lexington Avenue
to the southwest corner of Fort Washington Avenue and Haven Avenue
in 1928, affiliated with Presbyterian Hospital in 1938. The New York
State–owned Psychiatric Institute and Hospital was located near the
Neurological Institute. Finally, Maxwell Hall, an eleven-story building,
a residence for student nurses and the nursing school staff, was built on
the west side of Fort Washington Avenue directly across from the Harkness Pavilion, the part of Presbyterian Hospital used for private patients.
Construction of Presbyterian Hospital, Harkness Pavilion, Vanderbilt
Clinic, and Maxwell Hall cost many millions, and the entire complex had
the appearance of a tremendously solid state-of-the-art medical city.

Walker's start at P & S did not go unnoticed in Greenville; Uncle
Will wrote to his friend Charlotte Gailor, noting that "Walker has finally
lodged in the Medical School at Columbia and has a splendid room and
a very scrawny Negro stiff to work on"—a crude reference to the fact
that Walker was studying anatomy and performing autopsies under
Dudley Joy Morton, author of *The Human Foot*.[3] In the gross anatomy
lab, Walker and three other students stood around a table and probed
and dissected a cadaver. The first few weeks of school would force the
squeamish to reconsider their vocations and to come face-to-face with
their own mortality.

Walker soon settled into a routine. He moved into the eleven-story
Bard Hall, the P & S residence on Haven Avenue where he lived for four
years of medical school. His corner room on the tenth floor had a panoramic view of the Hudson River and the Palisades Amusement Park
on the New Jersey side. From one side window he could see all the way
south to the Battery at the tip of Manhattan. Walker was one of the
fortunate ones to have a suite.[4] Bard Hall had a spacious lounge on the
ground floor, a dining room directly below the lounge (breakfast and
lunch were cafeteria style, dinner was served), four squash courts (where
Walker lost some front teeth), a gym (where he would join in pickup
games of basketball), a moderate-sized swimming pool, as well as a social club for P & S students who belonged to the YMCA. Movies were

very popular and a screen was installed in the dining room. The neighborhood was a stable one of walk-up brownstones and medium-sized tenement buildings belonging mostly to families of Irish stock and recently arrived German intellectuals seeking political and academic freedom, a number of whom would find employment at P&S. During his four years at P & S, he would invariably park his Ford near Bard Hall; with its out-of-state license plate, the car attracted the notice of the local police and inspired numerous conversations. His car allowed him a certain degree of freedom, most notably to absent himself from the activities of his classmates, but most of the time his classmates noticed that it just sat there.

As Walker became familiar with the layout of the medical complex, he walked through the stem on the eighth and ninth floors of P & S to the back part of the complex. There he encountered Presbyterian Hospital, three wards on each floor that could accommodate up to twelve patients each; each ward also had a smaller four-bed unit and three or four one-bed rooms. In these years, patients throughout the hospital would not have had private health insurance. At the ends of the twelve-bed wards were solaria for the patients who were mobile and needed a change of scenery. Students took elevators from internal medicine on the eighth floor up to histology on the ninth floor, anatomy on the tenth floor, bacteriology on the twelfth floor, pathology on the fourteenth floor, and obstetrics/gynecology on the fifteenth through the seventeenth floors. Each floor had its own set of laboratories. The operating rooms were on the eighteenth and nineteenth floors, and though students did not wander into these rooms, Walker and his classmates spent time there when studying surgery. Walker could have access in a few minutes to lecture rooms, faculty offices, and various hospitals.

The faculty that Dean William Darrach began recruiting before his retirement in 1930 had a decided influence on Walker. Their full names still ring strong and loud in the ears of their former students: Samuel Randall Detwiler, author of *Neuroembryology: An Experimental Study*, Philip Edward Smith in anatomy, Hans Thatcher Clarke in biochemistry, Horatio Burt Williams in physiology, and Frederick Parker Gay in bacteriology. Other distinguished professors appointed before Darrach's tenure as dean included James Wesley Jobling in pathology, John Bentley Squier in urology, and Charles Christian Lieb in pharmacology. New appointees included Walter Walker Palmer in medicine, Allen Oldfather Whipple in surgery, Benjamin Philip Watson in obstetrics, and Haven Emerson in public health. Darrach's tenure as dean was followed in 1931 by that of Willard Cole Rappleye, who had been professor of hospital administration at Yale. When Walker entered P & S, changes were taking place that seem fairly standard today, but they were then innovative and had far-reaching effects on the way Walker learned to diagnose the illnesses that he saw and studied.

It was expected that the entering class of 1937 would take two years of basic or preclinical science, consisting mostly of lectures and laboratory work, followed by two years of clinical science, which involved progressively greater ward experience and actual contact with patients. In the first year the basic courses would be anatomy, biochemistry, embryology, histology, neuroanatomy, microanatomy, and physiology. In the second year there were courses in pathology, microbiology, and pharmacology, with physical and clinical diagnosis during the last third of the year. In the third year there were four major clerkships, each coordinated by a professor and guided by one or more "attending" physicians: medicine, surgery, pediatrics, and psychiatry, with minor clerkships in ophthalmology, dermatology, orthopedics, neurology, obstetrics, and gynecology. It was not unusual for students to take their ob-gyn clerkship at Sloane Hospital. To a great extent, the fourth year was repetitious of the third, though there were some additional electives taught at a more advanced level. Rotations in the fourth year tended to be shorter than in the third because of these electives. Students in their final year had a greater sense of making a transition as they discussed their patients with their professors and planned procedures for these patients. Also during the fourth year, students worked on what was called the chest service and the general medical service at Bellevue, gaining invaluable experience in one of New York City's more dynamic hospitals. Unknown to the 113 entering students, the marking system was rigid: the department heads had been requested to distribute the grades as follows: A to approximately 10 percent of the class; B to 50 percent; C to the rest.[5]

At registration Walker posed for a student ID mug shot, one apparently used during his four years at P & S. It shows a serious young man in a light jacket, with a striped tie, looking up and slightly off-camera. His lips do not betray a smile and there is a hint of intensity in the eyes. Among new classmates, the most visible group was the contingent from Princeton.[6] Walker made his own set of friends, particularly with Frederick Dieterlie, Gilbert H. Mudge, Habeen Z. ("Hobby") Maroon, Robert F. Gehres, Gustave A. Haggstrom, and Frank J. Hardart, Jr. As they swapped stories at such local hangouts as Curran's Armory Bar & Grill on Broadway (popularly known as "A, B & G" and transformed in The Last Gentleman into the Washington Heights Bar & Grill), Walker's classmates admired his laid-back humor. His casual dress reflected his inner spirit and put people at ease. Walker and his classmates could go to the Uptown Theatre on Broadway and West 170th Street for the latest movies, or Loew's State at 175th, or farther uptown at 181st to the RKO Coliseum.

Walker did not look on movies as an escape: "I'd go all the time to movies up at Washington Heights. I think at the movies I was getting to know how people looked at the world, what they thought—just as a doctor does. The movies are not just fantasies; for a lot of people they provide important moments, maybe the only point in the day, or even the week, when someone (a cowboy, a detective, a crook) is heard asking what life is all about, asking what is worth fighting for—or asking if anything is worth fighting for."[7] Medical students dubbed another movie theater in the Audubon Ballroom building at 166th Street the "Armpit." Walker always found it difficult to share much about himself with new friends; he usually kept a calm and pleasant demeanor, but was not averse to joining in the more spirited give-and-takes. He could always hold his own in any group.

Not all the students initially considered themselves part of some inner crowd. George L. Hawkins, Jr., given the nickname "Hawkeye," met a pleasant and determined Walker at registration.[8] (Walker soon picked up a new moniker—Rollo—which may have come about from a comic-strip figure, Rollo Rollingstone.) George had never before been east of the Mississippi River and he felt fortunate in having been selected as a P & S student. In George's view, Walker would have made an excellent physician—or anything else—since he seemed to have the qualities needed for success in any endeavor.

Frank Hardart, a native New Yorker, who was slightly older than Walker, lived across the hall from him in Room 1002.[9] Frank, a Roman Catholic, had attended the Jesuit-run Loyola School in Manhattan, and transferred to Newman School in New Jersey before he went to Notre Dame for four years to study economics. Frank felt so confident about being accepted at P & S, as he told Walker, that he did not apply to other medical schools. Frank's father directed the Horn & Hardart restaurants, a self-help chain of "Automats" famous for low prices and a series of windowed slots with food paid for by depositing a number of nickels. The restaurants—and the Hardart family—had been celebrated in the Irving Berlin and Moss Hart musical *Face the Music* and in the 1937 film *Easy Living*. (*The Last Gentleman* mentions the Automat near Carnegie Hall.) Sometimes Frank would take Walker and a few other classmates to the Automat on 181st Street, where they might get a free meal if Frank happened to be recognized.

Another student who soon became friends with Walker was Bert Mudge, an Amherst graduate who took a year of premed at Columbia

University.[10] Bert sat next to Walker in class, especially during their first two years; his meticulously kept notebooks paint a detailed picture of their days at P & S. Walker also met and got on well with Philip Knapp, a native New Yorker and a graduate of Phillips Exeter and Harvard, who came from a long tradition of doctors who specialized in eye medicine.[11] Walker felt comfortable with different groups of friends, some of whom did not interact with other groups. In fact, it was one of Walker's saving graces, because it allowed him to form friendships with individuals who had interests independent from other people he knew.

The basic courses were often taught in amphitheaters, with patients sometimes brought in for the purpose of demonstration; these lectures were followed by sessions in classrooms or laboratories. Each of the three amphitheaters looked like a model for Thomas Eakins's *The Gross Clinic*, with its steep steps and vertiginous sweep. Any note of levity—sometimes provided by Dr. Franklin Hanger—was greatly appreciated by the students as they strained to absorb the demanding lectures.

What Walker missed in this new setting was a sense of his own Southern roots, but he knew where to find it. He started visiting Uncle Will's close friend Huger Wilkinson Jervey, who had an apartment at 1150 Fifth Avenue. A native of Charleston, who had bought Brinkwood with Will, he would become during the next few years Walker's surrogate uncle.[12] Walker felt comfortable with the older Jervey not only because of his patrician background and long-standing relationship with Will but also because he was an esteemed professor of law at Columbia University, well versed in the pressures of academic life. He and Will Percy first met at Sewanee. After graduate study at Johns Hopkins, Jervey returned to Sewanee to teach until 1909. He entered Columbia Law School in 1910 and received his law degree in February 1913. His intelligence had not gone unnoticed; he became an editor of *The Columbia Law Review* in 1911. When admitted to the New York Bar in 1913, he joined the law firm of Satterlee, Canfield & Stone. (In this case, the Stone was Justice-to-be Harlan Fiske Stone, the former dean of Columbia's Law School.) Like Uncle Will, Jervey served in France during 1917–18, attached to the Judge Advocate General's Department. He joined the law faculty at Columbia as an associate professor in 1923 and a year later became a full professor and dean of the Law School. In the early 1930s Jervey served as the administrative head of the Parker School of International Affairs at Columbia, and in 1936 he started teaching the first-year course in equity, providing him with a second career that would continue for the next thirteen years. Walker profited from the companionship and advice of this seasoned veteran of Columbia; they often enjoyed dinners together and nights at symphony concerts.

Classes continued at a relentless pace. In mid-November, Dr. Smith gave four lectures on the structure of the endocrine glands and the female reproductive organs, while Dr. Aura Edward Severinghaus focused on the pituitary gland. Dr. Earl T. Engle complemented Dr. Smith's lectures by discussing the anatomy of genital systems. As the Christmas holidays approached, Walker sat through lectures by Dr. Magnus I. Gregersen on blood and circulation and Dr. Goodwin Foster on enzyme reactions and hematology. Before Christmas, Walker attended his regular classes, plus three by Byron Stookey on the neuroanatomy of muscle and skin, using case studies as he went along. When Walker finished his first semester, he could enjoy the Christmas respite and see Huger Jervey; he would receive his grade evaluations at the end of the academic year.

How could Walker begin to synthesize all this technical knowledge? How could he articulate a context that made good sense to him? He knew that his studies had to go beyond just factual information; Walker was particularly taken by the phrase "mechanism of disease":

Even the *dis*-order of *dis*-ease, which one generally takes to be the very disruption of order, could be approached and understood and treated according to scientific principles governing the response of the patient to the causative agents of disease. This response *was* the disease as the physician sees it! Of course, it was hardly a new idea, but, new or old, it was an exciting discovery for a young man who had always thought of disease as disorder to be set right somehow by the "art" of medicine.[13]

Walker's breakthrough occurred in discovering the role the patient had in responding to a disease. As he memorized more and more factual material, he would also look first and foremost at the patient to see what types of responses there were and what they indicated. The patients Walker saw then and afterward became his first literary protagonists.

In 1938 he took classes on nerve injuries, brachial plexus disorders, metabolism, and physical diagnosis. Late in January, Kenneth S. Cole continued lecturing on the physiology of nerves and their receptors. For a good bit of February, Henry Alsop Riley took his students through the functions of various parts of the brain. These and similar lectures about the brain caused Walker to think about the relationship of a person to the person's own actuating center, and eventually led Walker to look at the locus where speech originates, a subject of inquiry that fascinated him throughout his life. He would become one of the few literary writers who approached semiotics with a detailed awareness of the mechanisms of the brain.

As he absorbed all these lectures, Walker fondly recalled his Edenic Chapel Hill days—a world quite remote from the pressures he was facing. For Roy it would be his last chance—particularly as Eminent Archon of SAE—to put some order into what Sarah Farish considered a very disorderly fraternity house. These were carefree days for Roy, yet he would assume responsibilities and burdens after graduation he had not quite expected.

Walker's life was not without distractions as he became more familiar with what New York offered. With the repeal of Prohibition in 1933, some of the former speakeasy joints on "Swing Alley" along West 52nd Street turned into legitimate boîtes, especially Jack and Charlie's "21" Club. "Oh, let's go to *Ein und Zwanzig*," Walker would coax a group of friends trying to decide where to go for the evening. Frequenters of these clubs included a mixture from uptown and downtown—socialites, Broadway stars, latter-day flappers, and college and graduate students. Walker, Phil Knapp, and others sometimes went to the Famous Door, which featured Ella Logan, as well as to the Onyx across the street or the Hickory House just down the block. Since Frank Hardart and his father had an apartment on East 54th Street, Walker would sometimes join Frank at the Weylin Bar. On more formal occasions, there were evenings at El Morocco, the Stork Club, and the Rainbow Room. There were the tea dances at the Biltmore, often to the music of Horace Heidt, and relaxed dinners at Dempsey's. Walker had no difficulty attracting young ladies; they seemed to gravitate to his lanky good looks. Small groups from P & S would hear the great black singers of the day at the Plantation Club, Connie's Inn, Dick Wells's, or in any of the clubs that dotted 125th Street in Harlem. Walker would sometimes join his friends for jazz at the Black Cat in Greenwich Village. And the big Broadway movie theaters, especially the Roxy, the Paramount, and the Capitol were definite magnets. "Confessions of a Movie-goer" takes place in a movie theater noted for its stage shows—Radio City Music Hall, where Walker and Phil Knapp enjoyed going.

There was always that other reality to face, the daily grind. Though the tedium of attending classes could easily become a mechanical routine, it taught Walker the value of budgeting his time. Though he often described himself as lazy, prone to distractions, his work habits over the years indicate something of the opposite, like his penchant for constantly revising what he had written. His slack and hasty physician's penmanship failed to reveal the tireless dedication that resulted from highly professional training.

After an embryology exam in May, Walker could relax and enjoy the end-of-the-year skit and other activities in Bard Hall. The year concluded with a party in Bard Hall, and a rather raucous drive through Central Park in Frank Hardart's car. Walker had survived his first year, and his grades indicate that he was approximately a B student. The school year had been tougher than Walker had anticipated and he felt discouraged that he had not lived up to his own expectations. Uncle Will, whose health was steadily declining—so much so that he began to turn over his legal practice to Hazelwood Farish—wrote a philosophic letter to Walker with the intention of shaking him out of his doldrums:

My whole theory about life is that glory and accomplishment are of far less importance than the creation of character and the individual good life. What the world thinks of any one person is largely a matter of chance, but what we are in the eyes of ourselves and of the high Gods is a matter largely of our own making. I can very well understand how you feel that to be anything less than the greatest in your line would be failure. I used to think the same way about poetry. But now I do not regret having written it, although what I wrote does not rank with the greatest and may well be forgotten shortly. If I had thought this would be its fate, I would not have written, but now I am glad I did. It was the best I could give and if it is not the best somebody else could give, that is not my concern. This may be a poor philosophy and one bred from defeat, so don't take it too much to heart.[14]

This was the first indication to Walker that he could even give up medicine if the moment presented itself.

Unknown to students, P & S and Bellevue Hospital were making plans that would have a profound effect on Walker's life: Dean Rappleye made an official report at the end of the academic year about work being done in the field of tuberculosis. James Alexander Miller had continued the excellent instruction to the fourth-year students in tuberculosis at Bellevue Hospital. Under his supervision and in cooperation with the Trudeau School at Saranac Lake, a two-week graduate course in tuberculosis was conducted for seventeen students and physicians. Work on the C and D buildings for the tuberculosis service at Bellevue, which had 270 beds for medical patients and 47 for surgical patients, was completed in August. The surgical service at Bellevue had been materially augmented by the opening of the new surgical chest service under the auspices of Columbia University. The establishment of this service marked a great advance in pulmonary surgery: segregation of tuberculosis patients would now be possible, much to the advantage of the general service, as previously overcrowded conditions had made proper precautions for the protection of nontuberculous individuals impossible.[15]

Roy graduated from the University of North Carolina. In order to celebrate his completion of college, he drew on the remainder of the money Uncle Will had given him for his education and joined five classmates on a trip to Europe. In Paris they bought an old car for $75 and drove through England, Scotland, Austria, Germany, and Italy. In Vienna they saw the Brownshirts marching up and down the streets and witnessed the raw discipline of the storm troopers in Berlin. And in Rome they glimpsed Il Duce. "Yet," as Roy noted, "we were as interested in politics as we were about going to the moon." When Roy returned home at the end of the summer, eager to continue his education at Harvard Business School, Will told him point-blank that he was to be in complete charge of Trail Lake. His hopes for further studies were dashed at that instant.

Walker returned to Greenville for his summer vacation, and he and Shelby drove to Brinkwood in mid-June. On the way, they spontaneously decided to stop at Rowan Oak, the lovely home that belonged to William Faulkner at Oxford, Mississippi. As they drove into the driveway, Walker's reticence got the better of him: "I'm not going in there and bother that man. You can go in, I'll stay out in the car and read," he told Shelby. He had brought along a Raymond Chandler novel and *Gone with the Wind*.[16] Shelby knocked on the front door and was politely invited into the house, where he stayed and chatted with Faulkner. The novelist had just finished *If I Forget Thee, O Jerusalem* (later called *The Wild Palms*) that morning, and was in a talkative mood. He and Shelby discussed poetry, and when Shelby inquired where he could obtain a copy of *The Marble Faun*, Faulkner's 1924 book of poems, he was told to write to Leland Hayward, agent and play producer. As Walker read on in the car, he remembered that Faulkner had been told by Uncle Will he would never be welcome in the Percy house in Greenville, after his behavior on the tennis court. (Was it calculated revenge against Will Percy that Faulkner subsequently named one of the least attractive characters in *Light in August*—and perhaps in all his fiction—Percy Grimm?) Walker always regretted not accompanying Shelby into Faulkner's front parlor.

When Faulkner and Shelby emerged after two hours, they walked over to the car and Shelby introduced the famous author to "Will Percy's nephew." Walker and Shelby spent the night in Tupelo, Mississippi, and saw a revival of *The Birth of a Nation* at the local cinema.[17] Though Walker did not meet Faulkner again, that does not mean that the latter's literary influence on Walker was not profound. "Even though I've gone out of my way to avoid Faulkner," he once said, "in spite of my—because of my—admiration, nevertheless, I find myself thinking, 'Oh God, that sounds like him,' you know, when I write it. Faulkner is at once the blessing and curse of all Southern novelists, maybe all novelists."[18] And though Walker Percy struggled not to imitate Faulkner, Binx Bolling's wanderings about New Orleans might be related to Quentin Compson's travels about Cambridge and Boston. For Shelby, the chat with Faulkner provided a pivotal moment in his life; he had met one of America's most famous novelists at the peak of his career. He was later to visit Faulkner four or five times, staying over at Rowan Oak one night and touring the Civil War battlefield at Shiloh with him. It is not without a tinge of irony that Shelby's novel about this battle is dedicated to Walker.

Currin Gass, Mary ("Shep") Shepherd, Jervey Quintard, and Rosamond Myers—all attractive young women—stopped by Brinkwood that summer.[19] No wonder Caroline Gordon could say that Walker was remembered in Sewanee for "stirring up a lot of commotion in the dove cotes."[20] Walker was so taken by Shep, then a student at St. Mary's College in Raleigh, that he gave her his SAE pin. For a project that summer at Brinkwood, Walker and Shelby built a so-called teahouse made of fieldstone on the back side of the property on the way to Natural Bridge. Johnny Smith, his two boys, and most likely Alice Hodgson worked hard to cut the wood and lay a foundation for the four pillars and the small wall. Walker painted the shingle roof green, and took great pride in his work. When they finished, they wrote the date in the newly poured concrete: July 4, 1938.[21] In order to furnish the teahouse, Walker and Shelby carried down a heavy leather couch from the main house. It was painful for Shelby, bent over and trailing behind Walker, as the sharp edges of the couch banged against his insteps. When Will returned from a trip to Europe, he inspected the teahouse and was displeased with its design. He had the front and side walls lowered about a foot so one could see the surrounding countryside while sitting down. What upset him most was that the teahouse had been constructed on the concrete platform on which he liked to lie at night and watch the stars.[22] Will spent part of that summer at Brinkwood working on his memoirs.

Shelby had become a working man, thanks to the foresight of Dave Cohn and Uncle Will, who had invited Hodding Carter, Jr., to come to Greenville and edit *The Delta Star*.[23] After Huey Long was shot, his brother Earl verbally attacked Carter in Hammond, Louisiana, the town where the Carters owned the local newspaper, *The Daily Courier*. There had been bad blood between Huey and Big Hodding, and the feud with the Longs became exacerbated after Huey's death; it fired up again when Hodding ran for the state legislature. With little prospect of finding advertisers or state support for their newspaper, Betty and Hodding decided to sell it to three Long supporters. As he recounts in his *Where Main Street Meets the River* (1952), when Hodding met Dave Cohn at a literary conference in Baton Rouge he had urged Hodding to contact Will Percy and build up a new local paper in Greenville to replace the almost moribund *Democrat-Times*. In December 1935 Betty and Hodding drove to Greenville to meet with Will and Dave and some townsfolk who were willing to listen to Hodding's proposal. In the fall of 1937 Hodding's Greenville paper, *The Delta Star*, was launched, and a year later, after acquiring *The Democrat-Times*, it became *The Delta Democrat-Times*. As a token of his confidence in Hodding's operation, Will put up $20,000 in U.S. Steel stock. Hodding hired Don Wetherbee as copy editor, wire editor, and makeup editor, and, in the summer of 1939, Shelby, who had decided not to continue his last two years at Chapel Hill. Shelby's novel *Follow Me Down* is based on his experiences as a reporter. Shelby was amazed at the speed with which Hodding could write editorials and news stories. Because of his paper's policy on racial matters, and even because of the occasional inclusion of photographs of blacks, Hodding stirred up deep feelings of resentment. When Don traveled out of town to marry Virginia LaRochelle in the summer of 1938, he wondered if he would have a job when he returned.

That fall in New York, Walker resumed class with a man he would come to admire—pathologist James Wesley Jobling, who taught classes on the death of cells and muscle atrophy. For the most part, second-year classes centered on bacteriology, pathology, microbiology, pharmacology, and physical and clinical diagnosis. At this point, the curriculum emphasized the relationship between the underlying pathology of disease and its manifestation in clinical signs and symptoms.

Walker began around this time to think about becoming a pathologist—and equipping himself intellectually to look at literature from the standpoint of a physician making a diagnosis. "Part of the natural equipment of the doctor," he wrote in his study of Chekhov, "is a nose for pathology. Something is wrong: what is it? What is the nature of the illness? Where is the lesion? Is it acute or chronic, treatable or fatal? Can we understand it? Does the disease have a name or is it something new?"[24] A pathologist takes an organism and probes its every fiber, discovering its inner connections. Though initially a messy and awkward procedure, further reflection reveals patterns of symmetry. One of the greatest pleasures of a scientist is to look through a microscope at living cells and see the movement there, even though there might be disease present. Part of Walker Percy's genius was that he made connections between one discipline or aspect of life and another.

At Christmas, Phin returned to Greenville from the McCallie School in Chattanooga, Tennessee, which he had attended for the last three and a half years, as a local hero because his picture and an announcement of his application to the U.S. Naval Academy had been featured in the local paper. Though he had applied to the Academy, Phin really wanted to follow in his brothers' footsteps and go to Chapel Hill. But Uncle Will had other ideas. Roy had taken control of Trail Lake, and Walker would be a physician in the near future; thus, it was only logical that the third son should go into the military. This symmetry pleased Will (who had no desire to send anyone into the ministry—the other alternative); it had the aura of what an aristocratic family arranged for its young. In addition, Will had a premonition that war was imminent. "I have an appointment for you with Will Whittington, the congressman," he had told Phin, "and you can go to Annapolis after you graduate from McCallie. Or you can do this: you can go to Chapel Hill for a year, and then can get an appointment while there." Will added that he would not override Phin's decision to stay at UNC if he really liked it. In the fall of 1938, Phin took the exam for the Naval Academy at the local post office in Chattanooga and the results were so good that the headmaster said he would be exempt from his final exams at McCallie if he chose to enter Annapolis. Walker lent a sympathetic ear to Phin, who finally opted to follow Will's wishes, though he really had no inclination to be a naval officer.

During the holidays, the noted psychoanalyst Harry Stack Sullivan stayed with the Percys for a little over a month. He had been invited partly to talk to and observe Phin, who still was shaken over his mother's death.[25] Sullivan had traveled South from New York to study race relations under the auspices of the American Council on Education. Years later, Walker gave a tempered perspective to this visit:

One memorable visitor to my uncle's house, a regular stopover then for South-watchers, was the psychiatrist Harry Stack Sullivan . . . Being the genius he probably was, he didn't take the project very seriously and spent his entire stay in the pantry sipping vodka Martinis (a concoction unheard of in Mississippi at the time), passing the time of day with anybody who came along, and refusing to utter a single conclusion then or later about the "problem." His silence and his peculiar way of doing field work I can only interpret now as signifying not that there was not a "problem"—indeed the injustices were gross and grievous—but rather that the human condition, race relations especially, is a very complex business, shot through with paradox, rights thriving with wrongs, joys in the face of poverty, sufferings in the face of plenty—and that one has to look and listen hard and long before venturing the most tentative impression.[26]

Between the kitchen and the dining room, and armed with his pitcher of martinis, Sullivan listened to any and all comers, particularly blacks, who provided sufficient material to fill up any number of notebooks. Two aspects of this account are worth noticing. First, Walker Percy does not indicate that he had met Sullivan before this visit to Greenville. Second, if they had met previously and Walker Percy had been his patient, how appropriate is Sullivan's behavior as a professional psychoanalyst in front of one of his analysands? Internal evidence strongly indicates that Walker began seeing him as a patient only after Sullivan's visit to Greenville. Walker never did learn what this "brilliant and sardonic" upstate New Yorker discovered in Will's pantry, yet he took delight in Sullivan's unorthodox methodology. Sullivan's trip was interrupted when his close friend and collaborator, Edward Sapir, the linguist, died in February 1939.[27] Part of Sullivan's pantry discussions were written up, transformed into a professional critique, and included as an appendix in *Growing Up in the Black Belt: Negro Youth in the Rural South* (1941), written by the black sociologist Charles S. Johnson. Walker liked Sullivan and felt he could trust him, though he might have been dismayed by Sullivan's statement that he "did not succeed in establishing contact with any of those who were described by my informants as 'just average niggers.' "[28] Walker made contact with Sullivan, at Uncle Will's urging, when he returned to New York.

LeRoy Percy and Sarah Farish were married on January 3, a date partly chosen by the bride's mother, who knew that the two other Percy boys would be home at that time. It was a good time for a wedding because Greenville would be in a festive mood that time of year and it would not interfere with Christmas itself. At the evening ceremony in the First Presbyterian Church, Uncle Will was best man, and Walker, Phin, Shelby, and Don Wetherbee participated as ushers.[29] Sometime after the wedding, Walker wrote to Uncle Will saying how pleased he was with this marriage and how he wished his mother could have been there.[30]

Walker returned late for classes, which began on January 4. The academic grind resumed with a series of lectures by William Carson Von Glahn on cirrhosis of the liver and diseases of the pancreas. In the middle of February, as Dr. Whipple gave a talk on physical diagnosis of the abdomen, Walker took one of the most crucial steps in his life—he underwent psychoanalysis.

Because he was distraught about the death of Sapir, Harry Stack Sullivan felt that New York had little to offer him anymore, and within six months made plans to move to Bethesda, Maryland. Georgetown University's Medical School had offered him a post. Before Sullivan left New York, Walker saw him a number of times, once in a bar. They decided not to continue this professional relationship, no doubt because of the press of time. Walker then saw Dr. Clara Thompson at her office on East 83rd Street, until Sullivan finally recommended Dr. Janet Rioch.[31] "What you need is a nice, good-looking woman psychiatrist," he told Walker.[32] As Walker wrote, Sullivan did give him an insight into a key psychological problem in the modern world: "Anxiety—according to Sullivan the chief subject matter of psychiatry—is, under one frame of reference, a symptom to be gotten rid of; under the other, it may be a summons to authentic existence, to be heeded at any cost."[33] Walker was also impressed by another side of Sullivan: "In Harry Stack Sullivan's words, the mark of success in the culture is how much one can do to another's genitals without risking one's self-esteem unduly."[34] In his book *Walker Percy: An American Search*, Robert Coles quotes Walker on his relationships with his psychiatrists: "I had seen Harry Stack Sullivan, a friend of Uncle Will's. He suggested Dr. Rioch. He wasn't sure what ailed me, and I wasn't either. I must say that, after three years, five days a week, Dr. Rioch and I still weren't sure."[35] Once, in a letter to Coles, Walker said that he saw Dr. Rioch for two years, not three.[36]

Walker told Barbara King that he went through two years of Freudian analysis: "At the time, I thought maybe Freud was the answer, and he is indeed a great man. I certainly don't want to put him down, but I elevated him far beyond the point that even he would place himself."[37] Walker read carefully Freud's *Basic Writings* and *A General Introduction to Psychoanalysis*, both of which he bought in New York in 1939. These works would be indispensable not only for his classroom study of psychiatry but for those moments when he wanted to try to understand himself better.

The problems Walker talked about were his unresolved feelings about the suicide of his father and what he considered to be the suicide of his mother. In an interview with John C. Carr, he would recall a quote from Kierkegaard that was important to him: "Every man has to stand in front of the house of his childhood in order to recover himself."[38] He did not tell Roy about these sessions. By temperament Walker was naturally attracted to psychology and psychiatry, and his daily discussions with Dr. Rioch would help him understand personally the dynamics of this type of treatment—something he could not experience during a psychiatric lecture course at P&S. By being the patient, Walker could test constantly both the theory and the results on a personal level. Not surprisingly, none of his classmates knew or even suspected that when Walker paid a nickel for the subway it was in order to explore the more painful parts of his own inner psyche. They knew he liked to go to the movies alone, and they let it go at that.

Undoubtedly Janet Rioch had a profound influence on Walker's life, or else he would have soon broken off the relationship. Walker trusted her and her judgment, and he would always gravitate toward articulate, competent women who shared his insights into life. Dr. Rioch's first office was on East 50th Street, between Lexington and Third Avenue; while he was seeing her she moved to a ground-floor office at 17 West 54th Street. Each session lasted fifty minutes. For a woman of her time and circumstances, Dr. Rioch had a diverse family background and an excellent academic record.[39] During Walker's years at P&S, it would have been possible for Walker to see this tall, attractive, gray-haired, gentle woman, who wore simple dresses, in the hallways of the hospital. Walker later wrote Nancy Lemann, a struggling writer from New Orleans who had moved to New York, about his period of analysis: "Thinking about you up there in Manhattan reminds me of me in the 1940s, a neurotic med student at P&S who decided he needed psychoanalysis. I did need it since at that time I didn't believe in anything else. So I got fixed up with a very nice lady analyst, Janet Rioch, who looked a little like Ingrid Bergman. What I remember is not too much the analysis, which went on for a year or so, four days a week, but being nervous about being on time and arriving thirty minutes early and sitting at a bar somewhere on Madison Avenue and planning *what I was going to say*—so as to impress her and please her, etc. On the whole it was helpful."[40]

One person familiar with Dr. Rioch at various times in her career—as her student, as an analysand, then as someone under her supervision, and finally as a colleague who shared patients with her at the William Alanson White Institute in New York—is Earl G. Witenberg, M.D.[41] Dr. Witenberg came to consider Janet Rioch the best exponent and practitioner of Sullivanian therapy. She was crisp and clean about pulling together theory and practice, and she cherished the privacy of her patients, once even hiring a leading lawyer from the Nuremberg trials to defend, successfully as it turned out, her right not to reveal confidential information. It would have been her decision, not his, to see Walker five times a week.

Initially, she would have Walker survey in great detail all the people and events in his life he wanted to talk about. Dr. Rioch would have attempted to stimulate him to make associations among significant people and events so that he could recapture them. Building on her background in Sullivanian theory, she would have wanted Walker to articulate how past experiences struck him retrospectively. Though Sullivan's books were published after his death and were not available to Walker at this time, an article entitled "Conceptions of Modern Psychiatry" (1940) gives an insight into the type of therapy that Sullivan and Rioch employed.[42] In tracing the growth of an individual, Sullivan noted that the most peculiar behavior of a patient—and he has a schizophrenic in mind—is made up of interpersonal processes that are familiar to all of us. Before a child has developed a vocabulary, it is autistic in the sense that individual words have highly individualized meanings. Gradually it learns a degree of empathy with other people, especially its mother. Once a child is taught a series of restraints, including habits of cleanliness and eating, it begins to understand approval and disapproval.

An unexpected event, such as the death of a parent, can trigger feelings of anxiety—one of the central explanatory concepts in Sullivanian interpersonal theory. "Not only does the self become the custodian of awareness, but when anything spectacular happens that is not welcome to the self, not sympathetic to the self dynamism, anxiety appears, almost as if anxiety finally became the instrument by which the self maintained its isolation within the personality."[43] In the case of a person who commits suicide—and for Walker this meant *both* mother and father—the hostile attitude that one ordinarily directs to the outer world is now directed toward oneself with full force. In discussing the occurrence of suicide in the family of a child, Sullivan stresses that "if you know a family situation in which such an event has occurred, you will be impressed with the fact that the self-destruction had an evil effect, and may well have been calculated to have a prolonged evil effect on some other people."[44] Robert Coles notes that Sullivan emphasized loneliness as a major developmental issue; it was not a symptom but a state of mind that is a major influence in the lives of normal and psychiatrically ill people.[45]

Dr. Rioch's hypothesis would have been that what was troubling Walker was 97 percent unattended, and not necessarily repressed. As Walker became more open and found the words to level with Dr. Rioch, he would become more capable of accepting such bouts of anxiety. He could build also on any positive experiences that he remembered that could now help him to put his life together. With time and with increasing awareness, he could live more in the present, without triggering off memories and images that were traumatic in his past.

As his novel *The Last Gentleman* shows, Walker Percy continued to search within himself to find his most vulnerable point, and then used his quest for the missing father as the psychic source from which the novel takes its shape. When Walker was asked about the relationship of his fictional characters to real people (as I asked him on several occasions), he would shrug his shoulders and say that the inspiration to create a single character often came not only from one real person but from *several* people whose personalities were fused together. The point was to consider the dilemmas of his fictional people, not as actual situations of real people, but as plausible ones within the confines of the world he had created. In other words, his characters had to stand on their own. As a writer Walker Percy said he wanted to preserve the integrity of creative fiction and was averse to having it go through a process of biographical reductionism.

This does not mean that he did not have serious problems to discuss, but it does mean that his fiction should not be read as the equivalent of the notes that a psychoanalyst would take. On the other hand, Janet Rioch did reveal her methodology and how, in particular, she would try to help the child within her patient. A short paper she wrote during her tenure at Roosevelt Hospital gives a succinct view of how she would have dealt with the deaths of Walker's parents.[46] She held above all that the organic basis of any disorder in a child's life has to be explored first. A deaf child could be thought to be "lazy" or "indifferent" at first, though once the real problem was diagnosed, the results of that problem could be dealt with. The next important step is to assess the child, using formal psychometric tests. A psychiatrist cannot help a child without trying to have a total knowledge of the patient. Third, it is important to realize that a newborn is subject to a "bundle of capacities and tendencies which are unchanneled"—everything is brand-new and totally unknown. Language is absent and the ability to communicate is minimal, an aspect of a child's life related to social conditioning. "If we can study the social setting of the child with all the variations that, say, such a large city as New York can offer, we have an idea of the strains and stresses that this social environment has on the growth and developing independence of the child." Lastly, once these factors have been analyzed, the psychiatrist could study the child's interpersonal relationships, first with parents and then in ever-widening and overlapping circles. "The mental life of the child is enormously subject to influence. Various forms of cruelty, domination and repression can profoundly affect the development of the youthful personality . . . To understand the child one must learn to know the kind of parents and brothers and sisters he has grown up with." At Roosevelt Hospital, Dr. Rioch insisted that her patients be both examined physically and tested psychologically.

As would have been clear to Walker, Dr. Rioch was sensitive to any changes in self-esteem manifested by her patient. Her celebrated article on transference shows that she was not handicapped by the built-in transference notions of the Freudians, or (as Sullivan called them) "parataxic distortions." As he talked with Dr. Rioch, Walker realized that she saw herself, not as a patient's mother or father, but more as a teacher or some other significant person; she wanted to avoid the analysand's displacement of deep-seated feelings toward a mother or father onto herself. Clara Thompson once noted that one of Harry Stack Sullivan's contributions to psychiatry was to clarify the notion of transference: "Sullivan was one of the first to point out that there was such a thing as an irrational attitude towards your physician which should technically be called transference, and that there was a rational attitude towards your physician which was not transference, and that one had to help the patient distinguish between these two."[47] Janet Rioch attempted to do just that in relating how a patient's relationship to his mother and father can affect his relationship to his analyst.[48] Dr. Rioch would have wanted Walker to discuss what he was like as a teenager, since Sullivanian theory viewed adolescence as being more than a repetition of the Oedipal phase. However Walker would have phrased it, it is clear that he was abandoned by his father at the moment of his suicide. Then he was taken by his mother, roughly within a two-year span, to live with relatives he barely knew, before (as Walker quietly believed all his life) she committed suicide herself.

Since Sullivan considered guilt a theological construct, it was probably an area they did not dwell on. In her role as analyst, Dr. Rioch would have underplayed herself and not posed as a representative of some greater power. Above all, she put the emphasis on how people could change, not how they are stuck in the past. It should be noted that when Walker ended his relationship with her, something positive undoubtedly took place. It could have signified that no more of her specific therapeutic guidance was needed.[49] Afterward Walker went to see Dr. Gotthard Booth, a man who shared his interest in existentialism.[50] Once this relationship terminated, Walker did not seek further counseling in New York.

At the end of his second year, Walker was described by an anonymous professor in the Department of Bacteriology on the "Student Achievement and Character Report" as having an "outstanding intelligence." Dr. Franklin Hanger complimented Walker: "A fine type of student. Gentle and bright." Dr. Hanger (according to Dr. Flood) quickly grew to know his students personally, thus giving this evaluation extra weight. The Department of Pathology gave four stars to Walker as being cooperative, industrious, intelligent, an independent worker, logical thinker, pleasant and courteous. However, he received only two stars for being "inquisitive."

No medical student could really relax at the end of the academic year. It was a shock when Stalin made peace with Hitler. In late August, the German-Soviet nonaggression pact was signed in Moscow by Molotov and Ribbentrop, including a secret protocol about the fates of Estonia, Latvia, and Lithuania.

That summer Walker returned to Brinkwood, where he was joined for a week by Don and Virginia Wetherbee. Roy and a very pregnant Sarah soon arrived, and Sarah stayed on for most of the summer. Uncle Will received an honorary degree in June from the University of the South at Sewanee.[51] Walker and Shelby went to Memphis to see *Gone with the Wind*.[52] The Tates were at Monteagle that summer living in a rented house called Westwood (Caroline Gordon called it "Wormwood"), entertaining friends like Cleanth Brooks and his wife, Tinkum, Peter and Eleanor Taylor, and Brainard ("Lon") Cheney. In a letter to her friend Ward Dorrance, Gordon mentioned that Will Percy's nephew "Phinezy [sic] . . . bears up under it but of course he is on native heath and not pulled about from pillar to post."[53]

Most likely, it was during this summer that Walker met the attractive poet Barbara Howes, two years his junior. A native of Boston, Howes had graduated from Bennington College in 1937 and gone South with the American Friends Service Committee Work Camps for two summers; in the fall of 1939 she worked for the Southern Tenant Farmers Union in Memphis. She came to know Caroline Gordon and Allen Tate, and it was probably through them that she was introduced to Walker, who admired not only her quiet composure and beauty but also her poetic talents. Walker would continue seeing Howes whenever he could, and they even considered flying off to Mexico to get married. Walker never seemed to have mentioned this relationship to his classmates at P&S, even though he dated Howes in New York when she went to work for the new literary journal *Chimera*. After Walker had achieved some fame, he was instrumental in encouraging the National Institute of Arts and Letters to recognize Howes's talents. His relationship with Howes broke off sometime in 1940, when she met William Jay Smith, himself a rising poet; they were married the next year.[54] Howes always followed Walker's career and was pleased, as she told her husband, by his success.

In late June, Phin packed up his gear and entered the Naval Academy. When he arrived at Annapolis, he discovered that only the plebes were there; most of the upperclassmen were on summer cruises. On his first night, a midshipman in charge of the plebes gave the order to "sound off." Phin replied, "Midshipman Billups Phinizy Percy, Fourth Class." "What the hell kind of name is that? You're 'Al' for the rest of the year." To him Annapolis resembled a prison; he drilled a good bit, rowed on the Severn, ate his "square" meals, did push-ups, sang "Anchors Aweigh" endlessly, went through dehumanizing rituals, attended dull classes (except for math), and quickly realized that he was in the wrong place. He soon called Walker for advice.[55] Walker counseled as gently as he could: "I realize the upperclassmen are taking it out on you, but don't worry, it will get better. Just wait them out a bit longer. And call me in a month." When Phin called a month later, he received similar advice: "You said you might try out for the tennis team. Why don't you wait until tennis tryouts?" The ploy worked: Phin played on the tennis team for three years and never did hand in his resignation. Phin was grateful to Walker and later realized from what he said that he did not like medical school any more than Phin liked the Naval Academy.

On September 3, Great Britain and France declared war on Germany, while President Roosevelt proclaimed a policy of neutrality for the United States. For Shelby, as for many other young Americans, this meant considerable soul-searching; he finally decided to join the Mississippi National Guard as his way of fulfilling his patriotic duty. Though Private Foote spent weekends learning the skills necessary to be a fighting soldier, he never gave up his interest in writing. He finished his first novel, eventually entitled *Tournament*, and sent it off to Alfred A. Knopf. It was the story of a "young man's attempt to deal with what he imagined might have been his grandfather's life."[56] The editors at Knopf liked what they read but not enough to publish it, and counseled him to move on to a second novel, which they would like to consider. When his Greenville unit was called into service in November 1940, Shelby joined the 114th Field Artillery at Camp Blanding, near Starke, Florida, where he bought a white Oldsmobile convertible and paid for it by charging fellow soldiers for rides back to Mississippi. He went on to the Officer Candidate School at Fort Sill, Oklahoma, and finally served as a battery commander in the 86th Division.[57] During these years his writing career was put on hold.

When Walker returned to P&S in September 1939, there were 106 students in his class. On Long Island, the World's Fair and its symbols, the Trylon and Perisphere, proved to be a welcome distraction. As Walker, David Scott, and other friends moved from one exhibition to another at Flushing Meadow, they could see the innovations created by television and 3-D movies. In the midst of the war in Europe, there were some glimmers at the fair of new, undreamed-of cities built by creative engineers. Walker began his classes and took a series of major clerkships in medicine, pediatrics, surgery, and psychiatry, plus minor ones in oph-thalmology, ob-gyn, orthopedics, neurology, radiology, public health, otolaryngology. Much of the time would be spent in the wards, where resident physicians described the sicknesses of the patients and gave detailed analyses of the various options open for treatment.

In the fall Walker took a train to spend a pleasant weekend at Princeton with Caroline Gordon and Allen Tate, who had just accepted a two-year appointment at the university.[58] The Tates had invited Mau-rice Coindreau, the noted French translator of Faulkner's works, to din-ner and the conversation turned to Faulkner. When Walker told the story of Uncle Will and Faulkner's behavior on the tennis court, the Tates were not particularly amused. Walker further embarrassed them and invited ridicule by asking Coindreau, "Why bother with Faulkner?" With all the savoir-faire of the French, Coindreau knew how to deflate this awkward moment.[59]

In late September and early October, Walker met on several occa-sions with Leland E. Hinsie to study cases of schizophrenia, and with Nolan D.C. Lewis to observe cases involving child psychiatry and senil-ity. Throughout November, he focused much of his attention on psychi-atry, hearing lectures in the Psychiatric Institute and Vanderbilt Clinic from over a dozen experts in the field. Israel S. Wechsler lectured on neurology and gait disorders. The days seemed to go faster now that Walker became involved with patients.

In January 1940, Will Percy stayed in chilly Fort Walton, Florida, where he wrote the Harvard chapter and other sections of his book *Lan-terns on the Levee*.[60] On a trip to New York, he met with Alfred Knopf, who was quite enthusiastic about the book. Will wrote to Huger Jervey, "I shall possibly get my manuscript off to the publisher [in the fall] and it will be rotten and I don't care—nothing seems worth while but the war."[61]

Walker's marks for the third year were good, but not spectacular. At the end of the year, Walter Palmer of the Department of Medicine gave Walker a B and a short evaluation: "High up in the average group. Pleasant. Good student. Not a rule of thumb fellow." At the same time, Yale Kneeland of the same department gave Walker an A–, plus the comment: "Did a very good job." W. J. Madonick and S. Philip Goodhart of the Department of Neurology gave Walker a B and called him "reliable" and "interested." Louis Bauman, assistant professor of clinical medicine, wrote that Walker appeared "intelligent, looks as though his prospects were good." Louisianan Beverly Smith, a surgeon, wrote that Walker was "a pleasant boy and expect improvement." One of the more enjoyable moments after classes ended was a party and baseball game at the home of Bert Mudge in Northport on Long Island, which Walker thought resembled a set for *The Great Gatsby*.[62]

Those about to begin their fourth year felt more and more like real doctors and wanted to position themselves to intern in hospitals of their choice. After Walker had made an inquiry at the hospital's research division for chronic diseases on Welfare Island, Dr. David Seegal, who was on the staff of both P&S and the hospital on Welfare Island in the East River, wrote that he would be welcome to work there during that summer. Assistant Dean Vernon W. Lippard wrote to Dr. Seegal giving Walker a favorable recommendation: "Percy is apparently an excellent student and if his grades for this year are as good as they were for the previous years, he should stand in the upper quarter of his class. I hope that you will find it possible to take care of him."[63] Walker stayed in New York for part of that summer, apparently availing himself of Dr. Seegal's offer. (His unpublished story "Young Nuclear Physicist" is partially set on Welfare Island.)

In Greenville, Walker wrote to Dean Lippard to have his transcript sent to St. Luke's Hospital on Morningside Heights. Dean Lippard wrote to the director of St. Luke's: "He is a good student and a very attractive young man. He has a keen analytical mind and a pleasant personality. In relation to other members of his class, he stands in the upper third."[64] It must have raised Walker's spirits to know how much he had improved since the end of his first year.

Will headed off for the Grand Canyon to stay at the El Toval Hotel for about a month.[65] Undoubtedly spurred on by the German blitzkrieg and bombing of Britain, he wrote to the Department of National Defense Militia in Ottawa to offer his services in their army; he noted that at age fifty-five he was in good health and had an income of about $7,500 a year. Will was not interested in being paid for his services and indicated he would go wherever needed.[66] That fall Will came to New York mainly to talk to Knopf about the final draft of *Lanterns on the Levee*. His book was dedicated with great affection to Walker, Roy, Phin, Adah Williams, Charlotte Gailor, and Tom (undoubtedly his friend Tom Glasco), and it was due to be published the following February.

With the passage of the Selective Service Act, Walker had to face the issue of military service. In November, a letter informed Walker's draft board that he was a student in good standing at P&S and a candidate for an imminent M.D. degree. As Walker attended classes that fall, four of them were devoted to war neuroses, aviation medicine, military sanitation, and submarine medicine. American citizens were feeling tremendous waves of anxiety in the face of the invasion of Norway, Denmark, and the Low Countries and the collapse of the Maginot Line, after which the Germans entered Paris. For the latter part of his final year, Walker was one of 96 students who traveled back and forth to Bellevue for medicine, surgery, and tuberculosis rotations, taking patients' histories and following them through their stays in the hospital. His fourth-year evaluations showed positive judgments, like that of Hattie E. Alexander, a dynamic woman in pediatrics, who described Walker as "an attractive, serious-minded, good student—mature in reactions and judgment." Jerry H. Holmes of the Department of Medicine gave Walker an average grade of 85: "History taking = very good (90); Ability to analyze cases = mediocre (80); Personality and relationship with patients = good (85)." Alvan Barach of the Department of Medicine gave Walker a grade of A: "Good clinically. General point of view toward patients excellent. Good character." Joseph C. Turner of the Department of Medicine gave a grade of B+ and considered Walker a "bright, capable fellow." Walker graduated from P&S with roughly a B average and evaluations that depicted him as a potentially competent physician. He graduated 25th in a class of 104 students.

About this time Walker learned that Faulkner, who had been thinking about trying to reactivate his commission by applying for admission into the British Air Force (or if that failed, the U.S. Air Force), had come to talk to Uncle Will about it.[67] In a form Walker filled out in May for the local draft board, he indicated that he would be free to serve in the army beginning in January 1944. (Later Walker told Shelby that he had applied to be a navy doctor and had been accepted.) He also wrote that he had no intention of returning to P&S and was not transferring to another institution. His internship at Bellevue, he wrote, would be completed by December 1943; he placed first in the competitive exam for an internship at Bellevue for the Columbia division.[68]

He attended an engagement party given in May by Eleanor Mackenzie's Aunt Evelyn on East 93rd Street; later that summer, Bert Mudge and Eleanor were married in Cooperstown. Bert would start his internship in October at Presbyterian Hospital. A week before graduation, Walker's class invited the faculty to the annual party and lampoon show, where liquor flowed easily. A group, including Walker, went to Frank

Hardart's room on the top floor of Bard Hall and started tossing out paper bags filled with water as guests departed. Walker's bag fell on Chet Fairlie.[69] It took only a few minutes for the riot squad to come. The inevitable happened: the perpetrators spent several hours in the clink until they could sober up. It was an embarrassing lesson for Walker, as he drove back in silence with Huger Jervey, who had obtained Walker's release.

Uncle Will's poor health prevented him from attending Walker's graduation at the main Columbia campus on June 3. The day itself was bright and sunny as Walker and his classmates took the Hippocratic oath. Walker had the summer free and concluded arrangements to begin his internship at Bellevue the following January.

He drove home to Greenville alone in his Ford. He was joined in July by Frank Hardart, who arrived in his brand-new blue Buick convertible, a graduation gift from his father. Uncle Will so impressed Frank that he bought a copy of *Lanterns on the Levee*. He and Walker journeyed on a three-month car trip through the South and West—New Orleans, Texas, New Mexico, Utah, Wyoming, South Dakota, Iowa, and Illinois. From Chicago, Walker flew home and Frank drove to New York. During the trip, Frank went to Mass alone every Sunday, while Walker caught a few more hours' sleep. He kidded Frank about the "dirty Papists," but his friend never tried to proselytize and concluded that Walker wanted to keep the workings of his imagination and his life private. Nor did Walker tell Frank that he had once talked to a priest at St. Ignatius Church on Park Avenue.[70] In notes Walker jotted down in 1951 about Frank and another devout Catholic, he observed: "An untouched field: The Catholicism of an American businessman. A good man. The faint anti-clericalism, the Protestant veneer, the stoic embarrassed tightlipped quality."

At home, Walker went with Will to Brinkwood. One evening after dinner with friends, Will experienced an abrupt period of aphasia. He grabbed Walker and said, "Let's get out of here." Walker immediately called Dr. Henry Kirby-Smith, grandson of the famous Confederate general. Will's blood pressure turned out to be 280 over 150, a sign of malignant hypertension. Walker then flew with Will to Johns Hopkins for a checkup, and Will wrote a friend that he had been diagnosed with acute exhaustion and high blood pressure.[71] The prognosis indicated there was little to be done, so they returned to Greenville.[72] Not long after his return, Will began putting his affairs in order, specifying in his will that Roy was to receive all right and title and interest (being one-third) in Trail Lake.[73] Walker and Phin were to receive, equally, all the notes Will received for the sale of his interest in Panther Burn Plantation. Will bequeathed the remainder of his estate to his three adopted sons. Roy, in the role of faithful Aeneas bearing the legacy of a beloved Anchises, was listed as the executor.

Dr. Walker Percy began medical practice by working at Gamble Brothers & Archer Clinic in Greenville. Sensing a new and brighter future, he bought a green Packard convertible—Will's graduation present to him.[74] Approximately one million Mississippians between sixteen and sixty-five registered for the draft. The first contingent of 275 enlisted arrived at the local U.S. Basic Flying School; the final goal was to have 2,000 enlisted men, 200 officers, 475 flying cadets, and 200 BT-13 training planes on site.[75]

When Shelby returned from Camp Blanding in late July, knowing he would be seeing Walker less often, he had lots of news to share with his friend. Walker knew both Josephine Ayres and Archer, her sister, and occasionally would date Archer during his summers home from medical school. Under the nom de plume of Ellen Douglas, Josephine described Walker at this stage of his life as someone who "was removed from the world of action and decision, in which his family had always functioned, and turned in upon himself with the greatest intensity."[76]

During the fall of 1941, Walker's presence was greatly appreciated at the clinic, across from King's Daughters Hospital. In the mornings, Walker usually assisted pathologist Dr. Earl White with blood counts and urinalyses. A considerate man, well beloved in the community, Dr. White had been with the clinic since 1922.[77] Walker often accompanied Dr. Hugh Gamble in the afternoons to the Colored King's Daughters Hospital and would be of whatever help he could during surgical operations. Since the clinic hired only one medical assistant each summer (who did not officially see patients), no records were kept of what Walker did or who his patients were.

Dr. White taught one or two students at a time to become medical technicians. One of his most promising students, Mary Bernice ("Bunt") Townsend, soon caught Walker's eye. Bunt was not from Greenville but from Doddsville in neighboring Sunflower County—something that did not go unnoticed by some of the local families.[78] But her honesty, down-to-earth qualities, and good looks outbalanced everything else. Born in September 1921 to Pascol Judson and Nanny Boyd Townsend, Bunt grew up with her sister, Willie Ruth, and brother, Pascol Judson. She graduated from high school in Ruleville (where she had been a cheerleader)

and went to Sunflower Junior College in nearby Moorhead. Not as affluent as Greenville, Doddsville served as a central point for itinerant
workers connected with logging, the sawmill, and the railroad. The
Townsends had settled in Doddsville in 1912, living a mile outside town.
The area was sparsely settled, but by 1920 Doddsville was incorporated
and upgraded from a village to a town. Mr. Townsend served as the
first mayor. As with many others of her Depression generation, Bunt
knew she would have to strike out on her own and get the best education
she could with little financial support. While a student of Dr. White, she
first met Walker by taking a sample of his blood.

It was not long before Bunt and Walker started dating. They went
to the movies, had picnics, and sometimes went down by the river to
shoot at turtles with .22 rifles. Bunt was attracted by Walker's good
looks, his personality, and his genuine modesty. As their friendship developed, Walker took their relationship in stride. He did not invite Bunt
to Sunday dinners, probably because of Uncle Will's illness, though he
saw her afterward. Once, Bunt was summoned to the big house to draw
some blood from Uncle Will. It was a terrifying moment for her because
Will knew that she was seeing Walker. As she approached his bedroom
on the first floor, she felt intimidated by the presence of his old friend
Huger Jervey and by the fact that Will was dressed in his green Japanese
"coat" with its long sleeves.[79] Their friendship succeeded because neither
Walker nor Bunt forced it. They found they could not only talk easily
but also enjoyed moments of silent communication. Bunt rarely kept important issues to herself. She always spoke out honestly and clearly, using words that might have escaped Walker or words he had buried deep
within himself.

On December 7, no one was prepared for the brutal surprise attack
by the Japanese at Pearl Harbor. On that quiet Sunday morning, Bunt
was in her apartment waiting for Walker to pick her up to go to Lake
Ferguson. When he arrived he told Bunt the shocking news. They con-
tinued to Lake Ferguson, wondering what changes this news would
bring. It was not long before Bunt felt the impact of Pearl Harbor: one
of her friends at the clinic lost her brother in the bombardment. As the
Percys looked forward to what they hoped would be an uneventful
Christmas, Wake Island fell to the Japanese. Ensigns Phinizy Percy and
Kelton Lowry arrived in Greenville before Christmas from Annapolis, as
Bob Horton traveled from New Orleans and Huger Jervey from New
York to stay with Will during the holidays.[80] Shelby was home on leave
that Christmas and went fishing with Walker and Bunt and her friend
Liber Wood.

Will suffered a cerebral hemorrhage before Christmas and clearly could not survive much longer. The day after Christmas, as Winston Churchill spoke to a joint session of Congress, there was a massive Japanese air assault on Manila. Roosevelt and Churchill had decided that Allied forces would wage a united effort in North Africa before attempting to enter into direct combat in Europe. During one of the lowest moments of Walker Percy's life, he made plans to drive northward to an unknown future at Bellevue Hospital.

5

Illness, Recuperation,
and Decision
1942–46

Dr. Walker Percy started his internship at Bellevue Hospital in January 1942. This large, dynamic, inner-city hospital in mid-Manhattan on the East River gave young interns a chance to observe a wide spectrum of illnesses in a short amount of time. Bellevue was, in fact, a living medical textbook. Since the mid-nineteenth century, the immigrant poor who lived on the Lower East Side spontaneously made use of its medical and psychiatric services. It was well known that many of these patients, overworked and undernourished, were prone to get TB. Bellevue was divided into four divisions, three of which were affiliated with specific medical schools: Columbia's College of Physicians and Surgeons, for instance, directed the first division—the medical, chest, and surgical services; the medical schools of New York University and Cornell had two other divisions, the fourth and last being an open division with no specific university affiliation.

Walker had placed first in the competitive examination for a Columbia internship at Bellevue.[1] As an intern in pathology, his working day fell into a predictable pattern, which meant seeing individual patients, doing necessary lab work, and performing autopsies in the basement morgue, where he analyzed various deadly diseases and illnesses. Most of the corpses were known as "five-day cases" (bodies unclaimed after five days) or "murders and floaters," and most of the interns who performed autopsies worked without gloves or masks. Walker's days normally began at 7 a.m. and frequently lasted well into the night. Each morning house-staff teams (an attending physician, a resident physician, several interns, and a nurse) saw and discussed the progress of every patient. After lunch the interns would work in the outpatient clinics for two or three hours. In the evening they would work up new patients by conducting interviews, doing much of their lab work, and writing up summaries of the morning rounds. Every Wednesday, from ten to noon, there would be a conference in the theater joining the A and B buildings. (By and large, buildings C and D at Bellevue were reserved for the chest service, while A and B were reserved for the medical service.) For their labors the city of New York paid each intern a modest salary, in addition to room and board.

The popularity of interning at Bellevue can be gauged by the number of Walker's classmates who applied and were accepted there: Rector T. Davol, Marie Irène Ferrer, Gustave A. Haggstrom, Philip Knapp, Coles W. Raymond, John Ryan, C. Blake Skinner, and Richard F. Wagner. They looked forward to working together, and they enjoyed talking about their experiences. Phil Knapp had spent part of previous summers at both Roosevelt Hospital and St. Luke's in order to position himself for an internship in New York; he finally decided to go to Bellevue, mainly because he wanted to be with his friends. Before arriving in January 1942, he had traveled to the Mayo Clinic in Rochester, Minnesota, and worked as a pathologist. He often stood shoulder to shoulder with Walker in the Bellevue morgue. As an intern, he would spend half a year on the chest service, half a year on surgery, and the last year on internal medicine. Rène Ferrer, who lived at home, had done a summer elective at Johns Hopkins; she eventually rose to be chief resident at Bellevue. She felt welcomed at Bellevue, perhaps due to the fact that her mother was on the Women's Board of Trustees. Walker always felt comfortable in the presence of intelligent female physicians.

Though he was prepared to begin full-time work as a doctor, his thoughts naturally turned to his family, particularly the state of Uncle Will's health. Will had written Charlotte Gailor that he was confined for the most part to his bed, with good and bad days; he was clearly signaling to his dear friend that his days were numbered.[2] When his intestines began hemorrhaging, he was rushed to King's Daughters Hospital. His friend Dave Cohn and LeRoy and Sarah Percy realized that Will was in extremis; his aphasia became more acute and he now lost his ability to communicate. (He had once told Shelby Foote that Maurice Ravel had tragically died while suffering from aphasia, a fate he feared for himself.) He died, at age fifty-six, on January 21 of a cerebral hemorrhage due to cardiovascular disease. Roy had his own theory about the cause of Will's death: "In no uncertain terms it was the commencement of hostilities before and after Pearl Harbor that killed Uncle Will."[3]

The first person Walker called with the news was Phin: "Uncle Will has died." These words devastated Phin, who said, "I feel adrift. The anchor is gone. I never saw Uncle Will do a selfish thing. I can't say that about anybody else I've ever known."[4] Phin left the Naval Academy that evening, shaken because he had not previously realized the extent of Will's sickness, met Walker in Washington, and they flew home together. One thing Phin regretted was that he had once told Will he reminded him of Ashley Wilkes in *Gone with the Wind*; it was a comparison he now knew did not fit Will at all. Walker's calming words to Phin gave him the strength to bear up under the pressures of the funeral. Shelby was at the Officer Candidate School at Fort Sill, Oklahoma, when he received his mother's telegram with the sad news.[5] Shelby felt it was almost impossible to capture Will in words: "How could one ever combine the incidental petulance—mainly his boundless capacity for outrage—with the enormous compassion? I often think of the paradox involved in his sorrow from the conviction that his father never thought him a shadow of the man his dead brother would have been, though the fact is he was twice the man the Senator ever was."[6]

Walker wrote a letter to a cousin explaining Will's religious beliefs:

[Will] used to speak often in admiration of the Catholic Church—of her wisdom, noble tradition, esthetic beauty, etc.—but he would not have regarded himself as a believer. That is to say, he did not believe that God actually revealed Himself in time, through the Jewish people, through the Incarnation, through the Catholic Church. He would regard the Jews as a peculiar people whose mysterious role in history could be explained by natural cultural causes; he regarded Christ as a great ethical teacher (and would frequently list him along with Socrates, Gautama Budha [sic], St. Francis, [Robert E.] Lee, etc.); he regarded the Catholic Church as a purely human institution with a noble history and a great store of wisdom.[7]

Before his death, Will had written Walker that he considered glory and accomplishment of far less importance than the creation of character and the individual good life.[8] Hodding Carter wrote a moving front-page editorial in *The Delta Democrat-Times*: "I loved Will Percy for every reason that any of our numbered legion could have had: for the greatness of his spirit, the goodness of his heart, the courage that shone in his eyes and spurred his frail body, the honesty, the tenderness, the full catalogue of virtues that made him one of God's few saints." On January 22, a perfunctory funeral service was held in the Percy home. Roy thought that it was only fitting that a Catholic priest be invited, and the Rev. John J. Igoe gave a blessing, after which the cortege formed to take Will Percy's body to the cemetery. (Roy thought it odd that the priest never took off his overcoat in the Percy house.)

LeRoy, now the *paterfamilias* of the Greenville Percys, had decisions to make. Later that year he enlisted at the Greenville Air Base and became an instructor for three or four months at the Advanced Flying School in Columbus, Mississippi, and then went to Europe, where he flew approximately twenty B-26 missions. Roy took up the challenge that Will and millions of other Americans so keenly felt.

For Walker, it was a catharsis after the funeral to resume the practice of medicine. He was now working next to some of the outstanding physicians in the country, such as André Cournand, a decorated soldier who had served in World War I and who received his M.D. degree from the University of Paris before joining the P&S faculty in 1935. Dr. Cournand worked primarily in the chest service at Bellevue as part of a distinguished team that included Dickinson W. Richards, a pulmonary and cardiac specialist, and J. Burns Amberson, Jr., a 1917 graduate of the Johns Hopkins School of Medicine and a former tuberculosis patient.[9] Though a dry lecturer, Dr. Amberson nevertheless held his students' attention as he diagnosed patients and taught the finer points of interpreting X rays. (Cournand and Richards won the Nobel Prize in Medicine in 1956 for their experimentation with Forssmann's heart catheter.) As an expert in tuberculosis, Amberson warned his students about the dangers of TB, instructing them, in particular, to protect themselves from any fluids, even sneezing, that might emanate from a patient. He maintained that heavy droplets containing the tubercle bacillus usually fell to the floor and dried out, but that "the droplet nucleus—that is, the particle which loses its content of moisture, leaving a single bacillus or a small clump of bacilli—is so light that it floats in the air like smoke. This . . . is easily inhaled into the depths of the lung, and is responsible for the inception of the disease through primary infection."[10] TB can be transmitted from a diseased organ to a cut, however slight, on an intern's hand or arm. Tuberculosis, however, cannot be acquired merely by doing autopsies on those who have died and whose organic systems have shut down, since inert cadavers do not emit such deadly droplets into the air.

Busy schedules meant that interns had little time for socializing, but as the narrator of an early version of *The Moviegoer* says, an intern might stay up all night at McSorley's, drink beer, and talk about life, art, religion, and women. One popular activity was to drive across the Brooklyn Bridge, go roller skating, and grab a bite to eat before heading back to Bellevue. Once Walker dated a "brisk, swift, good-looking" Bellevue nurse by taking her to the Boo Snooker bar of the New Yorker Hotel, where, surprisingly, he sipped a mint julep for the first time. When the bartender suggested that Walker and his date switch to gin fizzes, Walker agreed, though later, as he was driving the nurse home to Brooklyn, his lips swelled as a result of an allergy to the raw egg albumen in the drink. Thus a lovely evening turned into a disaster: "Not only was kissing out of the question but my eyes swelled shut. I made it across the bridge, pulled over to the curb, and fainted."[11] This noble nurse drove Walker back to Bellevue, gave him a shot, and put him to bed.

That March, Walker started coughing in a noticeable way, a "nonproductive cough" accompanied by frequent head colds, sore throat, loss of strength, and slight fatigue.[12] Yet he suffered no weight loss, hemoptysis, night sweats, or pleurisy, though he had a slightly elevated temperature that fluctuated between 99 and 100 degrees. Walker did not feel particularly sick. His X rays, which he examined himself, and felt very strange doing so, revealed a small exudative lesion in his right lung, in the second intercostal space. He had contracted tuberculosis.

Though Walker clearly believed that for him the chief predisposing factor was having performed approximately 125 autopsies on TB patients at Bellevue, he probably contracted the disease from one of his living patients.[13] Walker was aware that his mother's sister, Anne Barrett, had died in 1936 of tuberculosis and he had been in contact with her in his early teens.[14] If she had infected him, the disease could have remained dormant. Except for catarrhal jaundice at twenty-five and being subject to attacks of anorexia with some nausea and vomiting, Walker regarded his medical history as unimportant. He was put to bed in a small private room that overlooked the East River. He had a bedside table and a chair, and soon there were books all over the place.[15] Though Bellevue had a small library, Rène Ferrer and Phil Knapp wondered where Walker got so many books. Walker listened to the sad reports about the fall of Bataan and the subsequent death march. The successful feat of getting army bombers, led by General Doolittle, across the vast Pacific on navy aircraft carriers, for a retaliatory air raid on Tokyo, provided the only bright news.

Once Walker was diagnosed as having TB, Huger Jervey called Roy and Sarah and insisted that Walker leave Bellevue and seek treatment in a sanatorium.[16] Walker resigned from the Bellevue staff on June 4.[17] One critical piece of information was given him by Dr. Amberson: since Walker worked for the city of New York, local government funds would pay for his future hospitalization and convalescence as a TB patient. He initially thought of going to Colorado to recuperate.[18] At this juncture,

Walker wrote Bunt saying he wished he, like Phin, had joined the navy; he added he would like nothing better than to see her.[19]

After Phin graduated from the Naval Academy on June 19—number 130 in a class of 615 after three years of concentrated study—he was commissioned an ensign and sent to the Torpedo Boat Training School in Melville, Rhode Island. His group picked up a number of eighty-foot Elco PT boats and brought them back to Bayonne, New Jersey, where they were to be shipped off to the Pacific. When Phin passed through New York, he visited Walker, who looked wan and still coughed considerably. (To cheer him up, Phin raced one of the boats wildly up and down the East River, hoping that Walker would spot him from Bellevue and be distracted from his moroseness.) Phin was destined to sail to the Solomon Islands by way of the Panama Canal. His squadron practiced maneuvers on the Pacific side of the canal, headed on a tanker loaded with PT boats for Pearl Harbor, sailed southwestward to New Caledonia, and then "on their own bottoms" to Tulagi. Phin was about to begin another long separation from Walker.

Sarah and Roy went to New York late that summer and helped Walker prepare for his trip to the Trudeau Sanatorium in Saranac Lake, New York. It was more commonly known as "the San," where Dr. Amberson had close professional and familial connections, including his own sister, who was a nurse. The president of Trudeau, James Alexander Miller, another graduate of P&S, who had been cured of tuberculosis, founded the Bellevue tuberculosis service in 1903. Before Walker left, Roy, who was stationed at Fort Hamilton, dined with his brother and Huger a few times a week. One night they wired Sarah, "LeRoy didn't show up for dinner"—their secret code indicating that Roy had been shipped to Europe.

The popular press often carried articles on tuberculosis; an issue of *Life* magazine in 1937, for example, had run a feature story with large photographs of patients at Trudeau and the nearby Will Rogers Memorial Hospital. Tuberculosis had dropped from the first to the seventh cause for all deaths in the United States; of the 600,000 cases of tuberculosis each year, there were 70,000 deaths. The article noted that no vaccine had been discovered to cure TB. "Once a man is seriously infected, his best chance for cure still lies in rest. He must be put to bed, the movement of his sick lung restricted. He is better off in a sanatorium than at home. If the infection is discovered early, he may be cured in a few months. If it is discovered only after hemorrhages, he must count on at least one or two years, perhaps five or six." One picture showed patients who had been wheeled out in their beds onto a porch at Trudeau, noting that they spent most of the day outside and sometimes the nights, in spite of temperatures as low as 20 degrees below zero—though patients could use electric blankets.

One treatment used at that time was by artificial pneumothorax, a medical procedure in which air is injected into the chest cavity, with the lung either wholly or partially collapsed, thus allowing the infected tissue to rest and heal. As the air was absorbed by the lungs, "refills" were given every week or so for a period of two to five years. If a more drastic solution was needed, then the ribs on the infected side were removed through a process called "thoracoplasty," and the infected lung was permanently immobilized.

While at Bellevue in July, Walker had a pneumothorax on his right lung; his treatment had begun. In early September, he boarded a train for Albany and Utica, where he switched to the Adirondack Division. Others, like "Laughing Larry" Doyle of the New York Giants—the first player to hit a home run out of the Polo Grounds—were making similar journeys to Saranac Lake that year. Doyle's teammate Christy Mathewson had traveled the same route years before. (Walker Percy later transformed his experience at Trudeau into *The Gramercy Winner*, a novel about tuberculosis, in which Joe Carey is based on Larry Doyle.) The long ascent from Tupper Lake to Saranac Lake—through green forests and past shimmering lakes, a rugged natural beauty captured in the paintings of Harold Weston—signaled the calm that awaited Walker, though he was hardly prepared for the strict regime that would eventually turn his muscles to tallow. On his arrival, he was taken to Josephine Smithwick's, one of the 150 "cure cottages" that dotted the village, until a bed became available at Trudeau.[20] Mrs. Smithwick, a kind and officious woman, according to former resident Elise Kalb, made sure that her guests were content and cared for; she and her daughter, Gertrude, feared a lack of income from unoccupied rooms.[21] Unlike the routine in the sanatoria, social activity in such a cottage was kept to an absolute minimum. "When I arrived at Saranac," Walker wrote, "I wasn't admitted to Trudeau right away. The sanatorium was crowded so I stayed in a boarding house, Mrs. Ledbetter's, and it was the eeriest time of my life. A woman came in to give me a bath; otherwise I saw no one."[22] Ledbetter (Mrs. Ledbetter actually owned a boardinghouse in Chapel Hill) was the name he gave to a fictitious infirmary in *The Gramercy Winner*, modeled on the real Ethel Saltus Ludington Memorial, an infirmary for acutely ill patients behind the baronial Main Building at Trudeau. Dr. John N. Hayes, a Pennsylvanian who had been in Saranac Lake since June 1920, became Walker's primary physician at Smithwick. A charming man who had once had tuberculosis, Dr. Hayes was always seen dressed in jacket and shirt and tie, even in the dead of winter.[23]

Saranac Lake, 300 miles north of New York City and 1,600 feet above sea level, is nestled partially on Helen Hill, located on the shores of Lake Flower, whose limpid waters are fed by the Saranac River. In addition to the cure cottages at Saranac Lake, other sanatoria, including the Will Rogers Memorial Hospital for consumptive entertainers, the state-run sanatorium in nearby Ray Brook, and Stony Wald on Lake Kushaqua, attracted thousands of patients to the region. In its heyday, Saranac Lake housed 2,000 to 3,000 patients a year. The beauty of the Adirondacks and Saranac Lake inspired writers like Ralph Waldo Emerson (who wrote his poem "The Adirondacks" after he visited the area with James Russell Lowell in 1858) and Mark Twain, who wrote "The Double-Barreled Detective Story" after a vacation on the Lower Saranac Lake. Robert Louis Stevenson, a tubercular patient, arrived in the fall of 1887 and remained until the following April, writing a series of essays for *Scribner's* magazine; his cottage near Moody Pond was later turned into a museum. Isabel Smith's book *Wish I Might* recounted her stay at Trudeau from 1928 to 1949 and revealed that the optimism Trudeau projected in its brochures usually led to boredom and discouragement. From Penfold Cottage, she could look down on patients, including Walker, who passed under her window. A youthful-looking and slightly balding Walker once stopped near her cottage to have his picture taken with Wesley Depp and pipe-smoking David Lawton.[24]

There was little for Walker to do but rest and read and listen to the news on his Hallicrafter. This ongoing near-death experience prompted him to ask some very basic questions about science, philosophy, and theology:

I was in bed so much, alone so much, that I had nothing to do but read or think. I began to question everything I had once believed. I began to ask why Europe, why the world had come to such a sorry state. I never turned my back on science. It would be a mistake to do so—throw out the baby with the bath water. I had wanted to find answers through an application of the scientific method. I had found that method a rather impressive and beautiful thing; the logic and precision of systematic inquiry; the mind's impressive ability to be clear-headed, to reason. But I gradually began to realize that as a scientist—a doctor, a pathologist—I knew so very much *about* man, but had little idea what man *is*.[25]

Walker did not hesitate to label his situation a "misfortune," and preferred to chronicle its effects in terms of the consequences on his inner life—"the area of the deepest convictions and the unspoken assumptions by which every man lives his life (and if a man thinks he has no such assumptions, they are all the stronger for not being recognized)."[26] In the pathology lab at Bellevue, where medicine seemed to come closest to the science it should be, Walker had seen the "beautiful theater of disease and even measured the effect of treatment on the disease process." Now the scarlet tubercle bacillus, which had lain crisscrossed like Chinese characters in the sputum and lymphoid tissues of his patients, took hold of him. He put aside Macleod's *Physiology* and Gay's *Bacteriology*, and took up the works of Søren Kierkegaard, Martin Heidegger, Gabriel Marcel, Jean-Paul Sartre, and Albert Camus.[27] Jimmy Sprunt called a few times and sent Walker the books he had requested.[28]

Walker, when asked how he became acquainted with the European existentialists, said, "I think it was probably through Sartre first, probably through reading *Nausea*. And then later going back to Kierkegaard and then coming forward to Heidegger and Marcel . . . But Kierkegaard is probably the one who deserves the most credit. He saw [the problem] most clearly."[29] Walker probably read Gabriel Marcel's *Homo Viator* after reading *Nausea*.[30] He kept in his library in Covington the two-volume Augsburg edition of Kierkegaard's *Edifying Discourses*, plus *Fear and Trembling*, *Repetition*, and *The Concept of Dread*—these last three books have his marginal notes—as well as Theodor Hacker's *Søren Kierkegaard*, parts of which he also underlined as he read. He advised anyone interested in Kierkegaard to begin with *Concluding Unscientific Postscript*.[31] Walker also read Farber's *The Foundation of Phenomenology*, plus works of Mann, Tolstoy, Dostoevsky (most likely *Notes from Underground* and *The Possessed*), and Jaspers—in addition to Ernst Cassirer and Susanne K. Langer in the early 1950s. (As he told Barbara King, he dates his reading of Langer's *Philosophy in a New Key* from his days at Saranac Lake, and associates this with his 1954 review of Langer's *Feeling and Form* for the magazine *Thought*[32]). Over the years he made a transition from Tolstoy to Dostoevsky, from Sartre to Marcel, from Plato to Aristotle to Aquinas and Maritain, and from Wolfe to Faulkner.[33] In general, however, patients at the San read mostly murder mysteries, current fiction, books about the Adirondacks, and other "light reading."[34] In order to help those who were confined to bed, Edward Worthington had set up a system whereby he would fetch any item, including books from the public library, that patients might request.[35] Shelby always considered Walker a Tolstoy man (Percy owned a twelve-volume set of the Russian's works) and himself a Dostoevsky man; Shelby felt that Tolstoy was the greatest "slick" that ever lived, while Dostoevsky really went to the heart of the matter. Years later Walker admitted to Shelby, "You were right."[36]

(In 1962 Walker said that Dostoevsky, Kierkegaard, St. Augustine, D. H. Lawrence, James Joyce, Gerard Manley Hopkins, and Marcel meant the most to him, in that order.[37]) Clearly these writers gave him a new and more global orientation. "The effect was rather a shift of ground, a broadening of perspective, a change of focus," as he considered the nature and destiny of mankind and the predicament of man in a modern technological society. "After twelve years of scientific education, I felt somewhat like the Danish philosopher Søren Kierkegaard when he finished reading Hegel. Hegel, said Kierkegaard, explained everything under the sun, except one small detail: what it means to be a man living in the world who must die." Saranac Lake offered Walker an opportunity to delve more and more into the deeper reaches of himself, to probe and discover what had always been there from his earliest days.

Though Walker received no visits from any member of his family while at Saranac Lake, both Henry Toole Clark, a friend from his Chapel Hill days, and Marcelle Dunning, who had been a resident physician at Bellevue while he was there, came to see him. They alerted him to, and invited him to attend, the "Cabot cases" held at the Walter B. James Cottage, which housed physicians and medical students for the most part. James was a substantial red-brick building, located near the South Gate, with five double porches, adjacent bedrooms and bathrooms, plus two sitting rooms and two living rooms. These discussions of real cases taken from *The New England Journal of Medicine* were analyzed and discussed by fellow physicians George Digman, Ronald Smith, Charles McGoey, Eugene Mullen, Roger Mitchell, and Henry Frazier Parry, among others.[38] Their sessions provided an opportunity for physician-patients and staff physicians to know one another, and they were often the high point of the week. The Lawrason Brown Memorial Medical Library at Trudeau contained nearly 7,000 volumes, thus making up-to-date research available. Walker and Henry Clark knew each other from various premed courses they had taken together and from the Alpha Epsilon Delta meetings and lectures, though their paths diverged when Clark went to study medicine in Rochester. Clark entered Trudeau in September 1940 and spent his three years there in James Cottage. Talking with Walker in Smithwick had inspired Clark to read *Lanterns on the Levee*. He said, "Three years at Trudeau was like four years at Chapel Hill from the viewpoint of reading good books," though he admitted that his literature course with Professor Harry Russell was most helpful in dealing with his tuberculosis at the San.

Walker was likewise glad to see Marcelle Dunning, a 1940 graduate of New York University's School of Medicine. In April 1942, she was found to have TB while doing a rotation through pathology at Bellevue.

At Trudeau in late September, she ran into Raymond Luomanen, a graduate of the Johns Hopkins School of Medicine, who had likewise been at Bellevue with her before going to New York Hospital, where he was diagnosed as having tuberculosis. He was counseled by Dr. Amberson to go to Trudeau, where he stayed in James for six months.[39] The Bellevue–Trudeau axis ensured that Walker was readily accepted, more than one might have expected.

During the Christmas holidays, Dunning invited her cottage mate Barbara O'Neil, a charming brunette who had been a medical student at Women's Medical College in Philadelphia, to join her in visiting Walker at Smithwick. As with Clark, Dunning and Walker reminisced about the old days, and sometimes the name of a former professor at P&S, "Uncle Willy" Von Glahn, would come up (perhaps imaginatively combined with Dr. Amberson to become Dr. "Wild Bill" Ambrose in *The Gramercy Winner*). Marcelle once commented to Walker that he had taken a risk in courting the favor of Uncle Willy, who, as everyone seemed to know, had his eyes out for handsome physicians. O'Neil and Walker enjoyed each other's company; she responded well to his quick wit and honesty. On occasion Dunning, O'Neil, and Walker would take short walks together.

It is unclear exactly how long Walker stayed in Smithwick Cottage before being transferred to Trudeau.[40] From a photo of him with Dunning and O'Neil, it is reasonable to assume that he arrived at Trudeau around January 1943.[41] In *The Gramercy Winner*, the narrator described arriving at the sanatorium, which had the appearance of a campus:

Sturdy little cottages were dotted at random under the trees, like fraternity houses, and young men lolled about in front. In the middle of it all there rambled away a fine old spa-hotel of a building with far-flung wings and high screen porches. They passed the craft shop; from within came a sound of whirring and a high clamor of talk. A pair of nurses came toward them, students in black stockings, their sleeves rolled up, their arms folded identically into their starched waists. They stopped and looked back as the convertible passed. A young man and a girl strolled hand in hand, he with a blanket thrown serape-wise over his shoulder. The sanatorium lay on a gentle hillside. Below, they caught glimpses of a green valley with a winding river. Above there stretched away a high mountain meadow dotted with clumps of shimmering poplars.

Walker's first stop was at the admissions porch in the Main Building, where he stayed for ten days to two weeks after his initial exam at Trudeau. While there were 200 patients at the San when Walker arrived, the medical community formed a special bond. During Walker's stay there in 1943 and 1944, 420 patients with pulmonary tuberculosis were discharged from Trudeau. Seven of this number remained in the San for less than thirty days. Of the remaining 413, 126 had minimal, 245 moderately advanced, and 42 far-advanced tuberculosis. Thirteen died during those two years. Of the 400 who left alive, 62 were discharged as "arrested," 18 "apparently arrested," 198 "quiescent," 97 "improved," and 25 "unimproved." Among those who were discharged 50 were physicians, 31 nurses and student nurses, and 17 medical students.

Walker's pneumothorax treatment was now abandoned because of the appearance of some fluid on top of his diaphragm, and his condition remained stable, though under careful observation; he remained this way until late that fall. He was assigned first to Ludington Memorial and then to one of the "up cottages" near Baker Chapel.[42] As might be expected of people who had a potentially deadly illness, Walker followed the prescribed rules and regulations of the San, intended to ensure maximum comfort.[43] "TB doesn't hurt," said Fanny Genden Lyons, a patient at Trudeau for many years. "You just cough a lot." Conversation between patients concerning their diseases, their symptoms, or any subject relating to illness was forbidden during meals, as it frequently led to mental depression. There was absolute quiet from two to three-thirty in the afternoon. Patients were expected to lead an out-of-door life—that is, to remain from seven to ten hours in the open air during the daytime. As for coughing, care was taken to use specially prepared, disposable gauze handkerchiefs, and sputum cups were collected each day and burned. Every Saturday, an exercise clinic was held in the Medical Building, and patients were expected to report there once every two weeks, bringing with them their daily record sheets. For the most part, exercise was defined as walking or even standing. In addition, patients were expected to be back on the grounds by seven, and in their cottages by nine, an hour before the normal time to retire. Lights spotted after that hour meant that someone needed assistance, and the night nurse investigated. Members of the opposite sex could visit on porches but not inside the cottages. Alcohol was forbidden—but not smoking. Since most patients were on diets, and wartime imposed rationing, liquor was rarely seen on the grounds, though it was not unknown for someone to produce the ingredients for a nightcap. In spite of these rules and regulations, a congenial atmosphere permeated the San.

Because of Phin, Walker followed the war in the Pacific closely.

When Phin first arrived in the Solomon Islands in the spring of 1943, he met twenty-five-year-old Lieutenant (j.g.) John F. Kennedy from Massachusetts. Phin liked Jack, who was a bridge player like himself and had also trained at his torpedo school; they both had spent time maneuvering near the Panama Canal.[44] When Kennedy—known as "Shafty" because he had been "shafted" so often by his superior officers—finally reached the New Hebrides in April, the U.S. Marines and Australian infantry had succeeded in gaining back Guadalcanal. But the Japanese presence in the central Pacific was strong and Admiral Chester Nimitz wanted to attack them outright. Kennedy commanded PT-109, his executive officer being Ensign Leonard Thom, a former Ohio State football player. Airpower was used during the day, and to combat the Japanese off Guadalcanal, destroyers were used at night. The steel-hulled Japanese *daihatsus*, however, knew how to defend themselves against the PT boats. In an effort to stop the Japanese, the biggest PT operation in the Solomons began on August 1. Fifteen boats divided into four groups and they followed hit-and-run tactics. That night, Phin, whose boat had been assigned to another captain and sunk, had already agreed to ride with someone else. As he went to be briefed by the intelligence officer, Byron R. White (the future Supreme Court Justice), he happened to run into "Shafty" Kennedy, who offered him a place on his PT-109. Phin thanked him, but said he had signed up with someone else. Kennedy finally assembled his crew that evening and went out looking for the "Tokyo Express" (destroyers) passing by Kolombangara. Using their zigzagging motions to evade large destroyers, PT-109 and PT-162 (Phin was aboard the latter, under the command of Lieutenant John Lowrey) disappeared temporarily into the darkness. Early on Monday, August 2, PT-169 joined them and they all thought the "Express" had escaped their net. Suddenly at 2 a.m., the *Amagiri* came out of nowhere, to Phin's astonishment, and attacked PT-109, cutting her in two. Under specific orders no other PT boat was allowed to rescue the sailors of the sunken PT-109. (As it turned out, eleven of the thirteen crew members survived.) Phin, distraught at the helplessness of his comrades, wrestled with the idea of mutiny. Fortunately, Kennedy led the survivors of PT-109 and they made their way to Bird Island, and eventually paddled to Olasana Island. The survivors were soon on their way to the base at Tulagi. When Phin met Lenny Thom at the dock at Lumbari, Thom said, "Percy, why didn't you come back and look for us?" Phin explained how infuriated he was that they had been ordered not to organize a search-and-find group. Phin left the Solomons in early 1944, eventually making his way back to the United States, where he volunteered for submarine duty. Phin once said the "biggest disappointment in Walker's life was that he couldn't participate in World War II." Walker felt as strongly about the Nazi and Japanese menaces as Uncle Will had.

The only visitor from Greenville who got to the Adirondacks to see Walker was Shelby. After leaving Camp Bowie in Texas, Shelby was in New York in July waiting to sail to England on the *Queen Elizabeth* for Northern Ireland with the 5th Infantry Division. He had time to take a train to Saranac Lake and reported: "There he [Walker] was, gaunt and pale. He was living the life of a hermit. I worried about him; I wanted him out in the world, near people. But he seemed happy where he was, flat on his back and holding on to those books for dear life."[45] Once, while out walking on Helen Hill, they spotted W. Somerset Maugham. Shelby recognized the famous author but hesitated to intrude upon his privacy, and they passed in silence.[46] Among other things, Walker mentioned to Shelby that he had seen a psychiatrist at Saranac Lake. After visiting for a few days, Shelby had to return to New York.

There was a steady stream of new arrivals at Trudeau and a fair amount of moving from one cottage to another as beds became available. Henry Clark, after making several brief trips to Rochester from Saranac Lake to catch up on his medical studies, finally left Trudeau in September to begin his fourth year of medical school. It was not long after his departure that Walker transferred to James Cottage, where he was greeted by his new second-floor porch mate, Frazier Parry, an open and thoughtful young man from Philadelphia who had graduated from Haverford College and the University of Pennsylvania Medical School.[47] (Dr. Parry subsequently had a long and distinguished career as a physician in Saranac Lake and came to know Dr. Hayes both as a friend and as a colleague.) Richard Libby, a quiet and elderly medical technician, shared the same porch when he was not working in the X-ray department. Walker also came to know Agrippa Roberts, M.D., a relative of Frazier through marriage, who lived with his wife, Mary, in a little apartment on the ground floor. After ten months at Trudeau, Walker, who had been working part-time on the staff, had a relapse and was confined to bed for three months at James. This might have been the result of overexertion while skiing at Lake Placid, as he mentioned to Shelby.[48] After this setback, he improved remarkably. On the porch at James, though there were those odd moments of tension when Frazier did not find Walker all that cheerful, he realized that Walker deep down maintained his sense of humor, even under pressure.

A patient who was not totally confined to bed could gradually begin taking short walks; such mobility meant a chance to socialize and enjoy the local scenery. As a handsome young man, the type women would like to hold on to and protect, Walker gradually became friendly with a number of women. Since the lives of patients were so restricted, formal dating was out of the question, but they did pair off—as "cousins." The more energetic and hearty could climb Mount Pisgah and have a brief tête-à-tête in the small gazebo there, appropriately named Cousinola. Though it was not unheard of for two patients to marry, "cousins" by and large were just good friends who did not become romantically involved. Walker had several, some of them at the same time, though none ever came to the porch at James. Undoubtedly his closest "cousin" was Barbara O'Neil. When she left in the fall of 1943, Walker was to be seen strolling about with a tall blonde named Marion Clawson.[49] Some of them went to the movies at the Pontiac or had dinner at Hennessey's or Downing & Cane's (called Shaughnessy's Restaurant and Downey's Bar in *The Gramercy Winner*). Those who were well on their way to recovery could spend an evening listening to Bryce LaVigne's combo at the Hotel Saranac. One advantage of "cousining" was that patients made good friends without feeling obliged to enter into serious commitments. While at Trudeau, Walker also carried on a correspondence with Rosamond Myers, whom he had known from his stays at Brinkwood.[50]

For Walker his life seemed remote and distant from the war in Europe. In October he replied to a letter sent from Alaska by Lieutenant Edwin T. Boone, Jr., a friend from his Chapel Hill days, about a forthcoming college reunion. Walker's note was cryptic, revealing his life at Trudeau minimally. Though he said he wanted dialogue, he did not seem to encourage it: "Apart from all meditations on the philosophic nature of time (à la Hans Castorp), I can't help thinking of the fantastic turns both our lives have taken . . . My lesion, as they call it, appears to be healed. I am still at Trudeau—really, the prospects are good, my only handicap being a colossal disgust with myself." Walker did not pick up on Boone's reference to H. E. Monro, a little-known poet whom T. S. Eliot once called "honest and bitter," but he did mention that Don Wetherbee had started medical school at Harvard. He added a muted request: "Would like to hear from you again."

While being X-rayed during the Christmas holidays, Dr. Edwin L. Kendig, Jr., who had done part of his medical training at Bellevue, met a sorry-looking Walker, yet they both laughed heartily when they said that, in spite of everything, they were still alive.[51] When Kendig went to James Cottage in February 1944, Walker was still in residence there. Kendig always suspected that his cottage mate had manic-depressive tendencies and thus he tried to cheer him up whenever possible. The two new friends got on well and took several trips together to New York

City, staying at the Roosevelt and seeing one show on each trip. Clearly Walker's health was returning and he was making sorties into life outside Trudeau.

When Shelby returned from Europe on the *Mauritania* in early August, he made a second trip to Saranac Lake. Walker was now living in a cure cottage outside Trudeau. His spirits had greatly improved, to the extent that he was trying to learn to play the piano on a cardboard keyboard. Walker brought up the subject of religion, and though Shelby did not relish this type of discussion, he listened intently, wondering privately whether or not his friend was about to become actively associated with a church. Shelby had his own story to tell, particularly about his war record. While serving as a captain of Battery A of the 50th Field Artillery, 5th Infantry Division, stationed in Northern Ireland, he began dating Teresa Lavery. Earlier that spring, Shelby had defended a soldier who was being browbeaten by his superior officer for not cleaning his equipment properly. Naturally such a confrontation produced ill will for Shelby from his superior officer. He was charged with falsifying a travel pass to visit Lavery, found guilty in a court-martial (an "Other than Honorable" discharge), and released from the army. Such a record was difficult to explain, especially for someone who had always revered military heroes. Before Shelby left, Walker said, "Shelby, I have a problem." He opened the drawer of his nightstand, which was filled with checks from the state of New York. "My God, Walker, why haven't you cashed them?" Walker found this difficult to explain. "Well, I didn't feel right about it because I don't really need the money." Shelby's advice was direct: "That doesn't have anything to do with it. Cash them immediately, and give the money to someone who might need it." Walker heeded Shelby's advice. In New York, Shelby worked until Christmastime on the local desk of the Associated Press.

After Shelby's departure Walker left Trudeau permanently, going to New York and staying with Huger Jervey. But Walker's health was still precarious and he had a series of X rays to monitor his condition.[52] There was a gradual increase in soft patchy infiltration in the first and second intercostal spacings, so his tuberculosis had not become as quiescent as he thought it had. With the encouragement of Jervey, Walker and Shelby went in the late summer to Atlantic City. It proved such a good move that Walker stayed on for a couple of months, and was joined there by Phin on his return to the United States. Now a recipient of a Silver Star, Phin began a new and exciting career consisting of three submarine patrols in the Philippine Sea, the China Sea, and around Japan, each lasting about seventy-five days. Before leaving for another stint at sea, he gave Shelby his Buick convertible in New York to put in storage.[53]

That fall Shelby introduced Walker to Tess Lavery, the twenty-year-old woman he intended to marry. They ate hearty German meals in Yorkville, went to movies, and spent hours conversing in Shelby's nine-dollar-a-week walk-up apartment on East 86th Street. After Shelby acquired the marriage license, they decided to have an afternoon wedding in the Church of the Transfiguration ("The Little Church Around the Corner"), just off Fifth Avenue at 29th Street. In the taxi on the way to the church, best man Walker led a hearty rendition of "Don't Fence Me In." At the service the Rev. Charles Weatherby spoke quietly to the groom: "Shelby, I have never seen two people about to get married looking so solemn." So bride and groom put on smiles and the ceremony was completed. The small wedding party had a laugh about this on the way out. Shelby and Tess lived for the rest of their stay in New York in Washington Heights. Two months later Shelby joined the Marines, went to boot camp at Parris Island, then to intelligence school at Camp Lejeune in North Carolina, and finally to California, where he worked on the construction of rubber boats to be used for a possible landing in Formosa—if not Japan.

In the fall of 1944, not long after the liberation of Paris, Bunt was still in Greenville working at the Gamble Brothers & Archer Clinic. She invited Virginia ("Jidge") Minyard, a new friend, to share a garage apartment near the clinic with her and another technician, whose husband was away at war. The tide of war had turned; Americans had landed at Leyte in the Philippines. Partly because of an increase in population (due to the air base), Jidge and Bunt were kept busy at the clinic, though they attended social events organized for the cadets. Jidge never met any of the Greenville Percys, and was aware that Bunt dated Dr. Lyne Gamble, the son of Dr. Hugh. In July, Jidge received a fellowship to Tulane and departed for New Orleans.

Walker's battle with tuberculosis was not finished. In 1945, on the day on which President Roosevelt died, Walker boarded a train for the two-hour ride to Wallingford, Connecticut. He was headed for the Gaylord Farm Sanatorium, conducted primarily for patients who could not afford private care (there were no private rooms). Gaylord helped to cut costs by having its own dairy farm; patients enjoyed seeing the cows and pigs and poultry, whose presence helped create a relaxed, stress-free environment.[54] Walker wrote to Bunt soon after he arrived at Gaylord, informing her that he had previously started to work as an instructor in pathology at P&S and then had a relapse and had to go to the sanatorium.[55]

In addition to its cure cottages, Gaylord was noted for the Enders Sleeping Porch, where a long row of patients slept on Adirondack Recliners. Gaylord's most famous patient had been Eugene O'Neill, who arrived in a blizzard on Christmas Eve in 1912 and stayed five months. There he wrote his early play *The Straw*. Walker took solace in thinking about becoming a writer like the Nobel Prize-winning playwright whose bed (he was told) he slept in. One of the first people Walker met, and came to like, was Howard Crockett, who had been there almost two years.[56] By the time Walker met him, he had run out of funds and asked Dr. David Russell Lyman if he could return to his job on Wall Street. "You can go if you like, but don't buy a new suit," Dr. Lyman replied. Crockett eventually stayed on at Gaylord as a fund-raiser. Walker also came to know and admire Stevan Dohanos, who became famous for *The Saturday Evening Post* covers that featured fellow patients.

Walker's 136 days at Gaylord gave him a chance to engage in a more intense level of reflection about his life, since he now knew for sure that he might always be prone to "breaks"—recurrences of tuberculosis—and thus might need periodic hospitalization. He also wondered if the only new friends he would make would be TB patients. "It was at Gaylord that my mind got the chance to establish itself, to digest and valuate the impressions of many past years in which one experience had crowded on another with never a second's reflection. At Gaylord I really *thought about* my life for the first time, about past and future."[57]

Because the admitting physician was busy when twenty-eight-year-old Walker was welcomed into Brooker Hall, he filled out his own admissions form. In general, his condition both on entering and on leaving was "good," and he felt that he had not really changed during the last three years. His last X ray, taken three days before entering Gaylord, showed a slight increase in the lesion in the second interspace on the right side. Other than that, Walker listed no other symptoms, seeming to downplay his condition, even though he was smoking five to ten cigarettes daily. The April 13 X ray taken at Gaylord by Dr. William H. Morriss found no bony abnormality. Later in reviewing Walker's condition, Dr. Morriss wrote that Walker had "no present complaint." He had weighed in at 130 pounds, five pounds more than his normal weight, and at Gaylord put on close to eighteen pounds. Walker had no swollen glands and his trachea was not pulled to one side—it was midline; it would have been otherwise if he were having severe lung problems. His heart was not enlarged; nor were there any murmurs. The right lung revealed a slight impairment above the third to fifth vertebral spaces, and there was some faint bronchovesicular breathing above the clavicle and scapula. Walker had no rales (or little fine sounds) while breathing.

His left lung was fine, though there were some linear markings and interlacing. In short, there was tuberculous infiltration from the apex of the right lung to the third to fifth vertebral spaces—and this is what concerned his doctors. By May 9, the day after V-E Day, a further X ray revealed that the infiltration in the outer first intercostal spacing was perhaps a little harder and more nodular. The change was very slight and possibly due entirely to the X ray machine itself.

On July 18 Walker wrote to Bunt giving some news about his condition. After a final X ray on August 23, in the wake of President Truman's announcement of Japan's surrender, Dr. Theodore R. Dayton found no change in either lung and, in fact, the slight density noted in the previous X ray was less evident. Walker was discharged with a diagnosis that his tuberculosis was "quiescent." In spite of the years of rest and recuperation, Walker would maintain that "TB is the best thing that ever happened to me."[58]

In the Pacific, President Truman had permitted an atomic bomb to be dropped on Hiroshima, and three days later another on Nagasaki, obliterating well over 100,000 people, not to mention towns and cities. As Phin headed back to Midway from a patrol off the shores of Japan, his submarine received the news of the bombing. The Japanese had surrendered; there would be no invasion. Phin's initial euphoria was tempered by feelings of anxiety about the postwar world.

Walker had his own serious questions to ask. What would America be like after the war? What to do now? "I wanted to go home," he told Robert Coles, "but I had no home . . . People wanted to settle down again; there had been too much excitement for too long. I guess I wanted to settle down, too—but at the time I didn't know that was what I wanted. I'd been alone in the woods so long, I was blinking at the strong sun, and all the people."[59] According to records at P&S, Walker had been scheduled to teach in the Pathology Department as an instructor, but he was forced to withdraw due to illness after teaching for a short period of time that fall.[60]

He headed for Greenville, the only place he could really call home. Since Sarah and her children were in the big house, Walker lodged in the apartment over the garage. After his discharge, Shelby returned to Greenville, where he lived with Tess, and started writing spot commercials for station WJPR.[61] For two months Walker secluded himself in his apartment, until six-year-old Billy Percy, his nephew, knocked on the door and was asked in. Surprised at the invitation, he entered and found an enormous present—a balsa replica of a P-40 "Flying Tiger." Billy couldn't wait to show it to everyone, but there was a slight catch: Billy's father had brought back a German 9-millimeter Luger, complete with a shoulder holster, which Walker wanted. Billy sold it to him for fifty cents. Walker told Billy he would sell it back to him when he reached his teens. Roy was furious over his brother's trafficking in arms with his young son. Years later, in recalling the incident, Billy realized that Walker never did keep his promise.

Walker and Shelby also bought a kayak kit, which they assembled. When they went to put on the outer skin, they found it was too short, and so they bought another piece, which they nailed on and painted. The kayak failed its maiden voyage and proved not to be trustworthy, and so they sold it. Not having come from a wealthy family like the Percys, Shelby was amazed by examples of Walker's indifference to money. In his dresser in the garage apartment, Walker kept handfuls of coins. "Walker, for God's sake, why don't you spend this money?" "Can't figure out what to do with it." Walker said that when he entered a store to buy something, he hated to count his change, and the last thing he wanted was for some clerk to count it out for him.

In October, Walker went to Brinkwood, where he had the companionship of Billy Percy, little Roy Percy, Huger Jervey, and Shelby.[62] Walker found that he had little to do; he became so bored that he amused himself by jacking up the car and rotating the tires. They went to see baseball games at Sewanee and visited Monteagle, where Caroline and Allen Tate had been living in their rented house, the Robert E. Lee. Their marriage was severely strained, and during the fall Gordon traveled North to see Robert Lowell and Jean Stafford, among others, because she felt so betrayed by Tate's infidelities. When she finally returned to Sewanee before Christmas, she wrote to her friend Ward Dorrance about her need to have more of her friends visit so that she would not be so obsessed by her own problems. "We have a great many friends and a great many people come to our house, but, though it sounds strange to say and may seem incredible to you—I have forgone many friendships that I would have enjoyed."[63] For his part, Tate worked assiduously that fall on editing *The Sewanee Review*, with Brinley Rhys, an occasional visitor to Brinkwood, as his assistant. Tate seemed to take the breakup of his marriage more serenely than did Gordon. It is quite possible that Walker saw either Tate or Gordon, or both, especially as Gordon wanted to become more social. Surprisingly, after the divorce in January 1946, Peter and Eleanor Taylor came to visit Allen Tate for a couple of months at Monteagle without knowing about the divorce. The Tates remarried in Princeton on April 8.

While he still needed to rest, Walker felt a desire to become involved in some literary activity. About the only reading matter that made a difference to most Greenvillians was Hodding Carter's editorials. Shelby's marriage to Tess became strained and they were divorced in 1946. After this, with Walker's encouragement, Shelby took out the typescript of his novel *Tournament*, which had been gathering dust in his closet, and reread it. He soon made an extract, entitled "Flood Burial," which he showed to Ben Wasson, who sent it off to Stuart Rose at *The Saturday Evening Post*. When Shelby received a check for $750, the first thing he did was to run to Walker's apartment over the garage and show it to him. Shelby awaited the story's publication the following September.[64] Bolstered by his success, he sent the *Post* another story, "Tell Them Good-by" (later retitled "Ride Out"), which appeared in 1947. The *Post* doubled his stipend. Shelby had found his métier and hoped he could earn a living by writing full-time. His third story, "Miss Amanda," which later became the Barcroft section of *Love in a Dry Season*, was returned with a note saying that the *Post* did not publish stories about incest.

When Roy (a recipient of the Bronze Star) came home at Christmas 1945 on a Liberty Ship by way of Boston, Walker had a bit more time on his hands. Roy had volunteered to go to the China coast from Liège, but his orders were canceled, and he became caught in the backwash at the end of the war, thus delaying his arrival in Greenville. Once he recouped his strength, Walker started visiting Josephine and Kenneth Haxton sometime in the spring. A small group formed and they read Shakespeare and acted out the plays of Shaw. Walker brought along some novels of Evelyn Waugh, which he was reading with great relish.[65] Kenneth Haxton was working in the family-owned Nelms & Blum, whose book department Walker and Shelby greatly appreciated. At one point Haxton made a wax recording of the group reading Shaw's *The Doctor's Dilemma*, which Walker considered a parable of his life. This "problem play" involving a tubercular painter focuses on man's limited knowledge—and his inability to make adequate moral judgments.

While Walker dated some of the young women from his high school days, his eyes seemed fixed on Laura Archer Ayres, Josephine's sister, who preferred to be addressed by her middle name. Smitten, Walker asked the lovely Archer to marry him; she refused. Secretly Josephine felt a strong attraction for Walker ("If I weren't already married, I would have taken out after him"). When writing about this period of Walker's life, Josephine (under the nom de plume Ellen Douglas) could only say, "After his bout with tuberculosis, he returned slowly, impeded by intermittent periods of illness, to the world."[66]

Senator Theodore Bilbo gave a fiery speech in May 1946, as he sought, successfully, his third term. It was clear to Walker and Shelby that the senator's target was Hodding Carter. "No red-blooded Southerner worthy of the name," candidate Bilbo screamed, "would accept a Poolitzer-blitzer prize given by a bunch of nigger-loving Yankeefied Communists for editorials advocating mongrelization of the race." Incensed, Hodding asked three friends, including Walker, to sign affidavits stating that Bilbo had made an anti-Semitic remark when he referred to "every damn Jew from Jesus Christ on down" rather than "every good Jew," as he maintained. Walker willingly signed his affidavit before a notary public on June 3.[67] Walker wrote to Bunt in Jackson about the Bilbo diatribe, adding a more personal note, "When am I going to see you again?"

During the academic year 1945–46, Bunt had decided to attend Millsaps College in Jackson, Mississippi, taking courses in English, history, physics, chemistry, French (from returning soldiers), and religion. Expecting to find Bunt in Greenville when he returned from Gaylord, Walker started making inquiries and, when he located her, resumed their relationship with some lighthearted letters: "Dearest Bunny, If you don't show up, I'll get me another blonde." After finishing at Millsaps, Bunt decided to live with Jidge in an apartment in New Orleans, while working for Dr. Maurice St. Martin, whom she had known in Greenville.

That summer Walker and Shelby drove along Route 66 to Tucumcari in eastern New Mexico in order to find a place where the climate would be salubrious for Walker. When they arrived at Santa Fe, they booked into the La Fonda Hotel. Santa Fe and nearby Taos had become resorts for artists and writers like Georgia O'Keeffe and Oliver La Farge, who felt drawn to Pueblo Indian culture. The adobe buildings, like an assortment of boxes randomly piled, stood out against the silhouettes of high mesas and the Jemez and Sangre de Cristo Mountains. Up the street from La Fonda was St. Francis Cathedral, whose first bishop, Juan Bautista Lamy, inspired Willa Cather's novel *Death Comes for the Archbishop* and Paul Horgan's biography *Lamy of Santa Fe*. At one point on this trip, Walker told Shelby he had read a good deal about religion and Catholicism, and wanted to begin to make the necessary steps toward a formal commitment. Shelby quickly retorted, "Walker, you are in full intellectual retreat," which infuriated Walker.

Driving south of Santa Fe one day, they stumbled on Seton Village. "I bet it is named after Ernest Thompson Seton," Shelby said. They knocked on the door of the naturalist's house, and Seton greeted them. He spent the afternoon telling them Indian stories. After making inquiries and driving around the countryside, Walker and Shelby located a place for Walker to stay—Jim Whittaker's Rancho La Merced located off the Old Santa Fe Trail south of Santa Fe. (Most likely, as locals believe, the name of the ranch is from the Spanish word for land grant, *el merced*, not the Spanish word for "thanks" or "favor.") Walker paid Whittaker by check for his lodgings on July 16. The ranch was difficult to find, even in the best of circumstances. Its most distinguishing feature was a big red barn, which dominated the sprawling landscape of piñon, sagebrush, chaparral, yucca, and ponderosa pine. Whittaker had gone to Yale before World War I, become an opera singer with an excellent tenor voice, toured a bit, and then, perhaps because he saw no future in his chosen career, set up La Merced to be used partially as a small dude ranch that could accommodate a handful of visitors.[68] Once Walker was settled, Shelby flew back to Greenville. Walker went to visit Alamogordo, the testing site for nuclear bombs; he mentions this obliquely in his essay "The Loss of the Creature," where he talks about Native Americans occasionally finding strange-looking artifacts on which are stenciled these words: *Return to U.S. Experimental Project, Alamogordo. Reward.*

At La Merced, Walker met forty-seven-year-old Marjorie McDonough, a former nurse in the African campaign, and Perrine Dixon, whose New Orleanian family once owned Camp Dixon in Covington, Louisiana.[69] McDonough immediately fell in love with Walker, though he did not return her affectionate advances. When not reading Marcel, Heidegger, Jaspers, and Sartre, Walker joined the other guests at La Merced for long walks and horseback rides (he favored El Capitán—even gallantly posing for a picture on this Southwest champion quarter horse). He visited D. H. Lawrence's Del Monte ranch and read his works (he thought *Lady Chatterley's Lover* silly but liked *The Rainbow*).[70] He studied Indian culture and beliefs. "I liked the people I met out there. I slept in an old barn. I went to the Grand Canyon. I went to the reservations. I'm afraid at times I didn't see all I was meant to see. Instead of looking at the Canyon all the time, or the Indian dances all the time, I would watch people watching the Canyon or the dances. That's the way I've always been, I guess."[71] La Merced proved to be another, though more active, cure cottage. He had still not emerged from his illness with a career or even prospects for a family life, and it bothered him. Never having had a "normal" family life up to this point, he made a resolution to bind himself to what he saw as becoming the basis of a future life: marriage, religion, and a job, most likely as a physician in a TB sanatorium, though in the back of his mind he did not rule out becoming a writer of some sort. As he later mentioned, "I just kind of washed up on shore—no home, hadn't fought in the war like the others my age, no profession, but had the scars of a mysterious illness I never suffered from."[72] Finally Walker called Bunt from La Merced: "I need to be with you, to talk with you."[73] He telegrammed: "I need you to be my wife. I am neurotic as hell. I need you to get me out of my state. I love you."

When Walker flew to New Orleans there was only one thing on his mind—marriage. He went to see Bunt in her apartment on Carondelet Street.[74] Though Bunt had been dating Jidge's cousin John Minyard, a medical student at Tulane, the relationship was not serious. When Walker's visit with Bunt had ended and he was waiting for a taxi to take him to the airport, he turned to Bunt and matter-of-factly proposed:

"I am going home to get a ring."

"A ring for what?"

"A ring for our wedding." Bunt was thrilled.

A week later, driving his new maroon Chevrolet convertible, Walker returned with his mother's diamond wedding ring in a Tiffany setting, which he had fastened to his inside pocket with a safety pin. He flew to Santa Fe with Shelby in order to pick up his Ford and gear and to pay their respects to Walker's friends Eleanor Brownell and Alice Howland, who frequently hosted literary soirees and had become attached to Walker. From a distance, Walker began making arrangements for the wedding, the wedding night, and the honeymoon. On September 14 he sent Bunt a letter: "Dearest Bunny, For the love of heaven, let me know if you are going to fly out here to Albuquerque and help me drive home. I think it would be really fine, but I doubt if there is much chance you could get time off, and it wouldn't be a great big thing for you as for me, since you couldn't spend much time here. I'm driving East the last week of September . . . I'm supposed to be there in New Orleans on October 1st when I have engaged a room on St. Charles. Don't know whether I'll be there a week or a year. I've written Tulane a couple of times, but I haven't gotten anything interesting from them."

When Bunt and Walker got together, they decided to spend time at Brinkwood after they were married. It was the only "home" that Walker and his bride could go to. On November 2, while in Nashville, he sent a telegram to Bunt: "Reserve double room or suite if available November 7 for three nights . . . St. Charles Hotel." He also made a list of what he himself needed to do:

> Get dog
> Get papers and bankbook
> Underwear
> Get Vanderbilt catalogue
> Write Phin

Call Bunt
Call Mrs. Harrison
Tennessee map
Write O'Leary
Write Perrine (?)
Airplane tickets
Pressure cooker
Railroad reservations

Walker returned to New Orleans just before the wedding. Since Bunt's mother had died in July, it was decided not to have the wedding in Doddsville and to proceed without wedding invitations or a rehearsal. On November 6, Bunt and Walker applied for a marriage license. The marriage took place the next afternoon in the First Baptist Church on the corner of St. Charles Avenue and Delachaise. Since Sarah was heavily pregnant with her third child, the Greenville Percys (at Walker's insistence) did not attend the wedding. Phin was stationed in Panama and could not make it in time. Bunt's side of the family was represented by her father and sister, Willie Ruth Cowan, and a cousin from Biloxi. Inside the fan-shaped church, chrysanthemums graced the sanctuary as the Rev. J. D. Grey performed the brief ceremony. A radiant Bunt, wearing a pearl-gray gabardine suit with a matching veil, carried a French bouquet of pastel-shaded flowers. Willie Ruth served as matron of honor.

Shelby, the best man, was pleased for both his friends: "Bunt was exactly the type of person Walker wanted. Everything about Bunt pleased Walker."[75] The small wedding party then headed out for a restaurant and dinner. That evening and for the next two nights, the newlyweds stayed in the bridal suite of the St. Charles Hotel in New Orleans—a gift of the manager, Michael O'Leary, a friend of Uncle Will. The next day Shelby took a train back to Greenville. He left a note: "Take care of yourselves on that empty mountain top." Little LeRoy Percy gave the newlyweds fifty cents as his present. Shelby's wedding present was two pairs of ski pajamas with fleece inside; they were to be much appreciated as Dr. and Mrs. Walker Percy left for a prolonged stay at Brinkwood.

6

The Apprenticeship Years:
Writing *The Charterhouse*
1947–53

The newlyweds arrived at Brinkwood soon after their wedding and settled in. The routine was predictable—a good amount of rest, reading, some walking and bird-watching (for years, Walker had enjoyed tracking birds, particularly a certain horned owl in Greenville). Bunt and Walker lived casually, not trying to anticipate the future until the time when he would be ready to stand on his own. In the kitchen Bunt had the assistance of Mrs. Frances Gibson, as well as the help of their caretakers, Mr. and Mrs. Harrison, and Imogene, their daughter. Walker liked his privacy—in their living room or on the porch—though he and Bunt took walks through the fields of purple spiderworts and the magenta swatches of wild geranium and visited some of the battlefields at Franklin and Murfreesboro.[1] On occasion, Charlotte Gailor, Robert and Mary Daniel, Cynthia Sanborn, Brinley Rhys, Bucky Johnson, Humphreys ("Ug") and Charlotte McGee, Marian Elliott, and other "locals" would drop by for a visit. The Percys saw Andrew Lytle, who was not far away, from time to time. Their friends knew Walker's medical history and respected his need for privacy and rest. The Tates were at Sewanee that Christmas with their daughter, Nancy, and her husband, Percy Wood, and their baby, Percy Hoxie Wood III, affectionately called "P-3." They had a picnic at Natural Bridge, near Brinkwood, and visited Bunt and Walker.[2] Percy Wood and Phin had been at McCallie together. Walker liked Allen's lively and polemical literary criticism; he was less familiar with the poetry. He also admired what he considered Gordon's well-written and highly structured novels (she had been secretary to Ford Madox Ford, an important influence on her work). His library contained many of Gordon's novels. Inspired by her admiration for Dorothy Day, the *Catholic Worker* movement, and by her own reading of St. John of the Cross, Gordon was converting to Catholicism; the conversion took place formally in New York City in November 1947. Her subsequent friendship with Jacques and Raïssa Maritain at Princeton—and the latter's desire to make their home a *centre de rayonnement*—introduced Gordon to Thomistic philosophy and theology. This in turn gave an intellectual underpinning to what proved to be an emotive spirituality. From her myriad letters, it is clear that Gordon enjoyed communicating with others about her newfound faith.

After three months at Brinkwood, Walker had another "break," signaling that his tuberculosis might become active again. He knew the prescribed routine and rested on the porch as much as he could. Though Brinkwood was a lesser version of Trudeau and Gaylord, it gave him the opportunity he needed to live an existence that would not overtax his strength. Soon after arriving at Brinkwood, Walker received a batch of books a bookstore in Nashville had been holding for him. He never lacked for scholarly books to read, since Sarah and Roy would bring whatever he wanted from Uncle Will's library. He also kept up with current fiction and enjoyed Robert Penn Warren's *All the King's Men* when it came out in 1946.[3] Prompted by a postcard from Shelby, Walker devoured *The Possessed*, and read many other great Russian novels, including *The Idiot*.[4] Once, Walker posed for a photo in front of the bookcases at Brinkwood with some furniture that was special to him—his mother's desk and his father's leather chair.

Walker quietly started a regime of reading and writing, working away at a manuscript that was his first attempt at a novel, *The Charterhouse*, named after the religious houses of the Carthusian monks. (In this instance the title may have been related in Walker's mind to Sir Thomas More.[5] The inspiration for the title might also have come from Stendhal's famous novel, which Binx Bolling refers to in *The Moviegoer* as he rides on a bus: "The romantic sits across the aisle, slumped gracefully, one foot propped on the metal ledge. He is reading *The Charterhouse of Parma*.") Walker did not realize that this writing project would take so much time and effort; he worked on it unobtrusively for almost five years and later burned the finished manuscript. While Bunt, Shelby, Phin, and the Tates read the novel, their testimony is of little help in reconstructing its plot. Bunt felt the novel was too Thomas Wolfean— the main plot and the subplots never really meshed. Shelby felt the novel did not jell and the style reminded him somewhat of both Kafka and Wolfe, with (on reflection) strains of Céline and Sartre. One thing Shelby could remember was that the young man vomited after each crisis or tribulation in his life. Robert Coles noted that its setting—a country club—was familiar to all readers of Percy's fiction, a twentieth-century replacement for the medieval church. Where else to go on a Sunday? What else to do but swim, play tennis or golf, or join one's neighbors and friends for meals and booze at the club?[6] Walker called the novel "a sort of Southern *Bildungsroman*, about a young man who's out of sync with the world."[7]

In summary, the plot had Ben Cleburne leaving a sanatorium called the Hermitage, and returning home to a city like Birmingham. Walker wrote Virginia Durr, Justice Hugo Black's sister-in-law, saying he had written a novel in which the statue of Vulcan in Birmingham was a "symbol of something or other."[8] Ben, the protagonist, visits the home of Ignatz Kramer, a Jewish convert to Catholicism, and learns from his mother that her son has left the seminary and considers himself a failure. There is interaction among Ben, Ignatz, and their mutual friend Abbie Lipscomb, some of which takes place on a golf course. Ignatz and Ben set out West, become separated, and Ben heads off on a pilgrimage, perhaps with Abbie, to South America. Halfway through the novel, one of the protagonists decides to operate a filling station in a desertlike location. Two men (Ben and Ignatz?) are sitting on a patio when a man named Adam comes by. Returning from a trip to his father's house, Ben tells Ignatz that he feels spiritually dead. He proposes to Abbie and they marry. In the last section, Ben feels he has not solved his spiritual problems and seeks the help of Dr. Betty Jane, a psychiatrist. (In one revision, she appears in the first chapter.) There is a scene in a jail and a funeral (probably the death of Ben's father). At one point, Ben and Adam play cards. Though we do not know the book's outcome, it is clear that it centers on a young man who wants to develop the spiritual part of his nature.[9]

There were kind words from a few publishers when Walker circulated the novel—"but no deal."[10] When Caroline Gordon finished her own novel *The Malefactors* in 1955, she wrote Walker about the parallels between their characters:

I have finished the novel I have been working on for over four years—all but about four thousand words I have yet to write. I often think of Ben Cleburne. My hero is just another incarnation of him. But it has taken me thirty years of pretty hard labor to know how to present him effectively and I'm not sure yet I've made it, though Allen, to my great joy, likes the book.[11]

Her hero is forty-seven-year-old Tom Claiborne, a Southerner who served in World War I and decided to become a poet and live with his wife in Bucks County, Pennsylvania. Except for his last name, he bears little resemblance to Walker's Ben Cleburne.

That year Walker listened attentively to the Sunday radio broadcasts of Monsignor Fulton J. Sheen, famous for having converted Heywood Broun, Henry Ford II, and Clare Boothe Luce, as he dramatically presented the tenets of Catholicism and the growing horrors of Communism. Though impressed by Sheen's forthrightness, Walker did not hesitate to mock his flamboyant manner of speaking. Yet he wrote to Sheen and asked if he could take instruction. Sheen replied that it was pointless for Walker to come to New York and suggested he contact the superior of St. Augustine's Mission House in Bay St. Louis, Mississippi, the largest seminary in the Diocese of Natchez. Informed by the seminary that its principal mission was to educate black seminarians, Walker was directed to contact the Jesuits at Loyola University in New Orleans.[12] In Bunt's mind, "Walker's conversion more or less eased up on him." "I took it as an intolerable state of affairs," he told an interviewer, "to have found myself in this life and in this age, which is a disaster by any calculation, without demanding a gift commensurate with the offense. So I demanded it."[13] He read St. Augustine's *The City of God* and Kierkegaard's "The Difference Between a Genius and an Apostle," which, as he told Charles Bell, "turned me into a Catholic (well, helped)."[14]

At this juncture in their lives, his wife also started thinking about converting to Catholicism. At first glance it might appear that Bunt was merely following in his wake. She loved Walker very much and did not want to alienate herself from what was important to him. Yet, as her family and friends all knew, Bunt had a mind of her own. Her close friend Jidge Minyard said of her, "If Bunt had any problems, they would have to come out. Bunt does not hesitate to express herself right away." One thing lacking was a Catholic environment congenial to those who were committed to the beliefs and tenets of the Catholic faith. Until the right moment came, Walker read for spiritual comfort the Gospel of St. John in the New-Century edition—a book that had once belonged to his father.

It turned out to be an exceptionally cold winter, and the furnace at Brinkwood was not working properly. Walker kept boots at the foot of the basement stairs to put on whenever he had to stoke the furnace. His Christmas gift to Bunt was a black cocker spaniel, Pal Joey (the Percys would always have a dog from that time on). That year Huger Jervey spent a good deal of time at Brinkwood, though he did not stay overnight with the Percys. Bert and Eleanor Mudge and Alexander Heard, a year behind Walker at Chapel Hill and a fellow SAE, stopped by briefly.[15] Heard had been working at the University of Alabama on a project involving Southern political science under the direction of V. O. Key, Jr., of Johns Hopkins University. For the most part, however, Bunt felt that she could not make elaborate plans or do much formal entertaining, though once she and Walker visited nearby Lost Cove Cave, where someone took a series of photos.

Now out of the navy, Phin was staying with Sarah and Roy. When he moved out to Brinkwood, he and Walker had a joyous reunion. With good reason, Phin always felt that he was special in Walker's life. That spring, Walker mentioned to Phin that there were rumors abroad about the Tates. Allen Tate and Caroline Gordon were in New York, their marriage on the rocks for the second time. Tate had taken a suite at the Brevoort by himself, but they resumed living together when he moved in with Gordon on Perry Street. Gordon taught at a writers' conference at the University of Utah, and at some point during the summer caught up with Phin at Brinkwood. They all played croquet on the spacious lawn and Allen inscribed one of his books for Phin: "To a noble and patient host." Never satisfied with the education he received at the Naval Academy, Phin attended summer school at the University of the South and opted to continue the following year, taking courses as a special student in English, history, political science, French, and Spanish. Because he did not want to stay by himself at Brinkwood during that academic year, he moved in with Ug and Charlotte McGee.

Walker showed Phin his manuscript of The Charterhouse (1,100 pages as Phin recalled), but after reading fifty pages, mostly about people at a party and what they were wearing, he handed it back to Walker: "Look, I am not a literary critic. You write beautifully, but it doesn't get to me. It's not moving me. I can't go on with it."[16]

While Bunt and Walker were at Brinkwood, Shelby felt it only fitting that he not be intrusive and remained for the most part in Greenville. In June, the founders of the Levee Press (Kenneth Haxton, Ben Wasson, and Hodding Carter) convinced Shelby to use their imprint for his story, "The Merchant of Bristol," which he dedicated to Walker, who had helped pick the title. The story—an extract of Shelby's novel Tournament, based partly on the life of Huger Lee Foote, Shelby's grandfather—centers on the suicide of Abraham Wisten, who could not repay a debt on his clothing store in a town not unlike Greenville. The scene of the suicide, similar to LeRoy Percy's death, might have caused Walker to wonder why the story had been dedicated to him. "He took the pistol in both hands and, making a little moaning sound of pure terror, put the barrel into his mouth. His teeth chattered against it, and his tongue jerked in reflex away from the slick metallic taste. Then suddenly the fear was gone and it was exultation, triumph, as he clamped down with his teeth, thrust his tongue against the metal, and with his thumb looped awkwardly through the guard in reverse, pulled the trigger."

In late August, Bunt and Walker (with Pal Joey) loaded the maroon convertible and drove to New Orleans. They had no plans, except to stay for a while at the fashionable Pontchartrain Hotel. They knew they wanted to contact the Jesuits at Loyola, since they were both ready for religious instruction. They even drove to Covington and Gulf Shores to see what housing was available. Walker spotted an ad in *The Times-Picayune* for a house for rent at 1458 Calhoun Street, a stone's throw from the lovely Audubon Park, across from Loyola University and its impressive Tudor Gothic church. Walker took to New Orleans quickly. "New Orleans is both intimately related to the South and yet in a real sense cut adrift not only from the South but from the rest of Louisiana, somewhat like Mont-St.-Michel awash at high tide. One comes upon it, moreover, in the unlikeliest of places, by penetrating the depths of the Bible Belt, running the gauntlet of Klan territory, the pine barrens of south Mississippi, Bogalusa, and the Florida parishes of Louisiana. Out and over a watery waste and there it is, a proper enough American city, and yet within the next few hours the tourist is apt to see more nuns and naked women than he ever saw before."[17] Bunt hurried over to the house with a real estate agent, learned that others were interested, and called Walker, who immediately telephoned the owner, Julius Friend. He was one of the editors of *The Double-Dealer*, a noted New Orleans literary journal that was in existence from 1921 to 1926.[18] Will Percy had published in this journal, and right away the Friends and the Percys liked each other.[19] Since his mother, Ida Weis Friend, had been in poor health, Julius decided to move his family into her ample house on Palmer Avenue. For Bunt and Walker, the house on Calhoun turned out to be perfect—a small yard in front protected by a wrought-iron fence, a patio in the back, and a screened-in porch on the driveway side. The Friends had installed two bookcases downstairs, one from floor to ceiling about ten feet wide, and a smaller one. Since many books had come into *The Double-Dealer* for review, Julius had built up quite a collection.

Bunt and Walker moved in as soon as they could. They hired Vivian Hunt as their cook, though she did not live in. Bunt and Walker dined at Palmer Avenue, and the Friends would come by Calhoun Street for animated chats. Julius gave the Percys a number of books, including an inscribed copy of *The Unlimited Community: A Study of the Possibility of Social Science*, which he had written with James K. Feibleman. Feibleman chaired the Philosophy Department at Tulane and was an officer of the Charles Peirce Society, an academic group that studied the works of a philosopher and semiotician whose name Walker probably read for the first time as he paged through *The Unlimited Community*. If Walker needed further information about Peirce's thought, he had only to consult Feibleman's *An Introduction to Peirce's Philosophy, Interpretated as a System*.

Within two weeks of moving into Calhoun, the Percys and Bunt's friend Jidge Minyard started taking instructions at Holy Name Church. The pastor, John J. McCarthy, S.J., greeted them and set up a group appointment. Father McCarthy, who had entered the Society of Jesus in 1910 and was ordained fifteen years later, had recently been appointed pastor of Holy Name. A matter-of-fact man, he was experienced in dealing with converts. In her own mind Jidge had already entered the Church and instructions were a formality; her grandmother had objected to her conversion, but her mother took it well. For Bunt and Walker, it was otherwise. Not only did they need to know more about the doctrines, but they had to become comfortable with liturgical rites in Latin. According to Jidge, Bunt had the greatest adjustment to make. Shelby maintained that what "Walker desperately needed at that time was the strength the Catholic Church could give him." Twice a week, from mid-September until December, the three catechumens talked with Father McCarthy. Jidge often showed up late; she was teaching at Sophie Newcomb College and found it almost impossible to leave her lab before 4 p.m., dashing to Thomas Hall just as discussions were beginning. Walker soon became enthusiastic about his newfound faith, and after each session would have a hundred questions for Jidge's beau, Salvatore Milazzo: "Walker was gung ho. He enjoyed every bit of the instruction."[20] Walker was aware of the intellectual and human dimensions that were part and parcel of his conversion:

One can write about conversion two ways. One way is to put the best possible face on it, recount a respectable intellectual odyssey. Such as: Well, my tradition was scientific. I thought science explained the cosmos—until one day I read what Kierkegaard said about Hegelianism, the science of his day: that Hegel explained everything in the universe except what it is to be an individual, to be born, to live, and to die. And for me this "explanation" would be true enough, I suppose. But then there is this. When I was in college, I lived in the attic of a fraternity house with four other guys. God, religion, was the farthest thing from our minds and talk—from mine at least. Except for one of us, a fellow who got up every morning at the crack of dawn and went to Mass. He said nothing about it and seemed otherwise normal. Does anyone suppose that one had nothing to do with the other? That is, thinking about Kierkegaard's dilemma and remembering my roommate's strange behavior—this among a thousand other things one notices or remembers, which, if they don't "cause" it, at least enter into it, at least make room for this most mysterious turning in one's life.[21]

Once Walker asked Father McCarthy about evolution, a complicated subject for a priest not particularly trained in science (his one claim to fame as a scientific writer was an article entitled "Catholics Who Are Eminent in Electrical Science," published twenty years earlier in *America* magazine). When Father McCarthy gave Walker a long essay he had typed out explaining the position of the Catholic Church, as he understood it, Walker was impressed by its lack of pretension and utter candor. At one point Walker said, "Father, I do have some money and I am anxious to do something for the Church." The reply: "My son, do not worry about that. We will get around to it in due time." Walker considered it a blessing to have Father McCarthy as his instructor.[22]

Walker preferred not to talk publicly about why he became a Catholic. He knew that his spiritual life was private and that discussions of religion, friendly or polemical, often ended up in confusion. The statements he did make are clear and unencumbered: "The reason I am a Catholic is that I believe that what the Catholic Church proposes is true."[23] He knew that educated opponents believed the "Catholic Church is not only a foreign power but a fascist power," and that the less educated, like an ex-member of the Ku Klux Klan, might shout that the "Catholic Church is a piece of shit." Not easily flummoxed, Walker knew how to rebut such statements politely, the first by examining the meanings of "power" and "fascist" and the second with some barbershop humor, like "Truthfully, Lester, you're something of a shit yourself, even for white trash." When he thought the question "Why are you a Catholic?" had a smart-mouthed edge, he simply asked, "What else is there?" Walker knew how to discern the background of the questioner and reply civilly. He believed both the old "modern age" had ended and that post-Christian generations had failed to grasp that they were "ensouled creatures under God, born to trouble, whose salvation depends upon the entrance of God into history as Jesus Christ." Nor did they recognize that they lived in "the most scientifically advanced, savage, democratic, inhuman, sentimental, murderous century in human history." Aside from grace, a gift and invitation from God, why Walker chose the Catholic Church among the Judeo-Christian religions would conjure up, he maintained, "old family quarrels among these faiths." And rather than wasting anyone's time, Walker preferred to retreat into silence by noting finally that he didn't have the authority to bear or proclaim the Good News.

Father McCarthy's method of instruction was simple: he would read a question from the Baltimore Catechism, and the three would recite the answer in unison. Hearing the strange religious words prompted many questions. When they had finally finished their instruction, Father McCarthy met with each one individually to verify each one's true intent. The three were baptized conditionally on December 13, the feast of St. Lucy, by Father McCarthy. It was the common practice in those days; there was no evidence that Walker had been previously baptized. At baptism, it is customary for Catholics to assume the name of a saint. Walker chose the name John, which was fitting for one who had been so influenced by the Evangelist.[24] Soon the three neophytes stood in line before the confessional booths—a decisive moment, though the anonymity of the confessional guarded their identities. They looked nervously at one another and Walker said, "Well, who will go first?" Jidge looked at Bunt, who had her sins written out on a slip of paper, and they replied in unison, "Not me." So Walker went first.

Walker later told Jidge that one thing that attracted him to the Church was the sacrament of penance and reconciliation. He also told Shelby that he once went to confession on another occasion to an old Irish priest in New Orleans and mentioned the lustful thoughts he had been having. "Don't worry about it," came the voice behind the screen. "It's the nature of the beast."

Between Jidge's baptism and her confirmation with the Percys in mid-April, she received another sacrament when she and Sal Milazzo were married on Easter Saturday in 1948. (Jidge said she felt like a Girl Scout gaining merit badges: five different sacraments in the course of three months.)

As a newcomer to New Orleans without any prospects of employment, Walker continued to lead a fairly quiet life. The Percys went to Mass daily, preferably the later ones, as Walker tended to sleep in whenever possible. They enjoyed dining out at restaurants like Galatoire's, Antoine's, Café Sbisa, and Commander's Palace in the Garden District.[25] Walker also liked a snack at Felix's Oyster Bar in the Quarter, a small restaurant favored by Binx Bolling and Kate Cutrer in *The Moviegoer*.[26] He frequented Manale's restaurant on Napoleon Street, where, like John Millington Synge in an Aran pub, he could mentally record the local dialect. Because he had a problem swallowing properly, Walker would sometimes have to leave a restaurant quickly and be driven to an emergency ward for immediate treatment.

In his trips about New Orleans, Walker became fascinated with cemeteries, such as St. Louis Cemetery No. 1 on Basin Street (where he once served as a pallbearer at a funeral) and Lafayette Cemetery No. 1 on Washington Avenue. The tombs—"modest duplexes," as Walker characterized them—form little cities, most active on All Saints' Day and All Souls' Day when families turn out to scrub, whitewash, or polish them. Walker fell in love with New Orleans; in typical Cajun fashion, he called it *mon amour*.[27] New Orleans, particularly under the administration of young Mayor DeLesseps S. ("Chep") Morrison, was the one city Walker could think of where a person who fell down in the street might be picked up, taken to a local bar, and revived with a shot of Early Times. The city is cut off from the Deep South and has developed its own culture, an exotic blend of ingredients—"a gumbo of stray chunks of the South, of Latin and Negro oddments, German and Irish morsels, all swimming in a fairly standard American soup." Or to use another Percy image, it was as if "Marseilles had been plucked up off the Midi, monkeyed with by Robert Moses and Hugh Hefner, and set down off John O'Groats in Scotland." As Walker said, the "occupational hazard of the writer in New Orleans is a variety of the French flu, which might also be called the Vieux Carré Syndrome. One is apt to turn fey, potter about a patio, and write *feuilletons* and vignettes or catty *romans-à-clef*, a pleasant enough life but for me too seductive."[28]

Not only could Walker stroll around Audubon Park with Bunt and Pal Joey, visit the nearby zoo, and have access to two university libraries, but he took great pleasure in the landscape and mindscape of New Orleans itself—St. Louis Cathedral and Jackson Square in the French Quarter, the New Orleans Museum of Art in City Park, the historical and colorful houses in the Garden District (made even more lovely by an abundance of bougainvillea, night-blooming jasmine, magnolia trees, and cascading wisteria), the rougher neighborhoods of the Irish Channel (the area between Constance Street and the Mississippi River, extending from St. Joseph Street to Louisiana Avenue), and Uptown and the long levees that were perfect for Sunday strolls. With its fashionable shops and movie theaters, strollers along Canal Street had much to choose from. Walker would take rides out to Elysian Fields toward Gentilly and Lake Pontchartrain and catch an afternoon movie at the Pitt (called the Tivoli in *The Moviegoer*). He also saw movies at the Prytania Theater, as well as in a now demolished theater on Freret Street near the Tulane campus. He became acquainted with the historic Toby-Westfeldt House, which he transformed into Aunt Emily Cutrer's house in *The Moviegoer*. He crisscrossed New Orleans by auto and streetcar until he made it his own.

When Bunt had not become pregnant at Brinkwood (there was no history of miscarriages), she and Walker talked about adopting a child.

After some counseling sessions with Mrs. O'Connor at St. Vincent's Infant Asylum, run by the Daughters of Charity, they decided to adopt a daughter, whom they named Mary Pratt after Walker's paternal grandmother. When the baby was baptized, Bunt asked Jidge to be the godmother. With the arrival of an infant in their lives, Bunt and Walker sensed a new stage in their relationship.

Walker still did not have a paying job. Toiling away at his novel, he considered moving to Santa Fe and doing work as a physician in one of the TB sanatoria in the area. For Walker, the house on Calhoun seemed "haunted" by history, and there were too many social invitations to allow him to do any consistently serious writing.[29] As Bunt and Walker looked about in late spring for a permanent home, they drove again to Covington. One of the first things that Walker heard about Covington was that it was "the second healthiest place in the world" (he never did find out the first), partly because of the curative properties of the "ozone" secreted by the pine trees in St. Tammany Parish. The irony is that Walker was allergic to pollen and would spend hours each year with a wet towel over his face; sometimes he had to drive to Florida and stay several weeks until his eyes dried up and he could continue a normal routine. "Though St. Tammany Parish is, by any reckoning," Walker once wrote, "a backwater in the larger currents of history and though unflattering things have been said about it—Governor Claiborne mentioned 'a great scarcity of talent' and 'virtuous men,' and Judge Ezekiel Ellis, one of the founders of the local Methodist church, is reputed to have called Covington 'the wickedest place on earth,' " it really suited the needs of Bunt and Walker.[30] Walker scouted the area and was attracted to the house on Military Road that had belonged to Joseph and Marietta Woodward, five miles northeast of town in the direction of the Bogalusa Highway. Set back from the road, the house had a guest cottage and a very large lawn, the back of which went down to the banks of the Little Bogue Falaya. The flowering dogwoods, redbuds, purple wisteria, azaleas, and camellias accentuated the quiet loveliness of the area. Occasionally, Walker would stop in and talk with Julius Tugenhaft at Tugy's Bar, a favorite watering hole of family friend Bob Horton. When Walker raised the topic in Tugy's whether the asking price of $30,000 was fair, Tugy said to offer "$20,000 tops," which is what Walker paid.

Shelby was hoping that his new work, then entitled "Child by Fever," would be accepted soon for publication. He was working at the same time on a novel, *Vortex* (later changed to *Follow Me Down*). He drew his inspiration from the 1941 trial of Floyd Myers for the murder of Imogene Smothers in Greenville. Though he had finished fifteen sections, Shelby expected to have an entire first draft by the end of the summer.

Bolstered by his accomplishments, Shelby put on his coaching hat and tried to encourage Walker:

No writer ever developed without hard work and disappointment, and I am willing to have my share of both. I even realize I may never have anything else—there have been plenty of such artists, and some of them have been the very best. If you are serious about wanting to write fiction you had better get to work. I honestly don't think it can be done without a background of four or five years of apprenticeship (probably more). Sit down with pen and paper and describe anything at all: do it again and again—either an object or an action—until you satisfy yourself. Then try telling a story that has a beginning, middle, and end. Then tear it up and do it over, and over, and over. Then try another one, and another one, and another one. Finally you may begin to feel like tackling something with strength to it (I hope you won't have felt up to any such thing before this, for if you have, you'll have made a botch of it) . . . But the most heart-breaking thing about it is: the better you get, the harder you'll have to work—because your standards will rise with your ability.

By September 1948, Shelby had completed a second draft of *Tournament*, which Walker had read in its initial stages and which was published a year later, thus launching Shelby's career as a writer.

On the last day of May, "John Walker Percy" bought the Woodward house for the price Walker had been urged to offer. Twice during the following years, he bought parcels of property adjacent to his so that he would have as much privacy as possible. Walker's income at that time was estimated to be about $18,000 a year.[31] Walker continued his strict routine of writing in the morning, eating a solid lunch, and then resting and working outside or running errands in the afternoon. Though living in a small town, Walker was not immune from the racial problems of the South. Covington, too, had its own Negro section, with a separate Catholic church for blacks. Walker wrote to Joseph Fichter, S.J., professor of sociology at Loyola University, thanking him for the newsletter "Christian Conscience." Walker had read about it in *America*. "It is wonderful to see such a publication in the Deep South," he wrote.[32] He also asked a friend at Loyola, "Why limit the paper to the students? Why not put it on a subscription basis and get a mailing list of Catholics and non-Catholics (especially Negroes)? I for one would like to subscribe to it, but I saw no provisions anywhere for subscriptions." This was his first contact with the Regional Inter-Racial Commission of the National Federation of Catholic College Students, founded to influence student life and defend the Christian principle of human equality. This group, composed of students from Dominican College, Loyola University, and

Xavier University, wanted to break down blind prejudice through a program of prayer, study, and action, much in the spirit of John La Farge's book *The Race Question and the Negro*. Walker also read Thomas Merton's *The Seven Storey Mountain* when it appeared in 1948, a book that "meant a great deal" to him.[33]

Walker had tapped into something that would change his way of thinking, as he came to learn about the efforts of Father Fichter and his colleague Louis J. Twomey, S.J., who arrived at Loyola in the summer of 1947 to begin his Institute of Industrial Relations.[34] On the advice of Gordon Allport and Samuel Stouffer, his mentors at Harvard University, Father Fichter gradually worked out a program for the integration of black students at Loyola, as a prelude to what would happen in the South and the country as a whole. In the fall of 1947, he invited black students from Xavier to meet with him at Loyola. Yet his plan to have blacks accepted at Loyola in the fall of 1948 did not succeed at first. The Church was ineffectual in race relations because of an excess of prudence and a failure of nerve. Father Fichter's experience convinced him to form a lay group to work for racial desegregation in Catholic educational facilities.[35]

Shelby tended to tweak Walker's nose about his conversion whenever he could. When he heard that the Pope had given a decoration to William Randolph Hearst, he wrote: "My advice is, get out now. The ship is fixing to founder. However, I suppose that you'll say that all the nasty things I've heard about Willy are Communist propaganda." In addition to attending liturgical services at St. Peter's Church in Covington, Bunt and Walker started going to the St. Joseph Abbey just outside Covington on River Road. The abbey church, with its strikingly bold murals by Dom Gregory de Wit, O.S.B., and its 1,100 acres, provided the Percys with a sense of peace and tranquillity. Walker first heard Gregorian chant there when he went to Mass with Jidge and Sal Milazzo.

When the Footes spent part of the summer of 1949 at Brinkwood, Shelby had no real notion of what Walker was writing. They missed the companionship of Huger Jervey, who died on July 27, just after having been appointed the first Charles Evans Hughes Professor of Law at Columbia. In early October, Shelby visited Fredericksburg to see the Civil War battlefield and began seeing possibilities in writing about this battle: "I could do a job on that fight." In the back of his mind, Shelby considered a longer project about the Civil War, but decided to hold off for a few more years. He drove to the University of Virginia in Charlottesville, where Phin was studying law, which he considered "almost as bad as medicine." Grandmother Nellie Phinizy, who had worn black since the day of Billups's death, died of leukemia in Athens on October 9. Roy's plane arrived late, forcing a delay in the funeral.[36] Walker, Roy, Phin, and other grandsons were the pallbearers at her funeral in Athens.

Bunt and Walker tended to remain by themselves, perhaps fearing that Walker might be perceived as a carrier of tuberculosis, but as Mary Pratt grew, they began to reach out to other families in the area with children. Gradually they met their neighbors, including the Jack Harringtons and Ottilie Lambert, a librarian by training who ran the Pine Burr, which she filled with crafts, knitwear, and clothing for children. Neighborhood children enjoyed skimming about in her old wooden canoe on the Little Bogue Falaya. About this time, Walker and Bunt met Frederick Stephen and Betty Ellis, Robert and Katherine Lobdell, Dr. Richard Faust and his wife, Mary, and Lawrence ("Chink") and Betty Baldwin. Four years younger than Walker, Chink had been raised in New Orleans and attended Holy Name Church. After his discharge from the air force, Chink decided to go into the car business, and by October 1950 started his own Lincoln-Mercury dealership. From the earliest days of their friendship, Walker bought his cars from Chink; he was particularly attracted by a 1951 Lincoln four-door sedan with a Mercury body and beefed-up chassis in Chink's showroom.

"Hey, that's a nice car. How much?"

"In the neighborhood of $2,500. Would you like to buy it?"

Walker soon sported a new car about town, much to the consternation of Miss Ottilie, who thought it was funereal.

The Baldwins had three children, all slightly older than Mary Pratt. One day Betty Baldwin answered her phone: "Mrs. Baldwin, my name is Bunt Percy, and I understand you have children, and I would like to have a party for my daughter, and would you come? My husband is tubercular, but he would not be at the party. He will stay in the house, so there is no need to worry." The Baldwin children enjoyed the party, and the Percys started visiting the Baldwins. Betty thought that Bunt was the best mother possible. As the children became close friends, the Baldwin youngsters secretly wondered what Walker did for a living. Mary Pratt soon revealed her father's occupation to Elizabeth Baldwin while playing cards: "Kings beat aces. My father is a philosopher and he told me that."

Gradually Walker deepened his knowledge of Catholicism not only by reading some classic Catholic writers but also through prayer and meditation. He had made his first retreat at Xavier Hall in Pass Christian, Mississippi, under the direction of Edward A. Sheridan, S.J., mainly because Matthew Virden of Greenville had convinced Walker of the value of three days of prayer.[37] After this first retreat, Walker went back to Pass Christian several times even when formal retreats were not scheduled. In early May 1950, he continued his practice of making three-day retreats, now at Manresa Retreat House in Convent, Louisiana. After the retreat, Walker told Jidge, "I thought it was going to be such a restful weekend. They put us through such awful paces!" To which Bunt added, "But make Sal go, because Walker's been a perfect angel since he came back."

In Greenville, Roy took on added responsibilities when he became president of the Greenville Compress, which ginned cotton from all over the Delta. In order to gain fuller control over the operation at Trail Lake, he offered to buy out Phin's and Walker's shares.[38] Walker received approximately $180,000 when he sold his share of Trail Lake to Roy. Additional income also came from partial ownership of a hotel and a hardware company in Greenville. With sound investing, Walker increased his income and provided for his family.

In the fall, Shelby and Walker carried on a discussion about Hawthorne (whom Shelby disliked) and the works of F. Scott Fitzgerald, whose stories "Absolution" and "Babylon Revisited" and novel *Tender Is the Night* Shelby praised—"The writing itself is as clear as Tolstoy's —he's a better writer than Tolstoy, too; or do you see yet what I mean by that?" He wasn't sure if Walker had read any Fitzgerald other than *The Great Gatsby*, and he had strong feelings about the Catholic Church's reputed treatment of Fitzgerald: "I'll never agree with the Church's view of him. Proscribing his books, for instance. That's not only wrong; it's stupid. And as for Fitzgerald himself, they ought to count him among the Saints."[39] He told Walker that if Mary Pratt ever wanted to be a writer, "hit her hard on the head with something heavy." Above all, Shelby wanted Walker to read and reread *Crime and Punishment, Jude the Obscure, The Cossacks, The Wings of the Dove,* and the Bard's *Measure for Measure.* He placed Henry James, Fitzgerald, Hemingway, and Faulkner on a level with his two favorites, Dostoevsky and Proust.

While in Covington, Shelby read a chapter of Walker's novel-in-progress, *The Charterhouse,* and congratulated him on his work so far. "It's much better than I had thought you'd ever let it be. If the rest is up to this . . . the book will be really good. I was most surprised to see that you kept your sense of humor; I hadn't thought you could. That is the best sign possible. What you have done stylistically is quite interesting . . . The thing is to keep working." Though excited that Walker had finally starting writing serious fiction, Shelby wanted to refrain from making an explicit judgment about the text. Revisions and rewriting would come later and it was best for him not to become bogged down in this early stage by adverse criticism. He consoled Walker, who at this point was distressed because the book lacked a discernible plot, by suggesting that he not worry about this and try to write scenes for their own sake. He sent Walker a copy of Flaubert's *Sentimental Education* because it had the same theme: "a young man in search of his soul—and he doesn't find it, either."

Walker now felt a need to get some distance from his writing—he and Bunt started planning a trip to Cuba. In January 1951, together with Roy, Sarah, and Phin, they flew from New Orleans to Havana by way of Miami. Phin had made arrangements to stay at the Hotel National, which was much more expensive than they anticipated. Roy took immediate charge by checking them into another hotel. Havana was full of discoveries, including jai alai and Cuban cuisine, especially Morro crabs. A guide took them around Habana Vieja, and after a stroll through the Parque Central, they decided to lunch at El Floridito. When he returned from the washroom, Roy asked, "Are you all fans of Hemingway?"

"Why do you ask?" said Walker.

"Because he's right there at the bar, drunk as a goat."

They peered in and there indeed was Papa H., wearing a fishing hat and sporting his famous beard. Walker got up, took a look at the noted author, and came back; not a word passed between them. Sarah and Bunt were bolder, and went over and talked to Hemingway.[40] Because they were worried about their daughter "Pie," left at home in the care of Mrs. Farish, Sarah and Roy returned earlier than the others. Phin, Walker, and Bunt remained in Cuba, touring the countryside together.

Returning in early February, Walker experienced difficulty in continuing with *The Charterhouse*. Three months later Shelby returned from New York with news that his book, retitled *The Dry Season*, would be published by Dial in the fall, and that *Shiloh* would be published the following spring, with a dedication to Walker. (Faulkner said of *Shiloh*, "It's the damndest book I have ever read and one of the best."[41]) Shelby wondered whether Walker had resumed writing. "I want to know if you've let your novel completely go," he wrote Walker on May 24. "Whether you like it or not, I think it's very bad to abandon a piece of work. Shorten it if you want, but don't just drop it. And by all means go on to another."

In the fall of 1951, Caroline Gordon, still married to Allen Tate and teaching a course at the College of St. Catherine in Minneapolis, readily agreed to read *The Charterhouse*. She told Walker that a "Catholic novelist who relies more on his techniques than his piety is what is badly needed right now. I wouldn't want to pass up the chance of discovering one."[42] She wrote to Flannery O'Connor: "I had a letter yesterday from Will

Percy's nephew, Walker Percy, who lives at Covington, Louisiana. He says he has written a novel which he guesses is 'a Catholic novel, that it has no conversion or priests in it.' I don't know that your paths are likely to cross, but if they ever should I imagine that you'd find it interesting to know each other. He has been in the church about five years."[43] Gordon had now received Walker's manuscript, or most of it.[44] "It is the best first novel that I have ever read," she wrote her daughter, Nancy. "There are certain things he doesn't know that he badly needs to know but I have no doubt that he can pick them up easily. But he has really got what it takes. I have never been so enthusiastic before about any manuscript that has come my way."[45] She wrote Brainard ("Lon") Cheney: "It is . . . a sample of what the next development in the novel will be, according to me! And it *will* be something new. At least something we have not had before. Novels written by people consciously rooted and grounded in the faith."[46]

Toward the end of October, Shelby took the finished manuscript of *Shiloh* to his publisher in New York. There he learned that his books were selling well, providing welcome income and putting him in the black. He sent Walker an alabaster relief of St. Fiacre, which he had picked up at the Cloisters. Shelby had read Graham Greene's *The End of the Affair* and found it cheap, banal, and morose: "Faith kills art. To have sure faith in anything but the efficacy of art is a sin against art, and the artist pays a terrible price for such sins." Walker, on the other hand, thought that *The End of the Affair* was Greene's best novel.[47] Shelby also showed an anti-Protestant bias: "All religions except the Catholic and the Jewish are absolute junk." Pursuing what by now had become an almost manic concern of his, he wrote Walker:

As I have said before, the best novelists have all been doubters; their only firm conviction, the only one that is never shaken, is that absolute devotion and belief in the sanctity of art which results in further seeking, not a sense of having found . . . One of the things I have most admired the Catholic religion for is its unwillingness to compromise and its essentially realistic outlook. But the Catholic intellectuals seem to destroy all this. Here we've been better than five hundred years (since *The Divine Comedy*—which, incidentally, is as much a spiteful paying-off of personal animosity as it is "Catholic") without a single devoted Catholic writer producing one big lasting thing in the field of poetry or fiction; and yet, mind you, these intellectuals insist that the advantage lies with writers with an orthodox background to fall back on; it gives them a scale of reference, they say. It ought to be true; it ought to—but look at the result. Graham Greene, or a bare handful of minor poets like Hopkins . . . Thou shalt have no other gods before you, is a dictum of art; and whoever departs from this is penalized to the degree of his departure.

They did agree on one thing—they both liked Salinger's *Catcher in the Rye*.

In early December Caroline Gordon sent Walker a telegram praising his novel. She also wrote that she had never before been so impressed by a first novel. "Perhaps it is having read so many that has sharpened my pleasure in your book. I am sick unto death of the sensitive young man lost in a Protestant *mystique*."[48] She complimented him on precisely the point that Shelby had made: his characters talked in a manner that is perennially acceptable. Walker had found his own voice. Gordon continued: "I have an idea that it is the first novel of its particular kind that's been written. I am happy to salute it! It is no small achievement to write a novel that is not like anybody else's novel." Walker once commented that Caroline Gordon "was the only literary person I knew. She wrote me a 30-page single-spaced letter. It was an extraordinary kindness. She told me everything that was wrong with the novel."[49] Did Walker ever take Gordon's advice? "Not really. The valuable thing was the relationship with her. She had an extraordinary personality." Gordon apologized for being didactic, but she wanted to instill in him the fundamental principles and techniques of the great writers, something that she spelled out in elaborate detail in her book *How to Read a Novel*. She felt that Aristotle's definition of a play ("an imitation of an action of a certain magnitude") also applied to the novel. In addition, following the advice of Henry James, fictional characters must solicit a reader's attention: "You must follow them to see what they are going to do but in the end, they don't make up the play as they go along. They play the roles assigned them in the action they themselves create. If you haven't read *The Poetics* lately you will find it very helpful to re-read it. After all, Aristotle said it all, once for all. And nobody, not even St. Thomas Aquinas, ever caught him off base."[50] Though Gordon praised the novel for its action, she noted a number of major technical faults, including the form of the book. She said she thought Ignatz was an important character, though Walker approached him too casually, especially as Ben's fate depends on Ignatz. She suggested he mention in one sentence that Ignatz did not finish his education at the seminary and recommended that he rewrite a few of the key scenes, particularly in describing Mrs. Kramer. Ben has been away for months, and not only he, but the reader, must sense through the description of the house that something crucial is to take place inside. Gordon felt that Walker wrote like a newspaper reporter in that he presented the important details first, rather than creating drama by building up to a climax. It would be better to explain what is going on through Ben's eyes and ears, not through his mind.

As Gordon reached the conclusion of this draft of the novel, she reiterated her major criticism: the need for action. Yet she praised Walker for having dramatized Ben's "defeat" as seen through the eyes of Ignatz. Such a rendering of the story adds irony and likewise solves a problem that escapes many writers. Likewise, she repeated her critique that Abbie was treated too cavalierly—turned on and off like an electric light. Though Gordon liked the name Ignatz, she thought when she first encountered this character that he was Jewish and that impression persisted throughout her entire reading of the book. Her penultimate suggestion was that Walker "lay off the semi-colon" until he understood how to use it. She concluded her long letter by giving him more encouragement:

And as I said at the beginning of this letter the only way one can really understand a fundamental principle of the craft is by an illustration from one's own work. It seems to me that you need to learn a few things—a few tricks of the trade, as it were. Once you have learned them, once you have got out of a few bad habits and set up in their place some good habits I do not see what there is to stop you. You have an enormous—an incalculable—advantage over most people writing today: you know what it is all about. The saints, the mystics are the proper companions of the fiction writer, for, as Jacques Maritain points out in *Art and Scholasticism*, "they alone know what is the human heart." And the mystics are, particularly, the artists of artists. But the Protestant is cut off from most of the saints. When one is writing out of the Protestant *mystique*, which is what everybody who isn't a Catholic is doing—even the Communists, I think—one has the responsibility of setting up a new heaven and a new earth as one goes. But a Catholic knows that God has already created the universe and that his job is to find his proper place in it.

Gordon lamented that Catholic fiction had not been good up to the present, since most Catholic writers were poor technicians. Her latest find, Flannery O'Connor of Milledgeville, Georgia, had written her first novel, *Wise Blood*, which had been accepted and edited by Robert Giroux at Harcourt, Brace. Years later Walker himself compared the two novels: *The Charterhouse* was a very bad novel and *Wise Blood* was a very good one. O'Connor wrote Walker one of her laconic letters after the publication of *The Moviegoer*: "That was a good story. I hope you'd make up another one."[51]

During the Christmas holidays, Allen Tate, himself a convert to Catholicism in 1950, finished reading *The Charterhouse* in Minneapolis. He had not read Gordon's commentary and his reaction was not filtered through her critique. "It is a most impressive job, and I hope that you will be able to do the revisions necessary to round it out. I don't think there is anything fundamentally wrong with the book, but I do feel that there must be more work in detail."[52] His comments dealt with the internal logic of the relationships within the novel. Tate tried to teach Walker the value of action in a story and advised him to stress not description but the moral qualities of his characters. He noted in the final scene that the perceptions of the characters, several girls and three boys, might logically be perceived by the hero, but the method Walker employed was artistically wrong. Even vagueness, he contended, could be rendered vividly. Like Gordon, Tate turned to *Madame Bovary* as a proof text. Flaubert, throughout this novel, knows and sees more than Emma does and that makes all the difference:

I am certain that you can almost at will actualize any portion of the novel, or any character: the minor characters, in so far as we know them at all, we know well. Miss MacGahee is wonderfully done—but what happens to her? She is, of course, the female version of Ben, and not too much could be done with her. I am sure that you oughtn't to make Ben's marriage to Abbie a partial realization of the righting of a wrong: he need not know the full meaning (i.e., the full "conversion") of the righting of this wrong, but a dim perception of it would give him greater dignity than he has at the end: he would be a man of stature whose imperfect "contrition" would give him a tragic implication.

Tate sincerely complimented Walker and said that he wrote with intelligence and power and that he would be a "valuable novelist." In a postscript, he added that the "satire of Sewanee [the University of the South] as a psychiatric retreat is wonderful—effective in itself, but write an added discussion for those of us who know Sewanee."

Instead of opening the novel with a long soliloquy, Caroline Gordon suggested in an undated letter that Walker begin with the character Dr. Betty Jane. She warned Walker that once introduced through Dr. Betty Jane and Ben's interaction, Ignatz should not be lost sight of. Apparently Gordon was seeking to transform an innocent brotherly relationship into one with homosexual overtones. In his portrayal of the sanatorium that Ben flees to, Walker need not depict it as if it never changes. Gordon saw Ben as reacting violently against both Dr. Betty Jane and the sanatorium, so much so that he wants to flee. In her critique, Gordon seemed to be following Walker's plot outline. She told him if there were any contradictions between her advice and that of her husband, he should follow Tate's. Above all, Walker should not feel indebted to the Tates.

She believed that Walker was well versed in the craft of writing fiction and it was much easier to help him than real beginners.

In January 1952, Walker sent Gordon $200 as thanks for all her editorial efforts. In return, she sent Walker an essay on Henry James that Allen Tate had encouraged her to expand into a book.[53] Walker had informed her that he was awaiting the results of another X ray and she wished him good health.

Gordon also wrote to Lon Cheney and shared her views about Walker and Flannery O'Connor with him:

I have put my money on a good many horses, in my time, as you know. Scatter-brained though I be, I occasionally get a glimpse of the wheels going around. I saw them revolving in this study several months before Christmas. When I was working on Flannery O'Connor's novel and when Walker Percy sent me his novel. He's got a lot to learn that boy, almost everything, but reading that novel was like suddenly getting down on your knees on a long dusty walk to drink from a fresh, cold spring. His novel and Flannery's suddenly convinced me of something that I had been feeling vaguely for a long time. The Protestant mystique (which is what everybody who isn't a Catholic, even Communists, are writing of, whether they know it or not) is outworn, sucked-dry, beginning to rot, to stink. That accounts for the curious dryness which almost everybody remarks in homosexual novels. There's no juice left in that orange. Everybody has suspected it for some time but the fact is now being brought out into the open. Flannery's novel—as grim a picture of the Protestant world as you can find—and Walker's novel, which is the story of a man's desperate effort to stay alive spiritually, will be sensations when they come out. They will show so clearly that the tide has turned.[54]

Later, in sharing some thoughts with her friend Ward Dorrance, Gordon again mentioned *The Charterhouse*: "There is a line of dialogue in Walker Percy's novel which I wish I'd written. Two young people who have been at the same mental rest-home meet at a party and the young gentleman accuses the young lady of backsliding in her psychiatric faith, to which she responds with a pout: 'I admit that I was pretty anal last year but I think I've been quite genital all Fall.'"[55] Gordon was carrying Walker's text around in her head.

When Shelby learned that the Tates had been advising Walker, he lashed out: "Another fact is that in the final analysis you can learn absolutely nothing from another—I mean another person, as a person. (That is why I scream against the Tates.) . . . These articulate people who can put their finger on the trouble, and tell why, are archfiends incarnate." A copy of *Shiloh* was sent to Walker in February. "I'll expect you,"

Shelby wrote, "to dedicate *your* fourth book to me." Perhaps intimidated by Shelby's productivity, Walker acknowledged that he was just lazy, an excuse that made his friend furious. "I'm the laziest man I know," Shelby replied, "always have been, always will be. It has nothing to do with writing . . . Your terrible reluctance comes from guilt at having reached thirty-five without dedicating yourself to at least the point of studying what you now recognize to be your vocation." Caroline Gordon returned the manuscript of *The Charterhouse* to Walker in February, along with a book Flannery had sent her. She said she considered Flannery O'Connor's work too bare, too stripped, reduced to an essential core of action, much in the style of Kafka—"everything in it stands for something and you only find out what it stands for after you've left the book and the events sort of explode in your mind."[56]

About this time Walker told Gordon about another new novel he was considering, one that would take place in New York with scenes in Bellevue Hospital, a novel that would eventually become *The Gramercy Winner*. In comparing Lon Cheney's novel with *The Charterhouse*, especially in mentioning "angelism," Gordon might have subconsciously planted the seeds for another novel that Walker would write, *Love in the Ruins*. "You said one thing in your letter of January seventh that made me shudder, that you were reluctant to give up your angelic escape from the mountain-top. One reason I shudder is that I think you are in danger of falling, as a writer, for what Jacques Maritain calls the sin of the age: angelism. The shudders in me come from the teacher." For the record, Gordon made her credo very clear: all novels must be about love; and love between a man and a woman is an analogue of divine love. She stated explicitly that this love is rooted in the incarnation of Jesus, the Christ. "Your business as a novelist is to imitate Christ. He was about His Father's business every moment of His life. As a good novelist you must be about yours: Incarnation. Making your word flesh and making it dwell among men." In backtracking a little, she suggested that Flaubert was a good model, and once one had mastered Flaubert's techniques, then one was ready to move on to James, who himself learned from Flaubert. "Your idea about an angelic escape from the mountain-top is an example of 'the fallacy of imitative form.' Like when Malcolm Cowley said to Bunny Wilson: 'Bunny, why is your novel so dull?' 'It's about dull people,' Bunny said. But that's no excuse. Jane Austen's Mr. Woodhouse, Emma's father, must have been one of the dullest people in the world but perfectly delightful in a book." Though Gordon had second thoughts about her suggestion that Walker's novel start in the sanatorium, she held to her notion that there should be a homosexual attraction between Ben and Ignatz, though her rationale for this undoubtedly struck Walker as a bit bizarre: the lack of the presence of a Heavenly Father, or, as the psychiatrists say, the absence of a "father pattern." Without venturing to anticipate Allen Tate's reply to a letter he recently received from Walker, Gordon continued her catechetical lesson, which undoubtedly failed to stir Walker's spiritual imagination. "Lord, I hope we are not lecturing you too much! We both want you to make as good a job of this book as you can, but remember that you'll write other books. One reason for writing one's next book is to avoid the mistakes one made in the last book." In a characteristic postscript, Gordon rewarded her young pupil by giving him and Bunt one of her pictures, such as the one of St. John on the island of Patmos writing the Book of Revelations.

Shelby informed Walker on February 29 that he and Peggy, the former Marguerite Dessommes, the daughter of a Memphis physician whom he had married in 1947, were getting a divorce in March. He would assume daughter Margaret's support and would give a percentage of all his future earnings in exchange for visiting rights with her. Irritable and needing companionship, he reached out to Walker: "I'd like to have talked with you about all this . . . I've got no church; all I have is myself, and I was coming apart at the seams." By early March, Shelby was in Harrisburg, Pennsylvania, seeking distraction from his pain by seeing double features. The divorce became final on March 6, and by the middle of the month, Shelby, dog-tired, had driven his red Ford as far as Hagerstown, Maryland.

In early March, Grandmother Mary Pratt Percy of Birmingham died in the Madison Sanitarium in Madison, Tennessee.[57] In a codicil to her will, she had designated Walker and Ellen Murphy as co-executors of her estate, which would ultimately be evaluated at $100,000. But Walker did not feel comfortable as co-executor, and in a letter dated March 11, 1952, he wrote to Judge Tom C. Garner of the Probate Court in Jefferson County, Alabama, asking that he be allowed to resign. He preferred that Aunt Ellen, then residing on Cliff Road in Birmingham, assume this responsibility. In time, Walker, Roy, and Phin were notified of a petition for the probation of the will: Ellen was to receive one part of the estate, and Walker, Roy, and Phin the other.

In a letter to Stark Young, Caroline Gordon mentioned that she and Allen Tate had been reading R. W. Chambers's life of Thomas More.[58] Her praise of Walker was boundless: "Walker Percy sent me the best first novel I have ever read. Walker is not only gifted but he is the most intelligent young man who has come our way in a long time. Allen and I are both rather bowled over by him. It's really wonderful to have a pupil who is smarter than you are!" In acknowledging the receipt of a letter from Walker about Chambers's book, Gordon said she was still

interested in *The Charterhouse*.[59] Walker had been troubled by the possibility of another break, but his X ray revealed that he was in good health.
Gordon indicated that while he had "retained" her to assist him, she did
not feel that Walker would need her services in the future. "I think you
are just getting along swimmingly."

Realizing that his counsel had been too apodictic, Shelby backed off
and encouraged Walker to move out on his own. "You go ahead any
way you want; everyone has to do it his own way and it's folly to argue
Art or method." Part of Shelby's liberating new stance came from the
fact that *Shiloh* had gone into a second printing one week after publication and a third would soon be ordered by the publisher.

Shelby came to visit Bunt and Walker in mid-May but stayed a short
time, mostly because he felt guilty about being away from his writing
desk. He may have meant to talk about *The Charterhouse*, but he never
brought up the subject. Shelby wanted Walker to discipline himself by
working four or five hours a day on his novel, perhaps from nine to
twelve and then for a few hours in the afternoon. Unbeknownst to
Shelby, it was probably the type of schedule that Walker was already
following. It pleased Walker that Phin had finished law school and only
needed to take the bar exam.

Walker had no intention of catching up with Shelby's literary out-
put. He decided to see *The Charterhouse* to completion and to place it
with a publishing house. But there was one letter Shelby wrote on July
20 that Walker could not back away from. The letter interpreted the
events of Walker's life, especially the death of his father and his conversion, and related them to Walker as a creative writer.

Really, Walker, you won't do. You take me most seriously when I'm joking, and
least seriously when I'm most intense. However, that's just the kind of thing any
writer must be prepared for: which is exactly why I say he must write for neither
angels nor sinners, but himself—like God when he created the world complete
with its pitfalls and filth alongside the sunset and the rose . . . Listen. The one
thing a writer must preserve above all others is his innocence, his "ignorance"
if you will, his capacity for wonder. The realization must come later, in the
process of creation; or even later, in the process of having created; or perhaps
never—he moves on. It doesn't matter, once the thing has been put down on
paper . . . I blame my father enormously for going into business; it took him to
Mobile, Alabama, where he had a date with a strep germ that took him off; he
left me to fight this world alone. It must be far worse in your case, whose father
left voluntarily and mysteriously—after which you were uprooted in a manner
I never knew . . . and then lost [your mother] in a brutal way that could make
a man hate God. As if this wasn't enough, as soon as you'd found how to live

with all this, or anyhow exist, then came TB—and with TB, conversion. The Church, doubtless, can give you highly satisfactory answers to all this, as far as they go. But the real answers, the answers that will bring you not peace but understanding, can only be found in art. (I truly worship at that altar, as you see.) . . . I do, however, look with horror at your approach in some respects— especially your desire to be "wise" in that bloodless way. It's ruinous, nothing less. You apparently want to work toward some preconceived answer, you want to prove something you believe; fine; but that's not the way to do it. The answers are implicit—but it's not the answers that constitute the solution; it's how you get them. That's why a man must sweat like a horse in learning his craft; the abstract must be reached through the concrete, and he must have the skill for refining the raw materials of life . . . I don't say your religion must go by the board simply because much that I believe is in opposition to it. Each in his own way; there is room for everyone in this big pool. But it seems to me that certain ground-rules must not be transgressed.

Shelby's final words of advice were succinct: work and more work.

In late summer, Caroline Gordon wrote to Walker from Princeton inquiring about the progress of *The Charterhouse*. Her chatty letter focused for the most part on Dorothy Day, whose *Catholic Worker* movement and sense of mission to the poor continued to impress her. She praised Day's farm in Newburgh, New York, where anyone, from Bowery bum to distinguished cleric, was welcome to reflect and pray. "Not a word of cant, not one platitude and the most lucid and at times brilliant exposition. It was frankly mystical in its approach."[60] Gordon saw other possibilities for Day's "House of Hospitality" that would include Walker's services. Gordon wanted to start a "School of the Holy Ghost," in which young writers of all faiths would have older writers as teachers, but "the real teaching will be done by the Holy Ghost." Allen Tate approved of the idea in general, but opposed using Dorothy Day's farm in spite of the fact that it could raise sufficient food for those who came. Gordon wanted Walker to mull over the idea and write. In the meantime, she was submitting *The Charterhouse* to her editor at Scribner's, Jack Wheelock, who had succeeded the late Maxwell Perkins, her original editor. Gordon told Wheelock to expect an eight-pound package of manuscript and she identified Walker as the "nephew" of William Alexander Percy, though a better writer. "In this novel you have a new attitude towards the South on the part of a Southerner, a brand new approach to the 'Negro problem' and—Allen and I both think—the most important talent to come out of the South since Faulkner."[61]

Walker was not too enthusiastic about the School of the Holy Ghost and Gordon took umbrage at his remark that if the artist "cleaves too

close to the liturgy he is liable to breed something quaint and cultish."
It was an anxious Christmas for Walker and Bunt as they awaited word
about the fate of Walker's first novel. On January 5, Jack Wheelock wrote
Gordon saying that he was reading Walker's manuscript and requested
more information about its author: "Can you tell me something about
the author, his approximate age, occupation, and past literary career, if
any? His novel sounds as though it were partly autobiographical and as
if the author had medical training or himself experienced a nervous
breakdown and learned a great deal about such illnesses from his own
experience." Gordon provided Wheelock with the information he requested. Shelby's instincts proved to be accurate when he told Walker
that Scribner's delay in accepting the manuscript was not a good sign.
Wheelock wrote Gordon that *The Charterhouse* showed flashes of great
talent, but there were serious weaknesses that Wheelock perceived in the
novel. On February 3, he informed Gordon that he had decided not to
accept *The Charterhouse*. Gordon wrote Walker of Wheelock's decision
and she could not hold back the pain she felt. "I enclose Jack Wheelock's
rather stupid letter, but you doubtless have one like it by this time. It is
absurd for him to go on about the novel's faults. Of course it has faults
—obvious faults. But what about the amateurish work of Jim Jones? It
is not the novel's faults but its theme that makes it unacceptable to Scribner's. They just don't get it. However, they are the mossbacks of firms.
There are plenty of other publishers. What do you want to do next? . . .
I believe that Allen's advice is to send it to Denver Lindley at Harcourt.
I'll enclose a letter of recommendation from Allen which you can send
along with the ms. to Denver."[62] She dutifully informed Walker that
Wheelock had forwarded the manuscript to Harcourt, Brace.[63] Denver
Lindley soon wrote to Walker, acknowledging a warm letter of recom-
mendation from Allen Tate and the receipt of Walker's manuscript.[64]

Allen Tate had been in New York on his way to give a series of
lectures in New England, and saw their friend Sue Jenkins, whom Caroline Gordon had written asking whether she would be interested in
taking over the practical details of placing *The Charterhouse* with a publisher. Sue Jenkins wrote Walker: "I could, if you wish, place your manuscript with one of the reputable literary agencies, with which I already
have connections. The Tates say your work has merit (and if they say so
I believe it has) so I should have little trouble in getting a good agent to
accept you as a client. My own pursuits will shortly cause me to see
Elizabeth Otis, of McIntosh & Otis . . . Allen tells me that the book is
now at Harcourt, Brace."[65] Walker was being pointed in a direction that
would take away a burden and leave him more time to write.

Sue Jenkins soon received word from Allen Tate that Denver Lindley of Harcourt, Brace was declining *The Charterhouse*. She then had the type-script hand-delivered to Malcolm Cowley, who asked to see it.[66] Gordon thought that the religious dimension of the novel would puzzle Cowley ("Malcolm simply does not know how to read a novel. He always has to have a handle to pick up a novel by"). After many weeks Cowley rejected it for Viking.

Walker felt depleted, and not wanting to remain fixed on the fate of his first novel, he told Gordon he had started writing a new one, *The Gramercy Winner*. Now three months into this new manuscript, Walker seemed not to want to look back.[67] With four rejections so far (Regnery had also considered it for a while), he naturally felt disheartened. Shelby, who had been through it before, wanted Walker to move off the shoals:

Sorry to hear you're in the doldrums. Apparently, though, it's part of the price we pay. All I hope is you'll come out of it the soonest possible; the way it usually happens is, you find yourself writing like fury—that's when you know you're cured. Me, I'm cured . . . That's unpleasant business, having your ms. kicked around from reader to reader . . . Maybe now, after two years' work, what you need to see BY WALKER PERCY is nice, clean-limbed type.

Thus *The Charterhouse* was put aside. It constituted a *rite de passage* for Walker and the experience taught him valuable lessons.

In Washington, after the signing of the Korean armistice at Pan-munjom by UN, North Korean, and Chinese delegates, Phin, now work-ing for the CIA, was told by his superiors that he had several options: he could go to Saigon and become a covert agent, or he could volunteer for Quemoy or Matsu, or he could learn Arabic and go to Beirut. As he sat in his Quonset hut office by the Reflecting Pool, he felt he should cash it all in. He did make one big step; he proposed to Jaye Dobbs and they were married on August 13 in the First Congregational Church at Bar Harbor, Maine. LeRoy, as best man, represented the Percy family. Since Jaye's stepfather, Alan Rinehart, was the son of Mary Roberts Rine-hart, a highly successful novelist and playwright, Phin became part of a distinguished extended family. After the ceremony, Jaye and Phin trav-eled for four or five months to Naples, Capri, and Paris. They dined with the Tates while Gordon was a fellow at the American Academy in Rome.[68] Caroline Gordon wanted Walker to come to Rome so he could learn about the Eternal City and some of her favorite saints. Since Jaye and Phin wanted to live in the South, they first visited Greenville and then New Orleans and Covington, where they stayed in the guest cottage until the following January.

That fall Mary Pratt entered Sister Maria del Carmen's first-grade class at St. Peter's School. When Walker came to pick her up after school, he had a present, a black kitten named Midnight. Mary Pratt now knew her father was a doctor who had no patients, and that he spent his time writing—almost every morning on his second novel.

7

From *The Gramercy Winner*

to *Confessions of a Movie-goer*

1954–58

In late January 1954, Walker was working hard on *The Gramercy Winner*. Only one typescript exists, and in this second attempt at a novel Walker transformed his hidden years at Trudeau into an American version of Thomas Mann's *The Magic Mountain*. The protagonist, William Edward Grey III, a twenty-year-old Princeton sophomore who lives on Gramercy Park in New York, begins a process of recuperation from tuberculosis in an Adirondack village in 1941. His battle to get physically well is set against the war being fought in Europe and the Pacific—and as the title implies, William emerges a success. As a TB patient in an attic room of a cure cottage, he spends his time reading books like *Subatomic Particles*. After six months in an adjacent room, Miss Allen, a young woman William has never seen, departs from the cottage to continue her therapy at the Lodge. What is remarkable about William's past life is that very little ever happened to him. When Lieutenant Laverne Sutter, a tall, scholarly-looking, talkative Southerner and a graduate of Birmingham Southern, moves into Miss Allen's room, William is no longer preoccupied solely with himself; he becomes concerned about Sutter's health (he suffers from a functional disorder of the ductless glands) and the psychological effect this is having on his wife, Allison, a Mount Holyoke graduate from Aiken, South Carolina. Almost every evening, the three of them play a card game—hearts. As Sutter's health declines, Allison awakens a hitherto unfelt sexuality in William, causing him to grapple with "the special set of allowances and defenses, mitigations and concealments" that made the mismatch of Sutter and Allison possible.

What William finds taxing is that his future might depend on the

Grey family loyalties rather than on himself. "He had died to one life and meant to come alive in another. Already he was awakening to a strange new world." Sutter hunted quail with his father in southern Alabama and duck along the White River in Arkansas; William is enthralled by his vivid accounts of these hunting expeditions. In Sutter and Allison, Walker created two characters who would be reincarnated later: Sutter Vaught in *The Last Gentleman* and Allison Huger in *The Second Coming*. These three create their own separate universe in order to cope with the sickness surrounding them.

Sutter suffers physical diminishment and is forced to seek hospital care. William takes advantage of this by inviting Allison to the Lake Placid Inn, where he becomes more animated. Even the world of nature seems to ratify their burgeoning relationship—the vireos in the treetops twitter: "Here you, *here* you." Undaunted by his medical situation, Sutter still has visions of being cured and returning to the South.

Halfway through the novel, after William moves to an "up cottage," the social and intellectual matrix of the novel escalates; William meets Cadet Zeno Kostic of the Yugoslavian Navy and two physicians—John Van Norden and his companion, Scanlon. Dr. Scanlon, a rosy-faced surgeon with curly brown hair, reacts negatively to Van Norden's theoretical views; he feels that every research scientist should be paroled into the custody of a clinician. Van Norden characterizes Scanlon as a pious person who believes in a mystical theory of disease, and wants miracles—without Christ.

Allison's relationship with William intensifies once she starts working as a volunteer at the Lodge. Like a young intern, William makes the rounds with the Lodge's medical staff. In one voluble exchange, Scanlon accuses Van Norden of "organolatry," of investigating all the pertinent scientific facets of tuberculosis, except for one thing: " 'You look at everything but Willy! Look at Willy here!' They turned around and looked at the blushing Willy. 'Here's the mystery right under your nose, man! Not Willy's lung but Willy himself.' " Scanlon, who becomes the author's *porte-parole*, expresses a view that Walker would develop in the coming years: science cannot utter a single word about what is distinctive in human behavior—language, art, and thought itself—in short, what it is to be born, to live, and to die as a human being.

As William and Allison become more involved romantically, they never achieve a true meeting of minds and hearts. In one scene they go picnicking: "Poor Billy—who did not dream she saw him whole or that he was whole, who imagined instead that he was legion and showed her whichever mysterious self he pleased—the Billy of the cave, of desire, of pilgrimage." The shock of recognition occurs for William, not while he is with Allison, but when he realizes that the cadaver in Benjamin Grebner's Funeral Parlor is Sutter.

As William's disease spreads and Dr. Scanlon realizes he will die soon, William moves into the Doctors' Cottage. Perhaps because he never found a sense of his place in this world, or perhaps because he refuses to accept its values, or perhaps even because he has an insight that reflects Oriental philosophical wisdom, William admits to Scanlon that the secret of life is that there is "nothing"—just silence accompanied by a nagging feeling of being homesick. It is like Sartre's Mathieu in *The Age of Reason*, who stops in the middle of the Pont Neuf and discovers that freedom is a pervasive nothingness.[1] Percy's novel concludes with a surprising reversal of roles: "Scanlon's face was in darkness. When it had grown light enough to see and if there had been anyone to see, he would have thought William, his eyes closed, his face rosy with sleep, the healthy one, and Scanlon the one sick unto death." In an epilogue, the reader learns that William died on August 4, 1943, after having been baptized by Scanlon two days previously. Van Norden married Allison. After a hiatus, Dr. Scanlon returned and worked as a resident physician at the nearby Our Lady-of-the-Woods. This movie-like ending not only provided a natural transition to Walker's next novel but clearly indicated the influence movies had on his imaginative life. In *The Gramercy Winner*, Walker introduced both Kate, a minor character who is a mental defective, and the name Bolling, used for one of William's friends. This novel, as Gary Ciuba has noted, follows William as a sickened wayfarer who learns that health and home depend on the orientation of the heart: "The 'real enemy' that unmindful soldiers and convalescents must overcome is a dulling and deadly abstraction, 'a dryness, not hatefulness, but a withering of souls, a drawing away from one another' . . . In Percy's earliest surviving novel, tuberculosis is an incipient stage of what Tom More, himself preoccupied with German slaughter, would discover in Percy's last novel as the thanatos syndrome."[2] Through constant diminishment to the point of nothingness, William's baptism implies that the totality of his life has meaning insofar as he has achieved a relationship with a hidden God.

By the third week of February 1954, just about the time that Shelby was pleased that Walker had taken a renewed interest in poetry, *The Gramercy Winner* was finished. For over a year Shelby was not sure whether the work was a series of essays or something else.[3] Walker received rejection slips from various publishers, sometimes with painful notes from editors.[4] As Shelby awaited advance copies of his latest novel, *Jordan County*, which he wanted Walker to read, he was pleased to learn that Jaye and Phin were able to "hook atoms, balance frets," showing how compatible they were, and that Bunt was pregnant—"partridge-plump" with child.

Bunt checked into the Touro Infirmary in New Orleans in advance so that she and Walker would not have to make the long trip at the last minute. Naturally, they had to prepare Mary Pratt for a new addition. On July 11 Ann Boyd Percy was born. She was baptized two weeks later in St. Peter's Church in Covington, with Betty Baldwin as her godmother and Chink Baldwin as the proxy godfather for Hughes Spalding in Atlanta.

Bunt had time to be with her daughters, thanks in large part to a succession of help: Bertha the cook, Priscilla the laundress, and Laura Allen and a woman by the name of Augustine, both housekeepers. Augustine would take Mary Pratt out to the Pawleys Island hammock and rock her gently while singing, "Up in an airplane / Smoking her sweet cigarette / She went way up in an airplane / Smoking her sweet cigarette." Walker liked the ditty and mentally recorded it for further use. Earlier, when Mary Pratt had become old enough to go to kindergarten, Bunt or Walker would drive her to Mrs. Lillian Reeder's on 17th Avenue. Eventually Ida Mae Griffin, nicknamed "Mousy" by Mary Pratt, started working for the Percys. Walker bought her a jeep and taught her how to drive, which meant, of course, that he had more time to devote to his writing and did not have to shuttle her constantly back and forth to her house on Stafford Road. On occasion, Mousy and Mary Pratt would take off in the jeep and go picking blackberries, or Mary Pratt would accompany her mother to Mrs. Jenkins's country store on Little Hill Road. The Percys also hired Mrs. Terah Guidry, who often worked at the rectory, to babysit for Ann; a beloved widow, she worked intermittently for the Percys for roughly ten years. Sam Booker, who worked in the yard a few days a week, had to mow the enormous lawn by hand until Walker bought him a small tractor.

Having put his novel aside, Walker wrote a review of Susanne Langer's *Feeling and Form* for the fall issue of *Thought*. Walker admired the editor, William Lynch, S.J.[5] For this essay Walker had also read Langer's *Philosophy in a New Key* and traced the progress of her thought from her first book to the second, noting that for her the new key in philosophy "is the universal symbolic function of the human mind." Writing with vigor and energy, Walker had found the philosophical companion he had been seeking for a long time:

Feeling and Form is written with all the power and contagious excitement of a first-class mind exercising a valuable new insight. In brief, it is an application to art of a general thesis that the peculiarly human response is that of symbolic transformation. The communication of meaning, positivists to the contrary, is not limited to the discursive symbol, word and proposition; the art symbol conveys its own appropriate meaning, a meaning inaccessible to the discursive form.

Walker was attracted to the notion that each art form symbolizes not a series of abstract thoughts but the felt life of the artist. He was surprised Langer failed to cite Jacques Maritain's *Art and Scholasticism* or *Creative Intuition in Art and Poetry*, yet noted with interest that Langer mentioned Charles Sanders Peirce in passing and Ernst Cassirer in detail. As Walker put it, this essay was for him the "open sesame" toward a writing career. In August, Jacques Maritain, recuperating from a coronary thrombosis in Princeton, thanked Walker for his thirty-page essay "Symbol and Magic Cognition," which he had read "with extreme interest."[6] Maritain was especially pleased by the innovative use of the idea that he had once proposed, namely, "of magic sign [sic] as a 'state' of human mentality." In his judgment of Langer's work, which in his opinion rescued the symbol from the "toils of idealism," Walker had used Scholasticism, informed by his reading of Marcel's *The Mystery of Being*. His review asked a question that embodied his concern about the mystery of language: "How indeed *can* a sensible, a vocable, an odd little series of squeaks and grunts, *mean* anything, represent anything?" For Walker symbolization constituted the essential act of the mind, whether in art, language, dreams, or logic. What he found lacking in Langer's argument was an articulation of how and why there is a basic human "need" for symbolization, especially as it relates to a hierarchy of knowledge—not as it fits a biological need but as it reveals truth. In this review he had unwittingly set his own future agenda.

Shelby felt that Walker was becoming existentially ethereal. Anticipating a Guggenheim fellowship and the wherewithal to travel to the important Civil War battle sites (Shiloh was the only one he knew) in order to write a history of the Civil War, Shelby was not clear about the direction Walker was taking. "You mentioned it once before but I couldn't understand. Are you organizing a book, or a series of essays?" Shelby found living alone in Memphis "a wretched existence, yet strangely satisfactory in certain ways." If all a writer needed was no money and nobody to love him, Shelby said he was overly qualified.

Walker also sent Caroline Gordon in Minneapolis a copy of his review; she replied that both she and Allen Tate, having originally read it in *Thought*, liked it very much.[7] She hoped to use some of it for a lecture she was planning to give at the University of Indiana in July, and encouraged Walker to write more essays. Gordon had just finished writing her novel *The Malefactors*. "I often think of Ben Cleburne. My hero is just another incarnation of him. But it has taken me thirty years of pretty hard labor to know how to present him effectively and I'm not sure yet I've made it, though Allen, to my great joy, likes the book."[8]

In early September, James Collins thanked Walker for his interesting essay, one clearly influenced by the works of Collins, Langer, William E. Hocking, Christopher Dawson, C. K. Ogden, I. A. Richards, Charles Morris, Freud, Kant, Heidegger, Kierkegaard, and particularly by Marcel and Sartre.[9] Collins's view of symbolism in the previous issue of *Thought* had made two essential points: that "in Cassirer and possibly Langer, there is a Kantian and idealist basis for the theory of symbol; second, that the findings on symbolization can indeed be detached from this context and placed in a realist one." The second chapter of Collins's book, *The Mind of Kierkegaard*, developed his views of the stages of existence and the purely romantic interpretation of symbol. "It seems clear," Collins continued in his letter, "that existentialism is not enough and empiricism is not enough. Yet each group has much to offer by way of insight into man and his relation to the world. There is no intrinsic reason for keeping these two approaches either in isolation or in conflict. Together, they can put us on the road toward a reintegration of the various knowledges about man. The only point concerns the means by which existentialism and empiricism can be brought into communication." Collins applauded the way Walker brought this about in his essay—through symbolic transformation. He had some suggestions about the structure and argument that Walker proposed for his next essay and hoped he would focus more on the personal factor in symbolism and leave out "the matter of development in interpersonal relations." He encouraged Walker to submit the essay to Marvin Farber at the University of Buffalo, editor of the quarterly *Philosophy and Phenomenological Research*. Walker's spirits were boosted by having the encouragement of one of the top philosophers in the country.

The citizens of Covington, both black and white, felt that steps toward achieving integration within their community should begin. As with many parents who lived in rural areas, Miriam Barranger had worried for years about the lack of buses to pick up and deliver children to their schools, both public and private, and for years her husband, Dalton, drove their son, Garic ("Nikki"), and some black children to school each day. For Nikki, a twenty-year-old sophomore at Yale, coming home to Covington that Christmas meant a chance to discuss with "Dr. Percy" the recent U.S. Supreme Court decision in the case of *Brown v. Board of Education*, which outlawed segregated education and overturned the

1896 *Plessy v. Ferguson* decision that maintained that separate but equal facilities were constitutional.[10] It also meant that he could join the Percys, his parents, and other couples to see avant-garde films that Robert and Olga Hess had rented from the Museum of Modern Art in New York for their Covington Film Study Group.[11] Walker showed Nikki some of the philosophical essays he was writing. Though Nikki was a student of the philosopher Paul Weiss, he was never really comfortable "talking shop" with Walker.

After Shelby had digested Walker's review of Langer's book, he was at a loss for words about semiotics, which he found totally incomprehensible. A statement like "Art is the creation of forms symbolic of human feelings" simply left him cold. "Are you joking?" he wrote to Walker in mid-January. "To me it's as if someone pronounced solemnly that the world is round." While Shelby had read William James and Henri Bergson, whom he considered more novelists than philosophers, he hated to think where Walker's interest in language would take him. As he dealt with the battle of Fredericksburg, Shelby had no difficulty uniting ordinary language with "poetic" touches.[12] His concern about Walker's growing interest in language theory took a cruel—and critical —turn.

One day as Walker and Bunt took Ann, then about six months old, out for some air, Walker spotted a copperhead.[13] He went back to the house to get his shotgun and returned and shot the snake. He and Bunt looked at each other and then at Ann, who seemed impervious to the blast: she had not reacted at all. "Walker," Bunt said, "something's wrong. Ann did not move." Back at the house Walker examined his daughter and realized that she might be hearing-impaired or even deaf. Though Ann was just an infant, they wanted the best care for her, even if it meant they had to dramatically change their lives. They consulted a pediatrician in New Orleans, and he confirmed that Ann was almost totally deaf. (Ann, during her best moments as a child, could hear and distinguish about ten spoken words.) They traveled to Atlanta to investigate a speech school run by the Junior League; Aunt Bolling assured Walker and Bunt that she would look out for Ann's welfare.[14]

The Percys also took an overnight train to St. Louis to check out the Central Institute for the Deaf. Founded in 1914 by Dr. Max A. Goldstein, it maintained that, regardless of the severity of hearing loss, deaf children could learn to speak and understand the speech of others without the use of manual signs. Bunt, Walker, Mary Pratt, and Ann also visited St. Joseph's School for the Deaf run by the Sisters of St. Joseph of Carondelet, the oldest of the twelve Catholic schools for the deaf in the United States. St. Joseph's had switched from teaching by manual signing to the exclusive use of the auditory-oral method. On the train back to New Orleans, Walker and Bunt and Mary Pratt discussed their options. If Ann was too young to be institutionalized, as they felt she was, then all three would have to make a serious commitment to educate her at home. Bunt told Jidge after they had gone to St. Louis, "I can't leave Ann there, because if we did, we would lose her. She would no longer be our child. She would belong to the deaf community." Shelby did some research of his own and gave Walker the name of Doris Irene Mirrielees in Pompano Beach, Florida, as an expert in the field.[15] When Walker returned to his writing desk in February, he informed Shelby that he was working on an essay for *Philosophy and Phenomenological Research*, a journal that Shelby scoffingly knew could not be located in all of Memphis. It was a far different Walker who started his fifth retreat at Manresa at the end of March; Ann Boyd's future was very much on his mind.

By the time Ann was eleven months old and reading lips, Bunt and Walker got in touch with Doris Mirrielees, who agreed to visit in order to instruct Bunt and Walker how to teach Ann. As one of her former students said of her, she was "an itinerant bearer of hope whose passion and devotion deeply touched every child and parent she encountered."[16] When this tall, thin, elderly Iowan arrived that fall—an avatar of Annie Sullivan, who wrapped her gray hair in a bun and normally sported white tennis shoes—she changed the lives of all the Percys. At her prompting, Ann's hearing was tested in December at the Tulane School of Medicine; it was minimal, to say the least. The Percys grew to be protective of the new teacher and her eccentricities. Once when Ann had a cold, Miss Mirrielees put a clear bag over her head, with holes cut out for her eyes, as a way of protecting herself. Yet the Percys stressed to their friends how original a teacher she was. In her unpublished auto-biography, entitled *The Teacher Rests Her Case*, she explained her method. Her approach to deaf children was, above all, both considerate and clear:

Little deaf children, too, can learn language naturally and in its natural forms when they are given the right opportunity to do so. The deaf child cannot speak language with full correctness as early as can the child who hears. But he can be led to understand it just as fully, and to transfer that understanding to the form of print, which is reading, and on the same level of comprehension as children of the same age who hear. And, later, he can become able to use oral language correctly without the waste of hours that should be spent on development of understanding and intelligence.

Rather than have a formal class for Ann, Miss Mirrielees showed the Percys how to reinforce Ann's daily experiences by talking about them to her, thereby increasing her vocabulary and giving a sense of sequence and connectedness through language to what was happening in her life. If a neighbor brought a cake to the house, for instance, Miss Mirrielees might act out through pantomime how the various ingredients were mixed and made into a cake. She then might talk about food in general, so that the child could learn that language can be used to express abstract ideas. Walker gradually entered Ann's world and developed an instinctual, private mode of communication with her. When he watched television with Ann, he turned the sound down and tried to read lips as Ann was doing; it was a habit that stayed with him all his life. One area of the kitchen was Ann's school, with its calendar, clock, and a blackboard on which the names of visitors were written before their arrival.

Shelby drove down to Covington in early December to spend the night with the Percys before they set sail on the *Alcoa Clipper*, a cruise ship that took them to Venezuela and back. Roy, Sarah, and little Roy joined the group. This voyage had one unusual result: having endured the death of his mother by drowning, Walker decided that whenever possible he and Bunt would travel separately, each taking one of the girls.

Walker's first original philosophical essay, entitled "Symbol as Hermeneutic in Existentialism," appeared in *Philosophy and Phenomenological Research* in June. He later called the title "comic-barbarous": "It sounds like the sort of article an academic type in a Mary McCarthy novel would write."[17] Walker tackled a daunting subject for one not trained professionally as a philosopher: the need for a way to bridge Anglo-American empiricism and European existentialism. He suggested that language provided this necessary bridge. "It is the discovery of the symbolic transformation as the unique and universal human response . . . radically different from the purely behaviorist or causal theory of meaning." Symbols denote things; they name things and thus they are not substitutes of one thing for another. He cited the story of blind Helen Keller's experience at the pump with Annie Sullivan. Previously Helen had used words as signals, but when Miss Sullivan spelled out "water" while pumping it over her hands, Helen "understood" for the first time that the word "water" denoted what she felt on her hands. By reflecting on the addition of an "I" and a "you" in this act of communication, Walker proclaimed his insight: *Symbolization is of its very essence an inter-subjectivity*, presupposing an obligatory triad. Walker probed the relationship of the individual and symbolism: "The one thing in the world which by its very nature is not susceptible of a stable symbolic transformation is *myself*! I, who symbolize the world in order to know it, am destined to remain forever unknown to myself." Was Ann Boyd the one who forced Walker to reflect on the irreducibility of self and symbol?

Shelby had no trouble following Walker's two-part essay entitled "Stoicism in the South," which appeared in *Commonweal* in July. In this essay, Walker ventured to discuss the subtle changes taking place in the South—not, as might be expected, concerning black emigration or the Supreme Court decision. Walker argued that the old alliance between blacks and the white gentry had disappeared; the greatness of the South had less to do with Christianity than it did with the old Stoa—the old Stoicism. Citing Faulkner, Walker saw that formerly the relationship between a white and a black was based on mutual respect and courtesy. But the white had lost his noblesse oblige and the black his manners; the result was tight-lipped defiance and resentment.

The Christian, in Walker's eyes, knows differently, that blacks have a "sacred right" to be treated as equals. Unfortunately, Southern Catholics had absorbed the local mores rather than trying to change the dominant culture. In defiance of Archbishop Joseph Rummel's pastoral letters, "Blessed Are the Peacemakers" and "The Morality of Racial Segregation," which boldly labeled segregation "sinful," many Catholics in the New Orleans archdiocese, led by Emile Wagner, a member of the Orleans Parish School Board, boldly resisted. They muttered about Communist infiltration in the Church, convinced that Church leaders should not make such statements on exclusively social issues. Father Louis Twomey mentioned to Walker that there were bitter debates even within the Jesuit community about racial issues.[18] New Orleans was in danger of becoming a magnolia ghetto. Walker believed that sooner or later the archbishop's challenge must be answered. Even though lacking a national voice, Walker had spoken out in a reputable journal of opinion, something that more recognized personalities feared to do. Walker possessed a deep sense of justice, which he communicated frequently in public. Shelby, who passed on the essay to Faulkner, thought that Walker had overrated the Old South as much as Uncle Will had; the old virtues, he noted, were more admired than lived by. Yet he agreed with Walker that Christianity provided the answer.

As Ann required more and more attention, Walker did not neglect Mary Pratt, who desperately wanted a horse, something that Walker felt the family could do without. In order to placate his daughter, he pulled out the Sears, Roebuck catalogue and found that he could order a burro by mail. When Mary Pratt and Walker drove to the Railway Express office, they found a dehydrated, sickly-looking creature, soon to be named Cocóla after a storybook animal. It had to kneel all the way home in the back of the Mercury station wagon. The first night, Cocóla broke into the feed sacks and ate voraciously. Mary Pratt, pleased with her new pet, often rode it bareback to the river and delighted in watching it swim. Walker once took pictures of Ann hanging on to Cocóla's tail. The burro liked to mount the front porch and watch television through a window.

The summer went by peacefully in Covington, unlike the tensions that were increasing in Hungary, as anti-Stalinist forces began to plan for an insurrection, causing a crisis that would reach its peak in mid-fall. The Percys, joined by relatives from Greenville, spent some weeks at Point Clear on the coast. The fall 1956 issue of *Partisan Review* featured Walker's "The Man on the Train: Three Existential Modes," which addressed the theme of alienation, though uncharacteristically about someone in a situation unlike Walker's—about the difference between an alienated commuter and a man on a train reading a book about an alienated commuter. Walker saw alienation as a "reversal of the objective-empirical"—what should normally satisfy a man objectively, like sex and food, but does just the opposite. He imaginatively follows the commuter going through Metuchen, New Jersey, only to discover that he is physically in that city for a short time, but not there mentally. In short, Walker depicted the act of zone-crossing, of going from one physical space to another, and of exploring a locale that is somewhat familiar but actually new. He noted that amnesia is the perfect device of rotation and is available to anyone and everyone—small hints that he might be thinking about his next novel. Shelby liked this essay very much, since it openly expressed Walker's belief that the questions posed by contemporary thinkers could be answered by art. He was particularly glad to see Walker's writing in print—the attractiveness of thoughts made visible by type and paper and ink. "Isn't it odd how much the sight can teach us about writing?" He felt commas really look like commas in print.

Shelby now admitted to Walker that he could not function outside the married state. He had been working steadily and anticipated the completion of the first of three volumes of his Civil War history in six months' time. He had also been seeing Gwyn Rainer Shea, the former wife of Dr. John Shea. Gwyn (a Sarah Lawrence graduate thought by some to be a Lauren Bacall look-alike) was a perfect match for Shelby. Reserved and thoughtful, blessed with wit and energy, Gwyn had made a tough decision in seeking a divorce because of her two children. In addition, as a Catholic, she wanted to abide by the canonical and moral teachings of the Church. Gwyn applied to the local marriage tribunal for an annulment, and to make sure that an evaluation was made fairly, she traveled to Rome and met with Church officials. Her annulment was granted, and she and Shelby were married in October.[19] Gwyn quickly became best friends with Bunt and Walker. "Friendship is so rare a thing," Shelby wrote to Walker, "it should never be neglected." Having endured two unsuccessful marriages, Shelby was determined to put every effort possible into this one.

In January, *America* carried Walker's two-part essay entitled "The Coming Crisis in Psychiatry," prompted by Walker's discussions with his psychiatrist friend William Sorum.[20] The essay began by questioning the meaning of the phrase "humanistic psychoanalysis" as developed by Erich Fromm in *The Sane Society*. Walker stated the problem directly: "The issue is simply this: Is psychiatry a biological science in which man is treated as an organism with instinctive drives and needs not utterly or qualitatively different from those of other organisms? Or is psychiatry a humanistic discipline which must take into account of man as possessing a unique destiny by which he is oriented in a wholly different direction?" For Walker, the sciences do not operate in a vacuum, and he wanted to demonstrate ways in which they should be more interconnected. He felt that "if Western man's sense of homelessness and loss of community is in part due to the fact that he feels himself a stranger to the method and data of his sciences, and especially to himself construed as a datum, then the issue is no longer academic." In particular, American psychiatry seemed indifferent to the themes developed by Kierkegaard and Marcel—particularly the sickness of modern man and the sense of homelessness that modern man has tried to transform into a happy place. Ironically, modern psychiatry, in Walker's view, was unable to take into account the predicament of modern man, since the social sciences in particular evaluate illness as a deviation from a biological norm. Fromm posited that guilt occurs when people feel that their lives are running through their hands like sand: "This is the age of anxiety because it is the age of the loss of self."

Since Freud and Jung had double standards and had not given Walker the answers he sought to the sense of deception experienced by modern man, he wanted to look elsewhere for a goal to human life that is beyond that of adjusting to the demands of society and consuming goods. The answer was to be found in the insight that there are certain human needs that the biological approach cannot deal with. Walker agreed with Pascal—and Fromm—who were aware that only a foolish person spends his entire life seeking diversions and is not aware that he is the center of some supreme mystery. Walker wanted to go beyond Fromm's secularized notion of transcendence. "Once we have tran-

scended animal nature, as Fromm describes it, and discovered goals beyond the biological, by what right do we apply biological yardsticks to
these super-biological goals?" Walker was posing questions similar to
those of Pierre Teilhard de Chardin, S.J., though his final words in this
essay, about man knowing he has lost something and being "sick unto
death with the loss of it," bore the distinctive mark of Kierkegaard.

In March, *Commonweal* published Walker's essay on the Civil War.
"The American War," as it is called, begins by asking a general question: what are the reasons for the revival of interest in the Civil War, as
witnessed in Bruce Catton's *This Hallowed Ground* and Shelby's *Shiloh*?
Walker maintained, contrary to accepted opinion, that Southerners do
not think about the Civil War until they find themselves among Northerners who bring it up. "It was the last of the wars of individuals, when
a single man's ingenuity and pluck not only counted for something in
itself but could conceivably affect the entire issue." Shelby was proud of
what Walker had written, and though he did quibble about some factual
material, he knew that his friend was far more knowledgeable than this
article revealed. In mid-July, Walker sent Donald Barthelme, the dynamic
editor of *Forum*, a quarterly published by the University of Houston, an
essay tentatively called "Symbol and Sign."[21] That Walker was industrious was underscored by the fact that by the time he was in communication with Barthelme, he had already written or promised articles for
The Personalist, *The Sewanee Review*, *Modern Schoolman*, *Thought*, and *The
Journal of Philosophy*. The problem, naturally, was how to structure these
articles without becoming repetitious. He intended to publish them in
his projected book tentatively entitled *Symbol and Existence: A Study in
Meaning*.

Walker's intellectual achievement had begun to attract attention, and
even some potshots. In the June 15 issue of *America*, Stephen R. Ryan,
the chairman of the English Department at Xavier University in New
Orleans, wrote that one is "startled, for example, to find an intelligent
Southerner like Walker Percy, certainly no racist, confidently stating that
the South's constitutional position was correct, while admitting that slavery was a mistake: this, mind you, in the year 1957." In his long letter
of reply, Walker took umbrage with Ryan, who considered him a liberal
Southerner who opposed segregation. He admitted he might not have
been all that clear as he initially presented his views: "Perhaps the War
was really and truly fought over slavery. But the other case can be made,
too. It is difficult to see the yeoman farmers who largely made up the
Army of the Tennessee and the Army of Northern Virginia as Southern
Bourbons. The South had some reason to regard the fight as the continuation of the American Revolution. After all, it was her soil which was

being invaded, and her independence which was being denied. The
South might even have the better of the constitutional argument; yet
what won out seems to transcend all the arguments. For it is that extraordinary thing, the American Union." Walker conceded that he had
made a "subversive remark in an otherwise patriotic and pro-Union article," but he really wanted to focus on the issue of segregation. Citing
Archbishop Rummel, who had written publicly that segregation is sinful
because it denies the unity and solidarity of the human race, Walker also
stated that the more recent decision of the U.S. Supreme Court should
be obeyed by all Americans—in short, his argument was based on two
traditions deeply honored in the South: "Christianity and the majesty of
the law." In addition, he reminded his readers of the Southern heritage
of a stable family life, sensitivity and good manners, chivalry, a code of
honor, and individual integrity. As Southern historian and sociologist
Wilbur J. Cash had noted, they go back to the South's rural beginnings.
Not afraid to caricature the Northern way of life, Walker opposed actual
mudslinging. The race problem, he felt, was not solely the exclusive
problem of Southerners. One benefit of black emigration was that the
North now shared in both the problem and whatever solution would be
reached. Above all, Walker wanted to keep the spotlight on the blacks
who suffer. He praised the tactics of Martin Luther King, Jr., and saw
the sometimes arrogant tactics of the NAACP as essentially self-defeating. The Christian Southern segregationist knows, Walker held, that his
position is theologically and legally untenable. Thus Walker used an attack on himself to discuss the philosophical and theological issues he felt
were the outcome of the Civil War.

    After spending part of the summer at Sea Island in Georgia, and
stopping in Birmingham to visit Aunt Ellen Murphy, Walker again settled into his routine of writing.[22] By early October he had received the
summer issue of *Forum*, which featured his article "The Act of Naming"—a development of his "Semiotic and a Theory of Knowledge,"
published in the May 1957 issue of *The Modern Schoolman*. He also complimented Donald Barthelme on publishing an article by James Collins,
whom he considered "that rare creature, a first-class philosopher who is
also a first-class writer."[23] Though Walker was aware of the neurological
and physical bases of uttering sounds, he sought to describe the process
of understanding words, since it is generally accepted that people who
share a common language understand the same words. "The essence of
the process is a series of events in space-time: muscular events in the
mouth, wave events in the air, electrico-colloidal events in the nerve and
brain." Walker stressed, not the behavior of animals, but the symbolic
and denotative dimensions of language. He began with this concept:

"Naming is unique in natural history because for the first time a being in the universe stands apart from the universe and affirms some other being to be what it is." Unless a person says that a certain word is a certain object, that person will never know either the word or the object. The Scholastics had a theory that we do not know essences directly, but indirectly—a knowledge mediated by symbols. "Man is not merely a higher organism responding to and controlling his environment. He is, in Heidegger's words, that being in the world whose calling it is to find a name for Being, to give testimony to it, and to provide for it a clearing." Though the formulation might be abstract and derivative, Walker clearly announced, without giving any specifics at all, what was at its deepest level one of the greatest problems of his personal and intellectual life.

In October, Ivor and Marie Trapolin invited Alioune Diop, a Senegalese living in Paris and editor of *Présence Africaine*, who had been invited by the U.S. State Department to lecture in the country, to their home in Uptown New Orleans. As president of the Young Men's Business Club, Trapolin was risking a good deal by inviting a black-skinned man to visit, especially when the city's hotels were still segregated. Walker considered Ivor "a young, struggling lawyer with a large family who displayed enormous courage by inviting a racially mixed group to his home at that time."[24] When the limousine provided by the State Department arrived to deposit the honored guest, the Trapolins knew that they could not hide the fact that they were hosting a racially mixed group for the evening. In fact, as Walker approached the Trapolin home, he felt as if he was going to see a Mississippi bootlegger.

As if to reinforce his letter in *America*, Walker wrote "The Southern Moderate," published in the December 13 issue of *Commonweal*. Here he offered some modest proposals concerning segregation. "The Southern moderate, let us say, is a man of good will who is aware of the seriousness of the problem, is searching for a solution, but disagrees that the solution is simple and can be effected overnight." The moderate is in a dilemma, since he wants to exercise responsibility and avoid the irresponsible positions of those on both sides of the issue. Gallup polls show, Walker continued, that the race problem is the biggest one facing Americans, and as blacks move to other parts of the country, all sections of the country will have to deal with a common problem—a point he had made previously. "It may be the suffering Negro himself who will save us all from what we have done to him." The role of the moderate, even as blacks become economically better off, "is not to press for a quick solution but to humanize, to moderate, the solution which is surely coming." If people feel that desegregation does not necessarily mean a mixing of the races, then their fears about social—and sexual—encounters will be alleviated. Creating public zones of tolerance and secure anonymity might not be all that bad, "until the time comes when they might wish to be friends." It is curious that Walker based his argument here, not on Scripture or theology, but on a sociological analysis.

Sometime during the late fall of 1957, Bunt and Ida Mae, who had been making the daily trek across the new causeway except on Thursdays, when Walker drove, had been involved in an accident when taking Ann to New Orleans for her speech therapy. It was an upsetting moment. Most of all, the hours spent in traveling were not helpful to Ann. Bunt and Walker decided to move to New Orleans so that Ann could be near her speech therapist, Mrs. Pauline Joseph at Tulane, and not be tired when she arrived. It also meant that Walker could extricate himself from some socializing that tended to consume his time.

For Christmas, Walker sent Shelby a record of Jelly Roll Morton's songs. "Let me hear from you," Shelby concluded his final letter of that year. "Roy says you found a house in N.O. . . . Are you settled there for the winter?" They had indeed found a cottage at 1820 Milan Street, not far from the Academy of the Sacred Heart, where Mary Pratt, then age ten, and eventually Ann, then age three, would go to school. Walker sold some of his Polaroid stock to purchase the house. At the same time, the Percys kept the house in Covington and would return to it most weekends.

With two houses at his disposal, Walker learned not to become dependent on one room in which to do his writing. Without daily access to his personal library in Covington, he had to delve more into his imagination to find stories, and he began writing a third novel, made up entirely out of his head, on the back porch at Milan Street.[25] During these early months of 1958, he experienced a feeling of elation as he wrote. Inspired by the novels and other creative works of Mauriac, Malraux, and Sartre, he began to translate the psychological and philosophical ideas he had been dealing with into fiction.

Reflecting on this experience, Walker saw it objectively years later:

And so it came to pass that he wrote a short novel in which he created a character, an amiable but slightly bemused young man of a certain upper-class Southern background, and sat him down in Gentilly, a middle-class district of New Orleans, in order to see what would happen to him. For he has given up on the usual verities, home, family, church, country, and instead elects a solitary existence of selling stocks and bonds to the local burghers, hiring a succession of lovely secretaries and going to the movies. He enjoys bad movies.

What happens to him is that in the very extremity of his despair, cool as it is—indeed as the very consequence of his despair—it occurs to him that a *search* is possible, a search altogether different from the scientific explorations mounted by scientists or by the most perceptive of psychoanalysts. So the novel, almost by accident, became a narrative of the search, the quest. And so the novel, again almost by accident—or was it an accident?—landed squarely in the oldest tradition of Western letters: the pilgrim's search outside himself rather than the guru's search within. All this happened to the novelist and his character without the slightest consciousness of a debt to St. Augustine or Dante. Indeed the character recreates within himself and within the confines of a single weekend in New Orleans a microcosm of the spiritual history of the West, from the Roman patrician reading his Greek philosophers to the 13th-century pilgrim who leaves home and takes to the road.[26]

Curiously Walker abstracted himself from the tether of the political and racial problems of New Orleans as he focused on the protagonist of his novel, Binx Bolling, who seems at home in the Big Easy. Living in New Orleans also meant that Walker could draw on the landscape of the city to express it as his own mindscape. While the exact date Walker started writing *The Moviegoer* is not certain, there is evidence that some of the earliest stages of the novel were typed on the back of his personalized Milan Street stationery. His remark in an interview with Barbara King ("I sat down one day in New Orleans and began to write *The Moviegoer*") implies that he wrote definitely on weekdays at Milan Street and most likely on weekends in his back office in the house on Military Road, since he was traveling back and forth most weeks. Walker remembered the first sentences he wrote: "This morning I got a note from my aunt asking me to come for lunch. I know what that means."[27] He felt it was right, that he had found his own voice:

One begins to write not as one thinks he is supposed to write, and not even to write like the great models one admires, but rather to write as if he were the first man on earth ever to set pencil to paper . . . When I sat down to write *The Moviegoer*, I was very much aware of discarding the conventional notions of a plot and a set of characters, discarded because the traditional concept of plot-and-character itself reflects a view of reality which has been called into question. Rather would I begin with a *man* who finds himself in a *world*, a very concrete man who is located in a very concrete place and time. Such a man might be represented as *coming to himself* in somewhat the same sense as Robinson Crusoe came to himself on his island after his shipwreck, with the same wonder and curiosity.[28]

Walker felt that a great deal of *The Moviegoer* (and *The Last Gentleman*) has to do "with the differences between me and my uncle. The whole thing is a dialectic between his attitude, which was a Southern patrician paternalism, and the attitudes of the two young men in these novels, a more detached, alienated point of view."[29] In large measure, Walker had not only located the genesis of his first two published novels but showed a relationship between them.

In order to prime the creative pump, Walker first sketched the barest outline of the plot and indicated some of the characters. From one jotting, it is clear that the theme would deal with the notion of "mediocrity" in various sectors of society and in the protagonist's life. Once Walker had made this initial step, which actually suggested the overall design, he then typed out a more formal outline, structuring the novel into six sections and an epilogue. In doing this, Walker followed the advice of Shelby, who thoroughly delighted in the architectonic development of the preliminary stages of a novel.

Whenever the weather was agreeable, Walker wrote in the open air as Ann played nearby. Sometimes Bunt or her housekeeper Annette would take Ann to the swings in Audubon Park when she was not attending Miss Hoffman's preschool in Uptown. Now in Mother Jane Dubrouillet's fifth-grade class, Mary Pratt started taking art classes with Sadie Irvine and music with Virginia Kock. In thinking about the development of his novel, Walker told Don Lee Keith: "I felt that it would be a fascinating idea to start out with a young man whose life was free of all ordinary worries, one with a good family, fair financial stability and things with which he should be aesthetically satisfied, but who, somehow, finds himself as one of the 'outsiders' about which existentialists talk."[30] Having written two novels that had not been published, Walker knew he could not allow his third to surface unimpededly from his imagination.

That spring *The Sewanee Review* published his essay "Metaphor as Mistake." He had been reading R. P. Blackmur's *Language as Gesture* and William Empson's *Seven Types of Ambiguity*, thinking about the ways people misnamed objects, misunderstood words, and misremembered past events. Metaphors often caused the most problems: they seemed to scandalize philosophers, including semioticists, who view them as linguistic devices that substitute one thing for another or assert an identity between two different objects. Philosophers might dismiss a black Mississippian calling a Seeburg record player a "seabird," while to others it's a richer word. The question is, how does a metaphor meet the inner needs of an individual? Following Cassirer, Walker stated that one cannot know anything at all unless it is *symbolized*. "The essence of metaphorical truth and the almost impossible task of the poet is, it seems to me, to name unmistakably and yet to name by such a gentle analogy that the thing beheld by both of us may be truly formulated for what it is." In this essay, Walker showed a sensitivity to language and a mastery of it. He also made a connection between the aboriginal act of pointing and the act of locating a metaphor in a poem. "The aboriginal naming act is, in this sense, the most obscure and the most creative of metaphors; no modern poem was ever as obscure as Miss Sullivan's name *water* for Helen Keller. A perfectly definite something is pointed at and given a name, a sound or a gesture to which it bears only the most tenuous analogical similarities." Metaphor, as the true maker of language, unites "something that I had privately experienced but which was not available to me because it had never been formulated and rendered intersubjective." Even mistakes in reading can shed light on how metaphor functions in language, since they open up our fundamental symbolic orientation to the world. Semanticists say that we name something and thus know it, but they do not explain *how* we know. Behaviorists imply that we respond merely to stimuli, but do not really know at all. Yet we do know, "as men who must know one thing through the mirror of another."

The adventures of Binx Bolling in New Orleans did not spring full-blown from Walker's imagination. It took him a while to conceive the characters. The structure, for the most part, originated from Walker's experiences in New York as a medical student. In the initial draft of *Diary of the Last Romantic*, entitled "Confessions of a Movie-goer" (as *The Moviegoer* was first called), a Princeton graduate spends his *Wanderjahr* in New York, as his father had done years before. Living at the West Side Y and spending time in Central Park with the evening paper, the narrator likes to go to the movies. As the story begins, the narrator is seen waiting in front of Radio City Music Hall to see a John Ford Western. He spots two former classmates heading for "21" for lunch and remembers they were in a photo with him in the Princeton annual as they queued up at a local movie house called "the Armpit." Not wanting to be seen entering a movie theater alone, the narrator sidles up to a young woman in front of him. Inside he sits next to her, just as the stage show finishes and the movie is about to begin. He is determined not to become distracted by what he knows about the actual life of the male star. "But here he is the center of everything and all beauty is in him. His tiredness is beauty, his sweat, the soreness in his eyes, his solitude, his silence, his watchfulness; but most of all it is the beauty of his solitude that I love.

The question has occurred to me: who is he? What is his identity in relation to me? Is he a comrade? Is he I?" The narrator mentally divides the cinematographic experience into the Man, the Escape, the Encounter, and the Ordeal:

I recognize him at last because, of course, he is I . . . He moves through their festivals like a ghost, the silent American, whose very being consists at once in his respect for their ways and his aloofness from them . . . For we live in a meaningful world. This moment, the moment of the movies, is the Significant Moment. Where we differ from other people is that they live this moment as if it were like every other moment in their lives, a routine affair as if things and people were not any more worth noticing now than at any other time. But *now* everything is charmed with meaning; everything is a Presence or a Power—that ordinary brownstone there, that man on the subway. If their significance is not clear immediately, it soon will be. At any moment, IT will begin. In the words of the movie, as the camera moves along the stark coastline and the gulls cry and off there is a cliff house, deserted now—"This is how it all began—." IT will begin any minute. I have only to wait . . . The most authentic moment of the movies and the moment of my purest happiness is the Escape.

It is the progressive amnesiac who has the perfect escape in the movies, since in one stroke all the past is discarded. "*Everything* becomes new and unfamiliar. Every turn of a corner brings one face to face, not with an old actuality, an old sadness, but with new possibility. Anything can happen, and the happiness derives from the possibility itself." From here, the narrator explains what he means by the Encounter (with a woman) and the Ordeal (such as a bomb exploding). Though we see the medical student enter the theater, we do not see him exit, and thus are left with the distinct impression that this young man feels most comfortable—most at home—in a dark, cavernous movie theater.

Once Walker had finished writing this vignette, he began sketching out *Confessions of a Movie-goer*, which begins one Wednesday noon when the narrator, Jack, encounters Eddie Ouillibert and Jack's cousin, Kate. An hour later, Jack's Aunt Emily asks him to help Kate, who has not worked for two weeks, to get her through a critical time in her life. Kate later tells Jack she cannot marry Walter; her dilemma is that she does not know what to do. The following day Kate (who now says she hates Aunt Emily) and Jack go to Mr. Giambattista's duck club. Later Jack thinks about taking her to a drive-in movie starring Dick Powell, but they wind up instead going to his apartment and then to a biology lab. Jack accompanies Kate home on the streetcar. At 5 a.m. on Friday, Jack takes a lonely walk and then returns home and calls Kate, who is asleep.

Early the next morning he drives his MG to the lake, where he goes to his mother's camp. While there on Sunday he calls Kate, goes to Mass with his half brothers and sisters, and above all consoles Lonnie, who is dying. Before leaving the camp, Jack again calls Kate and tells her, "I'm going to follow your suggestion." In the fifth part, we learn that Kate has attempted suicide by slashing her wrists, though Aunt Emily believes she will be all right. At this point, Walker intended Sherwood Anderson and William Faulkner to make cameo appearances in the novel. Once summoned back home from a trip to Chicago, Jack receives a note from Kate to meet her at Jackson Square at 2 p.m. on Ash Wednesday. The outline ends with a dialogue between Kate and Jack: "What are you going to do now?" "I'm going to take Aunt Em up." Once Walker outlined the plot this far, he allotted a certain number of pages for each section, intending not to overwrite any particular scene.

This novelistic treatment definitely felt the imprint of Camus's *The Stranger* and Sartre's *Nausea*.[31] "I admit," Walker once said, "I owed a lot more to Jean-Paul Sartre—his novels, his character of Roquentin in *Nausea*—than I did to classical Southern novels."[32] For Walker his fictional work was "existentialist." What he meant by that term "was, on the one hand, feeling in this predicament of 'everydayness' and using what Kierkegaard and also Heidegger would call 'inauthentic' refuges from it, which is 'rotation'—to escape from it either by the tube or by girlfriends or whatever. But the other side of it is the more subtle—what I call the 'scientistic' worldview."[33] He did not have to search for names. Binx's name was a variation of Bix, the nickname of Leon Beiderbecke, the American jazz cornet player, and the name that Roy had given to his springer spaniel in Greenville. Bolling, of course, was a common Phinizy family name; and as a variation Bobo is the nickname of one of Kate's former roommates. Rollo, the nickname of Binx used by Harold Graebner, is one that Walker had at P & S. The name Winky Ouillibert was probably inspired by Florence ("Winky") Chestnutt, an artistic friend of Walker. There were Cutrers in the Covington area and Schexnayders all over the South, one of whom, Maurice Schexnayder, was the Bishop of Lafayette, Louisiana. Walker's cousin, Newt DeBardeleben, most likely served as the model for Walter Wade. Noting that Binx's Aunt Edna is a theosophist would not have escaped the eye of Miriam Barranger. From one perspective the novel might be considered an interior monologue of Rory Calhoun (a real actor, like Walker a convert to Catholicism), who starred in the television series *The Texan*, popular in the 1950s.

It is worth noting that *Commonweal* carried Walker's review of the recently published *Owen Wister Out West*, the letters and journals of a novelist noted primarily for his novel *The Virginian*, which became the source of the famous television show. "What is it about *The Virginian* and the Western at its best that is healthful in the way that good art is always healthful?" Walker asked. We see in the Western hero a deracinated person who has no kin and who returns at the end of the show not to his hearth—but elsewhere. What we have in the Western is "the abstract locus of perfection, solitude, and violence." The values of the television Western are counterfeit ones. The moment of truth, after all, is just after the shooting, when the hero blows smoke out of his pistol and walks away, ignoring the crowd. It is no wonder, then, that Binx carries on a conversation with a Western hero who, when transformed into a military hero, shares much of Binx's unresolved anxiety:

Sometimes I write about the peculiar phenomenon which happens, I know, both from my own experience with a possibly fatal disease and from talking to people who've been in combat. Again, this is not a new observation, but something happens under conditions of ordeal, where people have been shot. And Tolstoy did a beautiful example of it in *War and Peace* when he has Prince André shot and wounded on the battlefield of Borodino. Until that moment, André had been a typical dashing Russian officer with all the joy of life and love in military and Russian society. And he's lying there; he's dying; he's going to die eventually. And he might even know it. But he sees the clouds for the first time. And he sees the beauty of the world for the first time. I mean, under conditions of extreme ordeal—and the imminence of death—some people will, to use Marcel's term, "recover being." I did that with Binx Bolling. He said the only time that he felt he was onto something was when he was shot in the Korean War. And he said: "I vow that when I get back to New Orleans, I will not lose that sense of being onto something." Of course, he did.[34]

We do know that Walker typed a complete version of *Confessions of a Movie-goer*, approximately 858 pages, on Eaton's corrasable paper; he punched holes in the side, placed it in a spiral notebook, and made corrections throughout.

In June he visited Greenville, where he read Phinizy Spalding's M.A. thesis on Uncle Will; he liked it and considered it "very solid and a workmanlike job and at the same time provocative and stimulating."[35] He particularly enjoyed the chapter in which Phinizy discusses writers Walker had previously recommended. Yet Walker had not known about Will's interest in the works of George Tyrell, a priest dismissed from the Society of Jesus during the turn-of-the-century Modernist controversy in the Church. He indicated his true feelings about his relationship to Uncle Will: "I might even say that everything I am interested in writing about is a result of the impact of Uncle Will's world-view upon me and what had germinated as a result of the ferment which followed (a fouled-up metaphor if I ever made one)."[36] For the most part, Walker spent the summer in Covington writing and coping with bouts of hay fever, brought on by the live oaks and the Spanish moss.

In July, *The Journal of Philosophy* published Walker's essay "Symbol, Consciousness, and Intersubjectivity." This article, a companion piece to some of the philosophical dimensions of *Confessions of a Movie-goer*, discussed two approaches to the subject of inquiry: the explanatory-psychological and the phenomenological, while all the time not overlooking the role of symbol in the story of consciousness. Denotation resolves the dichotomy: "Certainly, whether we approve or disapprove, something very momentous has taken place when a sign which has been received as a signal—go fetch the water—is suddenly understood to 'mean' the water, to denote something." Once again Walker cited Helen Keller's paradigmatic moment at the water pump. He saw that every "symbolic formulation, whether it be language, art, or even thought, requires a real or posited *someone else* for whom the symbol is intended as meaningful. Denotation is an exercise in intersubjectivity." In addition, a person is conscious of something for another and for himself—a process of knowing with someone else. "The act of consciousness is the intending of the object as being what it is for both of us under the auspices of the symbol." Thus Walker inextricably linked consciousness and intersubjectivity, which are, in fact, "aspects of the same new orientation toward the world"—the symbolic orientation.

In early August, Walker received a copy of *Forum* and a note from Donald Barthelme asking for another contribution. He said that if he felt he had something suitable, he would send it on.[37] The fall issue of *Forum* contained "The Loss of the Creature," in which Walker focused on the multiple ways of perceiving ordinary events in everyday life. He assumed the posture of a tourist at the Grand Canyon. "The highest point, the term of the sightseer's satisfaction, is not the sovereign discovery of the thing before him; it is rather the measuring up of the thing to the criterion of the pre-formed symbolic complex." To rediscover the originality of an experience once it has become too familiar or lost, one could take a detour to come upon it fresh, or one could try to see it through the eyes of others. A filmmaker knows that you have to approach the Grand Canyon from various angles—the Inside Track, the Familiar Revisited, the Accidental Encounter. Above all, Walker was concerned with the notion of recovery by various stratagems to discover what is authentic and inauthentic. He uses the example of an American couple and an ethnologist watching a corn dance in Mexico. Not sure of themselves, the couple watch the ethnologist to see if he is pleased by the dance; in fact, they transfer their sovereignty to the ethnologist. "Their loss is so absolute that they are not even aware of a loss. They do not even know what it is to be a sovereign person in the world." In short, some people do not allow themselves to see what is before and within them: "The dogfish, the tree, the seashell, the American Negro, the dream, is rendered invisible by a shift of reality from concrete thing to theory which Whitehead has called the fallacy of the misplaced concreteness. It is the mistaking of an idea, a principle, an abstraction, for the real. As a consequence of the shift, the 'specimen' is seen as less real than the theory of the specimen. As Kierkegaard said, once a person is seen as a specimen of a race or a species, at that very moment he ceases to be an individual. Then there are no more individuals but only specimens." Walker wanted his readers to be open to what is before them and to that which beckons them in order to assert the sovereignty of themselves as knowers.

That October, *The New Scholasticism* published Walker's "Culture: The Antinomy of the Scientific Method." Here again Walker validates several ways of knowing without giving a priority to scientific knowledge. Interiorly Walker was struggling to validate his career as a novelist. Would the average American, for instance, consider the knowledge one receives from reading a novel a valid type of knowledge, different from—but no less valuable than—scientific knowledge? Walker maintained that "the main elements of cultural activity are in their most characteristic moments also assertatory in nature. The central acts of language, of worship, of myth-making, of story-telling, of art, as well as of science, are assertions." In setting up his argument about various antinomies—in myth, language, science—Walker cited Kant's belief that when "pure reason" goes beyond the manifold of experience, it falls into an antinomy. Walker set up a tetradic relationship: a scientist communicates to another scientist, through symbolic assertion, a phenomenon that has been observed. In Peircean fashion, one sign leads to another, or in this case to a further question: "How may we deal scientifically with man considered precisely in those activities which distinguish him as a culture member?"

Walker believed science is limited in that it recognizes only functional linkages and yet "presupposes other kinds of reality, the intersubjectivity of scientists and their assertions, neither of which are space-time linkages and neither of which can be grasped by the functional method." In the last analysis, the assertatory behavior of man, whether true or false, mythic or scientific, should be considered on the same ontological

plane as the intersubjective enterprise of scientists. Walker called for a
radical anthropology: a human person is seen not merely as an organism,
a social unit or a culture member, but as one who makes assertions that
grapple with truth/falsity, right/wrong, and authenticity/inauthenticity.
In his own way, Walker was setting up a philosophical *ars poetica*.

8

A Career Launched:

The Moviegoer

1959–61

During the latter part of the 1958–59 school year, the Percys decided to travel to the dryer climate of Tucson, Arizona, since Ann was having middle-ear problems and infections. Helen Generelly's brother, who lived in Tucson, had offered his assistance in helping search for a suitable school for Ann. Unfortunately, in Tucson Ann lost whatever hearing she had. The area became enveloped by a rainy spell and Bunt decided to return to New Orleans rather than risk further ear problems. Shelby wrote Walker in mid-April: "Bunt said that Arizona didn't work out well for Ann, but that you plan to keep looking; also that you sold the house." In late May, Gwyn and Shelby (who had had his Guggenheim fellowship renewed) came to New Orleans for a long weekend. Shelby had an idea: he wanted Walker to collect his essays and send them to Random House for publication: "I think those pieces have much that has been missing from American writing for far too long; maybe even since William James—though I doubt if that will please you."

But Walker's first concern was not the essays but his novel. He finished *Confessions of a Movie-goer* in the spring of 1959 and sent it to literary agent Elizabeth R. Otis of McIntosh & Otis in New York. Walker had chosen well; Miss Otis represented, among other good writers, John Steinbeck and Flannery O'Connor.

On June 5 *Commonweal* published his essay "The Culture Critics," for which Walker received some fan letters and requests from two publishers to write a book on the subject.[1] His theme was the state of the world—things looked bad and people were afraid to talk about it. "There are the tremblers, and there are the professional gravediggers of the West. Western civilization might have had its virtues in the past, but now, in their eyes, the jig is up." He cited Thomas Griffith's *The Waist-High Culture* and Vance Packard's *The Status Seekers* in discussing society's state of malaise—the American sickness, whether psychological, economic, or both. "It is, as Griffith knows very well, a religious dilemma, in that ultimate goals are involved." The malaise is often embodied in the ethical secularist's speech. Americans no longer were interested in asking why they should not seek status; it seemed to be a given in society. Walker wanted to take the question beyond social stereotypes to the individual person with a specific history.

He thanked Donald Barthelme for sending him one of Dwight Macdonald's essays in the defunct monthly *Politics* that had appealed greatly to him.[2] Macdonald in turn had been impressed by Walker's "The Loss of the Creature" in *Forum* and requested back issues with Walker's earlier essays, since he believed they had parallel interests.[3] Shelby thanked Walker for the *Commonweal* essay, which he enjoyed, except for his characterization of faith: "God painted himself into a corner and inconsiderately disappeared." For Walker, faith had not disappeared; it needed a search to locate it.

Miss Otis, who worked in collaboration with Annie Laurie Williams (who handled plays and motion pictures), sent a copy of *Confessions of a Moviegoer* (now without the hyphen) to Stanley Kauffmann at the publishing house of Alfred A. Knopf.[4] Kauffmann had recently called on Miss Otis in her office, had tea with her, and asked her to send him only manuscripts she thought Knopf might publish. It was fated that Stanley Kauffmann would serve as Walker's first book editor. A man of many talents, Kauffmann had begun in the theater, acting with the Washington Square Players from 1931 to 1941. He served as an associate editor at Bantam from 1949 to 1952, followed by four years as editor-in-chief at Ballantine Books, as well as their consulting editor for another year, before he became *The New Republic*'s film critic. Kauffmann was himself the author of six novels—*The Hidden Hero* (1949), *The Tightrope* (1952), *The Philanderer* (1953), *This Time Forever* (1954), *A Change of Climate* (1955), and *Man of the World* (1956). Under the nom de plume Terry Kirk, he wrote a Western, *Shootout Canyon*, which was made into a movie. In the summer of 1958, he hoped to get one of his plays produced, but when the option was dropped in the spring of 1959 he called Knopf's editor-in-chief, Harold Strauss, and asked for an interview. He was hired in early June. "Here is a book," Miss Otis wrote him on June 24, when she sent him the manuscript, "which I myself like very much. The author has just completed some work on it at my suggestion, and I still think there may be some further work to do. But on the whole this seems to me to be a strong new voice and I hope you will agree." It is no wonder that Walker grew to like the diminutive Miss Otis.

Since Knopf had published *Lanterns on the Levee* and *The Collected Poems of William Alexander Percy*, and since both Blanche and Alfred Knopf knew Uncle Will personally, the firm was a natural publisher to approach. Over the years, as Walker well knew, Alfred Knopf made sure that his firm maintained its reputation for the highest literary standards.

When Kauffmann diligently read Walker's manuscript, it reminded him of Christopher Isherwood's clear declarative style. Not only was Isherwood a former medical student, but he had Gide's knack of using *fausses pistes* that entice the reader with empirical data whose ethical import is appreciated only in retrospect. Kauffmann agreed with Miss Otis that "Walker Percy is a strong new voice" and "a writer of undoubted and attractive talent."[5] Yet he felt compelled to return the manuscript: "For the first 150 pages or so, I felt this was a genuine and important find—a novel of wit, pathos, and a Candide-like bland-savage satire." But he thought it collapsed halfway through: Binx's change from an irresponsible to a mature individual was not convincing. Yet he recognized Walker's talent: "From the first page I knew I had found a real writer. From the first page I felt an added excitement, the chance to establish myself at Knopf. But my heart began to hurt as I continued. Percy never stopped being a real writer, but he had not written a satisfactory novel. I couldn't recommend it for publication. The worst of it was that some other publisher might take the novel as it was, risking loss, just to get the author."[6] In his three-page letter to Miss Otis, he explained his reservations straightforwardly:

Certainly Mr. Percy wants to give his novel a conclusion, but the present conclusion seems to me arbitrary. The change of heart in Binx seems mechanical (almost like those movies he's so fond of!).

It seems to me that the basic problem is this: Mr. Percy has given Binx such clear, penetrating insight into the frauds, pretenses, shallownesses of contemporary life that his conversion to a sense of purpose and responsibility *must* take place at that same piercing depth of honesty. It simply will not do for a man with, figuratively, 20–20 vision to get a message of salvation that would satisfy someone with only 10–10 vision. I cannot blueprint for him how to do this— and would not presume to even if I thought I knew how; but I believe that in order to make this the novel that truly represents his gift, Mr. Percy must rethink the second half of his book, making sure that every scene and every new character contributes to Binx's growth *at Binx's level of insight*. (For example, the only new character in the second half who is up to the level of the excellent characterizations in the first half is the spastic child, in my opinion.)

By examining his material as rigorously as Binx himself would do, by subjecting every new experience to the acid test that Binx would give it, Mr. Percy will progress, I believe, towards the ending the book needs—less smoothly perhaps, but more convincingly. The death of Jules and the conversation with the priest are insufficient testimony to make Binx want to re-engage with the world. It is not that, necessarily, the book needs a titanic explosion in its second half; but it certainly needs seeds planted earlier which can be harvested credibly at the end. At present the effect is as if someone had suddenly switched on a lot of rosy lights.

Kauffmann believed strongly enough in the book to mention the golden word "contract" to Miss Otis: "A further paradox of this situation is that if the author were less unusual, if the book were one at a more predictable and mechanical level, it might be possible to discuss a contract at this point. But what Mr. Percy has to do, must take place at such an internal and unpredictable level, I feel I must wait to see what happens with him (if, of course, he chooses to do anything at all) before proceeding here." The ball was now clearly in Walker's court.

Miss Otis forwarded Kauffmann's critique to Walker, who mulled it over and finally agreed to work on the text, but not without misgivings. Kauffmann was delighted when he heard the news and wrote Walker: "I want to assure you again of my enthusiasm for your talent and my confidence that, if you can bring to bear on the second half the qualities that make the first half scintillate, the result will be a happy one indeed."[7] Walker knew he had a hard task before him, and dashed a quick note to Donald Barthelme, signing it "Earl Long" and saying he was wrestling with a piece of fiction "and not doing too well."[8] Walker thanked Kauffmann for his efforts and indicated he would have another go at the novel, "at least another hard look-and-think, but your acute criticism (and Miss Otis's which has been much the same as yours all along) only confirms my own misgivings. I mean to say that all I can hope to do is please myself, so if you should see it again you need not worry that I have tried to fix it up to pass Knopf—much as I would like to do that. Right now, I'm not even sure the thing can be finished satisfactorily."[9] The crisis had momentarily passed with Kauffmann's discreet nudging.

In a discussion with Alfred Knopf, Kauffmann explained to his boss the nature of Walker's novel and said he felt they should offer the author an option. With nostrils flaring above his large mustache, Knopf replied, "What d'you mean, option? How much?" Kauffmann suggested $200 against a total advance of $1,000. As Knopf's eyes grew wider (he was always hard on editors), Kauffmann quickly added, "I think it's in order, after what he's done already. It's only a gesture, of course, a token. Nothing to do with subsidizing him. In fact, I've heard that he's a man of independent means." "In that case," Knopf retorted, "give him $250."

In reworking his text, Walker made some surprising twists in his story, particularly in the fourth chapter, about Binx's father. On the way to the funeral parlor to pay tribute to his Uncle Jules, Binx learns that his father, Dr. Jack Bolling, was a prophetic figure who got tired of Bayou Sara and the Kiwanis and visited Sam Yerger in New Orleans. "He was so far ahead of his time that we didn't understand him," Sam says. "We are just beginning to understand him now." In Sam's eyes, Jack Bolling was the first postmodern man who "knew exactly what the world was going to be like when the last modern man crawled out of his cave after the holocaust. He was the first man I ever knew who tried to grope his way beyond our Western tradition." Yet Dr. Bolling, a womanizer and an alcoholic, suffered from hideous depression. While visiting Sam, he would disappear for days and then mysteriously return to the Yerger carriageway; his absence could only be explained as some type of interior pilgrimage. "I think his real quest was for death. Death in combat." Dr. Bolling dies from jaundice in an army hospital after helping those who were mortally sick and having been AWOL for two months. "So he died a soldier's death," Grandmother Emily tells Binx. "Your father loved the company of women and the intellectual companionship of men. I believe I'm one of the few women he met on his own level." Nothing had availed Dr. Jack Bolling, not even the counsel of Father Dansereau, the priest in Bayou Sara.

In the fall of 1959, *Thought* published Walker's essay "The Message in the Bottle," more accurately a parable of modern man. Prefaced with quotations from Aquinas and Kierkegaard on the relationship of faith and knowledge, it concerns an isolated figure, an amnesiac castaway, who discovers thousands of bottles that have been washed ashore containing one-sentence messages. Walker pits a scientist against this islander who comes to realize that there is a difference between a piece of *knowledge* (which can be arrived at anytime and anywhere) and a piece of *news* (which cannot be arrived at by experimentation or reflection or artistic insight). "The movement of science is toward unity through abstraction, toward formulae and principles which embrace an ever greater number of particular instances," as it tries to figure out what they imply and how they can be verified, particularly when one considers the person of the news bearer. Walker does not preach the content of the Good News, but asks his readers to open themselves up to an invitation to seek or return to their spiritual homes.

In late October, Walker sent Kauffmann the revised 319-page typescript of his novel. The editor was pleased with the results, calling it a "superlative job."[10] But the revised text still needed work. He noted that Walker introduced the notion of the "search" early on and continued it progressively to the last page, but he felt it needed more definition and had to be expressed in Binx's idiom: "This theme is a kind of spine for the book, and at present that spine is a little limp." He found the "dismissal" at the end of the novel mildly irritating. Had it been implied earlier, it would have become moving at the conclusion and not a "frustrating" feature of the text. Walker had wholly altered the story line of the second half, which Kauffmann highly praised, though he felt the conclusion (the coda) lacked conviction. Kauffmann also liked the quarrel between the "grandmother" and Binx, but felt that the moment of reconciliation needed more emphasis. Nor could Kauffmann understand why Kate changed her attitudes toward life and marriage in the last section. Could it have been the result of the scene on the train? "Could it be that out of the frustration of that encounter, she is taken with a sense of compassion and possibility—and a feeling of a bond with Binx that a successful encounter might well *not* have created in a girl like her?"

Perhaps Kauffmann's most significant query concerned the relevance of Binx's search for his father: "And how is it satisfied by the last scene with the priest? This is not clear, I'm afraid, to me. After all this is, in a way, the crucial scene of the book. I'm not asking for a message: simply for a resolution in emotional, human, characterful terms." Like the good editor he was, Kauffmann put his finger on the novel's critical problem: "In a word, what takes the agony out of living for Binx and Kate? I repeat: not homily or pabulum but in terms of sheerest revelation or maturing or adjustment or emotional reawakening or anything else that seems valid to Mr. Percy." He concluded with six minor points that needed correction and clarification. If Walker would agree to these minor revisions, the firm was ready to offer a contract: $250 on signature, $750 on acceptance of the completed manuscript—the total to be considered an advance against royalties of 10 percent of the retail price on the first 7,500 copies, and an upward sliding scale thereafter—plus an option on Walker's next novel or book of nonfiction. Alfred Knopf even approved the plan to announce the novel in the fall 1960 catalogue, with a projected advance sale of 3,500 copies.[11] Kauffmann not only admired Walker's talent and wanted him on the Knopf list, but he kept the manuscript on his desk, awaiting further word on Walker's reactions.

The day after receiving it, Miss Otis thanked Kauffmann for his letter, which she forwarded to Walker, urging him to accept the editor's suggestions. Walker replied immediately to Miss Otis, expressing his gratitude to her and Kauffmann. A minor clarification: Walker wanted to know if he would actually have a contract with Knopf if he followed the suggestions, which he had intuitively anticipated himself. "Mr. Kauffmann's penetrating remarks act as a happy irritant and I use them as an occasion to do what I want to do."[12] But a problem remained: supposing Knopf did not like the changes, would he still have a contract or would they back out? Walker wrote Kauffmann that he thought it best not to sign the contract just then (he had no problems with the terms), but to make the final revisions first and then resubmit the book. His reasoning was simple: it might take weeks or months to accomplish the task and he did not want to rush in meeting a delivery date. "I have a hunch that the last thirty pages are going to take some figuring. Moreover, I have some obligations and distractions coming up in the next few weeks."[13] Kauffmann wrote indicating he would put no pressure on him to sign the contract, if Walker preferred not to do so. If the delivery date proved to be a sticking point, they could alter it. Kauffmann appreciated Walker's integrity in dealing in the way he did with both his agent and his prospective editor. "Nothing in the finished novel," Kauffmann explained, "will be one whit less your own because of the fact that you have had some comments from interested readers like Miss Otis and myself. But your concern in the matter is refreshing and, if I may presume to say so, admirable in an age when so many writers consider agents and editors an integral part of their writing apparatus. It could not be that way with you, of course. I know that much just from reading your novel."[14] Not wanting to miss the chance of his lifetime, Walker returned the signed contract to Miss Otis and she sent it on. The delivery date was changed to February 4, although Walker anticipated he would finish earlier. When the check for $250 arrived, he had palpable evidence that at long last he had become a writer under contract.

Shelby Foote, immersed in writing about Murfreesboro, a much bloodier battle than Fredericksburg, felt the need to establish greater contact with Walker. "Tell me something of how things are shaping up for you and all your women—particularly your work. Does it move? Is it combining, making a whole, moving toward some consolidated future?" Walker wrote in early December to Donald Barthelme that he would soon send to *Forum* "5,000 words of the curious adventures of my ingenious young moviegoer."[15]

Late into the fall 1959 academic year, the Percys, realizing that Ann needed further help, started making plans to drive to Florida. As Christmas approached, they first stayed in an apartment and then in the Purich house near Deerfield Beach just north of Pompano Beach. Christmas was celebrated on Sanibel Island. In Florida, Miss Mirrielees assisted Bunt and Walker in instructing Ann, while Mary Pratt attended seventh grade at Pinecrest School.[16] Once while the family was on the way to church, Walker was stopped for speeding. For Bunt this was a learning moment for Ann, and so she took out her notebook and started writing down the news story for her daughter: "Policeman stopped father. We are going to police station. They are going to arrest your father." Shocked, Bunt realized that she had left out a few steps in the explanation process.

In mid-January, Miss Otis received Walker's revised manuscript, which she forwarded at once to the publisher.[17] It was then distributed to several editors at Knopf, including Henry Robbins and Judith Jones, and they all discussed it at length. The upshot was that it still needed revisions. Stanley Kauffmann wrote Walker at Pompano Beach, asking him not to become discouraged. "All who have read the book here recognize a talent, a unique voice, and a viewpoint of pertinence and importance." He listed five issues: (1) Binx's search needed more definition, consistency, presence, and force. (2) Some of the characters and subplots are dropped and picked up arbitrarily. (3) Binx's memory of his father, and their relationship, was unclear as a force in the book and insufficiently resolved. (4) Characters such as Sam Yerger, Jimmy, and Joel were employed beyond their utility. In addition, the Mardi Gras party went on too long. Kate's reactions needed development and other characters, particularly those appearing for the first time, needed to be filtered through Binx's mind. (5) Kauffmann did not really understand Binx's statement at the end of the book. In addition, Binx's decision to go to medical school, handled well throughout the novel, was too suddenly sloughed off at the end.

What all the above comes to, essentially, is that instead of a collection of brilliant and moving scenes rather arbitrarily bound together as the author seems from time to time to remember to bind them, we would like to see a more organic, better composed work in which the author has all his thematic and plot elements well in hand from the start and is moving them towards a conclusion. Our feeling is that you discovered things about Binx and his relationships as you went along, rather than seeing them clearly in his spiritual and physical environment from the start and knowing exactly who this particular pilgrim is and what his progress is to be.

In short, the editors were asking for important rewriting. Walker was being asked to take a deep breath and plunge in again. "My own feeling," he wrote to Stanley Kauffmann, "is that I am getting pretty close to what I am aiming at. There are lapses and gaucheries here and there which need to be taken care of, some strained-for effects and some sophomore posturing, and I want to make a few additions. But it will come to no more than tinkering and polishing—I think."[18] Walker felt exasperated by the task ahead of him. While he did not disagree with specific criticisms, he thought that he had a far different concept of how the novel should end than they did. In addition, Kauffmann's thoughts about dropped characters and interrupted story strands did not strike a responsive chord within him. As he wrote Kauffmann: "*A Passage to India* is a much better constructed novel than *Nausea*, but *Nausea* would be wrecked by a revision along these lines. I suppose I am trying to say that the fragmented alienated consciousness, which is Mr. Binx Bolling, cannot be done up in a *novel* in the usual sense of the word. At least I would not have the stomach for the job." Walker said he would make whatever changes came to mind, but "truthfully I doubt if there is much use in resubmitting it to you, for even if you decided then to accept it, I hardly see how you all could take it on with the enthusiasm and unanimity without which I'd rather you didn't take it on at all." Walker still wanted to be published by Knopf, the publisher of Camus's *The Stranger*, which he considered "the greatest book of our time."

It was not an easy interlude for Walker, and he started feeling ambivalent about ratcheting up his imaginative forces to undertake still another draft of his novel. In March he acknowledged to Donald Barthelme that Knopf had paid him a small sum as an option on the novel, but that they had returned the typescript. He informed Barthelme that he was undecided whether to rewrite the novel or not, but once he had made up his mind, he would let him know and forward a part of the text to him for possible first serial use in his magazine.

A sense of Walker's character can be shown by the philosophical questions he pursued at this time. His essay "Naming and Being" was published in the April 1960 issue of *The Personalist* (it would be part of a book that Walker was working on entitled *Symbol and Existence*). It began with a question: what is naming? It then proceeded to look carefully at the notion of meaning, trying to provide an argument different from those used by semioticians. Building on the insights expressed in "The Act of Naming," even with some of the same examples, Walker stressed the importance of the copula of a sentence, the word "is," which creates an identity or pairing—a metaphysical position that went to the heart of Scholasticism in arguing the distinction between essence (*essentia*) and actual being (*esse*). Above all, Walker believed that the copula provides "an intentional relation of identity," which affirms a realism in life—leading to notions of authenticity or inauthenticity. "In the joy of naming, one lives authentically . . . No matter whether I give a name to, or hear the name of, a strange bird, no matter whether I write or read a line of great poetry, form or understand a scientific hypothesis, I thereby exist authentically as a namer or a hearer, as an I or a Thou—and in either case a co-celebrant of what is." It is curiously appropriate—in light of the difficulties he was experiencing with *Confessions of a Moviegoer*— that Walker mentions how fear and anxiety can cause diminishment and even destruction. Naming can take away anxiety; when Helen Keller went through the process of understanding what water is, she concomitantly wanted to know the makeup of the universe she lived in.

Walker again began choosing words and ideas that not only suited his philosophical equation but lifted him from the doldrums of repeatedly rewriting a novel: naming, knowing, symbolizing, discovering, and truth-saying—combining, like the primitive tribesman he mentions, the offices of poet and scientist. Quoting a passage from Heidegger's *Existence and Being* at the essay's conclusion, Walker felt the need to preserve the truth of Being no matter what may happen. "In sacrifice there is expressed that hidden *thanking* which alone does homage to the grace wherewith Being has endowed the name of man, in order that he may take over in his relationship to Being the guardianship of Being." Though superficially discouraged, Walker conceived of his role as namer, as novel writer, at the deepest core of his being.

By late April, the Knopf contract department decided to change the delivery date of the typescript to October 1, though it was hoped that Walker would send in the revised text before then. As a way of solving his problem, Walker took a detour. In May he sent one section, "Carnival in Gentilly," to Donald Barthelme with a note indicating he could use all or part of it in his magazine. When Walker heard from Barthelme that his story was accepted, he agreed to make the few corrections Barthelme had suggested, and noted that his weakness consisted in his tendency to "Platonize."[19] "It is gradually forcing itself upon me in the most painful way," Walker wrote, "that it is almost impossible to Catholicize, pro or con, without falling on your face. It is a terrible something to have by the tail. My revision will largely consist of removing Catholic licks (and all other licks). Plato is killing us. Back to things. *Zurück an die Sache* ["Back to the matter at hand"]—that's my motto from here on (a lesson of the Incarnation after all)." Barthelme's editorial acumen reached a high point with the summer 1960 issue of *Forum*. It carried, in addition to Walker's story (labeled as such—"Carnival in Gentilly: A Story"), literary and critical material by Howard Nemerov, Marshall McLuhan, Hugh Kenner, William Gass—excellent company all.[20]

Walker wrote Shelby in mid-May describing how hard he had

worked during the past winter and how he had accomplished what he set out to do five years earlier. He had written "a couple of dozen major articles" and his latest was scheduled to appear in the February 1961 issue of *Psychiatry: Journal for the Study of Interpersonal Processes* as "The Symbolic Structure of Interpersonal Process." But Walker felt that too few people were reading his labors: "The trouble is that this is all pissing in the wind, or rather peeing into the abyss." Even neighbors in Covington were beginning to regard Walker as a "deliberate egghead who writes unreadable things, and this is even drearier than not being known at all. Which is to say what I have always said, a writer writes to communicate and he needs recognition. Don't tell me otherwise."

The novel was another matter altogether. Word had gotten around about it and he had been approached by six other publishers, including Simon & Schuster, even though he had Knopf's "option contract."[21] "Yet I am deeply pessimistic," Walker lamented. He sent Shelby, an astute critic, the opening of the novel to read. Shelby replied that what he had read had "a fine tone and carries right along; I wished I had more. In spots it came home to me harder than anything I've read in a long time—the idiotic logic of the bit on Holden and the litterbugs, for instance, and the unsentimental reaction of the eight-year-old who was relieved to find that all he had to do was be a soldier; the cellophane-wrapped girl on the bus, the newlyweds, the soured theater manager. All came through just fine." Shelby did not think a rewriting was necessary: "Don't ever accept an editor's judgment on anything that has to do with literary matters." Shelby suggested that Walker fuse the two titles: *Carnival in Gentilly, the Confessions of a Moviegoer.* "I'm curious though about the length," he continued. "It seems to me it should either be quite short, say 50- or 60,000 words, or quite long, 200,000 even. Which is it?" Clearly Shelby had not been previously consulted about the novel, perhaps because Walker wanted to try to find his own writing voice for himself.

The précis that Stanley Kauffmann wrote for Blanche Knopf shows how the novel was taking final shape: "A novel about a young New Orleans war veteran of good family, now in a good job, disenchanted with life, who goes to the movies as one might take a drug to deaden the realities of life—only he does it consciously, humorously, without self-pity. The novel is the story, principally, of how he and a girl—his cousin—who is unhappy and maladjusted for different reasons—finally come together and how he gives up his drifting and goes to medical school."[22] Kauffmann found the novel's style easy, vernacular, funny, and even poetic. Though it was not imitative of J. D. Salinger, this comparison proved useful in the report. A niche was being opened for Walker in the American canon.

That summer the racial issue in New Orleans and the South in general began to become more intense as black Americans took more control of their fates. In 1956 the U.S. District Court in New Orleans had ruled that segregation in public schools was illegal under the *Brown v. Board of Education* decision of 1954. Federal judge J. Skelly Wright ordered the school board to make arrangements for the admission of children on a racially nondiscriminatory basis with all deliberate speed. The school board resisted this and delayed action for three years. Judge Wright revised his order and directed that a plan be presented by March 1960. Likewise in 1956 Archbishop Rummel had ordered that "white" and "colored" signs be removed from church pews, and declared that racial discrimination was against the laws of God. He announced that parochial schools would begin to integrate on a grade-by-grade basis beginning in September 1957; yet because of public protest, he delayed this integration for two more years.

One of those who protested the archbishop's decision was John P. Nelson, a lawyer and native of Gulfport, Mississippi, who had met Walker when he accompanied Father Twomey to the Percy house.[23] Father Twomey, whom Walker heard preach at Holy Name Church, ran the Institute of Industrial Relations at Loyola. Beginning in 1948, he started publishing his influential "Christ's Blueprint for the South."[24] "Father Twomey had the most influence on labor at that time," Nelson maintained. Nelson was also impressed by the compassion with which Walker spoke about blacks. Although the U.S. Supreme Court had ruled in 1956 that bus segregation in Montgomery, Alabama, was unconstitutional, Klan activity throughout the South continued unabated. Curiously, the racial and political tensions prevalent throughout the South seemed not to have had a direct impact on Walker's creative imagination at this time.

Shelby read the final version by early August: "It's a real good book. Partly this is because you're working from a point of view well beyond anything you've ever shown before. I take it as the best of all possible signs, a sort of breakthrough of the spirit. The genesis, I guess, was 'The Man on a Train' piece. But wherever it came [from] it came just fine. I take it, now, you are ready for whatever it is you want to do. I don't think for a minute you are anything like ready to give up fiction, as you said. This is more in the nature of a beginning; I think you must think so, too." Shelby particularly liked the sense of place—New Orleans and its suburbs. He found only two short passages he did not like and thought the "last third [of the novel] gets so caught up in the story itself and the excitement of the big change of scene, so self-involved, that it changes in tone as well." For one thing, Binx was no longer a real moviegoer except that he remembered Rory from time to time. Shelby also enjoyed the fact that Walker mentioned *Arabia Deserta*. "All I can say is I like it fine and I hope you keep on working in this very vein. I enjoyed it from start to finish and always with a sense of wonder. I congratulate you." The genuine approbation of his best friend pleased Walker greatly.

On the last day of August, Kauffmann informed the treasurer that both Alfred and Blanche Knopf had authorized picking up Walker's option.[25] He wrote Miss Otis at the beginning of September formally accepting the novel and enclosing a check for $750.[26] He also wrote Walker: "In addition to the enthusiasm we feel when a fine work comes our way, we're especially happy in this instance because of the long labor you've gone through to bring the book to its best shape."[27] Since nobody at Knopf liked *Carnival in Gentilly*, Stanley suggested the "perfect title," *The Moviegoer*—short, memorable, provocative, and in this case it had a "satirical-intelligent-serious implication." The new title would give ample grounds for promotional and advertising ideas. If they could find the right way to describe Binx in the context of the movie theme, they would have greatly widened the promotional net. Walker replied immediately, expressing relief that the book would finally be published and agreeing to the new title.[28] He listed some legal concerns with libel that bothered him. Was it libelous to put William Holden on Royal Street after filming a scene in the Place d'Armes? Was it libelous to say "as extinguished in her soul as Eva Marie Saint," when Walker had no idea of her private life at all? Was it libelous to make Uncle Jules Rex of Mardi Gras and Aunt Em the recipient of *The Times-Picayune* cup when they were not? Walker had also learned from Shelby that the Cutrer family name occurs in several of Tennessee Williams's plays, and that in *Suddenly Last Summer* a Mrs. Cutrer lives in the Garden district. He was willing to change the name, but wanted Kauffmann's input first. Once again Walker thanked Kauffmann for his patient and penetrating criticism and said he would attend to the final suggestions right away. (A discerning critic whom Walker consulted at this time about his health—and the world of literature—was Arthur Silverman, M.D., his physician.[29]) Not one to enjoy having his picture taken, Walker drove to Hazel Ogden's studio in Covington and sat for a series of eight portrait shots. The one he sent Knopf shows him wearing a rumpled shirt, eyes looking slightly off-camera, with a hint of a smile.

Kauffmann acknowledged Walker's letter and was pleased that he liked *The Moviegoer* as a title. He again raised his concern about a key issue in the novel—the search: "Its general area might be indicated, I think, so that no reader, no matter how well disposed, will finish the book feeling that you had either omitted to define it or had teased him. In other words, the absence of definition ought to be clearly an indication of its indefinability."[30] As for matters of possible libel, they posed no problem; in fact, their legal advisors, Sterns & Reubens, had assured him Knopf would not be subject to libel on any of the matters he had cited. He added that Shelby had the names confused; the woman in *Suddenly Last Summer* was Mrs. Venable and there were no Cutrers in the play. (Shelby realized he had seen the Cutrer name, actually Carol Cutrere, in another Williams play, *Orpheus Descending*.) It would not be long before Walker would actually hold in his hands, as Shelby termed it—borrowing a phrase from D. H. Lawrence—"the one bright book of life."

By mid-September, having acted upon all of Kauffmann's suggestions and adding a few changes of his own, Walker sent him the final text.[31] Kauffmann was pleased with all the changes: "The few pages about the search, the new material at the fishing camp, and the revised telephone conversation at the end—these in particular help very much indeed. In fact they contain some of the best writing in the book."[32] Walker talked a bit about the fishing-camp episode, indicating that Binx believes in the resurrection because Lonnie will be able to water-ski in heaven. Kate hears him but doesn't understand. "What he has told them is—they have asked him if there is going to be a resurrection and if Lonnie is going to be resurrected and is going to be fine. He says, 'Yes.' Now Kate hears this but she doesn't believe he means this. So this is how I, as a novelist, am being indirect with the reader. Is he being very nice with the kids or is he telling the truth?"[33] This passage is clearly Walker's salute to Dostoevsky; at the end of *The Brothers Karamazov*, Kolya asks Alyosha, "Is it true what religion teaches, that we shall all rise from the dead, that we shall live again and see one another again?" And Alyosha says, "Certainly, we shall be resurrected."

Kauffmann wondered if Walker would have any objection to being identified as a relative of William Alexander Percy; in fact, Walker was pleased to dedicate the book to Uncle Will.[34] In-house editors still had a few lingering comments about the novel. Ralph Woodward thought the novel "intriguing," though "puzzling," but "quite original in its point of view." It was a novel "with an 'open end' offering the reader (or demanding of him) a considerable latitude of understanding and interpretation of the ideas the author is playing with."[35] While it suffered from comparison with the works of Salinger, Buechner, and Updike, Woodward felt it belonged in the same ballpark with them.

In the face of these belated negative points, Walker's own assessment and interpretation of the novel placed it squarely within a European philosophical tradition:

Although philosophy is usually regarded in this country as a dry and abstract subject, it is one of the features of modern European thought that it focuses on concrete life-situations rather than abstractions. In particular, of course, it is mainly interested in the predicament of modern man, afflicted as he is with feelings of uprootedness, estrangement, anxiety and the like. It is quite natural, therefore, for philosophers like Sartre and Marcel to write plays and novels. It also seemed natural to me to express my ideas in a novel. And to give a more practical reason, people would rather read a novel than an article.

My novel is an attempt to portray the rebellion of two young people against the shallowness and tastelessness of modern life. The rebellion takes different forms. In Kate, it manifests itself through psychiatric symptoms: anxiety, suicidal tendencies and the like. In Binx, it is a "metaphysical" rebellion—a search for meaning which is the occasion of a rather antic life in a suburb of New Orleans (the action spans one week, Mardi Gras week, in New Orleans). The antecedents of this book are European rather than American: Dostoevsky, Rilke, and especially Albert Camus.[36]

Though Walker wanted to thank him in the book with a note of acknowledgement, Kauffmann demurred, since he did not want to distract the reader from the book's content, nor would it be fair to single him out when others had also read the typescript.[37] There was one more item to attend to: one of the editors at Knopf had suggested that the book start with a brief epigraph, possibly from Kierkegaard—"One brief piercing knife-thrust from Kierkegaard or another might do much to jolt alive the right nerves in the reader even before he gets to your first sentence."[38] Walker liked the idea and provided a quote from *The Sickness unto Death*: ". . . the specific character of despair is precisely this: it is unaware of being despair."

Walker met Shelby in Vicksburg on Friday, October 7, and they spent the weekend touring the battlefield and environs. Shelby looked forward to serving as tour guide for what he considered "about the most fascinating single campaign of the war."[39] But an unexpected battle was being waged within the Knopf offices.

Before leaving for Europe, Alfred Knopf decided to fire Stanley Kauffmann and deputized one of his assistants to confront him with the news. In an internal office memo, Knopf had already signaled his intention to have Angus Cameron replace Kauffmann: "When we come to make publication plans for Percy's novel *The Moviegoer*, please be sure to consult the editorial record and particularly Mr. Cameron's report on the manuscript."[40] Walker was dismayed to learn of Knopf's decision. Had it been made a year before, he wrote Kauffmann, "I'd have been the loser."[41] Kauffmann replied that for him a chief pleasure being at Knopf had been his association with Walker and *The Moviegoer*.[42] For Percy, he had proved to be an excellent, forthright, diligent editor and the first person to see his possibilities as a novelist. Angus Cameron quickly assured Walker he would try to be an effective substitute: "I feel sure I can be useful to the novel, since I am an admirer of it and have been close to Mr. Kauffmann's own interest and work with the novel."[43]

Having succeeded in getting his novel accepted for publication, Walker felt ready to leave their residence on Military Road and move closer to town. For one thing, it meant less commuting time to take the girls to school. The Percys sold their house to George and Louise Cross in March 1961, and by the second week of July were in the new house off Jahnke Avenue that had belonged to Clarisse Grima. Moving closer to town meant they would also see their friends more often, with the result that the girls acquired more playmates, something crucial for Ann's future development, especially as she had no deaf friends in Covington. The new house (for which they paid $65,000, half immediately, the remainder in five equal annual installments), built of brick in the style of an English château with the front door flanked by two floor-to-ceiling windows, had three bedrooms and a fireplace. Since Walker never liked a formal dining room, the screened-in porch that faced the Bogue Falaya functioned for both formal and informal meals when the weather was congenial. The house was close to Covington, yet far enough out of town to give the Percys all the privacy they needed. It was definitely a good move for Ann; she received all A's on her first-grade report card and missed only two days of school in the second semester. Though Mary Pratt was most reluctant to move, she was persuaded to do so by her father's bribe of water skis.

Walker made a retreat at Manresa—this time with his brother Phin and Dick Faust, under the direction of John A. Cronin, S.J.—during the first few days of December 1961. Though technically an Episcopalian, Phin liked and enjoyed the silence of the devotions, and even a chance to say the Rosary. Walker never put any pressure on Phin about Roman

Catholicism. Once Phin asked him, "If the head of the Mafia came for a retreat and went to confession and died, would he go to heaven?" Walker shrugged, "Oh, I don't know about any of that."[44]

After Christmas, Walker, while pondering his next novel, tentatively entitled *Ground Zero*, corrected the galleys. It was not a coincidence that, just as Walker was putting finishing touches on *The Moviegoer*, his essay "The Symbolic Structure of Interpersonal Processes" appeared in the February 1961 issue of *Psychiatry*. His research drew on the writings of David Rioch, Harry Stack Sullivan, George H. Mead, Edward Sapir, Charles Morris, Susanne Langer, Martin Buber, Paul Weiss, Ernst Cassirer, Lucien Lévy-Bruhl, and Alfred North Whitehead. In spelling out his thesis, Walker reached back to his days as an analysand. Though he believed in the primary role that social interaction played in the genesis of the psyche, it concealed a deep ambiguity he hoped to rectify. He thought it called into question the behavioristic theory of interpersonal processes, by outlining the generic structure of symbolic behavior and by examining its relevance for the therapist-patient relationship. Walker's conclusion almost seemed to put Binx and his own persona in the shadows. Although a patient may have failed and needed help, "he enjoys a privileged status vis-à-vis the people out there in the street. They don't know what we know. They don't even know about themselves what we know about them. Thus the we-community of scientists—I, the therapist, and you, the patient but also now the surrogate-scientist—can become the means by which the patient's low self-esteem is offset by Thalesian insights into himself and the society he lives in." It is not without biographical significance that Walker returned to the interaction in the psychiatrist's office at the very time he was exploring Binx's psyche.

By April 3, well before the official publication date (May 15), ten copies of *The Moviegoer* were shipped to Walker. Knopf had not banked on this novel becoming a best-seller, and the first modest run was modified to 5,000 copies, according to a "Planning Card" in their files.[45] Approximately ninety-five review copies were sent to newspapers and journals throughout the country, including copies to Dorothy Parker, Granville Hicks, and Ben Wasson in Greenville. Alfred Knopf received a phone call in early April from an elderly friend in New Orleans raving about the novel and calling it "the first American novel which can be called Existentialist which hasn't one word of philosophy in it."[46] This indicated to Cameron that the book would appeal to several generations of readers at the same time. Mr. Knopf told Cameron he was pleased with the novel too and asked him to do a write-up for the "Borzoi Quarterly" (a promotional newsletter put out by Knopf), which Cameron did by linking it with Uncle Will's *Lanterns on the Levee*. For her part, Miss Otis found the book's binding and typography "particularly pleasant," and added, "Let's hope and pray that it gets off the ground."[47] Walker said he was thrilled at seeing the books and thought the jacket "fine."[48] He was anxious to read the early reviewers. He sent and inscribed one of his copies to Stanley Kauffmann.[49]

One of the first printed comments came from Warren Miller, a fiction writer and critic for *Show*: "What a marvelous novel it is. It should win every prize going for first novels this year. Although it is absurd to talk about this book as a first novel, it has all the assurance and skill of a book written by a man who knows everything there is to know about the novel . . . What a fine writer he is! I hope you all realize that what we have got is a *Catcher in the Rye* for adults."[50] Cleanth Brooks, the eminent literary critic, visited Walker and Bunt just after the publication of *The Moviegoer* with his wife, Edith Amy ("Tinkum"), a member of the Blanchard family of New Orleans. Brooks recalled that during his afternoon with the Percys the "air was warm but fresh," and Percy's house "seemed a place capable of calling forth good talk and good stories. The Percys abounded in both."[51] To honor Walker and his new book, Jaye and Phin had a party at their home. The reviewer in the May 19 issue of *Time* declared the novel to be a success "clothed in originality, intelligence and a fierce regard for man's fate." The reviewer said the novel focused on despair attacking the inmost mind, and the author's style blended "seriousness and humor." Walker clearly passed the test of *Time*. Though Cameron felt that the low budget for a first novel adversely affected the amount of publicity it received, he also believed Knopf would spend more money on advertising if the reviews were good.[52] In an office memo, Cameron was pleased that *Time* had compared Walker's novel with Uncle Will's book, but unfortunately sales remained slight.[53] The reviews trickled in slowly. When he read the novel belatedly, novelist J. F. Powers wrote Walker a personal note of congratulations.[54] On April 1, *Kirkus Reviews* reported in its usual pseudo-academic jargon: "It is an unaccented but tantalizing projection—of the suspension of self in a limbo without responsibility—without reality, and there will be those who will find that this kind of 'dark pilgrimage,' the indifferent prowling, frittering, shadow-walking—'like Banquo's ghost'—is curiously fascinating while elusive." Charles Poore in *The New York Times* gave it a generally favorable review, and Robert Massie in *The New York Times Book Review* wrote that Binx was a "bewildered" but an "amiable hero." He noted that Walker's interest in psychiatry was evident in the way he probed the mainsprings of his characters. "Nothing is stated; everything is implied. The reader gets fragments of meaning and occasional glimpses of deep-rooted causes. Yet so expertly are these fragments fitted together and these glimpses sustained that Binx and Kate grow steadily in character throughout the book. A memorable last scene makes it clear what kind of people they are." He praised Walker for reproducing the flavor, spirit, and dialogue of New Orleans with "marvelous accuracy." When Caroline Gordon read *The Moviegoer*, she admired it and wrote the publisher from Princeton: "I think it is an important work and I will try to review it for some periodical."[55] She requested they send a copy to Seán O'Faoláin, a writer-in-residence at Princeton; it was dispatched the next day. A review by Lon Cheney that would appear in *The Southern Review*, written with insight and clarity, concluded that Walker had "restored for us here the image of God that was fragmented by the humanists." The novel was well received in Catholic journals of opinion. Harold Gardiner, S.J., noted in *America* that it was commendable for its "wonderful evocation of the spirit of time and place," and Edwin Kennebeck, writing in *Commonweal*, said that the novel leads us through "layers of soft dreams and crusty realities to discover in one man's soul the core of compassion." But the novel had not really garnered the widespread attention Walker had hoped for.

During the third week of May, Walker flew to New York with Mary Pratt, followed a day later by Bunt, to attend the wedding of his old friend Frank Hardart to Frances O'Connor. Walker had not seen Frank since their trip following graduation from medical school. Walker had much to catch up on, especially concerning Frank's war years in Japan. Fran, a graduate of Manhattanville College, who had studied for a year in Florence, was a perfect match for Frank. At the bachelor party, Walker met Fran's father, George, her brother, Tom, and some old friends from his P&S days, including Bob Gehres. Walker took Bunt and Mary Pratt to see *Camelot*, the musical with Richard Burton and Julie Andrews, Ionesco's *Rhinoceros* with Laurence Olivier and Joan Plowright, and *The Unsinkable Molly Brown* with Tammy Grimes.

Walker also met with Cameron and mentioned his nonfiction project, which was a bit indefinite, as well as his next work of fiction.[56] Cameron and Miss Otis were both upset by the lack of reviews, even though Knopf did run a small ad in the Sunday *New York Times*. It was during this trip that he and Stanley Kauffmann met at the Plaza.[57] "Yes, Walker," Kauffmann consoled his friend, "the reviews could have been better and more plentiful, but don't become distressed about it." They both realized they were going through a mutual therapy. Yet Kauffmann, remembering Browning's "There shall never be one lost good," knew that some goods take a long time before they are discovered.

The Hardart wedding party traveled to Waterford, New York, for the ceremony at St. Mary's Church. Unfortunately, Walker came down with a severe case of hives (among other things, he was allergic to kiwi-fruit), and decided to return to New Orleans for medical treatment.

The Moviegoer enjoyed popular appeal in the South (Flannery O'Connor, for one, was delighted with the novel), and there were signs that it might become popular outside the United States.[58] When William Koshland of Knopf attended the Frankfurt Book Fair in the fall, Woefestein Lieber of the firm of K.H.B. Rabinow of Frankfurt expressed an interest in the German translation rights, an indication that Walker would soon attract an international following.[59] By September, several people in Covington, including a librarian, told Walker that the novel was unavailable. "I'd greatly appreciate knowing what is going on— whether or not the book is obtainable and if not, how come?" Walker wrote to Cameron. "Is the printing sold out?"[60] A problem for Knopf was that its sales department had merged with that of Random House —but Walker was assured there was ample stock.[61] According to the Knopf Advertising Report that month, 5,500 copies were in print, of which 3,457 had been sold.

By this time Ann, age seven, and Mary Pratt, age fourteen, had established their own routines. Ann was becoming more independent and neighbors could see her riding her bicycle (she had two mirrors on the handlebars to watch out for traffic behind her). Mary Pratt started her freshman year in the fall at St. Scholastica's, staffed by the Benedictine sisters and a number of laypeople. Walker continued lunching with his cronies, a habit that started in the late 1950s, when William Gibert and Chink Baldwin called up Walker and the trio started a Wednesday lunch group Walker attended for the rest of his days in Covington. Its makeup varied from week to week and Walker felt comfortable with his peer group. These luncheons provided a touchstone to the concerns of the larger community. As years went by, Dick Faust and William Boatner Reily III joined, as did Paul Gibert and Phin; the group would change restaurants as cooks changed. A new coadjutor archbishop, John P. Cody, had been appointed to assist Archbishop Rummel, a sign that things might change for the Catholic community in New Orleans. Dick Faust, whose ideas reflected a good deal of the sentiment of Southern Catholics, perhaps in reaction that summer to the papal encyclical *Mater et Magistra*, felt that the views expressed by John XXIII on the relationship between Christianity and social progress were appropriate, but he had some disagreement with parts of the encyclical.[62] Faust was an ardent states' rights supporter. Walker viewed the situation from a historical perspective, evoked by the centennial of the Civil War. In his *Commonweal* article "Red, White, and Blue-Gray," he maintained that in "the popular media the [Civil] War is so friendly that the fighting is made to appear as a kind of sacrament of fire by which one side expresses its affection for the other." He acknowledged that the Confederate flag was not a racist symbol, though often used as one. "The symbol is the same, but the referent has changed"—words he would repeat later in a different context. As a born Southerner, he knew that states' rights and the Southern Way of Life meant different things to different people: "In New Orleans, which has a delightful way of life, the 'Southern Way of Life' usually means 'Let's Keep McDonogh [School] No. 6 Segregated.' " Above all, the Civil War reconciled Anglo-Saxons of both sides with each other. But with whom is a black man or woman reconciled? "Who would have supposed that a hundred years later Northern cities would have large, undigested and mostly demoralized black ghettos, which Conant recently described as the most explosive element of American life?" Though Walker hoped that the United States would ameliorate racial problems, he did not, like many Berliners, know where to begin to breach the wall that divided the nation.

9

Working on
The Last Gentleman
1962–65

Early in 1962 Walker could take heart over his new project. *Time* listed *The Moviegoer* as one of the ten best novels of 1961, calling the author a "natural writer." He worked on his second novel, *The Last Gentleman*, every morning and on his nonfiction in the afternoon. The prospects for both books interested Angus Cameron, his new editor, who feared that Knopf's contractual tether on Walker might become loose. At this point Walker was not convinced that either of his new efforts would amount to much: "Have known for some time what I want to do, but they still mightn't come off," he wrote to Cameron. "What I would like to do is reach a point in one or the other where I can see through to the end, or at least over the hump. Then send you what I've got."[1]

Shelby, delighted by the birth of his son, Huger Lee, also expressed interest in Walker's novel-in-progress: "Have you settled on *The Fall Out* [a tentative title]? Or wouldn't it whip into shape? I don't recommend a three-month goof-off, such as the one I just passed through, but it does do wonders toward putting things back into perspective." Walker made many notes for his novel, sketched out tentative scenes, and gave names to some potential characters—in short, he creatively doodled. His protagonist, Williston Bibb Barrett, travels from New York to Birmingham and Greenville (Ithaca), ending up in Santa Fe, four cities that figure prominently in Walker's life.[2] The novel was to be a symbolic and mythic voyage homeward for Will, leading to the City of Holy Faith. In Will he was creating a character very much like himself, making of the novel an exploration into the depths of his own psyche and drawing from his own life experiences. In Will Barrett, as both seer and seeker, there are glimpses of Walker Percy the person. Walker felt the title could refer either to Will Barrett or Will's father, Ed Barrett. Walker wrote to one critic,[3] indicating that he usually assented to any or all interpretations of his work and enumerating the relationships between real and literary figures:

1. Williston, the name of a famous Harvard Law School professor.

2. Bibb and Barrett, old aristocratic Alabama surnames.

3. Chandler Vaught, a connection with Chance-Vaught Aircraft, manufacturer of military planes.

4. Dr. Moon Mullins, after the comic-strip character.

5. Kitty, after memories of Kitty in *Anna Karenina*.

6. Sutter, derived from the man who made the first California gold strike ("Has Sutter found the gold Will is looking for?").

7. Val, modeled on Mother Johnette Putnam, O.S.B. (from her given name, Valentine).

8. Fannin, the name of a street in Shreveport, associated with the song "Fannin Street."

9. Milo Menander, reminiscent of Leander Perez, the notorious Louisianan segregationist.

10. Doc Holliday, an actual person from Georgia who later became a Wild West gunslinger.

11. Father Boomer, most likely suggested by a character in one of Graham Greene's novels.

12. The Engineer, perhaps an echo of Thomas Mann's Hans Castorp, who Walker remembered was called "the Engineer."

Walker also mentioned that the likely source of his title was not Tennyson's poem but Malory's *Le Morte d'Arthur* as filtered through Walter Scott (mainly *Ivanhoe*, and particularly *The Boy's "King Arthur"*). "It is impossible to overemphasize the influence of Scott on that and earlier Southern generations. Scott, as much as Harriet Beecher Stowe, was responsible for the Civil War." Walker was in touch with Perrine Dixon in Tesuque, New Mexico, who supplied the texts of the carved quotations he wanted on the monument in the city's main plaza.[4] (In the novel Sutter's ex-wife Rita lives in Tesuque.)

By the third week of February *The Moviegoer* was nominated for the National Book Award in fiction, along with ten others, including Joseph Heller's *Catch-22*, William Maxwell's *The Château*, J. D. Salinger's *Franny and Zooey*, Bernard Malamud's *A New Life*, and Isaac Bashevis Singer's *The Spinoza of Market Street*. When Walker heard this news, he phoned Stanley Kauffmann in New York:

"Stanley?" (pause)

"Walker?" (pause)

And they began laughing for a whole minute, as they remembered their last conversation. Walker also wrote Kauffmann: "Don't expect to win, but it's nice being a contender. Thanks to your heavy editorial hand. Am presently spinning my wheels."⁵ On March 8 Harding ("Pete") Lemay of Knopf wired Walker the astonishing news that he had won the award! Walker flew to New York, as did Gwyn and Shelby, and they all stayed at the Algonquin; Bunt remained at home to take care of the girls. Walker had a happy reunion in town with Kauffmann. He also paid a visit to the Frank Hardarts in their apartment near St. Vincent's Hospital. A pregnant Fran was delighted to greet their unexpected guest: "Walker, *why* are you here?" "Oh, they're doing some things about this book I wrote." "What things?" "Oh, I'm getting an award."⁶

Though Robert Loomis, Shelby's editor at Random House, gave a party honoring Walker, the heads of Knopf were remarkably cool toward the award to this author. The publishing gossip was that Mr. Knopf wanted *The Château* to win and was "miffed" about *The Moviegoer*. Blanche Knopf, who lived separately from her husband, had a small get-together for Walker, to which she invited a few of her friends and staff members, including Pete Lemay, but not her husband. At one awkward moment, Blanche pointed to her shelves of Knopf books inscribed by Thomas Mann, Willa Cather, Albert Camus, et al., but she failed to ask Walker to sign his book.⁷ When he later met his publisher briefly, Walker asked him, "Mr. Knopf, how do you think this book will sell?" Knopf replied, "I've been in the publishing business for fifty years and to this day I don't have the slightest idea why a novel sells when it sells or why it doesn't sell when it doesn't."⁸

The fiction judges of the award were critic Lewis Gannett and novelists Herbert Gold and Jean Stafford. It was Jean Stafford—according to her friend and editor, Robert Giroux, and the publisher of her first novel, *Boston Adventure*, in 1944—who was directly responsible for *The Moviegoer* winning the award, since Knopf had *not* submitted it to the judges (though they had submitted *The Château*). She told Bob that A. J. Liebling, her husband, who was in New Orleans researching a book on Earl Long, liked it so much that he sent it on to her. She was impressed with its originality and requested copies for her fellow judges, both of whom later agreed with her about its superiority.⁹ Alfred Knopf was said to have grumbled about "a conspiracy engineered by Joe Liebling," who was a disaffected former Knopf author. Jean Stafford laughed this rumor to scorn: she had no meeting or conversation with either judge prior to the vote and *The Moviegoer* won unanimously on the first ballot. The judges' citation, the first draft of which was Stafford's, was slightly emended by her colleagues and read as follows:

The Moviegoer, an intimation rather than a statement of mortality and the inevitability of that condition, is a truthful novel with shocks of recognition and spasms of nostalgia for every—or nearly every—American. Mr. Percy, with compassion and without sentimentality or the mannerisms of the clinic, examines the delusions and hallucinations and the daydreams and the dreads that afflict those who abstain from the customary ways of making do.

Walker was particularly pleased to win out over *Catch-22*. At the ceremony on March 13, editor (and future publisher) Seymour Lawrence was surprised to see Alfred Knopf rise abruptly from his chair and leave the Astor ballroom.[10] In his report on the ceremony, Gay Talese quoted Stanley Kauffmann: "I heard that Mr. Knopf was baffled and somewhat irritated by this novel, which I, and now some very distinguished people, think very beautiful."[11] In his speech at the ceremony, Walker thanked everyone concerned, especially Miss Otis and Kauffmann. He said he had not been to New York in twenty years. Mentioning his experiences at Bellevue, he noted that his intention was not to say our culture is dying or all that remains is an autopsy, as a pathologist might do; the novel was merely a story, and unlike pathology, its function was to give pleasure to readers. Yet the posture of *The Moviegoer*, he added, was the posture of the pathologist with his suspicion that something is wrong. In this case the pathology had to do with the loss of individuality and the loss of identity at the very time when words like "the dignity of the individual" and "self-realization" were being heard more frequently than ever:

Yet the patient is not mortally ill. On the contrary, it speaks well for the national health that pathologists of one sort and another are tolerated and even encouraged. In short, the book attempts a modest restatement of the Judeo-Christian notion that man is more than an organism in an environment, more than an integrated personality, more even than a mature and creative individual, as the phrase goes. He is a wayfarer and a pilgrim.

Immediately after leaving the ceremony, Knopf wrote to Stanley Kauffmann: "I want to congratulate you, even at this late date, on the early confidence you showed in Walker Percy," to which Kauffmann replied, "Thanks for your note. It's pleasant, of course, to have one's opinion substantiated."[12] President Kennedy also sent his personal congratulations to all three winners.

After Hugh Downs introduced "Dr. Walker" on the *Today* show, the Percy family and their friends in Covington hung on Walker's every word.[13] (John Chancellor was supposed to interview Walker on television, and had the Book Committee known that he could not be there, they would have canceled Walker's appearance.[14]) After the broadcast, a proud and beaming Mary Pratt showed up late for school. Roy told a reporter in Greenville that Walker had worked a year and a half on the book, writing eight hours a day.[15]

The next day there was a reviewers' seminar at Columbia University's School of Journalism. Walker, whose photo appeared in *The New York Times* that morning, said he had no knowledge of how he won the award.[16] A. J. Liebling of *The New Yorker* confirmed what his wife had told Bob Giroux; he said he had read a favorable review of *The Moviegoer*, bought a copy of it, and called it to the attention of his wife, who liked it very much. Yet the question lingered: did Jean Stafford put undue pressure on the other two judges? All three judges wrote to Walker saying they had voted independently of one another (Gold and Gannett were a continent apart when they read the novel).[17] Talese speculated, "Apparently [Stafford] convinced the other two fiction judges on the merits of the novel, it was learned on good authority," but the other judges refused to comment publicly on their choice.[18] After reading an unsigned editorial in the June issue of *Show*, Joe Liebling set the record straight.[19] He had not put pressure on his wife and knew that Gold and Gannett, "two independent souls," would make up their own minds. Liebling felt that Alfred Knopf had treated his new author at the ceremony "like an erring daughter with child at breast." At the Columbia seminar Liebling maintained that Knopf had not pushed *The Moviegoer* —something he later wished he had not uttered. When Liebling asked Talese where he had learned "on good authority" that Stafford had apparently convinced her fellow judges how to vote, Talese told him that his informer worked at Knopf.

It was not until March 19 that Walker read the Talese article in Covington. "This is the first inkling I've had of what happened," he informed Kauffmann.[20] His letter to Jean Stafford was his own attempt to set the record straight:

A lot of things are becoming clear to me for the first time. Due to the confusion of the occasion plus inherent social inhibitions, I failed to click on what must have been fairly obvious . . .

But what I mean is that while I received certain brain waves recording the suspicion that it was you who had a great deal more to do with the award than you allowed—I had no idea what the real story was. Nor when you told me Wednesday night during Mr. Liebling's speaking at the seminar at the Columbia Graduate School of Journalism did I make out what you were saying. It was only this morning—when I got back from a week-end at the Gulf Coast and got a letter from Mrs. Dudley of the National Book Committee enclosing a story by Gay Talese in the *Times* about Mr. Liebling's and your role in the award—that the light has at last dawned.

Knowing that you have already forgiven my obtuseness, I will ask you to pass on to Mr. Liebling the gratitude which I am only just now making out the dimensions of. (I'll call him Joe if you all come to Louisiana—right now the habit of literary respect is too great.) If I understand it correctly, had it not been for Mr. Liebling (and his recent interest in Louisiana) *The Moviegoer* might never, would never have been considered. To think then, that if it hadn't been for old Earl, etc. For the first time, I feel kindly toward the Longs.

As to Knopf's remissness, I know nothing of that—have no standards by which to compare his handling of the book—and after all am glad that he did publish it.

So even though I must have returned your and Mr. Liebling's kindness very shabbily . . . you and Mr. Liebling must once again accept my very great gratitude.

Aside from all that, it was also a great privilege to meet at last an old friend, the Boston adventuress.[21]

But the last word had not been heard. *Saturday Review* carried a statement by Stafford on October 6, defending her part in the awards: "The newspaper story was factually incorrect and its implications were irresponsible and misleading. I wish to correct the impression that my husband bossed me in the first place and I bossed Mr. Gannett and Mr. Gold in the second. The jury reached a unanimous decision to grant the award to Mr. Percy, whose novel all of us admire."[22] This controversy surfaced again in 1971 when Alfred Kazin brought it up in an article in *Harper's*. Stafford wrote the magazine a letter saying that Joe Liebling had no influence on her decision, even though she admitted they had similar tastes in many things. "Though he didn't like Henry James," she continued, "I made no attempt to convert him; he did try to convert me to Hemingway, with a singular (and rather noisy) want of success."[23] At a dinner party she and Joe gave in her apartment on lower Fifth Avenue, she discovered how "personally charming" Walker was.[24] In replying to Lewis Gannett in California, Walker tried to calm the critical waters: "As a reader of your book review column for many years, I can say that absolutely the last thought to enter my head is that you could have been influenced to a decision about anything by anybody. Miss Stafford has been very kind indeed, but I was made uneasy on your and Mr. Gold's account by *The New York Times* account of the small literary flap, and on the whole was glad to get back to my Louisiana bayou."[25] Whether or not it was unfortunate that such a flap occurred, Walker handled it as well as anyone could have done. Even Shelby commented on the situation: "Too bad old Alfred wouldn't get off his ass, but you know well enough money wouldn't make you happy."

No doubt Mr. Knopf was annoyed by reports of his behavior. He wrote Walker expressing the hope that he was not upset by what had transpired at the Columbia seminar. "We have been working hard on *The Moviegoer*, have put a lot of copies out into the bookstores—you know by now, of course, that [the stores] can return everything they don't sell after an all-too-short period of time—and [we] are printing another edition."[26] In replying to his Aunt Bo Spalding's congratulatory note, Walker revealed that the trip to New York had used up a good bit of the $1,000 prize money.[27] He mentioned that the paperback rights to the book had been sold to Popular Library, which was expected to publish between 175,000 and 250,000 copies in May at fifty cents a copy.[28] The sales for the cloth edition seemed to be picking up; in the last week of March, it sold 440 copies, after 1,300 for the week before. Another 2,000 were printed in the second week of April. By the end of May, the novel had sold 7,073 copies, and a third printing was in the works. By late fall over 300,000 paperback copies were printed and distributed. When Walker received his first copy of this edition, he thought Popular had done "a very pretty job," and was grateful they did not put a naked woman on the cover.[29]

When he returned home, Walker received a letter he would treasure: "I'm glad we lost the [Civil] War," Flannery O'Connor wrote, "and you won the National Book Award. I didn't think the judges would have that much sense but they suprized [sic] me. Regards."[30] A few months later, Walker confided to Caroline Gordon, in uncharacteristic fashion, that he needed all the help he could get on his new novel, since he had decided to shift from an "I" narrator to an omniscient one, thus discarding much of the armor Gordon had previously supplied:

Actually I do not consider myself a novelist but a moralist or a propagandist. My spiritual father is Pascal (and/or Kierkegaard). And if I also kneel before the altar of Lawrence and Joyce and Flaubert, it is not because I wish to do what they did, even if I could. What I really want to do is to tell people what they must do and what they must believe if they want to live. Using every guile and low-handed trick in the book of course . . .

The problem which all but throws me all the time is this: how does a Catholic fiction writer handle the Catholic Faith in his novel? I am not really writing to get your answer because I think I already know it—that you don't worry about it—do what Augustine said: love God and do as you please. But this doesn't help much. (Actually the only reason I can raise the question now is that I can see the glimmerings of an answer.) Dostoevsky knew the answer.

But to show you that I am not imagining the problem: *The Moviegoer* was almost universally misunderstood. Its most enthusiastic admirers were precisely those people who misunderstood it worst. It was received as a novel of "despair"—not a novel about despair but as a novel ending in despair. Even though I left broad hints that such was not at all the case. Jack Bolling says, for example, that as far as his search is concerned, he is not inclined to say how it came out, since like Kierkegaard he does not believe he "has the authority to speak of such things." Also, when one of the children asks him at the end if it is true Our Lord will raise up on the last day, he replies simply: yes.[31]

Walker's letter to Jidge Milazzo, written before he saw her in early May in New Orleans, likewise showed that he was concerned that the novel communicated a message of despair: "OK, Jidge, I got your message, which was very shrewd and hit home. *The Moviegoer* should be received as an account of how it was before, a kind of pre-Christian pilgrimage, which it was. Thanks for digging it. The response to the book has been very gratifying and confusing. My warmest admirers usually totally misunderstood the book. They usually read it as a novel of despair, rather than a novel about despair but with hope, which was my intention. I am not even sure I didn't get the prize for the wrong reasons."[32] Intuitively Walker realized that a genuine religious writer must learn how to shout in silence.

Once Alfred Knopf saw the increased sales figures, he considered Walker in a new light. In a letter written in late May, he asked, "Anything for me to read yet?"[33] Yet Walker had not sent either Angus Cameron or Miss Otis any of his new novel, mainly because he had very little to show ("Saying that one is writing two books at once sounds good, but it is also a good way of writing neither").[34]

Another reason Walker put off writing was that he took the family to a chilly Los Angeles to seek more help for Ann. They visited the HEAR Foundation and acquired a transistorized Vicon Hearing Aid, with halter and packet, that was attached to both of Ann's ears to create a binaural effect for any possible residual hearing. For Mary Pratt, it was the chance to acquire her own Hans Hauser guitar. When they returned, Walker kept up his daily routine, writing a review of three Southern novels for *Commonweal*. Now there were out-of-towners waiting to spot him going into the post office each morning or slipping into the side door at St. Peter's on Sunday; still, he believed he was less well known in his hometown than the local beer distributor. By early June, he had finished 148 pages of the new work, now called *Ground Zero*. He sent it off to Miss Otis and she forwarded a copy to Kauffmann for his critique. Kauffmann's perceptive reply was most encouraging:

You have a very good novel in the making here, I believe. Whether or not it is better than the last I couldn't possibly say or care . . . I'm not going to dilate just now on the virtues of the book, except to say a) it is almost completely moving and interesting; b) it is full of Percy-type insights and observations that both stab and tickle; c) you seem to have a greater degree of control this time as far as form is concerned. Let me proceed to a few general observations and a few specifics . . .

The book seems a sequence of adventures, a kind of *internal* picaresque novel, rather than a tightly constructed plot, or even a *fairly* tightly constructed one whose general dynamics are clear by this point. I don't have the faintest idea of what's going to happen from now on; but I, as reader, don't want to be let down. You can sustain the book in two ways (and forgive me if I sound magisterial). First, by having at this point a clear idea of where the action is going. Second, more important, by having the thematic action, the rationale, the purpose of the book clearly in mind. (That wasn't always so in *The Moviegoer*, was it?) I don't mean of course that the end should contain an "answer," necessarily; chopped raisins and nuts will save the world, or something. But at least, if there is no "answer" intended, you ought to have clearly in mind the shape of the question and exactly where you're going to put the question mark.[35]

Kauffmann cited particular scenes that needed attention, but his basic message was one of congratulations. Walker was grateful: "Most telling was your sense of unease that a serious premeditated action had not been planned. This can be cured, I think, by reworking the encounter of the young amnesiac with his new 'family.' I can see this was too hurried and slapped together."[36] Walker thought he needed a personal change of scene, to profit from what new locales and a new perspective would offer.

Looking somewhat like the Joads, the four Percys put their packed suitcases on top of their blue Rambler and drove out West. Their goal was to meet up with Sarah and Roy and three of their children at Jackson Hole, Wyoming. They drove from Covington toward Dallas and northward up through Utah, where Walker allowed Mary Pratt to take the wheel on occasion. When they arrived at White Grass Ranch, they spent a week in their cabin dwarfed by large rolling vistas with majestic snow-covered mountains. Ann enjoyed riding a large pinto named Bear Bait. Indoor activities included cooking pies and cobblers in the main lodge, where they took their meals. (The Greenville Percys did not fare so well; they became sick with ptomaine poisoning at a local inn and wound up going to the hospital.) On the return trip, Walker stopped at Santa Fe, where he was unable to find copies of his novel in the bookstores.[37]

Around this point Walker intuitively realized how he should conclude his new novel. If the street names of New Orleans (Annunciation, Elysian Fields, Terpsichore, etc.) had helped to create a *paysage imaginaire* as background for *The Moviegoer*, then Santa Fe could serve a similar role, especially as Will Barrett—and all that his first name implies in the philosophies of Schopenhauer and Nietzsche—ultimately finds himself in this City of Holy Faith. They continued to drive to Amarillo in the Texas panhandle. One memorable night was spent outdoors in Palo Duro Canyon. The Percys had pitched camp just after sunset, inflating their Abercrombie & Fitch tent. While Ann and her mother were sleeping in the car, the deaf daughter was unaware she had placed her foot on the horn. The following night it was Mary Pratt who slept in the car with her mother, and Ann and Walker in the tent. Next summer, as he envisioned a trip to Italy, he expected to have a less hectic time with his family and writing.[38]

In September, Walker received good news about the movie rights of *The Moviegoer*, which he had sold to Ransdell Cox, an architect from New York. Stanley Kauffmann agreed to act as a consultant on the script.[39] Walker was pleased about the film's prospects and agreed to help Kauffmann, though he felt that he had to yield control to the demands of another medium. He would try to remain indifferent to the outcome of the movie, as long as it stayed within the bounds of good taste. When Walker invited Cox and Kauffmann to Covington, the two scriptwriters came to see him in late November. At one point they considered the possibilities of casting the Canadian actor Christopher Plummer as Binx and actress Jane Fonda as Kate. When he read Cox's preliminary script, Walker hardly recognized his novel and conceded that the two media were profoundly different.

Some readers and critics of *The Moviegoer* thought the author had not grappled sufficiently with the character of Kate; she was not as well rounded as Binx. Did Kate, in fact, represent Walker's "real" attitude toward women? Of course not, given the tragedy of his mother's early death, but she did represent some dimension of it. After reading Bruno Bettelheim's "Growing Up Female" in *Harper's*, and Dick Faust's subsequent letter to the editor, Walker shared with Faust his thoughts about Bettelheim's position on women. He believed Bettelheim stated the problem well, "calling attention to the strain of grievance which is to be found in so many modern women. This is a remarkable phenomenon, and it is all the more pronounced in those very women who should, by modern expectations, be freer than ever of grievance. Moreover I thought [Bettelheim] was generally correct in locating the etiology of the grievance: namely in the emphasis among emancipated and educated women in discovering satisfaction from 'emotional relationships,' 'interpersonal encounters' and other such 'goals' of modern psychology."[40] Yet Walker rejected Bettelheim's solution, which seemed "to come down to the suggestion that a woman ought to cultivate a more 'creative' life outside her marriage. This is a rather feeble therapy for the critical dilemma which he posed." Above all, Bettelheim did not take into account the religious and sacramental character of marriage. "But to tell you the truth," Walker concluded, "the article was better than I expected. At least it is a sign of some progress when an analyst recognizes the failure of Freudian technique to come to grips with one's role in life."

One of Walker's real-life heroines was Flannery O'Connor, whom he met only once, due to Henry Montecino, S.J., professor of philosophy at Loyola, who had invited over the years such noted philosophers and writers as Christopher Dawson and Martin D'Arcy, S.J., to the college.[41] Father Montecino's honored guest in November was O'Connor, who spoke in Marquette Hall on religion and literature. Walker was completely bowled over by what she said and kept a copy of her lecture in the house for years.[42] At a party afterward in O'Connor's honor, Father Montecino overheard her and Walker as they talked glowingly about Katherine Anne Porter, even though Walker admitted he had some trouble with O'Connor's Georgia accent.[43]

Walker continued to have difficulty putting the residual presence of *The Moviegoer* out of his mind. Could it be that some unfinished material in *The Moviegoer* might find further expression in his new novel? For example, was the character of Lonnie Smith revisited in Jamie Vaught? As he wrote to Charles Bell, "Hope you do not have as much trouble as I putting your published novel behind you and getting on with something else. Son of a bitch, I'm just now getting with it. It takes a certain amount of neglect and solitariness."[44] Walker hoped that the new year would mean a really new start.

Due to *The Moviegoer*'s growing popularity, Walker's name appeared in the press more and more. Elizabeth Hardwick selected him as one of the twenty-one great American writers in the February issue of *Vogue*. In an issue of *Time*, which listed him as one of the notable new writers, Walker mentioned that his new novel, to be called either *Ground Zero* or *The Fallout*, had a hero who operates Macy's air-conditioning system from a control center seven floors below street level. Walker wrote three different versions; they more or less followed what became the final plot of *The Last Gentleman*, though in one draft Will married Kitty and became manager of her father's insurance company, after which we learn of Sutter's death.[45] In another draft, Sutter tried to kill Jamie by driving him off a bridge into an arroyo.[46] Sutter's notebook citations seem to be a late addition to the novel. One character, a young woman who has not spoken for two years, would develop into Anna in *Lancelot*.

In congratulating Allen Tate for his essay "Narcissus as Narcissus," Walker referred to his own state of mind: "Through a falling out of events which escape me, I find myself ridden by two incubuses who appear to have no necessary connection with each other beyond the fact that there they are together: 'the formal ebullience of the human spirit' of the Confederacy and the solipsism-narcissism of the modern intellectual. Indeed your pairing of these two in the 'Ode' has always struck me, until now, as a shotgun wedding." He ended his letter with a "salute by way of affection and admiration."[47]

When his hay fever began to get the best of him, Walker flew to Key West and spent most of three weeks reading Henry James's *The Golden Bowl*.[48] He brought back a dress for Bunt as a gift. Walker considered his physical problems to be secondary to his creative ones. On the one hand, Penguin had just bought the British paperback rights to *The Moviegoer* and it was also being translated into Italian and Danish; on the other, at midpoint with his second novel, he was experiencing the worst sort of trouble, not knowing how he would complete it.[49] Walker worked extremely hard that summer, so much so that Shelby wrote him in mid-August congratulating him on his progress: "I'm pleased to find you getting at the nub of the thing: what a novel really is. It's shape, a method of releasing experience, of relating words to life." Shelby was expecting publication of the second volume of his Civil War series in November, and he and Gwyn anticipated building a new house at Gulf Shores.

September saw the publication of Walker's essay "Do Fictional Manners Require Sex, Horror?," which explored the relationship in Southern literature of violence and sex.[50] The most obvious characteristic of modern fiction, he stated, is its emphasis on sex and violence—not horror. Has the contemporary novel simply cultivated a four-letter-word mentality? He compared *Gone with the Wind* with Flannery O'Connor's freak-filled stories:

Gone with the Wind is soap opera, extraordinarily well-done readable engaging soap opera, charming as you please, but soap opera, nonetheless, and therefore bearing no serious relation to literature. Not that there were not grand ladies and gallant gentlemen and lovable darkies in the Old South, but rather that *Gone with the Wind* failed to portray them. As for Flannery O'Connor, her stories are creations of the highest order, informed by a tough orthodox Christianity, and plunging like a sword to the depths of the human heart. The preoccupation of the modern novel with sex and violence is not, then, to be dismissed so simply, either by damning or praising. The current trend must be examined more closely, strands untangled, before the good can be separated from the bad.

Yet a problem arises when serious writers see fit to use language that some find offensive. "Sex and violence are used properly when they are used in the interests of the integrity of the work undertaken by the artist. (Incidentally, St. Thomas Aquinas said this first.) They are used improperly when they are calculated to pander indiscriminately to the base instincts—what Arthur Miller called the keyhole sexuality—of the reader." Walker thought that Faulkner's Nobel Prize speech, which deals with the human heart in conflict with itself, provided a good definition of a novel. *Little Women*, *Gone with the Wind*, and *The Cardinal* may all be nice novels, he maintained, "but, please, let us not mention them in the same breath with *The Sound and the Fury*, *Ship of Fools*, and *The Heart of the Matter*." Walker's approach, commonsensical and forthright, showed again that he was willing to take an unpopular position on issues that affected moral thinking.

For different reasons Walker was not at all prepared to like Charles Bell's novel *The Half Gods*, which "purports to be about the Leflores who seem rather obviously modelled after the Percys of Greenville, Miss. I . . . cannot be sure of making out your intention," he wrote to Bell. "What I want to know is what is in your mind. I do not know how to understand you."[51] Apparently Bell thought he had permission to transpose members of Walker's family into a *roman-à-clef*. Walker wrote him again at the University of Rochester: "Yours is a very big gun with a massive charge of powder and I hope you can fire on target without laying waste the surrounding countryside."[52] Walker needed time to cool off from his own interior upheaval: "What I found myself offended at was the suspicion that you were *signalling* to those who might have occasion to know . . . It seemed you might be saying to the reader not, this is the way it is in your life and mine; but, look here, if you live in such a place and know who I know, you know who I am talking about. And doing it moreover from the superior posture of artistic transcendence."[53] In short, he asked Bell not to mention either his first name or the Percy name anywhere in the book. "Well, aside from all this, good luck with the novel in any case, which is to say, more action and less qualities. Mine, I'm sorry to say, is going badly. Nothing is harder to learn than to learn from one's mistakes, I find." Though Walker had been hurt, he expressed his honest feelings without rancor.

Of all the annual retreats Walker would make, the one in late November would be the most memorable. At Manresa, he, Phin, Dick Faust, and Chink Baldwin were greeted by Father Edward Sheridan, the director of the retreat house, and Father Edward Donahue, the retreat master for this particular group.[54] When not in prayer, the retreatants had a chance to dip into theological books by such writers as Karl Rahner, Henri DeLubac, Yves Congar, and Edward Schillebeeckx, well known to many bishops and *periti* attending the Vatican Council. Suddenly the news flashed that President John Kennedy had been shot and killed. When Father Sheridan met the retreatants in the chapel, he explained what had happened, and invited them to watch television in the private Jesuit quarters. They were all shaken by the unfolding events. "No sense in staying here," Father Sheridan said forlornly, and those who drove home continued to listen to the shocking news on their car radios. In Covington, the Percys were glued to the television set as the footage of the doctors at Parkland Memorial Hospital, unable to treat the murdered President, was shown again and again. The death of President Kennedy poignantly reinforced something that Walker had thought a good deal about: medicine and surgical interventions cannot be the absolute savior of the world's problems. The experience of being involved in a personal search while on retreat and of grieving at the loss of a leader was bound to have an effect on the composition of his novel-in-progress; the moment and its aftermath were overwhelming. An era was ending as heads of state from around the world followed the horse-drawn caisson down Pennsylvania Avenue and three-year-old John Kennedy, Jr., saluted the slain leader. As Walker mentioned to the editor of *Shenandoah*, he had no intention of finishing his novel in the current year.[55]

In January, *The Southern Review*, which had been published from 1935 to 1942, announced that it was resuming publication the following year under the editorship of Cleanth Brooks and Robert Penn Warren. Donald E. Stanford wrote Walker asking for a submission, offering three cents a word for anything he might write for them.[56] He also heard from Jack English, a close friend of Caroline Gordon, who had become a Trappist monk at Holy Ghost Monastery in Conyers, Georgia, suggesting that he send *The Moviegoer* to Thomas Merton at the Abbey of Our Lady of Gethsemani in Kentucky.[57] (It would not be untypical behavior for Jack, who was an alcoholic, to write Walker out of the blue or call him at ungodly hours.) Merton's letter described *The Moviegoer* as "right on target."[58] "The reason that the book is true," he continued, "is that you always stop at the point where more talk would have been false, untrue, confusing, irrelevant. It is not that what you say is true. It is neither true nor false, it points in the right direction, where there is something that has not been said and you know enough not to try to say it." Merton considered Walker one of the most hopeful existentialists he had read: "I think you started with the idea that Bolling would be a dope but he refused to be, and that is one of the best things about the book. Nice creative ambiguities in which the author and the character dialogue silently and wrestle for a kind of autonomy." In jest Merton said he dared not show the book to his novices because of Sharon, one of the attractive secretaries in the novel. If Walker did not have a French publisher, Merton was willing to contact the publishing firm Le Seuil for him. He sent an inscribed copy of his poems, *Emblems of a Season of Fury*. Walker's reply was short and modest: "I am a slow writer, easily discouraged, and depend on luck, grace, and a good word from others."[59] *The Moviegoer* had now been published in Denmark, Italy, England, but not France. "Yes, tell the guys at Le Seuil!" Walker advised Merton, but after Le Seuil had seen it they said they wanted to wait for his *next* book. "Well, I love the French whether they love me or not" was Walker's reply.[60] Merton also sent one of his abstract calligraphic drawings, which Walker hung next to the Franz Kafka motto: *Warte!* ("Wait").[61]

On June 17 the Percys loaded their car and drove to Northampton, Massachusetts, so that Walker and Bunt could attend Marjorie E. Magner's class at the Clarke School for the Deaf, a private institution across from Smith College that concentrated on learning speech without the use of sign language.[62] They stopped in Arlington, Virginia, to visit President Kennedy's grave. In Northampton they met Mrs. Joan Kennedy, whose husband, Ted, was recuperating from the crash of a plane carrying him, Senator and Mrs. Birch Bayh, and a Kennedy assistant on a flight from Washington, D.C., to Springfield, Massachusetts. Mary Pratt served as Mrs. Kennedy's chauffeur a few times a week, going to and from Cooley Dickinson Hospital. Most of Mary Pratt's time, however, was spent in a typing class and an algebra class at Northampton High School; she also took advance-placement high school biology at Smith. Her sister, Ann, entertained Mrs. Kennedy one afternoon with Amos, one of the white mice she kept that summer, much to her mother's astonishment. Walker and Bunt enrolled in the Institute Program for Teachers of the Deaf, most of the students being teachers working toward certification or wanting a refresher course.[63] Marge Magner taught a course called Speech for the Deaf to approximately fifty adults. After the first class, when they asked her to tutor Ann, she said she was too busy. The next day Ann approached Marge and asked if she could borrow books from the school's library, and Marge was so taken with Ann she decided after all to tutor her.

Bunt and Walker looked on during a demonstration with a five-year-old boy, who had a limited attention span and no lip-reading skills. As the boy's process of association began to take place, Walker lit up as he watched an amazing breakthrough. For the next two years Walker tutored Ann on a daily basis; in Marge's estimation he was the one mostly responsible for the progress Ann was making. "Watching him quietly, methodically, painstakingly pursue his goals with his squirmy, temperamental, opinionated, brilliant daughter was a thrill to behold," said Marge. In spite of all their hard work, Bunt and Walker still had a lot to learn. Marge gave them a B for the course, but they did less well in Teaching Language to the Deaf, for which they got a C. Marge subsequently visited Covington, and one evening when they went to the movies Marge observed that Ann positioned herself where she could watch her father, who talked silently to her throughout the film, mouthing the dialogue on the big screen. Marge also saw that Ann and Walker had established a complicated language code between them, not completely penetrable, it seemed to her, by anyone else.

That summer, Walker worked on his novel in addition to serving as a consultant to F. Gentry Harris, M.D., at the National Institutes for Health. Dr. Harris, who had received his medical degree at the University of South Carolina and collaborated with Dr. David Rioch, the brother of Walker's analyst, had been impressed by Walker's 1961 essay "The Symbolic Structure of Interpersonal Process," and invited Walker to pursue with him the Helen Keller paradigm as it related to schizophrenics.[64] Harris wanted Walker to become "acquainted with the background of one to three families, one member in each of which carries the label 'schizophrenia,' and that thereafter at intervals of two months, [he] could furnish an analysis of the symbolic structure and functioning of each family with particular attention to changes in the patient's symbolic structure."[65] Using his background in therapy and in language theory, Walker was asked to interpret the speech of Harris's patients. In the early part of the year, Bunt and Walker listened to the tapes that Harris had sent; Walker took notes and carefully evaluated how individuals related both theoretically and practically to others in the group:

Mrs. [A.] has a flat Midwestern schoolmarmish way of saying things, in sharp contrast to Mr. [B.'s] colloquial Southern style. Mr. [B.], I judged, sounded much the same in the first family session as he did in the 100th, with his rather trite anecdotal barbershop style, his conventional noble sentiments and even conventional laugh, heh, heh, heh. All of which clearly irritates Dr. [C.]. Mrs. [A.] on the other hand is more responsive to the cues of the therapeutic game. She catches on so well that she often switches over to the therapeutic team.[66]

As Walker focused on the communication skills (or lack of them) of each patient, he offered positive suggestions to break down needless barriers in therapy. Dr. Harris was grateful for Walker's efforts, though Walker admitted that he was the one who profited, since the experience of decoding the language of schizophrenics would help him with his study of semiotics, particularly with the process of naming. In July, Walker flew to Washington to observe personally one of Harris's sessions. Walker's written response is indicative of the excitement he felt: "I don't believe I conveyed to you my overall impression of that session: the sense that muddy waters are clearing a bit and that relationships are becoming manifest. The G.'s were firing straight from the shoulder. Even J. with his stalling was quite aware of it as such."[67] Their friendship grew gradually, due in large measure to their visits and consultations in Washington, D.C., Covington, and San Francisco.

The Percys went to New York in August so that Walker could consult with Elizabeth Otis.[68] Patricia Schartle, a new member of McIntosh & Otis, read the typescript of Walker's latest draft and critiqued it heavily. She said that since so much of *The Last Gentleman* (now called *Centennial*) points to Jamie's death, the event should "be on stage" earlier. She advised some cutting and looked forward to receiving a completed typescript in November.

Walker was still brooding about ending his association with Knopf, but had not reached a decision, though Miss Otis was encouraging him. She was not ready to tell him that her candidate was Farrar, Straus & Giroux, where Robert Giroux was now vice president and editor-in-chief. Giroux had lunched with Miss Otis and told her not only that he was an admirer of *The Moviegoer* but that the firm had recently hired Henry Robbins, who was being groomed as his editorial successor. Giroux, who had met Walker through Jean Stafford and knew a great deal about him, told Miss Otis their firm was the perfect publisher for Walker.

Pat Schartle felt that the revised draft made a "fine novel," with certain scenes that were "brilliant, perfect"—"the most penetrating, original novel I've read in quite a long time . . . Perhaps that's why the reader becomes almost frustrated and disturbed by those elements which are not effective."[69] She suggested that Jamie die at Sutter's ranch and that his death needed to have a deeper meaning for the reader. "In Sutter's report, we have an abstraction about death itself, not Jamie's death . . . It is Jamie's effort to die well among the yellow birds that can move us and drive Sutter to the inevitable suicide . . . Jamie's death could be reported to the others by the engineer." She also thought that the material relating to President Kennedy's assassination should be changed. (As Walker himself said, the assassination had forced him to lose a year's work; and in fact it had changed the whole direction of *The Last Gentleman*. Between two to three hundred pages about Kennedy were subsequently discarded.[70])

One of the sadder aspects of the return trip to New Orleans was that the Percys could not meet again with Flannery O'Connor, who had died on August 3, after a long bout with lupus. Walker learned of her death from the obituary in *The New York Times*, though Caroline Gordon had previously told him of her serious condition.[71] Walker mourned the loss of O'Connor very much. He told Louise H. Abbott, "When I think about how she spent the last years of her life I feel even sorrier than ever, but then I invoke her and feel better."[72]

When Walker settled into his routine in Covington by mid-August, he addressed the pressing problem of finding a new publisher. During the National Book Awards ceremony, Walker had met Henry Robbins, an editor at Knopf and a good friend of Stanley Kauffmann. Robbins, a Harvard graduate, had been given his first publishing job by Bob Giroux, at Harcourt, Brace, in the early 1950s. Robbins had returned to Harvard for a master's degree and then worked at Knopf and elsewhere until he was hired as a senior editor by Farrar, Straus & Giroux. At Knopf, Robbins had read and admired *The Moviegoer* in its early stages and made editorial suggestions. He knew Walker was seeking a new publisher and, after consulting with Giroux, he wrote Walker: "If you *do* contemplate changing, I hope we can persuade you to do what I believe in all sincerity: that Farrar, Straus & Giroux would be the best in America for you to publish with."[73] Naturally, Walker was pleased to hear from an editor he knew at a house whose list of authors he liked. "Yes, I am doing my best to rassle a novel into shape. It would probably be very bad luck for me even to think about publishers when the thing isn't yet fit to publish."[74]

Robbins in turn showed Walker's letter to Robert Giroux, whom Roger W. Straus, Jr., had just made a partner in the firm; the company's name was changed to Farrar, Straus & Giroux (FSG) in 1963. Among the many famous authors Giroux brought to the list were Bernard Malamud, Jean Stafford, Robert Lowell, Flannery O'Connor, Isaac Bashevis Singer, T. S. Eliot, Susan Sontag, John Berryman, Elizabeth Bishop, Peter Taylor, Derek Walcott, and Seamus Heaney. One of Giroux's most successful

(above) Wedding photo of Walker Percy's mother, Mrs. Martha Susan ("Mattie Sue") Percy. The wedding took place in Birmingham, Alabama, on September 1, 1915. (right) Walker Percy (standing), his younger brother LeRoy, and their father, who was commissioned a second lieutenant in the U.S. Air Service in September 1918

(above) The Percy residence in Birmingham Alabama. Walker Percy lived here briefly a child *(courtesy Birmingham Public Library (left)* William Alexander Percy ("Unc Will") of Greenville, Mississippi, as a your man. He adopted Walker Percy and his tw brothers in 1933 *(from the Percy family paper courtesy Mississippi Department of Archiv and History, Jackson)*

(above) Trophy winners of the Mississippi High School Poetry Association. Walker is in the second row, wearing a light suit. His friend Don Wetherbee is in the center of the first row. (right) In the summer of 1934, Percy joined college classmates for a trip to Europe; later he decided to travel on his own

(top) Marcelle Dunning, Walker Percy, and Barbara O'Neil on the grounds of Trudeau Sanatorium, Saranac Lake, New York, in January 1943. All three were TB patients *(courtesy Raymond Hogan, M.D.)*. *(bottom left)* Navy Lieutenant Billups Phinizy Percy (left) and Air Force First Lieutenant LeRoy Percy (right), Walker Percy's brothers, in Greenville in 1945. *(right)* Marjorie McDonough and Walker outside Santa Fe, New Mexico, during the summer of 1946. Both were staying at Jim Whittaker's Rancho La Merced *(courtesy Marjorie McDonough)*

(top) The Percys and Ransdell Cox in Covington, Louisiana, in December 1962. Cox and Stanley Kauffmann were there to discuss *The Moviegoer* filmscript *(photo by Stanley Kauffmann)*. *(bottom left)* The Percys and their daughter Ann in their home. This photo was probably taken in 1960 *(photo by Reynal Ariatti)*. *(right)* Walker receiving a kiss from his daughter Mary Pratt, at the 1966 Delta Debutante Ball in Greenville, Mississippi

Eudora Welty and Walker Percy during the Frank Nelson Doubleday Lecture at the National Museum of American History, Washington, D.C., in 1983 *(courtesy Smithsonian Institution, National Museum of American History, and Doubleday)*

(top) Bunt and Walker, Jaye Percy, Sarah Percy, Billups Phinizy Percy (left to right), in September 1986 in the area of Tenants Harbor, Maine *(photo by LeRoy Percy)*. *(bottom)* Bunt, Jack Moores, Ann Percy Moores, Walker, and David Moores. This photo of the Percys, their daughter, and her two sons was taken in 1989 after the Jefferson Lecture in Washington, D.C. *(courtesy National Endowment for the Humanities)*

Walker Percy in front of his portrait painted by Lyn Hill, which he commented on at the conclusion of his self-interview, ''Questions They Never Asked Me.'' It appears on the jacket of Percy's collection *Signposts in a Strange Land (photo by Christopher Harris)*

books was *The Seven Storey Mountain,* written by Thomas Merton, his former classmate at Columbia College. Giroux had decided to leave Harcourt, Brace in 1955 after fifteen years, having profited from the counsel and friendship of Frank Morley and Donald Brace (who died that year). Giroux had been approached by Roger Straus, Sheila Cudahy, and John Farrar to make the change. While still serving in the U.S. Navy, Straus had begun planning in 1945 to start his own publishing firm. He and Giroux, also a navy officer, had met during World War II when the latter was stationed with Air Group Nine on the aircraft carrier *Essex,* one of whose pilots had been shot down at Truk. The U.S. attack on this Japanese base was so successful that the entire task force participated in the pilot's rescue from enemy waters. Giroux took the account he had written of this rescue to Straus, who was serving in the navy's books and magazine section. Giroux was impressed by his promise that *Collier's* magazine would not only take the piece but feature it as a cover story, which they did; thus their friendship was formed. Poet Donald Hall in an interview in *The New York Times Book Review* described Robert Giroux as "the only living editor whose name is bracketed with that of Maxwell Perkins."

That fall Professor W. J. Stuckey of the English Department at Purdue University in Indiana asked Walker to be a writer-in-residence in charge of a small group of students for a salary of $10,000.[75] (Caroline Gordon had held the post the previous year.) As Walker was about to make his decision to leave Knopf, causing him to feel an "ordinary, normal, every-day malaise," he continued his correspondence with Stanley Kauffmann by asking what was the process by which an author disassociates himself from a publisher. "I hope to have something to show to a publisher in a few months and don't know who to show it to. All I know is Mr. Knopf, who is a very distinguished publisher, is not going to extend himself in selling something I write, and even a writer likes to sell his poor wares."[76]

For the April 1965 issue of *Harper's,* celebrating the centenary of Lee's surrender to Grant, editor Willie Morris asked Walker to write an essay on the topic of "The South Today," with other contributions by William Styron, C. Vann Woodward, LeRoi Jones, Robert Coles, Whitney M. Young, Jr., Louis D. Rubin, Jr., Arna Bontemps, Jonathan Daniels, and Langston Hughes. Walker's essay was entitled "Mississippi: The Fallen Paradise." The issue of *Harper's* was reprinted as a book, *The South Today: 100 Years After Appomattox.* In his essay Walker wrote about two of the bravest Mississippians in recent years—James Meredith and Medgar

Evers—who were like men from Ole Miss who fought valiantly during the Civil War for their beliefs. Medgar Evers was gunned down—shot in the back—on the evening of June 11, 1963, by racist Byron de la Beckwith. In the South, except for an oasis like Greenville, times had changed. Gone were the old-style white moderates and their alliance with blacks —elements that had figured prominently in Mississippi since Reconstruction. Faulkner's Snopes clan had taken over society, replacing the more temperate Yoknapatawphans, like Gavin Stevens of *Intruder in the Dust*, with a generation of "good-looking and ferocious young brats" indoctrinated by the White Citizens Councils and racist politicians. Another change had been the emigration of blacks to the North, reducing the black majority in Mississippi to a minority presence for the first time in one hundred years. "Mississippi had not got any better, but New York and Boston and Los Angeles have got worse," Walker believed, and he felt that Mississippi had a chance of emerging from its long nightmarish history. But President Kennedy's appeal to the students at Ole Miss to allow James Meredith to enroll as a regular student fell on deaf ears, because to Mississippians Ole Miss was very much a private reserve. To restore peace in Mississippi, in Walker's view, meant putting into practice the Judeo-Christian ethic and opening the doors to all. When laws were enforced and reason and good prevailed, changes could be brought about. Walker had diagnosed the malady in Mississippi; about the best he could hope for was a depersonalized neighborhood where one could at least expect some degree of tolerance. On a more personal level, Walker was "so damn mad at Mississippi" because what had happened there was a perversion of the genius of the South.[77] He held no brief at all for the North. For Walker, the Yankee *pax* meant purely and simply what was already happening in the South—increasing prosperity, urbanization, and industrialization. He was sure of one thing: Uncle Will would have had no more use for the new lawbreakers than he did for the Snopeses in Mississippi.

On March 26 Walker went to hear seventy-six-year-old Gabriel Marcel speak about the myth of the death of God in contemporary thought. Educated at the Sorbonne, Marcel had received the French Academy's Grand Prize of Literature and the National Grand Prize of Letters—and he was one of Walker's existential heroes. In his lecture, Marcel countered Nietzsche's contrary statement by asserting that "God is very much alive," contending that Nietzsche's denial "must be considered exclusively in the light of the exceptional being who made it." He believed that we can ask ourselves "if the death of God might not finally be the projection of an inner aging, in contrast to the ceaseless innovations in the realm of technology . . . Let me add that this understanding must necessarily imply self-scrutiny, for I must then ask myself as a Christian—or as a being aspiring towards Christianity—to what extent is God a living reality for myself?" Marcel said experience has shown that conversion is possible only when an existential relationship is created between two people. It excludes any pretentiousness in affirming the reality of God.[78] Walker had a few words with Marcel after the lecture, though he found it difficult to carry on a conversation because of Marcel's heavily accented English.[79] Yet Marcel had given Walker a good deal to think about as he structured the scenes juxtaposing Sutter's notebooks with Jamie's baptism.

In Alabama, the distance from Selma to Montgomery is fifty-four miles, yet in March 1965 it represented a journey that could not be measured with ordinary measuring devices. When Governor George Wallace thwarted the progress of six hundred marchers after they crossed the Edmund Pettis Bridge, the response from around the country was outrage. Walker and Bunt visited Gwyn and Shelby at this time and Walker proposed to Shelby that they both should join the Selma march. Shelby was in sympathy but did not want to do this. "It was an about-face for Walker to want to do something like that," Shelby said, "but it did not surprise me."[80] By midsummer, President Johnson signed the Voting Rights Act.

In early May, Henry Robbins did not yet know whether Walker had decided to go with FSG.[81] Walker had not finished the novel or made his decision.[82] By late May the wait was over. Bob Giroux again had lunch with Miss Otis at the Carlton House and proposed terms for a contract that she accepted on the author's behalf. The final title of the novel was *The Last Gentleman*. Miss Otis had asked that the $5,000 advance be payable on request of the author rather than on signing the contract.[83] The novel would be delivered on April 1, 1966, and FSG would budget $20,000 for advertising and promotion. Walker would receive a 15 percent royalty on the retail price of all copies sold.

In the mid-1960s, Walker became involved with a group called the Academy of Religion and Mental Health, which met in the International House in New Orleans. Together with the Rev. John Stone Jenkins, assistant headmaster of St. Martin's Episcopal School; Margaret Sidney, a Unitarian leader; Miriam Barranger; Edward H. Knight, M.D., a prominent psychiatrist; Gene Usdin, M.D.; the Rev. Simon ("Augie") Salter; and Father Ed Sheridan, he discussed various questions concerning re-

ligion and psychiatry. Walker regarded the mental health profession
highly, but Dr. Usdin believed he considered many psychiatrists to be
off base. In Walker's eyes, the most that therapy could accomplish was
not removing or solving problems but bringing an individual to the point
where he or she felt able to make a decision.[84]

In June, Mary Pratt graduated from high school (voted the "best
singer" of the class, and Bunt had her picture in the yearbook, *The Dove*).
The family had previously taken trips expressly for Ann's sake and now
it was time for Mary Pratt to have her vacation—in Europe. Walker
wrapped up the manuscript of *The Last Gentleman* and shipped it to New
York. After the four Percys were vaccinated in Covington, they drove
north to Washington and had lunch in a Holiday Inn, where Ann saw
deaf people using sign language. She had never seen this form of communication before and wanted to know what they were doing. The Percys continued to Morristown, New Jersey, and stayed with the Milazzos.
They left their car in the Milazzos' garage and boarded the *Queen Mary*,
to which the Hardarts had sent a bottle of champagne and other "bon
voyage" gifts. They docked at Southampton, took a train to Victoria
Station, and in London saw Agatha Christie's long-running play *The
Mousetrap*. There was a July Fourth day trip to Cambridge to visit Roy
Percy, who was studying there, and a side trip to Ely Cathedral in
Cambridgeshire, as well as a visit to a manor house where outlawed
priests were hidden in "priest holes" during the reign of Elizabeth I. On
July 11 they celebrated Ann's birthday in a castle in Scotland.

They had not planned on going to Lourdes, but Walker's and Bunt's
devout faith impelled them to make this pilgrimage. Though the town
outside the shrine had far too many souvenir shops, the grounds at the
foot of the French Pyrenees were quiet and peaceful. Walker was fascinated by this site built to commemorate the 1858 apparitions of Mary to
Bernadette Soubirous. He obtained an official badge identifying himself
as a medical doctor and during their five-day stay worked as a *brancar-
dier*, pushing invalids on pallets or in wheelchairs from the church to the
bathing areas, where miraculous cures (approximately sixty by the time
he went there) had been reported over the years. Walker always identified himself, using simple but correct French: *Je suis un médecin américain*
("I am an American doctor"). Because of her Marian devotion, Bunt felt
awed to be at this holy place. For Mary Pratt the experience of illness
and participating in the day and night processions had an undesirable
effect; she was not prepared for the stench of death or the open sores,
or for the woman who had a seizure in front of her. Though she refused
to be bathed, she accompanied her sister and parents as Ann was
wrapped in a white sheet and placed in the cold water.

While Walker was still in Europe, both Robbins and Giroux wrote him agreeing fully on the excellence of *The Last Gentleman*. Robbins found the book fascinating, funny, very moving, wonderfully odd, and absolutely true:

I have finished *The Last Gentleman* for the first time and am starting to re-read on a technical level.

The book has great power and that power rests on your artistic integrity. Actually everything that you say in the epilogue is already implied.

Through genius you have had Bill burn Sutter's philosophical ramblings. Therefore they gain permanence through destruction. They are snatched away from the reader. Your comments when you get into Sutter's mind in the epilogue are anti-climactic to me. By now *I know* Sutter. He is the main character in the book. He attracts me powerfully just as he attracts Jamie, Val, Rita and Bill.

The death scene has absolute pitch, great delicacy, and is beautiful. It is all —nothing can come afterwards except that the engineer may wonder if he can now call Kitty, if Poppy Vaught is "through" with him since Jamie no longer needs him and he has lost the check. He should fade out in his own confusions and anxieties. He should be homesick for his falcon.

I wonder if you were thinking of the epilogue when you spoke of "trouble." It is not necessary for me nor for you. Whom did you write the epilogue for?

Bill wouldn't be able to take Lamar's job, think about Sutter going back, anyway not for promoting tolerance and improving (the city's) image.

Bill needs Sutter, not Kitty. The world is full of Kitties with rich fathers. He would haunt Sutter, cling to him the rest of his life without knowing or caring why. He would go back and marry Kitty only if Sutter consented to go too but not to do any such thing as swell the ranks of responsible professional people, just because he wanted Sutter to and Sutter because of the engineer's faithfulness to Jamie would go.

A short conversation between Sutter and Bill in which Sutter's violence and frustration and grief mingle with the engineer's confusion and disorientation and need blend lightly and as surely as the rest of the book is written.[85]

Before flying to Europe for a vacation of his own, Giroux zeroed in on the problem of the epilogue in the novel:

To take the biggest matter first, most readers are going to be dissatisfied with the epilogue. After that magnificent powerful scene of Jamie's baptism and death (bumptious Fr. Boomer is perfect too), the epilogue is an anti-climax. It is too brief and compressed, and settles the fates of the main characters too neatly. Yet you say things in the epilogue that are important—about Sutter, about Bill, about existence. I agree that they have to be kept in the book somewhere. It may be the *word* "epilogue" that causes some of the trouble: the book's over, but hold! there's an undelivered message. The Bill-Sutter colloquy could either come before Jamie's death, or there should be a final chapter in which there is some movement as well as talk, more in the manner of the rest of the book—casual, unforced, with the kind of surprises you're so good at: they are inevitable as soon as they happen. I have no single point more important to make; this is *the* editorial problem of the book.

The character of Rita is another kind of problem. She now comes out Lesbian. From what you told me on the phone, there was to be an espionage subplot; no doubt the deletion of the mail-drop and those Valentines to Kitty will clear a good deal of this up. She seems more important than she turns out to be.

Henry has done such a thorough job of detailed queries that I will confine this first letter to just one more general comment—on Sutter. He and Bill are the two main characters, but he is kept offstage quite a while, with such a terrific buildup of suspense that his first scene is anti-climactic a bit, "viewed" by Bill before their meeting. And the nun Val "comes on" a little later than she should.[86]

From Lourdes, the Percys returned to London. After spending a few days in Brown's Hotel in Mayfair, they flew back to the States from Heathrow in late July and drove to Nantucket, where they met up with Marge Magner, who helped by tutoring Ann twice a day for a week. When they arrived in Covington, Mary Pratt packed her bags to head off to Trinity College in Washington, intending to major in psychology. Though her marks that fall were lower than she had hoped for, Walker nevertheless encouraged her to profit from her education. "We are very pleased that you have responded so well to your 'emancipation' from the apron strings," he wrote to Mary Pratt at Cuvilly Hall after Thanksgiving.[87] "I have never doubted that you would, but your maturity is even more than I hope for . . . You are a lady and you are a Catholic and you know what it is to be both. Perhaps it is only necessary to add this: that you are coming of age in a more troubled time than usual. Standards are decaying, moral values are being questioned. Chastity is coming to be despised. More than ever it is going to be up to *you* to control a situation—where in former times, the whole society and culture reinforced moral values. But I suspect you already know this too. Your old man loves you and must be forgiven for being a bore." (In another letter, written that fall, Walker mentioned that Ann had been up at Albena Plantation the previous week to visit fiction writer Berry Morgan, her husband, Lee, and their children.)

Miss Otis had no high hopes of placing parts of Walker's novel in any magazine, but she promised first serial rights to *The Saturday Evening Post*; they made no offer.[88] Walker wrote her that he would have his final touches done by mid-November. His comments to Dr. Gentry Harris about his character Sutter Vaught show the imaginative struggle Walker faced: "He finally abandons pathology for pornography, because in his view the alienating forces of abstraction have become so powerful that the only mode of re-entry into the real is the sexual (cf., the genital orientation of popular culture). In the course of an ordeal, a suicide attempt, he recovers himself and experiences a conversion to a belief in God and His entry into space-time via Jews, Christ and the Church, the supreme scandal to the transcending posture of abstraction."[89] FSG decided to announce spring publication and started planning the design of the book. They asked for Walker's own ideas about publicity and the jacket: "My own feeling about publicity . . . is that I would like to say as little as possible. The dust jacket of *The Moviegoer* had such things as the fact that I was a doctor and got tuberculosis and took up writing afterwards; and that I was the nephew of William Alexander Percy, etc. It is my hope that it will be enough to say simply that I wrote *The Moviegoer*, that I live with my wife and two daughters in Covington, Louisiana. What do you think?"[90] By mid-October, Robbins had heard nothing from Walker about the revisions; he was beginning to be a bit anxious about the production schedule and hoped the final text would arrive by the end of the year.[91]

Walker was hard at work and expected to be finished well in advance of the date agreed on. His major problem was getting the script typed; he had injured his left hand and could type only with one finger of his right hand. He was wary about sending his unique copy to New York, and asked Robbins for the copy of the manuscript he had sent in the ring binder. He wanted it returned to him before giving the revised text to Betty Ellis, his typist.[92] He feared that the Ellis house might burn down (which it subsequently did). Robbins was delighted with the good news of Walker's progress, and he returned the ring-binder copy.[93] He also sent Walker a draft of the catalogue copy for his approval.

"For some reason," Walker replied to Robbins, "I find myself almost at a total loss when it comes to saying something about this novel. This comes no doubt from being stuck with it for the past three years. This job I willingly leave to you. Since Mr. Holland [the FSG publicity director] did insist that I say something, the best I can do is . . . the enclosed."[94] Walker's write-up, in fact, constitutes an important personal interpretation of the novel:

This novel is, among other things, an exploration of some of the qualities and possibilities of life in the post-modern age. It deals, I hasten to add, with the here and now and not with 1984. The assumption is made that we are presently living in the post-modern age, i.e. that the era which has been described as the Modern Age has ended and that we are now living in the as yet unnamed Time After. Some of the characteristics of the Modern Age which future historians may list are such familiar preoccupations as: love of nature, cultivation of one's personality, the practice of Science and Art as quasi-religious all-construing professions. The Modern Age will no doubt be recognized to be still specified by its religious connections with previous ages, even when these connections were manifested by the familiar conflict of "Science vs. Religion."

Life in the post-modern age is not the same. One might argue that Homais, the village atheist in *Madame Bovary*, was very much a modern man insofar as he still lived in Christian space and time. But does it follow that a man who is once or twice removed from cultural Christendom necessarily conceives himself as dwelling in the same familiar coordinates of historical time and at home away from home? What is the place of the Christian Church in the post-Christendom, post-modern age? Billy Barrett's dislocations vis-à-vis place and time, his amnesia and déjà-vus and his "upsidedownness" in the face of heretofore unquestioned values, are here set forward as figures of the new order of things.

The artistic validity of these hypotheses will depend altogether on the reader's recognition of what he has himself known to be the case but has not until now known that he has known.

Specifically this novel will differ from other similar undertakings, e.g., a Bergman film, as say Alabama differs from Sweden. Whereas, that is to say, Sweden, like Japan, may be the locus of the first pure post-modern societies, Alabama (and the South) as a locale is complicated by the persistence of a cultural Christendom of a certain sort and the persistence as well of tragedy and the strong savor of places and memories and other artifacts of the ancient Modern Age. This novel deals with these complications.

Billy Barrett has the secret suspicion that "It"—the world catastrophe which everyone fears will happen—has already happened. This fancy is set forth with ambiguity and may be understood with equal plausibility from either of two viewpoints: as a symptom of an illness (his "nervous condition") in the old Modern Age, or as a prophetic glimmering of what has actually happened. For in a sense, "It" has already happened and the modern world has come to an end. Billy's "illness" can be understood as the tentative probing of the possibilities of life in the strange new world.

Robbins found Walker's statement fascinating and provocative. He said it illumined aspects of the novel that he had responded to on a subconscious rather than conscious level: "While the statement doesn't really lend itself to use as 'copy'—I'm leery of suggesting (even though you emphatically deny it) that the story has to do with some impending future when actually the post-modern age is the here and now—it will be extremely useful with reviewers, etc. I guess it's the word 'post-modern' that worries me, because it unavoidably carries the connotation of 'after today.' "[95] Having learned the hard way from misinterpretations of *The Moviegoer*, Walker at least wanted to get himself on the record this time. By the end of November, he sent FSG what he considered the final text.

Walker was deeply concerned about the civil rights issue, and gradually, through friends and acquaintances, he had begun to make decisions about how he could personally contribute to the movement. Will D. Campbell, a Yale-educated Baptist minister working for the National Council of Churches, first met Walker at a conference on race in New Orleans in the late 1950s.[96] Over the years, Walker, Campbell, and Thomas H. Clancy, S.J., became friends.[97] Father Clancy, a tall priest with a booming voice who hailed from Helena, Arkansas, met Walker in 1957. When Tom (as Walker addressed him) finished his studies at the London School of Economics in 1960, he again visited Walker, who consulted Clancy whenever he had a question about Catholicism. In effect, Clancy—who considered Walker too tough on himself in living up to the commitments of his faith—continued where Father McCarthy left off.

Walker's essay in the December 1965 issue of *Katallagete*, published by the Committee of Southern Churchmen and edited by James Holloway, appeared under the title "The Failure and the Hope." This essay returned to the theme of black revolution: "The paradox lies in this: that the hope for the future . . . requires as its condition of fulfillment the strictest honesty in assessing the dimensions of our failure." The South's failure toward blacks has been "both calamitous and unremarkable." Yet no one was surprised at the failure. "The sickness of Christendom may lie in fact in this: that we are judged by the world and even to a degree have come to judge ourselves as but one of a number of 'groups' or institutions which have a 'good' impact on society." Concerning racial issues, churches are treated with respectful impartiality. The South, whatever its faults, is perhaps the only section of the country where public consciousness is informed by theological notions of sin and redemption, heaven and hell—the Christ-haunted South that Flannery O'Connor wrote about. More likely than not, a Southerner "has grown up in a place drenched by tragedy and memory, and to have known first hand a rich and complex world of human relationships which are marked by a special grace and a special cruelty and guilt." Thus it is all the more shameful that the failure of the South has been precisely a theological failure. Like Northerners, Southerners believed that reconciliation can be achieved through the mediation of God's love and the love of men for God's sake. "We strive for the same goals," Walker maintained. A Southerner might say that Northerners deceive themselves in imagining that they can accomplish these goals without God, but he really cannot; the failure, for Walker, is a sinful one, and churches have done little to rectify it.

Yet it was liberal humanists, members of CORE or COFO, agnostics, and Sarah Lawrence sociology majors who had come forward to shoulder the burden and had led the way. Walker believed that the "ultimate basis for racial reconciliation must be theological rather than legal and sociological. In the South, perhaps more than in any other region, the civil and secular consciousness is still sufficiently informed by a theological tradition to provide a sanction for racial reconciliation." The "fusion principle" maintained that blacks enjoyed more civil rights in the period following Reconstruction than at any other time—except recently:

This alliance, it is important to note, was struck between the Negro and the white conservative against the poor whites and the Radical Republicans. It has been this same white conservative leadership which in many parts of the South exerted a more or less consciously moderate racial influence even after it was politically overwhelmed by the latter-day Populist-racists, Vardaman, Heflin, Bilbo, and their followers. The old alliance with the Negro was in part politically motivated. But it also had a strong moral basis. It is the contention here that this morality was paternalistic and Stoic in character and that it derived little or none of its energies from Christian theology.

Christians have sinned against their own past and compromised themselves with their Ham-Shem theological sociology. Without mentioning Martin Luther King, Jr., Walker said that new social forces were alive in the South and the Christian laity seem to respond with the old cultural reflexes. "The bitterest pill for him to swallow is the fact, hardly to be contested and which in his heart he does not contest, that the Negro revolution is mainly justified, mainly peaceful (from the side of the Negroes) and mainly American." Ironically, it is the new "good" person, who suffers the urban problems of malaise and anomie, that Walker looks to for hope.

On December 9, Walker wrote Bob Giroux saying he had sent off the finished typescript and asked for Giroux's critical judgment. Giroux called him and thanked him for being so prompt; he thought Walker had done a splendid job.[98] At the sales conference for spring books, Giroux maintained that Walker's new novel might be one of the greatest that FSG would ever publish.[99] After Christmas, Walker sent Robbins some minor changes: "A question I have not altogether settled in my own mind is the best format style for Sutter's notebook inserts . . . Any suggestions?"[100] Robbins did have minor suggestions to make, but for all practical purposes Walker had brought his second novel to a conclusion as the year ended.

10

Working on
Love in the Ruins
1966–70

As 1966 got underway, FSG received an exclusive offer for the paperback rights to *The Last Gentleman* from James Bryans of Popular Library.[1] Walker's new novel was selected by the Literary Guild as a July alternate; there was a down payment of $5,000 against a royalty of twenty cents per copy on the first 500,000 copies.[2] With such activity, the year began well for Walker. He inserted a dedication ("For Bunt") in *The Last Gentleman* and sent two revised pages to Henry Robbins.[3] It was decided to set off the excerpts of Sutter's notebooks from the text, to indent them, and to use a slightly different type font. Robbins wanted to use quotes from reviews of *The Moviegoer* on the back of the jacket, along with the National Book Award citation, but he was reluctant to approach Knopf for this material. "Do you happen to have a collection of the reviews," he wrote Walker, "or do you have certain favorite comments that you'd like us to use?"[4] Since the copy editor had made a few minor house-style changes and added some marginal queries, Robbins sent back the first fifty-four edited pages for approval.[5] Walker's inexperience in these matters became apparent: he was not sure whether he could insert new passages at this stage or not.[6] Robbins said they normally dissuaded authors from making extensive changes in the galley proofs because it was expensive, but with a novel as important as this, he certainly did not want to discourage last-minute changes: "As for corrections that occur to you . . . before we actually send the manuscript off to the printer, we might just as well make them now rather than in proof."[7] Walker sent Robbins a few review clippings, but said he had no favorites. He requested that a few bound galleys be sent to him when ready, and he would ask a select group for responses, including Stanley Kauffmann.[8] Roger Straus alerted John Bright-Holmes of Eyre & Spottiswoode, who had published *The Moviegoer* in England, and promised him an early set of galleys.[9]

When Shelby read the typescript, making minor suggestions, he cited Dostoevsky's *The Idiot* as a model, an insight that Walker confirmed. Walker also admitted that he was influenced by Eric Voegelin's two senses of time.[10] Shelby praised the new novel (as did Gwyn), especially the immortalization of Lige playing cards: "It gets seriouser as it goes, tightens up just fine, and doesn't break at all in two." He tried to dissuade Walker from using a quote either from Kierkegaard or from Guardini's *The End of the Modern World*, since it implied the author wanted to establish a note of seriousness at the start. Walker was well aware that such quotes struck an overtly religious note at the outset and he decided to keep them.

Mary Pratt enjoyed a break from school by going skiing with a classmate in Windham, New York, just south of Albany. Walker fervently hoped there would be no accident on the slopes, because her insurance ran out when she came of age. He also strongly advised his daughter not to take any chances in Washington, especially wandering around at night: "WE LIVE IN UNSETTLED REVOLUTIONARY TIMES. A LARGE SEGMENT OF THE NEGRO POPULATION IS SO ALIENATED FROM THIS AFFLUENT SOCIETY THAT THEY ARE VERGING ON MASS CRIMINALITY. FOR GOD'S SAKE, TAKE NO CHANCES AT ALL." He signed himself *Deine liebende Vater* ("Your loving father").[11] Before long, Mary Pratt experienced academic problems. "I'm sorry to hear that you've been overtaken by the doldrums, ennui, malaise, lack of motivation, etc.," her father wrote. "It happens to us all."[12]

In early February, as four sets of galley proofs and a proof of the jacket were being shipped to Walker, he also received requests to attend autograph parties in Atlanta and Memphis bookstores.[13] Walker wrote to Jean Stafford in February about her book *A Mother in History*, calling it "deadly cool" and "funny."[14] It was about Mrs. Oswald, the strange mother of President Kennedy's assassin. "And it is the first [book] to give some horrible plausibility to the whole thing." It explained the assassin's family background and psychology better than anything Walker had read. Jean would never know that Walker had planned to incorporate the assassination story into his own novel and finally dropped it.

Miss Otis was not entirely pleased with Janet Halverson's design for the jacket of *The Last Gentleman* or his photo: "He [Walker] is such a nice-looking man, and this makes him look like a polio victim, but I don't suppose the picture matters so very much."[15] Robbins apologized to Miss

Otis about the stylized eye on the cover: "The eye may indeed be a bit disconcerting, but it's by the same token extremely attention getting. And it's certainly not inappropriate to the book, for the idea of the hero as a watcher—even an eavesdropper—runs all through it. You remember Walker saying that he once thought of calling the book *The Eavesdropper* . . . About the picture of Walker: the very oddness of the pose gives it a special appeal, much more interesting than the usual portrait photo. His eyes have a piercing and yet somewhat haunted look that I find extremely attractive."[16] For his part, Walker found the jacket "superb" and the blurb "fine," though eventually the colors used for the eye on the jacket were toned down.[17] In mid-February *Harper's* purchased an excerpt, which they planned to publish under the title "Before the Fugue" in their May issue.[18]

Walker asked that bound galleys be sent to Caroline Gordon, then writer-in-residence at Emory University, and to Robert Daniel at Kenyon College in Ohio. He planned on returning the corrected galleys by mid-February.[19] Excited about the possibility of seeing Caroline, Walker flew to Atlanta in early March, rented a car at Hertz, and visited the Trappist monastery in Conyers for a weekend with his old mentor.[20] Caroline and Walker stayed overnight at the monastery, Walker in the retreat wing and Caroline in a guest cottage.[21] This was Caroline's second visit to Conyers; afterward she stopped to see Regina O'Connor, Flannery's mother, in Milledgeville.[22] Father Methodius and Father Charles (Jack English) gave Walker and Caroline a tour of the monastery grounds, including the stained-glass workshop set up by Father Methodius. Anselm Atkins, one of the more academically oriented Trappists (he would write his dissertation at Emory on five authors, including Walker Percy), had written Walker that Jack English was not well.[23] Walker found Jack "nutty as a fruitcake" and had pity on the abbot who would have to deal with this monk.[24] Jack, who read Caroline's galleys of *The Moviegoer*, told her about a discovery he had made in the second novel: "Jamie is the 'last gentleman'—you recall Barrett's and the doctor's discussion on faith, the clue is buried there. All the characters lean on, draw from Jamie, who paradoxically is sick and searching (the man who searches or who wants to believe, already does—this is Catholic thought going back to St. Augustine). Yet in the end when Jamie accepts baptism, how beautifully that is done, and how the priest so business-like holds his hand through the awful death, Barrett and the doctor go their way to keep their pact of double suicide."[25] Jack wrote to Walker after he had read *The Idiot*.[26] He intended to write an essay on Walker's novel, inspired in part by Walker's positive review of Ralph McGill's *The South and the Southerner*.[27] Jack mentioned he was reading the novel with the notion that both Walker's father and grandfather had committed suicide—Jack Spalding, Walker's cousin, had told him this: "Technically Walker admits the validity of my interpretation. You once said that fiction writers dredge up [images] from the unconscious and incorporate them into their fiction and are not aware of this until the work is finished . . . I will use this information, but in a way Walker will not know." Walker stored away the memory of Jack English for use in describing his fictional priests.

Upon his return, there were quiet moments for Walker away from his writing desk. He and Shelby played chess with Ann and her friend Elizabeth O'Brien, who never had any difficulty understanding Ann (top honors went to Ann and Betsy in school that year).[28] Walker and Shelby sometimes stayed up late playing Scrabble, and when Bunt complained about being married to a "non-writing writer," Walker explained to her that he was sweet-natured, a notable exception to the rule, and that writing was always going on in his head.

Walker still had last-minute corrections to make. He had recently been in touch with David Scott, now an engineer at the White House, who was looking forward to reading the new novel. If possible, Walker wanted to change the first name of the character David Ross to Saul (he reversed himself later). Walker had been burned before by characters' names: *The Moviegoer* had appeared with a schizophrenic character who had the same name as a woman in Greenville. Walker also altered "Bill" to "Will" throughout, though Robbins wondered why Walker wanted this change at all.[29] It turned out that in only one place did Walker really want "Will" to replace "Bill."[30]

Robert Fitzgerald read the galleys; he thought the new novel twice as good as *The Moviegoer*.[31] Paul Horgan submitted some detailed criticism because he was sincerely taken by the novel: "These may seem small to make all this fuss over—but the book is so remarkable, the eye so fresh, the ear so miraculously attuned, the language so keenly refreshed throughout that I am jealous of preserving its freshness by avoiding repetitions of the sort which most often go unnoticed by authors when they read and reread again and again material so familiar to them that they sometimes do not note such details as I have caught."[32] Walker deeply appreciated Horgan's close reading and sent Robbins two pages of additional corrections based on the novelist's suggestions.[33] J. F. Powers called it "a novel with surface and depth, a curious, important book."[34]

Caroline Gordon reread her set of bound galleys: "I am delighted with it—simply delighted! Well, not simply. I have one and one-quarter's worth of adverse comment to make on it and will make that now and get it—or them—out of the way so I can discourse on my delight."[35]

Gordon had the same reaction reading this novel as she had had when she reread *The Sound and the Fury* ("not taking proper mechanical care of the reader," as she put it). In her opinion, Walker's novel starts more like *Crime and Punishment* than *The Idiot*. In spite of this bit of criticism, Gordon found the novel both original and profound: "The average reader is going to find it hard to follow you because he is not used to originality or profundity. He is used to leaping from one fictional *cliché* to another. He never knows how to read." Gordon said she was going to reread Walker's book a third time: "It is such a *rich* book! Enough in it to make a dozen contemporary novels." She guessed that writer John Howard Griffin might have been the germ for the pseudo-Negro and mentioned that writing about Jamie's death must have been difficult for Walker, though she thought it was a fitting climax to the book. "You will have to keep on writing novels, I guess. You seem to be our white hope." Gordon also conveyed her enthusiasm to Bob Giroux and sent a blurb: "If I read it right, this is the odyssey of a Southern Prince Myshkin through regions as strange as Odysseus ever visited."[36] Henry Robbins received the corrected proofs from Walker in late March and expected the plate proofs about ten days later. In Paris, Roger Straus met with representatives of Calmann-Lévy, who expressed an interest in Walker's works, as did the firm of Kirjayhtymä in Finland.[37]

Robbins suggested that Walker come to New York and do some promotional work. "Look Henry," Walker wrote, "about the publication of *The Last Gentleman*. Do you all really want me to come up there? If I thought there was any use in it, I'd come. But I've always doubted that this sort of interview publicity sold any books. In fact I've always wondered whether publishers did it to please their authors. It might be different if I had written a novel about abortion like Mrs. Laël Tucker Wertenbaker or about the Battle of Berlin."[38] If pushed, Walker agreed he would make an appearance.

He brought up the following criticism by Robert Fitzgerald: "What is needed for your 1985 definitive edition of *The Last Gentleman* is one short (one page) section in which Rita is unequivocally shot down. Barrett, after hearing her yarn in the park about her great concern for Jamie and the new herb cure for leukemia, calls Rita's friend, the doctor, who supposedly offered to treat Jamie. The doctor more or less denies the whole thing, making it quite plain to the reader that Rita's motive is simply to get Barrett out of the way (for Barrett is supposed to stay with Jamie during the dangerous herb treatment), so Rita will have a clear field with Kitty. I thought I had made this clear, but apparently did not."

At this stage Walker revealed he now wanted to write a nonfiction philosophical-semantic book growing out of his interest in Charles Sanders Peirce. He also had a vague idea about starting a sort of *1984–Brave New World* satirical science-fiction work.[39] He made preliminary lists as early as February 1966, according to one notation, for a novel that would focus on two young pagans, a medical student, and courtship; it would have alternating chapters involving a love affair and science fiction. He wrote that "Jew," "Christ," and "history" are to be considered dirty words, and that "child's story," "vernacular," "old lust," and "money" were somehow to be featured. Walker also made a note that seemed to indicate Jacob O'Reilly, a forty-year-old ex-Catholic from Birmingham, might be featured in the novel. In outlining his first chapter (it would take place in a swamp), Walker intended that Zulu beliefs would play a role in the book. The pot was boiling for what would eventually become *Love in the Ruins*, but some of these ingredients would be discarded.

Walker made sure that Thomas Merton received a copy of *The Last Gentleman*. "Now that I think about it," Walker wrote to Robbins, "it seems entirely possible that *The Last Gentleman* may accomplish the unprecedented. It may succeed in offending all groups of readers with the exception of American Catholic intellectuals" (who in his opinion numbered some sixty-seven people).[40] He felt it might even manage to offend the humanist intellectual, liberal and conservative Protestants, and the entire book-club readership. It certainly would offend 99 percent of Catholics.

Robbins did not want to bother Shelby for a quote, though his letter to Walker was a rave; however, he did send Shelby a copy of the book as a hint.[41] Though June 13 was the official publication date, Bob Giroux reread the book (something he rarely did) and thought, "It's as fresh and good and surprising as ever—one of the best novels I've read *or* published."[42] Walker wrote to Charles Bell after the publication of *The Last Gentleman* and said he thought about Charles in connection with Sutter Vaught.[43] Jack English wrote a long, rambling letter to Walker, indicating that he intended to review the novel for *The Sewanee Review*, but severe physical problems prevented him from doing so.[44] Bob Giroux received a letter from his friend Thomas Merton:

Walker Percy is one of the few novelists whose books I am able to finish. This is in fact a haunting, disturbing, funny and fantastic anti-novel structured like a long dream and relentlessly insisting that most of reality is unconscious. It ends up by being one of the most intelligent and sophisticated statements about the South and about America, but one which too many people will probably find so baffling that they will not know what to make of it. Even then, if they persist in reading it, they cannot help being affected by this profoundly wacky wisdom of the book. Precisely because of the wackiness I would call it one of the sanest books I have read in a long time.[45]

Walker replied to these perceptive words, stating that writing "is a poor thing for a grown man to spend his time doing." As proof of their enthusiasm for the book, FSG ran ads in *The New York Times* and other leading papers and magazines. Lon Cheney, living in Smyrna, Tennessee, wrote in praise of the novel: "The farce is grim, the tragedy grotesque, but it lays open our malady graphically, wittily and at times with real humor. And it is done as dramatically as the prevailing rites of Existentialism will allow. Barrett is the blind deck's real joker, behaviorism's hero."[46] Walker wrote Bob Giroux: "If you get any response from Protestants, Jews and unbelievers—good or bad—would also appreciate seeing. For one thing, they buy more books."[47] By publication date, Robbins was hoping to have 10,000 advance orders.[48]

The June 5 edition of *The New York Times Book Review* asked writers and noted Americans what they would do with their leisure during the summer. Walker said he would stay home. Having endured a bus tour of England and Scotland the previous summer, he vowed he "would never travel again, unless I could find a place as quiet as the Bogue Falaya, which is Choctaw for River of Ghosts." When Don Lee Keith visited Walker in Covington for an interview, they sat outdoors as Ann took her art lessons nearby. Keith mentioned that Walker was currently involved in a research project on schizophrenia conducted with clinical tape recordings. Walker said about his fiction: "I usually am not acutely aware of the logic at the beginning, but as the work goes along, it becomes more apparent. By following a predestined plan with outlines, like some writers, I could foresee the action and likely it wouldn't go veering off on another path. But I can't work like that. When I realize my logic is off base, I have to go back and begin again at the point where the interior logic took the wrong turn." In other words, Walker might discard hundreds of pages before getting it right. Keith published his essay/interview in the May–June issue of *The Delta Review*.

By mid-June a third printing of *The Last Gentleman* had been ordered, bringing the total number of copies in print to 18,500.[49] The original run had been 10,000. Signet would publish the first paperback edition in February 1968 with a rather racy cover that caused immediate comment from Walker: "I am truly pissed off by this cover."[50] Arthur Schlesinger, Jr., also objected to the cover.[51] In a personal letter from Sidney B. Kramer of New American Library, Walker was assured that the cover would be changed if the book was ever reprinted.[52]

Walker traveled to Greenville for a book-signing party at McCormick's Book Inn.[53] On June 19, Harriet Doar reviewed *The Last Gentleman* for *The Charlotte Observer*; she thought this second novel was more complex and more earthbound than the first. "Barrett's oddities make for a viewpoint detached but by no means unconcerned. They also make for a flickering play of humor, light and dark, usually ironic but sometimes fairly broad." On June 25, *The Times-Picayune* featured a picture of Walker at a luncheon sponsored by Tess Crager's Basement Book Shop and Library on Zimple Street; also honored were four other novelists, including Berry Morgan for her forthcoming *Pursuit*.[54] Ellen Douglas's review of the novel in *The Delta Democrat-Times* found it a difficult book, though it belonged to the tradition of a journey novel, like *Huckleberry Finn*; she also called attention to "The Man on the Train" as an article showing how Walker dealt with this theme in nonfiction. She found little fault with the novel, however, and called it "first-rate." Her pamphlet "Walker Percy's *The Last Gentleman*: Introduction and Commentary" (1969), written for the Seabury Press, is a more personal appreciation of the novel. The anonymous reviewer in *Time* praised it as "a restless rustling of faith, under the ironic humor and serenity a groping toward God." Peter Buitenhuis in *The New York Times Book Review* wrote that the novel is more than a random series of coincidences in its depiction of "the contradictory nature of reality." The novel's irony combines "the Southern writer's sense of style and history with a razor-sharp perception of the technological, consumer-oriented civilization that the North has invented." Benjamin DeMott in the *The Washington Post Book Week* gave a mixed review: "The novel's weaknesses include obliqueness, patronizing language, and reflective irony; its strengths are that it demonstrates kindness and intelligence as it addresses questions of goodness and love."

Walker was "emotionally exhausted and somewhat unstrung" after having finished this novel.[55] He was thoroughly sick of *The Last Gentleman*. Yet the reviews kept appearing. In *The Nation*, Joyce Carol Oates wrote that it "is one no critic should want to swipe at, for it is rare to encounter a work engaging in nearly every line." Walker particularly liked the comment by Peter Taylor, whom he had long admired.[56] Taylor said that it was one of only two novels he had read in the past ten years that he thoroughly liked (the other was Malamud's *The Assistant*).[57] In all, the reviews were quite favorable, leaving Walker with little or nothing to apologize for. In light of his achievement, Walker's alma mater offered him a post as writer-in-residence for the 1967–68 academic year. He declined: "I hesitate to make such a radical remove from my solitary life on the bayou."[58]

When Walker reread *The Last Gentleman*, he typed out a page of corrections for Henry Robbins to incorporate in the next printing.[59] Robbins replied that he would make sure the corrections were made in the third printing (FSG had just finished running off 2,000 more copies), for which comments and blurbs would be added to the dust jacket.[60] Stephen Donadio's review, which discussed the opposition between immanence and transcendence in the summer issue of *The Partisan Review*, was a pleasant surprise for Walker.[61] Inquiries were coming in from Germany and Switzerland about translation rights. Walker thanked Bob Giroux for nominating *The Last Gentleman* for a Pulitzer: "If, as seems most extraordinarily unlikely, it should win a prize, it will be nice to know it was my publisher's idea."[62] In August, *The Washington Post Book Week* listed the novel on their best-seller list and sales in hardback reached 15,414.[63]

The Percys, along with Sarah and Roy, Gwyn and Shelby, Jaye and Phin, went to Pawleys Island in August. From Charleston, South Carolina, they crossed the Cooper River Bridge and drove north to Georgetown; from there it was a short sprint to Lachicotte's Store and over a creek bridge to a summer colony, many of whose houses were built on pilings and surrounded by myrtles and yucca. When the breeze shifted, the residents of these houses moved around their porches to the cooler spots, observing the seabirds and shrimping boats. The Percys rented the Prevost Cottage about seven miles south of the South Causeway. Mary Pratt, who had been attending summer school at Tulane, flew up for a few days. When Walker inscribed a copy of *The Last Gentleman* for June and Jimmy Carr on Pawleys Island, he made "a promise of more Levittown and less Sutter in the next."

After returning home, the Percys traveled to Greenville, where Mary Pratt, escorted by William Davis, was honored by the Delta Debutante Club. For her academic future, Mary Pratt decided to transfer to Dominican College in New Orleans, majoring in speech and drama.[64] Not wanting to live at home and commute, she also decided to live in an apartment with two other students, and later resided in a dorm on campus. From time to time, she would see Father Tom Clancy at Loyola. That year Ann entered Leo Bourgeois's seventh-grade class at St. Peter's.

Walker still needed more time to unwind before turning to a new novel. In November his "Backlash Semantics," published in *The Clarion Herald*, examined the fascinating use of language in recent political campaigns, such as Governor John McKeithen's recent reference to the Klan in Bogalusa as "conservative." "If a Martian from outer space had visited Alabama during the recent campaign, he would have been impressed by the marvelous silence of politicians on the whole subject of the Negro. He might have returned to Mars with the report that Alabama voters were not interested in race as a political issue." Walker also opposed Lester Maddox of Georgia and Judge John Rarick of Louisiana's Sixth Congressional District, but clearly his métier was not biting political satire.

Accompanied by Bunt, Walker flew to New York in December to attend a promotional meeting of the Rockefeller Foundation, for which he was a consultant on a national project involving schizophrenia.[65] They stayed two nights at the Algonquin and went to the theater.[66] At year's end, The Last Gentleman made the "best books of the year" lists. Wilfrid Sheed gave Walker's novel a boost in the yearly roundup for The National Catholic Reporter, as he likewise did in The Critic ("one of the best-written books in recent memory"). It was expected that by Christmas 18,000 copies would have been sold.[67] On Christmas Day The Washington Post Book Week published "From Facts to Fiction," Walker's biographical essay, in which he recounts how it came to pass that a physician turned writer and novelist. In many respects it parallels the interview by Ashley Brown in the spring 1967 Shenandoah. "It is hardly a momentous or typical story. Nor can I imagine this account to be of any use to either would-be physicians or writers. I would not recommend to young writers that they serve an apprenticeship in medicine or to physicians that they take up novel writing." Walker recognized that writers need to find their own ways in their own times and be left alone to do it. His big discovery: that the more science progressed and even as it benefited man, the less it said about what it is like to be a man living in the world. "Every advance in science seemed to take it farther from the concrete here-and-now in which we live . . . Hegel, said Kierkegaard, explained everything under the sun, except one small detail: what it means to be a man living in the world who must die."

In early January, Ralph Ellison, chairman of the committee on grants for literature for the National Institute of Arts and Letters in New York, wrote to Walker informing him that he would be given, during the May ceremony, a stipend in recognition of his creative work in literature. Walker thought highly of Ellison's work, as he had of the early (but not later) work of James Baldwin. Francis Fergusson had recommended Walker for the honor, after he, Ellison, Richmond Lattimore, Bernard Malamud, Phyllis McGinley, and Allen Tate had read Walker's two novels.[68] By late January, Walker asked Robbins for the return of the typescript of The Last Gentleman.[69] He also asked that four publicity photos be sent to the National Institute of Arts and Letters. Along with Sheed's *Office Politics* and Malamud's *The Fixer* (both published by FSG), *The Last Gentleman* had been nominated for a National Book Award. Because of winning the award for *The Moviegoer*, Walker felt that he did not have a second chance of winning, mainly because "*The New Yorker* has no use for W. Percy's writings."[70] After the judges met in February, Walker received the news from Henry Robbins: "Well, you were right: Malamud it is. The jury met today, and we just learned the news, which didn't surprise me either, especially because I had known how highly Mark Schorer, one of the judges, thought of it. He was also a strong admirer of *The Last Gentleman*, so he was sort of 'our man at the NBA.' "[71]

In early February, Robbins began the process of acquiring from Knopf the paperback rights of *The Moviegoer* for the firm's Noonday imprint, for three years with automatic renewal.[72] Later that month, Lewis P. Simpson wrote Walker saying that *The Southern Review* was planning a Southern issue for spring of 1968. Would he contribute an essay on "What are the prospects of Southern fiction?"[73] For Walker he would raise the ante from three cents a word to five. He had consulted Charles East about bringing Walker to LSU as a "critical prognosticator" and hoped Walker would think favorably about it.

John William Corrington sent Walker the galleys of his novel *The Upper Hand* and tentatively asked Walker to think about teaching a course in American literature at Loyola University. Perhaps he could sit in on a class by Miller Williams, who had studied under Robert Frost at Bread Loaf and received the Henry Bellamann Poetry Award.[74] Walker seemed interested and asked Corrington to consult with the administration. In the end Walker agreed to teach one course the following year, though he felt somewhat inferior to the girl in Miller Williams's poem: "a girl, anonymous as beer/telling forgotten things in a cheap bar/how she could have taught here as well as I./Better." Walker noted that his course would be unlike any English course ever taught anywhere: a medical-pathological-psychiatric-anthropological approach to modern fiction that would begin with Dostoevsky's *Notes from Underground* and not include either Hemingway or Faulkner.[75] In a slightly more serious vein, he said that his seminar would focus on point of view in the modern novel, or what is known in Europe as "philosophical anthropology"—"the consequences for modern fiction of such generally pervasive views of man as modern scientific positivism and existentialism." He preferred that Corrington choose the students.

Walker said he was not sure he could teach "creative writing"; he might teach fiction one semester and supervise creative writing projects the next. By the end of June he had decided to teach only one semester at Loyola; his stipend would be $1,500.[76] Later that summer he mentioned his larger hope: "It is this: to hit upon the means—a precarious thing for me—of working into some sort of perennial association with y'all at Loyola—a connection I have not sought with any other university."[77] He was glad to hear that Bill and Joyce Corrington were thinking about moving to Covington and offered them a ride in his boat. From the bayous, they would get a totally different perspective of the area.

Walker, however, was going through a bout of melancholy and depression, and writing very little. Sometimes, as he wrote to Shelby, he thought that the creative urge comes from malice, a strong desire to attack one's enemies or at least those in the culture one considers to be wrongheaded and injurious.[78] He hoped to write the "Big One," a novel bigger than *Don Quixote* or *Moby Dick*, "which is the shortest path to melancholy and perdition, since as St. Theresa of the Little Flower used to say, the only road is the Little Way, viz., the only way to do great things is to choose to treat of little things well. The other path leads to grandiosity of spirit, flatulence of the creative powers and perdition in general." Walker had in mind a futuristic novel dealing with the decline and fall of the United States. He envisioned the country becoming polarized and rent into an almost hopeless state between the rural Knotheaded right (a phrase he would use in *Love in the Ruins* for the "old" Republican Party) and the godless alienated left.

Yet the flow of reviews of *The Last Gentleman* was reason enough to provide Walker with consolation. In March he read a batch of British reviews, the most thoughtful by Stephen Wall in *The Observer*.[79] In *The Sewanee Review*, Lon Cheney had a long review-essay of *The Last Gentleman* under the title of "Secular Society as Deadly Farce." Walker, in Cheney's estimation, presented grim material in farcical form, a correct and perhaps inevitable choice on his part. Cheney noted that the closing passage of the novel reflects hope—"hope that underpins all faith." It was the type of positive review that Walker had hoped to get for *The Moviegoer*. Nor did Walker fail to develop his own faith. With fifty-two other retreatants, he made his annual retreat at Manresa at the beginning of April under the direction of John Curley, S.J.

By the end of that month, his own creative juices began to flow once again, as he began typing the "Journal of a Bad Catholic at a Time Near the End of the World," an eighty-one-page excerpt that begins during a thunderstorm at midnight in Boguechitto (also called Bogachitto), Louisiana. This journal was written in bed by crazed John E. Smith (a widower whose wife, Doris, had previously abandoned him). He was an encephalographer by profession who had invented the Quantitative Ontological Lapsometer. This character is perhaps a development from Sutter's notebooks. Smith at length describes his "sin" machine, as others call it. It reads the levels of electromagnetic radiation from various levels of the brain stem, in order to discern personality types and disorders. Walker could draw on the actual observations of two friends. Bill Sorum and Gene Usdin had participated in 1952 in a series of meetings on schizophrenia conducted by the Department of Psychiatry and Neurology of the Tulane University School of Medicine.[80] Part of the methodology used in discussing the mind-brain problem was to describe the cortex as the mediator between the needs of a whole living organism and its efferent responses. One diagram featured in the proceedings of these meetings shows a cross section of a shielded room and an instrument room. In the shielded room a patient is connected to headphones that send data to the instrument room, which contains, among other equipment, an electroencephalograph. The patient is photographed when reacting to the electrical stimulating equipment. Curiously—and no doubt reflecting the Kennedy material Walker had cut from the previous novel—Bobby McCulloch, a friend of Smith, vows to kill the President of the United States if the President ever flew into nearby Hebert Field. *Love in the Ruins* (an early version is dated March 5, 1968) was now in its very early stages.[81] This novel had been brewing in Walker's mind since the previous fall, as he had mentioned to Ashley Brown.

As preparations went forward for the award from the National Institute of Arts and Letters, Roger Straus wrote Walker congratulating him and inviting him and Bunt to a dinner party on the evening of the ceremony in honor of Walker and David Wagoner, another FSG author. Walker was most grateful for the attention, and said his not so subliminal reason for accepting the grant money was that it would boost his bank account.[82] Bill Sheed was anxious to meet Walker, and asked if a rendezvous could be set up. Walker and Bunt graciously accepted Straus's invitation and arranged to have lunch with Sheed.[83] Walker was ready to bring his tux if Robbins thought it was needed.

Before Walker headed to New York, however, Roy P. Basler, director of the Reference Department at the Library of Congress and associated with its Poetry Office and Literary Functions, wrote asking if he would be willing to share a platform with John Updike for a stipend of $1,000 in November; Walker would be required to read from a work-in-progress and answer questions. James Dickey, consultant in poetry at the Library of Congress, would serve as moderator.[84] Walker declined because he expected to be involved with teaching responsibilities at the time.[85]

Lewis A. Lawson, a genial professor of English at the University of

Maryland, who had decided to write an essay using nonfiction to expli-
cate fiction, wondered if he could look at Walker's two unpublished
novels. Walker was astonished—and pleased—that Lawson had collected his essays. He refused, however, to allow Lawson to see the two
novels: "In fact, you put me in mind of it: since it might very well be
over my dead body that somebody sees them, I aim to get up to the attic
today and throw them both in the bayou. In short, they're very bad and
the less said about them the better."[86] In a volte-face, Walker, concerned
about his upcoming role as teacher, asked if Lawson knew of a good
critical study of Camus, especially of *The Stranger*. Except for following
the New Criticism, spearheaded in the 1940s by John Crowe Ransom,
Walker tended to withdraw from debates about critical theory. The New
Criticism tended to focus on an organic theory of literature rather than
the biography of the author or the social or political background of a
literary work.

On their journey by train to New York, when Bunt went into the
dining car for breakfast, she saw a woman whom she thought she should
know. They struck up a conversation, and afterward Bunt told Walker
she had just met Eudora Welty. Walker went to greet the noted writer,
whom he greatly admired, and they had a long conversation together.[87]
When Walker and Bunt arrived for the joint ceremony of the American
Academy and the National Institute on May 24, Walker delighted in
being in the company of fellow honorees: Philip Booth, Hortense Cal-
isher, Stanley Edgar Hyman, Bernard M. W. Knox, and David Wagoner.
Bunt and Walker had a chance to meet the newly elected Academy
members—Kenneth Burke, Henry Steele Commager, Katherine Anne
Porter, John Crowe Ransom, and John Hall Wheelock. Katherine Anne
Porter received the Institute's Gold Medal for Fiction, given every five
years. Walker was presented with his check for $2,500 and a certificate,
signed by the secretary, Leon Edel: "This writer has now published two
distinguished novels in which American predicaments and manners are
realized with clarity of insight, charm and power of imagination." The
citation was written by Robert Fitzgerald, who had written another sentence that was finally deleted because another committee member called
it "invidious": "No one is writing any better, with any more constant
pressure or more grace." Walker enjoyed the dinner at the Strauses' and
confessed to feeling guilty about staying so long because he was having
such a good time.[88]

In the May issue of *Harper's*, Norman Podhoretz, the editor of *Commentary*, and Harper Lee commented on "A Very Stern Discipline: An
Interview with Ralph Ellison," published in the March issue. Podhoretz

was incensed by what he read; Lee had the opposite reaction. Walker wrote to the editor and prefaced his comments by stating that Ellison spoke of the correct political activities of American intellectuals in a political atmosphere of hatred and abuse. He noted that Ellison compared the phenomenon of "free creative minds" running in a herd with what had happened in the 1930s.[89] Walker found it unusual that a black writer should make this embarrassing comparison, since blacks themselves were vulnerable to the sociological and political pressures that Ellison mentioned. A young black needed to avoid seeing himself through the sociologist's abstraction. "That is to say, maybe the American intellectual will not grow up until the Negro intellectual shows him how. And maybe Ellison marks his coming of age." In brief, Walker had written a fine, quiet commentary that affirmed Ellison's position.

Four days after the ceremony, Walker wrote from Covington to Lewis Lawson asking for material on Styron, Ellison, and O'Connor.[90] Lawson sent him a copy of René Girard's "Camus's *Stranger* Period," plus his own final exam for "The Modern Novel," which included a question about *The Moviegoer*. Walker thanked Lawson ("or, if I may, Lewis") for *The Added Dimension*, a volume on Flannery O'Connor that Lawson had co-edited. Walker wondered what Lawson would do in his essay on *The Moviegoer*. He said he would be glad to answer any questions to avoid speculative misinterpretations: "For example, when a friend-Trappist-critic told me the other day that he knew what happened after the last chapter of *The Last Gentleman*: that Will and Sutter went off to the ranch and shot themselves, I only opened and closed my mouth."[91] Later that summer, Walker read with pleasure a draft of Lawson's article entitled "Walker Percy's Indirect Communications," and wrote: "It is, of course, unprecedented in its scope, thoroughness and in its grasp of both the fiction and articles and the discovery of some basic themes appertaining."[92] He praised Lawson for his research on Kierkegaard, though he felt that he might have given a too strictly Kierkegaardian reading to the theology of *The Moviegoer* and *The Last Gentleman*. On a personal level, Walker could not agree with Kierkegaard that Christianity involves solely a leap into the absurd: "Your readings of the novels is by and large on the mark (this may not sound like a matter for astonishment, but it is—you would have to have been exposed to the extraordinarily diverse *misreadings* to value your achievement)." He suggested that Lawson balance his views by integrating a more Thomistic appreciation of these novels. In particular, Walker recommended that Lawson not begin with St. Thomas but with James Collins's *The Existentialists*. Walker considered this book first-class, as well as John Wild's *Introduction to a Realist Philosophy* and perhaps Etienne Gilson's *Christian Philosophy of St.*

Thomas.[93] From then on Lewis Lawson would concentrate a good deal of his critical energies on the works of Walker Percy.

By June, Miss Otis had more figures concerning *The Last Gentleman* for Walker: 17,317 copies sold through the end of 1966, with approximately 160 copies per month after that. Yet there were 1,320 returns, leaving a net sale through June 1967 of about 17,000, though hardback sales would diminish once the paperback edition was available from Signet.[94] In *The New York Times Book Review*, Walker reviewed Robert Coles's *Children of Crisis: A Study of Courage and Fear*. Walker felt that social revolutions are notoriously paradoxical. Things often get better even as they are getting worse, and America's racial dilemma was never more critical. But even as the conflict spread, there occurred a shift of battlegrounds that holds out the first real promise of hope in a hundred years. Walker believed that the South should not be the country's scapegoat on the race question; it was something the entire country had to address. Using a mock-Faulknerian tone, Walker indicated that, just a few years before, Coles could have gone to Roxbury, Massachusetts, to find racial exploitation; there certainly was no need to go South for it. Coles and the tragedies of the people he interviewed did not fit any mold. What is one to make of Ruby, Coles's prime example, the little black girl from New Orleans who went to school each morning walking past a jeering mob of white girls and women? And what of her parents, who could have been totally demoralized by what was happening to their daughter? And the white Catholic mother who sent her children to school after the other whites had removed theirs? Coles "is that rarest of creatures, the social scientist who keeps his theory and his ideological spectacles in his pocket and spends his time listening to people and trying to understand them. Like Freud he is humble before the facts." Coles treaded a narrow path between socializing and theorizing and emerged as a wise and gentle physician. "He is doctor to the worst of our ills." Letters were exchanged, and Walker invited Coles to drop by when he was in the area, since he wanted to know what happened to Ruby and the others, and to learn more about Coles's recent medical survey of poverty among blacks in Mississippi.[95] Temperamentally these two writer-physicians had much in common.

Walker also began to have an influence on younger scholars at this time. William Dowie, S.J., who had read *The Moviegoer* at St. Charles College in Grand Coteau, and more recently *The Last Gentleman*, had returned to New Orleans while a graduate student in English at Brandeis University to attend to his dying mother. He decided to stay in New

Orleans for the rest of the summer.[96] When Father Tom Clancy asked him if he would like to meet Walker, it was at a time Dowie was searching for a topic for a public lecture he was to give at Brandeis. When Dowie returned to Brandeis in the fall, he lectured on "Walker Percy: Sensualist-Thinker." Later, in a revised form, the lecture would appear in print.

Walker went to the Abbey of Our Lady of Gethsemani in Kentucky to meet Thomas Merton, along with Jim Holloway and the Rev. Will Campbell and other members of the Committee of Southern Churchmen who published the journal *Katallagete*. When Walker returned home in the second week of July, he wrote to "Father Louis" (Merton's name in the Trappist order) saying it was a pleasure to have met him. They had been left alone together one Saturday morning because, as Walker wrote, the others had wandered about the hillside and expected "that somehow some great Apostolic Catholic sparks would fly and *Katallagete* would be fecundated by many noble ecumenical ideas. When the truth is I haven't had an idea for months. Anyhow it was a pleasure meeting you and something I have aimed to do for some time."[97] Clearly no thunder-thinking had taken place as these two men grew to know each other. At the abbey, Walker found a robust Merton, dressed in jeans and a T-shirt that resembled a "Marine skivy-shirt." Merton poured Walker some bourbon and water as they sat in his hermitage. Walker was surprised to see large photos on the walls of the hermitage that John Howard Griffin had taken. Merton's *The Seven Storey Mountain* had meant a lot to Walker, especially as both of them were affected by "Columbia University agnosticism" and had acquaintances in common. Walker, who had previously listened to tapes of Merton at Manresa during one of his retreats, now wanted the name of a book on Bantu metaphysics that Merton had mentioned; it would help with a novel he was trying to conceive, which concerned "the decline and fall of the USA as a consequence of its failure with the Negroes. It takes place in a pleasant all-white 100 percent Christian exurb named Paradise. As a consequence of internecine conflict between right-wing 'patriotic' anti-Communist 'Christians' and left-wing scientific-artistic euthanasic psychedelic pagans, the country falls apart, the whites more or less kill each other off, leaving a black guerilla group in control of Paradise." Walker and the others had lunch in the refectory with the monks.

Merton wrote Walker that the book he referred to, *La Philosophie bantoue* by Redemptorist Placide Tempels, was difficult to find. He might try to locate instead the Grove edition of Jahainz Jahn's *Muntu*. Merton acknowledged the reason why he and Walker had been left alone: "But I enjoy talking to people (except about movements). I think the best thing is to belong to a universal anti-movement underground. The failure to deal with the Negroes properly and justly and humanly seems to be by now conclusive, irreversible, and your novel is acting itself out. Just keep a diary, maybe."[98] He signed his letter "Tom." Merton informed Walker that he was in his thoughts as he continued his explorations into Bantu myths and religious ideas.[99] Merton was reading Bengt Sundkler's *Bantu Prophets in South Africa*, which deals with the syncretism of Zulu religion and a kind of Evangelical Christianity found in South Africa. He suggested the types of questions that might interest Walker as he looked at the coming Bantu society in the United States: medical diagnosis, psychosomatic illness, questions of potency, interesting treatments, and resistance to nefarious influence of dead ancestors: "You could probably distinguish a high Church sort of set with very decorous unctions of the infirm, and a low Church set of more rollings, beatings, vomiting, etc. There might be heated controversies and even religious and ideological conflicts over crucial points concerning the dead: where they are, what they are doing, how they should be treated, fed, appeased, raised, not raised, kept quiet, etc. What about nefarious influence of Catholic and Lutheran ancestors? There is by the way an African Castor Oil Dead Church in which new life is acquired by laxatives. Interesting possibility of description of a mass revival meeting of a Church of this type." He also recommended that Walker read *Man*, one of the better anthropological journals. He sent Walker one of his latest mimeographed essays, "The Long Hot Summer of Sixty-seven," and mentioned that he was working on *The Geography of Lograire*, a long poetic work-in-progress.

Merton had sparked Walker's imagination: "Am most entranced by the prospect of a society of prosperous middle-class fallen-aways from the African Castor Oil Dead Church who will have taken over the Covington Country Club Estates in 1977 following the ideological wars among the Whites."[100] Walker said he had reservations about uniting race and Vietnam under the same rubric, since he regarded one as the clearest kind of moral issue and the other as murderously complex and baffling.

In reading the mimeographed material that Merton had sent him, Walker was struck by a statement made by Whitney Young: "You've either got to shoot all the Negroes or treat them with justice." Any ambiguity Walker might have had about the civil rights movement now took on a clear-cut perspective. In a letter to Mother Johnette Putnam, O.S.B., he reflected on this visit with Merton: "There is this perennial issue of activism vs. monasticism which he never really resolved—and which I certainly wouldn't even attempt to resolve . . . Considering his fiery revolutionary nature, I thought he was remarkably faithful. He never quit his vocation—despite the fact that for twenty years I heard repeated rumors that he was leaving or had left, was schizophrenic, has seen the folly of monkery, etc."[101] Again, Walker proved that he was an excellent reader of someone's character. In a playful gesture, Walker sent Merton a card in mid-October supporting Ned Touchstone for Superintendent of Education in Louisiana that had racial overtones. It would be Walker's last attempt to communicate with his friend, who died while attending an ecumenical conference in Bangkok in December 1968.

At this time, Walker began to experience the pressures and vagaries of fame. He was asked by the administrators of the National Book Award to be a judge for a new division on translations, and he wanted to recommend Robert Bly's translation of Knut Hamsun's *Hunger* for an award.[102] FSG sent him four other books in translation they had published that Walker might also consider.[103] In mid-September, Bob Giroux wrote to Walker about his first two novels: "The Noonday edition of *The Moviegoer* has given me a chance to reread a novel I liked very much when it first appeared. It seems even better on rereading, richer and deeper, and I even see (or think I see) a connection between the ending and *The Last Gentleman*."[104] Walker had not seen the new paperback; the only one he had at home was the Danish version.[105] Lila Karpf, in charge of subsidiary rights at FSG, feverishly tried to promote French editions of both of Walker's novels with Monique Nathan of Le Seuil.[106] Yet by mid-October, Walker was informed that FSG wanted to remainder some copies of *The Last Gentleman*; the Book Find Club bought 500 copies at sixty-nine cents each.[107]

At Loyola University his class of seven students met for the first of their two-and-a-half-hour seminars in a large parlor on the second floor of Cummings Hall.[108] Outside, the passing streetcars, lit up interiorly, pleasantly rumbled by. Dressed casually, Walker handed out a list of works they would be discussing, "novels of alienation," as he called them: *Notes from Underground, Nausea, The Stranger, The Fall, The Sun Also Rises, Light in August, Lie Down in Darkness, Invisible Man, The Pawnbroker* by Edward L. Wallant, *The Voyeur* by Alain Robbe-Grillet, and *Three* by Flannery O'Connor. He primed the pump by discussing Dostoevsky's work and asked questions about the implications of the view that a person is incapable of moral choice or unable to act. As he ranged through some of the positions of the existentialists, he apologized for not being a skilled teacher. If anything, he wanted the class to join in and share their own views with him. He talked about his correspondence with Flannery O'Connor and Thomas Merton, even showing them some actual letters.

On his way to class, Walker enjoyed stopping in at the Maple Street

Book Store, located a short walk from the Tulane campus. Started by
Rhoda K. Norman and Mary Kellogg, Rhoda Faust's mother, the store
boasted five rooms of paperback shelves. Because of the efforts of the
two founders, plus the diligence of Marigny Dupuy, the bookshop gradually came to be an oasis for many in Uptown New Orleans if they
wanted a copy of the latest novel by a local writer or a heady treatise
by an avant-garde European philosopher. (Walker once stopped by the
Maple Street Book Store with William Styron.[109]) Because he had known
Rhoda Faust since she was a little girl, they often drank coffee nearby.
Walker appreciated the fact that Rhoda promoted his books aggressively.

In mid-November, Walker participated in a literary symposium at
Loyola and Xavier University, along with Bill Corrington, Miller Williams, and outside speakers Frank Hercules, author of *I Want a Black Doll*
and *Where the Hummingbird Flies*; Seymour Epstein, professor of English
at Princeton; Robert Pack, poet; Dabney Stuart, professor of English at
Washington and Lee University; and John Williams of Denver, author of
the novel *Stoner*.[110] Walker's involvement in Catholic education no doubt
prompted him to write a letter to *The Clarion Herald* commenting on the
remarks by Lloyd Rittiner, a member of the New Orleans School Board.
He was reported as saying that, because religious schools instill religious
beliefs in their students, they are inferior to public schools. Walker said
he thought society had gone beyond making such bigoted accusations;
he was happy that Catholics did not go around saying public schools
are atheistic and inferior. In addition, Walker thought Catholics should
continue to support public schools through taxes. For Walker the sub-
stantive issue was how a public school system could be devised that was
not hostile to the Judeo-Christian view of man while at the same time it
respected the views of others who do not share these views. "How to
preserve the freedom of the parent to educate his child without sacrific-
ing the excellence of education?" Such issues would be solved, he believed, by intelligent people of goodwill.

That fall Noel Parmentel, a native of the area and a graduate of
Tulane, approached Ben C. Toledano, a lawyer from an old New Orleans
family, about the possibility of transforming *The Moviegoer* into a film.[111]
The option Walker had made with Ransdell Cox would expire in January. Parmentel had worked with the film company of Pennebaker-
Leacock in the late 1950s and had met Walker several times. After
graduating from the University of North Carolina, Toledano worked for
the States' Rights Party of Louisiana before studying law at LSU. When
he returned to New Orleans in 1961, he became involved in local politics

and ran for the state legislature as a Democrat in 1963. That experience prompted him to become a Republican, which, in turn, led to his meeting Phin and, through Phin, Walker. Their friendship developed when Walker took Ann to town for speech therapy; sometimes he would stop to see Toledano at his house on Camp Street. When they finally approached Walker about making a film of his novel, Walker explained that Randy Cox still held an option but he had not done much with it. Given this tentative nod, Parmentel started planning. He knew that Hal Prince was also interested in making the film, but he felt that he could accomplish the task himself with the aid of Richard Leacock, the cinematographer of Robert Flaherty's film *Louisiana Story*. "You will have a great deal of difficulty getting a script anybody will film," Walker told Parmentel. "Why?" "Because of the interior monologue." Parmentel retorted that Camus's *The Stranger* had been made into a film. Walker wrote to Toledano toward the end of November:

This will confirm our conversation yesterday. I do not want a misunderstanding of my position if I can help it. I would hope that Noel or you deal with my agent, whose address I gave you, now or after the first of the year as you please. It would have been better if Noel had done this in the beginning. That is why I have a film agent and pay her ten per cent. What I don't like is to transact business in this superheated personal atmosphere with implications of bad faith on my part if I don't do such and such. Noel must surely realize that Randy Cox is free to pick up his option any time between now and January 1. And that I am free to sell the property to anyone I please after that time or not to sell it at all. Having said this, I will say that if the property is on the market January 1 and if Noel makes a reasonable proposal, setting forth some sort of credible prospects of putting together people and money, I would think it quite possible to do business. But let's do it through my agent.[112]

Parmentel contacted a seasoned film veteran, agent Robert Lantz, who was not particularly interested but said that he would contact Mike Nichols. Lantz knew that financing and a good script were the first two essentials and Parmentel had neither. Parmentel then contacted Ulu Grosbard, a stage and film director responsible for the 1965 revival of Arthur Miller's *A View from the Bridge* at the Sheridan Square Playhouse, who liked Walker's novel but did not want to compete with anything that Mike Nichols might be considering. The waters were stirring, but not flowing in the same direction.

Walker wrote to Annie Laurie Williams at McIntosh & Otis in late December, reminding her that his "gentleman's agreement" with Randy Cox for *The Moviegoer*'s film rights would now expire. He had received inquiries about the rights: "One in particular I have reason to believe is a serious offer and I have accordingly asked the parties to get in touch with you . . . Mr. Parmentel did not spell out to me the terms of the agreement under which he wished to exercise the film rights of *The Moviegoer*. I suggested that he negotiate this with you. Mr. Parmentel has an understanding of the book and is, in my opinion, seriously interested in making a film."[113] Walker forwarded a copy of his letter to Toledano.

As the academic year came to a close Walker suggested to Loyola that they might like to hire Frank Hercules to teach next semester; his feelings would not be hurt if Loyola hired someone else.[114] Walker could relax after a tiring semester that had required more time than he anticipated. When the course finished before Christmas, Walker gave each student a paperback copy of *The Moviegoer*.

As President Lyndon Johnson ordered into active duty 14,787 navy and air force reservists to build up forces in Vietnam in January, Walker heard from Donald Barthelme that FSG was now his publisher too. Walker wanted Barthelme to stand in line, since he needed Henry Robbins's editorial help first.[115] Robbins inquired how Walker's new novel was taking shape: "I hope your doing all this judging of other people's writing isn't distracting you from the main thing."[116] It was a dry spell for Walker, as he wrote to Phinizy Spalding in the History Department at the University of Georgia; he had not taken pencil to paper in months.[117] While Walker had enjoyed his stint as a professor, he admitted it was a "mistake" to try to teach and write at the same time. In commenting on three student papers sent to him by Lewis Lawson, Walker found them better than what had been turned in at Loyola. Walker mentioned that he was surprised that many readers failed to make a connection between his fiction and his religious beliefs: "My work is really quite orthodox, by my calculation at least. The last couple of pages of *The Moviegoer* is a kind of re-enactment of the last two pages of *The Brothers Karamazov*."[118]

By mid-February, Walker thought his two friends had a green light for filming *The Moviegoer*: "Noel has the talent and the other necessary stuff to make a good film," Walker wrote Toledano.[119] Parmentel had agreed to give Walker approval of the final shooting script. Walker had no intention, however, of looking over Parmentel's shoulder and making suggestions. The last time he wrote to him at his Park Avenue address in New York, the letter was returned unopened. This was the first clue of this sort that Walker failed to recognize.

Walker gave his readers an indirect peek at the novel-in-progress in a commissioned article he wrote for the winter 1967–68 issue of *Katallagete*, entitled "Notes for a Novel About the End of the World." He began by stating that a "serious novel about the destruction of the United States and the end of the world should perform the function of prophecy in reverse. A novelist writes about the coming end in order to warn about present ills and so avert the end." Writers are not necessarily wiser than others, but they have a perspective on life or an "affliction" that gives them an odd point of view. In this context, Walker was not considering a Wellsian fantasy or a science-fiction show, or a novel that predicts the end of the world. It came down to the question: "Is the secular city in great trouble or is the novelist a decadent bourgeois left over from a past age who likes to titivate himself and his readers with periodic doom-crying?" Walker had in mind a novelist who is ultimately concerned about the nature of man and reality. Such a writer is "religious" in the sense that he binds himself to reality and deals, as do Dostoevsky, Tolstoy, Camus, Sartre, Faulkner, Flannery O'Connor, either with meaning or its absence. A novelist can function as a quasi-prophet in that he or she communicates something urgent, usually bad news. But care must be taken. "Nothing comes easier than the sepulchral manifestoes of the old-style café existentialist and the new-style hippy who professes to despise the squares and the technology of the Western city while living on remittance checks from the same source, and who would be the first to go for his shot of penicillin if he got meningitis." If the artist disagrees with views held by other Americans, he can either be considered as mistaken and foolish, or in an Orphic way what he is telling us might be of value.

The novelist, unlike the scientist, deals with mystery. Walker found it curious that the new novelist, not the new theologian, now judges the world, calls attention to catastrophe, and pronounces anathemas upon his permissive society. Above all, the novelist sees the massive failure of Christianity in the world today, and he witnesses individuals who have a penchant for catastrophe—not without hope, however. The desire for absolute loneliness cannot be separated from a rediscovery of community and reconciliation. It is as if a person arrives at a destination and then runs out of purpose in life. For Walker "the hero of the post-modern novel is a man who has forgotten his bad memories and conquered his present ills and who finds himself in the victorious secular city. His only problem now is to keep from blowing his brains out." Has man so realigned his energies that the Good News is no longer relevant to him? Many in modern society accept the "magical aura of science" as a way to deal with life's problems. The novelist of the apocalypse must try to change the reader's heart and mind.

As Walker worked on his new novel, he would deal, quite uncharacteristically, with racial unrest and juxtapose this with a parody of regulating behavior, much of it sexual, by means of electronic instruments.[120] Walker now turned his attention to the end time and the games people play as the moment of the apocalypse nears. He pushed the novel form to an extreme, partly to emphasize the direction that a self-destructive American society has the possibility of taking if it is not careful. In the early draft John Smith seriously contemplates making love to Moira Shaffner, who works with Ken Kiss in the Clitoris Clinic, as the Bantu revolution envelops them. While Walker went on to modify and develop these two characters, other characters were suppressed or deferred. One character, for example, the Rev. Martin Hebert, a light-skinned black who left the Church to marry and write a book, seemed even too much for Walker to develop. Father Hebert is depicted as a heroin addict who wants people in need of rehabilitation to return to a housing project. Another character, Harry Legion, M.D., is looking for 10 percent of the heavy sodium that had not been recovered from the French Quarter Project (an idea dealt with more fully in Walker's final novel). When first seen, Dr. Legion wants to make a proposal to Jack about his Lapsometer, since he possesses a drug at the National Institute of Mental Health that has curative powers. In another draft the protagonist talks briefly about his wife, Doris, and his daughter, Samantha, two important characters. Another draft was started on June 5, the day that Robert Kennedy was shot by Sirhan Sirhan in the Hotel Ambassador in Los Angeles. With all this cruelty at local and international levels, it was clear that humankind—neither total angel nor total beast—could not solve its problems, whether they be racial, sexual, familial, or social, through the application of machinery alone.

Stanley Kubrick wrote from England to Parmentel in March saying he had his own projects and could not work on *The Moviegoer* film.[121] Lucille Sullivan of Annie Laurie Williams's office gave Parmentel permission to proceed with the script until formal agreements were signed between him and Walker.[122] According to the agreement signed on April 1, he would pay $3,000 to Walker, with Annie Laurie Williams acting as an agent, for an eighteen-month option, which could be extended an additional six months for $1,000. Option payments would be applicable against a cash purchase of $15,000, and Walker would receive not less than 5 percent of the net profits of the film. Filming must begin within two years of the signing, or rights would revert. Stipulations for television were also included. Walker had the right to approve the final script.

Life on March 29 carried Walker's review of William Gass's collection of stories, *In the Heart of the Heart of the Country*. While Walker had found Gass's first book, *Omensetter's Luck*, dense and yet immensely rewarding, like a kind of transplantation of the Faulkner idiom to Midwestern soil, he considered this book a mixed bag. The stories "achieve at their best a superb union of manner and form, a dreamlike action yielding up meanings at several levels, the whole wrought in a poet's prose." Walker clearly admired Gass, particularly one story in the collection, "The Pedersen Kid."

Walker joined Curtis Thomsen of the Delta Primate Center, Charles and Suzanne Hill, Henry Randle, Jacqueline Pierre and her mother, Naomi, and others, including several Protestant ministers, in the Covington Community Relations Council, a biracial group that was more activist than other groups in the state. Out of this umbrella organization sprang the credit union and the federal job training program in Covington. Walker wrote to Father Twomey supporting the desire for a Head Start program and a day-care center and asking for Loyola's assistance.[123] A picture exists of Walker sitting in the middle of a group of nuns as Father Twomey spoke at St. Paul's about Head Start.[124] "It's funny," Walker recalled, "but I didn't see a single black face in the whole auditorium."

Walker paid attention to the writings of the Rev. Robert I. Guste, a diocesan priest: "I don't think he changed the minds of many of the older Catholics. But he affected young people. He strongly influenced me and Bill Sorum and Jack Nelson." What struck Walker about Father Twomey and his colleagues were their old-fashioned ways, with "a Protestant ethic," as he put it, of doing right and being proper, and yet having roots in Catholic and Southern Christianity—like a Georgia preacher with advanced ideas. Father Twomey told Walker that Loyola would sponsor the group in Covington. The violent murder of the Rev. Martin Luther King, Jr., in Memphis on April 24 shocked and rallied those concerned with civil rights. Father Twomey preached at a Mass at the abbey in honor of the slain black leader. Two days later, Walker declined an invitation to go to Washington University in St. Louis, explaining that he preferred not to leave Covington at present.[125]

That spring, Carlton Creemens published his interview with Walker in *The Southern Review*. Walker replied succinctly to a question about an article written by Eudora Welty in which she talked about the differences between a novelist and a civil rights crusader: "My own feeling: I don't mind saying or writing what I think on the social issues or the race issue in the South." He maintained that he was completely convinced of the rightness of the struggle among blacks for civil rights. "And when any writer in the South pretends he can write a novel and ignore the social issue of the Negro, something is wrong." The writer in the South finds himself caught between the right wing in the South and the intellectual herd in the North, who line themselves up clearly against all the things they oppose. It might be an advantage living in the South—Walker wasn't quite sure. He did feel that his task as a writer was to transmit universal truths of a particular sort. "And so, what the artist does, or tries to do, is simply to validate the human experience and to tell people the deep human truths which they already unconsciously know." Walker mentioned that his own writing involved many false starts and blind detours as he discovered where the novel was taking him. Creemens was able to extract a lively, engaging interview, as Walker ranged back and forth about the role of the novelist and various aspects of fiction, from the French novel to pornography to Jewish novelists.

Toward the end of June, Hodding Carter shared the news of his conversion with Walker. In his autobiography, *Where Main Street Meets the River*, Hodding said he had made retreats at Xavier Hall in Pass Christian: "Young Father Sheridan was a dedicated Jesuit shock trooper, slangily contemporary when it was appropriate, hypnotic, mystical and sure. I went the whole way—except for making a confession—fumbling through the rituals, at first self-consciously, from early morning to well after nightfall." He was received into the Roman Catholic Church by Father Sheridan and made his first communion at St. Joseph's Church near Gulfport.[126] That day he called Walker with the news.

In a letter to Lewis Lawson, Walker said he would be surprised if Lawson came across many writers influenced by Kierkegaard, except in the past few years. "It has seemed to me precisely a watershed between American and European fiction that the former has been largely innocent of radical or 'metaphysical' concerns—until quite recently. But this is only an impression."[127] Walker thought that Updike in *Couples* might fill the bill, but he wasn't sure. "*Couples* is evidently open to an obvious Kierkegaardian explication: e.g. fucking elevated to a kind of religion, SK's sphere of esthetic-damnation, and then transcended and discarded —for the ethical? for the religious?" Walker's own conversion clearly could not find a parallel in the works of other writers.

Those moments that Walker would take for private reading, observing, and note taking were his way of preparing for his next sustained writing project. One of his great strengths was his ability to size up people and situations—and the city of New Orleans was no exception. In September, *Harper's* featured Walker's article, entitled "New Orleans Mon Amour," which recorded his fascination with this city. The only other locale, outside the South in general, that Walker would have considered living in was Santa Fe.[128] New Orleans, as any visitor knows, is not an Atlantis rising out of the ocean. In this "marriage of George Babbitt and Marianne," Walker saw more than toleration, he saw people who enjoyed one another's company and had some habitable space. Walker was well aware of the patience of the blacks in New Orleans; as long as a black does not do anything, nobody notices, but if he does something, it is resented by whites. Though once known for its exploitive trade market, New Orleans had luckily hit upon jazz, "a truly happy and truly American sound which bears little relation to the chamber music of Brubeck and Mulligan." There is always a series of "and yets" when considering New Orleans—trade-offs that redeem any negative reality in the city. Walker praised Father Twomey for doing "more than any one man hereabouts to translate Catholic social principles into meaningful action." He praised the new archbishop, Philip M. Hannan, for being aware of the needs of the poor, and Harold R. Perry, S.V.D., the first black Catholic bishop in the United States, recently installed in New Orleans. "The peculiar virtue of New Orleans, like St. Theresa, may be that of the Little Way, a talent for everyday life rather than the heroic deed. If in its two hundred and fifty years of history, it has produced no giants, no Lincolns, no Lees, no Faulkners, no Thoreaus, it has nurtured a great many people who live tolerably, like to talk and eat, laugh a good deal, manage generally to be civil and at the same time mind their own business." In a time when tensions divided large cities and small towns throughout the United States, Walker provided an honest appraisal of a city he greatly admired. In his new novel, however, he would explore the terrain north and east of New Orleans, an area that Walker now considered his home territory.

Walker was still concerned about *The Moviegoer* film rights. He phoned Noel Parmentel, turning down his request to use a portion of *The Last Gentleman* in his script.[129]

Walker, John Hawkes, and William Styron had the task of selecting works to be included in the *American Literary Anthology/I*, published by Noonday (a division of FSG), featuring the best work from literary journals. Walker said in the preface, "Unlike the judges of beauty contests, I don't feel like saying how hard it was to choose from so many good-looking girls. Truthfully, there were quite a few dogs." The judges looked through 285 magazines for material. The first work of fiction they selected was Bill Corrington's "To Carthage Then I Came" from *The Southwest Review*. Walker felt buoyed by this type of literary engagement, though he had serious reservations about the political climate of the country. He was leaning toward Hubert Humphrey.[130]

In late November, Parmentel sent a copy of *The Moviegoer* to Irene Selznick in New York.[131] He wanted Katharine Hepburn to play Emily Cutrer, since he thought that Walker had her in mind as a physical model for this character; Myrna Loy was another possibility for this part. Since the script would be finished in December, Parmentel intended to get a second unit down to New Orleans in mid-February to shoot the Mardi Gras scenes, and thus the full company was tentatively scheduled to assemble there in late spring or early summer of 1969. Sam Waterston was Noel's choice to play Binx. A talented and rising actor, Waterston had played Prince Hal to Stacy Keach's Henry IV during the summer of 1968 in New York's Shakespeare in the Park. In addition, he had recently completed his first feature film, tentatively titled *The Three of Us*, based on an Irwin Shaw novel. Kate was still uncast, though Parmentel had written Katharine Ross through her agent in Los Angeles. Lewis Minor ("L.M.") Kit Carson had met Ross recently in Cuernavaca, and Parmentel hoped to send her a copy of the script in the near future. He was also considering Sam Peckinpah as a possible director.

Phin, Roy, and Walker all went to Aunt Ellen Percy Murphy's funeral in mid-November. Walker arrived late for the ceremony. Bunt and Walker had been to see her about two weeks before, at Hanover House, a nursing home on the south side of Birmingham. Walker and Phin had also visited previously.[132] Roy flew from New York to Birmingham to arrange for the funeral and the burial in Elmwood Cemetery. It would be one of the last times any of the Percy brothers talked about the old Birmingham days with Donie DeBardeleben. When Walker returned he made his annual retreat at Manresa in late November, along with Phin and seventy-five other men. The delightfully entertaining English Jesuit Bernard Bassett was the retreat master. The humor of this retreat might have prompted a feigning mood on Walker's part in early December, as shown in the letter he wrote to Mr. Fontanelle, business manager of Winn-Dixie in New Orleans:

I am a writer living in Covington. For my next book I am planning a socioeconomic study of a small Southern community, using my hometown Covington as a model. The tentative title of the book is *Small Town South* . . . The reason I am writing you is that in describing the local employment practices vis-à-vis race relations, I plan to cite the Winn-Dixie store here as a bad example. However, I do not wish to do so without checking the accuracy of my information with you.

My information from the Covington Community Relations Council is that your store here discriminates against Negroes in its hiring policy, that it has for one reason or another refused to employ Negroes as cashiers or in other responsible positions.

Frankly my present plan is to contrast your store here unfavorably with A&P which has shown good faith and nondiscrimination in its hiring. My book is to be positively oriented, however, stressing the comparatively good race relations which obtain in some Southern communities. Therefore I certainly do not wish to comment unfavorably on Winn-Dixie if it is in any way undeserved.[133]

Having read the letter, Henry Robbins replied to Walker: "Far from thinking you've gone batty, I think your news about *Small Town South* is very exciting. Of course, I have a certain regret that this means putting aside the novel for a little while, but apart from that, the book sounds like it will be fascinating and important."[134] But there was an angrier side to Walker's concern about the race issue.

On stationery of the Humphrey-Muskie Headquarters on Howard Avenue in New Orleans, Walker wrote Toledano about his review of Willie Morris's book. Walker considered it unwarranted in its negative criticism. When he lived in Mississippi, he said, "it took a lot of guts to buck the mainstream of good Christian racist businessmen and very few indeed did it, including my brother and Hodding Carter, and for their pains got obscene phone calls and garbage dumped in their driveway."[135] The answer to the present racial situation would be solved not by writers and intellectuals but by the churchgoing businessman. In late January 1969, after Richard M. Nixon was sworn in, having narrowly defeated Hubert H. Humphrey, the political temperament of the country was changing, and Walker's letter to Toledano shows growing irritation: "With your talents, intelligence, courage and integrity, and what with living in the South, you should not be attacking liberals like Willie Morris who, after all and whatever their faults, are on the right side of the big issue: race. For one thing, there are few if any liberals left in the South and a growing number of bastards on the right. Why don't you attack them?"[136] Toledano was flirting with trouble in Walker's eyes, and their friendship might not stand too much antagonism.

With two novels under his belt and a third in progress, he revealed to Charles Bell one of his deepest desires. Commenting on an essay that Bell wrote about Kierkegaard, Walker said, "My only reply might be expressed in the hope that I will in my old age write a theory of communication which will accommodate news as a form of communication and specify its relevance to various modes of existence. You express the standard scandal of the scientific-artistic mind to the imputation of significance to news beyond its particular significance. But I am a bad person to address these remarks to, since I am a bad Catholic, a lazy writer and a sinful man."[137] In effect, he had given Bell part of the subtitle of the novel that would be published in 1971. When Shelby's mother died that January, Walker went to the funeral in Greenville; he saw Josephine Haxton and together they discussed the old days in Greenville.

Toward the end of April, Kit Carson, who was finishing a book on cinema vérité while doing research in the Museum of Modern Art in New York, finished the script and sent a copy to Toledano.[138] Carson, a graduate of the University of Dallas, had read *The Moviegoer* soon after it was published. Through his friendship with Robert Alexander at Tulane, he went to see Walker, who directed him to his agent. When he went to see Annie Laurie Williams, he had ten copies of an early version of the script. She told him in no uncertain terms, "Professionals are involved in this, sonny." It was after Carson began writing film reviews, including one on the Pennebaker-Leacock documentary on Bob Dylan entitled *Don't Look Back*, which Noel Parmentel read, that he was invited to work seriously on his script. Carson had showed it to several people, including Robert Benton, one of the writers of *Bonnie and Clyde*. Parmentel now hoped that preproduction would start in the fall. Henry Robbins had heard marvelous reports about the screenplay of *The Moviegoer*, though he had not yet had a chance to read it. He had met Carson and seen his first movie, *David Holtzman's Diary*, and could see why he might be the right person to convert *The Moviegoer* to the screen.[139] In an early, undated version of the script, Carson noted that he struggled four or five days and nights with the streetcar scene and decided to omit it, mainly to keep the story line moving and to hold the audience's attention.[140] The monologue on the streetcar, he felt, was not enough to sustain dramatic tension. In addition, the "movie-in-Pirate's-Alley scene," as Carson called it, was extra and might not be filmed. Other than that, Carson felt that the scenes were "jumping along" at the right pace. Carson recommended that Parmentel see *Bullitt*, which had the type of action Carson used as a model.

When the spring issue of *Shenandoah* appeared, there were tributes to Eudora Welty from Ashley Brown, Malcolm Cowley, Martha Graham, Joyce Carol Oates, Reynolds Price, Diarmuid Russell, Allen Tate, Robert Penn Warren, and Walker. He considered Welty among the best of the living short-story writers (together with Katherine Anne Porter, Caroline Gordon, and Peter Taylor). What was extraordinary was that she had done it in one place—in the same house in Jackson, Mississippi. Walker had his novel-in-progress in mind when he wrote this tribute: "The question is: how can a writer live in a place without either succumbing to angelism and haunting it like a ghost or being 'on,' playing himself or somebody else and watching to see how it comes out?" Walker believed that the time was coming when the American novelists would tire of their angelism—of which obsessive genital sexuality was the most urgent symptom, the reaching out for the flesh that had been shucked—and wonder how to get back into a body, live in a place, at a street address. For such novelists, Eudora Welty would be a valuable clue.

In mid-May, Walker wrote to Bob Giroux thanking him for setting forth the particulars of Merton's death and for sending him Larry Woiwode's novel *What I'm Going to Do I Think*, plus the volume containing Flannery O'Connor's essays. "She cracked some very good enduring holy jokes."[141] He gave an update of his work: "All I can tell you and Henry is that I am doing what I am doing and it will come out the way it comes out." It is not surprising that as Walker wrote about race relations and became more involved in the local civil rights efforts, he and Bunt reached out to help the local Benedictine nuns by establishing a scholarship fund for Marilyn Abadie, known as Sister Marie when she entered the Benedictines.[142] Anonymously, they also gave a scholarship to a student at St. Scholastica's, who was told at one point who her benefactors were. Walker was upset about this breach of confidence and went to the school to complain, but not to withdraw the funds.

About this time, Walker drew closer to Vincent Malcolm and Christine Byrnes and their growing family: Laura, Mary, Walton Malcolm, Francis Joseph, Amy Clare, and Una.[143] (Walker later became godfather to John Martin Byrnes.[144]) A 1951 graduate of LSU, Malcolm, as he preferred to be called, served in the army for two years, returned to graduate school at LSU, married, and taught for two years at St. Paul's in Covington, starting in 1956. He eventually transferred to Tulane to continue his graduate work, and the family moved to New Orleans in 1958. Not only did Christine and Malcolm know Walker and Bunt from the days when Ann attended Mrs. Reeder's kindergarten (Mrs. Reeder was Christine's aunt), but Christine had contact with Walker through Head Start. In early 1966, the Byrnes family moved back to Covington, to an isolated farmhouse off Highway 190. Walker came to the house once for a family liturgy. Baptized a Catholic, Malcolm had been reared as a Protestant, but returned to the Catholic Church in the late 1940s. Vatican II had awakened within him a new realization of his own spirituality, but he did not expect much from the Catholic hierarchy. Malcolm felt that Walker was breaking out of a mold as he became involved in working for the underprivileged. "Walker had a whole lot of cool and he was very steadfast," Malcolm said. When the Byrnes children started going to St. Peter's, a controversy developed; the pastor, Rudolph Siedling, O.S.B., favoring integration, pushed for a two-tiered fee system at the school, depending on whether or not students were members of the parish. As a member of the school board, and deeply concerned about the plight of the poor, Malcolm objected to the new policy and eventually left the board. Naturally, Sister Frances MacIsaac, O.S.B., the principal, was distraught, and asked Walker to serve as a counselor. By that time, Holy Family Parish in Covington had closed its school and parish. Sisters

Johnette Putnam and Jeanne d'Arc Kernion went to the Percy home a number of times to discuss the issues with Walker and profit from his advice.

Just after finishing her senior year in college (though the actual graduation was put off since she had a few more courses to complete), Mary Pratt married Byrne Robert Lobdell, someone she had known all her life, with Father Siedling presiding at the noon ceremony on May 31. As she walked down the aisle of St. Peter's Church, Walker felt proud of the daughter he and Bunt had raised. He had always wanted a family, and now that phase of his life would change slightly as he contemplated Mary Pratt and Byrne's future together. After Shelby (soon about to start his account of Brice's Crossroads) and Gwyn flew back to Memphis after the wedding, Shelby wrote to Walker, "I thought Mary Pratt made a handsome bride and took it all with splendid aplomb."

Though Walker's novel-in-progress dealt with a Southern apocalypse, he was still very much interested in the relationship between art and technology, as he elaborated in a long letter to critic Nilo Lindgren: "You may turn out to be the fellow who can synthesize this crazy technological world. You are where it is and somehow you're one of the very few who *can* see it all."[145] Walker had portrayed his first protagonist as an engineer; he felt that a conception of the artist as a kind of playmate of the engineer in the latter's off-hours would be diametrically opposed to the views of every serious novelist he knew. While an artist like Robert Rauschenberg needed to cooperate with engineers to complete his work of art, Walker believed, other situations should be recalled, like Max Planck's wandering around the Tiergarten trying to figure out why a heated black body emits such a peculiar radiation jump or, on the other hand, Rilke and Robert Lowell sweating over one poetic line. Walker wrote: "The issue really stems from Dewey's assumption that science was work toward the pursuit of truth and that art was play in the interests of recreation. I would feel very strongly with Susanne Langer that art is very serious business indeed, and as passionately concerned with cognition and truth as science, though in a different dimension." He suspected that if we abandoned the truth-seeking cognitive goal of all serious art (the truth being what it is like to be a person in a certain place experiencing life), the artist would find it almost impossible to humanize a technological environment and restore a lost sense of community.

Project Head Start finally got launched during the summer when a group gathered under the moss-draped oaks of Regina Coeli Convent on Folsom Road outside Covington to implement a program that would serve economically disadvantaged preschool children. Originally started by the federal government as an eight-week summer program in 1965, it was designed to help break the cycle of poverty by providing preschool children of low-income families with a comprehensive program to meet their emotional, social, health, nutritional, and psychological needs. The local program initially served 125 children, with funding amounting to $45,000, which would be increased in subsequent years. Walker and Nikki Barranger served as registered agents for incorporation.

Walker reached out that fall in another way: after Hurricane Camille struck, he, Dominic Braud, O.S.B., and others helped the poor whose homes had been devastated.[146] Walker transported hundreds of gallons of water to help the homeless in Biloxi.

Walker finally read and approved (but not before he expressed displeasure) Kit Carson's film script, though he wondered why Noel Parmentel had not been much in evidence in New Orleans. "Did Noel die or get locked in the attic by his girl friends?"[147] A film of *The Moviegoer* meant that more of his novels would be bought and read, and he could continue to make a living from writing. He felt very committed to furthering this project.

In early October, Walker wrote to Elizabeth Spencer, a writer from Carrollton, Mississippi, then living in Montreal, thanking her for her recent praise of *The Last Gentleman*. "Yes, I expect you're right about the Catholic part not working. I was trying to write a novel about the sacrament of baptism and even though Flannery O'Connor said you can't do it now, I thought you could. You can't."[148] Walker concluded by saying that he was sunk in a "miserable novel" and did not know how to get out. In mid-November, Shelby, now fifty-three, served again as cheerleader, urging Walker to work on his new novel. "Book sounds great, affording as it does so many chances to wing it. Maybe that's a drawback in a way, because reading it over and looking back you'll always see how much more you could have made of it." Shelby had recently returned to Greenville to prepare his mother's tombstone and had a chance to see Trail Lake, for the first time in twenty-five years, and other sites he knew so well. "Weird feeling. All tenant houses gone, all woods, all Old South, *all* gone." Robert Holland, a Mississippi State University English professor, had started a campaign to save the old Percy home in Greenville, owned by two Greenville merchants willing to sell it for $26,500. The city had no use for the house and it was demolished at the end of the summer. "A skeleton. You can look right through the walls," Shelby wrote, "and see where we used to sleep and read, and the fireplaces where the fires were and where Mr. Will use to light his matches, padding around in fuzzy slippers and the robe that he couldn't keep the belt tied to . . . Do you realize he was then about our age?"

Lewis Lawson wrote to the editor of The Noonday Press in late December proposing that he collect and edit selected essays by Walker in addition to several interviews.[149] Henry Robbins sent the proposal to Walker, and added that he did not favor the proposed volume, though it did give rise to a question bandied about the office: what about publishing all of Walker's nonfiction in a single volume?[150] Walker liked Lawson's proposal, since he had received inquiries from various English professors about interpreting his novels. Walker gave his approval, provided that everyone understood that Lawson's proposed work would not prejudice in any way Walker's own plans to collect, revise, edit, and add to his own collection of essays, which he hoped to assemble in the near future.[151] Walker believed that Lawson showed a shrewd understanding of the themes of The Moviegoer. Robbins, however, wrote to Lawson saying that his projected volume would compete with the Noonday edition of the novel, thus rejecting the idea.[152]

Walker was marvelously steadfast in writing each day, so much so that by mid-January 1970 he had finished a long (650 sheets), fairly complete typescript, entitled How to Make Love in the Ruins: The Journal of a Bad Catholic at a Time Near the End of the World. This title was subsequently changed, he admitted to Lewis Simpson, because it sounded like a report from Masters and Johnson.[153] Walker would have one later version typed, which he would send off to his publisher. He felt he was too busy writing when he turned down Cleanth Brooks's invitation to lecture at Yale.[154]

Work on the film of The Moviegoer was progressing. When Ulu Grosbard read Kit Carson's script, he told Parmentel, "We'll have to throw it away." Parmentel decided otherwise, and Grosbard backed out of the project. Agnes Varda was approached as a possible director; in turn, she tried to get Warren Beatty interested in playing Binx, and when Parmentel objected (thinking that she might want Goldie Hawn to play Kate), she backed off from the project. Robert Redford read the script to see if he wanted to play Binx; he declined because of what he considered Binx's quirky nature. Katharine Hepburn decided not to play Binx's aunt. After many phone calls and letters, the shooting of the script seemed about to take place. Sam Waterston agreed to play Binx; Elizabeth Hartman to play Kate, and Bruce Dern to play Walter. William Hale joined the team as the director. Friends and relatives of the Percys were abuzz about the film. Sam Waterston—sporting long hair and a self-described "Percy addict"—flew to New Orleans with Parmentel to get a feel for the atmosphere of the city.[155] Waterston felt that Walker's fiction "accorded reality to all that he touched." Parmentel and Waterston went out to meet Walker, spending part of the time outdoors talking to him. Parmentel wondered whether Waterston was too intelligent to play Binx. Waterston had read *The Moviegoer* and felt, as a Bostonian, that his only problem would be to get the Southern accent correct; Walker made a recording of himself reading the first few pages of the novel and sent it to him. At the end of the tape, Walker signed off as they did on the television show *Mission Impossible*. He counseled Waterston to listen to Marlon Brando in the Goetz-Pennebaker production of *Sayonara*. When the shooting started, Walker refrained from visiting the various locations. Waterston stayed with Toledano and his wife, Roulhac, now living on Chestnut Street, and he learned about Toledano's political ambitions.[156] Once, after eating too many oysters, he became quite ill and was confined to bed.

Elizabeth Hartman had started as an actress in *A Patch of Blue* (1965) and *The Group* (1966), and then appeared on Broadway in *Our Town*, beginning in September 1969. After seeing the show, Parmentel went backstage and convinced her to appear in *The Moviegoer*. A few of Hartman's scenes were shot in front of the Café du Monde, near the river, and at one of the masked balls, thanks to the connections of John Hobson of New Orleans. They shot some of Dern's scenes in front of a warehouse where they were building floats for Mardi Gras. Cinematographer Ricky Leacock used a handheld 35 mm camera with color film and shot footage of Waterston and Hartman, wearing radio microphones, from the ballroom balcony.[157] Once Hartman became involved in the film, her husband, Gil Dennis, collaborated on the script. Waterston looked forward to acting in what he considered the novel's concluding key scene—when Kate receives instructions from Binx and together they seal a pact "of mutual redemption." Unfortunately, Sam never saw any of the rushes, including those shown at the Museum of Modern Art in New York, but he felt thrilled to have been part of this uncompleted film, even for a few weeks. Because of Parmentel's gross incompetence, the film was never completed, even after he solicited hundreds of potential backers, and even asked Norman Mailer to write on his behalf, but to no avail. For Parmentel a film that deserves to be made one day is *The Non-Making of "The Moviegoer."*

In nearby St. Tammany Parish Hospital, Walker and Bunt's first grandchild, John Walker Lobdell, was born on March 18. Mary Pratt (still a student) and Byrne were about to move to Fourth Street in Covington.

It is not surprising that Walker proved to be a doting and solicitous grandfather.

In late April, Walker contacted Harvey Core, president of the St. Tammany Parish School Board in Covington, because he felt that the black students at Covington High School had a legitimate grievance in protesting against the display of the Confederate flag at their school.[158] Walker was not ashamed of the Confederate flag; his ancestors had defended it for an honorable cause. But this flag had become an emblem of racism, white supremacy, and bigotry—and thus an insult to all blacks and whites. Walker urged the school board to direct the principal to remove the flag. To make sure his message was heard, Walker sent copies of his letter to Philip Burns, Theodore Talley, Curtis Thomsen, Bill Corrington, Cyprian Schoen, the superintendent of schools in St. Tammany Parish, and Louis Wagner, the principal of Covington High School. Walker also resigned from the restrictive Boston Club on Canal Street in New Orleans.

He gave testimony before federal district judge Frederick J. R. Heebe of New Orleans.[159] Walker, introduced as an expert witness, said that the Confederate flag did not mean the same thing today as it did a hundred years ago. "In Covington, I think it is a very common sight to see automobiles with Confederate flag bumper plates on one end of the car, and a Wallace for President sticker on the other end . . . I've seen it used at political rallies for avowedly segregationist candidates. I have seen it carried by white pickets, picketing newly integrated public schools, and I have known members of the Ku Klux Klan who make no secret of their allegiance to the Confederate flag." Thus Walker could not imagine any black group ever displaying this flag. Under questioning by Stanley A. Halpin, Jr., Walker responded that he had taken some courses in psychiatry in preparation for a career in that field. Julian Rodrique, the defense lawyer, who had known Walker for a long time, conceded that Walker was well versed in present-day conditions in the South; he nevertheless felt that Walker did not qualify as an expert "on the application of the thing or anything of a contemporaneous nature." The judge overruled Rodrique's objection, stating that Walker could testify and that he would treat his testimony "as a question of weight rather than admissibility." Walker mentioned how he dealt with similar issues in his fiction: that Will Barrett notices Confederate flag bumper plates when he returns to the South and that the racial situation of a black applying to a university in *The Last Gentleman* was drawn from the 1962 incident at Ole Miss. "But the point is," Walker testified, "the change in the meaning of the use of the Confederate flag in the past ten or fifteen years, specifically since the Supreme Court decision in 1954, after which time, in my opinion, the Confederate flag has come to stand specifically as a symbol of segregation, a symbol of opposition to desegregation of the public schools." In his testimony, Willie ("Butch") Wilson supported Walker's position. Mrs. Gloria May Stewart, a parent of a student in Covington, also testified that in her opinion the flag represented hatred. The plaintiffs asked that biracial committees be formed for each ward of the parish prior to the beginning of the 1970–71 school year so they could discuss ways of easing tension; they also asked that a black assistant principal be appointed at Covington High School.

Walker informed Shelby about the case: "So I got threatened by the Klan: bomb the house, etc.—we slept in the attic for two weeks—not that I thought there was one chance in 1,000, but didn't want Ann and Bunt to get blown up. Then I accused the local Catholic school of getting rid of the niggers, running a seg school with holy water thrown on it. Now the Catholics (most) are mad at me. And I do believe they're more unpleasant than the Klan. In my book *How to Make Love in the Ruins* (or *Love in the Ruins*, which do you like better, tell me no kidding), the niggers take over in Louisiana and become ten times more bourgeois and Republican ('Knothead' in book) than the whites." Walker even suggested to Shelby, however halfheartedly, that he and Shelby both buy houses at Gulf Shores: "If it weren't for Ann and her attachments here, in fact, I'd be long gone. After twenty-three years here, I am more of an outsider than the first day I arrived."

Walker finished his novel, thinking of *The Fall Out* as an alternative title after Shelby alerted him to the possible confusion with Browning's "Love Among the Ruins," and spent part of the summer playing golf (the first time since he played in Greenville before the war) and reading George Eliot's *Middlemarch* and *Silas Marner*.[160] Finished with fiction, Walker hoped to write a short seminal article on the symbolic process (this would ultimately be his claim to fame, he thought) and a short religio-political work damning the right and left in U.S. life. He also made time to see John Walker (called "Red Label"), who was living nearby with his parents and doing quite well.

On August 4 Walker mailed to Elizabeth Otis two copies of his novel, whose new title had been slightly altered: *How to Make Love in the Ruins: The Adventures of a Bad Catholic at a Time Near the End of the World*. He realized, when he returned from the post office, that for four years he had not played his stereo hi-fi, simply because he had been so focused on writing his novel. "Which is not to say I didn't waste 90 percent of the time—I did—but there is nevertheless this thing of not being able to do anything else," he wrote to Shelby. Walker kept one copy of the typescript, which Shelby could critique if he so wished. "What is it about?" Walker asked rhetorically. "Screwing and God (which all Catholic novels since Augustine have been about)—to use 'Catholic' somewhat loosely since you were right the other day about me not being a Catholic writer as Flannery was. Also about the U.S.A. coming apart between left and right." In his own mind, Walker still vacillated about the novel's title; *The Fall Out* might ultimately be excluded because of its association with Camus's *The Fall*; another possibility might be *The Center Did Not Hold.*

Walker gave Shelby a summary of the plot: Dr. More is a descendant of Sir Thomas More, "a Catholic but a bad one, unlike his ancestor a whisky head and horny all the time (which is not to say Sir Thomas wasn't, he well might have been since there was a curious period in his twenties when he wore a hair shirt and lived like a monk in the charterhouse and might have married not for love but to be relieved of horniness). The novel is also funny. It will please no one. It will infuriate Catholics, Protestants, Jews, Southerners, Northerners, liberals and conservatives, hawks and doves." Walker said he was now taking up golf and the philosophy of language "like all good Anglo-Saxon philosophers." He had whetted Shelby's appetite and Shelby was anxious to start reading.

By late August, Gwyn and Shelby had both read the typescript and liked it very much, though Shelby did send some tentative corrections, principally concerning the "reappearing carbine." Shelby felt Walker hit the right note throughout the entire novel and told Walker not to worry about offending anyone: "You know any bookreading Panthers or Kluxers? And mostly liberals don't consider themselves liberals of this type . . . As for your fellow Catholics, I guess you'll just have to settle for being considered immoral, like the rest of us modern writers." He particularly liked Art Immelmann. "Colonel Ringo's wounding was to me the funniest thing in the book—in the sense of laughing-out-loud I mean."

Though Walker wanted to write another work about religious extremism, he expressed his thoughts about the state of the Church more calmly when replying to Mother Johnette Putnam, who had sent Walker two papers she had written. "They were of particular interest to me," Walker wrote, "because your own thinking on the subject is much more advanced and specific than mine, which amounts mainly to vague forebodings, hunches that the conservatives may be wrong in one thing and right in another, that the liberals are the same, and that there is a *tertium quid.*"[161] Both Walker and Mother Johnette felt that a comparison of the contemporary state of religious life with that of the English Reformation was quite apposite. "While not disagreeing with your own prophetic view of the Church's failure in its responsibility to the Negro—disagreement! quite the opposite: the failure of Christendom in general and of the Catholic Church in particular has been so total as to be ironic." The Roman Catholic Church in the South has been too silent, Walker wrote, particularly in the area of morality. Walker found that in his writing he could only take "a rather bitterly sardonic and black-humor attitude, since nothing else seems to fit." Walker believed the Catholic Church was in big trouble, because it not only had no relevant social doctrine but had lost the intellectual excitement he felt when he converted. It boiled down to one complex question: has the Catholic Church simply failed to respond to the needs of the times, or are the times such that no matter what the Catholic Church may do or not do, the fact is that Christians are in for a long cold winter of faith? Walker did not know the answer. All he knew was that "we have come to the end of a world and that we are living in a new world which nobody yet understands, and that the tempestuous nature of the times is such that it is hard for me to conceive *any* expression of the faith, whether in the contemplative life or in social activism, which would not be received with something like a shrug in the modern consciousness." One might well argue that this "end of the world" mentality provided the axis upon which his new novel rotated. Walker was not sure where the changes brought about by the decrees of Vatican II would lead, especially for women who belonged to religious orders, but he reaffirmed his belief that Mother Johnette was on the right track in her thinking. Walker also found time to talk to twenty-three-year-old Sister Joan Ridley, O.P., who worked for Head Start. With Sister Paula Richard, O.P., a theologian, she would visit Walker and talk about her life as a professedly religious woman. Sister Joan found Walker's theology "conservative."[162]

About Daniel Berrigan, S.J. and his brother Philip, a member of the Josephite order, who had led a raid along with seven others on the draftboard offices in Catonsville, Maryland, Walker had definite opinions. Activist priests, especially those with vows of obedience, grated on Walker; he felt they were not loyal to the *magisterium*. In the September 4 issue of *Commonweal*, Walker's letter criticizing the Berrigan brothers because they violated federal law, destroyed public property, and terrorized government employees as a way of expressing moral outrage about U.S. foreign policy was clear and to the point. "It would follow, by the same logic, that a Catholic opposed to the use of public funds to promote population control could with equal propriety destroy the files of the Internal Revenue Service." Walker mentioned that the KKK

burned churches and scared people for God and country—allegedly to
save us from Communists—yet why should a Klansman be put in jail
and the Berrigans set free? "As it happens, I stand a good deal closer to
the Berrigans than to the Klan. The point is, however: God save us all
from the moral zealot who places himself above the law and who is
willing to burn my house down, and yours, providing he feels he is
sufficiently right and I sufficiently wrong." Walker's letter, and the one
from theologian Rosemary Ruether, less critical and more nuanced than
Walker's, were in response to Father Daniel Berrigan's published article
from the underground, "How to Make a Difference," in the August 7
issue of *Commonweal*. Walker's views about this particular priest had
changed over the years; in an unpublished review of *The Bow in the
Clouds: Man's Covenant with God* (1961), Walker found that Father Berrigan's writing showed "precision and abstemiousness."

When Roger Straus read Walker's novel, he was greatly pleased. "It
is a delight and joy, beautifully done, effective as hell, and wonderfully
readable. I think it is a ten-strike, and as you know from Henry and Bob,
we shall be publishing it with enormous enthusiasm and hope to give it
the kind of publication it so richly deserves."[163] Naturally, Walker was
pleased that Straus liked the novel, though he wrote Straus that it gave
him a good deal of trouble and that he still had minor changes he wanted
to make.[164] In a long letter to Walker, Henry Robbins expressed his feelings about the novel:

As you know by now from Elizabeth, Bob and I both read *How to Make Love in
the Ruins* with great delight and admiration. It's a marvelous novel, fantastically
inventive, covering an astonishingly broad range of experience, yet as compel-
lingly readable as a suspense novel. And it is completely original—different even
from your own two novels (except for certain notable characteristics of style and
theme). I hope I'm not stepping on your toes by saying that if it re-called any
other recent novel to me it was John Barth's *Giles Goat-Boy*, his attempt to tell us
what our world is coming to. But at every point and in every way that Barth's
novel failed (as I think it did), your novel succeeds. You convince us that this is
indeed what our world is coming to, but you do it with such grace and charm
and humor that we take the not-quite-apocalyptic vision smiling.

Dr. Thomas More—who seems like a hybrid between Sutter Vaught and
Will Barrett—is a superb character, and I did not see how any reader could help
being with him all the way through, even when he's satirizing cherished attitudes. (And there's hardly anyone whose cherished attitudes aren't satirized.)

As Elizabeth undoubtedly told you, the one flaw that both Bob and I find
in the book is the ending. The idea of a "Five Years Later" epilogue is fine, but
this epilogue seems to start up a whole new section of the novel, rather than

tying up the loose threads swiftly and surely. My own feeling is that this section should be more like fifteen or twenty pages rather than the 50 pages you now have. For one thing, I don't think it's necessary to find out what happened to all of the major and minor characters. Nor do I think it's a good idea to give so elaborate a picture of the "present" state of the nation and of Paradise. The various further twists on black-white relations and Knothead politics are amusing, but seem a bit redundant, mere variations on what you've already shown. Then, too, the account of Tom More's several patients (in Section 4) seems a discursive element, a sidetracking off the main line that slows down what should, I think, be a rapid movement to the novel's close.[165]

Walker agreed to take Robbins's advice about compressing the ending, though he was not sure how to proceed. Robbins could either send him the entire typescript or just indicate the pages that needed changes. He also wondered whether Robbins and Giroux liked the title (Walker suggested three: *Love in the Ruins, Last Days, The Last Days*).[166] "My talent is so fallible that I am exceedingly grateful for the opinion of those I respect."[167] Miss Otis voted for *Love in the Ruins*; she simply couldn't stand another book title with "Days" in it.[168] Neither Robbins nor Giroux was particularly troubled by Walker's original title, though they found *Love in the Ruins* a good alternative. Robbins mentioned he would send the typescript back to Walker with the "few minor things that bothered," so that Walker could deal with them as he pleased. Robbins would also mark up the epilogue for specific cuts.[169] Walker received an advance of $10,000, with a royalty of 15 percent, plus a fifty-fifty split of book-club advances to $10,000, with a sliding scale thereafter.[170]

By early November, FSG planned a paperback Noonday edition of *The Last Gentleman*, to be released, with corrections by Walker, about the same time as the new novel. The plan was to adapt Janet Halverson's jacket for the Noonday cover.[171] As became his habit, Walker delayed starting a new fiction project. Instead, he wrote what he called "a dull article" on Charles Sanders Peirce, someone entirely unknown to Shelby and most of his readers.[172] Walker was told he could make revisions on his new novel up to the last minute. He diligently finished the task by mid-November—and Robbins and Giroux were pleased with the new epilogue and the changes throughout.[173] Except for dealing with queries from the copy editor, the book was completed.[174] FSG scheduled the book for a May 1971 publication date, with a first printing of 25,000 copies and an initial advertising budget of $20,000. After prolonged negotiation, Eyre & Spottiswoode in London signed a contract to include the book in its summer list.[175] Robbins was eager to show Walker the Halverson jacket design for *Love in the Ruins*, which was just about finished.[176]

The November 13 issue of *The Vieux Carré Courier* featured an interview with Walker by Louis Gallo, accompanied by a photo by Franke Keating of Greenville.[177] In discussing politics, Walker predicted that the new mayor of New Orleans, Moon Landrieu, would do well in bringing blacks and whites together; he had a different opinion about Governor McKeithen, whose second term, unlike his first, had proved disastrous. "McKeithen has turned into a crybaby, going about the country complaining that the South is mistreated. This is beneath the dignity of a governor. McKeithen should get over his inferiority complex. The South is the best place in the U.S. to live, has the brightest future in industry and the best hope of race relations." Walker saw the Republican Party having a future in Louisiana because of the corruption of the Democratic Party. Landrieu had run against Ben C. Toledano, who would enter the race for the U.S. Senate, at the behest of Richard Nixon, in 1972.[178] The South of Faulkner and Flannery O'Connor had mostly disappeared, in Walker's eyes, but not that of Cormac McCarthy, whose *The Orchard Keeper* and *Outer Dark* he admired very much.[179] A future great novelist of the South, according to Walker, would probably be someone growing up in Thibodaux or Magnolia, attending Loyola or Tulane, and being ornery, tough, mean, and talented enough to go his or her own way.

In early November, Alfred Kazin visited Walker and Bunt for a weekend, had dinner in the French Quarter with his hosts, and even attended Sunday Mass. Ironically, Ann received a C– on a paper about Chaucer on which Kazin and her father had offered assistance.[180] Later, when she wanted to write a paper on William Blake, she went up to the attic and discovered Kazin's edition of Blake in the Viking Portable series. Her own efforts proved more successful. Kazin then headed to Greenville to see Roy, and finally to Memphis to see Shelby, who liked his "very Jewish New York" guest.[181] The two talked about the relationship of art and the South, though Shelby felt that Kazin really did not understand the relationship. When the June 1971 issue of *Harper's* appeared, it carried Kazin's article, under the title "The Pilgrimage of Walker Percy," which included some of the controversy surrounding the 1962 National Book Award for *The Moviegoer*, a novel Kazin considered "a lean, tartly written, subtle, not very dramatic attack on the wholly bourgeois way of life and thinking in a 'gracious' and 'historic' part of the South. But instead of becoming another satire on the South's retreat from its traditions, it was, for all the narrator's bantering light tone, an altogether tragic and curiously noble study in the loneliness of necessary human perceptions." Kazin saw the novel as pointing to the fact that Gentilly had become representative of an America in which people no longer knew how to look at anything. Kazin saw Walker as a Southern son who believed in the existence of a spiritual tradition of defeat and exile: "One might say that he knows exile and defeat in their purest American state." Kazin was intrigued by the fact that Walker watched television without any sound. For Kazin, Walker cultivated the art of restful sitting and lounging, of looking easy, in a way that kept conversation as casual as drifting through a summer afternoon. He seemed a most domesticated creature, intensely devoted to his family, and also at home with himself. Walker ended the year successfully; he had completed his third major novel and looked forward to changing the normal rhythm of his life.

11

Writing and Teaching
1971–74

As 1971 began, Walker had every reason to be optimistic about *Love in the Ruins*. Galley proofs were ready by late January and proofs were sent to several book clubs.[1] The Book-of-the-Month Club chose the novel as an "alternate" rather than a major selection, with an advance guarantee of $5,000; they printed their own edition.[2] Roger Straus had sent a set of proofs to Martin Luschei, a professor of English at California State Polytechnic College in San Luis Obispo, who was preparing a book for LSU Press.[3] (When Walker read with appreciation Luschei's *The Sovereign Wayfarer: Walker Percy's Diagnosis of the Malaise*, he nevertheless felt "a little like a laid-out corpse."[4]) A first run of 25,000 copies of the novel was available by May 17 at a retail price of $7.95.[5] Six weeks prior to publication, half the first printing had been sold. Elizabeth Otis was going to assign the film rights to a Hollywood producer, until she was asked by Walker to withdraw the offer; wary of movie executives, Walker likewise turned down both David Susskind and Lee Rosenberg, who made separate offers for the film rights.[6]

Walker now halfheartedly contemplated turning his attention to writing a full-length book about semiotics and Charles Sanders Peirce's theory of language. He felt linked to Peirce in a special way, and even considered elaborating a single theory based on their mutual insights into language. "I still think [such a book] would be as important as I told you," Walker informed Shelby Foote in early February. "I would even say that it is revolutionary: that 100 years from now it could well be known as the Peirce-Percy theory of meaning (not Pierce but Peirce and so pronounced Perce-Percy)." Walker proposed to take Peirce's semiotic insights, put them in modern behavioral terms, and "unhorse an entire generation of behaviorists and grammarians." For the present, all Walker could do was to content himself by writing an article on the subject, which he submitted to *Psychiatry*.

Walker thought about "making up a story"—as Flannery O'Connor had suggested to him before she died—though he felt her phrase for another novel was not quite right. More was at stake than Flannery implied. He even contemplated writing a proper planned-out Footean architectonic novel, about a man who finds himself amnesiac in a hospital for the criminally insane. "What he does not know, and has made himself forget, and pieces together later, is that he has killed his wife and infant son," he wrote Shelby. Amnesia fascinated Walker. With this new protagonist in mind, he started plotting his new novel, *Lancelot*. Watching the afternoon soap operas, particularly *Days of Our Lives*, Walker realized that amnesia is an attractive American theme, just as fornication is a favorite American sin. Dealing with an amnesiac would allow him to explore both the psychological aspect of growing old and the possibility of an amnesiac's being born again into a new world. Yet Walker did not want to write a novel that might be considered pornographic. He feared, as he told Shelby, that one of his novels might lead an impressionable teenager to commit fornication. Walker did not want that on his conscience. On the other hand, he did not think Christianity was the proper institution or force to regulate the moral standards of the *artistic* world. Walker was theoretically grappling with problems and situations that would make their way into *Lancelot*.

The winter doldrums had caught up with him and he was ready for some respite. He planned a trip to the Yucatán and invited Caroline Gordon, then in St. Petersburg, Florida, nursing her brother Morris, to join the group.[7] Walker had just finished reading Gordon's novel *The Glory of Hera*. He even contemplated a trip to Florida to see Caroline, but felt compelled to stay at home and tutor Ann. Walker also made reference in his letter to their mutual Trappist friend, Father Charles (Jack English), who, while drunk in some motel in Georgia, where he was traveling with a young man in a Volkswagen, had telephoned Walker. If he didn't sober up and go back to Conyers immediately, Walker told him, he'd be dead in six months. His relationship with this Trappist, sporadic and unpredictable, gave him ample reason not to have romantic notions about the Catholic or any other clergy. Walker revealed to Father Charles that he kept Caroline's introduction to the Harper edition of *Madame Bovary* on his desk, since he considered it the finest critique of a novel ever written.

Juxtaposed with Walker's honest reading of Father Charles was his admiration for Walter M. Miller's novel *A Canticle for Leibowitz*, the strange story of Brother Francis of the Albertian Order of Leibowitz. The Jewish-Christian coordinates in the novel created haunting resonances in Walker's own imagination. In his review in *The Southern Review*, he recommended the novel but with qualifications; he did not want to be perceived as a Malcolm Cowley rehabilitating Faulkner, since the merit of the book was at once "sub-literary and trans-literary." He considered it of more moment than other apocalyptic novels. "Like a cipher, the book has a secret. But unlike a cipher, the secret can't be told." The book had a mysterious quality that Walker wanted Miller's readers to ponder.

When *The Last Gentleman* was nominated for the 22nd Annual National Book Awards, Walker flew to New York, where he attended a dinner in his honor at the Four Seasons.[8] Roger Straus and his staff had invited an impressive list of writers, critics, and journalists, including Christopher Lehmann-Haupt, Martha Duffy, John Leonard, Geoffrey Wolff, Bruce Cook, Harriet Doar, Willie Morris, Jonathan Yardley, Gene Shalit, Marjorie Kellogg, Jean Stafford, and Alfred Kazin. Apparently Walker chatted with Elizabeth Hardwick and Randall Jarrell's widow without knowing initially who they were.[9] He also had a pleasant conversation with photographer Rollie McKenna of Stonington, Connecticut; while it snowed outside, she took some pictures of Walker.[10] Though always gracious at public functions, Walker sometimes appeared to invent conversation to cover a shyness that never seemed to disappear.

At one press conference, Herbert Kenny of *The Boston Globe* introduced four of the nominees: Hamilton Fish Armstrong, Jim Bouton, John Sack, and Walker Percy. They answered questions on a host of topics, ranging from international events and malaise in American society to baseball. When Walker's turn came to share his thoughts, he chose not to speak about *The Last Gentleman* but about his new, unpublished novel. As he adjusted his dark, horn-rimmed glasses, he was aware that his listeners had not read *Love in the Ruins*. He began his prepared remarks by stressing the role of the novelist and the need for the novelist to prophesy, "in order to be wrong."[11] The novelist, he explained, not merely rocks the boat but swamps it, just at the moment when everyone is talking about the dignity of the individual and the quality of life. Walker likewise felt a need to exaggerate slips in language and perception in order for everyone to recognize them. Though his new novel was a futuristic satire set in the United States, he did not want his listeners to associate it automatically with Orwell's *1984* or Huxley's *Brave New World*.

"What I was concerned with in this novel is something else altogether," he said. "What interested me is what can happen in a free society." He said everybody agreed with Orwell and Huxley but felt that something has gone wrong. His new novel dealt, not with the takeover of a society by tyrants or computers or whatever, but rather "with the increasing malaise and finally the falling apart of a society which remains, on the surface at least, democratic and pluralistic." Walker was again influenced by Kierkegaard in his writing. He had also considered using Yeats's line—about the center not holding—as an epigraph for the novel, but he did not want to suggest that the novel was political satire. In Walker's mind, the book was only incidentally about politics; it was really about the pursuit of happiness in Paradise Estates, where everyone generally succeeded but felt that something was wrong. "As one character says, we were all happy but our hearts broke." In portraying the lives of those who live in the ruins and who spurn 2,000 years of Christianity, he wanted to call a bluff. "The fact is that America is not immovable and indestructible." Walker told his audience there was something in the novel to offend everybody. He later chatted briefly with William Kennedy, a novelist from Albany, and sent him some material for his novel-in-progress.[12] Saul Bellow's *Mr. Sammler's Planet*, which Walker subsequently read, won the fiction award the next day.

Walker and Bob Giroux talked shop in his apartment in New York, including a conversation about their mutual friend Jean Stafford. When Walker returned to Covington he wrote to Stafford at her East Hampton home, mentioning a dream he had after reading one of her stories, "Children Are Bored on Sunday," in which a young woman goes to a museum, meets a man she knows, and finally has a drink with him in a bar.[13] Then Walker did something he had not done since he was a boy; he read a section of *Treasure Island*, as if trying to relive the story there. When finished, Walker went to the kitchen at ten in the morning and poured out a great belt of Early Times and drank a toast to Stafford, as if congratulating her for having taken him back to his imaginative, childhood roots. It is interesting to note that Lewis Lawson, in stressing *Love in the Ruins* as a sequel to Sinclair Lewis's *Arrowsmith*, suggests that most of Walker's novel represents Tom More's dream.[14] Walker once told a student of his that a fiction writer should not put a dream into a novel, unless he actually had it.[15]

Walker received printed copies of *Love in the Ruins* (dedicated to Shelby) in mid-April. (Years later, he allowed Emmet G. Lavery, Jr., to take out a film option on the novel.[16]) From FSG, Julie Coryn, Henry Robbins's secretary, forwarded reviews, including favorable ones in *The Saturday Review* and *Cosmopolitan*, as well as two negative ones in *Book World* and *The New Leader*.[17] Richard Schickel of *Life* informed Henry Robbins, who passed the word along to Walker, that he read the first

300 pages in a couple of days and then dawdled for a week over the last quarter of the book simply because he was enjoying the novel so much. He thought it would become some kind of American masterpiece.[18] Walker read William Kennedy's "nutty but favorable" review in the March 18 issue of *Look*. Anatole Broyard in the daily *New York Times* found Tom More a "charming fellow, an appealing tragicomedian." Ellen Douglas, Walker's longtime friend, wrote a review for the *The Delta Democrat-Chronicle*. That Walker was well known in Greenville only made her task more difficult. Douglas had kept tabs on this novel, as the Greenville Percys returned from Covington with reports of its progress—namely, that Walker was first writing about a fierce tribe of Bantus taking over the United States, then about a Masters-and-Johnson-type laboratory, then about a kind of Doomsday machine. As it turned out, all three reports proved correct. Douglas said Walker was indebted to the novels of Evelyn Waugh, the Toryism of Ford Madox Ford, the novel *A Canticle for Leibowitz*, Kurt Vonnegut, and Faulkner. Her observations about Faulkner's influence could be substantiated insofar as Walker gave dates to the chapter headings, much as Faulkner did in *The Sound and the Fury*. Though Douglas liked the book, she did have reservations, especially about the "dour and young and beautiful" Ellen Oglethorpe. Although an astute writer and critic, Douglas failed to do justice to the novel's complexity.

The reviews tended to be mixed, but seemed by and large to emphasize something positive about the novel. Martha Duffy, who visited Walker in Covington, noted in *Time* that this novel was an abrupt departure from Walker's previous ones, but it was shored up by "a rueful equanimity and a lingering hope."[19] In *Life*, Guy Davenport found the novel "a very funny book because it wets down so much solemnity and lets the gas out of so much arrogance." Like all superb satirists, Davenport concluded, Walker showed how absurd we are at our best, how very far we are from where we think we are, and how we still find it strangely delicious. The review in *The New York Times Book Review* by Thomas McGuane stressed Walker's "delineation of a comedy of love against a field of anarchy." In *The Clarion Herald*, Father Clement J. McNaspy wrote: "No amount of quotation can suggest the humor, the poignancy, the spoofing exposure, the prophetic judgment of one of the great (perhaps the greatest) American writers of our time in this, his greatest book thus far." Walker replied courteously to the priest the next day: "Your review meant more to me than I can say."[20] Walker particularly felt that David Anderson's review in *The Wall Street Journal* hit the mark. In a special piece in *The New York Times Book Review*, Wilfrid Sheed sounded an off-note when he reported his reactions to Walker's novel, lightly but lengthily scolding Walker and avoiding genuine praise. He discussed the book so obliquely that it was difficult to tell what the book was about. Walker once commented about this piece: "These guys ought to say what they do believe."[21] In response to Sheed, the title of Walker's subsequent review of Sheed's *People Will Always Be Kind* seemed most appropriate: "The Left Hand of Sheed." Walker found Sheed's novel about Brian Casey, a teenager felled by polio (as had happened to Sheed himself), "arresting, complex and enigmatic," but the account of Brian's life was almost impenetrable. One of the unsigned reviews of *The Moviegoer* was actually written by Max Gissen, the former book editor of *Time*, to whom Walker wrote after the appearance of the review. Gissen, living in Weston, Connecticut, was likewise enthralled by Walker's new novel.[22] On the whole, as Walker admitted to Roger Straus, "the reviews have been odd as usual. It's nice to get favorable ones, though—to tell you the truth—I learn more from the unfavorable ones, painful though they are."[23]

By June 6 *Love in the Ruins* placed ninth on the *The New York Times* best-seller list; the book, with 45,000 copies in print, was now in its third printing. Pocket Books had proposed a base bid of $75,000, which meant that bids would start at that figure and Pocket would have the opportunity to top others by 10 percent.[24] Yet Dell's offer was not topped and they acquired the paperback rights.[25] Walker was pleased but disturbed that such a windfall of money might mean he would have a tax problem that fiscal year. Michelle Lapautre, an American living in Paris and acting as the firm's *agent littéraire*, had received so many requests for the French rights to the novel that she wrote FSG asking whether they or Miss Otis represented Walker's foreign rights.[26] Miss Otis, of course, handled these rights. In the end, Alain Oulman of the Calmann-Lévy publishing house in Paris contracted for *Love in the Ruins*, translated into French as *Amour parmi les ruines*. They needed Walker's help on the meaning of colloquial phrases and passages, which he subsequently gave them.[27]

In a lull between books, Walker was interviewed at length by John C. Carr about Kierkegaard and Sartre, for the fall issue of *The Georgia Review*. When Philip D. Carter, Hodding's son, visited Walker in June, he described a "quiet man, spare, courtly and gray," who "rends the most optimistic and most apocalyptic observations with a nonchalant calm."[28] Later that month, interviewer Les Brumfield arrived without a tape recorder and sat with Walker on the back porch sipping iced tea. Their conversation ranged from the flight to the suburbs and exurbs and the decline in the city's tax base and the lack of jobs for the growing black population to *Love in the Ruins*. In passing, Walker mentioned he was reading *A Cry of Absence* by Madison Jones, writer-in-residence at

Auburn: "It's a good one. About race relations. Usually those novels are pretty bad." After reading Jones's novel, Walker wrote to editor David McDowell, expressing concern about the rather obtuse reviews of this novel. For Walker, Jones "accomplished the most difficult of tasks, that bête noire, that sure enough beast which lies there in front of every Southern novelist like a lion in the path, a successful novel about RACE—ugh, I don't like to say it. He is able to do it without falling victim either to ideology, liberal or conservative—again 'ugh' in both cases—or to Gothic clichés, simply because *A Cry of Absence* is first and last a well-wrought novel, a tragedy whose motion is swift, sure and inevitable."[29] Clearly this novel, set in 1957 in a small Tennessee town about to awaken to shifting racial and social attitudes and the resulting changes, deeply impressed Walker.

Elizabeth Spencer also met a quiet and courtly Walker that summer. A talented writer who had known about the Percys while growing up in Mississippi but had never met any of them, Spencer traveled to New Orleans to gather material for her novel *The Snare*.[30] Her friend David Burns suggested that she might like to meet Ben C. Toledano, who privately enjoyed collecting the works of certain authors. During dinner at the Toledanos', Ben C. brought up Walker's name. A few days later, Bunt and Walker drove to New Orleans and lunched with Spencer. When Walker later wrote her, he said he would be glad to send her *Love in the Ruins* but she would be better off sticking with Dickens.[31]

Walker told Henry Robbins that he was disappointed *Love in the Ruins* did not do better. "I thought it had a chance of taking off. I kept thinking of *Herzog*. If *Herzog* could take off, why not *Love in the Ruins*?"[32] Yet Walker knew the answer: the novel never really found its audience because its point of view, vis-à-vis Southern and Catholic novel buyers, was too eccentric. Family and friends knew that once Walker became irritated, they had better back off for a while. Surprisingly, *Love in the Ruins* won the 1972 award in fiction given by the Catholic Press Association.

In August the Percys spent two weeks at Hilton Head—a locale Walker associated with his imaginary Paradise Estates, as he told Zoltán Abádi-Nagy. Walker did not have a particularly good summer, suffering from hay fever and bouts of morning terror. "To tell the truth," he wrote Jean Stafford, "I've not been able to figure out whether the malaise was physical, psychic or spiritual. Just that I'm fed up with fiction."[33] Walker believed the New York literary critics had landed on him too hard and he regretted attending the NBA ceremony. He just wanted to be left alone. He told Stafford the reason he had tried so hard with the last two novels was to prove that *she* was not batty. "In a way, you and Joe are partly responsible for me, so I guess you'll have to put up with Kazin-Percy foolishness." Alfred Kazin's article about Walker in *Harper's*, in spite of Kazin's "epistemological savvy" about some aspects of *The Moviegoer*, had not pleased Walker and he wrote the author, pointing out minor factual mistakes. Yet Walker was grateful to Kazin for his letter of recommendation on behalf of his nephew, LeRoy Percy, who landed a teaching position at Fordham University.[34]

Walker fueled his depression by drinking, a subject he mentioned in a letter to Shelby: "You are a good drunk—peaceable, gentle, amiable and ecumenical, which speaks well for you. I am told I am a lowdown drunk, many sneers and insults to waiters, etc." Walker once made a bittersweet discovery after having problems with his large bowel, that too much drinking at the Boston Club had been the cause. Temporarily, he swore off drink and the bosky bite of bourbon he so enjoyed.

The financial fiasco over the filming of Walker's first novel did not alleviate Walker's malaise. It may have provided a seed for the next novel, *Lancelot*, which deals with destruction and a film crew. Kit Carson, then living in Irving, Texas, wanted to talk to Walker about his film project, but only after he really had something substantial to offer.[35] Carson was busy editing *The Future's Ours*, under an American Film Institute grant, and working on his own book, entitled *Fear's Diary*.[36] By early July, Walker had severed his relationship with Carson and gave complete control of the project to Noel Parmentel for the next three years. "Well, at least it's over," Carson wrote Walker. "I don't really understand what happened; but I guess it's one of those things called The Mysteries of Life. I'm putting Noel in touch with the various people I'd gathered for the project: Redford, some money-raisers, the cinematographer who just shot *McCabe* and is now shooting *Deliverance*."[37] Henry Robbins, who had followed the situation, was amazed and depressed, he confided to Carson, that Walker so trusted Parmentel; he suspected that the only way Walker could get Parmentel off his back was to let him have the film rights in exchange for the promise not to bother him.[38] Robbins's intuitions were quite correct. If anything could have revived Walker's spirits, however, it was the birth, on August 3, of his second grandson, Robert Livingston Lobdell.

Walker continued writing, whether he felt up or down. In declining to attend a party in his honor that Loyola professor Forrest Ingram, S.J., wanted to organize, Walker suggested he send Father Ingram, and through him to *The New Orleans Review*, an article entitled "Toward a Theory of Language," a companion to "Toward a Triadic Theory of

Meaning," to be published in the upcoming February issue of *Psychiatry*. Walker had been working on both for some years and attached more importance to them than to making up novels.[39] Willing to help others, Walker also recommended Jason Berry ("a talented, well-educated, idealistic and self-assured young man") as a candidate for a Rhodes scholarship.[40] Having graduated from Georgetown University, Berry worked in Mississippi as publicity director in Charles Evers's campaign for governor. Walker had read some of the young activist's writings and found that they showed "both the virtues and shortcomings of a young, exuberant talent." Berry visited Walker and they talked for several hours, especially about the dynamics of a young white man working among blacks.[41] Later Berry's and Percy's concerns seemed to merge as each, in his own way, wrote about pedophilia.

One big decision that Bunt and Walker made that summer was to allow Ann to spend her senior year of high school at Southeastern Louisiana University in Hammond, where she took courses in English, botany, and chemistry. The administration at St. Scholastica's was not particularly pleased with this arrangement. It was a time of trial and experimentation, since Ann would be totally on her own, though she would drive her red Gremlin back and forth to Covington whenever she felt a bit homesick. Without the distractions of Ann's girl friends popping into the house, Walker revived his interest in semiotics. "Though I know that this subject mystifies you through its seeming triviality," he wrote Shelby in mid-September, "the fact is after 5,000 years of Western learning and 500 years of modern science, nobody can explain how it is that people talk and animals don't. But Percy Knows!" With Ann away so much of the time, Bunt and Walker had less need of hired workers, though they still relied considerably on John Henry Walker, a trusted yardman who had first started working for them in 1957.[42]

Walker sent off a short list of corrections for the forthcoming paperback edition of *Love in the Ruins*.[43] His next reading project, as he informed Shelby, was to make his way through Thomas Mann's *Joseph and His Brothers* and then to begin Dickens's *Bleak House*. Once Walker finished "Toward a Theory of Language," he intended to clear the decks and see what would come his way. Though he kept his options open, he did not want to venture from his desk. He turned down an invitation from Lewis Simpson to lecture at LSU: "Thanks again—one reason I'd *want* to come would be to meet you and David Madden."[44] Simpson and his colleague Charles East were most welcome to come by for lunch in Covington any weekday but Wednesday, the day reserved for lunch with his male friends in town.[45]

Except for a sardonic "Letter to the Editor" to *The Vieux Carré*

Courier, in which he handed out end-of-the-year booby prizes to local politicians, Walker had little pressing on his agenda. To accommodate Marion Montgomery, a novelist from Georgia, he spent the first three days of January reading the script of Montgomery's novel *The Fugitive,* "with alternating astonishment, wonderment, bemusement and pleasure."[46] Ultimately, Walker felt that he could not judge what he considered a strange book.[47] Walker had favorably reviewed Montgomery's first novel, *A Wandering of Desire,* and he thought that Henry Robbins's editing of Montgomery's new novel might enhance the work, but it was declined by FSG.[48]

Walker now agreed to sit for Jill Krementz, the noted photographer, for a series of photos, one of which would be featured on the back cover of *Lancelot.*[49] Krementz took several photos of Walker lying on his bed with his writing board nearby. The crucifix above the bed intrigued his little grandson John Walker Lobdell, who asked him about it. "That's Jesus," Walker replied. From that day forward, John Walker—and the other grandsons—called Walker "Geegaw," a variant of the name they heard. (Bunt was named "Mimi" by her grandsons.) Krementz took several photos of Walker in a hounds-tooth jacket; noticeable now were his delineated features and receding hairline. For someone who did not like to have his picture taken, Walker seemed to enjoy the process, as he also did for those taken by local photographer Christopher Harris.[50]

Walker felt buoyed by the critical attention he was getting from his fiction. He read with pleasure Lewis Lawson's article "Walker Percy: The Physician as Novelist," as well as the dissertation Michael Cass had written at Mercer University in Macon, Georgia. One crucial sign of an author's success is whether graduate students decide to write in-depth criticism on a specific work—in fact, it may well be the true test for an author to enter into the American literary canon. "It is very well done," Walker wrote Cass. "But aside from the competent scholarship, what moved me—and what [makes] yours different from most such studies I've seen—is that you understood the religious sphere, as Søren Kierkegaard would call it."[51] Walker also appreciated the article that Simone Vauthier had written about *The Moviegoer* in *RANAM,* a French literary journal, which meant that Walker now had an academic European following.[52]

That spring, Bunt and Walker spent countless hours visiting Bunt's father in a local nursing home after he had an operation to remove a gangrenous leg. Between visits, Walker read in and out of *Bleak House,* but he could barely remember the plot; he was definitely more at home with a Robbe-Grillet novel. Walker's one chance for private reflection came when he made his annual retreat at the end of March at Manresa.

When Christopher Lehmann-Haupt, Martha Duffy, Joseph Heller, Joan Didion, and Larry Woiwode met in New York to discuss novels, including *Love in the Ruins*, for the 1972 NBA Award, they could not reach an immediate consensus.[53] Lehmann-Haupt admired E. L. Doctorow's *The Book of Daniel*, a fictional treatment of the Rosenberg espionage case, and when *Love in the Ruins* was brought up, he retorted, "Right over my dead body." The judges discussed Bernard Malamud's *The Tenants*, Mary McCarthy's *Birds of America*, and John Updike's *Rabbit Redux*. Joseph Heller asked if Sylvia Plath's *The Bell Jar* was eligible, since there was a rule that an author who had been dead for three years or more would not be eligible for an award. Heller also asked whether the committee wished to waive the rule and consider Flannery O'Connor's *The Complete Stories*. O'Connor had died in 1964, but some judges felt the collection would be a good compromise if they could not agree on another. Lehmann-Haupt finally voted with the majority for waiving the rule in O'Connor's case; she was now eligible. The night before the final meeting, Lehmann-Haupt talked to Joan Didion at a party and made a pitch for the Doctorow book. When the group met the next morning, there were five candidates, Flannery O'Connor's volume excluded, and Doctorow's and Walker's novels seemed to be prevailing. With two votes for *Love in the Ruins*, Lehmann-Haupt refused to cast the third for Walker because he had won before, and he said he did not consider the new novel superior to *The Moviegoer*. Flannery's collection of stories won. "It wasn't a bad choice, of course," Lehmann-Haupt admitted. Regina O'Connor, Flannery's mother, asked Bob Giroux (who edited all her books) to accept the award on behalf of the family. Walker did not attend the ceremony in Alice Tully Hall at Lincoln Center. When he heard the news, he wrote Bob Giroux: "Am delighted to learn from Henry that Flannery won the prize. And as you must know, I ain't just being a good sport."[54] Walker felt that Flannery should have received the recognition during her lifetime, but better late than never.

Yet Walker received several honors and awards that summer. He was elected a fellow of the American Academy of Arts and Sciences and also of the New York Academy of Medicine. He received an honorary degree from the University of North Carolina, having been nominated by Louis D. Rubin, Jr., a noted critic of Southern literature. Walker was surprised to see that the SAE fraternity house was a shell, as if it had been bombed. After Chapel Hill, Walker attended his induction ceremony into the Institute of Arts and Letters in New York. He had been nominated by Jean Stafford and seconded by Robert Fitzgerald and Glenway Wescott. Although William Maxwell at *The New Yorker* had initially been listed as the nominator, he backed out. At the reception in May,

Jill Krementz took pictures of Walker and Eudora Welty, who had received the Gold Medal for Fiction. After the ceremony, under a gigantic tent set up in the courtyard, Walker exchanged small talk with Truman Capote, looking like a little boy, and Norman Mailer, moving his shoulders around like a tough guy.[55]

To persuade Walker to accept an honorary doctorate at Loyola, three Jesuits—Joseph Tetlow, Clement J. McNaspy, and Francis Sullivan—drove to Covington to talk with Walker.[56] On the return trip, the battery of the Jesuit car went dead on the causeway, and after a fifteen-minute wait, Bunt and Walker arrived and drove their guests back to Thomas Hall.[57] Walker wryly smiled at their "erudition, charm, wit—and total mechanical incompetence."[58] At the commencement, Provost James Carter, S.J., slowed down so that the audience could catch the Latin of Walker's diploma, written by Father McNaspy: *Creamus et pronuntiamus doctorem litterarum humaniarum* ("We create and proclaim [Walker Percy] a doctor of humane letters"). In mid-June, Walker received another honorary degree at the College of St. Scholastica in Duluth, Minnesota, run by the Benedictine Sisters.

When Walker returned to Covington, he planned to work quietly. He wrote Shelby: "Would like to polish off one more linguistic article and then get down to something serious—like making up a story, i.e., a horrendous crime committed by a fellow who doesn't believe in sin (just reread *Crime and Punishment* for edification)." Walker envisioned a long, hot summer on the front porch drinking iced tea.

An article on the Rev. Will Campbell in *Life* included a short section on his relationship with Walker. This debonair, Gibson-guitar-strumming, licorice-flavored-Beech-Nut-tobacco-spitting, Yale-educated Baptist preacher had great affection for Walker, as glimpsed in the quiet photograph of these two friends accompanying the article. Will could share with Walker an honest, down-home view of the world that balanced the more traditional spirituality of the Dominicans, Benedictines, and Jesuits.

Walker's sensitivity to the spiritual and material needs of those around him, especially the poor, took a forward step during the summer. Under the directorship of Sister Anthony Balot, O.S.B., the Biracial Institute for Doing, Giving, and Enriching published a report, based on a survey of 320 families (about 50 percent of the population of 7,170) that targeted one-third of the population of Covington, mostly black. Walker was on the board of trustees. His own attitude toward poverty and racial issues can be seen in his long review in the *Tulane Law Review* of Albert Murray's *The Omni-Americans: New Perspectives on Black Experience and American Culture* and Gilbert Moore's *A Special Rage*: "The lesson for the black or white author who writes about black-and-white in the present perfervid climate is surely to write the unrhetorical and unfashionable truth as he sees it, even though he will almost certainly be misunderstood." Walker believed that Murray's book could well be the most important one on white-black relations in the United States, indeed on American culture, published in this generation.

Walker finished the second of his two articles on semiotics in mid-July, which he entitled "Why Don't You Linguists Have an Explanatory Theory of Language?" He felt it was so special that he had it copyrighted and placed in the Library of Congress: "In fact, it might be regarded as the final crystallization of maybe 20 years off-and-on between-novels worrying of the subject. It is important to me. In fact, if anybody remembers my name 100 years from now, it will be for this and companion articles."[59]

Walker seemed to be in the middle of emotional doldrums, as he informed Shelby. He had come to the "damnedest watershed" in his life—"done what I wanted to do in the novel, with linguistics, children gone, sitting down here with my old lady in the Louisiana autumn." Everything was quiet. What to do now? Walker found it all very spooky. "Life is much stranger than art—and often more geometrical. My life breaks exactly in half: 1st half = growing up Southern and medical; 2nd half = imposing art on 1st half. 3rd half? Sitting on bayou and repeating over and over like old Buddenbrooks: *kurios!* Actually, I know what I want to do for #4. It's a good idea, but must wait for the winds to pick me up out of these 56-year-old horse latitudes." Even well into the fall, Walker felt himself caught between thinking (linguistics) and imagining (literature), "a bad place to be." He felt that he should not write the first sentence of any work until he had the tone of voice exactly right.

Perhaps he was feeling the belated effects of the empty-nest syndrome. In the fall Ann enrolled at LSU, and since she could not talk by phone to her parents, she wrote her family ("Mom, Dad, and Fats") chatty letters. She shared college experiences, of being elected vice president of her dorm, meeting Frank Percy and his family from St. Francisville, and going to TGIF parties. One day she received eight letters. "What a surprise, have been bragging about it to everyone on my floor!!"[60] Bunt and Walker came to the Chi Omega parents' day events, which pleased Ann enormously.

As a member of the James Agee Memorial Library Committee at St. Andrew's School near Sewanee, Walker went to Monteagle, marveling at the dogwood, black walnut, sumac, and tulip trees displaying their fall colors. On October 14 he participated in a panel discussion with others who knew Agee (Andrew Lytle, Dwight Macdonald, Robert Fitzgerald, David McDowell, eighty-eight-year-old Rev. James Harold Flye, and Walker's old friend Robert Daniel). When McDowell asked the panelists about their relationships with Agee, Walker mentioned that although he had never known him, Agee had given him an insight into the technical aspects of writing. He compared Agee's writing style to the "inscape" of Gerard Manley Hopkins. He thought of Agee not in connection with Southern writers but with English and Irish writers like Hopkins and the early Joyce. The way that Agee crafted a sentence and used metaphors and sentence structure within a single paragraph—in short Agee's "poetic prose—had influenced him."[61] In his opinion Agee had been radicalized by the movies he had seen between 1945 and 1950—the worst ones Walker could remember.

Afterward Walker and Bunt drove out to Brinkwood for the first time in twenty-two years. Bunt wrote to Ann about her father: "He sounded brilliant whether he was or not. It was so strange to see where we spent our first year of marriage. The view from the teahouse Walker and Shelby built out of natural stone was beautiful."[62] Some of his mother and father's furniture was still in the house. The old barn and the split-rail fence looked just the same. That evening Walker had a chance to greet and talk to some of the other guests, including Lon Cheney, Madison Jones, film director John Huston, and Mia Agee and her son John.

When Walker returned to Covington, he helped aspiring writer Robert Milling III, whose novel he had read and considered first-rate. Walker complimented Milling by telling him he really did not need advice, since he was doing so well on his own.[63] Looking at the novel made Walker think about his own life as a writer: "It's funny looking back on it—living out on the Military Road, having chosen to exile myself from everyone I knew to an unknown town in Louisiana where I knew no one, for eight years, not in the least worried, existing in fact in a state of besotted confidence, believing that God must have some use for me, or at any rate that was not something that worrying would help."[64] Though their friendship grew slowly, Milling developed a deep affection for Walker, who, in the eyes of some, treated this Princeton grad as the son he never had.

Eudora Welty had the surprise of her life when she first met William F. Buckley, Jr., at station WMAA in Jackson for the taping of his show Firing Line. Buckley greeted her with heavy makeup on, and Welty was convinced that he had flown powdered and rouged from New York.[65] Walker joined Welty on the small stage, along with panelists Gordon Weaver from the University of Southern Mississippi, Jerry Ward from Tougaloo College, and Dan Hise from Millsaps College. Welty seemed quite at ease and wanted the discussion to stay as close to literary home territory as possible. In introducing Welty, Buckley said, "Eudora Welty is as interesting to New Yorkers as Mary McCarthy is to Alabamians." In introducing Walker, he said, "Walker Percy went out of Mississippi to go to college, all the way up to what Senator Claghorn once insisted should be called 'Upper South Carolina.' " Not unexpectedly, Walker maintained a serious demeanor and twiddled his thumbs when not part of the discussion. It was Welty, taking Buckley in stride and finding her own voice, who brought Walker into the conversation. "I think one of the advantages of being a Southern writer," he said, "is the advantage of a perspective—you are in a subculture in one sense, and in another sense you are able to look at the main culture from outside. I mean it is possible to see the forest better from the outside than from the inside." He maintained that the South was no longer on the defensive, and remembered growing up when the best brains in the Senate and the House from the South were devoted to devising parliamentary maneuvers to defeat the anti-lynch bill. And though Walker conceded that many facets of the culture of the North and South were merging, the South still had history, family life, storytelling, and tragedy. "I think the task of a novelist—and I would like to hope that maybe the Southerner, with his peculiar tradition, might contribute to this—is somehow to humanize the new American culture." Buckley rarely alluded to the important works of fiction written by his two eminent guests. When Walker and Buckley next met, at the black-tie gala sponsored by the Catholic Foundation of the Archdiocese of New Orleans, they greeted each other like old friends.[66]

By the end of January 1973 Shelby had about 200 pages left to his trilogy, which he anticipated would be finished by the end of the year.[67] He was narrating the events leading up to Lincoln's assassination. For Walker, the only bright note was that FSG finally obtained the paperback rights to *The Moviegoer* from Knopf in mid-February; Walker received $7,500 as an advance.[68] Caroline Gordon called Walker from Princeton, inviting him to be a judge for the creative writing program at the University of Dallas, where she was a professor.[69] He agreed on the condition that he could do it by mail. Eudora Welty, Seán O'Faoláin, and Peter Taylor were also on her list.[70] Later that month Walker, recently invited to serve as a judge for the NBA fiction award, flew to New York for his first committee meeting. It was clear that Leslie Fiedler and William Gass were old friends but the three others were strangers. At lunch, Walker shared his thoughts with the others: "Since Jonathan Yardley went to the trouble to get us in touch with each other, shouldn't we elect him chairman?"[71] To his surprise Yardley was unanimously elected. In the end, Walker and Yardley voted for Welty's *The Optimist's Daughter*, Evan Connell for John Williams's *Augustus*, and Fiedler and Gass for Barth's *Chimera*. It became clear that no book would get all five votes, so they decided to divide the award between *Augustus* and *Chimera*. When Yardley announced the award, it was not popularly received. *The New York Times*, noting falsely that the committee meetings had been noisy and argumentative, described Yardley as a "courtly young Southern critic" —not without some subsequent ribbing from Walker. Later that spring, Walker sent his new friend a paperback copy of *Love in the Ruins*: "To Jon, best of all judges (of wine anyhow) and books too—then how come, with the two best minds in the South, we didn't do better?"[72]

At this time, Walker met Robert Coles, M.D., who had started his work in the South in 1958, in large part due to his admiration for Anna Freud's work with English children during wartime.[73] His book *Children of Crisis: A Study of Courage and Fear* reveals that he had visited New Orleans in the early 1960s while chief of neurology and the psychiatry unit at the U.S. Air Force Hospital at Keesler Field in Biloxi. For six years, from 1958 to 1964, he lived in Mississippi, Louisiana, and Georgia. While doing a psychiatric residency, he read Walker's essay "The Man on the Train," which he showed to some friends, one of whom, a Catholic doctor, subsequently gave Coles the articles Walker had previously written for *Commonweal*. "The essays were a tonic, and I glowed: all the dreary, smug tautological reasoning of the social sciences pointedly exposed— all the secular, agnostic obsessions of self-preoccupied people for whom the mind was the latest fad, if not the last refuge and hope."[74] From Keesler, Captain Coles would speed in his sports car along Route 90 to Pass Christian, and through Gentilly to New Orleans, where he met with a fellow psychiatrist who wondered why he repeatedly saw certain films, especially those with Jimmy Dean. In 1960 Coles saw *Sunset Boulevard* three times in three days.

When Coles first read *The Moviegoer*, he was so totally absorbed by the novel that he phoned the air base to report sick so he could finish it. William Shawn at *The New Yorker* approached Coles about writing a profile on Erik Erikson of Harvard, which was later published in book form. When Shawn asked about another profile, Coles spontaneously suggested Walker's name. Though Shawn did not seem to know Walker's works, he agreed, and so Coles called Walker from Albuquerque to set up a loose interview schedule. In preparation Coles immersed himself in Kierkegaard, whom he had studied at Harvard under Perry Miller. He also read Walker's other favorite European writers. When Coles and Walker met finally, they took walks together and listened to Benny Goodman records. Walker was amazed that Coles did not use a tape recorder. Coles felt, on the other hand, that his training as a psychiatrist had prepared him to remember what questions had been asked and what answers given. Walker and Coles soon became spiritual kinsmen. Walker wrote to Shelby that Coles was both "sane and funny." Coles saw that Walker was willing to ask lots of questions about the nature of things and, at the same time, be unhappy with readily accepted answers.

Robert Coles had the ability to lift up Walker's spirits, as evidenced in Walker's review of his *Farewell to the South* in the *National Observer*. Coles had lived through the violent summer of 1964 in the South, yet preserved sympathy and understanding for the people, black and white, he came to know. Part of Coles's method was to keep in touch with the people he had interviewed. "How does it happen that Ruby," Walker wrote, "the little black girl who alone integrated a New Orleans school and was subject month after month to the vilest abuse, was not only not damaged by the 'trauma' but has grown up to be a very wise and mature young lady—while the son or daughter of an 'advantaged' middle-class Boston family turns out badly, suffers all manner of self-doubt, identity crises, and suchlike?" Walker considered Coles a physician in the larger sense of the word; he had taken on the nation's travail and used un-psychiatric words and phrases like "friendship," "refreshing," "laughter," "courage," and "getting along." Coles clearly spoke Walker's language.

In early March, Walker asked if Shelby would see Coles, who was making the rounds of Walker's friends and relatives. Coles went first to meet Roy and Sarah in Greenville, and then to Memphis. Shelby found him "a wonderful likeable man, but somewhat puzzling in that I couldn't tell what he had come for, what he was after; mainly I guess because he doesn't take notes or press you for information." Coles's visit prompted Shelby to encourage Walker, once again, to start a big novel, "big in every way, theme, content, length, wealth of characters, action, everything." Walker had become caught up, however, not in writing fiction, but in doing his homework for the Institute of Arts and Letters. He recommended to Howard Moss that the Institute consider for awards three novels that had been overlooked: Jack Matthews's *The Charisma Campaigns*, David Rhodes's *The Last Fair Deal Going Down*, and Ken Schiff's *Passing Go*.[75] When Walker attended the April meeting of the Institute, he ran into Willie Morris of *Harper's* magazine, who had visited him in Covington, and they went to the Hotel Blackstone bar. After a fairly boisterous time there with James Jones and William Styron, they moved on to P. J. Clarke's and stayed until it closed.[76] One person who distinctly remembered meeting Walker at sessions of the Academy-Institute awards committee was Paul Horgan: "In the most easy and casual way, he made a fine-grained and distinguished presence. Tall and thin, with something of a guarded posture of the former tubercular patient, he was direct and informal."[77] Horgan found their conversation fairly ordinary, but Walker's presence—"his civility of soul"—deeply impressed him.

Walker agreed to see Professor Zoltán Abádi-Nagy of Kossuth University in Hungary, who was studying black humor in American novels in preparation for a higher-level doctorate in his native land.[78] Since he had been doing research in the Southwest, he drove to Covington from Oklahoma, and because of car problems arrived late for his appointment. Embarrassed as he drove into the front driveway, Abádi-Nagy soon realized that Bunt and Walker were about to head out for the evening. Graciously, Walker called his hosts and said that he would not be able to make it; instead, he stayed home and talked to Abádi-Nagy. When the interview was published in the fall issue of *The Southern Literary Journal*, it showed that Abádi-Nagy was one of the best interviewers Walker would ever have.

Walker told Donald Barthelme that he had supported Welty for the NBA award, yet he had not been able to self-start his own engines. "I've had a rotten year," he wrote Henry Robbins, who was then recuperating in New York Hospital from a mild cardiac infarction, "with a good novel in mind and not being able to get a hold of it. So I'm thinking, so what? So the world doesn't get another novel? Big deal. It couldn't matter less—which doesn't exactly build up steam for writing a novel."[79] He had something else in mind—a collection of his essays.[80] Truth was that Walker felt lazy and did not want to be bothered by the editorial work involved.

After attending the wedding of Jimmy and June Sprunt's deaf daughter, Louise, to Robert Miera at the Sprunt plantation near Wrightsville Beach, North Carolina, Walker flew to Milwaukee to receive another honorary degree at Marquette University.[81] Professor Joseph Schwartz, chairman of the English Department, had been the one to recommend Walker.[82] In introducing him to more than 1,500 graduates and their families, Schwartz noted that the "predicament of man in a modern technological society" had been Walker's main concern as a novelist and essayist. Walker also received an honor from Yale; he had been appointed (with no obligations attached) as an associate fellow of More College for a term of five years.[83] When Walker returned, he told Charles East at *The Sewanee Review* that he would be willing to write an introduction to the paperback edition of Uncle Will's *Lanterns on the Levee*.[84] He felt it was the only productive thing he did that summer. "Quite an experience," he wrote Bob Coles.[85]

Walker and Bunt, joined by Shelby and Gwyn, vacationed at Gulf Shores in June; they rented the Bankston Cottage, which they hoped to return to the following year.[86] Walker read an absorbing volume entitled *Children of Pride* (the letters of the C. C. Jones family of Liberty County, Georgia, before, during, and after the Civil War).[87] He gave Shelby an inkling of what he was thinking about writing—a novel about a forty-five-year-old priest who has gone sour and is about to chuck the whole thing and take off with a twenty-year-old Bobby McGee type. He had even written the opening lines: "The morning after All Souls' Day, I stood looking down at my mother's grave in the Felicity Street Cemetery in old New Orleans and I came to myself in the middle of life and knew that I knew nothing and cared for nothing but following her." The female protagonist was singing:

> *Freedom ain't nothing, Lord but nothing left to lose.*
> *Freedom was all she left to me.*
> *Loving her was easy, Lord, when Bobby sang the blues.*
> *Loving her was good enough for me.*
> *Good enough for me and Bobby McGee.*

Walker considered it a "post-menopausal novel." He had even thought of two titles: *Lancelot* and *Lancelot in Hell*. Shelby was delighted that Walker was back on track; *Lancelot* would be fine, in or out of hell, as long as Walker caught him midway in the journey of his life.

That summer, James Hart ("Hooty") McCown, S.J., drove up to the Percy house and knocked on the door.[88] Graciously, Walker welcomed him, though he preferred not to be bothered during his siesta time, by anyone, including a rumply cleric. Soon Father McCown ingratiated himself with Walker; they would have heated discussions about the Church and the survival of the Jews. Father McCown savored one of Walker's better toss-away lines: "You know, Hooty, you can go from one end of New York to another and not find a single Hittite." Walker read and blurbed Father McCown's autobiographical book about East Africa, entitled *Elephants Have the Right of Way* (1974). On one of his visits, he asked Walker point-blank if he had ever considered suicide. Walker replied unhesitatingly, "No." Another time, Father McCown took Walker to the estate of Roy and Beverly Guste, the owners of Antoine's restaurant in New Orleans. Hooty McCown was another exceptional priest in Walker's life whose insights and wisdom, however wacky at times, he simply could not discount.

Walker read Lewis Simpson's *The Man of Letters in New England and the South* (he liked especially the section on the novelists of the antebellum South).[89] After reading *August 1914*, he recommended that Solzhenitsyn be nominated as an honorary member of the Institute of Arts and Letters.[90] In an interview, Louis Gallo wrote of Walker: "Intellectual but not pedantic, and serious but not morose, Percy speaks with a natural exactness, a subtle sense of humor, and a low-key but wry wit."[91] Walker mentioned he was having difficulty with his new novel, which takes place in Louisiana; it involved conflicting points of view and cultures, "the Anglo-Saxon/Greco-Roman Stoic point of view as against the Latin-Catholic-Mediterranean, or whatever." Walker told Gallo that Norman Cousins had approached him about writing on what is wrong with the American novel, but he had ducked the opportunity. When talking about Watergate, Walker called the co-conspirators "not very smart." Though a Democrat, Walker would not vote for Ted Kennedy (if nominated), and felt it would be presumptuous to judge President Nixon at this point.

On a Sunday in late September, when Lewis Simpson and his wife drove to Covington for a picnic with the Percys, Simpson brought up the possibility of Walker teaching a seminar at LSU. He also urged Walker to think of *The Southern Review* if he had anything ready for publication. Walker did have a forty-page essay in progress—"anti-Chomsky, anti-Skinner, anti-Lévi-Strauss theory of the nature of language and especially the acquisition of language."[92] Walker considered it probably the most important piece he would ever write and asked Simpson to look at it when it was finished.[93] Though eventually accepted by Simpson for publication in June 1974, Walker substituted "The Delta Factor" for it later on.[94] The real imaginative fires, however, had not started up again, he told Shelby:

I think what's got me down is that the novel is attempting the impossible: to write about the great traditional themes, sin, God, love, death, etc., when in fact these themes are no longer with us, we've left them, even death, or they've left us. I've been in a long spell of *acedia*, anomie and aridity in which, unlike the saints who write under the assaults of devils, I simply get sleepy and doze off. I'm also bemused by the reality of being the oldest male Percy in history (LeRoy doesn't count, he was too normal to be a Percy); so what lies ahead is virgin territory; imagine a Percy with arthritis! senility! Parkinsonism, shuffling along, fingers rolling pills, head agoing! . . . I don't know whether I'm looking forward to doing a great thing like Kant and Spinoza and Verdi in the 1980s or whether I'll jump in the Bogue Falaya next week with a sugar kettle on my head (lately it's been close to the latter). Yeah, my Catholicism is not very operative, as Nixon would say. It consists just now and mainly in the deepest kind of hunch that it all works out, generally for the good, and everybody gets their deserts—which is frightening. But I mean, artistically, there is no sweat. One waits. Not for the

Muse, fuck her, but until one finds a new language, because that's about what it takes . . .

It might have been just a gnawing feeling of aridity, but Walker questioned radically his adopted faith: "I think that culturally speaking I am still a gloomy Georgia Presbyterian." He believed in the "one, holy, Catholic, and apostolic church, etc.," but its intellectual manifestations made him feel awkward. He noted, too, that the "Great Beast of Bethlehem is coming back." This was a reference to Yeats's poem, but he may also have been thinking of his mother's image of "The Crouching Beast," in a letter written just before his father committed suicide, and was indeed entering a dark night of the soul.[95] Though Walker anticipated enjoying Christmas with his two grandsons, he was not sure he could pull it off: "If you're between novels, I do wish you luck," he wrote to Lon Cheney. "I am into one which is about to kill me—suffering depression and other symptoms."[96] Walker considered at this point in his life that writing was a "rotten profession."

After one of their visits to see Ann, Walker sat down and wrote her a letter. "It was great seeing you, although the food was lousy. You seem to have a lot of very nice friends."[97] Though he had a queasy gut, he was enjoying his golf games with Phin and George Cross. "I'm still in a period of interregnum (look it up!). Still have in mind the novel I spoke to you of, but it is in a period of gestation, like an embryo. It is just an idea but it hasn't taken shape." Strangely enough, Walker told Ann the most important thing about a novel is its *tone*—the feeling, flavor, smell, taste. He hadn't gotten hold of that yet. The question was how long to wait, whether to force it too quickly and get it wrong. Walker felt good about having written the two long articles on linguistics, which he believed not a hundred people might read in his lifetime.

On a sunny November day Walker welcomed Bradley Dewey to his house for an extensive interview on Kierkegaard. After sherry and lunch were served, Walker and Dewey strolled down to the bayou to have their conversation. When Dewey transcribed the interview, he added a running commentary that helps the uninitiated put the discussion in a larger Kierkegaardian context. Walker mentioned that *Either/Or* was the first book by Kierkegaard he read, and once into it, he thought it was a hopeless undertaking. He then moved on to *Sickness unto Death*, *Repetition*, then *Concluding Unscientific Postscript*, a text he found quite accessible, and then *Edifying Discourses*, which he thought quite homiletic in nature. Over the years, Walker dipped in and out of Kierkegaard's books, leaving them when he felt frustrated by the denseness of the arguments. Walker particularly admired Kierkegaard's essay "The Difference Between a Genius and an Apostle," which had helped him enormously in plotting out Binx's life and career. For Walker, Kierkegaard expressed his own feelings about the whole scientific synthesis—authors who pitted science against emotion and art and play discouraged Walker. What he found missing, whether in scientific or philosophical theory, was the study of an individual as an individual. Unfortunately, Kierkegaard never gave Walker a methodology for dealing with inter-subjectivity, unlike the works of Martin Buber or Harry Stack Sullivan. While Walker's creativity often diverged from Kierkegaard's in matters of content, Dewey felt they seemed to agree on matters of intent and form.

When Walker received Bob Coles's essay about him in December, he immediately sat down and read it with much emotion, gratitude, and wonderment that Bob should have felt it worthwhile to give so much time and effort to it. He would not presume to agree or disagree with Coles's findings, though he did tell Coles that in the main he was right —"that is, your readings and my intention, often foggy, by and large coincide."[98] Walker did correct some factual errors. He was glad that Coles had seen the differences between Uncle Will and Aunt Emily in *The Moviegoer*; too many critics had focused on the similarities. Later Walker reread the whole text: "Again Bob, I'm somewhat overwhelmed by what you've done. Would you believe that the best of it for me is this: somebody actually *read* all that, and *understood* it and *said* so in such a way that I cannot doubt it."[99] Walker felt like Helen Keller feeling the world with one hand and her friend's hand with the other. It was probably just as well that Coles had not known about Walker's spiritual and emotional state. As Walker told Lon Cheney, his novel was in "disarray."[100]

By Christmas, Walker seemed to see around the bend, as he wrote to Shelby: "Art here buggered, blowed and screwed. I'm certainly at the end of something and therefore *hopefully* at the beginning." His Christmas card to Caroline Gordon likewise seemed somewhat hopeful: "Nothing much at this end. I've run into a spell of anomie, *acedia*, plus plain old Percy depression. I trust, however, all these things work to good ends."[101] He sent a $500 check to the Gordon-Cowan School of Letters, the first novelist to make such a contribution.[102] But, in general, Walker did not enjoy this Christmas, especially going to parties where people talked about Watergate. The only happy moments were when he played Santy to the grandchildren.

Still not fully preoccupied with writing his new novel, Walker spent considerable time that winter helping some of the local nuns, especially Eucharistic Missionaries Joan Ridley, Madeleine Davis, and Stanislaus Langlinais, make a decision about the ultimate use of their property, Regina Coeli.[103] The nuns had stopped using the building as a novitiate and were looking to use it for other apostolic purposes.[104] Sister Joan lunched a few times with the Percys to discuss the problems of integration in Covington. Walker would occasionally ask her questions about theology and the current status of religious women. She appreciated Walker's ongoing efforts to help with their projects, especially Head Start. Walker was in charge of the transportation committee and once, while driving children home in a bus, one of the young passengers fell asleep. At the end of his route, Walker discovered the sleeping child, took him home, and waited until his parents could be contacted. Walker also came to a number of meetings during which the Eucharistic Missionaries assessed their work. A small group first met in early February at Regina Coeli.[105] Present were Robert Berlin, a land surveyor, and his wife, Aline, whom Walker knew from his earliest days in Covington.[106] Two of the black Baptist churches were represented by the Rev. Mallery Callahan and Deacon Henry Randle. The discussion focused on whether to sell the land to the city for possible industrial use or as a prison-farm site, or use it for housing, or build a vocational-technical school on the property. The committee finally endorsed a plan for the nuns to meet with Bob Berlin and the county supervisors of the Farmers' Home Administration, at which it became clear that families must be helped individually. The Eucharistic Missionaries then had to decide how much to retain for their community needs and how much to give away or sell.

Walker had his opinion, as he told Sister Joan; he believed that the sale of lots to poor people at reasonable prices would provide an opportunity not presently available (especially to black people) and also give the sisters the income they needed to take care of their own.[107] Walker never felt "too knowledgeable" about such matters, but that did not prevent him from giving his opinion.[108] Walker was also involved with the Berlins in attempting to make a subdivision of the property owned by the Benedictine nuns at St. Gertrude's Convent in Ramsey, which would have been financed partly by the Farmers' Home Administration. The subdivision had been laid out and the financing was in order, but it was blocked by the local Police Jury, a governing body in Covington. Another time the Berlins and Walker came together when a group of concerned citizens went to Americus, Georgia, to apply for a Habitat for Humanity affiliate, in order to explore this enterprise that promotes providing housing for the poor at modest prices. Once they had their affiliation, the local members built the first house at the end of

33rd Avenue. In subsequent years, Walker served on the board of directors of the Greater Covington Federal Credit Union, which began in a modest office on Van Buren and 31st Street. Under the leadership of Leroy Frick, Harvey Stalling, and Emily Diamond, the credit union would make loans amounting to over $400,000 by 1982. As Leroy Frick was fond of saying, the work of the credit union was "the most unselfish business in town." Though less active in future years on behalf of the poor, Walker nevertheless followed their plight and, when necessary, publicly made his opinions known.[109]

It is no wonder that by mid-February Walker was hopelessly stuck with his novel; he could not get it right and he would not let it go. For the present, all he had were some notes and another title, *The Knight, Death and the Devil* (from the Dürer engraving.)[110] Walker was willing to put these aside to host Jane and Bob Coles, once he had learned that Jane was ill.[111] His comforting words and gestures could only draw the Percys and the Coleses closer together. A Harvard professor, Daniel Aaron, and his student, Walter Isaacson, visited Walker about this time. When they arrived, they had some bourbon and hors d'oeuvres, and after some friendly conversation Walker invited them to stay for dinner, even though Walter had originally planned to take his adviser and the Percys out to dinner. Concerned that Isaacson would be overly influenced by the logical positivism and analytic philosophy then being taught at Harvard, Walker suggested that Isaacson read Camus and Kierkegaard as preparation for his senior honors essay, entitled "*The Moviegoer* as a Dramatization of Walker Percy's Early Philosophy," a version of which he tried to get published.[112]

Walker kept busy that spring. Donald Barthelme and Marion Knox flew down after Mardi Gras from New York to see the Percys.[113] Walker attended a party at the home of Bob and Olga Hess on Prytania Street in New Orleans.[114] During the first week of April, he drove over to Manresa to make another retreat.

Dressed as a rabbit, he ran into Dr. Susanne M. Jensen at the Mardi Gras parade in Covington.[115] Jensen, originally from a small German town in the Alsace-Lorraine region, would see the Percys at social functions and once visited them with her husband, Richard, their two sons, and her sister Gertrude Kronz. But after her appointment as associate director of the Student Mental Health Services at LSU, the Percys and the Jensens drifted apart. The Jensens, however, returned occasionally to stay at their twenty-acre hideaway "ranch" near Folsom. During their conversation at the parade, Jensen mentioned that the LSU faculty and staff met every Thursday for LSU's chancellor Cecil G. Taylor's Human Development Program, to aid the chancellor in thinking about ways to build up the university community. Walker expressed an interest in joining one of the groups. Since Walker was not on the faculty, a vote was taken when Jensen returned to campus, and he was invited to join a group soon that spring.[116]

Otis B. Wheeler, the chairman of the English Department at LSU, learned from Sue Jensen that Walker might indeed be interested in teaching there. Walker had been considering teaching either a long seminar once a week or a shorter one twice a week. He would not rule out a fiction-writing course, but was not really keen on that. He suggested that he and Wheeler have lunch, along with Lewis Simpson in April.[117] The lunch proved successful.[118] Wheeler contacted Chancellor Taylor, requesting that a contract for $12,000 be drawn up to bring Walker as a visiting professor of English for the following academic year.[119] Walker had to turn down Professor Dwight Culler's offer to lecture at Yale.[120]

On a blazing afternoon, after Walker ("lean and graying" with "milky blue, transparent eyes that, if not sad, seem somehow inviolably internal") talked with Barbara King from *Cosmopolitan*, she left with the sense that Walker, a rather shy, sensitive, brooding man, belonged here in these curiously Gothic surroundings, where ducks roamed about the back yard just outside his bedroom window. Walker's visit to Memphis in mid-May for a party celebrating the completion of Shelby's trilogy (which he considered an American *Iliad*) temporarily lifted his spirits. Shelby's completed trilogy was actually longer than Gibbon's *Decline and Fall*. When Walker returned from Memphis, he realized that he, too, needed an ambitious project, and thus he pulled together his essays, including "A Theory of Language," which he had submitted to *The Southern Review*. He sent the manuscript off to his agent, tentatively entitled *The Message in the Bottle or How Queer Man Is, How Queer Language Is, and What One Has to Do with the Other*.[121] Walker merely Xeroxed some of his published essays; in other cases he provided freshly edited typescript. Bob Giroux, who had become Walker's sole editor after Henry Robbins moved to Simon & Schuster, accepted Walker's volume of essays, with an advance of $4,000 for publication in the spring.[122]

As a change of pace, Walker then started reading the two-volume biography of Faulkner written by Joseph Blotner of the University of Michigan. He felt Blotner had left out some of the more "interesting stuff" because Jill Faulkner Summers and her mother, Estelle, were still alive. Bunt and Walker went to Gulf Shores in June; Ann stayed in Baton

Rouge, living in the Contempo Apartments on July Street and taking courses in summer school.[123] After his vacation, Walker continued reading and critiquing Shelby's final volume.

Toward the end of July, Walker ran a fever and checked into Ochsner Clinic.[124] Ann, who had brought home a college friend, John Moores, to meet her parents, was distraught because she thought her father's illness was worse than they told her.[125] The doctors ruled out a recurrence of TB; in fact, Walker had hepatitis. By early August, Walker still felt shaky and refused to read the manuscripts writers wanted to send.[126] Nor could he muster sympathy for Richard Nixon when he announced his resignation. By the end of the month, Walker considered his depression and hepatitis both better, as he informed Caroline Gordon: "Maybe one caused the other. Truthfully, I don't know whether I've been overtaken by a virus or male menopause or the devil—who, I am quite willing to believe, does indeed roam about the world seeking whom he may devour. Anyhow it takes the form in my case of disinterest, *acedia*, little or no use for the things of God and the old virtues. I'd rather chase women (not that I do, but how strange to have to come to this pass). I think it has something to do with laziness or at least the inability to give birth to a two-year-old fetus of a novel. I don't like it at all and keep tearing it up."[127] Clearly, some of the spunk was returning. "Liver mending. Back up to my *normal* depression," he wrote Shelby in early September.

After the ferocious winds of Hurricane Carmen had settled down, Walker started traveling to Baton Rouge each week to teach a seminar on the "novel of alienation" at LSU. He attended the faculty meeting dressed in a dark blue suit, but afterward appeared on campus in more relaxed attire. Bunt often accompanied him, auditing a photography course to keep herself occupied. When Ann was not busy with classes or homework, the three would have dinner together. Walker's seminar included a talented group, eager to learn. *The Daily Reveille* featured a story on Walker, accompanied by three photos of him in various moods; Walker said that, unlike an academic, he taught one year and took seven off. He preferred to think of himself in terms of Flannery O'Connor's work habits: "Flannery O'Connor used to say that she spent three hours a day working and the rest of the day getting over it." Walker met his class twice a week, on Wednesday afternoons and Thursday mornings. Not pretending to be a skilled teacher, Walker brought to his students a searching mind, commitment to the literary enterprise, and a desire to learn from his students. He valued directness in class. In addition to the assigned texts, he recommended James Collins's *The Existentialists*; *Existentialism from Dostoevsky to Sartre*, edited by Walker Kaufmann; *A Case-*

book on Existentialism, edited by William Spanos; Beckett's *Molloy*; and Styron's *Lie Down in Darkness*.[128] Walker put his own copy of Kierkegaard's *Looking at Unscientific Postscripts* on reserve in the library.

His opening classes in September were devoted to a discussion of alienation as estrangement or the distancing of the self from itself, from community, from work, or from society. With references to Kierkegaard, Nietzsche, Barth, Brunner, Jaspers, Heidegger, Sartre, and Harry Stack Sullivan, Walker outlined the development of this notion of alienation, relating it to anxiety, abandonment, and despair. He noted the high value of literature, now on the threshold of a breakthrough similar to physics at the end of the nineteenth century, and stressed its cognitive aspects, particularly how literature is related to other forms of knowledge. Yet what happens when the scientific method is applied to oneself? One could have admiration for the method, but he felt there was a gap: science leaves out the self. And using what technique could one explore the gap? By writing fiction. The existentialist writings of Kierkegaard, Sartre, and Marcel emphasize the uniqueness of the self and generally hold that the individual human being cannot be comprehended by any system or philosophy.

Thus Walker developed themes that he had expressed in some of his essays, though only the most dedicated student would have searched them out. The next two classes were devoted to Dostoevsky's *Notes from Underground*, followed by a discussion of Hemingway's *The Sun Also Rises* and Sartre. By early October, as the seminar focused on Camus's *The Fall* and *The Stranger*, Walker, sensing the obvious, raised questions that members of the seminar were no doubt asking themselves: why read depressing books? What are the writers of such books trying to say? What has gone wrong with society? What is the cause of alienation? Can one be happy in an absurd world? Is mankind a problem or a mystery?

At this point, Walker shared some insights of his own with the class. It is the task of the poet, he maintained, to discover the new terms, the new forms of expression. Walker suggested that among the problems those living in Western societies must address is not that Christianity is not true but that European culture is finished. Walker assigned a 3,000-word midterm essay, asking the students to reach inside themselves to evaluate those works that meant something to them in their everyday lives. Faculty and students often dropped by Allen 237-F to talk to Walker in private.[129] Walker welcomed Professor Barbara Sims into his class whenever she wanted to attend. Edith Babin, who taught English to Ann, and her husband, James, had lunch with Walker.

Once when Wyatt Prunty, a former naval gunnery officer from Athens, Georgia, entered into conversation with Walker, he was surprised to hear Walker mention something deeply personal: "The central mystery of my life is to figure out why my father committed suicide."[130] And in discussing Camus's *The Stranger*, Walker asked Prunty, "Why would a character behave this way?" Prunty answered, "Because he is an absolutist." Prunty felt that Walker posed questions about himself and the world through the eyes of an absolutist. Yet, when Prunty told Walker he was the sanest man he ever knew, Walker replied, "I just might be crazy"—and Prunty felt they were back to the "absolutist" way of looking at the world, which Prunty equated with "crazy." Using this back-looping logic, Prunty came away feeling that Walker was trying to communicate to him the notion that if there was no God, then nothing means anything at all. After graduation, when Prunty was about to publish his first book of poetry, Walker jokingly sent along two possible blurbs: (1) "Wyatt Prunty's poems are O.K., I guess, but his daughter Heather is a lot better." (2) "In Wyatt Prunty's poetry, familiar things and places, old things and new things, lost things, lost faces are recovered and illumined by a language both skewed and precise." Of course Prunty chose the second one.

Others, like Nancy Hargrove, preferred not to wait in line to see Walker.[131] As a teaching assistant, she shared an office with Anne Noctor and Ira Siegal, who were married to one another, and they critiqued Walker's classes in private. Rebecca Butler, on the other hand, enjoyed her conversations with Walker. Though at the dissertation stage, Butler was eager to take Walker's seminar and kept careful notes of what he said.[132] Another student, New Orleanian Huey Guagliardo, was so impressed by the course that he wrote a reminiscence about it.[133] For Guagliardo, Walker's course was one of the richest experiences of his life. "To say that I was impressed with Walker's novels would be a gross understatement. They struck a chord within me unlike anything else that I had ever read. And Walker himself was even more impressive than the novels. Not that he was the flamboyant man of letters. Far from it. He was painfully shy. In his quiet, unassuming way, he led the class through wide-ranging, fascinating discussions of the novels as well as the work of philosophers such as Kierkegaard and Charles Sanders Peirce." Walker reminded Guagliardo that through novels he could gain a sense of what it means to be a human being.

In October, *Partisan Review* asked to see "The Delta Factor," an essay in Walker's new book, which Bob Giroux thought would be good advance publicity for the volume.[134] Walker had already promised it to *The Southern Review*, where it was published.[135] He also took time to write a sympathetic review of Fred C. Hobson's *Serpent in Eden: H. L. Mencken and the South* for the fall issue of *The Georgia Historical Review*.

Walker would see Sue Jensen in her office periodically for what amounted to counseling sessions. They sometimes talked about aggression and destructiveness, about the possibility that fantasy behavior lies within all human beings, and about therapy as an opportunity to make the unspeakable speakable. Therapists, Jensen knew, are part of the culture and have the same blocks and inhibitions that other people have. "I think Walker's relationship with his mother stayed unresolved," she believed. Jensen maintained that when someone enters a therapist's office, he or she does not enter alone, but mentally brings in others. In general, however, Jensen did not see Walker's life as forming the bases of his novels. The nature of their relationship can partially be seen in the prologue that Walker wrote for one of the handbooks for the Student Mental Health Service:

As an organism, one responds to those sectors of one's environment to which one has learned to respond or been wired to respond. Other sectors are simply not noticed. A chicken responds to a shadow of a hawk but not the shadow of a swallow, but a child wants to know what a swallow is. A world unlike an environment is totally constructed by all symbol users, it has no gaps. For men, unlike other organisms, gaps have a label on them reading "gaps"; on old maps, unexplored areas are labeled "terra incognita."

Man has to work willy-nilly whether he likes it or not; in a world everything is accounted for one way or another. Realistically or nonsensically, mythically or scientifically, abstractly or concretely. Chickens have no myths, but man always knows or thinks he knows what is under the earth and above the earth and what is holding the earth up. The therapist, like other men, has a world whether he knows it or not or likes it or not. The patient also has a world. He cannot not have a world. The relationship, therefore, of the psychotherapist and his patient is not primarily that of the scientist confronted by an organism which he seeks to manipulate by this or that technique, but rather that of two human beings inhabiting a world and whose fate it is to understand or misunderstand each other.[136]

When Walker showed Jensen some of the preliminary material for *Lancelot*, he said he had been working for weeks on the first sentence. They also talked about the nonfilming of *The Moviegoer*. At one point Jensen was concerned about Walker's drinking, and suggested that he might write something about it; the result was his delightful essay on bourbon. Walker gave Jensen a book of poetry that Uncle Will had given him, inscribing it for her in German, *Nun für Sue* ("Now for Sue").

In the introduction to *The Art of Walker Percy: Stratagems for Being*, which Panthea Reid Broughton edited in 1979, she mentions that the first

letter she wrote to Walker contained an outline of her interpretation of
his fiction. Walker kindly replied that Broughton was basically right, but
"it's more complicated than that." An articulate scholar, well versed in
Faulkner and Southern literature, Broughton received her Ph.D. in English from Walker's alma mater.[137] Once when she approached him about
an interview, Walker replied that anything he said would be redundant.
"I've said all I want to about the N.B.A.—an unhappy affair—and as
for the state of the modern novel and my own work—UGH."[138] A native
of Owensboro, Kentucky, Broughton arrived at LSU in 1974 as a visiting
scholar to work on collecting essays about Walker's writings. She first
met Walker in late August at a meeting of the English Department.
Walker agreed to help with her project, which they discussed over an
occasional lunch in the Plantation Room in the Student Union with Bunt
and Ann. Sometimes Walker would visit Broughton in her office in Allen
Hall or in her rented house on Aberdeen Avenue, where they would sit
and talk. Because of the tensions with her husband, George Broughton,
she felt a good deal of anxiety in her life that fall; she sought out the
professional counsel of Sue Jensen. Walker dropped her several short
notes about her plight.[139]

By that time, Walker had met her husband and son, and he urged
Broughton to keep the future open: "The valuable thing, surely, is your
getting away and being alone and collecting yourself (recollecting yourself, Marcel would say), so that you can *see* what was there, is there,
what was valuable and what not. And seeing also what is valuable and
what not in the alternative one imagined for yourself." Broughton commissioned articles for her projected volume, and consulted Walker about
which ones to accept and which to drop. At Thanksgiving time she invited Joseph Davis and Bunt and Walker for a small dinner, during
which Mary Pratt and Byrne stopped by for a few minutes. She visited
the Percys at Christmas in Covington on her way to see her mother in
Tuscaloosa, Alabama. One of the gifts that Walker gave her was his
annotated copy of the Bollingen series of Maritain's *Creative Intuition in
Art and Poetry*, which contained his own bookmark: a dove in flight reading a book, together with his name and the Latin words *Veni Creator*
("Come, Holy Spirit").

When Jerry Kennedy arrived at LSU in 1973, after obtaining his English degree at Duke University, he was not really familiar with Walker's
works.[140] That changed when Walker moved into the office next to his.
Asked by Broughton to write an essay for her volume, Kennedy consented to do one on *Love in the Ruins*; he was fortunate enough to have
Walker critique it.[141] Kennedy found Walker shy and difficult to know,
though he did get to understand him a bit better when he participated

in the chancellor's discussion groups in the union. Walker once lectured to one of Kennedy's classes on *The Moviegoer*. He stressed that the key to Binx's search could be found in Binx's rejection of the Stoic tradition of history, the Catholic faith, and the discipline of science. In short, Binx begins from scratch. His dalliance with his secretaries is analogous to what happens in *Love in the Ruins*. "Marriage," Walker told his audience of students and some of their parents, "is the best expression of the ethical." Of the novels he had so far written, Walker felt most comfortable talking about *The Moviegoer*.

Walker sent Shelby the first few pages of his collection of essays.[142] Shelby liked what he had read: "Language may be the clue, but in my limited way I see it more in a gain of individuality." Though not quite an enthusiastic pat on the back, Shelby's philosophical attitude showed that he was warming up more and more to Walker's nonfiction. Walker and Bob Giroux spoke on the phone about the collection of essays. He asked for a copy of "The Delta Factor" from Giroux in order to make a few changes: "I know you sent me one a couple of months ago but I think I gave it to *The Southern Review*. Forgive my incompetence: am feeling somewhat disconnected in general. Actually I think it's pretty much O.K., except for some repetitiousness."[143] Giroux returned a copy of the essay to Walker along with his editorial comments.[144] Giroux said that a sketch for the cover would soon be ready; unfortunately, it looked like an Old Crow bottle with a mouth inside and Giroux rejected it.[145] Walker suggested that the new design feature a bottle washed up on a beach with a note inside on which was inscribed a triangle.[146] The new design featured a delta-symbol and a profile of an Indian head, which Giroux felt had a poster-like impact.[147]

Since Allen Tate, now married to the former Helen Heinz, would turn seventy-five on November 19, some of his friends gathered for a symposium at Sewanee to celebrate his birthday. Among the participants were Denis Donoghue, Cleanth Brooks, William Jay Smith, Doris Grumbach, Howard Nemerov, Lewis Simpson, Louis Rubin, and Eudora Welty. Walker had been invited, accepted the invitation, and attended the celebration, though he sidestepped all the photos taken of the group.[148]

The seminar continued. Toward the end of November the class analyzed both Robbe-Grillet's *Jealousy* and a play written by one of the students, Charles DeGravelles. They focused, too, on some of the problems resulting from the calculated ambiguity of Kafka's *The Castle*, as well as the relationship between Huck's journey down the Mississippi River and Kerouac's novel *On the Road*. During the first week of December, the discussion centered on *Mr. Sammler's Planet* and the relationship between abstract European philosophy and the more socially oriented, historical American philosophy. At the end of the semester, an appreciative seminar member gave him an LSU football shirt with "Percy" blazoned on the back.

Walker did have some reservations about his teaching ability, as he said to Bob Coles: "The trouble was that I wasn't at all sure I was doing the students a service, or at least some of them. After a long discussion of Sartre's *Nausea*, a girl came up to me and said, 'Mr. Percy, I feel like him sometimes, but all I have to do is go home to my folks' ranch in West Texas and I feel good.' Which is only to raise the question: can alienation, which I do in fact believe to be the peculiar legacy of this century, be by-passed by a few lucky or courageous souls, and if so, what business has a literary fellow telling them otherwise?"[149] On the other hand, Walker flippantly maintained that certain Southern girls do not pay much attention to literature.

Walker's academic responsibilities did not stop in Allen Hall. He sent Louise Cowan at the University of Dallas a long letter in which he critiqued the manuscripts that had been sent to him. Walker thanked Professor Cowan for the check she sent and indicated that he would be willing to fly to Dallas in early 1975. In a postscript he added, "Now that I think about it, it is hard to believe that these stories are the work of undergraduates. If so, they are not like any undergraduates I ever came across. As I say, they (three at least) are better than the graduate students I've seen writing fiction here."[150] Tired by the academic experience, Walker checked into St. Tammany Parish Hospital before Christmas for minor surgery, yet was home for the festivities. Professor Phil Bryant drove down to see him, a visit that pleased Walker immensely. Naturally Lewis Simpson was concerned that Walker would stay on another semester, and Walker showed no reason why he shouldn't: "The students were very rewarding and I found myself thinking a great deal about them and their futures. Selfishly, I look on this year as a 'crop rotation'—hopefully the field planted with soy beans can go back to make more and better cotton."[151] Walker finally decided that he would return next semester. To seek a change of pace, he flew to Las Vegas and, in a rented car, toured the Sierra Nevada.[152] He also spent part of his vacation, as he told Shelby, reading Richard Ellmann's biography of James Joyce.

12

The Message in the Bottle,
Lancelot, and The Second Coming
1975–80

Walker resumed teaching in January 1975 in LSU's Allen Hall with a diverse, new group of students—mostly juniors, seniors, and graduate students.[1] One student, Leo Luke Marcello, submitted sections of his rather gruesome novel-in-progress in order to be accepted. (In hindsight, Marcello wondered whether incidents in his novel, which dealt with a character named John who left a monastery, might have prompted some of the situations in *Lancelot*.) Since the class focused on creative writing, they normally analyzed the fiction of one student, copies of which had been distributed in advance. They might discuss Camus's notebooks, Dostoevsky's *Diary of a Writer*, or the aphorisms in Paul Horgan's *Approaches to Writing*.

Ruth Laney kept notes of their first class: "He [Percy] is fascinating. Left handed. A deeper Southern accent than I had expected. Funny that it takes him an hour and a half to drive here from Covington and another hour and a half to find a parking place. Very deadpan. I hate it when I admire someone because I want to absorb and soak up everything about him. It's exhausting. He asked that we give him ten pages a week and also that we read both Camus's notebooks and *A Happy Death*. He brought the latter to class and gave everybody a copy. I was very struck by this action."

Because the seminar demanded less formal preparation on Walker's part, he had more time for his own work. In mid-January he received sample type pages of *The Message in the Bottle*, a title that may have been derived from Poe's "Ms. Found in a Bottle."[2] The book's extensive bibliography indicates his wide reading in the area of semiotics. When he returned the corrected galleys, he noted that the subtitle, *How Queer Man Is, How Queer Language Is, and What One Has to Do with the Other*, had been omitted from the title page; he had meant it as a reader's aid, but had no objection if the omission was an editorial decision.[3] Bob Giroux reinserted the subtitle. Walker had no idea who would want to read his new book, but was nevertheless glad to have it published. In thanking Simone Vauthier for her essay on *The Moviegoer*, he mentioned that his own collection of essays was both bad-tempered and amateurish, being mainly directed against behaviorist and transformational linguists.[4]

He gave one set of galleys to Chink Baldwin, who could barely make his way through them. "It is a very odd collection," Walker wrote Bob Giroux, "but I think it will have a lasting value." As Bob concerned himself with the details of production, he needed an inordinate amount of time to obtain releases for essays reprinted from journals like *Thought* and *Psychiatry* that were reluctant to revert the copyrights to Walker, but they finally did at his insistence.[5] Bob sent galleys to Donald Barthelme, who in turn suggested Noam Chomsky, Ved Mehta, and Jeremy Bernstein of the Stevens Institute in Hoboken, New Jersey. Walker recommended that galleys be sent to Arthur Koestler (he had been influenced by Koestler's *The Ghost in the Machine* while writing *Love in the Ruins*) and George Steiner.[6] In addition, Giroux sent copies to Jean Stafford, Kurt Vonnegut, Wilfrid Sheed, and Caroline Gordon, who had been on leave from teaching because of illness.[7]

At this time, Shelby was anxiously awaiting the announcement of several prizes in history, including the Pulitzer, which was awarded to Dumas Malone. Because he felt Shelby had reached the pinnacle of his writing career, Walker brooded over the advent of his own sixth decade on earth and questioned himself about the future. He was in a definite quandary and yet for the time being contented himself with reading Joseph Heller's *Something Happened*.

He received his first copy of *The Message in the Bottle* on April 27. "It's nice to see it—a book!—but I can't say it's all that handsome," he wrote Rhoda Faust, who was planning a book-signing celebration at her store.[8] He was particularly disappointed over the size of the type. Copies were sent to relatives and friends, including Charles East, Panthea Broughton, Sue Jensen, and Maurice Natanson at the University of California at Santa Cruz.[9] When Shelby read the introductory essay, he said he was bewildered by the subject matter; he often had to stop and try to figure out what Walker was saying. (Ironically, Shelby preferred to stick with *Ulysses*, which he was now reading for the ninth time.) Chiding Walker for preferring Tolstoy to Proust, Shelby recommended that Walker begin anew his effort to read Dante. If he had done that earlier,

Shelby believed, he might have already been inspired to write his *magnum opus*. Walker replied that he was more interested in Homer than Dante. Shelby supplied Walker with texts by both authors, as well as Thomas Bergin's handbook, *Dante*, which Walker read. If he found that Dante was as good as Shelby claimed, he'd trade his New York edition of Henry James for Bergin's three-volume Dante. He could still boast of one reading triumph—he claimed to have read the *Summa* of Thomas Aquinas from cover to cover.

After Rhoda's book party, Marcus Smith, a professor of English at Loyola, broached the idea of doing an interview with Walker for *The New Orleans Review*.[10] Behind the scenes, Loyola was interested in bringing Walker to campus again as a visiting professor, something that Walker himself wanted. Negotiations began for the spring 1976 semester.[11] William Poteat at Duke, who planned on teaching a junior-senior seminar devoted exclusively to *The Message in the Bottle*, invited Walker to speak to his students.[12] Walter Sullivan at Vanderbilt offered Walker a position for the 1976 fall semester.[13] Given his desire not to travel too far from home, Walker turned them down.

Once classes had ended, Walker and Bunt and their daughters went to New York, staying at the Plaza. Ann and John Moores had become engaged, and Ann needed a trousseau. During their visit, the Percys saw the Scythian gold exhibit at the Metropolitan Museum of Art, as well as *Sherlock Holmes* at the Broadhurst Theatre and *Equus*, starring Anthony Hopkins, at the Plymouth Theatre. As they exited the Plymouth, Bunt turned to her husband and said, "Walker, that whole last act was in the nude." Walker replied that he, too, had noticed.

When he lunched at the Century Club in early June with Bob Giroux, he was informed that the book clubs had decided against *The Message in the Bottle*, since they usually preferred fiction.[14] Henry Robbins, now in charge of Simon & Schuster's Touchstone division, decided not to accept the book for paperback publication.[15] Early notices in *Booklist* and *Kirkus* called the volume "laborious but elegant rhetorical exercises" and "a deadly serious work"—which of course it was. Novelist Madeleine L'Engle wrote Bob Giroux saying that she greatly admired Walker's collection of essays.[16] The review in *The New York Times* by Thomas LeClair provided a fine analysis: "Despite their unity of focus and repetition, the essays remain discrete probes into what Percy calls the 'terra incognita' of language use. There is no map—just an open place for being." John Ciardi, writing in *The Chicago Tribune*, noted that the questions that Walker asked were worthwhile but he felt his ideas were disjointed and the volume lacked an overall shape. James Boatwright in *The New Republic* wrote that the book "demonstrates that for seriousness and keenness of mind, Walker Percy has few rivals in American letters." He commended the essays for their "richness, intellectual power, and coherence." In her review in *The National Observer*, novelist Anne Tyler accused Walker of faulty logic and said he wrote in an unnecessarily abstruse manner. Hugh Kenner in *National Review* praised Walker as a new Copernicus. Marcus Smith in *The Vieux Carré Courier* tried to discount hostile reviews by stressing that Walker, when explaining his philosophical views, appropriately inquired about the nature of language itself. Walker personally thanked Lon Cheney for his kind critique: "The reviews vary all the way from 'Copernican breakthrough' to 'amateur crackpot.' "[17] He mentioned that his new novel was "a different kind of misery than the mystery of trying to get hold of language—as you know."

Walker admitted in his correspondence with Will Campbell that the older he got, the more complicated life became. Years before, he had it all figured out—"liberal in politics, conservative in dogma, Dr. King was a saint and the Kluxers were all bastards."[18] He had still retained his conservative streak, approving of the Vietnam War, in spite of the political duplicity, deaths, and destruction. He likewise signaled to Campbell that something disturbing was happening in his life; as "a horny impotent" at age fifty-nine, he might just jump in a car and seek Will's counsel.[19] He did travel to Mount Juliet, Tennessee, to talk about his anxieties; with Ann about to be married, he and Bunt would face the "empty-nest syndrome" and a new stage in their lives together.

For part of the summer, he and Bunt vacationed at Point Clear with Roy and Sarah.[20] After a dove hunt at Trail Lake with Roy and nephews Billy and Robert (doing his residency as a physician in Jackson), Walker resumed work on his new novel in earnest in September and hoped to finish it within a year's time.[21] Through the good graces of James Boatwright, Walker gave a talk in October entitled "The State of the Novel: Dying Art or New Science?" at Washington and Lee University, as part of a two-day program that included a panel discussion with Donald Barthelme, William Gass, and Grace Paley.[22]

The panelists discussed their views on literature. "My own feeling," Walker stated, "is that it's primarily cognitive, whereas emotional transactions may take place in both the creation and reception of a work of art. I think, as Langer said, that what is transmitted primarily is not feelings but the forms of feelings and that involves an act of cognition." Lewis Simpson wanted to print this talk in *The Southern Review*, but Walker felt it had not been conceived for scholarly publication.[23]

After Sue Jensen had assumed the directorship of the Student Mental Health Services in September, Walker spoke at LSU on "Is a Theory of Man Possible?"[24] In this carefully prepared talk, he stressed Peirce's notion of triadic relationships—namely, that once human beings have crossed the threshold of language and symbolism a new world is literally opened up before them. Undoubtedly this talk came from deep recesses within Walker and indicated the direction his new novel would take. He had jokingly asked what his stipend would be; as recompense, Jensen went up to the podium and planted a kiss on his cheek.

Lyn Hill, a local artist, met Bob Milling at the Playmakers Theatre and invited him to visit her studio in a building adjacent to the St. Tammany Art Association. Walker, alerted by Bunt's enthusiasm for Hill's series of paintings on the psalms, had stopped by her studio three years before. Lyn, the same age as Mary Pratt, had studied art at Auburn University and the Art Students League in New York, married Thomas Hill, and moved to Tchefuncta Estates in 1970. After Bunt suggested to Walker—no doubt overwhelmed at times by the boisterous activity of his two grandsons—that he move into one of the studios, each of which had a small bathroom and a kitchen area, he soon ensconced himself in his new office, arriving with a vinyl couch and writing apparatus that looked like a hospital tray. He had a private phone line installed. (This was after someone called the Percy residence in the early hours of the morning: "Dr. Percy, I'm calling from Greenwich Village. I love your books. I'm about to commit suicide. You just wouldn't believe it, but John Updike is unlisted and Norman Mailer's line has been busy for a two lousy hours. Isn't that annoying?")

Walker kept to his routine: visiting the post office, working all morning, lunching either at home or at a fast-food restaurant, and typing in his office kitchen in the afternoon. Whenever Lyn Hill heard three knocks on the wall or radiator, she knew that he wanted to read a section to her; they would often laugh aloud at the funny passages. Sometimes Bob Milling dropped by to play his guitar or Trudy Lagarde brought sandwiches. At other times, to review submissions with Walker for an elementary school contest on the topic "Why I Love the Library," Sheila Stroup would come by with her daughter Claire, age three. Walker always enjoyed talking to little Claire.

In November he accompanied Ann down the aisle of the abbey church in the wedding ceremony, at which James Boulware, O.S.B., presided.[25] Walker liked John Moores, the quiet, considerate groom, who had grown up as a Methodist in Lafayette, Louisiana. It did not sit well at all with Walker that his daughter was marrying while still in her senior year at college. The newlyweds had to return to Baton Rouge afterward, so the wedding was kept simple. Since late adolescence Ann had distanced herself from the Catholic Church, yet she drew on her father's faith as she was about to assume the role of a wife. Though Ann would graduate in May 1976, John's graduation would be a year later; he would spend his last year of college taking courses at Southeastern Louisiana University in Hammond. When Ann and John returned to Covington for the Christmas holidays, John mentioned to Walker that he enjoyed his essay in the December issue of *Esquire* entitled "Bourbon." When it was printed later in a deluxe edition it bore a cryptic dedication to "S.M."—Susanna Maria, as Walker fondly called Sue Jensen.

As the year ended, Walker wanted to keep his focus with work on *Lancelot*. While it is difficult to determine the genetic origins of the novel, it might partly have had to do with the filming of *The Moviegoer*. Walker's subconscious desire may have been to destroy the film crew, which had failed to complete their important artistic undertaking. It may also have been prompted by Ann's departure through marriage, except that in *Lancelot* Siobhan becomes estranged from her father when he discovers she is illegitimate; or by Walker's interest in talented women like Panthea Broughton, Lyn Hill, and Sue Jensen; or, further back, by Walker's portrayal in *The Last Gentleman* of Margaret Rich, the young psychotic woman whom Will Barrett met at a sanatorium. Certainly the scene in the film *Cabaret* where the young Hitler Youth sings inspired Walker's depiction of Lancelot as a fanatic.[26] In his initial jottings, Walker seemed to have the names of the characters in mind, except for Percival, who was initially called John-Paul. There is a cryptic reference to "W.P." (Walker Percy) and "S.D.F" (Shelby Dade Foote), suggesting that they were quasi-models for the two protagonists. Walker considered various titles—*The Prisoner* (he wrote an unpublished story with the same title), *The Assistant Chaplain*, and *Lancelot: Death, Famine and the Knight*. Other notes indicate that he had been thinking about Bill Sorum and Val Ambrose McInnes, O.P., a Catholic chaplain at Tulane, who knew Walker and Bunt when they helped with the projects sponsored by the Louisiana Council of Music and the Performing Arts. He also counseled them a number of times in the mid-1970s to help them through marital difficulties.[27] But clearly Walker's important literary source was Camus's *The Fall*. "I tried to write *Lancelot* as a third-person narrative about two men, Lance and Percival," he wrote to Simone Vauthier. "It didn't work at all. I had to rewrite it, diminishing Percival to the near-anonymity of the auditor in Camus's *The Fall*. Yet I wanted to keep Percival, and I wanted the reader to see him through Lance's eyes. And to make sure he wasn't taken as a figment of Lance's imagination, I gave him a couple of words: 'Yes,' 'yes.' Yet this was not entirely successful. Some readers never quite believed Percival existed."[28] In replying to a query from William Rodney Allen, Walker said that he was not thinking of Eliot's *The Waste Land* when writing this novel.[29] Belle Isle in *Lancelot* was based on several plantations. First, Greenwood, built in the 1830s by William Ruffin Barrow, which Bunt, Walker, and Mary Pratt had once visited. Before World War I, Greenwood was sold to Frank Percy, a distant relative, who set about restoring it. During a summer storm in 1960, lightning struck the house, and as in a scene out of a Southern Gothic novel, it was consumed by flames, leaving nothing but the columns and the chimneys. Second, Houmas House, which Walker identified in interviews as the setting for the film *Hush . . . Hush, Sweet Charlotte*. The idea of the visiting film company, as Walker told John Baker, came to him from an article by Peter Bogdanovich about the impact the director's company had on a little Kansas town during the making of *Paper Moon*. Joyce Corrington, who was having marital problems with Bill, thought that the film company she and Bill had started, Corrington Productions, provided Walker with some material for this novel.

Lewis Simpson's "Faulkner and the Legend of the Artist" struck a deep chord when Walker read it. This essay prompted Walker to formulate a major theme of *Lancelot*: the incapacity of the postmodern consciousness to deal with sexuality. "Also, your taking seriously William Faulkner's dictum 'I am Quentin' serves to remind me that there is such a community as lonely artists—so lonely that one often forgets and needs to be reminded."[30] About this time Walker wrote an astonishing poem about how consoling it was to find a community of like-minded people outside the environment of his family:

COMMUNITY

Now comes the artist to his life's surprise—
A fond abstract middle-aged public man is he,
Come to a place in his time when he thought he knew something.
What?
Namely, that on the short lovely Louisiana afternoons,
The winter sunlight making spaces, pale gold above
And in the live oaks, a shafted gloom like rooms
Of moss and leaf and tenant squirrels and jeweled birds—
He trafficked in loneliness, little brother, cellmate
And friend to him, and even turned it to good use,
A commodity, a good business man selling solitariness
Like GM selling Chevrolets or Burns furniture.

A strange success, this selling to other selves the very
Sealed-offness of self from selves.

Now comes the surprise—
What?
That in the very things he had denied and done so well
Denying—
Friendship, laughter, good red wine (well, anyhow, Early Times)
Marichal [sic] merriness, Lyn loveliness—
All the good things we Catholics used to stand for
Until something went wrong—
Did I help them go wrong?
I hope not—I only named the wrongness
Which in a way is to make it right and turn it around.
But what a surprise!
Twenty years of solitariness and success at solitariness,
Solitary with his family like the Swiss family on their island,
Then all at once community.
Community? What, friends out there in the world?
Yes.

Though feeling his actual physical age, Walker mentioned to Simpson that he considered himself like someone in his twenties, in that he still hoped to make a beginning in the endless task of creating oneself and a world "from the poor makings of the bloody 'rootless ego.' " Walker's remark about his age piqued Lewis's interest. He later sensed that Walker had failed to develop the most important text of his life: "What had happened to the almost ecstatic writer who in 'The Delta Factor' had told about how he discovered the triadic breakthrough in Helen Keller's act of naming the liquid sensation in her hand that summer morning in the well house?"[31] Walker's life did not have the coherence he expected. Thus it is not surprising that Walker and Bunt went to Tallahassee in late January for a weekend workshop on transactional analysis. As he wrote Bob Hess: "Should be interesting."[32] But why such analysis? One clue is that after reading Joseph Blotner's biography of Faulkner, Walker agreed with Simpson that "loneliness" characterized much of Faulkner's life. Walker seemed genuinely interested in trying to understand the pain this great writer experienced.[33] If Walker needed any further insight into Faulkner, he had only to consult Cleanth Brooks or Noel Polk, another Faulkner expert, who had asked Walker about writing a biography of Uncle Will.[34]

By early February, Walker had finished a draft of *Lancelot*, but could not bring himself to read it. While he continued working steadily, he invited Bob Coles for a visit—perhaps another attempt to seek counsel: "I am suffering from angelism-bestialism, large bowel complaints and Bicentennial blues and find Early Times useful."[35] He traveled to Washington in early April, where he presented a version of "The State of the Novel: Dying Art or New Science?" at the Washington School of Psychiatry. Here Walker emphasized the differences between a creative writer and a psychiatrist, especially that psychotherapists might stand in need of novelists, or in need of a new way of looking at their subject matter—"a way that may serve as a kind of triangulation point, a means of locating such elusive phenomena and answering such questions as: what is pathological and what is quote 'normal' in the last quarter of the twentieth century?"

Perhaps working from his experience of writing *Lancelot*, Walker noted that more often than not novelists and psychiatrists find themselves either talking at cross-purposes or upstaging each other from carefully prepared vantage points. He also noted that the hero or antihero of the contemporary novel hardly qualifies under any of the conventional mental-health canons—emotional maturity, autonomy, and enhanced interpersonal relations. Was Walker thinking about himself as he stated that the modern hero "is more often than not a solitary, disenchanted person who is radically estranged from his society, who has generally rejected the goals of his family and his peers, and whose encounters with other people, friendships, and love affairs are regularly attended by misunderstandings, misperceptions, breakdowns in communication, aggressions, and withdrawals, all occurring in a general climate of deflated significance"? Walker used Heller's *Something Happened* to demonstrate some of the points he wanted to make.

Bunt and Walker and Betty and Steve Ellis spent Holy Week in Mérida on the Yucatán Peninsula. Having finished his novel by mid-April, Walker gave the script to Betty Ellis to be properly typed. (He called her Della Street, after Perry Mason's secretary in the mystery novels.[36]) When $20,000 was agreed upon as an advance, he asked for and received a contract that would prevent an undue tax burden for the fiscal year.[37] Bob Giroux suggested editorial changes in Walker's manuscript; he made them, adding some modifications of his own.[38] On May 23, Walker received an honorary degree from the University of the South at Sewanee ("novelist and essayist, gentleman first and last"), where he had a chance to talk with Jane and Walter Sullivan from Nashville.

When elderly Miss Otis read the completed typescript in June, she told Bob Giroux she had some reservations: "I have told Walker that I am in a state of utter confusion, but that doesn't mean that you will be.

I have to confess that a number of the present writers, such as Barthelme, leave me in the same fog so I don't put too much confidence in my own reactions."[39]

Walker now felt free to offer to teach the following fall at Loyola.[40] By the end of May, after lunching with Dawson Gaillard, head of the English Department, Walker was informed that his stipend would be $5,000, even though Dawson had learned that both Vanderbilt and Yale had previously offered Walker $25,000.[41] Johns Hopkins University, Walker later informed her, offered him $10,000 to teach fiction workshops in the 1977 spring semester.[42]

On the last day of July, Walker was the featured author at the Louisiana Authors' Day in New Orleans. He sat with his daughter Ann at a table near the hotel's entrance, wearing his name tag, which merely read "Percy." By midafternoon, Ann, who had become a seller of books and antiques, had sold thirty copies of her father's books. Ann and John had bought a house, desperately in need of repair, next to Walker and Bunt's. When Ann discovered she was pregnant that winter, she and John had to hurry to fix up the house, though John commuted every day to Hammond. With encouragement and financial support from her parents, Ann opened her North Lee Road bookstore, called the Kumquat, after a tree the Percys had on their property on Military Road.

On the last day of August, Walker began teaching each Tuesday evening in Loyola's Bobet Hall. He had accepted twelve students.[43] Alan Davis, who worked as a prison counselor, had seen a poster for the course and sent Walker some stories, with a synopsis of his novel entitled *Somewhere to Go*. George Judson, a journalist from Hartford, Connecticut, had come to New Orleans for a year to write a novel. Walter Isaacson, whom Walker had come to know and now a graduate of Harvard and a former Rhodes scholar at Pembroke College, worked as a reporter for *The States-Item*. Both Tim Gautreaux, a fiction writer who was working on a novel, and Larry Gray, who had received his doctorate from the University of Notre Dame, were on the faculty at Southeastern; they would drive together from Hammond to attend class. Valerie Martin, a former student of W. Kenneth Holditch, was working on her novel *Alexandra*. Martin went on to become the most famous novelist of any of Walker's students; in 1978, she published *Set in Motion*, which Walker called "remarkable for its honesty." Martin felt that Walker did not particularly like her novel-in-progress and she considered Walker a good teacher even if his heart was not completely involved in teaching. Ken Holditch had known Walker through his contact with Milly Barranger at the University of New Orleans, dating from the mid-1960s. Once the course had finished, Ken wrote a sympathetic evaluation of it for a local paper.[44]

At Loyola, Walker varied his style of teaching, allowing students to read from their works-in-progress. During the first class, Alan Davis recorded his impressions of Walker: "He exhibited a winning personality. Sixty or so, conservatively dressed, slender, and appears to look about fifty. Only the wrinkles in the folds between his fingers reveal his age. He spoke tentatively, suggesting possibilities for the course in a halting manner, although the course plans were well thought out. His remarks weren't planned, but anecdotal in nature and occasionally directed toward a question or another remark." During a subsequent class, Walker brought in a dozen or so novels and read the opening lines of each—his first test of a good novel.

After sending Bob Giroux a long list of changes in the typescript of *Lancelot*, Walker became annoyed again by the persistent hubhub over the filming of *The Moviegoer*. He had told Dawson Gaillard that the actress Karen Black, who was the wife of Kit Carson, had optioned "exclusive and irrevocable" film rights for $3,000 two years before.[45] And as he mentioned at Loyola to reporter Alan Citron of *The Maroon*, he did not want to deal anymore with this project: "If they do a great job, fine. It they botch it up, it's not my fault." Once, after class, Walker asked Ken Holditch if he could get him some marijuana. Ken performed the errand, but never found out what Walker did with it.

For the last weekend of September, Walker flew to Atlanta with Marcus Smith and Dawson Gaillard to attend the first annual conference of the Semiotic Society of America. One can only speculate as to why Dawson, more poet than semiotician, went. Was she also attracted to Walker? Colleagues at Loyola certainly noticed that her marriage was about to come apart. Those in attendance at the conference included Peirce scholars and semioticians John Deely, Umberto Eco, Carolyn Eisele, Kenneth Laine Ketner, and Thomas A. Sebeok.[46] Walker attended a number of lectures and panels on Charles Sanders Peirce; the conference gave him a chance to hear personally the Peirce agenda as expressed by trained semioticians.

When Bob Milling talked in late October with Lyn Hill about starting a discussion group, they weighed various possibilities and decided to read the works of Carl Jung. By discussing material presented on cassette tapes and in a series of booklets from Centerpoint in St. Louis, the participants tried to understand the concepts of ego, persona, shadow, as well as the various facets of the anima/animus. The idea of the Jung group appealed to Walker. Not only would he have a chance to understand theoretically his own problems but he could listen to the psychological views expressed by Bunt, Trudy Lagarde, Lyn and Tom Hill, Alyce and Charlie O'Brien, Lucy and Ed Ballard, and Charles P. Bigger III (a philosophy professor at LSU). They started meeting once a week in the evenings at Bob's house. Bigger on occasion lunched with Walker at Bechac's and stayed overnight with the Percys.[47] Thus Walker's growing social schedule—luncheons on Wednesdays and an evening Centerpoint discussion each week—was bound to interrupt his writing schedule.

The interaction between Charles Bigger and Ed Ballard dated from their friendship as graduate students at the University of Virginia. Over the years, Bigger watched Walker become increasingly interested in questions originating in European phenomenology, though, as a professional philosopher, he felt that Walker's approach was impressionistic. Walker had an insight into language, according to Bigger, and was looking for some way to express it. Bigger was aware that Walker had been influenced by Heidegger, Kierkegaard, and especially Whitehead's "misplaced concreteness" and the sovereignty of the "I," but he knew that Walker had not read Peirce critically. Though Walker latched on to the notions of "thirdness" and "irreducibility" in Peirce, he had little or no understanding or interest in Peircean mathematics or logic. At one point, Bigger explored the possibility that DNA was fundamentally a semiotic system, not a causal one, and that interpretative relationships provided the key. His approach, with data provided by his wife, a chemist, attempted to show the allegorical nature of science. Walker was intrigued by this form of investigation since he welcomed any imaginative constructs that might challenge his own. Bigger was so taken by his reading of Walker's nonfiction that he started writing "Logos and Epiphany: Walker Percy's Theology of Language" for *The Southern Review*. From another perspective, Walker sometimes complained to Ed: "What does studying Jung have to do with justice and my obligations to other people?"

"Percy," Bigger subsequently wrote, "offered a Kantian defense for us against our efforts to belittle or sublime ourselves by construing ourselves in terms of this or that object of compelling interest. Though Kant gave us 'Enlightenment' and freed science for positivism by eliminating its theological moorings, he also showed in the section on the Paralogisms in the *Critique of Pure Reason* that the self which is open to beings, including its own being, can never be an object to itself. This Open defines the context within which Percy's reflections on language are to be understood."[48]

After spending a few days in Greenville, Walker and Bunt drove to

Highlands, North Carolina, during the last week of October to enjoy the foliage.[49] Walker expected to have corrected the galley proofs of *Lancelot* in November and finished books by January 1977. Bob Giroux reported good news: for the first time the Book-of-the-Month Club had chosen a Percy novel as a main selection. *Lancelot*—which Gilbert Highet, one of their judges, considered a major work—would be their chief selection in March, for which they were paying an advance of $85,000.[50] Jack New-combe, who had visited Walker in Covington, and Wilfrid Sheed both wrote short essays on *Lancelot* for the club's newsletter, which was sent to its enormous membership. Shelby said he considered the new novel "a good book, sharp, incisive, mean as a booger." Walker worked on the page proofs in early December.[51] After the sales conference in New York, the first printing was set at 35,000 copies, with an initial advertising budget of no less than $30,000. Because of the book-club backing, there were inquiries from film producers. Roger Straus sent a copy to an agent in Hollywood, but soon asked (due to Walker's insistence) that it be returned.[52]

By early November, Walker decided not to return to Loyola the following semester, which greatly disappointed Dawson.[53] In one class, Walker talked about his visit to the Institute of Arts and Letters the previous week. He had agreed to replace Kay Boyle, who had been taken ill, on the Literature Award Committee, and served along with John Barth, Elizabeth Bishop, John Ciardi, Harry Levin, Dwight Macdonald, and Arthur Miller.[54] As a result, the Institute started sending Walker more works of fiction than he ever requested.[55] Walker took contemporary literature seriously and generously immersed himself, at great expense to his own writing, in the works of others.

While at Loyola, Walker received a series of phone calls from a stranger—Mrs. Thelma Agnes Ducoing Toole, whose deceased son, John Kennedy Toole, had written a novel she wanted Walker to read. Swamped by the work he had already accepted, Walker put her off a dozen times, but she proved to be incredibly insistent.[56] One day two women, who arrived in a limousine, went to Marcus Smith's third-floor office and asked for Dr. Percy. The one wearing a blue hat and veil and white gloves, and using a walker, claimed that she had an appointment. They were taken to a lounge and asked if they would like anything while they waited; Mrs. Toole wanted tea. After an hour and a half, Walker appeared and was introduced to his guests. Mrs. Toole immediately began explaining how her son, "the Genius," had written a marvelous novel and she wanted Walker to recommend its publication. He accepted the box she proffered, peering in at the faded onionskin typescript. He read a few paragraphs and wondered if the rest could be as good.

Thus began one of the more celebrated episodes in Walker's life; strangely enough, it grew out of a suicide. Born in 1937, John Kennedy Toole attended McDonogh School No. 14, skipping several grades. The summer after graduation from Fortier High School, he wrote *The Neon Bible*, an adolescent novel. Ironically, the other top scholar in his graduating class, Sandra Brenner, went on to become a professor of philosophy at Loyola University and a Peirce scholar; unfortunately, Walker never met her.[57] Toole studied English at Tulane, where he graduated, Phi Beta Kappa, in 1958. He taught briefly at Southwestern Louisiana University and at Hunter College in New York. In 1962 he was drafted into the army and sent to Puerto Rico to teach English to soldiers. Here he started writing his novel *A Confederacy of Dunces*, the picaresque story of Ignatius Reilly in New Orleans. When Toole returned home, he continued to work on his novel, finally sending it to editor Robert Gottlieb at Simon & Schuster. John Kennedy Toole's prolonged relationship with Gottlieb would have severely troubled any aspiring novelist. Toole started teaching at Dominican College in 1964 and in 1968 began doctoral studies at Tulane. The pressures of teaching, studying, and writing finally got to him: early in 1969 he climbed into his ten-year-old Chevy and drove to California, then to Milledgeville, Georgia (out of homage to Flannery O'Connor), and finally to a wooded area outside Biloxi, Mississippi, where he took his own life on March 26.[58] It was widely believed that he committed suicide because he had failed to get his novel published.

In early December, Walker wrote to Mrs. Toole at her home on Elysian Fields, reporting that he had finished reading *A Confederacy of Dunces*. He found it astonishingly original and thought it revealed an extraordinary display of mordant humor and an uncanny ear for the speech patterns of New Orleans. "Ignatius Reilly is an original—a cross between Don Quixote and W. C. Fields," he wrote.[59] With Mrs. Toole's permission, Walker passed the novel on to Marcus Smith, editor of *The New Orleans Review*. It was not long before Mrs. Toole started sending Walker little gifts, such as Toole's army belt buckle and boxes of candy. Bunt finally called a halt to the gift receiving after he was sent a pair of pajamas.

Walker received even more lucrative gifts at year's end: FSG signed a contract with Avon for a paperback edition of *Lancelot*. The advance was $250,000, and the book was to be released a year after the hardback edition. Avon also purchased the paperback rights to *The Last Gentleman* and *Love in the Ruins.*

As 1977 began, Walker wondered whether Karen Black was going to exercise her option and actually purchase the film rights for *The Moviegoer.*[60] She did so, paying approximately $40,000. Moviegoer Productions, whose directors were Kit Carson, Karen Black, and James McBride, signed an agreement on April 21 with Lasky-Weisel, Inc., for the production of the film. Carson and McBride were responsible for rewriting the script; Sam Waterston and Karen Black would be starred; Jim McBride would be the director. In an article in *The New York Times,* Guy Flately reported Karen Black's involvement with the film project: she, Carson, and McBride arrived in Covington sometime in the spring of 1978.[61] To Carson, Walker seemed indifferent to what was going on. All Walker would say was that he had been paid by Black.[62] A few sequences of Karen Black as Kate were shot (without Sam Waterston, who had given up on the project), but nothing substantial developed. Walker was impressed that Black picked up the accent of the Irish Channel after only two days in New Orleans.[63] What the Percys and the Barrangers remembered most, as the filming came to a conclusion, was Black nursing her infant son, Hunter, while visiting the Percys in Covington.[64]

Walker was determined not to let the Hollywood types get him down. He checked page proofs of *Lancelot* in mid-January and ten days later flew with Bunt to New York for a meeting of the Institute. He met with Roger Straus, Bob Giroux, and Herbert Mitgang of *The New York Times* about the forthcoming novel.[65] Giroux had done a line-by-line editing of *Lancelot* and was relieved to see it in its final stages. From New York, Walker and Bunt went to a snowy Cornell University, where Walker gave a talk entitled "The Novelist as Diagnostician of the Modern Malaise"—one of a series of ongoing lectures on Chekhov. The next day, he read from *Lancelot* to a group of students and faculty. James and Gladys McConkey hosted the Percys, and before the Percys headed back to New York, Professor McConkey took Walker to Cornell's ornithology lab so that Walker could see their peregrine falcons, then in the process of being reintroduced to the wild. After Walker returned home, he submitted the names of Robert Lowell, Katherine Anne Porter, and Tennessee Williams as candidates for medals to be awarded by the Institute.[66] A week later, he submitted three citations he had written on behalf of Anne Tyler, James McElroy, and Tennessee Williams.

Bound copies of *Lancelot* were sent from FSG to Walker's brothers, Shelby, Bob Coles, Robert Daniel, Dawson Gaillard, and Alison Lurie at Cornell.[67] Walker wrote Bob Coles that the main trick of the novel was to use Percival's "*silence* as part of a [process of] communication. In fact, the novel can be read as failing communication, plus a renewal of language (tapping on wall, Percival's muted *yes*, etc.)."[68] Without a clearly defined writing project before him, Walker faced a dilemma: should he go flat out, throwing caution to the winds, and write a dreamlike novel, "the Big One," exploring "the delights of the new consciousness," as he wrote Shelby, or write "a *Gulliver's Travels* sort of fable-satire, serious-unserious, easily read"? Actually a third option in the back of his mind concerned a long-term project about either Faulkner or some aspect of modern culture, which would demonstrate the truth of what he called the "Peirce-Percyan" semiotic. Walker was aware that, with a few exceptions, some theorists who read *The Message in the Bottle* simply shrugged their shoulders and said, "It ain't so." Shelby, as was his wont, advised Walker to go for the big one, since he thought that Walker's last two books, much as he enjoyed them, were really departures from the excellent work in *The Last Gentleman.* Shelby's advice no doubt stemmed from his own writing situation; he was finishing *September, September* and about to tackle what he called *Two Gates to the City.*

Lyn Hill started painting a portrait of Walker, which he had commissioned and which he hoped would be used on the back cover of *Lancelot.* The idea for the portrait, which Walker commented on in his self-interview for *Esquire,* came to her in a dream—Walker standing with his arms crossed as ivy grew up his legs; the ivy turns into roses and rose thorns. Hill felt that it truly portrayed the author of *Lancelot,* a violent book, in her opinion. Initially working from photographs, Hill asked Walker to pose for the final finishing touches. Walker sent Bob Giroux a photo of Hill's portrait, which had not been completed in time for use on the dust jacket.[69] For his part, Roger Straus tried to drum up publicity for Walker's new novel by encouraging William Shawn of *The New Yorker* to publish Bob Coles's profile of Walker, which rested in their files.[70]

Bob Giroux considered Lehmann-Haupt's dismissive review in *The New York Times* "outrageous." Robert Towers in *The New York Review of Books* noted that the novel depicted "a miniature allegory of the New South."[71] The review by Joyce Carol Oates in *The New Republic* greatly disturbed Walker; Oates asserted that the central problem of the novel was its confusion of tones, and the relationship between Lance and his wife was not clear. Lon Cheney's critique of *Lancelot* as a pornographic novel clearly did not sit well with Walker.[72] In *The New York Times Book Review,* John Gardner, who liked Walker's novels in general and critiqued *Lancelot* with verve, found that the novel included "gross esthetic mistakes," productive in the end of "typical bad art." Novelist Reynolds Price in *The Washington Post Book World* gave a favorable review as he analyzed Lance's rage and cri de coeur. Andre Dubus in *Harper's* complimented Walker for grappling with questions about the meaning of life that are difficult to answer; in *Lancelot*, Walker had produced a counterattack on the forces that threaten life. In *National Review*, Richard Ford, whose novel *The Sportswriter* apparently was influenced by *The Moviegoer* and which Walker hailed as a "stunning novel," looked at Walker's novel from two angles: his mastery of style might have been achieved at the expense of writing a novel of ideas. (Walker recommended Ford for one of eight awards of $5,000 to be given in 1987 by the Academy and the Institute.[73]) When Walter Sullivan mentioned to Walker that two of his novels, *The Moviegoer* and *Lancelot*, use movies in opposite ways, Walker became angry: "Yes, I always have to depend on critics to tell me what I've been doing."[74] In short, reviewers (and friends) were divided, perhaps a sign that Walker's "cautionary tale," as he considered it, disturbed in the right way.

Walker did his part to promote the novel. He and Bunt flew in late February to New York, just after Rhoda Faust had a successful book-signing party at her Maple Street Book Shop. The Book-of-the-Month Club had a luncheon party honoring Walker, which club officials and judges (including Wilfrid Sheed) attended, as well as Roger Straus, Bob Giroux, and other FSG staff members. Walker participated with Robert and Sally Fitzgerald on a PEN panel concerning the works of Flannery O'Connor that Richard Gilman organized. He was also interviewed at the Algonquin by John Baker for *Publishers Weekly*.

When he arrived back in Covington, he went directly to the Jung discussion group, where he switched gears and talked about Jung: "I do not think the notion of 'growth' is steady or inexorable." For some in the group, this comment represented his own reflection about the novel he had just completed. Though he reluctantly turned down Cleanth Brooks's invitation to visit Yale during the summer, he did travel to Ann Arbor, where he gave the Avery Hopwood Lecture at the University of Michigan.[75] His talk was published as "The State of the Novel: Dying Art or New Science?" in *The Michigan Quarterly Review*. One indication that he thought his life was moving in a new direction was that he began considering whether to donate or sell his papers to the Southern Historical Collection at UNC.[76] In effect, Walker was beginning to clear house.

There was still another indication of change. On May 5, Walker, Lyn Hill, Bob Milling, and David Leon Chandler met for the first of their regular Thursday luncheons at Bechac's restaurant in Mandeville.[77] Milling did not know Chandler, a former candidate for governor of Louisiana, recipient of a Pulitzer Prize in investigative reporting in 1962, author of both *Brothers in Blood: The Rise of Criminal Brotherhoods* (1975) and a subsequent profile of Walker in *People* magazine. Walker highly favored the idea of having a community of writers and artists meet each week, and before long the luncheon was formalized. Three weeks later they entertained Jed Harris, actor and Broadway producer of Thornton Wilder's *Our Town*, then visiting Mandeville. Each member of the group was allowed to bring a guest—another writer or artist. Gradually, the group expanded to include, at various times, Florence ("Winky") Chestnutt (artist); William E. Borah (then gathering notes for *The Second Battle of New Orleans*) and his co-author, Richard O. Baumbach, Jr.; William Binnings (sculptor); Les Landon (editor of *The St. Tammany Farmer*); John Kemp (reporter for *The Times-Picayune*); Rhoda Faust (bookseller); and Sheila Bosworth (fiction writer). Walker briefly entrusted the typescript of Ken Toole's novel to Bill Borah, who said, "This guy's ear for New Orleans dialogue is extraordinary, but it is unfinished." "Yes," Walker replied, "but it is worth publishing."

The lunch group called themselves the Sons and Daughters of the Apocalypse and met year-round. Bob Milling once jotted down some thoughts about this group: "We were a bunch of noisy, mostly irreverent, sometimes obstreperous idiosyncrats, each of us dedicated however loosely to writing or art. All was forgiven, I must say (or I must hope), by the tolerant folks known around here as Walker's 'Young Friends.' Twenty, thirty, forty years Walker's junior, we were tolerated because he liked us. Fact is he was delighted with us. It's hard to figure. Maybe he invented us?" In a roundabout and even elliptical way, Walker would communicate messages to his companions, but he never orated, promulgated, dictated, preached, or taught in any overt way. He mostly kept opinions to himself, though once he called Herman Melville's *The Confidence Man* "a bad book, period."

Off the hook from writing, Walker received an honorary degree, along with James Feibleman, philosopher and Peirce expert, at Tulane's graduation ceremony. A few days later, he attended the funeral of Aunt Bolling Phinizy Spalding. (This left Louise and Nellie as the surviving sisters of the five Phinizy girls.) He flew to New York for a committee meeting and award ceremony of the Institute and the Academy in late May, and when he returned, he asked that Shelby's *September, September* (Walker considered it "a winner") be sent to his fellow judges at the Institute.[78] A few months later the members received a communication from Dwight Macdonald that, according to Walker, "put down" Shelby's novel "with vehemence." An irritated Walker wrote to his colleagues: "Foote is one of two people I nominated for the regular award. I did not do it lightly. He is, in my opinion, long overdue for some recognition from this body. He is sixty years old, a distinguished novelist and the author of the three-volume *Civil War: A Narrative*, a work twenty years in the writing and generally recognized as an extraordinary achievement, a rare union of the historian's scholarship and the novelist's art."[79] Walker, alas, would not live to see either the television series based on Shelby's Civil War narrative or his eventual induction into the Academy.

Before leaving for Europe on July 13 for a three-week trip, Walker mentioned to local reporter Hugh Mulligan that he was impressed by the new moral tone of President Jimmy Carter and his sense of sin: "I was thinking the other night that what makes Southerners different is that they are more complex, more indirect, capable of much more corruption and evil and maybe much more moral goodness. All it means is the two, evil and good, can be very close. Morality implies a sense of sin and corruption."[80] In Europe, Walker and Bunt, accompanied by Ed and Lucy Ballard, particularly enjoyed their stay in the Pigonnet Hotel in Aix-en-Provence, as they visited with Phin (then on sabbatical) and Jaye. Walker sent Shelby a risqué French postcard, signed "Fi Fi." In Avignon, Bunt and Walker had a chance to catch up with Betsy O'Brien, Ann's friend, who was pursuing graduate work. The Percys and the Ballards continued on to Venice.

Before leaving for Europe, Walker had sent John Kennedy Toole's typescript of *A Confederacy of Dunces* to FSG. Roger Straus wrote a memo to Bob Giroux in late July saying that he agreed the firm should not publish it.[81] Bob relayed his feelings to Walker: Toole's novel was an extraordinary book in many ways, but it was also seriously flawed, much too long, and could not be properly corrected, since the author had died. How could it be cut, edited, and perhaps rewritten without authorial approval?[82] The typescript was returned to Walker, who eventually sent it to LSU Press.

Back from Europe, Walker lunched with the Thursday group in early September, bringing along a copy of John Gregory Dunne's *True Confessions*, which he thought had a good bit of narrative drive. He also talked about a recent conversation he had with Joan Didion, Dunne's wife. Soon afterward, the luncheon group had memorable visitors: James Mason and his wife, who arrived in their limousine with a police escort. Mason had come to talk to Walker about purchasing the film rights to *Lancelot*. When Walker mentioned to Mrs. Mason that he had enjoyed seeing her once in a movie, Clarissa reminded him that he probably had mistaken her for James's first wife, Pamela.

As Ann's bookstore, the Kumquat, prospered, she could count on her father to sign books; she could also count on other nearby stores, such as Granny's Kitchen, Country Clutter, and Lagniappe, to attract townsfolk and tourists alike. After David was born, Ann and John were anxious to learn about the extent of his hearing. They waited until the appropriate time to have him tested, and when the reports arrived that there was some loss, Ann was devastated. It was now her turn to summon up all the strength and courage she could. Bunt and Walker again began calling on the skills they had learned from Miss Mirrielees. Aware that Ann and John might need a larger house for their growing family, Walker bought property before long from Theodore J. Moses at the intersection of Marigny Avenue and Claiborne Street in Mandeville, not far from the Pontchartrain Yacht Club.

When Walker saw Cleanth Brooks, who was giving a talk in early October as part of the Jambalaya series at the New Orleans Public Library, he mentioned that he was working on another "cautionary tale."[83] Brooks had followed Walker's writing career closely, even writing an essay on Gnosticism in Walker's fiction for Panthea Broughton's volume of essays. (After reading her collection of essays, Walker uncharacteristically wrote to a number of the contributors.[84] He especially appreciated the subtlety of an essay by Weldon Thornton that, at times, was critical of Walker's semiotic theory: "What makes me particularly grateful is that you have treated my amateurish forays into semiotics, particularly the semiotic approach to psycholinguistics. Though I worked pretty hard in this area, I've found that the fruits have pretty well fallen into a kind of no-man's-land: critics are not generally interested in linguistics and linguisticians consider all outsiders trespassers.") Walker felt less the tug of Gnosticism and more the desire to probe the triadic relationships of Charles Sanders Peirce. At a meeting of the Jung group in late October at Lyn Hill's house, each member of the group created an object that, no doubt, was revelatory of something deep within his or her personality: using Styrofoam and wire, Charles Bigger made a face with the eyes turning inward; Bob Milling made a theater with lions and tigers; Lyn Hill made a dollhouse; and Walker made a pyramid with an ankh and a spider in the middle of it—an artifact whose triadic shape remained mysterious to the group.

For the moment, Walker was "worrying at (rather than writing) a novel"—eventually entitled The Second Coming.[85] "Worrying" was probably an appropriate term. In spite of expectations and advance interests, Lancelot, in Walker's estimation, "fizzled saleswise." He had thought it was going to make him richer and feared just the opposite after Bob Giroux informed him that the number of returned books was "horrendous."[86] (Walker eventually ordered 1,000 remaindered copies of Lancelot for the Kumquat.[87]) Deeply upset, Walker tore up his novel in late November and started over again.

Yet the year did not end with a bust. His self-interview, "Questions They Never Asked Me So He Asked Them Himself," published in the December issue of *Esquire*, proved to be one of the most delightfully sardonic and incisive pieces he ever wrote. At the end, he reflected on himself: "So he keeps his own counsel, except for the faintest glimmer in his eye—of risibility, even hope?—which says to the reviewer: *I doubt if you know what's going on, but then again you just might. Do you? Do you understand?*" Or, as he said more matter-of-factly, "I've managed to live here for thirty years and am less well known than the Budweiser distributor"—the type of throwaway line that made Walker so appealing to his readers.

Walker continued working on his novel and the Ferdinand Phinizy Lecture that cousin Phinizy Spalding had invited him to deliver in mid-February at the University of Georgia. Well aware that he would have to inform as well as perform, he was ready to meet with the English faculty in Athens, followed by a similar session with the history faculty. At a formal dinner at the Taylor-Grady House, Walker introduced a select group of relatives and guests to Bunt, Ann, and John. After his lecture the next morning, which centered on the changing South, over one hundred cousins and friends from as far away as Texas, California, and New Jersey dined at Greer's restaurant, where Marion Calhoun Hendrix led the usual cheer: "Ra, Ra, Re, Re—Phin, Phin, Phinazee." Walker's lecture was an unqualified success. "I appreciate so much your consenting to be our lecturer, particularly when I realize how it must have been a strain for you and how it must have interrupted the writing schedule that you keep (whether something comes or not)," Phinizy wrote afterward.[88] All the festivities so exhausted Walker, as he mentioned to Panthea Broughton, that he went into a "Jungian funk," though he had every expectation of coming out of it to continue his novel about a "schizophrenic girl and a middle-aged golfer."[89] Not to disappoint friends at Vanderbilt, especially Allen Tate and his new wife, Helen, Walker agreed to be the leading speaker toward the end of March at the Gertrude and Harold S. Vanderbilt Visiting Writers' Forum.[90] Before leaving, he sent Dwight Macdonald his choices for the Institute awards, reaffirming his support for Shelby.[91]

In light of Shelby's estimate of taking five years to write his new novel, Walker was forced to consider his own plans. He had lived longer than any other Percy he knew and thus was entering uncharted territory. Still, he handled his feelings about his own mortality with wit and balance. When Lucy Ballard became irritated with Charles Bigger and

Walker at a Jung meeting and decided not to return, Walker said that the incident had depressed him.[92] Walker also talked briefly at one of the meetings about the disparity between the promises one makes during a wedding ceremony and subsequent realities. It was clear that Walker was referring not only to Lucy and Ed but to the marital difficulties he and Bunt were having over the mutual affection between Lyn Hill and him; gossip, not easy to quell in a small town, had already begun to circulate. (When an ex-Moonie who had come to the Thursday lunch was asked why he had ever joined the cult, his answer—"Because they gave me unstinting love"—floored Walker.)

By July, no decision had yet been made by Les Phillabaum at LSU Press about the Ken Toole novel, though *The New Orleans Review* had excerpted a section for its May issue.[93] *The New Yorker* was preparing to bring out Bob Coles's profile of Walker in a two-part series in October; it would subsequently be converted into a book. Walker congratulated Coles:

Am, of course, overwhelmed by "The Search" plus news of your forthcoming book on that obscure Louisiana novelist. I read the foreword with a strange mixture of pleasure and anxiety—pleasure at the depths of your understanding, anxiety at being the subject. The anxiety, I think, derives from a vague sense of fraudulence on the part of the subject and a fear of getting caught (e.g. I hope Coles doesn't look too close—he'll find there's nothing there). Now Bob, I must be severe with you. You seem to have taken on a responsibility toward me vis-à-vis this Profile as if somehow you owed it to me to get it published.[94]

Walker did not want Coles to reproach himself and worry about having the profile published. After receiving a copy of his book, Walker again congratulated him: "Its splendor is daunting, yet makes me feel proud."[95] But Walker's true feelings were a bit different, as he informed Shelby; he was grateful for Coles's genuine interest in his life and work, but he did not recognize himself in the book. "I think it is because he is projecting a good deal of himself, a kind of good-hearted Colesian decency which may apply to him but not exactly to me."[96] Walker felt that he was more malevolent, oblique, phony, ironical, and definitely more entertaining.

By mid-September, as Shelby was tuning up for *Two Gates to the City*, Walker was writing the conclusion of a handwritten draft of his new novel. He felt it was still "a mess" but he did see some "glimmers of virtue" in it. As he was typing out another draft of the novel a few weeks later, he declined for the second time to travel to either Australia or India for the U.S. Information Agency, though he would consider going to Poland, the Soviet Union, and Germany, should they propose such a trip.[97] It was not difficult for him to refuse other such offers, as he had done for offers from the University of Delaware in Newark, the University of California at Irvine, and the University of Notre Dame.[98]

Perhaps because of the steady progress on his novel, as well as the birth of his fourth grandson, John Percy Moores, in December, Walker seemed relaxed at the end of the year. Yet when he finished the typescript of *The Second Coming* in mid-January 1979, he was not sure whether he liked it.[99] Father Tom Clancy's essay "Feeling Bad About Feeling Good," which Walker read, might have helped with feelings of depression or desolation. As he informed Shelby, beginning a novel is "like the onset of a chronic illness, something to be suffered and gotten through, if possible in one piece." He was pleased "to have gotten through to the end without a catastrophe." For the time being, he would put it aside. The title had been derived in part from Yeats's poem of the same name. While he was writing *The Second Coming*, he was in contact with both Charles Bell and Norman O. Brown of the University of Rochester in New York. Bell felt that Brown's writings, particularly *Love's Body*, were an inspiration to Walker in writing this novel.[100] (Another possible source might have been Robert Penn Warren's sixth novel, *The Cave* [1959], which takes place in Tennessee in the 1950s. Walker was aware that cave imagery goes back to Plato's *Republic*.)

Upon close examination, it turned out that young Jack Moores did not have any hearing loss. This did not diminish the family's abiding concern about the value of oral education for the hearing-impaired. *The Times-Picayune* published a letter by Walker protesting the CBS show entitled *And Your Name Is Jonah*, which portrayed sign users as the good guys and the oral teachers as the villains: "I am astonished that you could jump into this complex matter in such a simplistic dim-witted fashion. How did you get sold such a bill of goods, by some fanatical sign-pusher?" Ann also wrote a letter of her own to the newspaper: "I hope you have it on your conscience that you may have led some parents of deaf children to take the sign language route who might otherwise have had an oral education and enjoyed a happy and independent life, instead of being trapped within a deaf community, forever dependent upon interpreters whenever they ventured out into the hearing world. For shame!" Too much was at stake for both Walker and Ann not to be loud and clear about this.

Subconsciously Walker, who was ill at ease for not liking Bob Coles's book about him, felt he had to make it up to Coles when he arrived in the South to speak on Flannery O'Connor at LSU during the first week of April. He wrote Coles in advance of the trip, offering to act as chauffeur and companion "willing to listen to the problems of your own mid-life crisis."[101] He informed Coles that he was hard at work on a disedifying novel that owed more to Erica Jong and Jerzy Kosinski than Kierkegaard—in fact, much less, since he had agreed to write a review of a new edition of Kierkegaard's letters, edited by Henrik Rosenmeier, only after he had substantially finished the novel. On a more serious note, Walker mentioned that Ann Percy, his nephew Billy's wife, had to decide whether to stay in an apartment in New Orleans and continue seeking psychological help at Touro or return to Greenville and commute. "A sore subject and one I hope they will resolve with some success but doubt; it may be that they might be better off divorced but I don't know enough to counsel." It is interesting to note that just as he finished a draft of a novel that dealt in part with a woman in a mental institution, he was faced with a similar situation in the extended Percy family.

In the "special message" he wrote for the signed Franklin Library edition of the novel, Walker addressed a problem about his female characters, perhaps trying to head off criticism that they were unbalanced. "A psychologist might say that women are so enigmatic and the male novelist is so isolated, shut up in himself, that the only way he can create a flesh-and-blood female is to encounter the woman in himself. Every man has his anima, his feminine self, and if we're lucky we'll stumble over her and recognize ourselves in her." He clearly wanted to communicate that Allison Huger was indeed close to his heart (Shelby thought she was based on Nancy Lemann, though Charles Bigger believed the Will–Allie relationship was based on the growing marital tensions of Lucy and Ed Ballard, and Ed's involvement with one of his female students).[102] There could have been some truth in each hypothesis, since Walker knew well both Lemann and the Ballards. He first met Lemann, a native New Orleanian, when, as a college student, she went with Phin's son Will to see Walker in the mid-1970s. Lemann was so struck with Walker that she went home and wrote a five-page account of their meeting. She would go on to become a noted fiction writer, writing to him from New York with some regularity about the problems she encountered in her life. Walker once mentioned to both Ken Holditch and Linda Hobson that the genesis of the novel derived from the visit of a friend from Chapel Hill, who, after retiring to North Carolina, had nothing of value in his life and could not tell his wife he had made a mistake.[103] He boarded a Greyhound and went south to seek Walker's counsel. After writing 100 pages of this novel, Walker realized that he had actually gone back to Will Barrett. Once he realized that, he felt free to move on. The novel's title, in Walker's mind, had three connotations: the return of Jesus the Christ, the rebirth of Will Barrett, and "a sexual event—e.g., the first violent 'coming' is the father's shotgun-in-mouth suicide and the second is Will's choice of Allie over suicide."[104] Surprisingly, none of his close friends seemed to think that this novel might have been based on Walker's own life and his need to seek female friends outside his home.

In mid-February, Walker attended another meeting of the Literature Award Committee of the Institute and subsequently wrote citations for James Still, Barry Hannah, and Robert Persig "for bringing off the most difficult of tasks: translating the perennial debate about the Great Ideas into a narrative prose as fresh and sharp as the mountain air of *Zen and the Art of Motorcycle Maintenance*."[105] Walker also nominated two others for awards, Reynolds Price and Shelby Foote.[106] He was concerned, too, about LSU Press's reaction to John Kennedy Toole's novel. LSU Press wanted to publish the book, but even with a financial subsidy Les Phillabaum feared they might just about break even with a hardback edition. For the sake of formality, he was asked to submit an evaluation. Shortly thereafter, Les received Walker's views of this 480-page typescript:

John [Kennedy] Toole's novel, *A Confederacy of Dunces* is, I can say without hesitation, a fantastic novel, a major achievement, a huge comic-satiric-tragic one-of-a-kind rendering of life in New Orleans. No one has ever or ever will capture the particularity of the backstreets, middle- and lower-class whites, blacks and other ethnics of New Orleans as Toole has.

I have never come across a novel in manuscript which has impressed me as this one has . . . This is true comedy, by no means the hilarious madcap variety but rather more a great rumbling farce of Falstaffian dimensions . . . But Toole's greatest achievement is Ignatius Reilly, slob, intellectual, ideologue, deadbeat, goof-off, who should repulse the reader with his gargantuan bloats, his thunderous contempt and one-man all out war against all of modern times, T.V., B-girls, Freud, homosexuals, heterosexuals, and the assorted excesses of democracy. Imagine a Thomas Aquinas gone to pot, transported to New Orleans—from which he makes one wild trip through the swamps to Baton Rouge and the LSU history department where his jacket is stolen in the faculty men's room—where he is afflicted with mammoth gastro-intestinal problems—his pyloric valve closes on him whenever things go wrong, causing volcanic eructations—assaulting modern society in the name of various mad Quixotic ideals, such as having the "proper geometry and theology"—and in the end escaping his foes and his momma by taking off for New York in a Volkswagen with his girlfriend Myrna Minkoff for God knows what new adventures.

It is a great pity John Kennedy Toole is not alive and well and writing. But he is not, and there is nothing we can do about it but make sure that this gargantuan tumultuous human comedy is at least made available to the reader.[107]

(Ironically, this novel went on to win the Pulitzer Prize for fiction, an honor that always eluded Walker.) He had recommended to Thelma Toole that the text *not* be edited, though she might supply words that Sandra Ariatti, a secretary at Loyola, may have incorrectly transcribed when she retyped the text.[108] To assist Mrs. Toole with legal problems, Nikki Barranger was informed of the novel's existence. At this time, too, Dawson Gaillard was looking to leave Loyola and had made an appointment with Les Phillabaum to work at the press. "I don't know what you or she are looking for," Walker wrote Phillabaum, "but let me say that you couldn't do better than to latch onto her."[109] Walker considered Gaillard a "super-gal" and "super-nice." What he failed to note, if he knew at all, was that Gaillard had multiple sclerosis.

In addition to speaking at Robert Daniel's literature seminar at Kenyon College in Ohio and making another three-day retreat at Manresa, Walker watched Steve Owens's construction crew build a new and expanded Kumquat bookstore across Lee Lane in the early spring.[110] When the building was finished that summer, Ann hired some local women to work for her part-time. Bunt helped out when she could, but she was careful not to usurp Ann's decision-making role. Walker gathered up his little Sony 510 stereo radio and Craig speakers, his box of fifty tapes, his books, including Troyat's biography, *Tolstoy* ("truly credible and incredible"), *The Death of Ivan Ilyich*, which he had recently finished reading, Ellen Douglas's novel *The Rock Cried Out* ("The girl is steadily getting better and better"), and a writing manual that VISTA worker Rosemary Kenah had sent him, and transported them to his rather claustrophobic new office above the Kumquat, which he reached by climbing spiral stairs. A disadvantage of such a move was that customers could now wait for him to arrive at the store so they could talk with him. One such loquacious customer followed him around and ended up carrying on a conversation with him through the bathroom door!

Walker planned on spending the summer in Covington completing his novel, though he was convinced, as he wrote Shelby, the times were never worse for novelists, in the sense that somehow "the straight narrative form is in default and so one must resort to all manners of tricks, cons, blandishments, obfuscations, curses, lies, jokes, animadversions." When he got this novel in final shape, he hoped to spend a few years figuring out how television rots the brain ("nobody knows"). In late June, he spoke to Lewis Simpson's National Endowment Summer Seminar at LSU.[111] Walker mentioned that he was writing about Will Barrett in North Carolina, "surrounded by 100 percent so-called Christian society and would almost rather be like Sartre, or a Camus agnostic. This present book, if I ever get it right or finish it, will probably be understood as an anti-Christian statement in that sense." He sent Les Phillabaum his foreword to the Toole novel, now in production thanks to a publication grant from the National Endowment for the Arts. "Please edit this ad libitum," Walker wrote, which Martha Lacy Hall proceeded to do with skill and care.[112]

Hall had known Walker since 1970, when he called quite spontaneously and said how much he liked one of her stories published in *The Southern Review*. (He would later write a blurb for her collection of stories, *Music Lessons*.) When she visited her sister Elizabeth, a librarian in Covington, she would stop to see the Percys, and gradually, over the years, their lives overlapped with the Simpsons, Dawson Gaillard, and Charles and Sarah East. Once, when Martha suffered from writer's block, she drove to Covington and Walker shared with her some matter-of-fact advice about writing.

Sometime that summer the Rev. L. Jerome Taylor, Jr., an Episcopal priest from Belvedere, New Jersey, visited Walker.[113] Father Taylor, or Jay, as he preferred to be called, felt comfortable in Walker's presence, as if he were talking to an old friend. In 1972 he had sent Walker a copy of his dissertation, written under the direction of William Poteat at Duke, on the relationship between Walker's works and Kierkegaard. At lunch, Father Taylor mentioned he had attended the Naval Academy and served in World War II. More recently, he had taught theology at St. Andrew's Seminary in Quezon City in the Philippines. As Walker talked about his novel-in-progress, he said that he was struggling with Will Barrett's conversion. When Father Taylor later read *The Second Coming*, he thought maybe he had been the inspiration for the Episcopal priest in the novel, Father Weatherbee, who once had ministered to a remote community in Mindanao.

Walker sent a copy of the completed typescript of *The Second Coming* to Shelby in late August. Shelby had some suggestions, especially to straighten out the differences in the chronology between *The Last Gentleman* and *The Second Coming*. Having finished this novel, Walker was bewildered as to the direction to take. All he knew was that he did not want to write another novel "now, maybe ever." "A novel," he mentioned to Shelby, "is an incredible ordeal, which gets worse and worse, requiring all manner of alternate despairs, piss-offs, deaths and rebirths, too much for an aging infirm novelist." No other book had so drained Walker of his energies. Only a few people, including Walker's agent, had seen it, and though Bunt seemed to like it, she felt that Barrett should not have been so ugly to his daughter. Walker had also sent it to Robert Daniel, who, in spite of recovering from a cataract operation, found it compelling. Since Walker had recently received a payment for the film rights to *The Moviegoer*, and thus did not need the new funds just yet, he asked Miss Otis not to submit it yet to Bob Giroux. He seemed content just to sit in his garret office looking at "the tin roof, a camphor tree, a patch of sky and listening to people downstairs buying Jackie O and *Scruples*." Though he might feel like a dinosaur, as he said, he took pleasure in walking around town with his three-iron.

By October, the Jung group had run its course, though some felt a need to continue having some sort of discussion group. As before, a new group, one that followed the Great Books program, gradually came into existence: Walker, Bunt, Nikki Barranger, Father James C. Boulware, Gabrielle ("Phena") Keti, M.D., Nicole and Richard Spangenberg, George Riser, M.D., Lucy and Ed Ballard, the Rev. William H. Barnwell, an Episcopal priest who knew the Ballards, and occasionally Lyn Hill, Winky Chestnutt, and Ann Trousdale, Bob Milling's former wife. Though Steve Ellis came to meetings for a few years, and others attended sporadically and at different times, the group remained fairly stable, meeting every other Monday evening.

With his writing board cleared for the moment, Walker took a respite from his usual routine. He wrote to Father Boulware at the abbeyseminary, mentioning that he would like to teach there, not for the salary, but to be closer to the Benedictine life and community.[114] He said he lacked a formal association with a traditional spiritual community. Participating in the liturgy at the abbey certainly gave him a sense of belonging to the Benedictine tradition, but once the monks retreated to their rooms Walker was left alone to get in his car and drive home. During the years that Father Boulware served as an active Benedictine monk, he grew in his understanding of Walker's personality in ways different from Walker's other close friends; in particular, he thought that Walker overworked a good deal of the philosophical material he used. Yet, like Walker, his strong faith did not necessarily contain all the answers to life's problems. James asked himself whether Walker's cynicism and open-mindedness ultimately proved to be reassuring or elevating. He asked hard questions that many others would have answered quite differently. Walker himself began to question the ongoing integration of the Benedictine community into modern society; he seemed to be having second thoughts about teaching at the seminary. Maybe his original offer, as he wrote James, had originated because of a "hankering to become a Benedictine, which ain't exactly practical." Nor was he able to say whether this hankering was a consequence of "1) writer's neurosis, writers being notorious subject to strange possessions, 2) male menopause, 3) true vocation, 4) none of the above."

Linda Whitney Hobson, a Percy scholar and recent divorcée who was wildly overdressed for the occasion, drove across the causeway to Bechac's to join the Thursday lunch group (Father Barnwell had brokered the invitation). Terrified when she walked through the doorway, Hobson blurted, "I'm a chicken-shit Ohioan." Walker laughed, the only one in the group to pick up the reference to *Love in the Ruins*. Walker immediately liked Hobson and stayed with her a couple of hours after the others had gone. "In a way," Hobson reflected, "Walker was possibly the father I never had." From then on, whenever Hobson joined the group, she never felt like a stranger. Walker cherished his younger friends and saw no reason to leave Covington to lecture at Boston College, Stanford, Harvard, or the University of Michigan.[115]

Walker had no complaints as he finished out the year. Roger Straus had read *The Second Coming* in late November and considered it "a triumph."[116] Bob Giroux also expressed approval, and by late December, Walker had begun sending him revisions, as well as a photo taken by Christopher Harris of Hill's portrait, which was never used.[117] Walker contracted for an advance of $75,000, of which $25,000 was payable on signing.

Once 1980 got underway, Walker wrote a letter of reference for Huger Foote, Shelby's son, and sent a copy to Shelby with an accompanying note.[118] Walker was at a stage in his life, he said, where he would be perfectly happy to be let alone for the rest of his life so that he could write about semiotics. He had no desire to travel to New York or publicize his latest novel. And though Walker felt guilty about this and wanted Shelby's understanding, he felt determined by now to start his study of semiotics—a subject that remained an "utter mystery" to his friend. Not long afterward Walker found a focus for what he thought would be a sequel to *The Message in the Bottle*: a semiotic investigation of the self, "the stranded consciousness," which is left over after a person has fallen prey to the immanentism of science.[119] He wanted to consult Bob Coles about his project, especially the latter's thoughts on Carl Sagan, the Cornell astronomer.[120]

By late February, after Walker had rewritten a new chapter about Allie and the big stove, *The Second Coming* was in proofs.[121] Walker's financial resources were quite sufficient to tide him over; the Book-of-the-Month Club advanced $50,000 for the novel (half of which went to Walker). Calmann-Lévy (France), Suhrkamp (Germany), and Secker & Warburg (England) all expressed interest in publishing the novel abroad. FSG did a limited edition (450 signed copies) and the Franklin Library agreed to publish an edition of 250 signed copies, for an advance of $10,000 (half of which went to Walker).[122] In effect, the novel was off to a good start. Walker's financial success bolstered his good spirits, seen in his essay "Why I Live Where I Live," published in *Esquire*. It gives a delightful account of Walker's at-easeness in Covington.

Walker delivered the second Flora Levy Lecture, entitled "How to Be a Novelist in Spite of Being a Catholic," at Southwestern Louisiana State University in Lafayette, and three days later showed up at Thelma Toole's book-signing party for *A Confederacy of Dunces* sponsored by Rhoda Faust at one of her bookstores, as well as his own book-signing at Dolpen's on Royal Street that Linda Hobson arranged. But his heart was elsewhere as he made plans to study semiotics in Toronto. When Hobson interviewed Walker for *Horizon* magazine, he said he already had a title for this nonfiction book, *Novum Organum*.[123]

Walker now asked Father Boulware to be his spiritual advisor. Though he had vacillated about taking this step, he sat down and outlined ten general areas for discussion, from the nature of faith in Jesus to the nature of marriage. Having gone through therapy as a medical student, he knew the benefits of counseling, and it became more and more obvious that the only way to do this was to bounce his "perplexities" off this intelligent Benedictine.[124] Because he would be out of town when Father Boulware received the letter, he knew he would not receive an immediate reply. By the time Walker participated in an FSG sales conference in late May, the recently published *The Second Coming* was in its second printing.[125] By the end of July, FSG estimated they had 70,000 copies in print with 55,000 sold. In addition, Pocket Books bought the paperback rights for $40,000 ($22,500 went to Walker).[126] *Book Digest* agreed to reprint an excerpt in late fall for $2,500. By the end of August, the novel was in its fourth printing and FSG appropriated another $10,000 for advertising.[127] In New York, Walker was interviewed by James Atlas for *The New York Times Book Review* and Marc Kirkeby for *The Los Angeles Times*. He also asked the new president of McIntosh & Otis, Patricia Schartle Myrer (she now used her married name), to serve as his agent.[128]

Bunt and Walker traveled to Toronto, where Walker gave an interview to Henry Kisor, the insightful (and deaf) book editor of *The Chicago Sun-Times*. As a child, Henry had been tutored by Doris Mirrielees, the woman who had also tutored Ann after the Percys discovered she was deaf. During the course of their interview, Walker shed some light on the autobiographical nature of his protagonists: "I am more like Binx than Will Barrett," thus downplaying to some extent his relationship with the hero of *The Second Coming*.[129] Shortly afterward, he echoed Flaubert when he told another interviewer: "Allison was a woman, and she is me."[130] Walker noted that *The Second Coming* was a breakthrough for him, a form of celebration in that he saw in his characters a way out of alienation.

Walker had met Professor Thomas A. Sebeok of Indiana University four years before at a conference in Atlanta and had read his *Sight, Sound and Sense*.[131] As the oldest student in Sebeok's class, he audited the monthlong course, "Introduction to Semiotics," at Victoria College. Walker had a second reason for coming to Canada, as he explained to Sebeok; he wanted to consult a specialist in Toronto who could possibly help young David with his hearing problem. Sebeok treated Peirce only in a historical context and tended to stick to a syllabus as outlined in an appendix to his book *The Sign & Its Masters* (1979). The class relied on two main texts, Sebeok's yearbook of semiotics, entitled *The Semiotic Web*, and Umberto Eco's *A Theory of Semiotics* (1976). At lunch with Sebeok and his wife, Jean Umiker-Sebeok, Walker said he had a strong personal aversion to Eco; he was more taken by Jakob von Uexküll, a German biosemiotician (someone Walker had discovered independently of Sebeok), as well as Aquinas, Maritain, and John Deely, a former student of Sebeok, who was knowledgeable about the Scholastic views on semiotics. In Sebeok's eyes, Walker had a narrow conception of semiotics and worried about certain issues that were not mainstream; he had rather prematurely and uncritically grasped at Norman Geschwind's idea of the triadic structure of the symbolic act existing in the cortex of the brain.[132] Yet as Walker read and took notes on semiotics, he now had more information with which to explore new ground and make his semiotic-literary synthesis.

From Canada, the Percys went to Highlands, North Carolina, where they were joined by Steve Ellis and his second wife, Haydée, whom he had recently married (Betty had died in January 1978). Dannye Romine interviewed Walker, who denied that Linwood in *The Second Coming* was based on Linville, North Carolina, since it had no caves, he said, like the one he described. Yet it is a fact that the Linville Caverns were well known in the area. It is most likely, too, that the golf course at the Eseeola Lodge was the model for the one in *The Second Coming*, as was Broughton Hospital (with its imposing glass-inclosed greenhouse) in Morganton for the psychiatric hospital where Allie stayed.

The Percys were back home in mid-July. Walker signed books, first at the Kumquat and then for four hours at Rhoda Faust's bookstore on Prytania Street. Thelma Toole sent a bouquet of flowers.[133] She had also given Faust two copies of her son's unpublished juvenile novel, *The Neon Bible*.[134] Walker's third book-signing was at DeVille's Book Store. Faust had recently joined a second Great Books group in Covington in which

Walker, Philip and Jan Melançon, Trudy Lagarde, Wilson and Celia Krebs, Bob Milling, David Metzner, M.D., Lyn and Tom Hill, Verne Clark, and others also participated. This meant that Walker had two Great Books groups (as well as two lunch groups) going at the same time, an incredible drain on his time and energy.

Once the book signings were finished, Bunt and Walker went back to Highlands briefly before returning to Covington in August, where Father Boulware's reply awaited him. In a strange sort of way, he would relish being targeted with Walker's array of paradoxes, axioms, and questions. "I don't know the peculiar anxiety of a writer," he wrote Walker, "but try on sometime the peculiar anxiety of a professional 'holy figure.' At least your American Express card doesn't have 'Reverend' on it."[135] If anything, their subsequent relationship showed that Walker was trying to grow in his faith and perhaps shed some of the puritanical feelings he sometimes communicated.

Before long the reviews of *The Second Coming* appeared. Edmund Fuller, who had interviewed Walker by phone, liked the novel, calling it the "most life-affirming of all of Dr. Percy's distinguished novels." Fuller wrote in *The Wall Street Journal* that he felt that Walker's perceptive eye scans American culture like radar. John Romano, a professor at Columbia University, wrote in *The New York Times Book Review* that he had reservations about the theological burden Walker had undertaken, yet he considered this novel "among recent novels, masterly and superior." Benjamin DeMott in *The Atlantic Monthly* praised the book as an imaginative work exploring a broad range of experiences, from hope and despair to kindness and idiocy: "The case is, ladies and gentlemen, that we have before us a novel in which a woman of grace, beauty, talent, and wit falls believably in love with a man who's vigorously athletic, competent, sensitive, funny, unillusioned, and loving at his core." The review in *The New Republic*, written by Richard Gilman, was most laudatory, stressing that the writing is "shrewd, lovely, wholly original." Doreen Fowler in *The Memphis Commercial Appeal* noted that Walker asks the right questions and provides a convincing answer, love. *Newsweek*'s critique, written by Walter Clemons, declared that Walker's "worst novel, this one, is still more interesting than most other writers' best shot." Clemons said that he felt heartsick that such an intelligent and sympathetic writer as Walker could write a novel as "bad" as this one. Paul Gray, a critic Walker admired, wrote for *Time* that in spite of character flaws in the hero Walker blended the past with the present in an unobtrusive but "meticulously crafted narrative." Gray noted that the "novel survives the weakness of its hero because Percy is as genial and humane as Will is obsessed." *The Washington Post Book World* carried a favorable review by Monroe Spears, who considered the novel "an unsentimental and unrhetorical affirmation of love against death." Thomas Bonner, Jr., wrote in *The Times-Picayune* of some of the correspondences of this novel with works by Faulkner, Plato, Blake, and Hemingway. He emphasized that this novel "reflects the malaise of the modern world in its sun belt, success-oriented Southern landscape while reminding us of the possibilities of hope. Robert Towers in a long review in *The New York Review of Books* refused to put critical labels on Walker, and tried to evaluate this novel on its own terms. In the last analysis, Towers found the novel "unsatisfactory," as "the story-line wavers between a realistic ordering of events and the contrivances of allegorical romance." The review in *The New Yorker* by Whitney Balliett gave a plot summary and then dismissed Walker's fiction. In the November–December edition of *Chronicles of Culture*, Joseph Schwartz of Marquette University praised Walker's "profound vision" and "vigorous ideological thrust" and considered *The Second Coming* to be "major fiction." He noted that a faint odor of incest hangs over the story because of a number of misleading hints that Will may be Allie's father. Professor Schwartz was most taken by Walker's diagnosis of "the sickness of this poor, whipped century," and the way the author managed to convey this in fiction "with aesthetic grace." Schwartz found an inconsistency between *The Last Gentleman* and *The Second Coming*: "Surely, Jamie's agonizing and glorious death is not a nonevent in Will's life as *The Second Coming* suggests. That kind of bitter irony would be possible to consider only if Will, in the later novel, actually committed suicide finally. Is Percy fooling with the notion that we have alternate destinies?" Walker briefly replied that Will really did not know what was going on with Jamie's baptism and death.

After being interviewed by Jerry Kennedy and Ben Forkner, Walker was surprised by two visitors, Louis P. River III, M.D., and his wife, Jacqueline, who had flown to New Orleans from Chicago to discuss making movies. Walker was adamant about not selling them the film rights to his novel. About two weeks later, Dr. River unexpectedly arrived again in Covington with the bizarre advice that Walker must not commit suicide but should forgive his father for trying to kill him. Walker thanked his visitor, who showed signs of mental instability, and said he had no intention of killing himself, though he still kept the 12-gauge Greener shotgun in his bedroom. (A few years later, the Rivers made a homemade, noncommercial movie based on Walker's novel.)

By September, Walker had relaxed sufficiently to begin thinking about his new work, as he informed Shelby. He would first list some of the familiar oddities and anomalies of modern times, such as the rise of boredom and suicide, the longing of people for UFOs and trivial magic, the eroticization of society, and why people applaud frantically on the Johnny Carson show when their hometowns are mentioned. Then he would set forth his own semiotic theory and, finally, discuss any "disparate left-overs and oddities"—arraying them like so many dancers in a ballet. "As you can see, this is not an entirely serious book, and yet it *is* serious. What it is getting at is, of course, my old hobbyhorse that science is extraordinarily stupid about people as people and the consequence of this stupidity (combined with an instinctual confidence in science) is going to do us all in if we don't do something about it." Bob Giroux had once given him some advice when Walker complained that when nothing he wrote seemed good enough, he had to back up and start over. Giroux said, "Well now, why not just keep writing? You know it's your métier." Walker tried his best, but said he was becoming very tired as he went along.

That fall Walker and Bunt visited and dined with Frank and Fran Hardart and their children, Frank Jr., George, Richard, Marie Thérèse, Christopher, and Michael, who had flown to New Orleans for a Notre Dame football game (young Frank was a Notre Dame freshman). Walker was Richard's godfather and always felt a bit guilty when seeing him. He lunched in early October with Dawson Gaillard and Martha Hall at Bechac's to discuss the status of *A Confederacy of Dunces*, particularly how he might help promote the book.[136] Walker said he would do what he could, within reason. He also responded to questions from the Rev. George Madathiparampil of Kerala, India, who was writing his dissertation on the notion of prophecy in Walker's fiction at the Catholic University of America.[137] Likewise that month, the Percy brothers, their spouses, relatives, and friends attended Hughes Spalding's sixty-third birthday in Atlanta. In December, Shelby and Gwyn drove to New Orleans for Shelby's periodic checkup at Ochsner and stopped to see the Percys. Before Christmas, Walker made a quick trip to the West Coast to receive the *Los Angeles Times* book award in literature for *The Second Coming*. Each of the honorees received a $1,000 prize.[138] *The Second Coming* also received a Notable Book Citation from the American Library Association in 1980.[139]

By the end of the year, Walker, exhausted and unwilling to consider outside lecturing or teaching, nevertheless decided to write about the choices one faces in reentering the world from outer space, of finding again a human community. In a sense he was expanding the questions he posed to Father Boulware. When the Benedictine decided to leave the active priesthood, Walker looked within himself for the answers. "What I'd like to do is write a book," he wrote Robert Coles, "on why it is we can do such things as send Voyager 2 to Saturn only forty-five seconds late and twelve miles off course (after a three-year journey) and yet manage to be in so much trouble on earth. A small order, right? A tentative title: *The Last Self-Help Book / or, Why it is we know so much about Jupiter and so little about ourselves / or, Why it is Carl Sagan can be so smart and so dumb.*"[140] Thus Walker had his agenda set out before him for the following year.

13

Before and After

Lost in the Cosmos

1981–85

In January 1981, Walker and Bunt felt the need to change—and simplify—their lives. With architect Arthur Middleton, they set about designing a new house next to the château—a comfortable Cajun cottage with a full porch facing the driveway. Walker wanted a tin roof to lull him to sleep during the evening rainstorms; Bunt favored floor-to-ceiling windows in the living room and dining area, to provide an unobstructed view of the Bogue Falaya. When it was finished and they moved in, Ann and John Moores occupied the big house next door where Ann had lived before her marriage.

As was his wont, Walker plotted out *Lost in the Cosmos* by making sketches and diagrams. He tentatively considered a number of titles: *The Last Self-Help Book, or why it is you don't know anything about yourself and are not likely to learn, and have not been able to help yourself much despite a hundred thousand self-help books* and *The Last How-to-Know-Yourself-and-Be-Happy Book*, and *The Unknown Self*. He finally opted for *Lost in the Cosmos: The Last Self-Help Book*. He began this book with a thesis: "The problem is that in an age of acute self-consciousness and an age of the objective scientific knowledge of things, the relationship of the knower to himself is that he cannot know the first thing about himself." If anything, this thesis is but a variant of what had been providing Walker intellectual stimulation for years. Consequently, Walker believed there was a growing gap between one's objective knowledge of the world—which is reliable—and the subjective knowledge of oneself—which is not only *not* reliable but more than likely wrong. Thus the self perceives itself as left-over in a world that otherwise can be accounted for. "The irony is that the left-over, the self, cannot be left out." One strong impetus to write this book came from Thomas Sebeok's course in Toronto. Another was Walker's desire to improve himself, as he indicated in his correspondence with Father James Boulware. Though seemingly monochromatic, *Lost in the Cosmos* actually functions on different levels. It was both a reply to Carl Sagan's *Cosmos* and another of the popular self-help books that dominated the market. It was also an update of St. Thomas Aquinas's *Quaestiones Disputatae*, a comprehensive psychological study of American culture, and a catalogue of the ideas and attitudes that motivated Walker's own fictional characters. Walker seemed to have little difficulty composing the text. Above all, he considered the semiotic "intermezzo," which decenters the volume to a great extent and gives it a philosophical grounding, to be the most important section.

Walker wrote *Lost in the Cosmos* with ease because he felt confident that his other work, especially his fiction, was receiving greater attention, not only in America but throughout much of the world. In Germany, for instance, Suhrkamp bought the rights to *The Last Gentleman* and *The Second Coming*, and Droemer planned an edition of *Lancelot* for the following year. In America, Avon was about to publish a paperback edition of *Love in the Ruins* (for which a contract was also signed by a Swedish firm). Contacts were also made to publish and promote Walker's work in Finland, Holland, and Brazil.[1] Because of all this activity, Walker felt less inclined to call attention to himself. He felt absolutely no compulsion to travel or lecture, and decided not to attend the first PEN/Faulkner Award ceremony in Charlottesville, Virginia, when he learned that *How German Is It* by Walter Abish beat out *The Second Coming* (PEN had decided to boycott the American Book Awards, a successor to the National Book Awards, which, in the opinion of many, had become too commercial).[2] There was one exception: Walker accepted an invitation from Gene Usdin to address the members of the Department of Psychiatry at Ochsner.[3]

Another indication of the ease with which he wrote *Lost in the Cosmos* can be seen in his willingness to be away from his three-ring spiral notebook. In addition to playing golf and attending the symphony in New Orleans with some regularity, the Percys and the Ellises visited Marcelle ("Nootsie") Couhig, a relative of Haydée, who owned Asphodel Plantation, a modified Greek Revival home near Jackson. The Percys joined the Footes for a week's vacation at Point Clear in late March, something they had been anticipating for months.[4] Walker made his annual retreat at Manresa in early April.[5] Later, he participated in a two-day literary program, along with Margaret Walker Alexander, Cleanth Brooks, Andrew Lytle, and Eudora Welty, at the University of Tennessee in Chattanooga.

As he worked on his self-help book, and asked his potential readers to consider options that confront various personality types—such as the "amnesic" self, the "nowhere" self, the "fearful" self, and the "misplaced" self—Walker remained constant in his opposition to one option facing many women: abortion. Though his position, as manifested in his support for Mercedes Wilson and her book *The Ovulation Method of Birth Regulation*, conformed to the mandates of the *magisterium* of the Catholic Church, it found little favor among "pro-choice" factions. Pleased by his stance against abortion, Mercedes Wilson later asked Walker about ways to seek funds for WOOMB-USA and the Billings Ovulation Method of Natural Family Planning.[6] Still later, calling on his association over the years with the MacArthur Foundation, Walker wrote to its president, John E. Corbally, complaining about giving grants to such organizations as Planned Parenthood. He wished to call attention to Wilson's Family of the Americas Foundation and hoped that the MacArthur Foundation would fund such humane and noncontroversial methods of family planning.[7] Walker felt he had nothing to lose in making such an appeal. After reading Walter Isaacson's pro-abortion article in *Time*, Walker wasted no time upbraiding his former student:

What dismayed me was your conclusion, not merely favoring the "pro-choice" folks but draping them in the august mantles of "a pluralistic society," democracy, the Constitution and so on . . . I don't think you realize the consequences of favoring the abortionists. Once the traditional Judeo-Christian principle of the sacredness of life is breached in the name of whatever sanction of convenience, public welfare, efficiency and so on—I'm afraid you may have turned loose some devils you may not want to have around later. Once abortion is sanctioned, for whatever good and humane reasons, I don't see why we can't get rid of the aged and useless and infirm for similar reasons.

And since you make a point of "leaving such decisions to individuals"—well, of course, such decisions are always up to individuals, just as it is your decision to shoot me if you like. The question is whether the law should condone your doing so. The danger is that if the majority rules and the majority wants to do away with life in whatever form, who is to say they're not going to try to do away with the likes of you and me.[8]

Walker was concerned that his position might have a negative impact on how a select group of literary judges—the Eastern Literary Establishment—might vote when considering his work. Gradually, at the continued urging of Mercedes Wilson, he spoke out publicly, and in the years to follow, Walker continued to support Wilson and her cause whenever he felt she came under attack.[9] Walker's letter published in the June 8 edition of *The New York Times* called abortion "yet another atrocity in a century where atrocities have become commonplace." His message to pro-abortionists was clear: it looked as if they might get their way, but they were not going to have it *both* ways: "You're going to be told *what* you're doing." Walker's letter caught the eye of George F. Will, who argued in *Newsweek* that "abortion cannot be about the beginning of human life," but about "the status of life at various early stages" of fetal development. Will believed that any civilized sensibility would be troubled by jeopardizing life during the later stages of pregnancy.

As Walker was busy packing his books to move into the Cajun cottage and completing the final pages of his new work, he was honored in early June by the Mississippi Institute of Arts and Letters for *The Second Coming* at the awards banquet in Jackson.[10] He looked elegant in his tux (the same one he had worn in his college days) as he greeted friends and admirers in the Mississippi Museum of Modern Art. Not long afterward, he attended the graduation ceremony at the University of the South, where Shelby received an honorary degree.[11] In spite of these professional and social commitments, Walker finished by late August a corrected first draft of *Lost in the Cosmos*. He sent a copy to Father Tom Clancy to see if there was anything objectionable in it from a theological point of view.

Since Ann's life was stable and she and her family were now living comfortably in the château, Walker and Bunt set up an *Inter Vivos* trust, so that their share of the property in the Robindale subdivision would be equally divided between John Walker and Robert Lobdell, which would terminate once they reached the age of twenty-five. The primary purpose of the trust was to provide for the education, college or otherwise, of the two Lobdell grandsons. Walker also wanted to make sure that his literary papers would be cared for properly: he contacted Carolyn Wallace, director of the Southern Historical Collection at UNC, in order to pursue a disposition, either by loan, purchase, or gift, of his manuscripts and typescripts.[12] (Shelby had already put on deposit the manuscript of his Civil War history and Bob Coles would eventually house his papers there too).[13]

Since Walker had prior commitments, he could not attend Bob Coles's Levy Lecture that fall at Southwestern Louisiana University on *A Confederacy of Dunces*. Strangely, while Coles referred to Dorothy Day, Flannery O'Connor, and Simone Weil in his talk, he failed to cite Walker's crucial role in having this novel published. When Coles read a typescript copy of *Lost in the Cosmos*, he could hardly restrain his enthusiasm for Walker's work: "The space ship story is *Love in the Ruins* to the 10th power—futurism updated to the final moment."[14] Coles was particularly amazed, as was his son Bobby, by the statistics Walker had amassed. Such positive feedback gave Walker a chance to sort out his own thoughts about this book, which constituted a new stage in his development as a writer—one that had its pitfalls. While vacationing at Gulf Shores, he had to decide whether to go ahead and have it published, or put it aside for a while and see if he could transform it into a larger work on semiotics. Part of his hesitation came from the fact that Pat Myrer at McIntosh & Otis was personally offended by the "male-chauvinist-pig" attitude in the book. She told Walker he should lay off the San Francisco gay scene and instead bear down on those in favor of nuclear warfare.[15] Walker still was undecided in late October, though he informed Bob Giroux that his firm would get first crack at the book; for his part, Giroux, then busy with his book on Shakespeare's sonnets, encouraged Walker to work at his own pace and not rush the rewriting.[16]

In arranging approximately 3,000 books (Walker's estimate) in the new ground-floor study of the Cajun cottage, Walker reread "a couple of hundred" letters that Shelby had written him, some going back to the late 1940s. "If I've learned anything over the years," he informed Shelby in November, "it is that if you let things alone, they come out in the end. You don't write books, they write you." Walker would take a fresh look at his work-in-progress in a month or so before making any final decision. "The funny thing is I don't have the slightest desire or even the prospect of ever writing fiction again." To test the waters even further, he provided copies of his new work for Rhoda Faust and Bob Milling to read. "Like I told you," he wrote Faust, "I have reservations about it. I think it is in places too glib, smart-ass and maybe even mean, and I don't really enjoy shocking conventional folk with foul language."[17] Milling informed Walker that *Lost in the Cosmos* elicited strong discussion among his friends, especially during the past month at the Thursday luncheons; Dr. Patricia Maykuth from Atlanta, a psychologist friend of Lyn Hill, had reservations about the book. Hill told Walker that *Lost in the Cosmos* was not publishable, mainly because she saw that he was angry at women.

Walker, in her mind, was passive-aggressive toward women, no doubt stemming from the loss of his mother. "Her death was the ultimate abandonment," Hill believed. "Walker had a good deal of anger because of it," and she felt he simply had not faced up to this issue.[18] As a whole, the lunch group felt that Walker was retreating from them. Gossip had spread in certain quarters that he and Hill were perhaps too familiar with each other. His friends knew he was attracted to articulate, younger women—and that the feeling was often reciprocal. Not one to hide her feelings, Bunt began to put pressure on Walker not to see Hill, even at the luncheons; if he did, some would interpret it as a cause for scandal. In a letter to Bob Milling, Walker did not address directly his interest in Hill:

Thanks for your good letter. And the advice on *Lost in Cosmos* which I intend to take. I've put it out of sight and mind and hope after a couple of months to come back and see it afresh. It's really not good enough. My objection to it is not the same as L.H.'s [Lyn Hill] and P.M.'s [Patricia Maykuth]. My objection is that it is in places too heavy-footed, rancorous, glib and even preachy. The trick of the satirist, as Swift well knew, is to use the rapier not the sledge, and slip it in without the reader even knowing. And above all to stay light-footed . . . No, I'm not mad at those two girls. On the contrary: I have the greatest affection and respect for both of them. They're the best and the brightest of their generation, albeit in totally different ways. One is ninety-nine percent located in her left brain—to use a current metaphor—the other ninety-nine percent in her right. And I suspect that part of their offense at *Lost in Cosmos* is ontological; that is, that it arises from the challenge to a certain absolutizing of self and reality in each case.

The left-brained girl is scandalized by particularity, by the serious suggestion that a particular event, person, thing might have any other significance than as a datum from which an abstraction can be drawn. The right-brained girl is offended by assignment of serious, even crucial significance to a reality outside the self, to history, to a real world, to a God who is out there as well as in here, to any density in this life which cannot be engulfed and recycled and attenuated by an absolute self. The interesting thing is that as extreme as each case is, each girl senses dimly in the other their own dormant cortex—and that I think is part of the basis of their friendship. My only credential for speaking this way is not that I am smarter than they are—each one is far superior to me in the right and left—but age—I've got thirty years on them.[19]

Walker concluded that he had not retired from life, the human race, or friendships. He would continue to have lunch occasionally on Thursday with his friends for another year or so, until Bunt's insistence finally prevailed.

Shelby thought *Lost in the Cosmos* not only a very funny work but timely as well. He suggested that Walker might deal more specifically with what he considered the underlying notion, that Sagan knows everything about everything and nothing about nothing. How did Walker feel at this point? One gets an indirect glimpse from his reply in the

December 6 edition of *The New York Times Book Review* to the question of what book he would most like to have written and why. Walker selected *Don Quixote* because of the happy conjunction of narrative and satire. He could imagine how good Cervantes must have felt to have hit upon telling a superb, funny, tragic adventure and at the same time getting in his licks at what's wrong with society. "Now there's a happy man."

When Walker was informed that UNC had received a preliminary appraisal of $30,000 for his papers, lower than what Carolyn Wallace had expected, he nevertheless welcomed Walter ("Tim") West, who arrived to pick up the first installment.[20] In sorting out his papers and books, Walker had decided not to sell his original New York edition of Henry James's works. Shelby had his eye on them: "Very astute refusal on your part, I now realize, but don't forget I'm planning to outlive you just long enough to read straight through the twenty-six volumes." Lewis Lawson indirectly asked Walker (now, at age sixty-five, older than most other male ancestors he could remember) for permission to write a full-length study of his works that would have a strong biographical underpinning.[21] Walker soon informed Lawson to feel free to engage in his project, and even stop by Covington if he wished. Walker had no interest in writing an autobiography, though he would be most willing to answer any *factual* questions Lawson might have.[22] Not long after, Walker received a copy of the French journal *Delta*, edited by Jerry Kennedy, on Walker's works (Simone Vauthier, Lewis Lawson, and I had articles in this journal).[23] Kennedy had made overtures about writing a biography of Walker, but had been put off.[24]

Waiting seven months into the new year before sending *Lost in the Cosmos* to Bob Giroux, Walker looked about for subject matter for his next book. Perhaps due to exhaustion from work, he took a long hiatus from his normal routine of writing. If his friendship with Lyn Hill was raising eyebrows, his friendship with thirty-one-year-old Jo Marie Gulledge was hardly noticed. After graduating with an M.A. in English from Clemson University, Gulledge had moved the previous summer to Baton Rouge with her husband, Tom. She found employment at *The Southern Review* and started doctoral work under Lewis Simpson, who provided an introduction to Walker. In mid-February, Walker invited Gulledge to lunch at Bechac's with Chris Wiltz, an aspiring fiction writer, Rhoda Faust, and others of the Thursday group.[25] He was charmed by Gulledge, and when she arrived in Covington the second time, she talked briefly with Walker at his office in the Kumquat, where he informed her that he was working on a lecture, on which she made a few suggestions, as she later did on a typescript of *Lost in the Cosmos*. Thereafter, Gulledge and Walker occasionally took walks through Fontainebleau Park or lunched together when Bunt was away with Ann on one of their buying trips for the Kumquat.

When Gulledge was considering applying to law school that summer, Walker—thinking she might also apply for doctoral studies in English—suggested she might consider editing a volume of Uncle Will's letters as a dissertation. Walker wrote to Uncle Will's relative, Janet Longcope's daughter, and his brother Roy about this possible venture: "I hope you will sign the enclosed permission. Jo is a very nice lady . . . Highly intelligent and an admirer of WAP [Will], and a good scholar. I think she will do him [Will] proud."[26] Walker encouraged Gulledge to consider this project, and even brought up the possibility that she might think about writing his biography, something she declined to do. Once, after reading *A Band of Prophets*, which contained an essay by Lewis Simpson, Walker wrote Simpson a congratulatory letter and made this passing reference to Jo Gulledge: "She's not only beautiful but smart."[27] As their friendship grew deeper, Gulledge took a number of photos of Walker; one was featured in Lewis Baker's *The Percys of Mississippi* and another in an article on Uncle Will by Walker in *Architectural Digest*. Over the ensuing months, Gulledge wanted him to feel that he had met a woman who respected him wholly, not just as a writer. Walker told Gulledge she was hiding behind her wedding ring, and she replied he was hiding behind the rituals of the Catholic Church. Gulledge believed that he was looking for some type of commitment, one way or another, from her.

In the presence of Eudora Welty at Millsaps College in Jackson, Walker gave the inaugural address for the Eudora Welty Chair of Southern Studies on March 15. It was announced that Cleanth Brooks would be the Welty Professor in the spring of 1983. In Walker's address, published as "Novel-Writing in an Apocalyptic Time," he showed he had been thinking about a new novel when he mentioned that, while the world witnessed some of its greatest advances in science, it had not made the expected quantum leap toward the betterment of mankind. He cited the Holocaust and the banality with which the world accepted such an atrocity. The challenge, as Walker saw it, was for the novelist to humanize life, "to formulate it for someone else, to render the interstates, to tell the truth, to show how life is lived, and therefore to affirm life, not only the lives of poor white people and poor black people in the Georgia countryside and in Mississippi towns and hamlets," but also the lives of middle- and upper-class Americans who spend time on golf courses. In this talk he clearly articulated themes he would draw on for his next novel.

Another side of Walker, one rarely seen by his friends, became apparent at income-tax time. He was deeply concerned about his finances, especially the fact that his publisher retained a "Reserve for Returns" account of $40,000 in his name. If a payment of at least $30,000 was not made immediately, Walker would have to borrow money. While he was very fond of his publishing house, Walker was not sure he could afford to live by their returns policy.[28] Pat Myrer did her homework, corroborating Walker's financial figures, and wasted no time contacting Roger Straus, who made the sum available.[29]

Before heading off with Bunt to Charlottesville for the PEN/Faulkner Award, Walker made his annual retreat with the Olivier Provosty group at Manresa. Novelist Mary Lee Settle had asked him to serve as one of the judges, and he said he would do anything, even lick stamps if need be. (When Settle later called him because she was depressed, he said, "Honey, I can't help you because I suffer from it too.") One Sunday, the Percys and Richard Bausch and his wife went to Mass at St. Thomas Church, which was guarded by an exotic Buddha-like statue of Christ made of car bumpers. Though he shook his head in wonderment, Walker never wavered in his commitment to the post-Vatican II Church, however bizarrely it manifested itself.[30] He had no problem with Vatican II because he believed in the Holy Spirit being with the Church.[31] Often considered conservative by his Catholic friends, Walker nevertheless applauded the maturing process brought about by the council. Though many Southern Catholics were shocked by his novels, he said, "the strange thing is that I am a Catholic writer and I have less readership among my fellow Catholics than anyone else."

Walker next headed to Southwestern Louisiana University, where he gave the 1982 Flora Levy Lecture, which he entitled "How to Be an American Novelist in Spite of Being Southern and Catholic." Clearly admitting he was a Southern novelist in a Christian tradition, Walker had the advantage of seeing the South from the inside and thus the rest of the country from a unique perspective, one that opens itself up to satire, "always launched in the mode of hope." The possibilities of failure and default for a Southern novelist were unlimited, he said, and not being a prophet, he tended to be pessimistic.

Going home to Greenville during the last weekend in April, Walker would have a chance to measure how far he had come since his days in high school. A group of writers, artists, and musicians who had lived in Greenville returned to their native city for a civic and artistic celebration called "The Time Has Come"—the title came from a weekly newspaper column written by Ben Wasson, who, though infirm, followed the events closely. For Walker, Shelby, Josephine Haxton, and Charles Bell, as photographed together by Noel Workman for *Delta Scene Magazine*, it would be the last reunion of this sort. At one of the sessions, Shelby said he was there because growing up in Greenville "was really as good as I think it was." Bell agreed: "One wouldn't come back and address this audience if he didn't believe that Greenville was distinctive." Walker took a different tack, noting that he had never sat around the courthouse or swapped stories with the old-timers because he had heard his early stories at a country club in Birmingham. In fact, Walker never particularly liked going back to Greenville, most likely because Uncle Will's house had been torn down. Yet the trip gave Walker a chance to reflect on Shelby's achievements, and he nominated him for the Institute of Arts and Letters in literature. (Eudora Welty, C. Vann Woodward, and Donald Barthelme seconded the nomination. Later Paul Horgan, seconded by Cleanth Brooks and Richard Wilbur, nominated Walker for the Academy's Gold Medal for Fiction. Neither nomination proved to be successful.)

One of Walker's admirers, Jeffrey D. Wilson of Street, Maryland, characterized his work in a new light. "You are the most Augustine-like writer I have ever read," Wilson wrote. "More specifically, your body of fiction resembles *The City of God*. In that work, St. Augustine tried to come to terms with the sack of Rome and the imminent fall of the Western empire, in God's eternal plan . . . You are immersed in your culture, as he was in his. You try to deal with the imminent demise of our culture as St. Augustine did with his."[32] He asked, "Are you an Augustinian?" Walker replied that though he had not been conscious of being an Augustinian, nevertheless he clearly admitted the influence of *The City of God* on his work. "It stretches matters a little, however, to compare my work with his."[33] If Wilson needed any further evidence, he had only to look at a quote from St. Augustine—"O God, I pray you to let me know my self"—that Walker added to later editions of *Lost in the Cosmos*. If Walker's Augustinian star was rising, his Kierkegaardian one was diminishing asymptotically as he developed his own open-ended, American-based spirituality. Walker's ongoing correspondence with Jan Nordby Gretlund, a scholar of Southern literature who taught at the University of Odense in Denmark, served as a reminder to Walker of his spiritual roots, even as he pushed the abstracted logic of Kierkegaard farther back on the shelf.

When the Percys visited June and Jimmy Sprunt at their lovely house on Grandfather Mountain in North Carolina, Walker gave them a copy of the typescript of *Lost in the Cosmos*.[34] He also sent a copy of the typescript to Tom Sebeok, and called his attention to the section about the semiotic history of the cosmos. Sebeok would probably object to

Walker's tendency to agree with Ernst Cassirer, but he wanted Sebeok's imprimatur, if possible. "I am figuring," he concluded his letter to Sebeok, "that since you venture into literary forms such as dialogues with Maeterlinck, you can forgive a novelist for trespassing into semiotics."[35] Sebeok in turn alerted the director of Indiana University Press about the new book. "About the *Cosmos*," Sebeok informed Walker, "my personal views are, roughly, identical with those of John Archibald Wheeler, but these, too, hark back to Peirce: 'The Universe as an argument is necessarily a great work of art, a great poem—for every fine argument is a poem and a symphony—just as every true poem is a sound argument . . . That total effect is beyond our ken.' . . . And further: 'Mind is First, Matter is Second, Evolution is Third . . .' "[36] Sebeok understood what Walker was doing, but did not give him the unqualified praise he was seeking.

The revised text of *Lost in the Cosmos* was forwarded to Bob Giroux. "Brilliant" was Bob's first word to describe the book. "It's funny, bitter, satiric and in places as savage as Swift. It will certainly do better than *The Message in the Bottle*, because of its *humor*. It's hard to assess its potential because you offend established religious positions in every direction."[37] Encouraged by this response, Walker sent his editor many corrections, insertions, and deletions.[38] Bob Giroux's instincts proved correct; when it was published, *Lost in the Cosmos* found an immediate and dedicated following, eventually outselling Walker's other books.

Enormously pleased by his publisher's response, Walker felt the need of a vacation. The Percys and the Footes headed for the West Coast, flying first to Chicago, where they boarded the Twentieth Century Limited. Once they reached Ogden, Utah, the train came to a halt at 1 a.m., due to a strike. The conductor announced, "Everyone off the train." Walker, who had spent the day reading a novel by Shusaku Endo, adamantly refused to budge from his bed. A porter came and stood over Walker: "We are going to disconnect the air-conditioning and you will be very uncomfortable." "What you do to me is your own responsibility," Walker retorted. The beleaguered passengers waited for three hours until buses arrived for them. After spending the night on the train, the Percys and Footes flew from Salt Lake City to San Francisco, where they stayed at the St. Francis Hotel until September 24. They visited Monterey and Robinson Jeffers's Tor House in Carmel before touring Hearst's San Simeon Castle. Determined that justice be done, Walker received a refund for his train ticket from Amtrak.

On his return from Los Angeles, Walker learned from Zoltán Abádi-Nagy that his translation of *Lancelot* would be published in Hungarian.[39] Since Abádi-Nagy had no American colleague at Kossuth University in

Debrecen, he sent Walker six pages of inquiries about American colloquialisms, and the response was fifteen handwritten pages. In passing he mentioned that *Lost in the Cosmos* would be published the following May. "It is a kind of satire on U.S. self-help books, so popular, and the best seller is *Cosmos* by Carl Sagan, which professes total knowledge of the cosmos, including man."[40] FSG had paid an advance of $35,000 and was empowered to handle translation rights.[41] In addition to a print run of 35,000 copies (the book was dedicated to Walker's four grandsons, "fellow space travelers"), there was a limited edition of 300 copies at $60 each. In customary fashion, Walker continued submitting emendations into the late fall.[42]

Walker looked about for something to occupy his time. One day that fall, as he chatted in a doctor's waiting room with Pius Lartigue, O.S.B., president-rector of St. Joseph Seminary College, he expressed interest in offering a course at the seminary. "We would be most happy to have you do this. I would like to meet with you to discuss this possibility," the Benedictine replied.[43] With Shelby's encouragement, Walker also started reading Dante. Walker received an invitation from Monsignor Charles Murphy, rector of the North American College in Rome, to lecture there.[44] He kept his options open about going to Rome ("It would be for me an extraordinary experience"), though he hesitated to make an actual commitment.[45] He refused outright to serve on the board of trustees of Gallaudet College in Washington in mid-October when he learned that Gallaudet students used sign language exclusively. Walker also flew again before Christmas to Washington, where he met with officials of the National Endowment for the Arts, and then to New York City in order to participate at a sales conference for his book at the Gramercy Park Hotel.[46] Before leaving, Roger Straus provided him with a copy of the French version of *The Moviegoer* (it was called *Le Cinéphile* in France), informing him that Pandora in Paris had agreed to publish *Lancelot*.[47] Even after a delay of twenty years, Walker was proud that the French would be able to read his work.

In mid-January, Walker set about reading the galleys of *Lost in the Cosmos*.[48] He made a few corrections and soon returned them.[49] He turned down Rhoda Faust's invitation for a book-signing party: "It ain't worth the hassle and watching p.o.'d people standing in line and getting the dry grins."[50] But he would be glad to go to her store and sign any number of books. Bunt had confidence in the book; she called FSG and ordered 500 copies for the Kumquat.[51] As Walker corrected the page proofs, which he completed by the end of February, he lunched with Jo Gulledge during the second week of January. As they spent part of the afternoon strolling around a park outside Covington, they talked about

Uncle Will's poetry. He gave Gulledge a Xerox copy of Will's poetry to discuss at their next lunch in mid-February.[52] Gulledge wrote: "You brought up an interesting idea, *Lost in the Cosmos* as a religious book, probably more so than realized, raised by the seemingly amusing question, why is Carl Sagan so lonely? An idea directed at scientists in general who try to dissolve the universe of man and make him like all other species . . . While evolutionists don't pretend to see their view as eternal truth, scientists like Sagan see the status of evolution as the logical theory, even though it too is not provable in the traditional method."

Walker agreed to give the commencement address at the seminary and started making plans to teach a course on the modern novel there during the fall semester, one that would be based on *The Individual and Society*, one of the Great Books courses.[53] When he submitted his syllabus, he indicated the course would be a sampling of twentieth-century fiction (with some precursors in the nineteenth century) toward a general goal of the use of fiction as a cognitive tool in the understanding of the relation of the individual to society, with particular emphasis on the dislocation and alienation of twentieth-century Western man.[54] Walker requested there be no tests or papers, unless required by the college. Naturally the seminary's administrators were anxious to comply with Walker's requests. Because he had committed himself to teaching at the seminary (and building a pool next to the new house for his grandsons), he refused Marion Montgomery's offer to be considered for a visiting professorship at the University of Georgia.[55] "The reason you're better known in Crawford than I am in Covington," Walker wrote Montgomery, "is that writers rank somewhere behind used-car salesmen in Louisiana."[56] Stanley Lindberg, the editor of *The Georgia Review*, had prompted Montgomery to contact the author when he read the galleys of Walker's book, a portion of which would be featured in their summer issue, and also in *Vanity Fair* and *Omni*.

As Rhoda Faust and Bob Milling went through the throes of breaking up, they called Walker and asked him to lunch. Since he faced his sixty-seventh birthday, he said he was too old for "sexual shenanigans" and might show up in a wheelchair. He always remained supportive of these friends: "Allow me to say to you what I said to Rhoda," he wrote Milling. "I value your friendship, and since I don't have many, I aim to hang onto it. You won't be rid of me so easily."[57] Never a robust man, Walker checked into the hospital in March for a sigmoidoscopy, an examination of his rectum and colon.[58] When Dr. George Riser reviewed Walker's medical records, he decided that Walker was in good shape at this point in his life.[59]

Walker's address to the graduating class at the seminary on May 10 concerned "today's church, today's priesthood, today's vocation problems." Archbishop Hannan of New Orleans, Abbot Patrick Regan, O.S.B., students, and their guests listened to Walker as he explained both his attachment to the Benedictine tradition and his expectations of the Catholic clergy. (Like Jacques Maritain, who, toward the end of his life, lived with the Little Brothers of Jesus in their monastery near Toulouse, Walker would eventually become a member of the Benedictine tertiary order, and after his death, he was buried in the abbey cemetery.) His planning for his next (and last) novel had begun.

The Thanatos Syndrome, a novel that takes place in the late 1990s, reveals that in the Catholicism of the future only the radical, prophetic clergy—dressed, most likely, for the liturgy in chinos, sneakers, and sweatshirts—would really understand what is truly traditional.[60] In comparing the role of the future parish priest with that of the creative writer, Walker set out an agenda for himself and the seminarians he addressed: traditional formulaic patterns of expression about the spiritual nature of humanity and the world we live in would not necessarily suffice in the future. Walker told the seminarians that they could barely imagine in the present how they would share the Good News in the future. Unlike the Rev. Shegog in Faulkner's *The Sound and the Fury* and Father Arnall in Joyce's *A Portrait of the Artist as a Young Man*, who preach in a style expected by their congregations, Father Simon Smith in *The Thanatos Syndrome* remains aloof, unpredictable, and at times even obnoxious. His preference for the Tridentine liturgy signals that he had not adapted to the changes in liturgical practice since the Second Vatican Council. Yet he finds a niche within himself, rooted in his experiences in Nazi Germany, where he once lived. The larger concerns of Feliciana Parish, especially the dire effects of heavy sodium in the water supply, seem not to invade his inner sanctum the way they do Dr. Tom More's. Walker's last fictional priest acts and speaks in a shockingly new way, which nevertheless is consistent with his prophetic calling within the Church. His life dramatically calls attention to evil in the world and the need to protect and heal those who cannot voice their needs. Walker's address to the seminarians was received politely; few recognized the boldness of his approach, or the years of prayer and reflection that had gone into it.

When Phin received his copy of *Lost in the Cosmos* in May, he called it "a blockbuster."[61] He felt that Walker's smile as revealed on the back cover said it all. "Aside from its originality and high humor, its most remarkable quality is its dazzling display of intellectual range without a trace of ostentation or pomposity." After Ann had read the book, she asked what her father would do next; he replied he didn't know. When Walker asked her advice, she answered with characteristic Percyan humor that he should attempt only that writing project in which he could be "most obnoxious."[62]

Shelby praised the book: "It makes clear—and mainly by demonstrations, which as you know I much prefer in any choice between show and tell—a great deal of what you have been saying all along." But more than that, Walker had done it in high good humor and an ever-present savageness that lay just below the surface. Though buoyed by the praise of relatives and friends, Walker reread the book with a critical eye, and in mid-July sent in corrections he hoped could get into the second edition.[63] His nagging concerns were allayed when he was informed that FSG sold the paperback rights to Pocket Books for $82,500.[64]

Walker lectured, as did Eudora Welty and C. Vann Woodward, on "Arts, Letters and Americans" in the Frank Nelson Doubleday Lecture series on May 17 at the National Museum of American History in Washington. His rambling talk focused on Herman Melville; along the way he made some gibes at "deconstructionism." At times, Walker seemed to be commenting on his own work rather than Melville's: "The freedom and happiness of the artist is attested to by his playfulness, his tricks, his malice, his underhandedness, his naughtiness, his hoodwinking the reader." When Walker returned home, he wrote to Elizabeth Spencer: "I think I am through with this foolishness, giving lectures, etc. I intend to sit here in my swamp, more or less in a funk, and hope that something comes to mind and won't mind much if it doesn't."[65]

Soon the reviews started appearing. Writing in *The New York Times*, Anatole Broyard found that Walker worries about "all the right things and expresses his fears with a naturalness and elegance that are all his own." Linda Hobson in *The Times-Picayune* said that this work defies categorization: "It is designed to shock the complacent, bored reader out of his own predicament and loss of the self, and it certainly has the effect desired." Having recently completed her dissertation on Walker's use of the comic and Christianity in his fiction, Hobson called attention to this dimension in this work. Gene Lyons in *Newsweek* found that Walker's work was getting, like Alice talking about mad hatters and Cheshire cats, "curiouser and curiouser!" But deep down, he postulated that Walker's readers would be "challenged and amused." R. Z. Sheppard stipulated in *Time* that Walker's voice in this work was "beguiling" and "civilized." Jack Beatty in *The New Republic* found the book crackling with "thought, ideas, exotic information." He praised Walker's wit and found him to be a "maestro of fear and trembling." In *Gambit*, a local paper, Jesse Core, a longtime correspondent of Walker, found that the work "stands brilliantly alone as a work of non-fiction." As Walker had suspected, the reviews showed a wide spectrum of criticism. In writing to Cleanth

Brooks, he said he was well aware of the critical reception of *Lost in the Cosmos*: "It is a somewhat mischievous book and it has elicited already considerable irritation as well as approval from reviewers."[66]

Partly because he wanted more privacy in which to start his new writing project, he moved in mid-May from his office in the Kumquat to 433 North Columbia, which had a side entrance on Lockwood Street. The new office—which he would occupy for the next twelve months, was on the ground floor, just off a quiet courtyard with a fountain. It was a square room in which he kept a daybed and a small refrigerator. Because of the persistent gossip about him and Lyn Hill, he almost never went to lunch on Thursday. Though he still attended the original Great Books group, he dropped out of the second one.[67] During this period, Walker and Bunt were most concerned about Lucy Ballard's failing health. They wrote to her daughter, Suzanne, asking if they could help in any way.[68] In the weeks that preceded her death on July 4, they read Peter Matthiessen's *The Snow Leopard* to her.

Walker continued seeing Jo Gulledge in his new office that summer.[69] In late July, Gulledge wrote a long synopsis for Walker of the life of Tom More, which could link up his first and second More books, an indication that Walker had started planning another novel. Another indication that his literary juices were flowing was his request to Joan Massey, Bob Giroux's assistant, asking for the best book concerning the Three Mile Island disaster.[70] He informed Shelby in early August that he had returned to the adventures of Tom More, this time placed more precisely in and around St. Francisville, Louisiana.[71]

Walker's summer was not without its interruptions. He read a screen treatment of *Love in the Ruins*, which he found "very interesting."[72] The author, Michael Hargraves of Los Angeles, was informed by Walker's agent that producer Evarts Ziegler of Hollywood would read the script.[73] Unfortunately, neither this film nor the one optioned a year later by Learning in Focus of New York for *The Last Gentleman* ever got off the ground.[74] Walker allowed David Duty of the Austin Independent School District to pursue working on a PBS series based on *The Message in the Bottle* and *Lost in the Cosmos*.[75] Walker had learned not to put his hopes in such ventures. But a more public incident, involving the improper use of his name in the press as one of the supporters of the hospital at the American University of Beirut, irritated him enormously. Together with prominent locals, including Marcus Smith, Walker signed a petition lamenting the kidnapping in Lebanon of David Dodge, the university's acting president. But Walker objected when his name appeared as one of the signatories of "An Open Letter from American Writers Concerned About Lebanon" in *The New York Review of Books*. Deeply upset, Walker, contemplating legal action, asked both Marcus Smith and Roger Straus to look into the situation. Smith assured him he had nothing to do, "absolutely and categorically," with the unauthorized use of his name. Walker learned that the person who had placed the ad admitted that he was not authorized to use it and a correction was published soon after.[76]

To obtain additional background material for his novel, Walker, Bunt, and the Ellises went to St. Francisville one weekend in early September, visiting Ellerslie, where they met a Percy relative, Lucy Maddox. Walker had previously met Lucy Parlange, wife of the owner of Parlange Plantation.[77] Though the first name of his character in the novel may have been inspired by either woman, Dr. Lucy Lipscomb's willingness to assist Dr. More probably came from Jo Gulledge's attentive nature. In late September she and Walker lunched and had a chance meeting with Rhoda Faust and Bob Milling, who stopped by Walker's office with books for him to sign. Gulledge was still on Walker's mind when the Percys vacationed during the first ten days of October, with the Ellises and William and Nell Pape Waring, both physicians from New Orleans. With the Percys' Boston bull terrier, Mardi, they climbed Mount Satulah and went to Ellicott's Rock. Bunt relaxed by reading *Sophie's Choice*. Walker called Gulledge when they returned and they had another rendezvous at Fontainebleau Park.

Walker began teaching English 49 at the seminary in September. His first words were succinct and direct: "I'm Walker Percy. I'm a writer. It's a tough way to make a living." They met each Monday afternoon for two and a half hours on the second floor of the library; he had specifically requested no salary.[78] Father Scott Underwood had spread the word that he wanted qualified students in the seminar; ten of the dozen who were admitted to the course were seniors.[79] The following week, as they discussed Flannery O'Connor's stories "The River" and "Circle of Fire," the students sensed Walker's lack of ease—the slight stuttering, the hesitation to follow through on a point—but he seemed more relaxed after a number of sessions. Clearly the best student was Mark David, a philosophy major, whom Walker liked to engage in conversation. David felt that Walker was "too self-effacing," though he enjoyed Walker's changing the direction of the conversation when it got bogged down or when he probed the underlying meaning of the story they were reading.[80] Scott Collier and Kyle Scafide felt that Walker's gift to his students was that he taught them to be critics of literature. Walker got along, too, with Steven ("Blaze") Leszczynski, a down-to-earth young man who had no hesitation sharing his thoughts. Tom Eldringhoff was pleased to be in the course, but he had no idea who Walker was or what he had written (some in the class thought Walker was a dentist). Another student, Lawrence Bouchea, O.S.B., perceived something that had escaped the others: "Walker had a hole in his heart he could not plug, and writing was an attempt to fill that hole."

Walker endorsed Zoltán Abádi-Nagy's application for a fellowship with the National Humanities Center in North Carolina. Walker thought that Zoltán's project on post-Pynchonian American fiction held "considerable promise."[81] Though Abádi-Nagy did not receive the fellowship, Kent Mullikin, who had misplaced Walker's original letter of recommendation, wrote Walker the following year saying that Abádi-Nagy had again applied for a fellowship.[82] Would Walker write another letter? "It was a strong recommendation," Walker replied, "but I have better things to do than rewrite letters to people who lose the first. I realize this response may not help Mr. Abádi-Nagy's application, but it will be a matter of your conscience not mine."[83] Mullikin came back with a civilized appeal and sent a copy of *The Last Gentleman* to be signed. "You're right," Walker replied. "That was a shitty letter. I apologize."[84] Walker admitted he was in a bad mood and sent Mullikin a second favorable letter of recommendation.

In late November he accepted a second *Los Angeles Times* Award, this time for *Lost in the Cosmos*.[85] With Shelby and Gwyn, the Percys took the Sunset Limited train to Albuquerque and then proceeded in a rented car to Santa Fe, where they spent four or five days at the La Fonda. They visited the Bandelier National Monument and stopped at Jim Whittaker's ranch and then at Ernest Thompson Seton's house, but learned Seton had died many years before. Walker sent a postcard to Jo Gulledge: "Lovely hiking here if it weren't for the snow storm."[86] When the four arrived in Los Angeles, they met Bob Giroux at the New Itari Hotel. When Giroux returned to New York, he again congratulated Walker on his award and sent him galleys of Padgett Powell's *Edisto*, which Walker liked well enough to write a blurb.[87]

Before Christmas, Walker made a decision: he would not teach at the seminary during the spring semester, mainly because writing his novel now took priority.[88] But the transition from "smart-aleck" nonfiction to fiction was troubling, as he wrote in a letter to Elizabeth Spencer, whose *The Salt Line* he had just received. "I don't seem to know anything about novel-writing except to deplore what seems to be the fashion now: writing flat-out *romans-à-clef*, cataloguing one's affairs, etc."[89] Later, he wrote that he was getting deeper into the quicksand of a "1,000-page novel" and saw no way to extricate himself.[90] Part of the difficulty was that he was preoccupied with reading 300 proposals and manuscripts for the National Endowment for the Arts.[91] But another was that he was still seeing Gulledge. The winter issue of *The Southern Review* published a lively, in-depth interview between Walker and Gulledge, featuring one of Gulledge's photos. The question naturally arose: would Walker seek further counsel about his marriage? When asking Gene Usdin's advice about an internist, Walker also talked to him about psychiatry, which he thought highly of even though he felt that many psychiatrists were off base. The most therapy could accomplish, in Walker's view, was not to solve problems but to bring an individual to the point where he or she was able to make a decision, however "disastrously."[92]

As Walker read in English Proust's *In Search of Lost Time* (Shelby had been through the text eight times), he mentioned to Shelby how women were attracted to him—a topic quite uncharacteristic of him:

I think often about Huggie [Huger, Shelby Foote's son] and how different it is with him from us—even though we were comparatively liberated, as they say. What I am curious about is whether the far more open, relaxed and casual sex of Huggie's generation does not lead to a totally different view of life itself once the old itch, which used to lay at the bottom of all itches or we thought it did, is scratched at will. Or whether it is proper that the old itch remain what it was, the alpha/omega or joy/sin transcending—or lying under—all others?

The irony is how we, our generation, got crossed up in any case, going in two generations from a genteel repressed Southern Presbyterian sexuality—with barely enough room for an awkward piece maybe twice or three times—all the way to Huggie and girlfriend and the blue-grey rooftops and chimney pots, like Rudolfo and Mimi. It's enough to make a fellow wonder.

The comedy is where the new Bohemia catches up, too late, with us literary seniors. Explain why it is that the girls did not exactly knock each other down to get at me when I needed them most but that in this my sixty-eighth year to the Lord, I am propositioned regularly by handsome thirtyish lady-girls, three in recent months, an editor, a photographer, a P-R lady—who have in common only that they don't fool around at all. Their seductions have been almost totally unsuccessful. One of the dubious comforts of age is that what one might not have been able to resist by the practice of virtue, one can more easily resist by means of the prospect of incapacity and, worse, making a fool of oneself. Explain women. Have women gone crazy? What does a handsome, fine-assed, thirtyish lady-girl want with a skinny, bald-headed, sixty-seven-year-old writer? Given the positions in reverse, I'd want no part of it. Has it something to do with lit-ee-ra-choor?

Walker's question was not rhetorical: he knew literary success or celebrity attracted too many women.

In late February he received a "treasure trove" from Kenneth Laine Ketner, the Charles Sanders Peirce Professor of Philosophy at Texas Tech University.[93] Ketner was so taken with Walker's writing that he wanted to share with him an article he had written on Charles Sanders Peirce. Walker responded favorably to Ketner's friendliness. Their correspondence and Ketner's essays, reproduced in *A Thief of Peirce: The Letters of Kenneth Laine Ketner and Walker Percy*, assisted Walker in planning the book on semiotics he had long wanted to write.

Walker received an award at Loyola University in Chicago, during the Loyola-Mellon Humanities Convocation in the newly opened Edward Crown Center. He had been recommended indirectly by Jo Gulledge.[94] On a blustery February 28, Walker spoke on "Remembering Chicago," a short talk about the various times he had visited Chicago as a youth. Except for passing through Chicago or changing planes there, Walker had not been in the city since he was a boy. Afterward, Bunt, Walker, Dr. Alice B. Hayes, Professor Paul Messbarger of the English Department, and invited students lunched at Arrupe House, one of the Jesuit residences. Once again, Gulledge proved to be a go-between, in early May, when she accompanied the Polish scholar Elzbieta Olesky to Covington for an interview with Walker. Walker was upset later because he heard Professor Olesky was sending her interview to *The Paris Review*, when she had told him it was for a Polish literary journal. "The moral," Walker informed Gulledge, "is don't give any interviews except to someone you know and trust, i.e, J.G."[95]

By mid-May, Linda Hobson was writing a master bibliography of Walker's works. Walker wrote the introduction, one that really did not please Hobson because of its flippancy.[96] "What else to do," Walker had written, "in a society which believes that Shirley MacLaine has discovered the Secret of Life and that Jane Fonda knows the secrets of politics and health? What to do? One does not speak ill of fellow writers. What to say about them—that both have great legs." Nor did Hobson like Walker's writing that most of the current theorists of language "are up shit creek and can't get out without crawling over eight-year-old Helen Keller in North Alabama." Soon after, Walker withdrew from the project, since he still had to read the materials the NEA had sent him.[97] He nevertheless admired Hobson's bibliographic skills, as he told her when they had lunch.

After a rainy vacation on Lake Sequoia in Highlands, Walker returned to work on his novel.[98] He put off assisting Jo Gulledge in sorting through Uncle Will's letters until early October, after the final meeting of the NEA judges. He also hoped to have his novel under control, describing it as "a metaphysical rendering of the theme of *The Invasion of the Body Snatchers*, e.g., people don't seem to be themselves."[99] He shared some of his novel-in-progress with Shelby. By late fall, he informed Roger Straus he was working on "a real mess of novel," which might, in fact, succeed.[100]

Walker wrote to Ken Ketner on August 8 asking him for more information on the difference between dyadicity and triadicity and other Peircean semiotic categories. It is not difficult to sense Walker's frustration in dealing with Peirce: "Sometimes I could genuflect before CSP [Charles Sanders Peirce] for his genius and for seeing, before his time and *before our time still*, the difference between dyadicity and triadicity. Other times I could kick his ass for his deliberate withdrawal into logical games." Ketner responded by sending him some Peirce essays as well as more of his own writings. Walker again wrote Ketner in early September; he felt he was beginning to make exciting breakthroughs into Peirce's thought.

As Walker revived his interest in semiotics, he backed off from becoming involved in a controversy over John Kennedy Toole's *The Neon Bible*. Rhoda Faust claimed Toole's mother had promised her book rights. The stakes were considerable, as Toole's first novel had sold 50,000 hardback and 500,000 paperback copies. Through her lawyer, Brian Begue, Faust filed for either a fulfillment of the promise or damages of $250,000. Since Mrs. Toole was hospitalized and at death's door, she refused to comment on the situation; according to the law in Louisiana, she did not have exclusive copyright to this work, since it belonged partly to Toole's uncle and four cousins on his father's side. Walker read the typescript and thought that it should be published, given the popularity of *A Confederacy of Dunces*; yet he felt he could not take sides in such a complicated legal suit.

Sheila Bosworth had finished her novel *Almost Innocent*, for which Walker gave a blurb ("a lovely achievement, a superior one").[101] He would have recognized the last name of one of her characters, De-Bardeleben. He certainly recognized himself in a slightly disguised cameo appearance in the opening pages as the writer from Covington dining at Galatoire's. When the proofs were ready in June, they had lunch and Bosworth had a request: "I am not asking you to do anything but read the prologue. If you want to continue reading, I'm honored. If not, I am still honored that you have had it in your hands." Walker agreed to read just the first fifty pages and soon telephoned her: "I called to ask if your husband would mind if I gave you a hug." Bosworth felt that Walker seemed fascinated with the workings of women's minds. He was struck with wonder at the things women implicitly know and instinctively do. After the book was published, Walker called her again: how a woman could manage to raise children, run a household, and write a novel was beyond his powers to comprehend.[102] And then he wrote her a long congratulatory letter, stressing in part her religious faith: "Your Catholicism is part of the air you breathe because you were born in this faith and you lived it all your life. Not so for me. I am a convert. And it all came to me late in life, yet I do incorporate it into what I think and write." Bosworth also had an insight into Walker's fiction that not all other women writers could accept: "An odd thing about the truth Walker Percy wrote in his fiction is that so much of that truth concerns women. Women *signify* in Percy's work." In short, Bosworth found Walker both an intellectual writer with ever-growing awareness of the complexity of life around him and a man whose faith gave comfort to others.

Walker had good and bad news from Roger Straus: novelist Peter Handke's translation in German of *The Last Gentleman* would appear the following spring.[103] Yet because Handke wanted to work on his own fiction, he could translate only one more of Walker's novels. Walker answered a letter of inquiry from Handke concerning Southern colloquialisms. A new translator was lined up: Harry Rowohlt, the translator of Powell's *Edisto*.

It was a quiet fall. Walker stuck to his routine of writing in the morning, having lunch either at home or at Wendy's, followed by taking a nap. (His last essay, two short paragraphs on the Waffle House in Covington, was published posthumously in the *Condé Nast Traveler*.) He seemed to be reaching for greater peace in his life. In the afternoon he might play golf with Bunt and the Ellises or simply take a walk with Bunt. These were times for renewal and reflection on their life together. Walker took particular strength from seeing the loving relationship between Steve and Haydée; both had raised families in separate marriages and both, like the Warings, were professionals. Sometimes Bunt and Walker would sit on the porch before heading off to the chapel at St. Paul's for the late-afternoon liturgy.

Walker seemed more accepting of his limitations—the slowness in writing, the time taken to respond to demands placed on him by others, and negative criticism of his work. He even had to live with the nagging suspicion that it was no longer possible for him to write a novel.[104] He corresponded with Wendell ("Whit") Jones, a graduate student at UNC just beginning to write his M.A. thesis on the relationship of *The Last Gentleman* and *The Second Coming* to the Faulkner canon.[105] Walker was delighted when students of literature read his novels with insight; he seemed to sense that they had explicitly discovered something he knew only intuitively. Whit's thesis concerning the failure of the code of honor as a way of understanding the broad changes in Western consciousness provided a corrective to some of the views on Stoicism developed by Lewis Lawson. For his part, Walker believed there was "a good deal" about the Southern ethos and "modern consciousness" in the two Barrett novels; not only was *The Sound and the Fury* crucial in interpreting these two novels, but "it would not be too much to say that they can be read as a version of what Quentin Compson would do if he had opted for life instead of death."[106] Yet after reading Patricia Poteat's *Walker Percy and the Old Modern Age*, Walker felt that she was on the wrong wavelength because she compared his novels with his essays—and thus dealt with two different genres. "Poteat thinks I am OK as a novelist and all wet as a semioticist," he wrote Jo Gulledge.[107] "She thinks it is dehumanizing to try to figure out what is going on in someone else's head . . . She is 1, partly right, 2, partly a victim of the old humanities-science split."

Shortly before the end of the year, Nancy Lemann went to Bechac's to see her hero. "Hi, doll," Walker greeted her. During lunch, each person present told what he or she most desired during 1985. Lemann wanted, among other things, a house and a palmy garden somewhere in the South; she also hoped to find Mr. Right and, above all, peace of mind and heart. "You won't get it," Walker said. "None of us will." Rhoda Faust wished she would start a detective agency. Bob Milling wanted to sail his boat and write and live well. Walker wished he would finish his new novel, which had been driving him crazy for the last few years. When he had finished, Lemann noted in her journal, they all bunched up and said what they wished for Walker: "We think you should spend more time with your friends." He looked at them sideways, askance, with his knowing blue eyes.

His wish for himself came true seven months later. For the first time, unlike his previous novels, the new work would probe unspeakable evil—a subject that needed reflection, discernment, and control. In an interview with Jan Nordby Gretlund in late January 1985, Walker said he was halfway through this novel. In contrast to his other fiction, where "boy falls in love and marries girl," the new protagonist "is not doing too well in his marriage right now. His wife is not happy with him. They have fallen on difficult times." After a family skiing trip to Vail, Colorado, he continued working on his "maddening novel," as he wrote to

William Rodney Allen.[108] In response to a question Allen had sent, he said he had read Ernest Becker's *The Denial of Death*; he was not particularly interested in his thesis that Freud's major theoretical shortcoming was that he failed to see that our first suppression is of the awareness of death rather than of sexual desire, but he was definitely interested in Freud's late idea of the "death instinct," which he was using in *The Thanatos Syndrome*. "It has to do socio-comically with Tom More's several encounters with the death-in-life."

Walker still felt ambivalent about his relationship with Jo Gulledge. They sparred in strange ways and used words obliquely, because what they enjoyed would be dispelled if said directly.[109] Yet Walker was less than indirect in thanking her for her Valentine's Day card: "I had to laugh because it reminded me of you, not your good looks, but your disposition. Love. Walker."[110] At the same time, he lashed out at certain female theologians and nuns in a letter to the editor in *The National Catholic Reporter*:

I am experiencing an ever-increasing pain in the ass at the likes of Rosemary Ruether and her fem-lib chic, which doesn't do much for the liberation of women or men—for example her statement [*NCR*, January 11] in support of the "22 other American religious women" who signed the "pluralistic" statement in *The New York Times*.

Not only are all the buzz words there—"autonomous consciences," "nuns to support reproductive choice," "hostility to sexual women"—there is also the undisguised hatred of the Holy Father—"the current papacy," "the monarchical chain of command," "a monolithic church." . . . In short, I submit that this tiny contentious minority of American nuns—whatever their psychological traumas, political grievances and what I believe to be their latent sexism—might do well to take men less seriously. American men, religious and clergy included, need all the help they can get. The church too. Women too. And this kind of bitchiness is not helping anybody.

He publicly held up Mother Teresa as a model of a modern woman serving the Church, even though he knew that most men and women settled for less ambitious endeavors. The gap between the Gospel ideal and ordinary life triggered in Walker unresolvable smoldering frustration.

Except for a short stay in St. Louis in mid-April to receive a literary award, Walker spent most of his time on his novel. He followed the troubled political scene in Central America, especially in the wake of the election of José Napoleón Duarte as President of El Salvador. Farther south, in Nicaragua, the Sandinista government had been accused by

President Reagan of betraying the revolution; many in Washington felt that Soviet aggression in this region was a threat to the national security of the United States. Walker had appreciated the two-part documentary shown on WLAE in New Orleans, but he had no use for the Sandinistas or their clerical apologists. Rather, he supported Bishop Obando y Bravo of Managua.[111] Walker's sympathy went out to the poor people of Nicaragua, who were victims, in his mind, purely and simply of the Marxist-Leninist left.[112]

In late May, Walker sent Gulledge a copy of his unfinished novel, saying, "This novel is downright bizarre. You'll hate it."[113] As she read, Gulledge felt that she, indeed, was the model for Dr. Lucy Lipscomb. Walker's feelings about the novel might be glimpsed in a short piece he wrote in *The New York Times Book Review*. He noted that *Don Quixote* contained the best opening of any novel: "Here is Cervantes, a failed writer in his late fifties, who has come to that fateful pass when failure is just that, defeat, or by some mysterious dispensation reverses itself and confers a freedom all its own. 'What the hell,' one can imagine Cervantes saying to himself, 'I've tried it their way all my life. Now I'll amuse myself. What's to lose?' " Walker discussed his novel in New York with Bob Giroux during the first week of June before receiving an award in Brooklyn.

On Friday, June 7, the Percys and Eudora Welty took a cab to the Cathedral-Basilica of St. James in Brooklyn, where Walker was honored with the Compostela Award. When Welty had been a recipient in 1984, she recommended that Walker be considered for the award. This oldest Catholic church on Long Island honored distinguished men and women each year. Fathers Dennis Corrado and James Hinchey had traveled to Covington to see Walker. During the course of two days, they registered their interview on four ninety-minute tapes, undoubtedly the most comprehensive interview that Walker ever gave. He mentioned that he was writing a novel about "the euthanasia program in Germany" that started before the mass destruction of the Jews, inspired partly by Frederic Wertham's *A Sign for Cain*. In preparation for the ceremony, Bob Coles wrote the citation: "It is an occasion, surely, when one of the wisest persons in the United States is being applauded by his grateful and edified readers—we who do, indeed, know how healing a particular physician-novelist's pilgrimage has been for so many of us who have felt privileged to have counted him among us: a wayfarer who has reminded us of a clue or two—who has reminded us, in a special manner, of Him who came here long ago to give us those clues." As Walker gave an impromptu interview to a BBC film crew that showed up unexpectedly,

Bunt talked to Bill Beutel, co-anchor of ABC's *Eyewitness News*, and his Southern wife, Adair.

About this time, as Pat Myrer began to experience some problems with her health, lawyer Eugene H. Winick took over McIntosh & Otis, causing Walker to ponder whether or not he should switch agents. He consulted Roger Straus, who said, "Winick is well thought of as a lawyer, but no one seems to think literature is his thing."[114] Winick first met Walker in Covington as Walker was working on *The Thanatos Syndrome*, but since the book was not finished, they really did not talk business.[115] They developed a good relationship, but not a particularly warm one, and one of Gene Winick's first official acts as Walker's agent was to advise him about an option with Blackhawk Enterprises for the motion picture rights to *The Second Coming*.[116] "What do you think?" Walker wrote. "My main concern is this: I'd be delighted to have Frank Perry make the film. He is a fine director—what I fear is that he may not do it and may sell it to somebody who would screw it up. Why don't you recommend what we ought to do?"[117] Like all the other film options Walker signed, this one would come to naught.

Walker shared with Tom Jenks of *Esquire* his thoughts about living in Covington: "I chose to live in a small town. One reason is that people here don't take writers very seriously and accordingly I don't either." One disadvantage was that Walker was more likely to be read as a "regional" writer in the bad sense of entertaining literature about exotic and bizarre types. Still, his comments reaffirmed his desire to continue to live in Covington. Walker finished the first draft of *The Thanatos Syndrome* on July 12 and vacationed with Bunt, the Ellises, and the Warings in Destin, Florida.[118] When he returned, he found time, as usual, for younger writers and scholars. He read with appreciation Gary Ciuba's essay on *Lancelot*, which had appeared in *American Literature*.[119] Ciuba would become one of Walker's best literary critics. He also received a letter from Richard R. Schulze, a student at Trinity College, Oxford.[120] His background would naturally interest Walker. Schulze was born into a wealthy family in Savannah. His parents eventually divorced, but that did not prevent him from getting a degree in English from Princeton and acceptance by the University of Virginia Medical School. Schulze decided to defer his entrance to medical school for two years in order to study at Oxford. He had written a thesis on Faulkner at Princeton and contemplated writing another at Oxford, but after reading Walker's published interviews he decided to write about his novels. Before doing so, he wanted Walker's guidance and a chance to talk to him. "Thanks for your letter," Walker replied. "I experienced a *déjà vu* reading it."[121] Walker recommended

Concluding Unscientific Postscript as being Kierkegaard's "most accessible and comprehensive statement." He also recommended Sebeok's books and essays, "although he misses out, I think, on the unique role of the symbol. For this, you'd have to consult the old master, Peirce, or somebody like Susanne Langer's *Philosophy in a New Key*." Knowing that a dialogue was possible, Schulze met Walker the following January in Covington.

Jo Gulledge was one of the organizers of the fiftieth-anniversary celebration of the founding of *The Southern Review* at LSU. It was the last gathering of the Southern literary eagles (Walker termed them the "Southern Geritol Group"): Robert Penn Warren, George Core, Cleanth Brooks, Lewis Simpson, Louis Rubin, James Olney, Eudora Welty, Donald Stanford, Elizabeth Spencer, Walter Sullivan, and Ernest Gaines, plus fledglings Houston A. Baker, Jr., Henry Louis Gates, Jr., and Gloria Naylor. On the afternoon of Thursday, October 10, in the Union Theater, Walker read from *The Thanatos Syndrome*. I was in the audience sitting next to Betty Carter, who said how much she had liked what Walker had read. As he mingled with the audience, Walker asked graduate student Charles Fister, "Well, what do you want of me?" Fister replied, "Isn't that what Raymond Burr says to Jimmy Stewart during the confrontation scene of *Rear Window*?"[122] Walker laughed. "Yeah, I guess that's true. Okay, I'll talk with you." Awkward at times in front of admirers and well-wishers, Walker was always polite, though it was not difficult to sense that he wanted to be elsewhere.

Before the end of the year, Walker had two final bits of business to attend to, no doubt prompted by seeing so many distinguished (some elderly) creative writers and historians at LSU. First, he wrote out a will by hand in late October, designating Bunt as the executrix of his estate; he left to Ann his community interest in the house and land where she and John resided and to Mary Pratt his community interest in his literary papers on loan at UNC and all other books and manuscripts in his possession. His intention was that what his daughters received be of equal value, and if that was not the case, then adjustments should be made accordingly. Second, since Elizabeth Spencer was now a member of the Institute, Walker wrote to her about proposing Shelby once again for membership: "I think it is a scandal he is not in the Institute. *The Civil War: A Narrative* is emerging as one of the great American works of this century. I've nominated him in the past without success. Maybe my colleagues think I'm pushing a friend—logrolling."[123] Shelby himself felt disheartened over the reception of his *magnum opus*. Historians would not read it because it lacked footnotes and liberal-arts professors would shun it because it was history. "I fall between two stools," he wrote

Walker, "and mainly find my following composed of 'buffs,' a sorry lot who know little or nothing of either history or literature." In December, Shelby had been to a clinic, where he learned that his prostatic tumor had gone into the prostate itself. He felt in relatively good health and knew, as did Walker, that cancer of the prostate was common for men of their ages.

14

The Thanatos Syndrome and the Final Illness 1986–90

During the last four and a half years of his life, Walker finished his final novel and began a major work on semiotics. He accepted an honor offered only to eminent authors in the humanities when he delivered the prestigious Jefferson Lecture in Washington. During his declining months, he suffered greatly from cancer of the prostate. From January to the end of March 1986, he focused his attention on his last novel, *The Thanatos Syndrome*.[1] As he wrote, he often returned imaginatively to the summer he spent in Germany while a college student, in an attempt to unlock the great horror of the century, the Holocaust, as it related to another great evil, child abuse and pedophilia. It was a voyage into the heart of ineffable darkness, where no maps or guides existed. As he stated in an interview with Phil McCombs, the character of Father Simon Smith feels compelled to warn his parishioners about Satan, the Prince of Liars, the eternal enemy who wages his war of destruction. Father Smith embodies the crucial insights and judgments that sustain this novel; it is clear from the various typescripts that Walker allowed this character to grow as the novel developed. He had to locate the character within himself, and what he ultimately discovered was so radically disturbing that, in his judgment, only an alcoholic, prophetic priest could be the vehicle to announce it. A three-page holographic insert in the first typescript reveals that his original concept of Father Smith was as a teacher at Spring Hill College in Mobile, Alabama. Perhaps this suggests that the inspiration was based on Father Hooty McCown, but this Jesuit and the fictional priest do not share the same psychological or spiritual profile. Another, more likely candidate would be the Trappist Father

Charles (Jack English), who had been a prisoner of war before entering religious life.

In the novel, Father Smith lives rather bizarrely in his fire tower as a presbyterial spiritual Semite in the tradition of the Old Testament prophets. When he presides at the liturgy (albeit in Latin), he believes he might be able to transform the modern world by diminishing diabolical evil. The end of the novel, like the end of *Love in the Ruins*, hints at a positive resolution as events and situations appear to fall serendipitously into place. It could, however, be argued that when Walker uncharacteristically manipulated the conclusion, it reflected his own conscious effort to restore his relationship with Bunt. In the novel, Ellen More, the doctor's wife, distracted from her marital duties (by playing in bridge tournaments), resumes her life with her husband, even traveling to Disney World with her family. And though we finally hear Dr. More say, "Well well well," we wonder whether his voice can override that of Father Smith, himself sobered by Flannery O'Connor's brand of Southern mysticism, which never loses sight of evil. "Tenderness leads to the gas chamber"—a phrase from O'Connor—echoes throughout the novel. Walker had actually driven to the prison at Angola, hoping to get a firsthand glimpse of prison life and Death Row, but the guards would not allow him inside.[2]

In an interview with Charlotte Hayes, Walker commented on his religious views. He maintained that contemporary society had entered a post-Christian age ("a time when there is really no Christian consensus, as there was even in the nineteenth century"). He said when he had first moved to Covington, for example, it was common to see nuns almost every day, yet only recently one of his grandsons had to be informed who they were. In addition, this post-Christian age had no room for those fundamentalists who wished to promote Christianity in ways that rejected the findings of modern science. Walker did not know a single scientist of repute, as he wrote in *The Times-Picayune*, who denied biological evolution. "If one believes in God, it hardly diminishes the glory of God if He chose to create man and other creatures through this or that process of evolution." Walker's theology, though rooted in the past and lived in the present, looked mostly to the future, perhaps to the type of spiritual work done by the Rev. Benedict Groeschel, the founder of the newly constituted Franciscan Friars of the Renewal, with whom Walker once spent an afternoon.[3]

The Catholic Book Club recognized Walker as a religious writer when in early February it presented him with the Campion Award, named after St. Edmund Campion, S.J., a recusant man of letters and a martyr executed brutally during the reign of Elizabeth I. Representing the club's editorial board, I welcomed Walker and Bunt, their two daughters, and their families to the Jesuit community at Loyola University in New Orleans. Walker told me he was particularly pleased to receive an award previously given to Paul Horgan. In the Danna Center, after presenting Walker with a medallion and a scroll, I asked him if he would like to join me and Father Tom Clancy and perhaps one or two others for a roundtable discussion to be televised on the local CBS affiliate owned by Loyola. He seemed hesitant about doing this, and suggested an interview instead. His excuse: television made him look like Dracula.[4]

After another skiing trip, Walker finished the first draft of *The Thanatos Syndrome*, typing the last page on March 27. Except for his annual retreat at Manresa, he spent most of April revising his text.[5] An exhausted Walker relaxed by touring Vicksburg with Bunt, Gwyn, and Shelby; they stayed in an antebellum home, Anchuca. His renewed efforts to build up his marriage meant that he and Bunt would learn to focus their attention on each other in ways sometimes neglected in the past. It would be a slow process requiring effort from both parties. Malcolm Jones, writing in *The New York Times Magazine*, visited Greenwood Plantation with him and caught some of the spontaneous give-and-take between him and Bunt. "Each looks after the other with unobtrusive fondness." Bunt and Walker had aged gracefully, though as Covington journalist Ray Broussard remarked, the polished dome of Walker's forehead was now dusted by fine, ashlike hair.[6] Walker's eyes remained, as before, a study of quietude and affability. Mainly because of his absences, the Thursday lunch group had dwindled considerably, and Lyn Hill, Sheila Bosworth, and Bob Milling all missed Walker's amiable presence. "Well, there we were," Milling recounted to Walker. "Just three of us. A depressingly small number. Lyn said, 'Percy called to say he couldn't decide whether to come to lunch today or slide over to Taco Bell.' 'Finished his book, has he, Lyn?' 'It's at the typist. Can't even decide about Taco Bell,' she said."[7]

Walker took his time before replying to Milling, well aware of the lingering rumors about Hill and him. "I will admit only to fear of becoming just another old fart (which I am), ogling good-looking young (well, fairly young) ladies, which I do."[8] Later, tongue in cheek, Walker amplified his remark: "One reason I can't come regularly is that our four (five?) girlfriends are so ravishingly attractive that after two of Joe's J.D.'s, I am almost certain to behave badly . . . You know as well as I that such behavior ill-befits the illusion of wisdom, maturity and virtue an aging writer should project."[9] Walker gave copies of his novel to Milling, Zoltán Abádi-Nagy, and Linda Hobson. Milling most of all enjoyed the humor and incongruity of certain scenes.[10]

After Walker sent Bob Giroux the corrected typescript in mid-May, he had nothing explicitly pressing to do while he waited for galley proofs. In the meantime, he gave a short talk at a conference organized by the American Booksellers Association.[11] Afterward Bunt and Walker mingled with friends and acquaintances at the New Orleans Museum of Art before having dinner at Sbisa's with Roger Straus, accompanied by Helene Atwan and Bridget Marmion from FSG, who had flown down from New York. One bit of news pleased Roger: Walker said he was thinking about putting together a collection of essays as his next work.[12]

Walker rested during the summer, expending his energies sparingly, in part because of a cataract in his right eye.[13] He again nominated Shelby (seconded by C. Vann Woodward and Elizabeth Spencer) for admission to the Institute of Arts and Letters and read with appreciation Mary Deems Howland's dissertation relating his work to certain themes of Gabriel Marcel.[14] He said he was most grateful to Elizabeth Dale Johnson, another student of Lewis Lawson, who understood what other critics, particularly Patricia Poteat, failed to see: "That because I start with the observables of psychology—uttered words, people (utterer, listener), it doesn't follow that I am a 'behaviorist' or 'deterministic' or whatever."[15] He allowed Professor John Edward Hardy of the University of Illinois at Chicago to read the galleys of *The Thanatos Syndrome* for the book he was writing on Walker's fiction.[16] But he put off until August responding to seventy questions sent to him by Professor Abádi-Nagy.[17]

Before leaving for a short vacation on Pawleys Island with Bunt, Roy, and Sarah, Walker wrote to Cleanth Brooks, saying that he had heard from several sources that Tinkum was not in the best of health.[18] Brooks and his wife were among his "all time favorites," and Walker was distressed to learn that her cancer had spread.[19] Walker called Brooks, proposing that he and Bunt fly to New Haven and take the Brookses on a tour of New England to see the fall foliage. Brooks was deeply touched, but said that in her weakened state Tinkum could not leave the house. Brooks never forgot the affection that Bunt and Walker showed during these dark hours of his life.[20] Walker told Brooks he needed to find some relief from the "postpartum depression and disorientation" he was experiencing after having written "an arduous novel." (If a photo taken of Walker by Monsignor Elmo Romagosa at the fiftieth anniversary of his ordination is any indication of Walker's physical state, then his comments to Brooks were on the mark.)

Though suffering the letdown that accompanies the completion of a book, Walker took one self-corrective measure to get his creative juices flowing again. He wrote a humorous letter in late August to Henry Ford III about the trials and tribulations of changing a tire on his new Mercury

Marquis brougham. He seemed back on track and sent Gwyn and Shelby a smudged typescript of *The Thanatos Syndrome*. He also laid out his future plans: "I have two small tasks to accomplish: (1) write a good novel, (2) correct the Cartesian mind-body split which has screwed up the West for 300 years. Actually (2) will be easier than (1)." He took another vacation in Maine in late September with Bunt, his two brothers and their wives, staying mostly in the area of Tenants Harbor in Penobscot Bay and absorbing the natural beauty of the rocky coastline and the offshore islands. He decided not to accept an invitation to visit Russia, which Yassen N. Zassoursky, dean of the faculty of journalism of Moscow University, had also extended to Eudora Welty and Elizabeth Spencer. His excuse had nothing to do with ideology but with large-bowel complaints.[21] He had visions of combing Moscow for a jar of Metamucil (to which he was addicted) and speaking to students while being overtaken by flatulence. Nor was he inclined to accept an invitation to travel to France, for that matter, to lecture on *The Moviegoer* to English majors at a half dozen universities throughout the country. To prepare these students, the Presses de l'Université de Paris-Sorbonne published a collection of essays on Walker (and Dashiell Hammett) under the title *Deux Regards sur l'Amérique*. Peggy Castex (who had interviewed Walker in August 1981) and Daniel Charbonnier (who would subsequently visit Walker in Covington, camcorder in hand) were among the contributors of informative, scholarly essays in this book.[22] Walker did agree to a discussion, via a satellite hookup, between him and a distinguished panel of French scholars of American literature. I subsequently lectured in France as Walker's substitute. Had he decided to make these two trips, he might have had an interesting impact on Russian and French intellectuals.

Determined to begin his semiotics work, Walker wrote to Professor John N. Deely of Loras College in Dubuque expressing his gratitude for the magnificent translation of John Poinsot's *Tractatus de Signis* by Deely.[23] Walker said he had no competence to deal with the original Latin text.[24] He also felt that the works of Viktor Shklovskij might prove a valuable resource.[25] He received a long letter from Ken Ketner, who attempted to define "novel science" as it pertained to Walker's interest in the Helen Keller phenomenon. Using the categories of Charles Sanders Peirce, Ketner informed Walker that he had depicted in his semiotic essays in *The Message in the Bottle* a series of "dyadic" relationships incorrectly to form a "triadic" one. In effect, Ketner had spotted a key weakness in Walker's understanding of Peirce.[26] Ketner's letter clearly provided a learning moment for Walker, one he could not afford to dismiss. In fact, Ketner reiterated his critique a year later to impress its significance upon Walker: "You seem to be saying, then, that a triadic relation (the whole diagram?) can be made up by a combination of three dyadic relations. Peirce has arguments and considerations all over the place aimed at showing that such cannot be done."[27] Reluctant to change his modus operandi, Walker shifted the discussion back to the notion of the "interpretant," the one word in Peirce's vocabulary he most wanted to understand.

He needed more time to think through his Peirce project as 1987 began. He read and responded favorably to Rodney Allen's *Walker Percy: A Southern Wayfarer*.[28] He lunched in early February with Elinor Ann Walker, a student at Sewanee, and contributed short reflections on Catholicism to two religious periodicals, *Crisis* and *The New Oxford Review*.[29]

Another essay, in *The U.S. Catholic Historian*, which focused on "American Fiction and Catholic Culture," gives a glimpse of what he wanted to develop in his Peirce project: "Being a novelist, a trafficker in words, I find it natural to think of the novelist's task in terms of a semiosis, a dealing, that is, with signs and symbols and sentences." In past golden ages literature and science offered clear and positive answers, but he asked: what sentences remain in a post-Christian age when even scientific sentences have played out? Are any sentences valid? Should one consider Samuel Beckett the modern-day prophet? His characters either say nothing or make no sense to each other. "Here is where it becomes possible for the novelist to entertain the notion, admittedly in a fashion so indirect as to be collusive, that another sort of sentence has begun to acquire validity for his characters, for the post-modern consciousness, even as the positivist propositions fade. It is the sentence conveying news of a certain sort." A novelist, Walker maintained, needs to break out of the solipsism that has haunted the West since Descartes and Kant, even though a novelist has no such authority to "tell" anybody anything—except how it is with his characters.[30] In these remarks, Walker retraced familiar ground; the task before him was to design his arguments carefully using a Peircean template. This was different from starting a novel: he could not let a thesis unravel on its own; he needed to control it in advance. His intermittent attempts to deal with various aspects of his inchoate thesis worked against producing a coherent whole.

Because thousands of French students were studying *The Moviegoer* during the spring semester, the noted publisher Claude Gallimard, at Roger Straus's urging, informed Michelle Lapautre, his firm's representative in France, that he wanted to publish *The Thanatos Syndrome*, *The*

Moviegoer, The Last Gentleman, and *Lancelot* in that order. Lapautre, however, had previously arranged with Editions Rivages to publish *The Moviegoer* and other Percy novels.[31] Since Walker had agreed to the contract with Rivages, Straus told Yannick Guillou at Gallimard how badly he felt that they had made so great an effort to acquire the Percy novels but to no avail.[32] Walker indicated to Straus that he did not want to delay the publication of his books in France—a point of honor with him. Claude Gallimard was of course disappointed that his firm's efforts were totally in vain.[33] Though the decision had been made, Antoine Gallimard wrote to Lapautre rehearsing the sequence of events; on March 17 Gallimard had made a firm offer for *The Thanatos Syndrome* (50,000 francs) and for *The Moviegoer* (30,000 francs). So that Lapautre might clearly understand his feelings, he wrote: *Je regrette que vous n'ayez pas cru devoir le faire et que nous ayons, de ce fait, déployé tant d'efforts en vain* ("I regret that you did not believe there was a need to do this and as a result we have spent so much effort in vain").[34] In reply, Lapautre indicated she had called Yannick Guillou and told him that although Rivages had already made an offer she would consider Gallimard's offer. As it turned out, Gallimard had offered less for *The Thanatos Syndrome,* though more for *The Moviegoer,* than Rivages. Knowing that Rivages agreed to publish three books instead of two (though Gallimard offered an option on the third), Lapautre ended her letter to Gallimard: *Peut-être avons-nous tous eu tort?* ("Were we perhaps all wrong?")[35] In the long run, Walker, who tracked these negotiations carefully, suffered most because he lost the great prestige of being published by Gallimard.

Aside from this situation, Walker had reason to be optimistic about the success of *The Thanatos Syndrome.* He had received an advance of $100,000 from FSG, who planned a first run of 75,000 copies. Contracts for publication in England, Italy, Holland, Germany, and Denmark were also being negotiated. In late spring Fawcett paid an advance of $260,000 for the U.S. paperback rights. The Book-of-the-Month Club agreed to an advance of $7,500 for a dual selection in May, and the Franklin Library contracted to publish a signed first edition.[36] Sensing a potential bestseller, Harcourt Brace Jovanovich had sent one of their senior editors to Covington, but Walker refused their reported offer of $250,000.[37]

As he awaited publication of his novel, Walker replied favorably to my request to become his biographer. During my visit in early March, he gave me free rein to talk to anyone and collect any information I wanted.[38] Formal address soon disappeared and we called each other by first name. As far as he was concerned, his life was an open book. When I returned to New York, it took me a few days to get over the shock of the absolute trust and graciousness of this man toward someone who was a relative stranger.

A week later Henry Kisor of *The Chicago Sun-Times* and his wife, Debby, visited with the Percys to discuss a proposed book about his own deafness and Miss Mirrielees. Unlike Kisor, Ann Percy Moores never felt the need for periodic therapy as an adult. Walker asked Gene Winick to act as Henry Kisor's agent.³⁹ Winick, in turn, sent the manuscript to Roger Straus, who published the book with a foreword by Walker as *What's That Pig Outdoors?: A Memoir of Deafness.*⁴⁰

Walker sat on the porch of the Kumquat for four hours on Saturday, March 28, signing copies of *The Thanatos Syndrome* (dedicated to Bob Coles) for nearly six hundred admirers. When not ringing up sales, Bunt, Simonne ("Woo") Brown, Sheena Dooley, and Irène Rathe took care of sandwiches, cookies, fruit, twenty gallons of punch, and cheese snacks. Walker also signed books at Hugh McCormick's bookstore in Greenville. It was not long before the reviews started appearing. Walker fully expected to receive some hostile ones "since the book is certainly calculated to offend in places."⁴¹ Professor George Garrett of the University of Virginia noted in *The Chicago Tribune* that the detective work by Dr. Tom More and Dr. Lucy Lipscomb paralleled that of epidemiologist John Snow as he searched for the causes of the 1849 cholera epidemic in London; he called the novel a "delightful mystery at the core of the art and craft of Walker Percy." Paul Gray in *Time* wrote a fine review: "The pages Percy devotes to establishing and then fleshing out this mystery are as gripping as any he has ever written." Gray felt the novel embodied Walker's most detailed, explicit attack on contemporary materialism and science. In *The Atlantic Monthly*, Douglas Bauer likewise wrote a laudatory review, saying that "with a little harmless pharmacology these vigilantes of morality are accomplishing in Feliciana parish a kind of, yes, Utopia"—a kind of farcical ordering of one's life. Above all, he found that, in spite of Byzantine melodrama, "the droll Dixie anthropology, the pitch-perfect comic dialogue, the sheer intelligence" were alive throughout the novel. In *America*, I called it Walker's "best and most probing novel to date," since the axis upon which the literary imagination rotates was co-natural with the hermeneutics used in contemporary theology and philosophy. To me, the novel's ending was reminiscent of those in Shakespeare's later comedies since "the Resurrection . . . renders divine all human situations even when they are not perceived this way." I felt the novel revealed outstanding wit, probity, and creativity—hallmarks long associated with Percy's writings. "Nobody presently writing has so keen an eye for the surreal quality of our cultural topography," wrote Sven Birkerts of Harvard in *The New Republic*. *The Thanatos Syndrome* was Number 9 on the *New York Times* best-seller list by April 13. In *The New York Review of Books*, Robert Towers found that the novel lacked the substance of achieved literary art as it spun out of control in the last third, yet he found the book "exhilarating" and likened Walker to a "cool Dostoevsky" and "the adult's Kurt Vonnegut." On the whole the reviews were certainly not as negative as Walker had expected.

In early April, Walker made his twenty-third and last retreat at Manresa ("a lovely period of total silence, recollections, five-mile walks on the levee, plus the old rigorous Ignatian exercises"), this time under the direction of Harold Cooper, S.J.[42] He would not have been such a faithful retreatant had he not experienced these weekends as grace-filled days in which to discover and discern the significance of what he professed.

Because he was known publicly as a Roman Catholic, Catholic editors naturally approached him. In the foreword to Dan O'Neill's *The New Catholics: Contemporary Converts Tell Their Stories*, for example, Walker discussed his own conversion as part of a pilgrimage of grace. He also made his position clear about certain fundamentals of his religious beliefs in a collection entitled *If I Were Pope*: "I think John Paul II is a great Pope and I'd wish to be half as good. In a word, I'd say I agree with his goals of trying to realize the gains of Vatican II while at the same time saving what John XXIII called 'the sacred deposit of faith.' Toward that end I'd take about the same stand as John Paul II toward the enemies of the church, both inside and out."

It was not out of character for Walker to be upset by the op-ed piece in the March 26 *Times-Picayune* by Raymond A. Schroth, S.J., associate professor of communications at Loyola, who initially questioned whether it was appropriate to spend enormous sums for the papal visit to the United States in September. In addition, Father Schroth, a former college dean, felt that a larger issue should be addressed by the Pope and the American bishops: academic freedom and the control of Catholic colleges and universities. For the past two years there had been debate over the efforts of the Vatican's Sacred Congregation for Catholic Education to impose standards and conditions on the 235 Catholic colleges and universities in the United States, norms that, if implemented, would have disastrous consequences, in Father Schroth's mind, for academic freedom, public imaging, and funding. At Catholic University in Washington, for example, attempts were being made to remove the Rev. Charles Curran from his teaching post, even though he was a respected moral theologian. "Many Catholic intellectuals who are dismayed by some of the Pope's policies respect his office, love him as a brother, and admire his vigor, physical courage and concern for the poor," Father Schroth wrote. "They know no moral leader tells people only what they want to hear." Father Schroth suggested that a symposium take place at Xavier University, where the Pope was to address Catholic university presidents from across the country during his visit, rather than having religious and academic leaders read a series of papers to one another. In a democratic society, Father Schroth concluded, truth is most likely to be discovered when it emerges as part of a process of dialogue. Walker would not let this act of apparent disloyalty pass. "It is unusual," he wrote Father Schroth, "to hear a Jesuit refer to a Pope as 'a religious leader' undertaking a 'multi-million-dollar grand tour.' "[43] Walker had always considered the Jesuits the strong right arm of the Apostolic See and he now believed, at least with some American Jesuits, this was no longer the case. "Indeed to judge from the public pronouncements of some Jesuits, they seem more bent on promoting a schism in the U.S. Catholic Church than in advancing the mission of the one, holy, Catholic, apostolic, and Roman Church." Father Clancy wrote Walker saying that Father Schroth's radicalism came strictly from the gut and there was not much point in carrying on a debate with him.[44] Father Schroth replied to Walker, saying he was both honored and saddened by Walker's reaction—honored that he would take time to write him (they had met in 1962 when Walker won the National Book Award) and saddened because Walker did not see what many others saw: "A deeper loyalty to the Pope—a loyalty that dares to try to tell him what he may not want to hear."[45] Father Schroth did not believe that the Church could effectively spread the word of Christ by attempting to silence good men and women who love the Church but may disagree with Rome.

Not unexpectedly, Father Hooty McCown entered the fray. He theorized that the Church of Vatican II was vastly different from the earlier Church. The Church is no bigger than human history, he wrote Walker, and she is moved by the tides and currents of that history. The age of absolute monarchies is gone and the monarchical model of the Church inspired by the model of the Roman Empire was crumbling.[46] Father McCown felt the Pope was an archconservative, trying to turn back Vatican II while saying that he was really implementing it. Very little that the Pope said in his encyclicals, Father McCown maintained, was addressed to the American populace or really stirred anybody. "The Holy Spirit works in them [the bishops], not just in the mind of Pope John

Paul via Cardinal Joseph Ratzinger. All this from-the-top-down correction of theology will paralyze creative thinking, and we are going to be back in the frozen eras before good Pope John." Father McCown knew that Walker had examined the Roman Catholic Church at the time of his conversion, but subsequently the Vatican Council made changes that Walker had not foreseen. Yet "some of the new things, like the new spirit among the Jesuits, do not fit your cherished picture of the church and the Jesuit order." Father McCown maintained he loved the papacy and would die for the institution because Christ established it, but he prayed the present Pope would change his views. Walker appreciated such honesty and had no desire to attack his friend personally: "My only gripe with you," he wrote Father McCown, "was that, with all your denunciations of U.S.-as-imperialist, Pope-as-monarch, etc., you never once uttered one murmur of complaint against the Sandinistas (e.g., attack on civil liberties, closing down of *La Prensa*, etc.)."[47]

Before the Pope's visit to New Orleans, Walker had a chance to give him counsel in an issue of *America* devoted to the topic "If I Had Five Minutes with the Pope": "Do not suppress the Society of Jesus at this time. While it may be true that the Jesuits as a body no longer seem to enlist themselves in the defense of the primacy of the Holy Apostolic See, as they have done traditionally since Loyola and Xavier, it does not necessarily follow that most American Jesuits are working for a schism in the U.S. Catholic Church. Most, I think, are not." Walker felt that the Pope was well understood by Catholics in Louisiana: "We may not know much about such things as 'the importance of the affirmation of social structures and empowerment rather than conversion,' but we understand you." Suffused by common sense, directness, graciousness, and humor, Walker's wisdom appealed to the wide *America* readership, many of whom thought he was addressing their personal concerns and interests.

Though hesitant about a publicity tour, Walker finally gave the thumbs-up.[48] Deirdre Donahue of *USA Today* and Phil McCombs of *The Washington Post* approached Helene Atwan for interviews with Walker.[49] Walker agreed to Bridget Marmion's scheduling: "You must tell me sometime how you do a 45-minute reading in a bookstore. Where do people sit?"[50] In reply, Marmion wrote that anyone standing during Walker's reading would rather be standing there than sitting anywhere else on earth.[51] The Percys flew to New York on April 13. At a Book-of-the-Month Club luncheon the next day, Walker chatted with their staff, as well as his agent Gene Winick and his friend Wilfrid Sheed.[52] Roger Straus III (his father was out of the country), Kristin Kliemann, Helene Atwan, Bridget Marmion, and Bob Giroux represented FSG.[53] That evening Walker read from *The Moviegoer* at Books & Co. on Madison Avenue.

Bunt and Walker flew to Washington for a book signing at Kramerbooks & Afterwords. He was back in New Orleans two days later to deliver his talk, "Another Message in the Bottle," to a session at the Superdome sponsored by the National Catholic Education Association. A bleeding ulcer caused him to cancel further book signings in San Francisco and Seattle.[54]

Jay Tolson, an associate editor of the *Wilson Quarterly*, met with Walker a number of times, and found that the material he had gathered could be used for a biography.[55] Walker had agreed to talk to Tolson, and gradually he began to share aspects of his life, as he also did with Bertram Wyatt-Brown, a professor of history at the University of Florida. Though Tolson and I occasionally met each other, we both sensed that we had different approaches to the subject. Such interest in his life was a sign of Walker's new stature in the literary world.

He and Bunt made their way to Hilton Head, staying with the Milazzos a few days, though Walker grew tired. A low-grade fever persisted most of the summer—a faint signal that his health was slowly about to decline. Walker's general irritability could be seen in a number of letters, but especially in the one he wrote his old friend Dick Faust, attacking his support of President Reagan: "Why do [you] feel obliged to make out Ron Reagan as perfect? Nobody has been perfect since Hitler and Stalin. I find it more useful to think of conservatives as ordinary fucked-up humans with perhaps a good idea or two, and of liberals as perhaps even more fucked-up and hardly an idea beyond good intentions."[56] Part of Walker's malaise was due to his inability to attack the problems of working seriously on his book on semiotics. When Thomas A. Underwood of Harvard interviewed Walker about Allen Tate, Walker told him he now had three possible titles for his book: *The Delta Factor, Thirdness,* or *Contra Gentiles.* He dropped the last title when he realized some readers might think he was writing about the "gentle Contras" of Central America.[57] He mentioned to another interviewer, Robert Cubbage, that he just might write another novel, though his voice lacked conviction. Cubbage found Walker "slightly stooped" when they had a crawfish lunch outside Covington. Walker and Bunt accepted an unexpected invitation to enjoy Chesapeake Bay crabs at the White House in early September at a dinner honoring Prime Minister Ingvar Carlsson of Sweden, vacationed in Maine in October with the Ellises, and attended a family gathering in Atlanta for Hughes Spalding's seventieth birthday.

Seven months had elapsed since Walker had his book-signing party at the Kumquat for *The Thanatos Syndrome* and he began to feel uneasy about the gap between talking about his book of nonfiction and actually writing it. He thought of buying a word processor in order to "settle down to a serious semiotic study," which he now decided would begin not with Peirce but with Poinsot.[58] He did buy a word processor, but gave it to his grandsons. Since Poinsot's Latin and Deely's translation proved difficult to knead into his own prose, Walker reverted to Peirce in developing his thesis:

Charles Sanders Peirce's Thirdness, triadicity, properly understood and properly applied, can go a long way in pointing some right directions for the current mess in which the social sciences find themselves. Or, as Thomas Kuhn puts it in his *The Structure of Scientific Revolutions*, the traditional scientific paradigm (Cartesian and Newtonian), which has been so extraordinarily successful in the physical, chemical, and biological sciences, has proved quite as spectacularly unsuccessful in the so-called social sciences, i.e., the sciences of man *qua* man. As Kuhn expresses it in his own mild way: "Today research in parts of philosophy, psychology, linguistics and even art history, all converge to suggest that the traditional paradigm is somehow askew."[59]

Walker felt stymied by the impenetrable prose of both Peirce and Poinsot. "I wish these goddam semioticists has taken a course in ordinary writing—or had read Hemingway."[60] He wanted someone to draw him a picture—not about the latest theory in the neurology and electrochemistry of the synapses, some nonchemical, nonelectrical agent that one might call a mind or a soul, but about the way the brain operates when someone speaks. Understandably, as he was about to launch into his new work, he decided that his best course would be to read serious books about the problems that Kuhn addressed. Showing great eagerness to be helpful, Ken Ketner quickly provided the appropriate titles.[61]

Walker met with Texan David Duty, with whom he had corresponded intermittently since 1978. Impressed by Duty's comprehension of *The Message in the Bottle*, Walker offered to send him a chapter or two of *Thirdness* to critique.[62] Because Walker never typed this material in final form, it was never sent. In a letter to Jay Tolson in early December, Walker mentioned he was still preoccupied with the Cartesian problem, and as a result, he turned down an invitation to be a principal speaker at the forthcoming Charles Sanders Peirce Sesquicentennial International Congress at Harvard.[63] Was it timidity or insecurity that prompted him to refuse what could have been a major address to prominent semioticians throughout the world? The invitation arrived at the precise moment he was most prepared to communicate his heartfelt convictions on a topic that had preoccupied him, one way or another, since he first published his critique of Susanne Langer's book in 1954. He was convinced, as he wrote to the author of *Altarity*, Mark Taylor, that Derrida and his followers had not succeeded in polishing off Western philosophy but rather had been treed themselves—indeed, they were up an old tree, a split oak named Descartes.[64] For Walker to have succeeded at Harvard, he would have had to acquire new arrows in his semiotics quill, especially a knowledge of Peirce's works on logic and mathematics—a daunting task for even the most devoted scholar. Not long afterward, he informed Roger Straus he was writing a book on semiotics that, in his estimation, would sell "at most 200 copies."[65]

In early December, Cardinal Paul Poupard invited Walker, in the name of the Pope, to become a member of the Pontifical Council for Culture in Rome.[66] This letter was forwarded by Archbishop Pio Laghi, Nuncio in Washington, to Archbishop Hannan, who had recommended Walker in early October to the five-year post.[67] Hannan called Walker just before Christmas and, after having received his positive reply, forwarded the invitation with his own note of congratulation.[68] Walker penned a brief letter of acceptance: "It is an honor and I hope I can be of some use."[69] Walker also wired Cardinal Poupard his acceptance, and asked if Bunt could travel with him at his expense (the Vatican paid for Walker's trip), to which the Vatican agreed. Father Clement J. McNaspy, who had visited Rome the previous year, mistakenly thought that he had been the intermediary securing Walker's nomination to replace Theodore Hesburgh, C.S.C., the recently retired president of Notre Dame University. In this instance, the Vatican functioned more formally than Father McNaspy supposed.

Before flying to Rome in January he called Sheila Bosworth to inquire whether, in her judgment, Bunt should wear a black mantilla when greeting the Pope. Bosworth said she could hear Bunt in the background: "Oh, I'm just a convert. The Pope can't expect me to know all that protocol." In Rome, Walker made his way daily from the Hotel Columbus to 16 Piazza San Calisto, the council's headquarters, where he met the other male representatives (from Egypt, Italy, Benin, Germany, India, Spain, France, England, Peru, and Poland), plus two women (from Japan and Nigeria). Walker now realized, more than ever, that he was part of an international church. To start the meeting, Cardinal Poupard reported on the previous year's activities and then, one by one, each representative spoke. When Walker's turn came on the fifteenth, he began by considering U.S. culture from the perspective of evangelization, and his talk focused on using television as a practical means for this, something Protestants had been utilizing in the South for years. "Americans, I have read, watch five or six hours of television a day—their children even more." The Church had known for a long time the value of television, but because the Catholic sacramental system united matter (water and wine, for example) with words, it tended not to use television to communicate the Good News. Since Walker saw the challenge of secularism, he felt the Church should use television in a manner totally different from that of manipulative televangelists. "By the very virtue of its technique, its instant transmission of word and image, its near total access to the entire population of a modern society, it would be difficult surely to imagine a more perfect instrument through which the Church can teach, inform, indeed evangelize." After they had all spoken on Friday, the members of the council (and family members accompanying them) had a private audience with the Pope. Walker and Bunt shook the Pope's sturdy hand and felt honored to meet a person they had long admired.

Walker caught a rotten cold on the return flight, which was rerouted to St. Louis because of high winds. As a result, he was laid up temporarily with bronchitis.[70] He gave a brief evaluation of his trip to Rhoda Faust: "I'm afraid I didn't learn much from the Pope—who, however, was an impressively sweet, tough man."[71] Walker informed Father Tom Clancy that he went to Rome with a mission: "J.P. II wants advice on what to do about Jesuits."[72] (He shared more about his visit with Father Clancy when they watched their annual football game together.) "I don't have the feeling that I accomplished anything," Walker wrote Monsignor Elmo Romagosa, "but it was more than interesting, meeting fellow Catholics from all over the world, all the way from a lovely black Nigerian to a British lord, straight out of Evelyn Waugh."[73] Walker later corresponded with his fellow councilman Norman A.F. St. John-Stevas, author and chairman of the Royal Fine Arts Commission in England, whose views on religion and society coincided with Walker's.[74]

Since I had received a visiting professorship in English at Loyola, I could now see Walker on a regular basis. Two days after he returned, we lunched at the Winner's Circle. Still basking in a certain glow from having met the Pope, he asked me what I thought of him. I replied that, while I admired him tremendously, I had mixed feelings about the manner in which he became involved in the internal affairs of the Society of Jesus in the early 1980s (it was not a particularly joyous moment for many Jesuits). This answer was not the one he wanted to hear. "You know, Walker," I finally said, using a golf metaphor, "I am in the middle of a sand trap, and no matter what club I use I won't get out gracefully." He laughed and the matter was put aside.

During the first few months of the new year, Walker felt anxious about Mary Pratt, who was experiencing marital problems. Byrne had quit working for Delta a few years before the birth of their first son and started his own business repairing trucks and working on vintage cars; he also dealt in freelance real estate and worked for Baldwin Motors. As a senior at St. Paul's, the last thing their son John Walker wanted to see was his parents' divorce. Walker had to reevaluate his theological stance in trying to be supportive of his daughter.

Because he felt run-down after his return from Rome, Walker had a medical exam, during which a nascent prostate tumor was detected.[75] A general exam at Ochsner Clinic in New Orleans in 1987 had not revealed any medical problem that needed attention. In late January, Walker had a radical prostatectomy, the removal of his prostate—"a dull business," he wrote. "I don't recommend it to anybody."[76] Afterward, Walker lacked energy and needed to rest; he felt "like something the cat dragged in."[77] After an old friend, Georgia Fisher of Greenville, had contacted Walker, he sent her, for the William Alexander Percy Library, one of his three-ring binders from his days at P & S, plus holographic notes of *Thirdness or The Delta Factor*.[78] It is interesting that he parted with this preliminary material, when his habit had been to keep and rework it.

Senator Albert Gore, Jr., had recently asked Walker's support for the nomination of Faye Wattleton ("an extremely distinguished and articulate spokeswoman on abortion and family planning issues," Gore wrote) to the Biomedical Ethics Advisory Board Committee. Even though Walker considered Gore his choice to be the next President of the United States, he adamantly refused to endorse Wattleton.[79] As if his position were not clear enough, he sent to James McFadden of the Human Life Foundation in New York an unpublished letter that he had written to *The New York Times* on January 22 (and again on February 15) concerning the fifteenth anniversary of *Roe v. Wade*, for which he received no acknowledgment. He hoped that McFadden would publish this correspondence.[80] McFadden, in turn, suggested that Walker write a book on the topic.[81]

Bothered by the fact that he needed to urinate frequently, often getting out of bed to do so in the middle of the night, Walker was referred to James Roberts, M.D., a urologist and member of the Tulane medical faculty, who after tests informed Walker that he had cancer and needed an operation; but before that could be done, he needed a preoperation clearance from an internist. On March 8, Walker went to the office of Dr. George Riser in Covington, where further diagnosis revealed that the carcinoma had spread from the area of the prostate to his testicles; five out of six lymph nodes on the right testicle had cancer, as did five out of eight on the left. Walker's reaction to the news seemed matter-of-fact; he did not shy away from discussing his illness. This put his family and friends at ease, especially when he used appropriate medical terminology, which tended to reassure them that he understood the problems and risks involved. Above all, Walker wanted to know the exact nature of the carcinoma, so that he could make any necessary decisions. When he entered St. Tammany Parish Hospital, a short drive from his house and just down the street from Mary Pratt's house, he learned that he had a Grade Three abnocarcinoma. The scale measuring the tumor-node-metastasis stages (TNM) went from one to four, and though Walker's condition was clearly a serious one, his physicians felt that surgery would provide definitive therapy for the cancer, because an evaluation, including a bone scan, indicated that the cancer was localized. Dr. Roberts performed the operation. Dr. Riser, assisted by his partner, Dr. Thomas A. Franklin, carefully monitored Walker's condition on Station Five of the second floor. Word quickly spread about the operation to family and friends, and only those closest to Walker contacted Bunt. Walker went home about a week after the operation. Unfortunately, the operation failed to check the spread of the cancer and further tests revealed that it had entered other lymph nodes. His condition was now serious—at Stage D (the Whitmore-Jewett system measured from A to D). His brief note to Rhoda Faust reveals how well he accepted his condition: "As we used to say in medical school, it always gets you in the end."[82] While at home, Walker had a catheter in place to relieve any discomfort or pain.

In spite of this operation, he continued as much of a normal routine as possible; he saw a few visitors and, as was his custom, drove to town almost daily for his mail. Nor had he given up on his writing, as he informed Ken Ketner: "I am thinking of writing something smart-alecky, presently entitled *Contra Gentiles*. Thesis: The great superstition now is not religion, as generally held, but science or scientism, i.e., the real fuck-up of applying 'dyadic' science to human behavior."[83] He was readmitted to St. Tammany Parish Hospital and had an orchiectomy, the removal of both testicles, on March 24. When I saw him at home a week later, he looked wan, though clearly holding his own; certainly none of the graciousness had disappeared from his demeanor. Though he kept on reading the material that Ken Ketner sent him, his cryptic replies to Ketner (and Charles Fister of Amherst, Massachusetts) did not tell the entire story. "I'd have answered earlier but they threw me down and took out my prostate. Seems to be working out, but it laid me out in good style."[84] By this time, Bunt's genius for coping with Walker's sicknesses had kicked in; she knew instinctively how to create an environment so that he could function and make decisions important to him.

When I lunched with them on May 6, Walker seemed stable. Though the doctors were still trying to decide on the next step of treatment, in no way did Walker indicate that his life was threatened. In fact, I had the opposite impression; a few days earlier he had dined with Ben C. Toledano and Cleanth Brooks; he had also seen Jay Tolson, who was in town interviewing Walker's friends. Curiously, Walker wrote at this time to Don Wetherbee, his high school classmate, relating his condition—a way for him to alert his former friends that his life was, in fact, in jeopardy.[85] He distracted himself by reading and commenting on term papers from one of Ken Ketner's classes.

When I met Walker and Bunt in Jackson on May 26 at the Mississippi Museum of Art, he looked distinguished in his tux. He mingled easily with the guests, including Sarah and Roy; at one point, he carried on a short conversation with two visiting Japanese graduate students, who finally worked up enough courage to ask him to pose for photographs. Since Josephine Haxton, the mistress of ceremonies for the evening, had invited me to accompany her to the banquet, I sat at the head table with her, Bunt and Walker, Eudora Welty (who received a lifetime achievement award), and Suzanne Marrs, a Welty scholar at Millsaps. Welty and Walker spent a good deal of time talking about growing up in Mississippi. After dinner, Haxton introduced Walker, the awardee for fiction. "I still don't know how to answer that perennial question," Walker said. "Why it is that Mississippi produces so many writers. I have no idea, and yet I do not doubt that if I had spent these same years in California or Ohio, I would not be a writer." Throughout his career, Walker disliked being labeled a "Southern writer": yet, except for sections of *The Last Gentleman*, his writing was decidedly Southern, but with an originality that gave a distinctive flavor to his work. Four days after this banquet, Walker, sprawled out on the sofa in his living room, told me that the doctors thought he was making progress. He felt so encouraged that he intended to study more carefully the works of Allan Bloom, whom he admired, in order to integrate his findings into his semiotics project.

In late May, Walker agreed to accept the 18th Jefferson Award in Washington, one of the highest intellectual honors the U.S. government can bestow on a citizen, carrying a stipend of $10,000. Ellis Sandoz, a distinguished professor of political science at LSU, editor of Eric Voegelin's *Autobiographical Reflections*, and a consultant for the National Endowment for the Humanities, had recommended Walker at the urging of Lewis Simpson. Lewis shared this good news with Jo Gulledge, who now lived south of Washington.[86] Walker also felt strong enough to accept Governor Buddy Roemer's six-year-term appointment of him to the board of supervisors for LSU, after Bob Milling's sister-in-law had proposed Walker's name.[87] He was so stunned by the political brokering that took place at a meeting of the new board in June that he quickly submitted his resignation. As a result, Walker's mail decreased as students realized he would no longer be in a position to influence the awarding of LSU scholarships.

For six nights in mid-July, Walker and Bunt retreated to Eseeola Lodge as part of a three-week vacation in the mountains of western North Carolina; they wanted to visit the Sprunts on Grandfather Mountain and the Spangenbergs in Cashiers, yet have a certain amount of privacy at the same time. Jaye and Phin managed to spend some time with them too. Sadamichi Kato, associate professor at the Center for Linguistic and Cultural Research at Nagoya University in Japan, traveled to Highlands to interview Walker.[88]

Walker's health was not improving, and by late August he was getting over a bout of fever.[89] By early September, he wrote to Dannye Romine that he seemed physically better. "Seems as of now they got it all out. At any rate no signs of recurrence."[90] But there were more tests at Ochsner and a low-grade fever that made him feel constantly "crummy."[91] Though tired from babysitting David and Jack, while Ann and John went to the mountains for a week, Walker felt strong enough to start writing his Jefferson Lecture. "I am working on a lecture-article," he wrote Ken Ketner, "presently entitled 'Science, Religion and the Tertium Quid'—the Tertium Quid being Peirce's triad being considered as an *event*, e.g., an eighteen-month-old naming for the first time, the assertion of any sentence."[92]

Walker again took out his tux to receive the T. S. Eliot Award, one of the Ingersoll Prizes in Literature and the Humanities, at the Drake Hotel in Chicago on the evening of November 4. John A. Howard, president of the Ingersoll Foundation, and Thomas Fleming, executive director, had met with Walker in Covington on different occasions to encourage him to receive the award and a check for $15,000. Walker's talk, "Physician as Novelist, or Why the Best Training for a Novelist in These Last Years of the Twentieth Century Is an Internship at Bellevue or Cook County Hospital, and How This Training Prepares Him for Diagnosing T. S. Eliot's 'The Waste Land,' " provides a fine summary of his career. "But let us speak of vocations," he began. "What one ends up doing with one's life is surely one of God's mysteries. A good deal of luck, good luck and bad luck, is involved as well as, I firmly believe, God's providence." Essentially an autobiographical talk, Walker avoided using the word "I" and posited, instead, a stranger—novelist, pilgrim, news bearer—to be the vehicle for his views. "Like all artists, he is interested, not in edifying, but in discovering and pointing out and naming certain sectors of reality, both within oneself and outside oneself, which had gone unnoticed. Whereupon he, the novelist's character, is free, as only a man can be free, to act accordingly." The import of Walker's conclusion most likely escaped his listeners: a novelist who has studied medicine has a nose for pathology, and when he sees that something is wrong, he can diagnose it, toward the end that "the patient might at least have hope, and even in the end get well."

Walker labored over the composition of his Jefferson Lecture. In early December he sent Ken Ketner a forty-one-page draft, a text that would differ considerably from the lecture he finally delivered. At this point, Walker was not sure whether he should stick with a lecture on Peirce's semiotic or write something lighter about storytelling.[93] Before Christmas, he made an important decision: rather than write a book on semiotics, he would gather occasional pieces. As he wrote to Martha Lacy Hall, it "doesn't look like a book to me, or not a real book. So I'm marking time."[94] Not long afterward, he spoke by phone to Michael Swindle, who was writing an essay for the *New Orleans* magazine, "At Court with Walker Percy," indicating that he was working on a collection of essays and talks on semiotics that had not been included in *The Message in the Bottle*. When I lunched twice with Walker before the end of the year, both times I found him alert and responsive, and especially eager to see President Reagan step down from office.

Walker and Bunt spent five days in early January 1989 with Sarah and Roy, who were celebrating their fiftieth wedding anniversary at a condo on Perdido Key, not far from Pensacola, Florida. When he returned, Walker mailed off three short pieces on Catholicism (first, an essay entitled "Holiness of the Ordinary" to the alumni magazine at Boston College, and second, a foreword to *The New Catholics*, edited by Dan O'Neill). In his third, a reply to "Why Are You a Catholic?," written for a collection of essays entitled *Living Philosophies*, edited by Clifton Fadiman, Walker had lost none of his honesty and humor:

When the subject of religion does arise, at least in the South, the occasion is often an uncivil one, a challenge or a provocation or even an insult. It happens once in a while, for example, that one finds oneself in a group of educated persons one of whom, an educated person of a certain sort, may venture some such offhand remark as

"Of course the Roman Catholic Church is not only a foreign power but a fascist power"

or, when in a group of less educated persons, perhaps in a small town barbershop, one of whom, let us say an ex-member of the Ku Klux Klan—who are not bad fellows actually, at least hereabouts, except when it comes to blacks, Jews, and Catholics—when one of them comes out with something like

"The Catholic Church is a piece of shit,"

then one feels entitled to a polite rebuttal in both cases, in the one with something like, "Well, hold on, let us examine the terms, power, foreign, fascist—" and so on, and in the case of the other responding in the same tone of casual barbershop bonhomie with, say, "Truthfully, Lester, you're something of a shit yourself, even for white trash—" without in either case disrupting, necessarily, the general amiability.

His major preoccupation was in writing the Jefferson Lecture, a draft of which he showed to both Jay Tolson and me. Tolson, in turn, shared his copy with friends. As part of the preparation for writing this lecture, Walker had begun reading *Semiotic and Significs*, the correspondence of Peirce and Victoria Lady Welby.[95] His work was interrupted, however, by a short stay in the hospital, where doctors dealt with his chronic stricture of the esophagus ("probably too much Early Times in UNC," he wrote Ken Ketner[96]). Still feeling "somewhat poorly," Walker was pleased that Ketner wanted to dedicate to him a volume containing Peirce's Cambridge Conferences Lectures.[97] Upon reflection, Walker had some second thoughts about this dedication. "As you well know, I am not a student of Peirce. I am a thief of Peirce. I take from him what I want and let the rest go, most of it. I am only interested in Peirce insofar as I understand his attack on nominalism and his rehabilitation of Scholastic realism."[98] If Ketner wanted to dedicate the book to him, he could do so with the understanding that Walker admired, at the most, 1 percent of this collection (about two pages), and with the understanding that such a dedication would cause Peirce to spin in his grave. In spite of this, Walker relished the idea of using Peirce as the foundation of his Christian apologetic, still "tentatively entitled (after Aquinas) *Contra Gentiles*."

In early March, Walker sent his twenty-eight-page lecture to John McGrath at the NEH in Washington.[99] Yet it was far from finished, since it would go through a process of careful revision by Walker and others.[100] But it was too late to incorporate some of the ideas about the relationship between semiotics and the structure of the brain that he read in the book-in-progress by Robert Eckert of Rochester, New York. In Eckert, Walker recognized a projection of himself. "You remind me of me—one can really get hooked on this."[101] In some ways, the questions that Eckert asked were closer than Ken Ketner's to the ones that Walker grappled with, precisely because Eckert was trying to find connections between semiotics and neurology—a subject at the heart of Walker's quest. Likewise, John R. Hadd, who had worked nearly thirty years as a senior policy analyst for the federal government, wrote to Walker out of the blue about semiotics and the contemporary creationist-evolutionist argument: "At the point where origin of human language comes to the fore, I want to include the strongest possible reference to *The Message in the Bottle* and its impact. How would you suggest the influence of *The Message in the Bottle* be characterized?"[102] Though Walker had finished writing his Jefferson Lecture, he still liked this type of dialogue, but he found it fatiguing to respond in depth. He read with great interest Hadd's book-in-progress, entitled *Pointing* ("the best summary I've seen of the case against mechanistic Darwinism"[103]). Like Eckert, Hadd entered Walker's life too late for him to undertake a fruitful correspondence; these exchanges do reveal, however, that Walker intellectually desired to grow and discuss topics that sincerely interested him.

That spring Paul Horgan proposed (and Cleanth Brooks and Richard Wilbur seconded) the nomination of Walker for the Gold Medal for Fiction at the American Academy. In addition, Horgan asked Walker to write an afterword to his fictional "Richard Trilogy." "I am happy to do it and only hope I can do them justice," Walker replied.[104] Walker was glad to learn that Horgan was well. "I'm perking along," he said about his own health. His tribute to Horgan's trilogy was written with reverent admiration.

At the Chattanooga conference of Southern writers in early April, Walker, in an interview with Rebekah Presson, discussed Binx Bolling in a new way, one reflective of both his TB recuperation at Trudeau and his present deteriorating health: "So maybe my character in *The Moviegoer*, Binx Bolling's moviegoing was something like my lying in bed in upstate New York for two years. There was a crisis in life in the sense of what to do with one's life. You raise an interesting question of whether the background of death has something to do with it."[105]

In Washington, NEH staff member Susan Metts greeted Bunt, Walker, Ann, and her two sons and escorted them to the Henley Park Hotel on Massachusetts Avenue.[106] Plans had been made for a private lunch with Lynne V. Cheney, chairwoman of NEH, in addition to a forum with members of the Council on the Humanities and the NEH staff. William Bennett, the drug czar, requested a meeting with Walker in the West Wing of the White House. There would be interviews with Danielle Herubin of the States News Service and Brent Short, a librarian at the Catholic University of America. The Percys had also arranged to have dinner with Betsy O'Brien. Though Walker was accommodating, Bunt thought maybe too much had been planned.

The Jefferson Lecture in the Humanities was established in 1972 to provide an opportunity for an eminent scholar or writer to explore matters of broad concern. Among the previous lecturers in the series were Robert Penn Warren, Saul Bellow, and John Hope Franklin. From my perspective in the last row of the large auditorium on Constitution Avenue on May 3, it looked as if every seat was taken. It was not difficult to spot celebrities, including Judge Robert Bork and Secretary of Defense Dick Cheney. At 8 p.m., Walker walked onstage with Robert Hollander of Princeton and Lynne Cheney. The audience applauded enthusiastically. As he formally introduced Walker, Hollander mentioned that he had gone to the Firestone Library at Princeton and found that all of Walker's works had been checked out—a sure sign of popularity. As he approached the podium, Walker looked a bit lost. Behind him were three empty chairs and fourteen pillars, creating the appearance of a large Roman temple. He adjusted the microphone, shifted his posture a bit, and fidgeted with his glasses several times. He read from his prepared text, rarely taking cognizance of the audience. At times, he slurred a word here and there. It was a long and serious lecture. It took a while for the audience to catch the drift of his argument, but once they did (if they did), they settled back.

His title was "The San Andreas Fault in the Modern Mind," a comprehensive summary of his approach to semiotics. It might be considered an outline of the book on semiotics he had desperately wanted to write. He began with two propositions: "One is that our view of the world, which we get consciously or unconsciously from modern science, is radically incoherent. A corollary of this proposition is that modern science is itself radically incoherent, not when it seeks to understand things and subhuman organisms and the cosmos itself, but when it seeks to understand man, not man's physiology or neurology or his blood stream, but man *qua* man, man when he is peculiarly human. In short, the sciences of man are incoherent. The second proposition is that the source of the incoherence lies within science itself as it is presently practiced, and that the solution of the difficulty is not to be found in something extra-scientific, like New Age religion, but within science itself."

With the word "science" Walker referred to its root meaning—the discovery and knowing of something that can be demonstrated and verified within a community. Walker was not raising the standard humanistic objections to science—that it is too impersonal, detached, or abstracted, or that it does not meet human needs or take into account such human experiences as emotions, art, or faith. He did not want to challenge science in the name of humanism. "No, my purpose is rather to challenge science, as it is presently practiced by some scientists, *in the name of science*." Above all, Walker wanted scientists to consider language not as a formal structure but as a natural phenomenon, asking where it came from and what to make of it in anatomical, physiological, and evolutionary terms.

He also wanted to find the linking entity between mind and object. "Peirce's insistence on both the reality and nonmateriality of the third element—whatever one chooses to call it, interpretant, mind, coupler— is of critical importance to natural science because its claim to reality is grounded not on this or that theology or metaphysics but on empirical observation and the necessities of scientific logic." Walker desired to link all of this not in terms of a theological premise, nor as an item in a linguistic structure, but from the stance of natural science, the science of man, as something out there to be made sense of as one makes sense of a sunset or a bird migration. When he finished, the audience gave him a standing ovation. Few could doubt that Walker had presented his case clearly and without any rhetorical flourishes, but *The Washington Post* reported the next day that for most listeners it was over their heads. As Phil McCombs wrote: "It was one of them innerleckshul speeches, and not everyone got it." McCombs felt that Walker "got off some nice lines," but "those triad and dyads, and Heidegger, Marcel, Sartre, Buber—ye gods, minds were reeling all over the Departmental Auditorium." An unfortunate hillbilly piece in a prominent newspaper.

Not far from me sat the young novelist Madison Smartt Bell. "For what to me is a long, long time," he wrote Walker, "your essays have had a central place in what I like to call my thinking. So it was a pleasure to get to hear some of the same ideas delivered live and in person."[107] After the lecture, many in the audience walked across the street to a reception held in the Smithsonian's National Museum of American History. Clearly the evening had fatigued Walker; Bob Giroux asked Bunt to persuade Walker to sit down. He both stood and sat as he greeted an endless queue of well-wishers.

For weeks Ken Ketner had looked forward to his meeting with Walker. The day after the lecture, he and his friend Herbert Huser arrived at the Henley Park an hour in advance of their rendezvous. Ketner and Huser had lunch in the hotel restaurant, and almost missed meeting Walker, who walked by them unnoticed. Fortunately, Ketner and Walker were able to spend an hour together in Gompers Park, though Ketner felt awkward in the presence of someone he so admired. Walker later told Bunt how pleased he was with his conversation with Ketner: "Bunt, this man knows what I'm getting at."

Again showing courage and graciousness, Walker and Bunt traveled to the University of Notre Dame in order that he might receive the Lae- tare Medal at the commencement ceremony. There was an additional reason for going—it gave the Percys a chance to meet with classmate Frank Hardart and his family. Walker had telephoned Hardart in advance: "Hey, Sping, do you know anything about this Laetare Medal? A guy at Notre Dame called me up and wants to give it to me." (Walker's great-uncle John Johnson Spalding [1865–1939], a successful Atlanta lawyer, had been presented the medal in 1928.) After sitting through a lengthy graduation ceremony, Walker was finally introduced by Edward A. Malloy, C.S.C., the president of the university, and presented with the famous medal. In his brief words of acceptance, he recalled that his father loved football and would get tickets to many university games— Alabama, Georgia, Ole Miss, Tennessee—and then one came for Notre Dame. "What is that?" Walker asked. "I don't recall his giving me any satisfactory explanation of what it meant." When Walker mentioned that his friend Frank Hardart had graduated from Notre Dame, the Hardart cheering gallery screamed. Walker found it touching that a university, a community of scholars, and a great football team are all identified by the same two words: Our Lady.

The first thing Walker did when he returned to Covington was to meet with students in the Senior Advanced Placement English Class at St. Paul's.[108] Walker read a passage from *The Thanatos Syndrome*. When he finished, he asked, "What's going on here?" The students glanced around nervously and their looks said, "You wrote it. Why ask us?" Then someone ventured an opinion: "You're talking about loss of self and the things that make one essentially human." "Could you interpret the book as being a warning?" their teacher, Judith LaCour, asked. "You're damn right," Walker said. "We need to be wary of our technology. My job is just to raise a few questions, to annoy some, to irritate some. If I can get under some people's skins, I'm satisfied." As he concluded, Walker looked around the room. "This is where the hope lies— with you guys, not with us." It was the last class that Walker ever taught.

During May, Walker had a CAT scan at St. Tammany Parish Hospital, which revealed enlarged lymph nodes, and thus he was placed on a drug, Flutamide, which regulated the development of male hormones as a way of counteracting the progressive cancer.[109] Subsequent tests in early June showed that the Prostate Specific Antigen (PSA) had increased from twenty-eight to thirty-eight. When I spoke to him on June 10, he told me that prostate cancer was one of the easiest cancers to cure. He felt well enough, he said, to work on his afterword to Paul Horgan's book. But the medical situation was actually less optimistic. Prostate cancer that does not respond to hormonal treatment is, in fact, difficult to treat. Walker was referred to the Mayo Clinic for additional therapy.

His report to Shelby Foote was a truer evaluation: "Not much good news here. I've been having some abdominal and back pain for the past few weeks. Thought it was my periodic diverticulitis. Went to hospital last week for exam. Colon was normal, but there were masses around the aorta and along the spine. Don't know what it is, but presumably it's metastases from prostate carcinoma or pancreatic." Further exams revealed that he had also developed cancer in one of the lumbar vertebrae. Shelby sent Walker a copy of Chekhov's "The Bishop," which Walker considered "nothing short of miraculous." Since Walker began to see that he could not work on his semiotics project, he encouraged Ken Ketner to pick up the gauntlet and write a biography of Peirce.[110]

By early July, Walker was on chemotherapy. "I feel O.K.," he wrote Ann Trousdale, "and don't mind it but I need time to write a book."[111] To secure a second opinion, Walker and Bunt flew to Baltimore, where a urologist at Johns Hopkins Hospital confirmed Dr. Roberts's prognosis. At this point, Dr. Riser phoned Ronald W. Lewis, M.D., a friend on the staff of the Mayo Clinic in Rochester, Minnesota. Dr. Lewis replied that at Mayo physicians were using a new protocol involving interferon and he would be glad to see Walker. Though not an oncologist, Dr. Riser understood the experimental nature of the research being conducted at Mayo. Once Walker started going to Mayo, Dr. Riser did not consider himself his primary physician. Either medicine would cure Walker or it would not; he resigned himself to God's will. On July 27, he called his friend Father Val McInnes, who had written to Walker about seeing the sun whirl in Dubrovnik after visiting the site of an apparent Marian apparition. "Yes," the Dominican reiterated to Walker, "the sun spun in a counterclockwise way, with beautiful colors trailing off from the spin." Walker was deeply moved—and mystified—by these words, but he asked for no miracles. On July 29 he gave Shelby an honest evaluation of his situation:

No, we're headed for Mayo's tomorrow—on the strength of a new drug combo (something called interferon and 5-FU [5-fluorouracil]) said to be promising in some cancers . . . I'll tell you what I've discovered. Dying, if that's what it comes to, is no big thing since I'm ready for it, and prepared for it by the Catholic faith which I believe. What is a pain is not even the pain but the nuisance. It is a tremendous bother (and expense) to everyone. Worst of all is the indignity. Who wants to go to pot before strangers, be an object of head-shaking for friends, a lot of trouble to kin? I know the answer to this, of course; false pride—who are you to be too proud to get the way of all flesh—or as you would write on the chart at Bellevue: "—the patient went rapidly downhill and made his *exitus*."

. . . Like I say, it's too damn much trouble, this running around looking for a cure. I'm content to sit here and try to finish *Contra Gentiles*, a somewhat smart-ass collection of occasional pieces, including one which should interest you. "Three new signs, all more important than and different from the 59,018 signs of Charles Sanders Peirce." You want a copy?

The seven trips that Walker and Bunt took to Mayo were naturally filled with apprehension for both. Assigned to Dr. Lawrence Kvols, Walker initially explained that he had pain in his back and legs and that he had lost two or three pounds during the previous month; the morphine he had been taking seemed to be working. Dr. Kvols found his patient to be in good spirits, and at every step, he included Bunt in their discussions. One good sign was that a bone scan at Mayo came out negative; it was thought that pinched nerves might be the cause of the pain in the back and legs. Since Walker understood the nature of the pilot study he was part of—to see what doses of interferon and FU-5 could be administered effectively to human beings—he willingly accepted the risks of this first eight-day treatment. At Mayo, Walker felt the side effects of these treatments: temperature spikes, sometimes elevating his temperature to 102 degrees, followed by chills, lethargy, and fatigue. In spite of this, he had a revelation when he saw children with cancer waiting in the patients' lounges. He knew then and there that he would continue the treatment at Mayo as long as he could, so that the results of his treatment might someday be of value to others.

Scholars, many of them known to Walker, participated in the first international conference on Walker Percy in Sandbjerg, Denmark. Organizers Jan Nordby Gretlund and Karl-Heinz Westarp had invited Walker, who of course could not come. He wrote in the foreword to the published proceedings that, if he had come, he would have felt like Banquo showing up at Macbeth's feast.

After Walker had blood tests at St. Tammany Parish Hospital to monitor his condition, Dr. Riser called Dr. Kvols to say that Walker's pain was better and he seemed to be responding well to treatment. By the time of his second visit to Mayo in early September, his PSA count had fallen from sixty-five to twenty-one. Rather than stay at the Kahler Hotel, Bunt and Walker roomed in the Clinic View Inn, which had a kitchenette and offered more privacy. During this visit, Dr. Riser flew to Rochester to consult with Dr. Kvols. In flying back with the Percys in a private plane that Roy had secured, Dr. Riser briefed Walker about the tests that would be administered locally. By mid-September he felt that his doctors "seem to be doing some good" and he was determined to return to Mayo.[112] By the time of his fourth visit in late October, Dr. Kvols reported to Walker that his system was tolerating the interferon well and that he need not stay for the entire eight days—good news for the family, who now knew that their time with Walker was precious.

Shortly before Thanksgiving, Jonathan Potter, a graduate of Whitman College in Walla Walla, Washington, made his way to Covington. He had written Walker twice, with the hope of being able to talk to him, but had received no reply.[113] When he arrived by bus, thick fog and rain enveloped the town. Undaunted, he walked the streets, imagining he was Helen Keller in search of Annie Sullivan. By chance he spotted the Kumquat, where Sheena Dooley told him that Walker was not well but still signed books on request. When he arrived at the bookstore the next day, Sheena said she had just spoken to Walker, who was coming to town for a dental appointment and would stop by. Potter waited and waited and decided Walker would not come. Disheartened, he walked to the filling station to wait for the bus. Suddenly a pickup pulled over and a figure inside asked, "Is this where the bus comes?" Potter went over and introduced himself.

"Well, let me park over here and we'll go inside. Did you get my letter?" Walker asked.

"No, I must have missed it."

"I have to apologize for my bad behavior."

"Oh no, not at all."

"This old cancer cropped up a while ago."

As they talked in the gas station, Walker said the only writing he was doing was "a journal he kept during Lent last year"—the offshoot of his Peirce project. For Bunt this was one of his most inspiring efforts; she called it his *Lenten Journal*. Walker asked Potter what he was going to do now.

"Well, catch the train in New Orleans tomorrow and go to Florida."

"I mean, what are you going to do with your life?"

"Probably finish my M.A. degree and then find a teaching job."

"I'm glad I caught you before you left. Say hello to your father for me. He sent me your essay on *The Moviegoer*." When the bus arrived, Potter gathered up his pack and tried to say something memorable, but could only stammer inarticulate syllables. He climbed aboard and looked back as Walker departed into the rain. When Potter opened the copy of *The Moviegoer* Walker had placed in his hands, it was inscribed: "For Jonathan Potter, All best, from one pilgrim to another—(i.e., *re* Search)."

During Walker's fifth trip to Mayo after Thanksgiving, Dr. Kvols realized that Walker might not be responding as well as he had hoped.

The question became crucial: how long should treatment be continued? By late December, the answer had been partially given. Though Dr. Kvols stopped the use of oral morphine, it was clear that Walker could not continue indefinitely flying to Mayo for the monitoring of his treatment. It was simply too taxing on his system. When Walker checked out of the Kahler and flew back with Bunt to the subfreezing weather in Covington, he knew that he would have little chance of recovery.

As 1990 began, St. Tammany Parish Hospital announced that it had inaugurated the Hospice of St. Tammany to provide alternatives for traditional acute care for the dying. Nurses, social workers, clergy, and trained volunteers would assist the primary-care physicians in the treatment of their patients at home. It was welcome news to the Percys, though they were not quite sure they would have to call on the hospice. As they did the previous year, Bunt and Walker and Sarah and Roy spent a few days at Perdido Key.

Walker and Bunt made their seventh, and last, trip to Mayo, leaving New Orleans in late January. During their stay, Walker continued having night sweats and back pain. Dr. Kvols ordered a sputum test to see if there was a recurrence of TB. A CAT scan showed the extent to which cancer had penetrated the lymph nodes, and a bone scan showed that it now was present in the thoracic vertebrae. As a result, chemotherapy, interferon, and 5-FU were discontinued. Primary in the minds of all concerned was the quality of life that Walker would experience throughout this ordeal and how to create a therapy that would give him most of what was needed. After further consultation, Dr. Kvols told Walker that Ochsner could provide local radiation, a sign that indicated that Mayo had given him all the therapy they could. Radiation was a treatment of last resort for Walker. During March he received twenty-five separate radiation treatments; it meant that he spent most of that month on the causeway driving back and forth with Bunt or George Cross. To control the pain on a continual basis, Walker was provided with a small pump and catheter, which sent small doses of morphine directly into his spinal cord.

Walker and Bunt had been received as oblate members of the Benedictine order at the abbey in mid-February. Because of their new affiliation, they were able to purchase a plot in the abbey cemetery.[114] More so now than ever before, Bunt kept vigil, monitoring phone calls and requests for visits. Naturally, close friends and relatives were welcome. Yet Walker attended one of the regular Wednesday lunches and managed to go to Nikki Barranger's for one of the Great Books discussions. Archbishop Hannan paid a visit. I was invited to dinner on Palm Sunday, April 8; Walker talked freely about his health and showed me the catheter pack. At table, the conversation flowed back and forth quite normally. Maur Robira, O.S.B., assistant pastor at St. Peter's, administered the sacrament of the sick to Walker at home on April 27.

When word came that Walker had taken a turn for the worse and needed more and more bed care, Gwyn and Shelby arrived, and stayed at the Holiday Inn. Sarah and Roy drove from Greenville and stayed upstairs in the Cajun cottage. Mary Pratt and John Walker Lobdell, Ann and Jack and David Moores discreetly helped as much as they could, fixing meals and answering the phone. Robert Lobdell was away on naval maneuvers. Haydée and Steve Ellis, too, were generous with their time and energy. When John Moores spoke to Walker, he told him something that he had wanted to say for a long time: he had converted to Catholicism. Phin and Jaye drove over every afternoon and Camille and Will, their grown children, would often bring soup and catered foodstuffs. Partly to distract Walker from his pain, Will persuaded Walker to write to Bruce Springsteen, the rock singer, but the letter remained unanswered.

Because Walker tended to face the wall in his bed in the master bedroom, he was moved to the second bed in the room. All waited patiently, entering the bedroom when appropriate but never intruding. Bunt made sure that either she or Roy or Phin was attentive to Walker at all times. Since Valium had been dissolved and administered with his intravenous liquids, Shelby sometimes could not tell whether Walker was awake or asleep. Though in and out of consciousness, Walker listened to radio talk shows, as he had done most of his adult life. As nurse Barbara Dominique and three aides spelled one another, they were met at the front door by the two dogs: Sweet Thing, a corgi, and Luke, a Doberman pinscher. Keenly attached to Walker and sensing that something was wrong with him, Luke once bit Mrs. Dominique.

Prompted by a letter he had received, Walker rallied sufficiently to call Gene Winick two days before he died to inform him that he had given the dramatic rights to *Lost in the Cosmos* to William Sessions of Georgia State University and his friend Thomas Key, who had long been fans of Walker.[115]

Walker died at 3:40 on the afternoon of May 10 of metastatic carcinoma of the prostate, attested to by Dr. Riser, who signed the death certificate. His "legacy," a word that Ann had inscribed above the front door of the Kumquat, would be far-reaching. To cite but one example, the year after he died, a Walker Percy scholarship was established at St. Paul's and given first to Timothy D. Kimbrell. The memorial plaque reads: "This is where the hope lies—with you guys, not with us."

APPENDICES

NOTES

BIBLIOGRAPHY

INDEX

APPENDICES

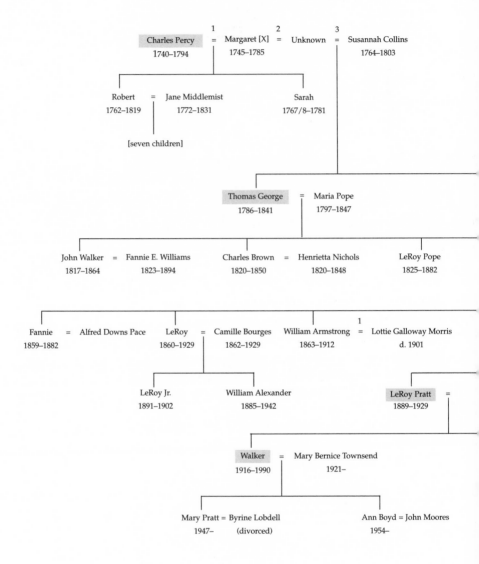

Percy Family Genealogy (Selective)

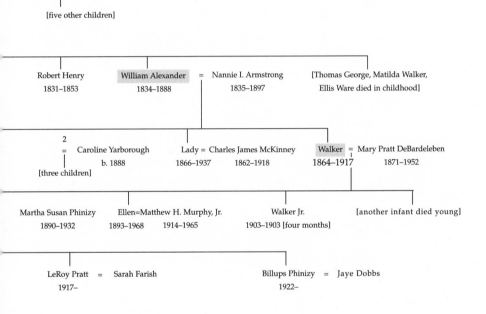

[five other children]

Robert Henry · 1831–1853

William Alexander · 1834–1888 = Nannie I. Armstrong · 1835–1897

[Thomas George, Matilda Walker, Ellis Ware died in childhood]

2 = Caroline Yarborough · b. 1888
[three children]

Lady = Charles James McKinney · 1866–1937 · 1862–1918

Walker = Mary Pratt DeBardeleben · 1864–1917 · 1871–1952

Martha Susan Phinizy · 1890–1932

Ellen=Matthew H. Murphy, Jr. · 1893–1968 · 1914–1965

Walker Jr. · 1903–1903 [four months]

[another infant died young]

LeRoy Pratt = Sarah Farish · 1917–

Billups Phinizy = Jaye Dobbs · 1922–

Percy Family History

William ("Will") Alexander Percy portrays himself in *Lanterns on the Levee* as writing a "pilgrim's script" or "one man's field-notes of a land not far but quite unknown"—a theme that greatly influenced Walker Percy in his novels. This book was published less than a year before Will's death in January 1942. Will Percy wanted to tell the story of "his people": "So while the world I know is crashing to bits, and what with the noise and the cryings-out no man could hear a trumpet blast, much less an idle evening reverie, I will indulge a heart beginning to be fretful by repeating to it the stories it knows and loves of my own country and my own people."[1] Though he focused on the demise of the Reconstruction governments in the 1870s and the rise of populism twenty years later, reflecting the last hold of the cult of the Confederacy on the South even as Northern businessmen were creating new industries and class divisions, he nevertheless felt, particularly as his health declined, an inner imperative to communicate his family history.[2]

The Percy name itself (with variants of Pearcy, Peirsey, Percey, Percie, Percye, Persie, Piercy, and Piersey—perhaps even Peirce, as in Charles Sanders Peirce) is one of the oldest in English history, dating back at least to Manfred, a Dane, and his son Galfred, who settled in the Province of Maen in Normandy.[3] Will Percy once visited one of the Northumberland Percys, but they could not establish any relationship.[4] We do know that in 1776 Charles Percy, who was born in the British Isles, sailed to St. Eustatius (Dutch West Indies) with Dr. Robert Dow and later became an *alcalde* (local judge) under the Spanish government, in what is now Wilkinson County, Mississippi, near Fort Adams. In September 1779 the King of England granted him 600 acres of land.[5] Before long, he set about clearing the lands that had been granted to him, planting indigo and other crops.[6] Charles's first wife, Margaret, thought to be French, was born in 1745, died in London forty years later, and was buried there with her daughter,

Sarah (according to the Register of Deaths of St. Giles Parish). They also had a son, Robert, born in 1762 in Kilkenny, Ireland, who entered the British Navy as a young boy.

Robert started his career in 1770 as a captain's helper on the HMS *Canceaux*, which arrived in Boston the following August. Plying back and forth during the American War of Independence between England and New England and Canada, he served on the *Albany, La Sophie, Prince William Henry,* and other ships until finally he became commander of the *Lord Nelson*, whose service he left in 1801. In a letter written from London to Dr. Dow in New Orleans, dated September 25, 1791, Robert relates an unfortunate situation: "I have been struck off the List of Lieutenants for not being home last year, agreeable to the advertisements from the Lords of the Admiralty, they have been pleased to restore me again with my rank but have stopt nine months half-pay that was due me."[7] In 1796 Robert married Jane (sometimes referred to as Jean) Middlemist, a native of Edinburgh, Scotland, in London's St. George's Church. They had seven children. After his naval service, Robert sailed again to the United States in 1802 on the chartered schooner *Bilboa* and settled near Fort Adams. He eventually moved to West Feliciana Parish, Louisiana, acquired a 2,200-acre plantation called Beech Woods (located on the west bank of Big Bayou Sara, about twelve miles from St. Francisville on the old Percy Road), and became a cotton farmer.

In January 1823 Lucy Blakewell Audubon, the wife of the famous naturalist and artist, arrived at Beech Woods at the invitation of widow Jane Percy. She and her son, John, remained there for four years, partly through the good graces of William Provan, M.D., who had married Sarah Percy and arranged a post for Lucy as mistress of the plantation school.[8] Audubon was not always a welcome presence at Beech Woods, perhaps because his portrait of the two Percy girls was negatively criticized by Mrs. Percy; she thought Audubon had given her daughters jaundiced complexions.

Robert Percy was also created a Spanish *alcalde* by Governor Don Carlos de Grand Pré and participated in the West Florida Rebellion of 1810 against Spanish rule. He became a member of the first high judiciary of West Florida, along with Fulwar Skipwith and Shepherd Brown.[9] Though Baton Rouge, Natchez, and the Mississippi Gulf Coast were considered part of Louisiana during the French colonial period, Spain claimed this territory as belonging to West Florida at the close of the French and Indian War. Since the boundaries of Louisiana were not determined by the Louisiana Purchase, the United States likewise did not hesitate to claim these lands. American settlers (without the right to a political vote) made up the majority of the West Florida population. A group of American settlers in West Florida began meeting at Bayou Sara to negotiate their status with representatives of the Spanish government at Baton Rouge. Some seventy men under the leadership of Philemon Thomas plotted to take control of what they considered their territory.[10] As one historian notes: "But when the English-speaking residents learned that the Spanish governor was not playing fair with the people of West Florida, and that their necks were in danger, Judge Percy, with other patriots holding responsible positions, ordered Gen. Philemon Thomas to take the fort at Baton Rouge, which was done after a spirited night of battle in which several of the Spanish garrison were killed, and the celebrated Lone Star flag of West Florida first unfurled as the royal ensign of Spain disappeared from that part of the United States forever."[11] In September 1810 St. Francisville became the capital of a small, spunky, and short-lived nation—the Free and Independent Republic of West Florida. Since the descendants of the original Anglo-Saxon settlers did not want to live under the Spanish, they waited seven years as government officials tried to decide whether the region constituted part of the Louisiana Purchase. Walker Percy relied on his knowledge of Robert Percy, who died in 1819, and the West Florida Rebellion in writing the foreword to *The Thanatos Syndrome*.

Nothing is known about the second woman in Charles's life, except that they supposedly met in Bermuda (no records of a marriage have survived).[12] He and his next wife, Susannah (or Susanah) Collins, whom he married in 1780, had seven children: Charles, Thomas George, Sarah, Susannah, Catherine, Luke, and William (the latter two died in childhood). The senior Charles, who subsequently acquired a fortune in lands and slaves and was the master of Northumberland House on Buffalo Creek, is best known for the manner of his death, which occurred by drowning in a bayou in late January 1794, in the aftermath of French and Spanish troops gathering to assault Natchez.[13] Will Percy cavalierly sketches the life and apparent suicide of this ancestor in his *Lanterns on the Levee*, and links it to the totally unexpected appearance of Margaret, who presented him with their son:

Don Carlos settled down on his plantation and married him an intelligent French lady from the other side of the river. The Lord blessed him with progeny, and things seemed to be going well and quite respectably when a lady suddenly appeared from England and said to Don Carlos: "I am the long lost wife of your bosom." As if that was not enough, she added: "Behold, your son and heir!" Whereupon she tendered him, not a wee bairn, but a full-grown Captain in the English Navy, also yclept Charles [sic]. Certainly a discouraging business all round. It is not recorded that Don Carlos slapped the lady, but of course, he was thoroughly provoked and everybody immediately began suing everybody else. Somewhere during the commotion Don Carlos walked down to the creek with a sugar kettle, tied it round his neck, and hopped in. The creek is still there and it is called Percy's Creek to this day. His will left his holdings, not to his English, but to his American family, whether from pique, outrage, or affection I can only surmise.[14]

In a letter from New Orleans, dated February 12, 1794, to Charles's son Robert, Dr. Dow matter-of-factly relates the manner of Charles's death:

There is every reason to think that your father put an end to his existence himself. His body was found in a creek with a large tin pot tied around his neck, his pistols were removed from the place, where they were accustomed to hang—I suppose he had reflected within himself that the noise of a firearm would alarm his family, and consequently fell upon the other plan, which was done in the night time, and his single footsteps were traced to the fatal place, where his body was in the morning found immersed in a place in the creek beyond his depth, where he was obliged to walk a considerable way before arriving at it.[15]

One of the causes of Charles's suicide, Dow believed, was that Charles was severely despondent over the death of one of his children, not the unexpected appearance of a son, as in Will's version. The inventory of Charles Percy's estate in 1794, including fifty-five slaves and 5,000 acres of land, was worth approximately $22,400. Though Robert signed a release that he would not bring claims against his father's estate, he later breached this agreement. By 1804, after Susannah had died on the family plantation in Wilkinson County, the estate, excluding the land, had risen to $42,634 (part of this was based on the estimated price of seventy-six slaves). It would seem that Robert, after considerable efforts to prove that he was a legitimate child of Charles, finally inherited $5,075 and 500 acres of land at Bayou Sara before returning to Europe.[16] He died in 1819 and was buried at his plantation next to Jane, who died in 1831. Robert left an estate worth $20,000, plus fifty slaves valued at $14,580 and livestock worth over $2,000.

Walker Percy descends from the "illegitimate side" of the Percy family—that is, from Thomas George Percy, the third of the seven children of Charles and Susannah Percy. Thomas George was born prior to 1790 in Wilkinson County and died in 1841 in Huntsville, Alabama, where he lived for many years and where a monument was erected in his honor in City Cemetery. A graduate of what would eventually be called Princeton University, he is noted partly for an unsavory incident in his life. In 1815, he was the correspondent in a divorce suit between George Poindexter, an important political figure, and his wife, Lydia.[17] After living in Kentucky, he eventually moved to Madison County, Alabama, and in 1816 married a Huntsville woman, Maria Pope, the daughter of Colonel LeRoy Pope and sister of Matilda Pope, the wife of John Williams Walker, a friend from his college days. John Walker was elected a U.S. senator in 1819. The newlyweds settled in Huntsville, where they lived on their estate, Belfeld. Thomas George helped develop the Planters & Mechanics Bank of Huntsville. Colonel Pope, president of the bank, had served as General Andrew Jackson's provisions officer in 1813.[18] Thomas George and Maria Percy had a large family: John Walker, Charles Brown, LeRoy Pope, Robert Henry, and William Alexander (1834–88)—three others (Thomas George, Matilda, and Ellis Ware) died in childhood. After her husband's death, Maria Percy, along with her sons William Alexander Percy, Dr. John Walker Percy (and his bride, Fannie Williams Percy), and Dr. LeRoy Pope Percy, moved in the mid-1840s from Huntsville to Washington County, Mississippi, where Thomas George owned property near Deer Creek, on part of the site of present-day Leland. About this time, another son, Charles Brown Percy, and James C. Jones also bought 1,440 acres near Deer Creek; shortly afterward, Richard L. Dixon bought Jones's interest in this property. This property was divided in 1853; Dixon took the west section and named his property Sycamore Plantation; the Percys called their property Percy Plantation or Percy Place.[19] The author of *Lanterns on the Levee* often spent weekends at Percy Place as a young boy; the ramshackle slave quarters were still there, along with the main house, with its enormous cool and drafty hall.

The rich alluvial soil of the Delta, the hot sun, and careful management ensured that crops grew on the Percy plantation. Dr. John Walker and Fannie Percy had a daughter named Maria.[20] In *Lanterns on the Levee*, the rather eccentric Fannie is portrayed as if stepping out of Thomas Nelson Page's story *Marse Chan: A Tale of Ole Virginia*. As a young bride, she almost caused a duel: "She gave a house-warming, a large affair, with dancing and champagne and a nougat from New Orleans. In selecting her guests she flatly refused to invite a prominent planter because he openly and notoriously lived with a Negro woman." Though hurt, the planter did not challenge his hostess and moved away. As a widow, she lived with her son-in-law, Captain J. S. McNeily, who edited *The Greenville Times* from 1869 to 1892, after his service in the Confederate Army. For the last twenty years of her life, Fannie was prone to taking a small dose of morphine daily. She died in Greenville in 1894.[21] Yet a far more tragic death should be noted. Suffering from paralysis for part of his life, Dr. LeRoy Percy, a bachelor stricken with paralysis, ended his life by taking laudanum in 1882 in Eureka Springs, Arkansas. His death, it is reported, came about because of his ineffectual treatment of a relative, Fannie Percy Pace.[22]

In 1858 William Alexander Percy (a graduate of Princeton University and, in law, from the University of Virginia) married Nannie Irvin Armstrong. In *Lanterns on the Levee*, Nannie Percy is called "Mur," and depicted as a stalwart individual who alone had to care for three children while her husband, "a luke-warm slave-owner," was away fighting in the Civil War. Her husband, nick-named "Fafar," argued unsuccessfully against secession, entered the Confederate Army in 1861, and served on the staff of General John S. Bowen at the battle at Iuka. He later served under General A. L. Long, commander of artillery of the Second Corps of the Army of Northern Virginia. During an intense period of fighting in the war in May 1864, William Alexander saw action in the battle of the Wilderness, as Lee's army moved to block Grant at Spotsylvania Court House. He saw more bloodshed than he would ever care to remember, as 7,000 Union troops died in an hour. And he would have much to relate, particularly about his participation in General Jubal Early's march up the Shenandoah Valley toward Washington, and the subsequent routing by Union General Philip Sheridan. Toward the end of the war, just before he returned home, he saw action with Brigadier General Edward Alexander's First Corps Artillery. His last assignment was as assistant adjutant general on the staff of General G. B. Hodge, tracking enemy movements and trying to keep, if at all possible, morale high. His spirits sank as he learned of the destruction of the levees after Grant's capture of Vicksburg. While her husband was away at war, Nannie managed in 1864 to put down a slave uprising on Percy Place and even cajoled the slaves into harvesting the crop. "When the war was ended," concludes her grandson's portrait, "and my grandfather returned penniless, his family managed to live for more than a year or more on the proceeds from the sale of that cotton crop. At that time my grandmother was twenty-nine, very pretty, with a keen sense of the absurd, and how she could play Strauss waltzes!"[23]

After the war, the task was to regroup and rebuild. In particular, those who had land and were educated were looked to to provide local leadership. Known with good reason as the "Gray Eagle of the Delta," William Alexander Percy returned to Deer Creek, practiced law with William G. Yerger in nearby Greenville, and was elected a member of the Mississippi legislature in 1875 and 1877. Since the levee district established before the Civil War needed to be revived, he helped to establish a new one for Washington, Bolivar, and Issaquena counties. As told by his grandson: "That work required courage, tact, intelligence, patience; it also required vote-buying, the stuffing of ballot-boxes, chicanery, intimidation. Heart-breaking business and degrading, but in the end successful." He later served as Democratic Speaker of the House. From 1870 to 1888, he grew in prominence as carpetbaggers made inroads into Delta society, continually calling for reform measures in state politics. After Christmas 1876, Percy Place had to be rebuilt after a heavy snowstorm collapsed part of the roof.[24] Eventually, William Alexander moved his family to Greenville. Possessed of great personal magnetism and a champion of the levee interests, he went to the Democratic national conventions in 1880 and 1884 determined to address the problems of a postwar society. He died after a week's illness in January 1888 and was buried in the Percy family plot in the Greenville Cemetery.[25] A stained-glass window in nearby St. James's Episcopal Church, prominently featuring an eagle, commemorates this noted Percy ancestor. In addition, a window in the same church dedicated to his wife carries the inscription: "And I saw a new heaven and a new earth" —a fitting inscription for the great-grandmother of a novelist very much influenced by the notion of the apocalypse.

The five children of William Alexander and Nannie Percy (Fannie, LeRoy, William Armstrong, Walker [November 18, 1864–February 8, 1917], and Lady) were all familiar in one way or another to young Walker Percy from the time he moved to Greenville in 1930. Fannie married Alfred Downs Pace in 1878, but had no children; as mentioned, she died in her early twenties at Eureka Springs.[26] Unfortunately, Downs had a roving eye and a penchant for gambling. Once, when distraught because his life was in a shambles, he approached Senator LeRoy Percy and said that he ought to end his troubles. "Well, Downs," said the Senator, "there is a loaded .45 in my desk. And I think you have a good idea." The Senator walked out. Downs of course did nothing.[27] After graduating from the University of the South at Sewanee in 1879, LeRoy read law with his father. He subsequently entered the University of Virginia and graduated in 1881, when twenty-one years old. His father and his two brothers (William Armstrong and Walker) likewise took law degrees at the University of Virginia.[28] LeRoy then became a member of the law firm of Yerger & Percy in Greenville and grew active in local and state politics, especially concerning the management of the levees. He married Camille E. Bourges (b. 1862), a Roman Catholic, in 1883, and had two sons: William Alexander (b. May 15, 1885), and LeRoy Jr. (b. 1891), who died in 1902 when a childhood friend shot him accidentally in Hot Springs. A window above the altar in St. Joseph's Roman Catholic Church in Greenville, depicting the boy Jesus, is dedicated to him.

Camille's father, Ernest Bourges (1837–1906), known locally as Captain Bourges, was a cotton broker in New Orleans before running a bakery in the Delta.[29] His wife, Marie Camille Generelly (1841–1903), came from a prominent New Orleans family. Their four daughters lived at one time or another in Greenville. The Bourges family were active socially in Greenville, though they visited friends and relatives in New Orleans on occasion.[30] During his summers as a youth, Will Percy's parents would take him to visit his Aunt Nana and her husband, George Pearce, at their home called Roxbury in Virginia. George Pearce was noted for making cocktails of a kingly color that tasted like the "snow and honey concoctions of the Greeks, just sweet enough and just sour enough and altogether Olympian." Will's Aunt Rita Mount seems not to have had all that happy a life. When she was about to give birth, one friend of the family noted: "Poor little Rita, alas, it makes me sad to see her. She is to be a mother, in addition to her other misfortunes."[31]

Will Percy clearly had great affection for Marie Camille Bourges, his plump and blue-eyed maternal French grandmother, whom he called "Mère," a wonderful woman with a rather small English vocabulary. When her husband, Ernest, called "Père" by Will, "unexpectedly appeared one nightfall with an number of friends who had been bear-hunting with him, she first said to him: '*Mais, Ernest*'—and he quailed, for it was one of her favorite phrases and it could mean all manner of things, but it always *meant*—then she observed to her guests: 'Welcome, messieurs, I can eat you but I cannot sleep you.' She was a remarkable woman, and very firm."[32] Père was distinguished by his long silky beard, which gave him a look of "benign ferocity" when it was hooked over his ears. From New Orleans, he took his family (his daughter, Camille, had been educated at the Convent of the Sacred Heart) and sailed to the Delta to make his fortune at Woodstock Plantation near Deer Creek.

In many ways, Will's father, LeRoy Percy, could be considered the Henry Grady of the Delta; he wanted to bring order and wealth to an impoverished region of the country, but not, as it turns out, without serious controversy. Beginning in 1898, he, O. B. Crittenden, and Morris Rosenstock, a prominent Jew from Greenville and Shelby Foote's grandfather, leased land from the heirs of Austin Corbin with the intention of importing Italian immigrants to work on the 11,000-acre Sunnyside Plantation in Chicot County, Arkansas, across the Mississippi River from Greenville. LeRoy also wanted to implement a similar practice on his own 3,343-acre Trail Lake Plantation south of Greenville, named after a "dilapidated-looking slough which meandered halfheartedly into the center of the place," which he had acquired piecemeal over a period of ten years. His intention in bringing in this particular labor force was to balance the need for adequate medicine, low cotton prices, and the shortage of workers.[33] LeRoy, as his son notes, "started with a batch of virgin timber and cleared that. Next he won in the cotton market and put the winnings into that section of Doctor Atterbury's, good land and mostly in cultivation. Then he added the desolate-looking deadening along Deep Slough. At last he bought the Cheek Place and the Ross Place." He sent in Billy Hardie, a young manager from Arkansas, to run Trail Lake. Like scores of other planters in the area, LeRoy felt that Italian laborers were preferable to black laborers, and by 1907 he had managed to settle 158 families at Sunnyside. Responding negatively to this new form of peonage, the Italian government pressured the Roosevelt administration to investigate the local scene.

Mary Grace Quackenbos, a sharp-eyed special assistant in the U.S. Attorney General's office, drew up a list of serious offenses, many unfair, that focused on the period from 1904 to 1907, though her findings differed from those of Professor Albert Bushnell Hart from Harvard, who seemingly looked at Sunnyside with a less critical eye. LeRoy resented Quackenbos's intrusion, especially her modus operandi, and personally asked President Theodore Roosevelt, whom he had entertained at a Delta bear hunt in 1902, to assist in resolving the problems created by importing immigrant labor.[34] Above all, he wanted a fair-minded investigator. Bertram Wyatt-Brown observes: "Percy wanted to attract freemen who were supposed to accept a degree of debt servitude in return for the chance to start life over. The chief problem was the scarcely hidden presumption that the Italians deserved to be categorized as less than full citizens, better than blacks, but not truly freemen. For that reason the experiment ultimately failed—as well it should have. The problem was less Percy's, however, than the historical and economic situation itself."[35] When Crittenden was indicted for peonage by a federal grand jury, but not convicted, LeRoy (as his attorney) stood by his friend. By 1913 LeRoy had sold his shares in Sunnyside, which eventually adopted the sharecropping system.

LeRoy Percy is most noted, however, for his political career. Opposing Governor Anselm J. McLaurin, who backed Judge Andrew H. Longo, an advocate of "free silver," he supported in 1896 General Thomas C. Catchings and the gold standard, though he felt that the real issue concerned the construction and maintenance of the levees. In July, Catchings was unanimously declared the party's nominee. The same returns showed that LeRoy had been reelected to the district executive committee, thus further involving him and racist James Kimble Vardaman in the internecine wars of Southern politics. McLaurin (now a U.S. senator) died in December 1909, and Governor Edmund F. Noel appointed Colonel James B. Gordon as his replacement. LeRoy subsequently opposed Vardaman's candidacy for the Senate, and thus he entered the race himself. At that time, U.S. senators were still chosen by the state legislature. LeRoy went to Jackson, Mississippi, in early January 1910, bringing with him Camille, Will, campaign manager William Crump, and their supporters, J. T. Atterbury and State Representative Van Buren Boddie.[36] Showing fraternal solidarity, Walker Percy of Birmingham, along with his other brother, William Armstrong of Memphis, joined LeRoy's successful senatorial campaign against Vardaman. Endorsing the national Democratic platform, LeRoy devised strategies to counter Vardaman's offensive actions. He favored "equality to all, equal privileges, honest taxation, limited appropriations," and a wise use of revenues.[37] Governor Noel entered the fray by threatening to throw his support to Colonel Gordon if the legislature failed to elect a new senator.[38] By late February, those candidates opposing Vardaman withdrew from the race in an act of magnanimity (after the fifty-seventh ballot) to support LeRoy, who won the Senate seat by eighty-seven to eighty-two votes. LeRoy and Camille went to Washington in March 1910, knowing that Vardaman was still a powerful force. They also knew their battles were not finished. In Mississippi, Theodore G. Bilbo, a Vardaman supporter, claimed that LeRoy's campaign had been corrupt, and though LeRoy was vindicated of this charge, he was emotionally and physically exhausted by the charges and countercharges in the newspapers.

As a senator, LeRoy aligned himself with the problems of the Delta planters and sought to denounce the practices of cotton speculators who kept the price of cotton artificially depressed. Will said that his father fought the Civil War pensions racket, opposed the breach of faith with Great Britain in the Panama tolls case, helped with the levee legislation, and contributed significantly to a survey of the nation's immigration laws. President Taft liked and trusted him in spite of the Senator's friendship with the former President. Vardaman, on the other hand, campaigned for the interests of the hill farmers. At a rally at Lauderdale Springs in July 1910, the Senator, accompanied by his brother, Walker, and son, Will, spoke out against the tactics of Bilbo and Vardaman. Walker was so distraught that he suggested murdering Bilbo, much to the consternation of his nephew. "Uncle Walker," Will wrote, "came to my room after midnight to say that one of our group would have to kill the bribe-taker in the morning as he was to attend our meeting and was scheduled to denounce Father. At six we met in the cold dreary dining room for breakfast, Uncle Walker, his seventeen-year-old son, LeRoy, and I sitting at a table to ourselves. I had target-practiced most of the night in front of the mirror, so as not to forget to release the safety." Having decided *not* to kill Bilbo, LeRoy settled for a temporary victory—the approval of the crowd at the rally.

In June 1911, while campaigning at Rose Hill, Mississippi, LeRoy was stabbed twice in the back—a sign of the violence that had plagued his political life in Mississippi. As it turned out, neither LeRoy nor another contender, Charlton Alexander, would face Vardaman in a runoff, since Vardaman polled an overwhelming majority. To make matters worse, Bilbo was elected lieutenant governor. To rest and escape from troubles at home, LeRoy, Camille, and Will traveled to Italy, Albania, and Greece. In late December 1912, Senator Percy sold Percy Place for $70,000 to a group of four men, who changed the name of the property to Deer Creek Planting Company.[39] Will tended to see his father and his cronies in an epic mode, as being destined to be elected because they had superior intellects and characters.

The Percys in Birmingham likewise had considerable prestige and wealth, due mainly to their relationship with the DeBardeleben family. Mary Pratt DeBardeleben, wife of Senator Percy's brother, Walker, was a member of a family instrumental in founding the city of Bessemer, Alabama. Known as "Pratt," she came from old and distinguished Alabamian stock, and the DeBardelebens had every right to be as proud of their heritage as did the Percys. The roots of the American DeBardelebens go back to the time of Frederick II, who furnished Great Britain during the American Revolution with thousands of Hessian soldiers.[40] Arthur Franz Ferdinand von Bardeleben from Kattenburgh, Germany, and his brother John Heinrich arrived in New York in 1776. After the Civil War, as the DeBardelebens flourished, Henry Fairchild DeBardeleben, a Confederate veteran, organized and became president of the DeBardeleben Coal & Iron Company and the Pinckard & DeBardeleben Land Company in 1885. These properties, whose worth was estimated at $13 million, formed the largest industrial undertaking in the South at that time. In March 1886, Henry Fairchild pointed to a spot twelve miles southwest of Birmingham and said to a reporter, "Here is where I am going to establish a young city."[41] The DeBardelebens were reaching the zenith of their power and prestige just as Walker Percy, a Democrat and Episcopalian, came to Birmingham in 1886 to live and practice his vocation.[42]

The fourth child of William Alexander and Nannie Armstrong Percy, Walker Percy was respected during his lifetime as a corporation lawyer, a drafter of the commission form of government for Birmingham, a city leader, and an advocate for eliminating the fee system in Alabama. He was an important person in Birmingham's upwardly mobile society. Born on November 18, 1864, in Leland, Mississippi, he grew up on Percy Place.[43] Once Walker had left for the University of the South in Sewanee in 1879, he returned often to Mississippi for hunting and fishing. He journeyed south to Birmingham during his college days and became acquainted with the DeBardeleben family.

In the exquisite Episcopal Church of the Advent in downtown Birmingham, Walker Percy married Mary Pratt DeBardeleben on April 17, 1888, in a ceremony presided over by the Rev. Thomas J. Beard.[44] The merger of these two families solidified the positions of both Mary Pratt and Walker in Birmingham society; it also meant that the accumulation of wealth and power could expand. After the wedding, the young couple visited the Percys in Greenville. Of Pratt and Walker's four children, two lived: LeRoy Pratt (born June 23, 1889), and Ellen (born January 12, 1893), who eventually married in 1912 lawyer Matthew Hobson Murphy.[45]

Walker proved to be a gifted counselor and legal advocate, though he showed reluctance at first about entering the world of politics. He formed a law partnership in 1889 with James Weatherly, a graduate of Sewanee and the University of Alabama. Their practice lasted only a few years and then they parted amicably.[46] After the dissolution of Weatherly & Percy, Walker practiced law alone while residing at 1921 Avenue J between 19th and 20th Streets. Once Weatherly left the firm, Walker looked for a new partner. He formed a partnership in 1895, known as Percy & Grubb, with William Grubb, who later became a U.S. district judge; this firm lasted until 1905, the same year Grubb left to become a partner in the firm of Tillman, Grubb, Bradley & Morrow. As new firms were created and lawyers looked about for better positions, Walker continued practicing in the Woodward Building as counsel for the Alabama Council of the Tennessee Coal & Iron Company (TCI), which had merged with the enormous DeBardeleben steel interests. Understandably, his legal business increased and he earned a reputation, during this time of expansion—and controversy— as a fine trial lawyer.[47] Eventually he sold a good portion of his real estate and mineral resources to Enoch Ensley, who purchased them for TCI.

Pulsating with the life and times of Birmingham and the vacillating fortunes of the DeBardelebens, Walker was anxious about Henry Fairchild DeBardeleben's attempt to gain control of TCI's stock, which, when Henry Fairchild failed to do so, proved to be the catalyst for the financial decline of the DeBardeleben family, reflecting the lean years for Bessemer. By 1891, the DeBardeleben Coal & Iron Company had merged with the Henry Ellen Coal Company and the reacquired Eureka Company to form a large corporation that owned seven blast furnaces, seven coal mines, and 140,000 acres of land producing coal and iron. A year later, TCI had increased the value of its stock and exchanged it for all of the DeBardeleben stock. With 400,000 acres of land, seventeen blast furnaces, and a daily coal capacity of 13,000 tons, TCI soon became the largest coal and iron company in the South, and Henry Fairchild, no doubt exhausted and exhilarated at the same time, was its largest individual stockholder. When TCI moved into Jefferson County, a conflict developed between Thomas Hillman, who did not like being a minority stockholder to Enoch Ensley, and TCI stockholder Colonel Alfred M. Shook. Since no stockholder, including Henry Fairchild, had an absolute majority, John Inman of New York and Henry Fairchild agreed that Nathaniel Baxter, Jr., an Inman friend, would be president and Henry Fairchild vice president. Yet the stakes were too high not to push relentlessly forward; it took two years and a $2.25 million stock deal for TCI to absorb the Pratt Coal & Iron Company. Henry Fairchild DeBardeleben was now one of the richest men in the South.

The fortunes of the DeBardelebens, however, slowly began to decline. By February 1893, Henry Fairchild desperately wanted to control TCI. Yet, through various deals that soured within six weeks, he lost an estimated $2.5 million. By the end of March, he had sold 25,000 shares to Inman, who was trying to gain control of the company. Inman had all of Henry Fairchild's stock by May, and when Henry Fairchild reached a low peak in his life, he could not count on others to bail him out. In October 1894, Henry Fairchild resigned and went into retirement, though three years later he mustered his strength once again and tried to regain control of his former company.

Overshadowed to some extent by the money brokers and the major players, Walker and Pratt needed courage in the face of the declining DeBardeleben power, wealth, and prestige. During this time, the Percys sought spiritual strength at St. Mary's-on-the-Highlands, and Walker served in 1894 as a delegate to a convention of the Episcopal Church.[48] He never seemed to slow down. During the latter part of the decade, he held posts that showed that he could make important decisions outside his law office. In 1897 he was vice president and secretary of the Bessemer Land & Improvement Company.[49] Likewise that year, he stepped forward and advised that something must be done to reorganize the Ensley Land Company in order to satisfy its creditors.[50] At a gathering in Feb-

ruary 1898 of the representatives of seven furnace companies whose purpose
was to maintain equity in pricing, he declared their desires were actually contrary to the Sherman Antitrust Act. In addition, he made his presence felt on the
board of trustees of the Alabama Steel & Shipbuilding Company, which was
organized to build a steel plant.[51] The crucial question naturally arose for those
who lived and worked with Walker: how could he continue to respond at full
steam to all the burdens that he had accepted? Edward L. Ayers, the Southern
economic historian, maintains that the Southern iron industry's late start, its re-
liance on outside expertise, and the slow market for steel in the South conspired
to keep Birmingham from what seemed so promising in the early 1890s.[52] For
those who worked in the coal and steel industries in Birmingham, the doors
leading to growth and development, whether financial, social, or psychological,
would be, at best, difficult to find and open. Though his own life seemed stable,
Walker thought about his own death as he dealt with the final phase of Henry
Fairchild's career. William I. Grubb and Andrew Jordan witnessed Walker's Last
Will and Testament on May 11, 1898; he cited his brother, LeRoy, in Greenville
and his wife as executors, and son, LeRoy, and daughter, Ellen, as his eventual
heirs.

Gradually Birmingham and Bessemer made a recovery. Walker Percy was
president of the Berney National Bank in 1900, after having served a number of
years as a director; later, after its incorporation into the First National Bank, he
served on that board. He was also president of the Ensley Land Company.[53] The
Bessemer Land & Improvement Company, now under the direction of Henry L.
Badham, Walker Percy, and R. E. Evans, pledged themselves in 1901 to the improvement of residential and industrial construction.[54] As Birmingham struggled
to find a new road to prosperity, it attracted more and more outside interest.
About this time, too, the Walker Percys moved to a large house, originally known
as the Westover House, near the fashionable Five Points South section on 2217
Arlington Avenue.[55] It was a large, imposing structure built of brown stone with
sloping wood-shingle roofs, surrounded in the front and on one side by a tiled
terrace with white picket railings. Though the house was impressive, it would
contain its fair share of grief. On September 16, 1903, Walker Percy, Jr., born the
previous May and baptized at home, died. He was buried in Oak Hill Cemetery.[56]

In spite of such a personal loss, Walker continued to meet his legal obligations. After Grubb left the firm in 1905, he formed a partnership with Augustus
Benners, the son of Judge Alfred H. Benners, the chancellor of the Northwestern
Chancery Division for many years. Walker was appointed District Attorney for
the Illinois Central Railroad Company in March 1906.[57] During 1907 he represented the U.S. Steel Corporation, which had purchased the nearly bankrupt TCI
when it was under investigation by the U.S. Justice Department. In 1909 Percy
and Benners asked Borden Burr of Talladega to join their firm, to be known as
Percy, Benners & Burr.[58] Walker's talents and successful collaborative efforts gave
him considerable recognition both locally and nationally, and his managerial skill
and legal services were constantly in demand by the DeBardeleben enterprises,
the Ensley Land Company, the Republic Steel Corporation, the Birmingham

Southern Railroad, and *The Birmingham News.* A member of the Southern Club, the Roebuck Golf & Auto Club, the Birmingham Athletic Club, and the Birmingham Country Club at Lakeview, he pursued a life that merged his interests with the other elite of Birmingham.[59] He was president of the country club in 1909. From all appearances, the Percys led a most comfortable life, and Walker's activities reveal a personality that showed that he managed to integrate family and social life with unstinting professionalism, particularly as TCI and similar operations in Birmingham faced one crisis after another. Thus it is not surprising that Walker Percy was elected to the state legislature, where he wrote and helped pass a bill in 1911 that permitted Birmingham to change its form of government from a mayor-aldermen form to a commission form that had been popular during the Progressive era.[60] His efforts served the city well, and this form of government lasted until 1963, when Birmingham was on the brink of bankruptcy and needed to update its form of governance.

As Walker Percy rose to prominence in Birmingham, young Will Percy was receiving a carefully crafted education in Greenville. After attending St. Rose of Lima Grade School, Will had a series of tutors: Judge Griffin (a neighbor); Rev. P. J. Korstenbrock (for Latin and Greek); Mr. E. E. Bass, Jr. (the local superintendent of schools, for other subjects). Father Korstenbrock heard Will's first confession, gave him his first communion, and prepared him for confirmation. Will entered the University of the South at the turn of the century when he was just fifteen. "Until I came to Sewanee," he wrote, "I had been utterly without intimates of my own age." At Sewanee he met new friends, including Huger Jervey, a professor of romance languages and "brilliant and bumptious then, brilliant and wise now, and so human." Once a month he went dutifully to the Catholic church in Winchester. He went through a change that Catholics sometimes experience during early adulthood; he felt that no priest could absolve him nor could any church direct his life. With a newfound interior freedom, Will took a break from his college studies and went to Paris with his parents. When he returned home, he entered Harvard Law School, not because the world of law would supply the challenges he was seeking, but because it was a respectable occupation. The ulterior motive for choosing Cambridge was that he would have access to first-class music and theater in Boston. Yet he reduced his three years of balancing legal studies with his love of art, music, and literature to a curt dismissal: "Boston meant nothing to me. Cambridge meant nothing to me." And so, at age twenty-three, he returned to Greenville, after teaching at Sewanee for a semester.

Living at home, Will carved out an interior niche into which he could retreat when the demands of law or the presence of family or friends proved too taxing. He found consolation and satisfaction in writing poetry, which earned him a national reputation, though he was never able to break into the ranks of the first-rate poets of his day. His own career as a teacher of literature was short-lived; he taught at the University of the South for one semester after his mentor, John Bell Henneman, died in 1908. He taught there again in 1920 and was elected to the board of trustees, but once the administration discovered that he had been raised a Roman Catholic, his affiliation was terminated.[61] Will viewed the university's move as a sign of religious intolerance. In March 1925 he and Huger Jervey purchased Brinkwood, near Sewanee, as a place of retreat.[62] Since Will was an inveterate traveler, his life in Greenville lacked a familial core, and perhaps for this reason he opened up his house and welcomed three young cousins and their mother and shared with them whatever he had.

NOTES

Codes

AB: The Athens (Georgia) *Banner*
AB-H: The Athens (Georgia) *Banner-Herald*
AC: Angus Cameron
AK: Alfred A. Knopf
APM: Ann Percy Moores (WP's daughter)
BA-H: The Birmingham (Alabama) *Age-Herald*
BCT: Ben C. Toledano
BD: Ball Diary
BPP: Billups Phinizy Percy (WP's brother)
BPS: Billups Phinizy Spalding
CB: Cleanth Brooks
CBP: Camille Bourges Percy
CG: Charlotte Gailor
CGB: Charles Greenleaf Bell
CGT: Caroline Gordon Tate
DB: Donald Barthelme
DDDA: Donie Drane DeBardeleben Allison
DD-T: The Delta Democrat-Times (Greenville, Mississippi)
DHS: Daniel Hughes Spalding, Jr.
DTH: The Daily Tar Heel (newspaper of UNC)
EO: Elizabeth Otis
ER: Monsignor Elmo L. Romagosa
ES: Elizabeth Spencer
FO'C: Flannery O'Connor
GD-D: The Greenville (Mississippi) *Delta-Democrat*
GU: Gene Usdin, M.D.
HK: Henry Kisor

HR: Henry Robbins
JC: Julie Coryn of FSG
JE: Father Charles, O.C.S.O. (John English)
JG: Jo Marie Gulledge
JHM, SJ: James Hart McCown, S.J.
JJS: Jack J. Spalding
JWC: John William Corrington
KLK: Kenneth Laine Ketner
LAL: Lewis A. Lawson
LEP: Les E. Phillabaum
LK: Lila Karpf of FSG
LP: Senator LeRoy Percy of Greenville, Mississippi
LP-B: LeRoy Percy of Birmingham, Alabama (WP's father)
LP-G: LeRoy Percy of Greenville, Mississippi (WP's brother)
LPS: Lewis P. Simpson
LSU: Louisiana State University
LWH: Linda Whitney Hobson
MBTP: Mary Bernice Townsend Percy (WP's wife)
MF: Mitchell Finch
MPPL: Mary Pratt Percy Lobdell (WP's daughter)
NJ: Nell B. Johnson
NL: Nancy Lemann
NP: Noel E. Parmentel
PRB: Panthea Reid (Broughton) Fischer
PSM: Patricia (Schartle) Myrer
PS, SJ: Patrick H. Samway, S.J.
RC: Robert Coles, M.D.
RDDDA: Records of Donie Drane DeBardeleben Allison
RERCB: Real Estate Records for the City of Birmingham, Alabama
RF: Rhoda K. Faust
RG: Robert Giroux
RM: Robert Milling III
RS: Roger Straus
SF: Shelby Foote
SFP: Sarah Farish Percy (wife of LP-G)
SK: Stanley Kauffmann
SMH: Records of St. Mary's-on-the-Highlands Church in Birmingham, Alabama
THC, SJ: Thomas H. Clancy, S.J.
TM: Father Louis, O.C.S.O. (Thomas Merton)
UNC: University of North Carolina at Chapel Hill
WAP: William Alexander Percy
WP: Walker Percy
WP-B: Walker Percy of Birmingham (WP's grandfather)
ZAN: Zoltán Abádi-Nagy

1. The Birmingham Years, 1916–29

1. When asked to sketch his family background by John Griffin Jones in 1980, WP did so accurately but without revealing any significant details (*Conversations*, p. 250).

2. In making preliminary notes for *SC*, WP traced some of his family history. SHCUNC, series I: E-1a (ii).
3. WP to SF, Aug. 4, 1970; SF to WP, Aug. 5, 1970.
4. WP to RF, Jan. 20, 1990.
5. SHCUNC, addition of May 1992, folder 3, p. 87.
6. George Howe Colt, *The Enigma of Suicide* (New York: Summit Books, 1991), p. 226.
7. Bertram Wyatt-Brown, "Walker, Will, and Honor Dying: The Percys and Literary Creativity," in *Looking South: Chapters in the Story of an American Region*, edited by Winfred B. Moore, Jr., and Joseph F. Tripp (Westport, Conn.: Greenwood Press, 1989), pp. 229–58.
8. *Conversations*, p. 300.
9. John F. Desmond, "From Suicide to Ex-Suicide: Notes on the Southern Writer as Hero in the Age of Despair," *The Southern Literary Journal*, 25 (Fall 1992), p. 91.
10. *AB*, Sept. 2, 5, 1914. Billups Phinizy and Nellie Stovall were married on April 21, 1886.
11. *AB*, Sept. 19, 1914.
12. *AB*, Oct. 16, 27, 1914.
13. *AB*, Nov. 19, 1914. DDDA told PS, SJ that it was probably one of Mattie Sue's sisters who, after visiting Birmingham socially on various occasions, provided the initial introduction of Mattie Sue to LeRoy. WP once told NL that his parents met at the Greenbrier. Interview: NL.
14. Interview: JJS.
15. *History of Athens and Clarke County* (Athens: McGregor Company, 1923) and James K. Reap, *Athens: A Pictorial History* (Norfolk, Va.: The Donning Company, 1985), p. 151.
16. After the death of Nellie Stovall Phinizy in 1949, the Thomas Tillmans lived in the house until it was rented to the Kappa Sigmas and eventually sold to the Chi Omega sorority in 1960. The house was torn down and a new Chi Omega house was built. See *Athens: A Pictorial History*, p. 72, for a picture of this house and information about Billups Phinizy. For a chatty but informative tour of post-Civil War Athens, see the facsimile reprint of Sylvanus Morris, *Stroll About Athens During the Early Seventies* (Athens: Athens Historical Society, 1969); also *Strolls Around Athens* by William Tate (Athens: The Observer Press, 1975). A picture of the Phinizy house can be found in *Strolls Around Athens*, facing p. 50. Also Frances T. Thomas, *A Portrait of Historic Athens and Clarke County* (Athens: University of Georgia Press, 1992), p. 148.
17. *AB*, May 2, 1915.
18. The Rev. Eugene Lott Hill also presided at the marriages of Anne Barrett Phinizy to E. Hammond Johnson in the First Presbyterian Church on Nov. 10, 1910, and to Josiah Billing on Nov. 15, 1923; Robert Malcolm Fortson and Nellie Phinizy on Jan. 7, 1918; Thomas Tillman and Louise Phinizy on Nov. 12, 1930. Except for the first wedding, the rest were held in the Phinizy home in Athens. E. Hammond Johnson died a mysterious death during World War I. (Sources: Records of the First Presbyterian Church in Athens and JJS.) When Bolling and Hughes Spalding married on Feb. 7, 1912, wags said that the outfit of the Bishop of Natchez was prettier than the bride's. Hughes Spalding told the story of stepping through the bowed bay window into the ballroom just in time for the wedding procession. The bishop was using the room that Hughes would have waited in, and since Hughes might have seen his fiancée if he waited in another room, he decided to make his own dramatic entrance. A photo of the Phinizy house seems to confirm the existence of such a window, later replaced by a plate-glass one (BPS to WP, Dec. 28, 1988). The Spaldings trace their Catholic roots back from Atlanta to Bardstown, Kentucky, and finally to St. Marys County in

Maryland. Mother Catherine Spalding, co-founder of the Sisters of Charity of Naza-reth, and her cousin, Archbishop Martin John Spalding of Baltimore, were part of this Kentucky branch of the family.

19. *AB*, Sept. 2, 1915.

20. *AB*, Sept. 12, 1915.

21. *AB*, Oct. 15, 23, 24, 27, Nov. 4, 1915.

22. On Jan. 19, 1918, LP-B was assessed taxes for this property.

23. Source: LAL's unpublished lecture "The Origin of Will Barrett's 'Exceptional States.' "

24. GH. When WP was admitted to Gaylord Farm Sanatorium in Wallingford, Connect-icut, on April 12, 1945, the physician on duty asked him to write up his own case history, which he did. This document provides an unusual evaluation of WP's medical history in his own words.

25. *BA-H*, July 30, 1916.

26. *BA-H*, Oct. 3, 8, 1916.

27. SHCUNC, series I: A-4, p. 247.

28. For information about the history of the Independent Presbyterian Church, I am in-debted to Marvin Yeomans Whiting's authoritative *The Bearing Day Is Not Gone: The Seventy-fifth Anniversary History of Independent Presbyterian Church of Birmingham, Ala-bama, 1915–1990* (Birmingham: Independent Presbyterian Church, 1990).

29. James Bowron's views of Dr. Edmonds can be seen in Robert J. Norrell's *James Bowron: The Autobiography of a New South Industrialism* (Chapel Hill: UNC Press, 1991), pp. 209 ff.

30. See *The Independent Presbyterian Church, Birmingham, Alabama* (Birmingham: Guild of the Independent Presbyterian Church, 1950), pp. 76–77, for a list of names of first members. The "Minutes of Session" of the South Highland Presbyterian Church for March 16, 1916, record that it was ordered that a parishioner be dropped if that person also appeared simultaneously on the membership rolls of the Independent Presbyte-rian Church. No Percy is mentioned in these minutes either as being in good standing at South Highland Presbyterian or as a new member of Independent Presbyterian.

31. *GD-D*, Nov. 13, 1916.

32. WAP to Carrie Stern, Dec. 10, 1916.

33. *BA-H*, Feb. 3, 1917. Interview: DDDA.

34. GH. In these records, WP also used the same word to describe his mother's death. Curiously, *BA-H* carried a report on WP-B's life insurance policies. He had $120,000 in total coverage, of which $60,000 was in accident coverage; he had carried most of these policies for over ten years, and some as long as twenty years. The policies, mainly with Mutual Life, New York Life, Equitable Life, and National Life, were incontestable, inasmuch as they all had been in operation longer than a year. There was one exception: in November 1916, WP-B had canceled one accident policy with the Fidelity & Casualty Company of New York City for $50,000. In petitions to dis-tribute the estate of WP-B and probate his will, which had been originally drawn up in May 1898, Grandmother Pratt is listed as the sole beneficiary. LP-B, age twenty-seven, and his married sister, Ellen Murphy, age twenty-three, were designated as "heirs and distributees."

35. *LL*, p. 168.

36. See *Harvard's Military Record in the World War*, edited by Frederick Mead (Boston: Harvard Alumni Association, 1921), under "LeRoy Pratt Percy" and "William Alex-

ander Percy." Also George M. Cruikshank, *A History of Birmingham and Its Environs,* Vol. 2 (Chicago: Lewis Publishing Company, 1920), pp. 357–58.

37. *BA-H,* March 10, 1918.
38. Interview: LP-G.
39. WAP to LP, Aug. 31, 1918. For other letters of WAP to his mother and father from this time period, see the appendix to BPS's M.A. thesis entitled "William Alexander Percy: His Philosophy of Life as Reflected in His Poetry" (University of Georgia, 1957).
40. WAP to CBP, Sept. 13, 1918.
41. WAP to LP, Nov. 15, 1918.
42. WAP to CBP, Feb. 2, 1919.
43. Records of the Independent Presbyterian Church dated Feb. 1, 1919.
44. Interview of WP by Jan Nordby Gretlund in *Conversations,* p. 206.
45. SF to WP, Oct. 7, 1949.
46. WP to SF, Jan. 29, 1979.
47. Undated letter from WP to Ann M. Burkhardt of the Birmingham Historical Society (though written before July 12, 1982). Burkhardt notes that the records of the Birmingham Fire Department during the period of Walker's youth are not available.
48. A corrected version of this review can be found in *Faulkner's University Pieces,* edited by Carvel E. Collins (Tokyo: Kenkyusha Limited, 1962), pp. 66–68. Two articles evaluating WAP by BPS are "A Stoic Trend in William Alexander Percy's Thought," *The Georgia Review,* 12 (Fall 1958), pp. 241–51, and "Mississippi and the Poet: William Alexander Percy," *The Journal of Mississippi History,* 27 (February 1965), pp. 63–73.
49. Interview: Leon K. Koury.
50. Privately printed in pamphlet form. Also LP's "The Modern Ku Klux Klan," *The Atlantic Monthly,* July 1922, pp. 122–28.
51. *LL,* p. 232.
52. WP to Virginia Durr, Dec. 12, [1962].
53. LP-B to LP, March 29, 1922.
54. LP-B to R. B. Claggett, April 12, 1922.
55. LP to Caroline Percy, Feb. 3, 1923.
56. LP-B to LP, Feb. 17, 1923.
57. LP to the Ponce de Leon Hotel, March 3, 1923.
58. LP to Bell Hebron, March 5, 1923.
59. LP to William Percy McKinney, April 2, 1923.
60. WAP to CG, May 16, 1923.
61. WP's comments in "A Symposium on Fiction," *Shenandoah,* 27 (Winter 1976), pp. 22–23; also WP's comments in his essay "Metaphor as Mistake," in *MB,* p. 64.
62. RERCB.
63. LP to George Alexander, Oct. 30, 1924; LP to Mrs. C. J. McKinney, Oct. 30, 1924.
64. LP to LP-B, Nov. 21, Dec. 27, 1924.
65. *The Birmingham City Directory* lists the DeBardelebens as living in Shades Mountain from 1926 to 1932. If the 1926 directory indicated where people lived the previous year, as would seem likely, then the DeBardelebens moved in 1925.
66. After Henry Fairchild DeBardeleben's son, Henry Ticknor, graduated in 1892 from Alabama Polytechnic Institute, he became superintendent of a number of companies: the Alice Furnace Division of TCI in 1894, the Gracie-Woodward Iron Company in 1896, and the Woodward Iron Company from 1897 to 1899. While at the Polytechnic Institute, he met Lulie Thomas, daughter of William Bailey Thomas and Lulie Ann

Speer Thomas of Athens, Georgia, who was living then with relatives. Henry Ticknor and Lulie married after six years of courtship in Atlanta on April 21, 1896, at St. Luke's Episcopal Church, and subsequently had four children. In 1899, Henry Ticknor moved to Clarksville, Tennessee, to manage the Red River Furnace Company; then, in 1904, to Allen's Creek, Tennessee, where he managed the Bon Air Coal & Iron Company; then, in 1907, to Anniston, Alabama, where he served as vice president and manager of the Woodstock Iron & Steel Corporation. Finally, in 1909, he became president of the Russellville Iron Ore & Metal Company and returned to Birmingham to become vice president of the Alabama Fuel & Iron Company, president of the DeBardeleben Coal Corporation, and manager of the Warrior River Section of the Mississippi-Warrior River Service under the U.S. War Department. Lulie Thomas DeBardeleben died on Jan. 18, 1910, in Birmingham. On April 19, 1911, Henry Ticknor DeBardeleben married again, this time in Clarksville, Tennessee, to Lulie's close friend Donie Drane, daughter of Dr. Henry Tupper Drane and Betty Thomas Drane of Clarksville. Henry Ticknor and his second wife had two children: Donie, born in November 1912, and Newton, born in January 1915. Donie DeBardeleben married William Mills Neal on Oct. 14, 1937; after his death, she married Charles Johnson Allison, Jr., on Jan. 2, 1960. Newton DeBardeleben, who married Virginia Dunwood Swann on April 10, 1940, and Betty Cahill on Oct. 4, 1975, died on April 23, 1979. Though never particularly close, Newton and WP would be fellow students at UNC. Shortly before both DDDA and WP died, they looked back on their friendship with great fondness and affection.

67. RERCB.
68. Interview: Margaret Gresham Livingston.
69. *BA-H*, Aug. 16, 1925.
70. Interview: William M. Miller.
71. Glenn T. Eskew, "Demagoguery in Birmingham and the Building of Vestavia," *The Alabama Review*, 42 (July 1989), pp. 192–217; also LAL, "Will Barrett and 'the fat rosy temple of Juno,'" *The Southern Literary Journal*, 2 (Spring 1994), pp. 58–76.
72. WP's review of *A World Unsuspected*, *The New York Times Book Review*, Oct. 11, 1987, p. 41.
73. WP, "Another Message in the Bottle," in *SSL*, p. 358.
74. WP to SF, Nov. 20, 1971.
75. WP, "Questions They Never Asked Me," *Esquire*, 88 (December 1977), p. 186.
76. *The Birmingham City Directory* lists 2144 Highland Avenue for Miss Stillwell's School in 1926 and 1927. Interviews: WP, LP-G, DDDA, Hill Ferguson, and Ernest Oliver, M.D.—all of whom attended Miss Stillwell's. Also Leah Rawls Atkins, *The Valley and the Hills: An Illustrated History of Birmingham and Jefferson County* (Woodland Hills, Calif.: Windsor Publications, 1981), p. 88.
77. WP to Charles Barrett, April 10, 1980.
78. Information about BUS and the Percys derived from several interviews: Morris C. Benners, Beach Chenoweth, M.D., William M. Miller, Paschal G. Shook.
79. Brochure in archives of PS, SJ. Tuition was $200 for the first and second forms, $250 for the third and fourth forms, and $300 for the upper forms. See an ad for the school in *BA-H*, Sept. 4, 1927.
80. Interview: LP-G.
81. Interview: BPP with John Jones (April 17, 1980). MDAH. Interview: PRB.
82. WP, "Bourbon," in *SSL*, p. 105.
83. GH.
84. Interview: LP-G.

85. LP to E. L. Sharkey, Nov. 23, 1925; LP to Vanderbilt Hotel in New York City, Nov. 23, 1925.

86. LP to James Sexton, Jan. 15, 1926.

87. RERCB.

88. RERCB (dated May 12, 1926).

89. A map of Rockridge Park, including the Percy lot, can be found in Marilyn Davis Barefield, *A History of Mountain Brook, Alabama, and Incidentally of Shades Mountain* (Birmingham: Southern University Press, 1989), p. 160.

90. *The Independent Presbyterian Church, Birmingham, Alabama*, p. 79.

91. LP to Charles Burch, Aug. 11, 1926.

92. John F. Baker, "PW Interviews: Walker Percy," *Publishers Weekly*, March 21, 1977, p. 6.

93. "Altamont Heritage: The History of The Altamont School," *Altamont Alumni*, Winter 1987, pp. 4–7.

94. Noel Workman, "Forty Years Ago the Rampaging River Brought the Cry . . . De Levee Done Broke!," *The Delta Review*, 4 (March–April 1967), p. 24. BD also gives a firsthand account of this flood. A native of Washington County, Mississippi, Henry ("Harry") Waring Ball, the son of Dr. and Mrs. Spencer Ball, edited *The Greenville* (Mississippi) *Times*.

95. Interview: Hill Ferguson. Information derived from a 1925 Camp Winnepe brochure.

96. WP's talk "Remembering Chicago," given after receiving the 1984 Loyola-Mellon Humanities Award at Loyola University, Chicago, Feb. 28, 1984.

97. WP, "Physician as Novelist," a reply upon receiving the T. S. Eliot Award, Nov. 4, 1988.

98. William Stage, "Street Talk," *The St. Louis* (Missouri) *RiverFront Times*, April 24–30, 1985.

99. Interview: Robert McDavid Smith.

100. *The House of Percy*, p. 253.

101. Mrs. LeRoy Pratt Percy of Birmingham to LP, "Thursday night," [n.d.].

102. In at least one conversation in the early 1980s, WP mentioned that BPP was present just after his father shot himself. Interview: JG.

103. LP-G has no recollection of his father's funeral, and thus believes he and WP were not there. Source for train schedules: *The Official Guide of the Railways and Steam Navigation of the United States, Puerto Rico, Canada, Mexico and Cuba* (New York: National Railway Publishing Company, July 1929).

104. Interview: Dr. and Mrs. Ernest Oliver of Birmingham. This rumor also persisted in Greenville. CGB, *The Half Gods* (Boston: Houghton Mifflin Company, 1968), p. 519.

105. SHCUNC, series I: A-4, Chapters 4 and 5.

106. SHCUNC, series I: B-2, p. 268.

107. WP to RC, Thursday, [probably early December 1973]. Archives of RC. In discussing his relationship with WP, RC raised a caveat: "But do one scene in *The Last Gentleman* (the recollected suicide of Will's father) and one scene in *The Second Coming* (Will's potentially suicidal descent into a cave) constitute a preoccupation?" ("Shadowing Binx," in *Literature and Medicine*, Vol. 4, edited by Peter W. Graham [Baltimore: Johns Hopkins University Press, 1985], p. 158.)

108. For a fine analysis of this event, see J. Gerald Kennedy, "The Semiotics of Memory: Suicide in *The Second Coming*," *Delta* (Université Paul Valéry, Montpellier, France: November 1981), pp. 103–25.

109. WP to PS, SJ, March 15, 1981.

110. Unpublished interview of WP by LWH (May 9, 1980). In this same interview, WP admitted that he was not haunted by his father's suicide the way Will Barrett was for years. He stated that *SC* was not a *roman-à-clef*.

111. "Walker, Will, and Honor Dying: The Percys and Literary Creativity," p. 232.

112. Mattie Sue Percy rented out the home in 1929 for $1,200; in 1930 and 1931 for $3,600 each year; and in 1932 for $225. From May 1, 1932, to April 30, 1933, Gilbert S. Bright rented the house. Eventually, Margaret Bush bought the house, gradually remodeled it, and lived there with her daughter, Gage. Records of Jefferson County Probate Court in Alabama, especially those of Jan. 9, Nov. 15, 1933. The three Percy boys inherited the Country Club Road house, worth more than $30,000, after their mother's death. A postcard, dated May 15, 1973, in one of LP-G's books in his library in Greenville, from WP to LP-G cryptically states: "I agree, hold out for 140 G on Birmingham property."

2. Athens and Greenville, 1929–33

1. LP to WAP, Aug. 12, 1929; LP to Mattie Sue Percy, Aug. 13, 1929.

2. Ferdinand Phinizy's regiment landed in Savannah, Georgia, engaged in fighting the British there, and eventually fought at Newport, Philadelphia, and in the battles leading up to the surrender of Cornwallis. He was discharged from service on Jan. 14, 1784, married Margaret Condon, an Irish woman from Rhode Island, settled in Wilkes County, Georgia, then built a home, called China Grove, in Stephens (Bowling Green), Oglethorpe County, and finally took up residence in Augusta, where he became a merchant. He and Margaret had five children: Sarah, Jacob (1790–1853), Eliza, John, and Marcoe. After Margaret's death in Augusta in August 1815, he married Mary Hudson Sanders, a widow. Ferdinand Phinizy, a convert to Methodism from Roman Catholicism, died at age fifty-seven on Oct. 19, 1818. His eldest son, Jacob, married Matilda Stewart, the daughter of General John Stewart, on June 25, 1813, in Augusta. Together they had six children: Ferdinand (1819–89), Marcoe, John Thomas, Jacob, Sarah Matilda, and Margaret. A captain in the military and a planter in Oglethorpe County, Jacob moved his family to Athens to take advantage of the university there. Jacob's son Ferdinand married Harriet Hays Bowdre of Augusta on Feb. 22, 1849, and they had eight children: Ferdinand Bowdre, Stewart, Leonard, Mary Louise, Jacob, Marion Daniel, Billups (born Feb. 27, 1861), and Harry Hays. Ferdinand was a partner in Augusta in the cotton firm of Phinizy & Clayton, which eventually became F. Phinizy & Company, and a director of the Georgia Railroad & Banking Company. For a long time he was an agent for the Southern Mutual Insurance Company in Augusta. During the Civil War, he was a financial officer for the Confederacy and transported cotton through the Federal blockade. After Harriet died on Feb. 7, 1863, he married again, this time to Anne Barrett, and had three more children: Savannah, Barrett, and Charles Henry. Though Ferdinand had been financially hurt by the war, he invested wisely and was known as one who adapted with ease to the new order in the New South. He owned an extension of the Cobbham section of Athens later developed as Lynwood Park. At the time of his death in Athens, he was reputed to be a millionaire, one of the wealthiest men in Georgia. For further information about the history of the Phinizy family, see Dr. Ferdinand Phinizy Calhoun, Jr., *The Phinizy Family in America* (Atlanta: Johnson-Dallis Company, n.d.), as well as the work his son compiled, *Grandmother Was a Phinizy* (privately printed, 1991). August Longstreet Hall, *Annals of Athens, Georgia, 1801–1901* (Athens: Banner Job Office, 1906), pp. 392–93;

also *A Portrait of Historic Athens and Clarke County* (Athens: University of Georgia Press, 1992), p. 103.

3. BPS to WP, Jan. 16, 1979.

4. Nellie's mother, Martha ("Mattie") Stovall (Jan. 15, 1836–Feb. 1, 1906), died in Athens. Her mother, Jane Smithey Wilson, the heroine of Edyth Kaigh-Eustace's tribute *The Tragedy of Mosega*, and her father, Dr. Alexander Erwin Wilson, worked among the Matabele tribe 1,000 miles northeast of Cape Town, South Africa. Mattie Wilson was shipped to Richmond, Virginia, as a young girl to live with her aunt and grandmother. She married Bolling Anthony Stovall of Augusta on Sept. 19, 1856, and they moved to Athens about 1872. Their daughter Nellie married Billups Phinizy. In 1846, Sarah Matilda Phinizy, the daughter of Jacob and Matilda Stewart Phinizy, married John M. Billups, a descendant of George Billups, who was born in 1755 in Gloucester County, Virginia. Like the names Walker and LeRoy, the name Billups has an old and distinguished history of its own. (See "In Memoriam: Mrs. M. W. Stovall" in the Rare Book Room of the Ilah Dunlap Little Library at the University of Georgia in Athens.)

5. Malcolm Jones, "Moralist of the South," *The New York Times*, March 22, 1987, Section 6, p. 46.

6. Interview of WP by Dorothy H. Kitchings, *More Conversations*, p. 9.

7. Interview-essay by Ray Broussard in *The St. Tammany* (Louisiana) *News-Banner*, March 25, 1987.

8. Interview: Mattie L. Marshall.

9. For a fictional account of John Houghton, see *LG*, p. 199.

10. Interview: JJS.

11. WP's introduction to LWH, *Walker Percy: A Comprehensive Descriptive Bibliography* (New Orleans: Faust Publishing Company, 1988), p. xviii.

12. Interview: JJS.

13. Unpublished interview of WP by Sr. Park Jeong-Mi, R.S.C.J.

14. Interview: Leon Southerland.

15. Interview: NJ.

16. *AB-H*, May 19, 1930.

17. GH. WP mentions specifically that he was in contact with Aunt Annie B. while she had tuberculosis.

18. Interview: Dolores Elizabeth Artau.

19. English II, taught by Miss Sarah Matthews, for which he received a 93; Latin II, taught by Miss Martha Comer (88—his grade for Latin I at BUS had been 92); Algebra I, taught by Miss Mattie Jane Kimbrough (97, for one-half credit); civics, taught by Miss Comer (96), and ancient history (92). Academic records are from the Clarke County School Board in Georgia and the Greenville High School. Interview: Melvin D. Brown, Class of 1933 from Athens High School.

20. WP, "Going Back to Georgia," in *SSL*, p. 27.

21. MF to J. B. Hebron, Oct. 12, 1929.

22. MF to W. A. Percy in Los Angeles, Oct. 19, 1929.

23. MF to James G. McConkey, Nov. 11, 1929.

24. WAP in Memphis to Malcolm Davis, Dec. 2, 1929.

25. *AB-H*, May 18, 1930.

26. *AB-H*, May 14, June 4, 1930. Interview: WP.

27. WP's introduction to the reprint of *LL* (Baton Rouge: LSU Press, 1973), pp. vii ff.

28. *DD-T*, June 9, 1930.

29. *DD-T*, June 24, 1930. Interview: SF.

30. *DD-T*, July 1, 1930.

31. *AB-H*, June 16, 1930.

32. *AB-H*, July 13, 24, Aug. 6, 1930.

33. *AB-H*, July 22, 1930.

34. For another sympathetic account of Greenville, see Hodding Carter, Jr., "The Broad-sword Virtues," *Southern Legacy* (Baton Rouge: LSU Press, 1950), pp. 1–15. For a more up-to-date account, see Tony Dunbar, "What Is It About Greenville?," *Delta Time: A Journey Through Mississippi* (New York: Pantheon Books, 1990), pp. 208–18.

35. Interview: JJS.

36. CGB, "The Symbolic Landscape," *The Delta Review*, 1 (Winter 1963–64), p. 16.

37. *The Pica* (newspaper of Greenville High School), April 13, Nov. 24, 1933.

38. *DD-T*, Oct. 14, 1962.

39. Interview: RC.

40. WP to CGB, Nov. 15, 1968.

41. CGB, *The Half Gods* (Boston: Houghton Mifflin, 1968), p. 122.

42. Interview: CGB.

43. Chapter 24 of *LL.*; also "William Alexander Percy and the Fugitives: A Literary Correspondence, 1921–1923," edited by JG, *The Southern Review*, 21 (April 1985), p. 415.

44. WP to Jean Stafford Liebling, March 29, 1971.

45. Unpublished interview of WP by Sadamichi Kato.

46. Hodding Carter, Jr., *Lower Mississippi* (New York: Rinehart & Company, 1942), p. 406.

47. WP, "Uncle Will's House," *Architectural Digest*, 41 (October 1984), p. 44.

48. David L. Cohn, "Eighteenth-Century Chevalier," *The Virginia Quarterly Review*, 31 (Autumn 1955), p. 571.

49. BPS, "William Alexander Percy: His Philosophy of Life as Reflected in His Poetry" (M.A. thesis, University of Georgia, 1957), p. 5.

50. Interviews: BPP and SF.

51. Interview: WP.

52. Interview: SFP.

53. *The Pica*, Oct. 11, 14, 1930.

54. Interview of WP by John C. Carr, in *Conversations*, p. 56; interview of WP by John Griffin Jones in *Conversations*, p. 259.

55. WP at "The Time Has Come" Conference in Greenville in 1982.

56. BD, Oct. 25, 1930.

57. Interview: Leon K. Koury.

58. *DD-T*, Nov. 28, 1930.

59. *DD-T*, Nov. 11, 1930.

60. Interview: SF.

61. *DD-T*, Oct. 2, 1930.

62. Interview: SFP.

63. Holmes Adams, "Writers of Greenville, Mississippi, 1915–1950," *The Journal of Mississippi History*, 32 (August 1970), pp. 229–43.

64. "Eighteenth-Century Chevalier," p. 562.

65. Hodding Carter, Jr., *Where Main Street Meets the River* (New York: Rinehart & Company, 1952), pp. 264–65.

66. Ellen Douglas at "The Time Has Come" Conference in Greenville in 1982.

67. Rabbi Leo E. Turitz and Evelyn Turitz, *Jews in Early Mississippi* (Jackson: University Press of Mississippi, 1983), pp. 65–72.

68. Lillian McLaughlin's and Ben Wasson's tributes to Caroline Stern, *DD-T*, June 18, 1939; June 15, 1975.
69. *The Pica*, Nov. 12, 1930.
70. For data about the earliest published material by WP, see Stuart Wright, *Walker Percy: A Bibliography: 1930–1984* (Westport, Conn.: Meckler Publishing, 1986), p. 33; also *Conversations*, p. 31.
71. WP to SF, May 26, 1989.
72. WP to SF, March 4, 1978.
73. Interview: Eudora Welty.
74. SHCUNC, series I: A-8, p. 8.
75. Interview: SF.
76. Interview: SF.
77. Interviews: WP, SF, and Margaret Kirk Virden.
78. Interview: WP.
79. WP to SF, Aug. 9, 1986.
80. *DD-T*, Jan. 10, 1931.
81. *DD-T*, Feb. 10, 1931.
82. "William Alexander Percy and the Fugitives: A Literary Correspondence, 1921–1923," p. 416.
83. "Eighteenth-Century Chevalier," pp. 572–73.
84. Arnold Rampersad, *The Life of Langston Hughes*, Vol. 1 (New York: Oxford University Press, 1986), pp. 231–32. Also *Conversations with Shelby Foote*, edited by William C. Carter (Jackson: University Press of Mississippi, 1989) p. 236.
85. Jonathan Daniels, *A Southerner Discovers the South* (New York: Macmillan Publishing Company, 1938), pp. 172–80.
86. SF to WP, Dec. 24, 1977.
87. *DD-T*, March 5, 1931.
88. BD, May 7, 1931.
89. Interview: SF.
90. *The Pica*, March 30, 1931.
91. *The Pica*, April 29, 1931.
92. WP to SF, Sept. 3, 1980.
93. *The Pica*, April 25, 1932.
94. WP, "The Books That Made Writers," *The New York Times Book Review*, Nov. 25, 1979, pp. 7, 80.
95. Interview: SF. "The Books That Made Writers" and the interview of WP by W. Kenneth Holditch in *More Conversations*, p. 25.
96. Ann Waldron, *Close Connections: Caroline Gordon and the Southern Renaissance* (New York: G. P. Putnam's Sons, 1987).
97. *The Percys of Mississippi*, pp. 117–18; also "William Alexander Percy and the Fugitives: A Literary Correspondence, 1921–1923," pp. 415–27.
98. Interview: CGB. Also his essay entitled "The Old Life" in the William Alexander Percy Library in Greenville, Mississippi.
99. Interview: William Alexander Percy II of Greenville, Mississippi. Dudley Percy, "Change Comes to the Plantation," *The Atlanta* (Georgia) *Constitution*, July 19, 1988.
100. For a study of Trail Lake in the mid-1930s, see Raymond McClinton, "A Social-Economic Analysis of a Mississippi Delta Plantation" (M.A. thesis, UNC, 1938).
101. Interview: SF.

102. *The Pica*, Oct. 9, 1931.

103. SHCUNC, series I: A-4, pp. 199, 230.

104. *The Pica*, Nov. 25, 1931.

105. *The Pica*, Jan. 27, 1932.

106. *The Pica*, Feb. 24, 1932.

107. *The Pica*, March 17, 1932.

108. Interview: John ("Buddy") Branton.

109. Bertram Wyatt-Brown, "Walker, Will, and Honor Dying: The Percys and Literary Creativity," in *Looking South: Chapters in the Story of an American Region*, edited by Winfred B. Moore, Jr., and Joseph F. Tripp (Westport, Conn.: Greenwood Press, 1989), pp. 237–38; also *DD-T*, April 2, 1932.

110. Interview: NJ.

111. BD, April 3, 1932.

112. Interview: NJ.

113. Interviews: NJ and JJS.

114. Interview: JJS.

115. Interview: WP.

116. GH.

117. WP told at least two people, both of whom I interviewed, that he thought his mother committed suicide. One person has asked not to be identified; the other is PRB. Once, after CGB had brought up the matter of Mrs. Percy's death with RC, and RC had related the conversation to WP, RC suspected in his heart that WP believed that his mother had committed suicide. RC and WP, however, never explicitly discussed Mrs. Percy's death. Interview: RC. WP once posed the troubling question to his daughter Ann: "Why didn't Mother ever get out of that car?" Interview: APM.

118. Interview: SF.

119. Interview: RC.

120. Interview: Lyn (Hill) Hayward.

121. *The Pica*, April 25, 1932.

122. *The Pica*, April 25, 1932.

123. WP to Mary Eloise Jarrell, [n.d.].

124. *The Percys of Mississippi*, p. 166.

125. *The Pica*, Oct. 5, 1932.

126. Interview of LP-G by John Griffin Jones, MDAH.

127. *The Pica*, Oct. 28, 1932.

128. *The Pica*, Oct. 28, 1932.

129. See WP to SF, Feb. 7, 1972; also William W. Starr, "A Diagnostician of the Human Spirit," *The Columbia* (South Carolina) *State*, Nov. 5, 1980.

130. Information on a form filled out by Mary Shields for "The Time Has Come" Conference in Greenville in 1982.

131. "Twilight of the Lives" was originally published in the Oct. 5, 1932, issue of *The Pica* and then repeated in the Nov. 23, 1932, issue.

132. WP, "Physician as Novelist," a reply upon receiving the T. S. Eliot Award, Nov. 4, 1988.

133. *The Percys of Mississippi*, pp. 146–47.

134. *LL*, pp. 280–81.

135. Interview: SF.

136. WP, "Mississippi: The Fallen Paradise," in *SSL*, p. 46.

137. WP, "Bourbon," in *SSL*, p. 105.

138. Interview: Mary Kathryn Finlay.
139. Notebook of RM concerning a meeting of the Jung group, Jan. 10, 1979. WP said that the girl's father owned a hardware store; most likely he was trying to think of a drugstore, but confused it with Wetherbee's Hardware Store.
140. SHCUNC, series I: B-4, pp. 311 ff.
141. Interview: WP.
142. WP to SF, June 25, 1983.
143. Talk by WP at the Mississippi Arts and Letters Award ceremony, May 26, 1988. Archives of Noel Polk.
144. *The Pica*, April 13, 1933.
145. SF to WP: April 29, 1975.
146. Interview: LP-G.
147. WP, "Remembering Chicago," a talk given after receiving the Mellon Humanities Award at Loyola University in Chicago, Feb. 28, 1984.
148. WP to Edwin T. Boone, Jr., Nov. 16, 1973.
149. Personal Information Sheet for Admission to P&S, Jan. 14, 1937.
150. Anne Abernathy and Maggie Bryan, "Dr. Walker Percy: Novelist," *Pathways*, Fall 1972, p. 23.

3. The College Years, 1933–37

1. *DTH*, Oct. 12, 13, 1934. Unless noted otherwise, *DTH* is the source for references to campus and fraternity activities.
2. For material on Howard Odum, I am indebted to Fred Hobson, *Tell About the South: The Southern Rage to Explain* (Baton Rouge: LSU Press, 1983), pp. 180–202.
3. Interview: LP-G.
4. Alumni record at UNC, dated September 1933.
5. Interview: Donald Wetherbee, M.D. For a partial view of UNC recounted by a left-wing student whose days at Chapel Hill overlapped with WP's, see Junius Irving Scales and Richard Nickson, *Cause at Heart: A Former Communist Remembers* (Athens: University of Georgia Press, 1987).
6. WP, "From Facts to Fiction," in *SSL*, p. 187.
7. *More Conversations*, p. 104; also SF to WP, Aug. 28, 1952.
8. *DTH*, Sept. 27, 1933.
9. Interview of WP by Dannye Romine, *Conversations*, p. 200.
10. Interview: LP-G. Wasson's version is in his *Count No 'Count: Flashbacks to Faulkner* (Jackson: University Press of Mississippi, 1983), pp. 59–63. WP mentions this visit in "Uncle Will's House," *Architectural Digest*, 41 (October 1984), p. 50. WP once repeated versions of this story to RM, Richard R. Schulze, Jr., M.D., and W. Kenneth Holditch (*More Conversations*, p. 25). Also *The Percys of Mississippi*, p. 162. This story has been repeated often, and thus become vivid in the minds of many Greenvillians, so much so that some, who were certainly not present, believe that they actually witnessed the event. LP-G did hear Faulkner speak on May 15, 1952, when Faulkner gave a speech on the campus of the Delta State Teachers College in Cleveland, Mississippi. WP had great admiration for Faulkner as a writer, yet WP never felt intimidated by Faulkner or his writings.
11. WP, *The New York Times Book Review*, June 3, 1979.
12. *DTH*, Sept. 22, 23, 1933.
13. WP to Ansley Cope, Sept. 24, 1987. Interview: Ross G. Allen.

14. *DTH*, Sept. 27, 1933.

15. *DTH*, Sept. 22, 1933.

16. SF to WP, Feb. 8, 1951; Elise Winter, *Dinner at the Mansion* (Oxford, Miss.: Yoknapatawpha Press, 1982), p. 84.

17. William W. Starr, "A Diagnostician of the Human Spirit," *The Columbia* (South Carolina) *State*, Nov. 5, 1980.

18. *DTH*, Oct. 12, 1933.

19. *DTH*, Jan. 14, 1934.

20. *DTH*, Feb. 22, 1934.

21. Interview: Henry W. Lewis, who has a copy of the photograph.

22. Interview: James D. Carr.

23. WP to Ansley Cope, Oct. 8, 1961.

24. WP to Mr. and Mrs. James D. Carr, May 19, 1973.

25. *DTH*, March 2, 1934.

26. *DTH*, March 11, 1934.

27. *DTH*, April 8, 1934.

28. I am grateful to Manfred van Rey, archivist of Bonn, for verifying the accuracy of this material. WP indicated to PS, SJ that he believed this building was the one he lived in, at least briefly, while in Bonn.

29. Interview: WP. Also interviews of WP by Jan Nordby Gretlund in *Conversations*, p. 208, and in *More Conversations*, p. 104, and Phil McCombs in *More Conversations*, p. 190.

30. Interview: WP.

31. *The Pica*, Jan. 23, 1934.

32. *The Pica*, Oct. 10, 1934.

33. For a description of these typescripts, see my article "Two Conversations in Walker Percy's *The Thanatos Syndrome*: Text and Context," in *Walker Percy: Novelist and Philosopher*, pp. 24–32.

34. Interview: WP.

35. *The Pica*, May 30, 1934.

36. Mentioned in a letter from LP-G to DHS, July 18, [1988]; also DHS to LP-G, July 21, 1988. Interview: DHS.

37. Interview: James D. Carr.

38. Interview: James D. Carr.

39. *DTH*, Oct. 9, 1934.

40. Interview: SF.

41. *DTH*, Nov. 16, 1934.

42. *The 1935 Yackety Yack*. Interviews: Jean Brock Hawley, Edward Clement, and Clay Clement Pitlick.

43. Interviews: Henry W. Lewis and SFP.

44. *DTH*, Jan. 25, 1935.

45. Interview: John E. Cay, Jr.

46. SF to WP, Feb. 2, 1977. Interview: SF.

47. Interview: SF. Also the letter of SF to WP, Feb. 2, 1977.

48. Interview: Louis Shaffner.

49. WP to Joseph Schwartz, Jan. 14, 1981.

50. Interview: James D. Carr.

51. Interview: SF.

52. Interview: James L. Sprunt, Jr.

53. Interview: WP.

54. Interview: SF.

55. Interview: James L. Sprunt, Jr. WP to SF, March 17, 1989.

56. Interview: Louis Shaffner.

57. Clare Jupiter, "Walker Percy of Covington," *The* (New Orleans) *States-Item*, June 21, 1975.

58. WP's admission records at P&S.

59. These letters of reference are part of WP's admission records at P&S.

60. Interviews: SF and James L. Sprunt, Jr.

61. "Walker Percy: The Chapel Hill Years," by Lynn Roundtree (privately published).

62. *DTH*, May 23, 1936.

63. WP listed his membership in Phi Beta Kappa on the "Author's Questionnaire" he filled out for Knopf on Sept. 16, 1960, as well as on the Faculty Information Sheet for Loyola University, New Orleans, Oct. 15, 1967.

64. Interview of WP by Dannye Romine in *Conversations*, p. 200.

65. In the version of the essay entitled "The State of the Novel: Dying Art or New Science?," which WP delivered at Washington and Lee University, he mentions visiting this campus while studying at UNC.

66. Interviews: James L. Sprunt, Jr., and James D. Carr.

67. Interview: SF.

68. Interview: SF.

69. WAP to CG, May 27, 1936. Also *The Percys of Mississippi*, p. 159.

70. Interview: WP.

71. Interview: Thomas A. Underwood.

72. WP to Thomas A. Underwood, May 12, 1987.

73. Birmingham Tax Assessor's Report, Oct. 21, 1936.

74. *DTH*, Sept. 24, 1936.

75. WP to SK, [n.d., circa March 1962].

76. Interview: WP.

77. A note on WP's transcript indicates that a copy of his transcript was sent to Harvard Medical School on Jan. 16, 1936. I believe this is an error, and the year should be 1937; most likely a clerk in the Registrar's Office confused the old year with the new year, as often happens during the month of January. Interview: RC.

78. WP to Charles A. Flood, M.D., March 11, 1937.

79. Interview: Louis Shaffner.

80. Interview: WP.

81. Interview of WP by Malcolm Jones in *More Conversations*, p. 173.

4. The Medical School Years, 1937–41

1. WP to SF, Nov. 10, 1981.

2. For background on P & S, see John C. Dalton, *History of the College of Physicians and Surgeons in the City of New York* (New York: Columbia University Press, 1988), and Charles A. Flood's unpublished memoir *P&S: The College of Physicians and Surgeons: Columbia University*.

3. WAP to CG, Sept. 22, 1937.

4. Timothy Wagner, "The History of Bard Hall," in the program entitled "An Evening of Celebration: Columbia University: Bard Hall, Dec. 4, 1991."

5. "Report of the Dean of the School of Medicine of Columbia University for the Period

Ending June 30, 1938," Augustus C. Long Health Sciences Library of Columbia University. Unless otherwise noted, data mentioned in passing about P & S will come from these annual Dean's Reports.

6. Interview: Chester Fairlie, Jr., M.D.

7. Quoted in *Walker Percy: An American Search*, p. 63.

8. Letter from George L. Hawkins, Jr., M.D., to PS, SJ, Aug. 18, 1987.

9. Interview: Frank J. Hardart, Jr., M.D.

10. Interview: Gilbert H. Mudge, M.D. WP kept his medical school textbooks and notebooks first at Brinkwood and then in a shed at his brother LP-G's house (SF to WP, Oct. 31, Nov. 1, 1950), but eventually they disappeared.

11. Interview: Philip Knapp, M.D.

12. For information about Huger W. Jervey, see *A History of the School of Law: Columbia University*, by the staff of the Foundation for Research in Legal History under the direction of Julius Goebel, Jr. (New York: Columbia University Press, 1955), pp. 275–305, 330–31, 361.

13. WP, "From Facts to Fiction," in *SSL*, p. 187.

14. Letter reproduced in BPS, "William Alexander Percy: His Philosophy of Life as Reflected in His Poetry" (M.A. thesis, University of Georgia, 1957), p. 13.

15. "Report of the Dean of the School of Medicine of Columbia University for the Period Ending June 30, 1938," pp. 37–38, 39, 45.

16. Interviews: SF, WP, and William E. Borah. *Conversations with Shelby Foote*, pp. 147–48; Julia Reed, "The Last Southern Gentleman," *U.S. News & World Report*, March 16, 1987, p. 76; Robert L. Phillips, *Shelby Foote: Novelist and Historian* (Jackson: University Press of Mississippi, 1992), p. 21; interview of WP by Zoltán Abádi-Nagy in *Conversations*, p. 85, where the encounter is said to have taken place when WP was in college; this version does not coincide with the completion of *If I Forget Thee, O Jerusalem* (*The Wild Palms*) in June 1938. In a letter to ES, dated Oct. 2, 1969, WP wrote that he and SF were on their way to Chapel Hill when they stopped at Rowan Oak; he added in reference to Faulkner, "I never met him." Also Tracy Lee Simmons, "Ken Burns' 'Civil War' and the Future of Literature: A Concluding Walk with Shelby Foote," *Crisis*, 10 (January 1992), p. 34, and Willie Morris, *Faulkner's Mississippi* (Birmingham, Ala.: Oxmoor House, 1990), pp. 63–64. In a letter to SF, dated Oct. 6, 1972, WP expressed an interest in returning to Faulkner's house, taking a look inside, and then continuing to the battlefield at Shiloh. WP remembers reading *Gone with the Wind* as he mentioned in an interview with W. Kenneth Holditch in *More Conversations*, p. 25.

17. *More Conversations*, p. 35.

18. *Conversations*, pp. 275–76.

19. *The House of Percy*, pp. 294–95.

20. CGT to Brainard Cheney, Dec. 31, 1951.

21. WP to SF, Aug. 4, 1987; SF to WP, Aug. 8, 1987.

22. WP to Robert Lokey, M.D., March 7, 1990.

23. Interview: Betty Carter. Ann Waldron, *Hodding Carter: The Reconstruction of a Racist* (Chapel Hill, N.C.: Algonquin Books, 1993), pp. 60–126. I gratefully acknowledge my indebtedness to this book and to Mrs. Waldron for sharing with me, on several occasions, her insights about Greenville and the Hodding Carters.

24. WP, "Diagnosing the Modern Malaise," in *SSL*, p. 205.

25. Source: Conversation between Lyn Hill (Hayward) and WP.

26. WP, "A Doctor Talks with the South and Its Young Heroes," *The National Observer*, Sept. 16, 1972, p. 14.

27. Helen Swick Perry, *Psychiatrist of America: The Life of Harry Stack Sullivan* (Cambridge, Mass.: Belknap Press, 1982), pp. 374–75.

28. Harry Stack Sullivan, M.D., "Memorandum on a Psychiatric Reconnaissance," in Charles S. Johnson, *Growing Up in the Black Belt: Negro Youth in the Rural South* (Washington, D.C.: American Council on Education, 1941), pp. 328–33. In *The Thanatos Syndrome*, Dr. Thomas More pays tribute to Dr. Sullivan: "My psychiatric faith I got in the old days from Dr. Harry Stack Sullivan, perhaps this country's best psychiatrist, who, if not a genius, had a certain secret belief which he himself could not account for. Nor could it be scientifically proven. He thus transmitted it to his residents. It seemed to him to be an article of faith, and to me it is as valuable as Freud's genius . . . *Each patient this side of psychosis, and even some psychotics, has the means of obtaining what he needs, she needs, with a little help from you.*"

29. *DD-T*, Jan. 4, 1939.

30. Interview: SFP.

31. Interviews: Nicholas Dellis and Susanne M. Jensen.

32. Interview: WP.

33. WP, "The Coming Crisis in Psychiatry: II," *America*, 96 (Jan. 12, 1957), p. 416.

34. WP, "The Man on the Train," *The Partisan Review*, 23 (Fall 1956), p. 494.

35. Quoted in *Walker Percy: An American Search*, p. 63.

36. WP to RC, Thursday, [Dec. 20, 1973].

37. Interview of WP by Barbara King in *Conversations*, p. 94.

38. Interview of WP by John C. Carr in *Conversations*, p. 67.

39. Born in India in 1905, Janet Rioch grew up in missionary surroundings; her father, David, headed a sect of a Christian denomination in Damoh known as the Campbellites. Her mother, Minnie Henly, was a missionary doctor. Educated both at home and in an Indian girls' school, Janet eventually left India for her higher education. In 1932 her parents returned to Boston, where they joined up with David, Janet's brother, who was then teaching anatomy at Harvard Medical School. Janet received her undergraduate degree from Butler College in Indiana and her medical degree in 1930 from the University of Rochester, interning for two years in medicine and surgery. She then did research in 1932–33 in the Department of Physiology at Harvard. During 1933–35, she lived in Towson, Maryland, working as a psychiatric resident at the Sheppard and Enoch Pratt Hospital; here she first met Clara Thompson, who became her friend and colleague. At meetings of the Washington-Baltimore Psychoanalytic Society, Dr. Rioch met Harry Stack Sullivan, William Silverberg, Karen Horney, Frieda Fromm-Reichmann, and Erich Fromm—all interested in discussing and exploring the recent developments in psychoanalysis. These contacts proved to be important in her life, as she participated and took a stand on the positions of her colleagues. On Dec. 4, 1933, Lucile Dooley, Ernest E. Hadley, and Sullivan formed the William Alanson White Psychoanalytic Foundation. Janet Rioch would eventually found the New York Branch of the Washington School of Psychiatry with Clara Thompson and Erich Fromm. Her brother also played an important role in the institution. In 1935, she came to New York City and moved into an apartment at 605 West 112th Street and opened her office on East 50th Street. She worked for two years as a research assistant in the field of psychosomatic medicine at Presbyterian Hospital. In 1936, she collaborated with H. Flanders Dunbar and Theodore P. Wolfe in investigating and reporting in considerable detail on the psychic component of the disease process in cardiac, diabetic, and fracture patients. Her colleagues said, however, that she felt most comfortable as an attending pediatric psychiatrist at Roosevelt Hospital.

40. WP to NL, Feb. 28, 1987.

41. Interview: Earl G. Witenberg, M.D.

42. Harry Stack Sullivan, M.D., "Conceptions of Modern Psychiatry," *Psychiatry*, 3 (1940), pp. 1–117.

43. "Conceptions of Modern Psychiatry," p. 10.

44. "Conceptions of Modern Psychiatry," p. 12.

45. *Walker Percy: An American Search*, p. 18.

46. Janet Rioch, M.D., "The Function of the Child Guidance Clinic," *The Roosevelt Review*, 12 (1941), pp. 15–16.

47. Lecture by Clara Thompson, M.D., for the Harry Stack Sullivan Society, March 15, 1955. Archives of the William Alanson White Institute, New York City.

48. "A patient cannot feel close to a detached or hostile analyst and will therefore never display the full intensity of his transference illusions. The complexity of this process, whereby the transference can be used as the therapeutic instrument and, at the same time, as a resistance, may be illustrated by the following example: a patient had developed intense feelings of attachment to a father surrogate in his everyday life. The transference feelings towards this man were of great value in elucidating his original problems with his real father. As a patient became more and more aware of his own personal validity, he found this masochistic attachment to be weakening. This occasioned acute feelings of anxiety, since his sense of independence was not yet fully established. At that point, he developed very disturbing feelings regarding the analyst, believing that she was untrustworthy and hostile, although prior to this, he had succeeded in establishing a realistically positive relationship to her. The feelings of untrustworthiness precisely reproduced an ancient pattern with his mother. He experienced them at this particular point in the analysis in order to retain and to justify his attachment to the father figure, the weakening of which attachment had threatened him so profoundly. The entire pattern was elucidated when it was seen that he was reëxperiencing an ancient triangle, in which he was continuously driven to a submissive attachment to a dominating father, due to the utter untrustworthiness of his weak mother. If the transference character of this sudden feeling of untrustworthiness of the analyst had not been clarified, he would have turned again submissively to his father surrogate, which would have further postponed his development of independence. Nevertheless, the development of this transference to the analyst brought to light a new insight." Janet Rioch, M.D., "The Transference Phenomenon in Psychoanalytic Practice," *Psychiatry*, 6 (1943), p. 152.

49. WP, "The Symbolic Structure of Interpersonal Process," *Psychiatry*, 24 (February 1961).

50. Sources for sequence of psychiatrists: WP and William Sorum, M.D.

51. WAP to CG, May 8, 1939.

52. Interview: SF.

53. Ann Waldron, *Close Connections: Caroline Gordon and the Southern Renaissance* (New York: G. P. Putnam's Sons, 1987), pp. 185–87; also letter from CGT to Ward Dorrance [n.d.] in the Ward Dorrance Papers. SHCUNC.

54. Interview: William Jay Smith.

55. Lecture: BPP, Orleans Club, New Orleans, Feb. 2, 1991; records of the U.S. Naval Academy, Annapolis, Maryland.

56. *Conversations with Shelby Foote*, p. 197.

57. Susie James, "Shelby Foote Visits Buddies at Barbershop," *The Oxford* (Mississippi) *Eagle*, Aug. 6, 1976.

58. Interviews: Thomas A. Underwood and Cary Peebles; also mentioned in the unpub-

lished version of WP interview with J. Gerald Kennedy and Ben Forkner (Aug. 5, 1980).

59. Interview: Maurice Edgar Coindreau.

60. WAP to CG, postmarked Jan. 29, Feb. 19, 1940.

61. WAP to Huger Jervey, June 14, 1940; "William Alexander Percy: His Philosophy of Life as Reflected in His Poetry," p. 57.

62. WP to Gilbert H. Mudge, M.D., Aug. 30, [no year, probably 1974].

63. Vernon W. Lippard, M.D., to David Seegal, M.D., May 23, 1940.

64. Vernon W. Lippard, M.D., to C. W. Munger, M.D., Sept. 12, 1940.

65. WAP to CG, Sept. 19, 1940.

66. WAP to Department of National Defense Militia, Oct. 1, 1940; "William Alexander Percy: His Philosophy of Life as Reflected in His Poetry," pp. 231–32.

67. WP to Jesse Core, Feb. 17, 1988.

68. "Author's Questionnaire" for Alfred A. Knopf, Inc., Sept. 16, 1960.

69. WP to Gilbert H. Mudge, M.D., Aug. 30, [1974].

70. Source: Benedict Groeschel, C.F.R.

71. WAP to CG, [n.d., from "Johns Hopkins"]; *The House of Percy*, p. 285.

72. Interview of WP by John Griffin Jones in *Conversations*, pp. 263–64.

73. The Last Will and Testament of WAP, dated July 17, 1941.

74. Interview of WP by John Griffin Jones in *Conversations*, p. 268.

75. *DD-T*, Oct. 5, 1941.

76. Ellen Douglas, "Walker Percy's *The Last Gentleman*: Introduction and Commentary by Ellen Douglas" (New York: Seabury Press, 1969), p. 8.

77. Interview: Earl White, M.D.

78. For the role the Townsends played in Sunflower County, see Marie M. Hemphill, *Fevers, Floods and Faith: A History of Sunflower County, Mississippi, 1844–1976* (Sunflower County Historical Society: Indianola, Mississippi, 1980), pp. 343 ff.

79. Interview of WP by John Griffin Jones in *Conversations*, pp. 266–67.

80. *DD-T*, Dec. 21, 28, 1941.

5. Illness, Recuperation, and Decision, 1942–46

1. "Author's Questionnaire" for Alfred A. Knopf, Inc., Sept. 16, 1960.

2. WAP to CG, Jan. 3, 1942.

3. Interview: LP-G.

4. Interview: BPP.

5. *Conversations with Shelby Foote*, pp. 164–65.

6. SF to WP, Dec. 11, 1973.

7. WP to BPS, May 30, 1957. For a portion of this letter, see BPS, "William Alexander Percy: His Philosophy of Life as Reflected in His Poetry" (M.A. thesis, University of Georgia, 1957), p. 97.

8. WAP to WP, May 4, 1938. For a portion of this letter, see "William Alexander Percy: His Philosophy of Life as Reflected in His Poetry," p. 108.

9. Source: L. Fred Ayvazian, M.D.

10. J. Burns Amberson, M.D., "A Retrospective of Tuberculosis: 1865–1965," *The American Review of Respiratory Diseases*, 93 (March 1966), pp. 343–51.

11. WP, "Bourbon," in *SSL*, p. 106.

12. GH.

13. "Author's Questionnaire" for Alfred A. Knopf, Inc., Sept. 16, 1960; the number of autopsies is mentioned in Herbert Mitgang, "A Talk with Walker Percy," in *Conver-*

sations, p. 148; also discussed in the unpublished interview of WP by Sr. Park Jeong-Mi, R.S.C.J.; also "A Conversation with Walker Percy," *Compostela Award Journal,* June 7, 1985.

14. GH.

15. Interview: Marie Irène Ferrer, M.D.

16. Interview: SFP.

17. Records of Bellevue Hospital, New York City.

18. Interview-essay by Ray Broussard in *The St. Tammany* (Louisiana) *News-Banner,* March 25, 1987.

19. Interview: MBTP.

20. Records of the Saranac Lake Society for the Control of Tuberculosis (now the Saranac Lake Voluntary Health Association).

21. Interview: Elise Kalb Chapin.

22. For information about Saranac Lake and the Trudeau Sanatorium, see Mark Caldwell, *Saranac Lake: Pioneer Health Resort* (Saranac Lake: Historic Saranac Lake, 1993); Mark Caldwell, *The Last Crusade: The War on Consumption, 1862–1954* (New York: Atheneum Publishers, 1988); Philip L. Gallos, *Cure Cottages of Saranac Lake: Architecture and History of a Pioneer Health Resort* (Saranac Lake: Historic Saranac Lake, 1985); Robert Taylor, *Saranac: America's Magic Mountain* (Boston: Houghton Mifflin Company, 1986). The quote is taken from *Saranac: America's Magic Mountain,* p. 233.

23. Source: L. Fred Ayvazian, M.D.

24. Photograph given to PS, SJ by Raymond Hogan, M.D., husband of Barbara O'Neil Hogan.

25. Quoted in *Walker Percy: An American Search,* pp. 65–66.

26. WP, "From Facts to Fiction," in *SSL,* pp. 186–90.

27. *Conversations,* pp. 12, 106; also *Walker Percy: An American Search,* p. 66.

28. Interview: James L. Sprunt, Jr.

29. Rev. L. Jerome Taylor, Jr., "Walker Percy and the Self," *Commonweal,* 100 (May 10, 1974), p. 233.

30. WP to Mary Deems Howland, Aug. 25, 1980.

31. WP to Stephen Kanaga, May 27, 1981.

32. Interview of WP by Barbara King, *Conversations,* pp. 92–93.

33. *Conversations,* p. 270; also *More Conversations,* p. 63; also Ellen Douglas, *"The Last Gentleman:* Introduction and Commentary" (New York: Seabury Press, 1969), pp. 8–9; also the unpublished interview of WP by Sr. Park Jeong-Mi, R.S.C.J.

34. WP could have borrowed books from the small Mellon Memorial Library with over 8,000 volumes at Trudeau or from the public library in the village, though Edna Bea Sprague, the librarian in 1943, indicated that the library had few holdings in philosophy. Interview: Edna Bea Sprague Edwards, R.N.

35. Interview: Edward Worthington.

36. "Walking Easy with Shelby Foote," an interview of WP by Tracy Lee Simmons in *Crisis,* 9 (December 1991), p. 19.

37. *Conversations,* p. 5.

38. Photograph taken in 1942 of WP's fellow physicians. Archives of Henry Frazier Parry, M.D.

39. Interview: Raymond Luomanen, M.D.

40. Interview: Francis B. Trudeau, Jr., M.D.

41. Date of January 1943 on a photograph given to PS, SJ by Raymond Hogan, M.D.

42. Interviews: Marcelle Dunning, M.D., Henry Toole Clark, M.D., and Vincent Montalbine.

43. Official "Rules and Information for Patients" pamphlet.

44. Nigel Hamilton, *JFK: Reckless Youth* (New York: Random House, 1992), pp. 497–602.

45. Quoted in *Walker Percy: An American Search*, p. 66.

46. *Saranac: America's Magic Mountain*, p. 237.

47. Interview: Henry Frazier Parry, M.D.

48. GH.

49. Interview: Helen McDonald Grossman.

50. *The House of Percy*, pp. 305–6.

51. Interview: Edwin L. Kendig, Jr., M.D.

52. On Sept. 5 in Atlantic City, on Nov. 3 in New York City, and on Jan. 11 and April 9, 1945. GH.

53. Interview: SF.

54. GH.

55. WP to Mary Bernice Townsend, July 18, 1945.

56. Interview: Howard Crockett.

57. Michiko Kakutani, "Hospital Remembers Rebirth of O'Neill," *The New York Times*, Oct. 18, 1982.

58. Interview of WP by Patricia Rice, "No 'Happily Ever After' for Walker Percy's Characters," *The St. Louis Post-Dispatch*, April 23, 1985.

59. Quoted in *Walker Percy: An American Search*, p. 67.

60. WP mentions teaching at P & S in a letter to CGB, "Friday," [no year]; also the author's bio in WP, "The Symbolic Structure of Interpersonal Process," *Psychiatry*, 24 (February 1961), p. 39.

61. Interview: SF. Also Robert L. Phillips, *Shelby Foote: Novelist and Historian* (Jackson: University Press of Mississippi, 1992), for details of Foote's life and career.

62. Interviews: MBTP and William Alexander Percy II.

63. CGT to Ward Dorrance, Dec. 7, 1945.

64. WP to SF, Feb. 28, 1987.

65. Interviews: Kenneth Haxton, Jr., and Josephine Haxton (Ellen Douglas). Interview of Ellen Douglas by John Griffin Jones in *Mississippi Writers Talking II*, edited by John Griffin Jones (Jackson: University Press of Mississippi, 1983), pp. 50–52. *Conversations*, p. 46. For WP's comments on Waugh, see Joe Larose, "Novelist Likes 'To Do a Number on the Experts,' " *The* (New Orleans) *Clarion Herald*, Dec. 15, 1988.

66. *"The Last Gentleman*: Introduction and Commentary," p. 9.

67. Hodding Carter, Jr., *Where Main Street Meets the River* (Jackson: University Press of Mississippi, 1983), pp. 182–84; also *Conversations*, pp. 268–69.

68. Interview: Mr. and Mrs. David C. Davenport.

69. Marjorie McDonough to PS, SJ, Aug. 7, 1991.

70. Interview: SF.

71. Quoted in *Walker Percy, An American Search*, pp. 67–68.

72. LWH, "Man vs. Malaise, In the Eyes of Louisiana's Walker Percy," *Louisiana Life*, 3 (July–August 1981), p. 54.

73. Interview: MBTP.

74. Interview: Salvatore Milazzo.

75. Interview: SF.

6. *The Apprenticeship Years: Writing* The Charterhouse, *1947–53*

1. WP to Paul Whyte Ferris, July 2, 1972.
2. Interview: Thomas A. Underwood.
3. WP to William Rodney Allen, Feb. 3, 1985.
4. "A Conversation with Walker Percy," *Compostela Award Journal*, June 7, 1985.
5. See the reference to Sir Thomas More and the English charterhouse in WP to SF, Aug. 4, 1970.
6. *Walker Percy: An American Search*, p. 143.
7. Interview of WP by Dannye Romine Powell in *Parting the Curtains: Interviews with Southern Writers*, interviews by Dannye Romine Powell, photographs by Jill Krementz (Winston-Salem, N.C.: John F. Blair Publisher, 1994), p. 243.
8. WP to Virginia Durr, Dec. 12, [1962].
9. Interview: WP.
10. WP, "Physician as Novelist," a reply upon receiving the T. S. Eliot Award, Nov. 4, 1988.
11. CGT to WP, June 10, 1955.
12. Interview: Virginia Milazzo.
13. Robert Cubbage, "Writing in the Ruins," *Notre Dame Magazine*, Autumn 1987, p. 30.
14. WP, "Foreword," *The New Catholics: Contemporary Converts Tell Their Stories*, edited by Dan O'Neill (New York: Crossroad, 1987), p. xv. WP to CGB, Jan. 19, 1969.
15. WP to Gilbert H. Mudge, M.D., Aug. 30, [1974].
16. Interview: BPP. Also an unpublished interview of BPP by John Jones. MDAH.
17. WP, "New Orleans Mon Amour," in *SSL*, pp. 11–12.
18. Interview: Joseph Friend.
19. "William Alexander Percy and the Fugitives: A Literary Correspondence, 1921–1923," edited by JG, *The Southern Review*, 21 (April 1985), p. 416.
20. Interview: Salvatore Milazzo.
21. WP, "Foreword," *The New Catholics: Contemporary Converts Tell Their Stories*, p. xiii.
22. Interview: WP.
23. WP, "Why Are You a Catholic?" in *SSL*, pp. 304–15.
24. SF to WP, Aug. 5, 1970.
25. Constance Casey, "Literary New Orleans," *Publishers Weekly*, May 9, 1986, p. 155.
26. LWH, "Literary Landmarks: Walker Percy's New Orleans," *Diversion Travel Planner*, 15 (January 1987), pp. 38–39, 42.
27. WP, "New Orleans: Mon Amour," in *SSL*, pp. 10–22.
28. WP, "Why I Live Where I Live," in *SSL*, p. 9.
29. "Literary Landmarks: Walker Percy's New Orleans," p. 39.
30. WP, "Foreword," *St. Tammany Parish: L'Autre Côté du Lac*, by Frederick S. Ellis (Gretna, La.: Pelican Publishing Company, 1981), pp. ix–xi.
31. Interview: MBTP.
32. WP to Joseph H. Fichter, S.J., Nov. 13, 1948.
33. Unpublished interview of WP by Sr. Park Jeong-Mi, R.S.C.J.
34. Interview: Joseph H. Fichter, S.J. Source: John R. Payne, S.J. (author of "A Jesuit Search for Social Justice: The Public Career of Louis J. Twomey, S.J., 1947–1969" [Ph.D. dissertation, University of Texas at Austin, 1976]). Unpublished interview of WP by Father Payne, April 9, 1974.
35. Joseph H. Fichter, S.J., *One-Man Research: Reminiscences of a Catholic Sociologist* (New

York: John Wiley & Sons, 1973), pp. 76–79. Father Fichter's *Southern Parish*, Vol. 1: *The Dynamics of a City Parish* (Chicago: University of Chicago Press, 1951), a study of Mater Dolorosa Parish, is an unparalleled sociological treatment of Catholicism in New Orleans for this time period.

36. Interviews: JJS and NJ.
37. Interview: Edward A. Sheridan, S.J.
38. Interview: LP-G.
39. SF to WP, March 3, 1951.
40. Interviews: LP-G and SFP.
41. Malcolm A. Franklin, *Bitterweeds: Life with William Faulkner at Rowan Oak* (Irving, Tex.: The Society for the Study of Traditional Culture, 1977), p. 59.
42. CGT to WP, [n.d.].
43. CGT to FO'C, [n.d., circa late September 1951], quoted in Sally Fitzgerald, "A Master Class: From the Correspondence of Caroline Gordon and Flannery O'Connor," *The Georgia Review*, 33 (Winter 1979), p. 830.
44. Perhaps it was a bit longer since it later grew to become a 942-page manuscript. Jack Wheelock to CGT, Feb. 3, 1953.
45. CGT to Nancy Wood, [n.d.].
46. Ann Waldron, *Close Connections: Caroline Gordon and the Southern Renaissance* (New York: G. P. Putnam's Sons, 1987), p. 285.
47. *More Conversations*, p. 29.
48. CGT to WP, the feast of St. Damasus, [Dec. 11], 1951.
49. *Close Connections: Caroline Gordon and the Southern Renaissance*, p. 284.
50. CGT to WP, the feast of St. Damasus, 1951.
51. *Conversations*, p. 232.
52. Allen Tate to WP, Jan. 1, 1952.
53. CGT to WP, [n.d., circa late January 1952].
54. CGT to Brainard Cheney, [n.d., circa mid-February 1952].
55. CGT to Ward Dorrance, [n.d.].
56. CGT to WP, [n.d., circa late February 1952].
57. Both Grandmother Pratt Percy and Aunt Ellen Murphy had histories of psychological problems. Ellen Murphy suffered a mental decline that initially caused her to rest in a local sanatorium in Birmingham. By January 1943, she was officially declared non compos mentis, and a temporary guardian was appointed for her by the Probate Court of Jefferson County (Probate Records, Jefferson County, Alabama, Jan. 23, Feb. 2, 9, 1943). Soon afterward she was admitted to Bryce Hospital and declared to be "mentally unsound to the extent that she is incapacitated, irresponsible and not capable of responding to process of law and incapable of transacting any matter of business in her present mental condition." Eventually her uncle, Henry T. DeBardeleben, became her guardian. By Oct. 16, 1943, Ellen was declared "restored to sanity," though less than two years later Grandmother Pratt Percy again petitioned the court on Ellen's behalf since Ellen had a recurrence of her previous condition and needed to be returned to Bryce. Ellen stayed there through mid-December 1945 and was again released. Grandmother Percy felt the strain of her daughter's illness; she sold some of her property on Henrietta Road to Mary Harris Wood (RERCB, Aug. 31, 1944). Unfortunately, Grandmother Percy herself suffered from manic-depressive psychosis, though she seemed to rally when Ellen needed her care and attention (GH). In late June 1946, the old Percy house on Arlington Avenue in Birmingham, which had once

been owned by LP-B and Mattie Sue, was sold to Mrs. Hener Bruce Byrd, who agreed to pay WP, LP-G, and BPP a sum of $12,500, at a rate of $75.75 a month (RERCB, June 21, 1946).

58. CGT to Donald Davidson, Ash Wednesday, [March 5], 1952; CGT to Andrew Lytle, Ash Wednesday, [March 5], 1952; CGT to Stark Young, [n.d.].
59. CGT to WP, Holy Saturday, [April 12], 1952; CGT to WP, [n.d., circa late summer 1952].
60. CGT to WP, [n.d.].
61. CGT to John Wheelock, [n.d.].
62. CGT to WP, [n.d.].
63. CGT to WP, [n.d.].
64. Denver Lindley to WP, Feb. 17, 1953.
65. Susan Jenkins to WP, March 17, 1953.
66. Susan Jenkins to WP, [n.d.].
67. CGT to WP, June 28, 1953.
68. CGT to WP, [n.d.].

7. *From* The Gramercy Winner *to* Confessions of a Movie-goer, *1954–58*

1. WP, "Symbol as Hermeneutic in Existentialism," *Journal of Philosophy and Phenomenological Research*, 16 (June 1956), p. 529.
2. *Walker Percy: Books of Revelations*, p. 33.
3. SF to WP, Feb. 19, Sept. 12, 1954; SF to WP, April 13, 1955.
4. WP, "From Facts to Fiction," in *SSL*, p. 189.
5. "A Conversation with Walker Percy," *Compostela Award Journal*, June 7, 1985.
6. Jacques Maritain to WP, Aug. 21, 1954.
7. CGT to WP, [n.d.].
8. CGT to WP, June 10, 1955.
9. James Collins to WP, Sept. 3, 1954.
10. Interview: Garic Kenneth Barranger.
11. Interview: Olga Hess.
12. SF to WP, Jan. 31, 1955; Feb. 18, [no year].
13. Unpublished interview of WP by Henry Kisor.
14. Interview: JJS.
15. SF to WP, Saturday, [n.d.].
16. Henry Kisor, *What's That Pig Outdoors?: A Memoir of Deafness* (New York: Hill & Wang, 1990), p. 24. Interview: Henry Kisor.
17. WP to RC, Thursday, [n.d., circa early December 1973].
18. Unpublished interview of WP by John R. Payne, S.J., April 9, 1974.
19. Interview: Gwyn Foote.
20. Interview: William Sorum, M.D.
21. WP to DB, July 10, 1957.
22. Interview: MPPL.
23. WP to DB, Oct. 2, 1957.
24. Unpublished interview of WP by John R. Payne, S.J.
25. Malcolm Jones, "Moralist of the South," *The New York Times*, March 22, 1987, Section 6, p. 46.
26. WP, "Novelist as Physician," a reply upon receiving the T. S. Eliot Award, Nov. 4, 1988.

27. Interview of WP by Dannye Romine Powell in *Parting the Curtains: Interviews with Southern Writers*, photographs by Jill Krementz (Winston-Salem, N.C.: John F. Blair Publisher, 1994), p. 246.

28. WP, "From Facts to Fiction," in *SSL*, p. 190.

29. Interview of WP by Barbara King in *Conversations*, p. 91.

30. Don Lee Keith, "Walker Percy Talks of Many Things," *The Delta Review*, 3 (May–June 1966), p. 38.

31. For other possible sources to this novel, see *More Conversations*, p. 142, and Allen Shepherd, "Percy's *The Moviegoer* and Warren's *All the King's Men*," *Notes on Mississippi Writers*, 4 (Spring 1971), pp. 2–14; William Rodney Allen, "Walker Percy's Allusions to *All the King's Men*," *Notes on Mississippi Writers*, 15 (1993), pp. 5–9.

32. "A Conversation with Walker Percy," *Compostela Award Journal*.

33. "A Conversation with Walker Percy," *Compostela Award Journal*.

34. "A Conversation with Walker Percy," *Compostela Award Journal*.

35. WP to BPS, June 28, 1958.

36. WP to BPS, May 30, 1957.

37. WP to DB, Aug. 4, 1958.

8. *A Career Launched:* The Moviegoer, *1959–61*

1. "Author's Questionnaire" for Alfred A. Knopf, Inc., Sept. 16, 1960.

2. WP to DB, June 15, 1959. Heather Moore, "Walker Percy's 'The Moviegoer': A Publishing History," *The Library Chronicle of the University of Texas at Austin*, 22 (1993), pp. 123–43.

3. Dwight Macdonald to DB, March 23, [no year].

4. EO to SK, June 24, 1959.

5. SK to EO, July 9, 1959.

6. SK, "Album of the Knopfs," *The American Scholar*, Summer 1987, pp. 377 ff.

7. SK to WP, July 16, 1959.

8. WP to DB, July 17, 1959.

9. WP to SK, July 20, 1959.

10. SK to EO, Oct. 21, 1959.

11. "Trade Editorial Publication Proposal" of Alfred A. Knopf, Inc., Oct. 27, 1959.

12. WP to EO, Oct. 26, 1959.

13. WP to SK, Nov. 6, 1959.

14. SK to WP, Nov. 9, 1959.

15. WP to DB, Dec. 4, 1959.

16. Doris Mirrielees to Dr. and Mrs. Walker Percy, [n.d.].

17. EO to SK, Jan. 11, 1960; SK to WP, Feb. 5, 1960. Interview: SK.

18. WP to SK, Feb. 11, 1960.

19. WP to DB, Friday, [n.d.].

20. It should be noted that at the conclusion of "Carnival in Gentilly," the editors stated the following: "The long section offered here is a portion of his [Percy's] forthcoming novel titled *Confessions of a Moviegoer*." In submitting this material to *Forum*, WP referred to "Carnival in Gentilly" as a "separate story." A second (partial) copy of this story, most likely the printer's setting copy, indicates clearly that the story had been longer than the published version. SHCUNC.

21. Nelle Haber of Simon & Schuster to DB, July 13, 1960.

22. SK to Blanche Knopf, July 20, 1960.

23. Interview: John P. Nelson.

24. WP, "Preface" in *At Face Value: A Biography of Louis J. Twomey, S.J.*, by Clement J. McNaspy, S.J. (New Orleans: Institute of Human Relations, Loyola University, 1978).

25. SK to Joseph C. Lesser, Aug. 31, 1960.

26. SK to EO, Sept. 1, 1960.

27. SK to WP, Sept. 1, 1960.

28. WP to SK, Sept. 3, 1960.

29. Arthur Silverman, M.D., to PS, SJ, July 19, 1994.

30. SK to WP, Sept. 3, 1960.

31. WP to SK, Sept. 15, 1960.

32. SK to WP, Sept. 20, 1960.

33. Unpublished interview of WP by Sr. Park Jeong-Mi, R.S.C.J.

34. WP to SK, Sept. 28, 1960; SK to WP, Sept. 23, 1960.

35. "Reading Report," Oct. 3, 1960.

36. WP to Judith Serebnick, New York City, Dec. 14, 1960, Pattee Library, Penn State University. Also Judith Serebnick, "First Novelists—Spring 1961," *Library Journal*, 86 (Feb. 1, 1961), p. 597.

37. SK to WP, Sept. 29, 1960.

38. SK to WP, Oct. 4, 1960.

39. Interview: SF.

40. Internal memo from AK, Sept. 2, 1960.

41. WP to SK, Oct. 28, 1960.

42. SK to WP, Oct. 24, 1960.

43. AC to WP, Oct. 27, 1960.

44. Interview: BPP.

45. According to LWH, *Walker Percy: A Comprehensive Descriptive Bibliography* (New Orleans: Faust Publishing Company, 1988), 1,500 copies were initially printed.

46. AC to EO, April 7, 1961.

47. EO to AC, April 13, 1961.

48. WP to AC, April 22, 1961.

49. WP to SK, May 1, 1961.

50. AC to WP, May 1, 1961.

51. CB, "Walker Percy: In Celebration," *Humanities* (National Endowment for the Humanities), 10 (May–June 1990), p. 5.

52. AC to WP, May 17, 1961.

53. AC to Julian McKee, May 22, 1961.

54. J. F. Powers to WP, May 11, 1976.

55. CGT to "Dear Sir," May 25, 1961.

56. AC to WP, June 5, 1961.

57. Interview: SK.

58. FO'C to "A," *The Habit of Being: Letters of Flannery O'Connor*, selected and edited by Sally Fitzgerald (New York: FSG, 1988), p. 442.

59. Thomas Lowry of Alfred A. Knopf, Inc., to McIntosh & Otis, Nov. 6, 1961.

60. WP to AC, Sept. 1, 1961.

61. AC to WP, Sept. 13, 1961.

62. Richard Faust, M.D., to WP, Oct. 18, 1961.

9. *Working on* The Last Gentleman, *1962–65*

1. WP to AC, Jan. 31, 1962: AC to WP, Feb. 14, 1962.
2. WP to Charles Barrett, April 10, 1980.
3. WP to Simone Vauthier, March 21, 1975. Archives of PRB. In addition, other references and situations are worth noting: Jamie Vaught is cared for in what is most likely Presbyterian Hospital in Washington Heights, where WP worked; Ed Barrett, like LP, hunted ducks at Lake Arthur, Louisiana; mention of the (Horn & Hardart) automat on West 57th Street in New York City (Frank Hardart, M.D., was a good friend of WP); mention of Mary Roberts Rinehart (related through marriage to WP's brother BPP); Dr. Dahanos most likely refers to Stevan Dohanos, the artist at Gaylord; one character is named Perlmutter (Irwin Perlmutter, M.D., graduated with WP from P&S); David Ross is based on David Scott, though his last name probably was borrowed from Ross Allen, a former SAE from Chapel Hill, who lives in New Orleans; Sadler Stovall is named most likely for Harry Stovall, again a former SAE from Chapel Hill; D'lo was originally called Arceel in the typescript (Arciel worked for WAP); John Houghton is based on John Houghton, who worked for Grandmother Phinizy in Athens; Alice Bocock is probably based on Alice Finlay, WP's former Greenville High School classmate; Gen. Kirby Smith had relatives in Sewanee whom WP knew; Rancho Merced is based on Rancho La Merced outside Santa Fe; Miss Mamie Billups shares a name with WP's youngest brother; Senator Oscar W. Underwood was a friend of LP-B.
4. Perrine Dixon to WP, Wednesday, Jan. 27, [no year, probably 1965].
5. WP to SK, Feb. 15, 1962.
6. Interview: Dr. and Mrs. Frank J. Hardart, Jr.
7. Interview: RG.
8. WP's talk at a meeting of the American Booksellers Association in New Orleans, May 24, 1986; also WP, "A Symposium on Fiction," *Shenandoah*, 27 (Winter 1976), pp. 16–17.
9. Interview: RG.
10. Interviews: Seymour Lawrence and RS. RS heard about AK's preference for Maxwell's book soon after the ceremony.
11. Gay Talese, *The New York Times*, March 15, 1962.
12. AK to SK, March 13, 1962; SK to AK, March 14, 1962.
13. Interview: Hugh Downs.
14. Margaret W. Dudley to WP, March 16, 1962.
15. Mary McCormick, "Walker Percy Carries Literary Torch Lit by William Alexander," *DD-T*, March 25, 1962.
16. For various material on the award ceremony and its aftermath, see *Publishers Weekly*, 181 (March 26, 1962).
17. Harriet Doar, "Walker Percy: He Likes to Put Protagonist in Situation," *The Charlotte Observer*, Sept. 30, 1962.
18. Martha MacGregor, "The Week in Books," *The New York Post*, March 17, 1962.
19. "Letter to the Editor," *Show*, 2 (August 1962), p. 4.
20. WP to SK, March 19, 1962.
21. WP to Jean Stafford, March 19, 1962.
22. Jean Stafford, "A Statement" [dated March 19, 1962], *Saturday Review*, Oct. 6, 1962, p. 50.

23. Jean Stafford, "Letter to the Editor," *Harper's*, Oct. 10, 1971. Norlin.

24. Interview: RG.

25. WP to Lewis Gannett, March 30, 1962.

26. AK to WP, March 21, 1962.

27. WP to Bolling Spalding, March 30, [no year].

28. William A. Koshland to WP, May 7, 1962.

29. WP to AK, June 1, 1962.

30. FO'C to WP, March 29, 1962.

31. WP to CGT, April 6, 1962. Archives of Ashley Brown.

32. WP to Virginia Milazzo, [n.d.].

33. AK to WP, May 21, 1962.

34. EO to WP, April 5, 1962; WP to AC, April 9, 1962; AC to WP, April 13, 1962.

35. SK to WP, June 8, 1962.

36. WP to SK, June 14, 1962.

37. WP to Marion Montgomery, Sept. 14, 1962.

38. WP to William Jay Smith, Nov. 8, 1962.

39. The Letter of Agreement was amended (and extended) on Jan. 22, July 23, Nov. 19, 1963; May 29, Nov. 24, 1964; and May 29, 1965. Each time, WP profited from the extension of the option. The letter of May 29, 1965, stipulated the following: "This additional payment of FIVE HUNDRED DOLLARS ($500.00), as well as THREE THOUSAND SEVEN HUNDRED AND FIFTY DOLLARS ($3,750) previously made by me shall be applicable against the cash purchase price as defined in Paragraph ELEVENTH of the Purchase Agreement attached to and made part of the aforesaid Option Agreement of July 30, 1962." For general information about these letters of agreement and contractual material, see Catalogues 44, 47, and 51 of Joseph the Provider, Santa Barbara, California; also WP to SK, Sept. 17, 1962. Interview: SK.

40. WP to Richard Faust, M.D., Dec. 22, 1962.

41. Interview: Henry R. Montecino, S.J.; interview of WP by Phil McCombs in *More Conversations*, pp. 205–6.

42. WP to LAL, June 27, 1967.

43. WP to BPS, March 1, 1963.

44. WP to CGB, Dec. 12, 1962.

45. SHCUNC, series I: B-4, Chapters 8 and 9.

46. SHCUNC, series I: B-4, p. 208.

47. WP to Allen Tate, Feb. 17, 1963.

48. WP to MBTP, March 25, 1963. Also WP to Jean Stafford, Oct. 27, 1971.

49. WP to Malcolm Bell, Jr., May 13, 1963.

50. *The* (New Orleans) *Clarion Herald*, Sept. 12, 1963.

51. WP to CGB, Oct. 30, 1963.

52. WP to CGB, [n.d., circa November 1963].

53. WP to CGB, Nov. 6, 1963.

54. Interviews: Edward A. Sheridan, S.J., Lawrence Baldwin, and Richard Faust, M.D.

55. WP to James Boatwright, Nov. 20, 1963.

56. Donald E. Stanford to WP, Jan. 15, 1964.

57. For evidence of correspondence between JE and WP, see FO'C to CGT, Nov. 16, 1961, JE to CGT, Friday, [n.d.]. Interviews: WP, Thomas Sullivan, Father Methodius, O.C.S.O., and Father Anthony, O.C.S.O. Also Thomas Sullivan, "Jack English—Trappist Monk and Catholic Worker Editor," *The Catholic Worker*, January 1973.

58. TM to WP, [January 1964].

59. WP to TM, Feb. 14, [1964].

60. TM to WP, March 31, 1964; WP to TM, April 11, [1964].

61. WP to TM, Feb. 27, [1964].

62. WP to Walter Sturdivant, June 13, 1964.

63. Source: Printed talk by Marjorie E. Magner, Monday Afternoon Club, Northampton, Mass., Nov. 5, 1990.

64. F. Gentry Harris, M.D., to WP, Aug. 23, 1963, Harris archives. Because of the confidential nature of the correspondence between WP and Dr. Harris, which began in August 1963 and lasted to May 1989, I have decided not to refer to it except in passing. It should be noted, however, that WP devoted hundreds of hours to listening to tapes of counseling sessions and evaluating them. WP used, for the most part, Peirce's theory of signs as the basis for these evaluations. Undoubtedly, *SC* and *L*, in particular, were influenced by WP's interpretations of the psychological problems he analyzed (see, for example, WP to F. Gentry Harris, M.D., Aug. 21, 1965).

65. F. Gentry Harris, M.D., to WP, Oct. 2, 1963, Harris archives.

66. WP to F. Gentry Harris, M.D., Jan. 29, 1964, Harris archives.

67. WP to F. Gentry Harris, M.D., July 15, 1964, Harris archives.

68. EO to WP, Aug. 7, 1964.

69. Patricia Schartle to WP, Aug. 6, 1964.

70. Interview of WP by Carlton Creemens in *Conversations*, p. 19.

71. WP to BPS, June 7, 1965. Interview of WP by Phil McCombs in *More Conversations*, pp. 205–6.

72. Louise H. Abbott to PS, SJ, March 9, 1992.

73. HR to WP, Aug. 28, 1964.

74. WP to HR, Sept. 8, 1964.

75. W. J. Stuckey to WP, Nov. 18, 1964.

76. WP to SK, Feb. 11, 1965.

77. WP to Ansley Cope, Easter Sunday, [n.d.].

78. Joan Treadway, "Christian Focus: Marcel on Nietzsche," *The Loyola Maroon*, April 2, 1965, pp. 1, 5. Also the interview of WP by Gilbert Schricke in *Conversations*, pp. 245–48.

79. Source: W. Kenneth Holditch.

80. Interview: SF.

81. HR to EO, May 7, 1965.

82. EO to HR, May 10, 1965.

83. Interview: RG. Margaret Nicholson of the FSG contract department to Mary S. Abbott, July 2, 1965; Margaret Nicholson to EO, Aug. 10, 1965.

84. Gene Usdin, M.D., to PS, SJ, Aug. 14, 1992.

85. HR to WP, Aug. 6, 1965.

86. RG to WP, Aug. 6, 1965.

87. WP to Mary Pratt Percy, Monday, [Nov. 30, 1965, on envelope].

88. EO to HR, Sept. 10, 1965.

89. WP to F. Gentry Harris, M.D., Aug. 21, 1965, Harris archives.

90. WP to Richard D. Holland of FSG, Sept. 13, 1965.

91. HR to WP, Oct. 13, 1965.

92. WP to HR, Oct. 16, 1965.

93. HR to WP, Oct. 20, 1965.

94. WP to HR, Oct. 31, 1965.

95. HR to WP, Nov. 9, 1965.

96. Interview: Rev. Will D. Campbell.

97. Interview: THC, SJ.

98. RG to WP, Dec. 9, 1965.

99. LK to Irv Goodman of the Literary Guild, Dec. 21, 1965.

100. WP to HR, Dec. 28, 1965.

10. Working on Love in the Ruins, *1966–70*

1. LK to James Byrans, Jan. 21, 1966.

2. Records of FSG, January 1966.

3. HR to WP, Jan. 3, 1966.

4. HR to WP, Jan. 4, 1966.

5. HR to WP, Jan. 5, 1966.

6. WP to HR, Jan. 10, 1966.

7. HR to WP, Jan. 11, 1966.

8. HR to SK, Feb. 23, 1966.

9. John Bright-Holmes to RS, Jan. 11, 1966.

10. Interview: SF. Ashley Brown, "An Interview with Walker Percy," *Shenandoah*, 18 (Spring 1967), p. 6.

11. WP to Mary Pratt Percy, Jan. 28, 1966.

12. WP to Mary Pratt Percy, Feb. 14, [no year].

13. WP to HR, Feb. 2, [no year]; HR to WP, Feb. 4, 8, 1966.

14. WP to Jean Stafford, Feb. 26, [no year; March 2, 1966, on envelope].

15. EO to HR, Feb. 9, 1966.

16. HR to EO, Feb. 11, 1966.

17. HR to EO, Feb. 14, 1966; EO to HR, Feb. 16, 1966.

18. Memo of HR, Feb. 18, 1966.

19. WP to HR, Feb. 11, 1966.

20. WP to TM, May 29, 1966.

21. WP to CGT, Feb. 11, 1974.

22. Guest book at the monastery; CGT to RG, March 11, 1966.

23. WP to CGT, Feb. 11, 1966; WP to CGT, Feb. 23, [no year].

24. WP to CGT, Tuesday, [n.d.].

25. JE to CGT, March 30, [no year].

26. JE to CGT, Monday, [n.d.].

27. JE to CGT, Friday, [n.d.]; JE to WP and CGT, Friday, [n.d.].

28. WP to Mary Pratt Percy, Tuesday, [March 15, 1966, on envelope]. Interview: Elizabeth O'Brien.

29. WP to HR, March 3, 1966; HR to WP, March 7, 1966; WP to HR, March 7, 1966; HR to WP, March 10, 1966.

30. WP to HR, March 10, [no year].

31. RG to WP, March 14, 1966.

32. Paul Horgan to RG, March 16, 1966.

33. WP to HR, [n.d., but received March 21, 1966].

34. J. F. Powers to RG, April 11, 1966.

35. CGT to WP, March 7, 1966.

36. CGT to RG, March 11, 1966.

37. LK to EO, April 5, 11, 1966.

38. WP to HR, April 20, 1966.

39. WP to HR, April 28, 1966.

40. WP to HR, April 28, 1966.

41. HR to WP, May 2, 1966.

42. RG to WP, May 4, 1966.

43. Interviews: CGB and WP.

44. JE to WP, May 13, 1966 (CGT Collection, PU); JE to CGT, Tuesday, March 1, [no year]; JE to Dorothy Day, [n.d.], MU.

45. TM to RG, May 22, 1966; WP to TM, May 29, 1966.

46. Brainard Cheney to RG, May 25, 1966.

47. WP to RG, May 30, 1966.

48. HR to WP, June 1, 1966.

49. RG to HR, June 16, 1966. The first printing of the novel had 409 pages; when reset it had 393 pages. Except for the correction of some typos, there is no difference in the text of various printings (John Peck of FSG to Acquisitions Department, Gleeson Library, University of San Francisco, Oct. 28, 1966).

50. WP to HR, Sept. 23, 1968.

51. LK to Edward Chase of New American Library, Oct. 3, 1968.

52. Sidney B. Kramer to WP, Oct. 22, 1968.

53. Interview: Hugh McCormick.

54. Tess Crager to RS, May 8, 1966. *Pursuit,* a winner of the Houghton Mifflin Literary Fellowship Award, appeared on Oct. 10, 1966, with a blurb by WP. WP to Joel Wells of *The Critic,* July 28, 1966. Catalogue 73 of Ken Lopez, Bookseller, Hadley, Massachusetts. Also Don Lee Keith, "The Woman Who Is Troubled by Experience," *The Delta Review,* 3 (July–August 1966), pp. 57, 70–71.

55. WP to Edwin T. Boone, Jr., June 30, 1966.

56. WP to RG, Sept. 28, [no year].

57. RG to WP, [n.d.].

58. WP to Edwin T. Boone, Jr., June 30, 1966.

59. WP to HR, July 7, 1966.

60. HR to WP, July 12, 1966.

61. WP to RS, Oct. 13, 1966.

62. WP to RG, Aug. 6, 1966.

63. RG to WP, Aug. 19, 1966.

64. WP to CGB, Oct. 25, 1966.

65. HR to WP, Sept. 11, 1967; Ashley Brown, "An Interview with Walker Percy," p. 5.

66. WP to HR and RG, Dec. 5, 1966.

67. HR to WP, Dec. 6, 1966.

68. Ralph Ellison to WP, Jan. 10, 1967, AA/NIAL.

69. WP to JC, Jan. 19, 1967.

70. WP to HR, Sunday, [n.d.].

71. HR to WP, Feb. 24, 1967.

72. HR to Margaret Nicholson, Feb. 2, 1967.

73. LPS to WP, Feb. 27, 1967.

74. WP to JWC, March 7, 1967; JWC to WP, March 13, 1967.

75. WP to JWC, April 10, 1967.

76. WP to JWC, June 24, 1967.

77. WP to JWC, July 9, 1967.

78. WP to SF, Sunday [before Mardi Gras, no year].

79. HR to WP, March 7, 1967.

80. *Studies in Schizophrenia: A Multidisciplinary Approach to Mind-Brain Relationships,* by the Tulane Department of Psychiatry and Neurology, reported by Robert G. Heath, M.D. (Cambridge, Mass.: Harvard University Press, 1954).

81. WP to Carolyn A. Wallace, Nov. 16, 1981.

82. RS to WP, April 20, 1967; WP to RS, April 22, 1967; HR to WP, April 26, 1967.

83. WP to HR, April 29, 1967.

84. Roy P. Basler to WP, May 2, 1967.

85. WP to Roy P. Basler, May 12, 1967.

86. WP to LAL, May 16, 1967.

87. Interview: MBTP.

88. WP to RS, June 12, 1967.

89. WP, "Letter to the Editor," *Harper's,* 234 (May 1967), pp. 8–9.

90. WP to LAL, May 28, 1967.

91. WP to LAL, June 27, 1967.

92. WP to LAL, July 9, 1967.

93. WP to LAL, Sept. 1, 1967.

94. HR to EO, June 28, 1967; EO to HR, June 29, 1967.

95. WP to RC, July 3, 1967.

96. William Dowie, "Encountering Walker Percy," *Southeastern Magazine,* 1 (Summer 1984), pp. 17–18.

97. WP to TM, July 13, 1967.

98. TM to WP, July 20, 1967.

99. TM to WP, Aug. 24, 1967.

100. WP to TM, Aug. 27, 1967.

101. WP to Mother Johnette Putnam, O.S.B., Aug. 27, 1970.

102. WP to HR, Sept. 8, 1967.

103. HR to WP, Sept. 11, 1967.

104. RG to WP, Sept. 21, 1967.

105. WP to RG, Oct. 3, 1967.

106. LK to Herbert Lottman in Paris, Oct. 31, 1967.

107. LK to Sharland Trotter of the Book Find Club, Oct. 13, 1967; Sharland Trotter to LK, Nov. 3, 1967; HR to WP, Dec. 21, 1967.

108. Interviews: Martin and Ralph Adamo and Carol Livaudais.

109. *The Times-Picayune,* Nov. 7, 1980.

110. *The Loyola Maroon,* Oct. 20, 1967.

111. Interviews: BCT and NP.

112. WP to BCT, Nov. 21, 1967, archives of BCT.

113. WP to Annie Laurie Williams, Dec. 28, 1967, archives of BCT.

114. WP to JWC, Dec. 16, 1967.

115. WP to HR, Jan. 21, 1968.

116. HR to WP, Feb. 1, 1968.

117. WP to BPS, Jan. 21, 1968.

118. WP to LAL, Jan. 21, 1968.

119. WP to BCT, Feb. 11, 1968.

120. SHCUNC, series I: C-3.

121. Stanley Kubrick to NP, March 18, 1968, archives of BCT.

122. Lucille Sullivan to NP, March 26, 1968, archives of BCT. See Catalogue 44, Joseph the Provider, Santa Barbara, California, for a list of other documents relating to this film script.

123. WP to Louis J. Twomey, S.J., April 3, 1968; Susan Veal to WP, Aug. 14, 1967.

124. Unpublished interview with WP by John R. Payne, S.J., April 9, 1974. On March 19, 1964, Raynol Ariatti took a picture of WP at one of Father Twomey's lectures in Covington.

125. WP to Jarvis A. Thurston, April 26, 1968, WU.

126. House Diary of Xavier Hall, Pass Christian, kept by Edward A. Sheridan, S.J. Interview: Edward A. Sheridan, S.J.

127. WP to LAL, June 25, 1968.

128. WP to CGB, Jan. 19, 1969.

129. WP to NP, Sept. 3, 1968, archives of BCT.

130. WP to Ansley Cope, Nov. 18, 1968.

131. NP to Irene Selznick, Nov. 27, 1968, archives of BCT.

132. SMH. Interviews: MBTP and BPP.

133. WP to HR, Dec. 13, 1968.

134. HR to WP, Dec. 18, 1968.

135. WP to BCT, Dec. 18, 1968.

136. WP to BCT, Jan. 26, 1969.

137. WP to CGB, Jan. 19, 1969.

138. L. M. Kit Carson to BCT, April 20, 1969. Interview: L. M. Kit Carson.

139. HR [probably] to WP, April 14, 1969.

140. Archives of BCT.

141. WP to RG, May 19, 1969.

142. Interview: Sr. Jeanne d'Arc Kernion, O.S.B.

143. Interview: Mr. and Mrs. Vincent Malcolm Byrnes and family.

144. Interview: John Martin Byrnes.

145. WP to Nilo Lindgren, June 29, 1969.

146. Interview: Dominic Braud, O.S.B.

147. WP to BCT, Sept. 12, 1969.

148. WP to ES, Oct. 2, 1969.

149. LAL to Editor of Noonday Press, Dec. 19, 1969.

150. HR to WP, Feb. 5, 1970.

151. WP to HR, March 10, 1970.

152. HR to LAL, March 16, 1970.

153. WP to LPS, March 19, 1971.

154. CB to WP, Jan. 20, 1970. Interview: CB.

155. Interview: Sam Waterston.

156. Interview: Roulhac Toledano.

157. Ricky Leacock to PS, SJ, March 31, 1993.

158. WP to Harvey Core, April 17, 1970; also material from the archives of BCT.

159. *The* (New Orleans) *States-Item*, May 11, 1970.

160. WP to SF, July 25 [no year].

161. WP to Mother Johnette Putnam, O.S.B., Aug. 27, 1970.

162. Interview: Sr. Joan Ridley, O.P.

163. RS to WP, Sept. 21, 1970.

164. WP to RS, Sept. 23, 1970.

165. HR to WP, Sept. 28, 1970.

166. WP to HR, Oct. 2, 1970.

167. WP to HR, Sept. 30, 1970.

168. EO to HR, Oct. 5, 1970.

169. HR to WP, Oct. 8, 1970.

170. HR to Margaret Nicholson, Sept. 23, 1970.

171. HR to WP, Nov. 4, 1970.

172. WP to Simone Vauthier, Sept. 22, 1970; SF to WP, Sept. 30, 1970; WP to HR, Nov. 6, 1970; HR to WP, Nov. 9, 1970.

173. HR to WP, Nov. 10, 1970.

174. HR to WP, Nov. 16, 1970.

175. John Bright-Holmes of Eyre & Spottiswoode to RS, Nov. 23, 25, 1970.

176. HR to WP, Nov. 23, 1970.

177. Interview: Louis Gallo.

178. Interview: BCT.

179. Albert Murray, *South to a Very Old Place* (New York: McGraw-Hill, 1971), p. 207.

180. WP to Alfred Kazin, April 15, 1971, Berg.

181. SF to WP, Nov. 23, 1970.

11. Writing and Teaching, 1971–74

1. HR to WP, Jan. 12, 20, 27, 1971; WP to HR, Feb. 1, 1971.

2. LK to James Ellison of BOMC, Jan. 18, 1971; internal memo of FSG, March 3, 1971.

3. Martin Luschei to JC, May 30, 1971.

4. WP to Martha Lacy Hall, Dec. 7, 1972.

5. HR to EO, April 21, 1971.

6. RS to David Susskind, Jan. 18, 1971; Lee Rosenberg to LK, April 6, 1971; LK to Lee Rosenberg, May 3, 1971.

7. WP to CGT, Feb. 6, 1971.

8. JC to WP, Feb. 22, April 2, 1971; Edward Tribble of *The Washington Evening Star* to JC, March 11, 1971; WP to JC, March 14, 1971.

9. WP to Jean Stafford, March 29, 1971.

10. Rosalie Thorne McKenna to JC, March 15, 30, 1971; JC to Rosalie Thorne McKenna, March 19, 1971.

11. WP, "Concerning *Love in the Ruins*," in *SSL*, pp. 247–48.

12. WP to JC, March 6, 1971.

13. WP to Jean Stafford, March 29, 1971.

14. LAL, "*Love in the Ruins*: Sequel to *Arrowsmith*," in *Following Percy: Essays on Walker Percy's Work*, pp. 164–77.

15. Interview: Elizabeth Dubus Baldridge.

16. Shirley Fisher to RG, Oct. 11, 1978.

17. JC to WP, May 12, 1971.

18. Richard Schickel to HR, April 25, 1971.

19. WP to HR, April 10, 1971.

20. WP to Clement J. McNaspy, S.J., June 4, 1971.

21. WP to CB, April 1, 1974.

22. RS to WP, May 17, 1971.

23. WP to RS, May 21, 1971.

24. HR to WP, April 27, 1971.

25. Eunice K. Boehle of Dell to LK, June 29, 1971.

26. Michelle Lapautre to Peter Hinzman of FSG, May 11, 1971.

27. Alain Oulman to Peggy Miller of FSG, Sept. 13, 1971.

28. Philip D. Carter, "Oh, You Know Uncle Walker," *The Washington Post*, June 17, 1971.

29. WP to David McDowell, July 5, 1971, Robert W. Woodruff Library, Emory University.

30. Interview: ES.

31. WP to ES, May 23, 1971.

32. WP to HR, Sept. 27, 1971.

33. WP to Jean Stafford, Oct. 27, 1971.

34. WP to Alfred Kazin, April 2, 15, 1971.

35. L. M. Kit Carson to WP, June 29, 1971.

36. L. M. Kit Carson to HR, June 30, 1971.

37. L. M. Kit Carson to WP, July 9, 1971.

38. HR to L. M. Kit Carson, July 14, 1971.

39. WP to Forrest Ingram, S.J., Sept. 17, 1971.

40. WP to T. N. Marsh of Centenary College, Shreveport, Louisiana, Oct. 28, 1971, Amstid Collection, Tulane University.

41. Jason Berry, "The Last Gentleman," *The Baltimore Sun*, May 19, 1990.

42. Interview: John Henry Walker.

43. WP to HR, Nov. 1, 1971.

44. WP to LPS, Nov. 22, 1971.

45. WP to LPS, Jan. 3, 1972.

46. WP to Marion Montgomery, Nov. 5, 1971; WP to Marion Montgomery, Jan. 4, 1972.

47. Marion Montgomery to WP, Jan. 7, 1972.

48. WP to HR, Jan. 12, 1972.

49. Interview: Jill Krementz.

50. WP to Martha Lacy Hall, May 28, 1972.

51. WP to LAL, Jan. 24, 1972; WP to Michael Cass, Feb. 26, 1972.

52. WP to Simone Vauthier, March 12, 1972.

53. Christopher Lehmann-Haupt, "Confessions of a Book Award Judge," *The Saturday Review of the Arts*, April 7, 1973, pp. 33–35.

54. WP to RG, April 12, 1972.

55. WP to ES, March 26, 1985.

56. Michael F. Kennelly, S.J., to WP, March 28, 1972.

57. Interview: Joseph Tetlow, S.J.

58. WP to Michael F. Kennelly, S.J., March 30, 1972.

59. WP to EO and HR, July 14, 1972.

60. Ann Percy to Dr. and Mrs. Walker Percy, Sept. 18, 1972, plus assorted other letters in the archives of APM.

61. Transcript of panel provided to me by David Madden. Also *Remembering James Agee*, edited by David Madden (Baton Rouge: LSU Press, 1974).

62. MBTP to Ann Percy, Saturday, 4 p.m., [n.d.].

63. Interview: RM.

64. WP to RM, Oct. 17, 1972.

65. Interview: Eudora Welty. Transcript made available from Southern Educational Communications Association of Columbia, South Carolina; videotape of show available at the Museum of Television and Radio, New York City.

66. *The Times-Picayune*, Jan. 1, 1985.

67. SF to WP, Jan. 26, May 13, 1973.

68. Financial records of FSG, Feb. 20, 1973.

69. CGT Collection, Box 38, Folder 9, PU.

70. CGT to Richard Wilbur, April 13, 1973; also press release from the University of Dallas, dated Aug. 10, 1973.

71. Jonathan Yardley, "The Verdict of Walker Percy, *The Washington Post*, May 14, 1990. WP to SF, May 1, 1975.

72. After reading through so many novels, WP made a list of the works that had most influenced him, as requested by Paul Whyte Ferris, a retired assistant managing editor of *The Chicago Sun-Times* living in Murfreesboro, Tennessee: 1. Dostoevsky's *The Brothers Karamazov* ("The first prophetic novel of the 19th century and foreshadowing the 20th"). 2. Faulkner's *The Sound and the Fury* ("The great opening gun of Southern and U.S. fiction in this century"). 3. Twain's *Huckleberry Finn* ("Perhaps the seed of the best U.S. fiction"). 4. The poetry of Gerard Manley Hopkins. 5. Eliot's *Middlemarch* ("The English novel of manners and country folk at its best"). 6. Sartre's *Nausea* ("The first stylistic triumph representing 20th-century malaise"). 7. The works of Kierkegaard ("The most important and 'modern' philosopher of modern times, especially *Concluding Unscientific Postscript*"). 8. The Bible ("Especially Genesis, Isaiah, the Gospel of St. John and the Epistles to the Romans and Ephesians—the unique Judeo-Christian truth as news [Gospel]"). 9. St. Augustine's *The City of God* ("The first and best statement of the linear rather than the cyclical view of history"). 10. Pascal's *Pensées* ("The first and maybe the best statement of the modern predicament"). 11. The works of Gabriel Marcel ("Perhaps the best modern existentialist"). 12 and 13. Shakespeare and Tolstoy ("Of course, no comment necessary"). WP to Paul Whyte Ferris, April 16, 1973.

73. Interview: RC.

74. RC, "Shadowing Binx," in *Literature and Medicine*, Vol. 4, edited by Peter W. Graham (Baltimore: Johns Hopkins University Press, 1985), p. 153.

75. WP to Howard Moss, March 25, 1973.

76. WP to SF, Wednesday, [April 26, 1973, on envelope]; interview of Willie Morris by John Griffin Jones, *Mississippi Writers Talking II*, edited by John Griffin Jones (Jackson: University Press of Mississippi, 1983), pp. 98–99.

77. Paul Horgan, "For Walker Percy: 1916–90," *America*, 164 (May 11, 1991), p. 508. Interview: Paul Horgan.

78. Interview: ZAN. WP to ZAN, April 24, 1973.

79. WP to HR, May 14, 1973.

80. Bradley R. Dewey to the Editor of FSG, May 8, 1973; HR to Bradley R. Dewey, May 10, 1973; WP to Rev. L. Jerome Taylor, Jr., Aug. 1, 1973.

81. Interview: Mr. and Mrs. James L. Sprunt, Jr.

82. John P. Raynor, S.J., to WP, Feb. 1, 1973, MU; WP to John P. Raynor, S.J., Feb. 7, 1973; WP to Joseph Schwartz, May 6, 1973.

83. Henry Chauncey, Jr., to WP, June 3, 1973.

84. WP to Charles [East], May 23, 1973.

85. WP to RC, Sept. 15, 1973.

86. WP to SF, June 13, [no year].

87. WP to Ansley Cope, Aug. 1, 1973.

88. Interview: JHM, SJ.

89. WP to LPS, Sept. 5, 1973.

90. Margaret M. Mills of the AA/NIAL to WP, Feb. 19, 1974.

91. Louis Gallo, "Walker Percy Struggles with Unbelief," *The Vieux Carré Courier*, Sept. 21–27, 1973.

92. WP to LPS, Oct. 4, 1973.

93. WP to LPS, Oct. 14, 1973.

94. Interview: LPS; WP to LPS, May 20, Sept. 30, 1974.

95. Mrs. LeRoy Pratt Percy of Birmingham to LP, Thursday night, [n.d.].
96. WP to Brainard Cheney, Nov. 14, 1973.
97. WP to Ann Percy, Sunday night, [n.d.].
98. WP to RC, Dec. 1, 1973.
99. WP to RC, Thursday, [n.d.].
100. WP to Brainard Cheney, Dec. 2, 1973.
101. WP to CGT, Christmas card, [n.d.].
102. Undated draft of letter by CGT, PU.
103. Copy of a letter of Sr. Joan Ridley, O.P., et al., to WP, Jan. 25, 1974.
104. Interview: Sr. Joan Ridley, O.P.
105. WP to Sr. Joan Ridley, O.P., Feb. 11, 1974.
106. Interview: Mr. and Mrs. Robert Berlin.
107. WP to Sr. Joan Ridley, O.P., March 10, 1974.
108. WP to Sr. Joan Ridley, O.P., Feb. 1, 1974.
109. WP, "Letter to the Editor," *The Times-Picayune*, Sept. 6, 1984. WP to Lawrence Baldwin, Dec. 1, 1986.
110. WP to CGT, Feb. 11, 1974.
111. WP to RC, Feb. 14. 1974.
112. WP to LPS, March 11, 1974. Interview: Walter Isaacson.
113. Interview: Marion Knox Barthelme.
114. WP to Robert D. Hess, Friday, [March 23, 1974, on envelope].
115. Interview: Susanne M. Jensen
116. Interview: Philip A. Bryant; Philip A. Bryant to PS, SJ, Feb. 9, 1995.
117. WP to Otis B. Wheeler, March 28, 1974. Interview: Otis B. Wheeler.
118. WP to Otis B. Wheeler, April 21, 1974.
119. Otis B. Wheeler to Cecil G. Taylor, April 29, 1974.
120. WP to CB, April 1, 1974.
121. WP to PRB, May 25, 1974.
122. RG to WP, Aug. 2, 1974.
123. WP to Jason Berry, May 28, 1974.
124. Otis B. Wheeler to WP, July 25, 1974.
125. Ann Percy to Dr. and Mrs. Walker Percy, [July 25, 1974, on envelope].
126. WP to Jason Berry, Aug. 8, 1974, Amstid Collection, Tulane University.
127. WP to CGT, Aug. 30, 1974.
128. WP to Otis B. Wheeler, May 18, 1974.
129. "Campus Correspondence" memo of WP to PRB, [n.d.].
130. Interview: Wyatt Prunty.
131. Interview: Nancy Hargrove.
132. Interview: Rebecca R. Butler. I gratefully acknowledge using the class notes of Rebecca R. Butler.
133. Interview: Huey S. Guagliardo. Huey S. Guagliardo, "Remembering a Gentleman and a Teacher: Walker Percy (1916–1990)," *Notes on Mississippi Writers*, 23 (June 1991), pp. 59–61.
134. RG to WP, Oct. 4, 1974.
135. WP to RG, Oct. 11, 1974.
136. WP, "Prologue" to *Welcome: Student Mental Health Services, Baton Rouge, Louisiana, 1987–1988*, by Susanne M. Jensen (privately reproduced and distributed by the Student Mental Health Services, LSU).
137. WP to PRB, June 25, 1971. Interview: PRB.

138. WP to PRB, May 28, 1973.

139. WP to PRB, Thursday, [n.d.]; WP to PRB, Oct. 27, 1974.

140. Interview: J. Gerald Kennedy.

141. WP to J. Gerald Kennedy, Dec. 15, 1974.

142. WP to SF, [n.d., but probably November 1974].

143. WP to RG, Oct. 27, 1974.

144. RG to WP, Oct. 31, 1974.

145. RG to WP, Nov. 13, 1974.

146. WP to RG, Nov. 15, 1974.

147. RG to WP, Nov. 21, 1974.

148. Interview: Eudora Welty. Walter Sullivan, *Allen Tate: A Recollection* (Baton Rouge, LSU Press, 1988), p. 45.

149. WP to RC, Dec. 26, 1974.

150. WP to Louise Cowan, Dec. 9, 1974, CGT Collection, PU.

151. WP to LPS, Dec. 21, 1974.

152. *The House of Percy*, p. 328.

12. The Message in the Bottle, Lancelot, *and* The Second Coming, *1975–80*

1. Interviews: Elizabeth Dubus Baldridge, Raymond T. Cothern, Leo Luke Marcello, Ruth H. Laney.

2. RG to WP, Jan. 13, 1975.

3. WP to RG, Feb. 10, 1975.

4. WP to Simone Vauthier, Jan. 10, 1975.

5. George Fletcher of Fordham University Press to RG, March 6, 1975; Rhoda Gamson of FSG to Gloria Parloff, managing editor of *Psychiatry*, March 19, 1975.

6. WP to RG, Feb. 15, March 31, 1975.

7. RG to WP, April 24, 1975.

8. WP to RF, April 28, 1975.

9. WP to RG, April 28, 1975.

10. Marcus Smith to WP, May 30, 1975. Interview: Marcus Smith. Marcus Smith to WP, Oct. 21, 1975; WP to Marcus Smith, Oct. 25, 1975; Dawson Gaillard to William Byron, S.J., May 30, 1975. Interview: William Byron, S.J.

11. Robert J. Ratchford, S.J., to Dawson Gaillard, June 19, 1975.

12. William H. Poteat to WP, Sept. 4, 1975.

13. Walter Sullivan to WP, Sept. 29, 1975.

14. WP to RG, May 14, 1975; RG to WP, May 19, 1975.

15. HR to Richard Kelley, July 10, 1975.

16. Madeleine L'Engle to RG, June 18, 1975.

17. WP to Brainard Cheney, Sept. 22, 1975.

18. WP to Rev. Will D. Campbell, June 7, 1975.

19. WP to Rev. Will D. Campbell, June 25, 1975.

20. Benjamin Ladner to WP, Sept. 17, 1975.

21. WP to RC, Sept. 15, 1975.

22. "A Symposium on Fiction," *Shenandoah*, 27 (Winter 1976), pp. 3–31, plus a notation on the typescript of "The State of the Novel: Dying Art or New Science?" indicating that it was delivered at Washington and Lee University; also WP to James Boatwright, Feb. 1, 1976, archives of Washington and Lee University.

23. WP to LPS, March 22, 1975.

24. *SSL*, pp. 111–29.

25. Interview: Mr. and Mrs. John David Moores, Jr.

26. *More Conversations*, pp. 79–80.

27. Interview: Val Ambrose McInnes, O.P.

28. WP to Simone Vauthier, Nov. 4, 1980.

29. WP to William Rodney Allen, Aug. 1, 1981.

30. WP to LPS, Jan. 10, 1976.

31. LPS, 1991 Flora Levy Lecture at the University of Southwestern Louisiana.

32. WP to Robert Hess, Jan. 21, 1976.

33. WP to LPS, Feb. 8, 1976.

34. WP to Noel Polk, June 13, 1976.

35. WP to RC, March 22, 1976.

36. WP to RG, April 19, 1976.

37. WP to RG, July 11, 1976.

38. WP to RG, April 23, 1976.

39. EO to RG, June 1, 1976.

40. WP to Dawson Gaillard, April 29, 1976.

41. Dawson Gaillard to WP, May 28, 1976; Dawson Gaillard to Lee Gary of Loyola's Development Office, June 3, 1976.

42. Charles Newman to WP, Aug. 1, 1976.

43. Interviews: Alan Davis, Tim Gautreaux, Larry Gray, W. Kenneth Holditch, Walter Isaacson, and Valerie Martin. I gratefully acknowledge the use of Alan Davis's class notes.

44. W. Kenneth Holditch, "The Last Gentleman Grades Papers," *The Vieux Carré Courier*, Jan. 20–26, 1977.

45. Dawson Gaillard to Lee Gary, June 3, 1976. Copies of agreements between WP and Karen Black and other pertinent documents in the archives of David Kappes.

46. *1976 Proceedings of the Semiotic Society of America*, edited by Charles Peason and Hope Hamilton-Faria (Atlanta: Georgia Institute of Technology, 1977).

47. Interview: Charles Bigger III.

48. Charles Bigger III, "Language That Opens Us to the Truth of Being," *Faith and Culture* (Baton Rouge, November–December 1990), pp. 5–6.

49. WP to ES, Oct. 17, 1976.

50. Vilma Bergane of BOMC to RG, Oct. 22, 1976.

51. RG to WP, Nov. 30, 1976.

52. RS to Herb Jaffeuhy, Nov. 17, 1976.

53. Dawson Gaillard to WP, Nov. 5, 1976.

54. Margaret Mills to WP, Sept. 24, 1976.

55. *John Keats* by Walter Jackson Bate; *The Killing Jar* by E. M. Beekman; *Adequate Earth* by Donald Finkel; *Farmer* by Jim Harrison; *Midnight Was My Cry* and *The Ungrateful Garden* by Carolyn Kizer; *Amputations* and *Transplants* by Cynthia Macdonald; *The Survival of the Bark Canoe* by John McPhee; *Giraffe* by Stanley Plumly; *Hush* by David St. John; *Selected Poems* by Robert Watson; *Hard Freight* and *Bloodlines* by Charles Wright; *Collected Poems* and *Diversifications* by A. R. Ammons; *The Follies* by Daniel Mark Epstein; *And Morning* by Roland Flint; *What Thou Lovest Well, Remains American* and *The Lady in Kicking Horse Reservoir* by Richard Hugo; *Half-Lives* by Erica Jong; *The Page-Turner* by David Shapiro; *The Great Railway Bazaar* and *The Family Arsenal* by Paul Theroux; *Mysteries of the Horizon* by Lawrence Raab; *Alehouse Sonnets* by Norman

Dubie; *Rattner's Scar* by Don DeLillo; *Plus* by Joseph McElroy; *Celestial Navigation* by Anne Tyler; *In Sepia* by Jon Anderson, and *Avenue of the Americas* by James Scully.

56. Dannye Romine, "Her Only Son, the Author . . . The Dead Author," *The Charlotte* (North Carolina) *Observer*, May 25, 1980.

57. Interview: Sandra Brenner Rosenthal.

58. The Gottlieb-Toole correspondence and biographical information from various articles in the John Kennedy Toole Collection, Tulane University Library.

59. WP to Mrs. John Toole, Dec. 7, 1976.

60. Interview: L. M. Kit Carson. WP to LAL, Jan. 9, 1977; option agreement between WP and Karen Black. Interview: David Kappes.

61. WP to PRB, March 31, 1978.

62. WP to PRB, March 4, 1979.

63. Notes taken by Celia Gittelson, Feb. 1, 1977, Berg.

64. On April 21, 1977, Moviegoer Productions (Carson, Black, McBride) signed an agreement with Lasky-Weisel, Inc., for the production of this film, but nothing really ever came of this venture. Three years later, on Aug. 8, 1980, Raymond R. Homer Productions of New York City paid $56,000 for the rights to the film from Black, although Homer was so convinced that the film would be made that he did not purchase the rights in his own name, but in Black's. Were the picture to be produced, Kit Carson and Jack Baran would be hired as the producers of the film. Due to Homer's personal and financial problems, the rights "reverted" to Black after a lapse of two years, and the fate of this film drifted toward an asymptotic conclusion, though Avenue Pictures signed an option for the film after WP's death.

65. RS to Herbert Mitgang, Jan. 19, 1977; Anita Halton of FSG to Herbert Mitgang, Jan. 27, [1977].

66. WP to Margaret Miles of AA/NIAL, Feb. 9, 1977.

67. WP to "Dear Anita or Celia," Feb. 7, 1977.

68. WP to RC, Feb. 7, 1977.

69. RG to WP, Feb. 17, 1977.

70. RS to William Shawn, March 23, 1977.

71. RG to WP, March 15, 1977.

72. WP to Brainard Cheney, May 24, 1977.

73. Margaret M. Mills to WP, March 7, 1986.

74. Walter Sullivan to PS, SJ, Jan. 10, 1993.

75. WP to CB, April 9, 1977.

76. WP to Carolyn A. Wallace, March 1, 1977.

77. Kathleen A. Mulhill, "A Bechac's Tradition," *The Times-Picayune*, Oct. 30, 1983.

78. WP to Lydia Kaim, June 5, 1977.

79. WP to "Dear Colleagues" at the AA/NIAL, Sept. 22, 1977.

80. See *The Times-Picayune*, July 10, 1977.

81. RS to RG, July 20, 1977.

82. RG to WP, Sept. 13, 1977.

83. WP to PRB, Oct. 27, 1977.

84. WP to J. Gerald Kennedy, Oct. 7, 1979; WP to Max Webb, Oct. 31, 1979 (archives of PRB); WP to Weldon Thornton, Nov. 6, 1979; WP to LAL, Nov. 14, 1979; WP to Simone Vauthier, Dec. 24, 1979.

85. WP to LPS, Nov. 24, 1977.

86. RG to PSM, Nov. 24, 1980.

87. WP to RS, June 4, 1979.

88. BPS to WP, Feb. 23, 1978.

89. WP to PRB, Feb. 23, 1978.

90. WP to Allen Tate, March 18, 1978.

91. WP to Dwight Macdonald, March 4, 1978. WP voted as follows: "Regular"—Alison Lurie, Paul Fussell, Edward Hoagland, Shelby Foote, Albert Murray, Toni Morrison, Elizabeth Cullinan, David Wagoner, James Seay, Lerone Bennett, Jr.; "Rosenthal"— Diane Johnson (not listed for Rosenthal but she met the criteria. Toni Morrison was listed and Walker would vote for her even though she is a "commercial success"); "Loines"—Barbara Howes (first choice), John Peck (second choice); "Zabel"—Joan Didion; "Prix de Rome"—John Peck, Barbara Howes (second choice), Michael Mewshaw (third choice).

92. WP to RM, March 9, 1978.

93. LEP to WP, July 10, 1978.

94. WP to RC, Aug. 17, 1978.

95. WP to RC, Dec. 1, 1978.

96. WP to SF, Jan. 29, 1979.

97. Willis Sutter to WP, Nov. 28, 1978.

98. Kevin Kerrane to WP, Sept. 29, 1977; Oakley Hall to WP, Dec. 6, 1977; Edward Vasta to WP, Jan. 20, 1978. WP turned down a chance to lecture at Auburn University in the fall of 1978, as well as to accept visiting posts at Emory, the College of William and Mary, and the University of Alabama at Birmingham. Before Christmas, WP declined to be the William Belden Noble Lecturer at Harvard during the 1979–80 academic year and to give a series of lectures at the University of Chicago. Taylor Littleton to WP, March 29, April 7, 1978; J. Paul Hunter to WP, March 8, 1978; LeRoy W. Smith to WP, July 13, 1978; Alan D. Perlis to WP, April 26, 1978, and May 8, 1978; Peter J. Gomes to WP, Dec. 7, 1978; Peter Kountz to WP, Dec. 19, 1978.

99. WP to PRB, Jan. 12, 1979.

100. Interview: CGB.

101. WP to RC, Feb. 17, 1979.

102. WP to CGB, March 26, 1980.

103. *More Conversations*, pp. 17–19.

104. WP to Robert Lokey, Feb. 1, 1981.

105. WP to Lydia Kaim, March 14, 1979.

106. WP to AA/NIAL, April 27, 1979.

107. Archives of LSU Press.

108. WP to LEP, March 2, 1979.

109. WP to LEP, April 11, 1979.

110. *The Mount Vernon* (Ohio) *News*, Feb. 23, 1979; WP to PRB, March 4, 1979.

111. WP to LPS, May 21, June 11, 1979.

112. WP to LEP, July 26, 1979; Martha Lacy Hall to WP, July 31, 1979.

113. Interview: Rev. L. Jerome Taylor, Jr.

114. WP to James C. Boulware, O.S.B., Sept. 22, 1979. Interview: James C. Boulware.

115. Francis Sweeney, S.J., to WP, June 6, 1979; Mary Jayne Whittington to WP, Oct. 5, 1979; Jon Barwise to WP, Nov. 26, 1979; Monroe Engel to WP, Nov. 26, 1979; Terrence Sandalow to WP, Dec. 6, 1979.

116. RS to WP, Nov. 27, 1979.

117. WP to RG, Dec. 19, 23, 31, 1979.

118. WP to Richard G. Cashwell, Jan. 28, 1980.

119. WP to LAL, March 4, 1980.

120. WP to RC, March 6, [no year].
121. RG to WP, Jan. 14, 1980; RG to EO, Jan. 17, 1980.
122. John Hawkins of the Franklin Library to RG, Feb. 26, 1980; Nancy Miller to Shirley Fisher, April 3, 1980; RG to Frances Perle of McIntosh & Otis, Nov. 20, 1980.
123. LWH to Stanley Lindberg, July 10, 1980. Interview: LWH.
124. WP to James Boulware, O.S.B., May 20, 1980.
125. Samuel Kam of FSG to Evelyn Jackson at the Plaza Hotel, March 20, 1980.
126. RS to Siegfried Unseld in Frankfurt am Main, Germany, July 31, 1980; RS to Frances Perle of McIntosh & Otis, Nov. 20, 1980.
127. RS to WP, Aug. 28, 1980.
128. PSM to RG, Sept. 11, 1980.
129. Interview: HK. I am grateful to HK for allowing me to listen to the unpublished portion of the tape of this interview.
130. *Parting the Curtains: Interviews with Southern Writers*, interviews by Dannye Romine Powell, photographs by Jill Krementz (Winston-Salem, N.C.: John F. Blair Publisher, 1994), pp. 241–49.
131. Interview: Thomas A. Sebeok.
132. Thomas A. Sebeok, *Semiotics in the United States* (Bloomington: Indiana University Press, 1991), p. 35.
133. WP to Thelma Toole, July 26, 1980.
134. RF to Custis, Hyde, Mooney & McEachin of New Orleans, July 12, 1980, LSU Press archives.
135. James Boulware, O.S.B., to WP, ["Sometime in July 1980"].
136. Memo from LEP to Otis B. Wheeler, Oct. 2, 1980.
137. WP to Rev. George Madathiparampil, Oct. 8, 24, 1980.
138. RS to Art Seidenbaum of *The Los Angeles Times*, Dec. 22, 1980.
139. Mentioned in Paul Horgan's 1989 nomination of WP for the Gold Medal for Fiction.
140. WP to RC, Dec. 28, 1980. As usual, WP turned down requests to lecture at UNC, the Library of Congress, the University of Missouri, the University of California at Berkeley, the Writers' Workshop at the University of Iowa, as well as an invitation from Paul Horgan to lecture at a writers' conference, an invitation to be a writer-in-residence at Southeastern Louisiana University, and an invitation from the USIA to lecture in Japan, Korea, and the Philippines. John B. Graham, M.D., to WP, May 13, 1980; John C. Broderick to WP, July 8, 1980; M. Gilbert Porter to WP, Aug. 5, 1980; Ginger Richardson to WP, Aug. 14, 1980; Connie Brothers to WP, Aug. 25, 1980; Paul Horgan to WP, Nov. 4, 1980; Wiley H. Sharp, Jr., to WP, Dec. 4, 1980; Jennifer Newton to WP, Dec. 17, 1980.

13. *Before and After* Lost in the Cosmos, *1981–85*

1. Nancy Miller to WP, Feb. 3, 1981; Dagmar Henne of Agence Hoffman in Munich, Germany, to RS, Feb. 3, 1981.
2. WP had no desire to give the Wade Memorial Lecture in Philosophy at St. Louis University in the spring of 1982, or lecture at Harvard, or give the Surtz Lecture at Loyola University in Chicago. He turned down, too, an honorary doctorate from the University of Santa Clara in California. Later, he declined an offer to be a writer-in-residence at the Woodrow Wilson International Center for Scholars at the Smithsonian in Washington, D.C., and the first occupant of the Welsh Chair in American Studies at the University of Notre Dame. E. O. Hawkins to WP, Jan. 5, 1981; Marianne M.

Childress to WP, Jan. 5, 1981; Mark C. McPherson to WP, Jan. 15, 1981; J. Patout Burns, S.J., to THC, SJ, Feb. 2, 1981; WP to William Rewak, S.J., March 11, 1981; James H. Billington to WP, July 17, 1981; Donald P. Costello to WP, Sept. 22, 1981.

3. WP to GU, Feb. 18, 1981.

4. WP to SF, Jan. 5, 1981.

5. WP to PS, SJ, March 15, 1981.

6. Sula J. Hurley to WP, Sept. 10, 1981.

7. WP to John E. Corbally, Feb. 12, 1987.

8. WP to Water Isaacson, April 11, 1981.

9. Sula J. Hurley to WP, Sept. 10, 1981. WP's "Letter to the Editor," *The St. Tammany* (Louisiana) *News-Banner*, Oct. 25, 1984, and the unpublished one to *The New York Times*, Sept. 5, 1985, archives of Mercedes Arzù Wilson.

10. *DD-T*, May 31, 1981.

11. WP to SF, June 21, 1981.

12. WP to Carolyn A. Wallace, Aug. 21, 1981.

13. Walter West to WP, June 25, 1982.

14. RC to WP, Oct. 18, 1981.

15. WP to RG, Oct. 23, 1981.

16. RG to WP, Oct. 27, 1981.

17. WP to RF, Nov. 4, 1981.

18. Interview: Lyn (Hill) Hayward.

19. WP to RM, Nov. 11, 1981.

20. Carolyn A. Wallace to WP, Dec. 1, 1981.

21. LAL to WP, Jan. 19, 1982.

22. WP to LAL, Jan. 23, 1982.

23. WP to J. Gerald Kennedy, Jan. 29, 1982.

24. At this time, WP declined an offer to be a visiting writer-in-residence at Lehigh University in Pennsylvania. During the following year, he turned down the Visiting Fannie Hurst Professorship at Washington University in St. Louis. Novelist Richard Ford wrote from the English Department at Williams College in Massachusetts asking that WP accept a professorship for one or two semesters, at $30,000 a semester. WP waited a while before turning Williams down. Irving Lo of the Department of East Asian Languages and Cultures at Indiana University in Bloomington invited WP to go to China in late spring as official representative of the U.S. government. WP also turned down offers to lecture in Graz, Austria; to give the Lamar Lecture at Wesleyan College in Macon, Georgia; to lecture at a U.S.-Chinese Writers' Conference at UCLA; to be the Brown Foundation Fellow at the University of the South; to lecture at Stanford University in California; and to give a Regents' Lecture at the University of California at Santa Cruz. James R. Frakes to WP, Nov. 30, 1981; Daniel B. Shea to WP, Jan. 8, 1982; Richard Ford to WP, Jan. 18, 1982; Vincent Barnett, Jr., to WP, April 30, 1982; Irving Lo to WP, March 31, 1982; Klaus Hoffer and Alfred Kolleritsch to WP, March 1982; Corawayne Wright to WP, June 2, 1982; Robert A. Rees to WP, June 22, 1982; D. E. Richardson to WP, Aug. 24, 1982; Susan H. Jones to WP, Aug. 25, 1982; Robert L. Sinsheimer to WP, Aug. 30, 1982.

25. WP to JG, Feb. 14, 1982; also JG to WP, Feb. 20, 1985. Interview: JG.

26. WP to LP-G, June 30, 1982.

27. WP to LPS, July 10, 1982.

28. WP to PSM, April 5, 1982.

29. PSM to RS, April 9, 1982.

30. Interview: Mary Lee Settle. Richard Bausch, "Nuns, Prophecies, Communists, the Bomb, the Dread of Angels, Reason, Faith, and the *Summa Theologica*," in *A Rumor of Bliss: Contemporary Writers on Saints*, edited by Paul Elie (New York: Harcourt, Brace and Company, 1994), pp. 74–91.

31. Comment referred to in a letter from Sister Park Jeong-Mi, R.S.C.J., to PS, SJ, May 13, 1992.

32. Jeffrey D. Wilson to WP, May 17, 1982.

33. WP to Jeffrey D. Wilson, Aug. 22, 1982.

34. Catalogue 60 of Ken Lopez, Bookseller, Hadley, Massachusetts.

35. WP to Thomas A. Sebeok, Aug. 13, 1982.

36. Thomas A. Sebeok to WP, Aug. 17, 1982.

37. PSM to RG, Aug. 13, 1982; RG to PSM, Aug. 25, 1982.

38. WP to RG, Sept. 7, 1982.

39. ZAN to WP, Oct. 8, 1982.

40. WP to ZAN, Oct. 16, 1982.

41. Elizabeth Besobrasow to PSM, Sept. 14, 1982.

42. WP to RG, Oct. 5, Nov. 8, 13, 1982.

43. Pius Lartigue, O.S.B., to WP, Oct. 11, 1982.

44. WP to ER, Dec. 2, 1982.

45. WP to Msgr. Charles Murphy, Dec. 29, 1982.

46. WP to JG, Dec. 4, 1982.

47. RS to WP, Dec. 3, 1982; Michelle Lapautre to Kristin Kliemann, Dec. 6, 1982; RS to WP, Dec. 16, 1982.

48. RG to WP, Dec. 27, 1982.

49. RG to WP, Jan. 25, 1983.

50. WP to RF, Jan. 26, 1983.

51. FSG memo by Joan Massey, April 19, 1983.

52. WP to JG, Feb. 10, 1983.

53. Scott Underwood, O.S.B., to WP, Feb. 24, 1983; Pius Lartigue, O.S.B., to WP, Feb. 24, 1983; WP to Pius Lartigue, O.S.B., March 8, 1983.

54. WP to Scott Underwood, O.S.B., March 20, 1983.

55. Marion Montgomery to WP, April 18, 1983.

56. WP to Marion Montgomery, May 3, 1983.

57. Interview: RM. WP to RM, May 12, 1983.

58. WP to JG, March 29, 1983.

59. Interview: George M. Riser, Jr., M.D.

60. *The Fiction of Walker Percy*, pp. 225–28.

61. BPP to WP, June 1, 1983.

62. WP to SF, May 10, 1983.

63. WP to Joan Massey, June 23, July 15, 1983.

64. Karen Everett of FSG to WP, June 30, 1983.

65. WP to ES, May 22, 1983.

66. WP to CB, June 25, 1983.

67. Interview: RM.

68. WP to Suzanne Ballard Dowouis, June 9, 1983.

69. JG to WP, June 30, 1983.

70. WP to Joan Massey, July 29, 1983.

71. SF to WP, August 10, 1983.

72. WP to Michael Hargraves, July 5, 1983.

73. PSM to Michael Hargraves, July 14, 1983.

74. Catalogue 51, Joseph the Provider, Santa Barbara, California.

75. WP to David Duty, Dec. 7, 1984; WP to David Duty, Jan. 25, 1986.

76. WP to RS, March 17, 1983.

77. Interview: Lucy Parlange.

78. WP to Pius Lartigue, O.S.B., Aug. 23, 1983.

79. Interviews: Lawrence Bouchea, O.S.B., Thomas W. Eldringhoff, Gary P. Pate, and Kyle J. Scafide.

80. Mark David to PS, SJ, Dec. 27, 1988.

81. WP to Kent Mullikin, Nov. 11, 1983.

82. Kent Mullikin to WP, Oct. 24, 1984.

83. WP to Kent Mullikin, Oct. 26, 1984.

84. WP to Kent Mullikin, Nov. 5, 1984.

85. WP to THC, SJ, Nov. 13, 1983.

86. WP to JG, Nov. 23, 1983.

87. RG to WP, Nov. 29, 1983.

88. WP to Pius Lartigue, O.S.B., Dec. 20, 1983.

89. WP to ES, Jan. 19, 1984.

90. WP to Martha Lacy Hall, Feb. 18, 1984.

91. WP to JG, Jan. 8, 1984.

92. GU to PS, SJ, Aug. 14, 1992; WP to "Sophie," Feb. 18, 1984, archives of GU.

93. KLK sent WP the first draft of the lectures subsequently published in *Reasoning and the Logic of Things*, plus a draft of his essay entitled "Identifying Peirce's 'Most Lucid and Interesting Paper': An Introduction to Cenopythagoreanism."

94. WP to Francis L. Fennell, July 23, 1983; WP to JG, Jan. 31, 1984. Interview: Francis L. Fennell.

95. WP to JG, June 27, 1984.

96. WP to RF, May 15, 1984.

97. WP to RF, [n.d.].

98. SF to WP, "D-Day, plus 40," [June 6, 1984].

99. WP to ES, July 12, 1984.

100. WP to RS, Nov. 12, 1984.

101. Interview: Sheila Bosworth.

102. Sheila Bosworth, "Women in the Fiction of Walker Percy," *The Double Dealer Redux*, 1 (New Orleans, Winter 1993–94), p. 15.

103. RS to WP, Nov. 2, 1984.

104. WP to ES, [Christmas card: n.d.].

105. Wendell Jones, Jr., to WP, Nov. 14, 1984. Interview: Wendell Jones, Jr.

106. WP to Wendell Jones, Jr., Dec. 18, 1984.

107. WP to JG, Jan. 17, 1985.

108. WP to THC, SJ, Feb. 1, 1985; WP to William Rodney Allen, Feb. 3, 1985.

109. WP to JG, Feb. 4, 1985.

110. WP to JG, [n.d., after Feb. 14, 1985].

111. WP to Jerry R. Romig, Oct. 17, 1984.

112. WP to JHM, SJ, May 7, 1985.

113. WP to JG, May 25, 1985.

114. RS to WP, June 10, 1985.

115. Interview: Eugene H. Winick.

116. Catalogue 28, Waiting for Godot Books, Hadley, Massachusetts.

117. WP to Eugene H. Winick, Oct. 13, 1985; Catalogue 28, Waiting for Godot Books, Hadley, Massachusetts.
118. *Walker Percy: A Comprehensive Descriptive Bibliography*, p. 60.
119. WP to Patricia Rogan, Aug. 5, 1985.
120. Richard R. Schultze, Jr., to WP, Aug. 31, 1985. Interview: Richard R. Schultze, Jr., M.D.
121. WP to Richard R. Schultze, Jr., Sept. 5, 1985.
122. Charles Fister to PS, SJ, Oct. 5, 1992. Interview: Charles Fister.
123. WP to ES, Dec. 5, 1985.

14. The Thanatos Syndrome *and the Final Illness, 1986–90*

1. Kim Heron, "Technical Hubris," *The New York Times Book Review*, April 5, 1987, p. 22.
2. Interview: John Martin Byrnes.
3. Interview: Benedict Groeschel, C.F.R.
4. WP to THC, SJ, Feb. 6, March 3, 1986; WP to PS, SJ, Feb. 17, 1986.
5. WP to ZAN, April 20, 1986.
6. Ray Broussard, "Profile: Walker Percy," *The St. Tammany* (Louisiana) *News-Banner*, March 25, 1987.
7. RM to WP, "Friday, April 1986."
8. WP to RM, June 16, 1986.
9. WP to RM, Jan. 16, 1987.
10. RM to WP, Jan. 15, 1987.
11. WP to RG, May 19, 1986.
12. Interview: Helene Atwan. LPS to WP, May 27, 1986; RS to WP, May 14, 1986.
13. WP to Dr. and Mrs. Gene Usdin, June 20, 1986.
14. Mary Deems Howland to WP, June 6, 1986. Interview: Mary Deems Howland.
15. Interview: Elizabeth Dale Johnson. WP to Elizabeth Dale Johnson, June 21, Sept. 6, 1986.
16. WP to John Edward Hardy, Aug. 9, 1986.
17. WP to ZAN, July 7, 1986.
18. WP to Mr. and Mrs. James D. Carr, June 30, 1986; WP to CB, July 18, 1986.
19. WP to LPS, June 8, 1985.
20. Interview: CB.
21. Hunter Cole to WP, Sept. 25, 1986; WP to Hunter Cole, Oct. 13, Nov. 12, 1986; WP to ZAN, Nov. 17, 1986.
22. Interviews: Peggy Castex and Daniel Charbonnier.
23. WP to John N. Deely, Oct. 27, 1986.
24. WP to John N. Deely, June 8, 1987.
25. WP to Thomas A. Sebeok, Oct. 29, 1986; Thomas A. Sebeok to WP, Nov. 4, 1986.
26. KLK to WP, Nov. 26, 1986.
27. KLK to WP, Nov. 26, 1987.
28. WP to William Rodney Allen, Jan. 31, 1987.
29. Interview: Elinor Ann Walker. WP to Elinor Ann Walker, March 3, 1987.
30. WP to Rev. Hugh Miller, July 6, 1986.
31. Gilles Barbedette of Editions Rivages to RS, March 12, 1987; Claude Gallimard to RS, March 17, 1987; RS to Claude Gallimard, March 17, 1987; RS to Michelle Lapautre, March 17, 1987.
32. RS to Yannick Guillou, March 18, 1987.
33. Claude Gallimard to RS, March 23, 1987.

34. Antoine Gallimard to Michelle Lapautre, March 30, 1987.
35. Michelle Lapautre to Antoine Gallimard, April 6, 1987.
36. FSG internal memo, Aug. 28, 1986.
37. Interview: RS.
38. WP to PS, SJ, Jan. 8, 1987.
39. WP to Eugene H. Winick, March 25, 1987.
40. HK to WP, May 11, 1987.
41. WP to RF, April 7, 1987.
42. WP to NL, April 7, 1987.
43. WP to Raymond A. Schroth, S.J., April 7, 1987.
44. THC, SJ to WP, April 8, 1987.
45. Raymond A. Schroth, S.J., to WP, April 8, 1987.
46. JHM, SJ to WP, April 15, 1987.
47. WP to JHM, SJ, May 16, 1987.
48. WP to Helene Atwan, Jan. 27, 1987; internal memo by Bridget Marmion, Feb. 18, 1987.
49. Helene Atwan to WP, Feb. 12, 1987.
50. WP to Bridget Marmion, [n.d.].
51. Bridget Marmion to WP, March 26, 1987.
52. Helene Atwan to WP, April 7, 1987.
53. Helene Atwan to WP, April 2, 1987.
54. Bridget Marmion to WP, Feb. 23, 1987.
55. Interviews: RG and Jay Tolson.
56. WP to BCT, Aug. 14, 1987; WP to Richard Faust, M.D., Aug. 14, 1987.
57. Interview: Thomas A. Underwood. Thomas A. Underwood to WP, Aug. 14, 1987.
58. WP to ZAN, Oct. 12, 1987; WP to Thomas A. Sebeok, Oct. 13, 1987.
59. WP to KLK, Oct. 20, 1987.
60. WP to KLK, Nov. 5, 1987.
61. KLK to WP, Oct. 24, 1987.
62. David Duty to WP, July 8, 1988.
63. WP to Jay Tolson, Dec. 9, 1987; WP to KLK and Hilary Putnam, Dec. 14, 1987.
64. WP to Mark Taylor, Dec. 15, 1987.
65. WP to Mr. and Mrs. Roger Straus, Jan. 9, 1988.
66. Cardinal Paul Poupard to WP, Dec. 3, 1987.
67. Archbishop Pio Laghi, Dec. 11, 1987.
68. Archbishop Philip M. Hannan to WP, Dec. 17, 1987. Interview: Archbishop Philip M. Hannan.
69. WP to Archbishop Philip M. Hannan, Dec. 24, 1987.
70. WP to Ann Trousdale, Jan. 28, 1988; WP to Susanne Ballard Dowouis, Jan. 31, 1988.
71. WP to RF, Jan. 29, 1988.
72. WP to THC, SJ, Jan. 9, 1988.
73. WP to ER, Jan. 31, 1988; WP to Jay Tolson, Feb. 11, 1988.
74. WP to Hervé Carrier, S.J., Feb. 24, 1988.
75. Interviews: George M. Riser, Jr., M.D., and Larry K. Kvols, M.D.
76. WP to Martha Lacy Hall, Jan. 30, 1988.
77. WP to NL, Jan. 30, 1988.
78. WP to Georgia Fisher, Feb. 3, 1988.
79. Senator Albert Gore, Jr., to WP, Jan. 22, 1988; WP to Senator Albert Gore, Jr., Jan. 31, 1988.

80. WP to James McFadden, Feb. 25, 1988.

81. James McFadden to WP, March 8, 1988.

82. WP to RF, March 17, 1988.

83. WP to KLK, March 18, 1988.

84. WP to KLK, April 30, 1988; WP to Charles Fister, May 1, 1988.

85. Interview: Donald Wetherbee, M.D.

86. LPS to WP, June 2, 1988; LPS to JG, June 13, 1988.

87. RM to WP, July 27, 1988.

88. Sadamichi Kato to PS, SJ, Jan. 14, 1991; unpublished transcript of taped interview of WP provided by Sadamichi Kato.

89. WP to KLK, Aug. 21, 1988.

90. WP to Dannye Romine, Sept. 5, 1988.

91. WP to LPS, Sept. 6, 24, 1988; WP to Dale Vree, Sept. 18, 1988.

92. WP to KLK, Oct. 20, 1988.

93. WP to KLK, Dec. 14, 1988.

94. WP to Martha Lacy Hall, Dec. 24, 1988.

95. WP to Jay Tolson, Jan. 6, Feb. 2, 1989; WP to LAL, Jan. 17, 1989; WP to KLK, Jan. 17, 1989.

96. WP to KLK, Jan. 29, 1989.

97. WP to KLK, Feb. 13, 1989.

98. WP to KLK, Feb. 27, 1989.

99. WP to John McGrath, March 2, 1989.

100. There are nine versions of this lecture: (1) Original version called "Science, Religion and the Tertium Quid," sent to KLK on Dec. 8, 1988. (2) "The Fateful Rift: The San Andreas Fault in the Modern Mind," with holograph insertions; this is closer to the final version than the original version. I believe this is the copy both Jay Tolson and I saw. (3) Copy entered into NEH computer and printed out; it was proofread by members of the staff. (4) A second NEH version. (5) Copy on file at McIntosh & Otis that resembles Number 4. (6) Copy with corrections made by WP on Number 4. (7) Reading copy given to John McGrath after the lecture; this version has a new lead-in. (8) "Official" N.E.H. version distributed to the press. (9) Taped version on television.

101. Robert Eckert to WP, [n.d.]; WP to Robert Eckert, March 11, 1989; Robert Eckert to WP, [n.d.]; WP to Robert Eckert, March 28, 1989; Robert Eckert to WP, [n.d.].

102. John R. Hadd to WP, May 1, 1989.

103. WP to John R. Hadd, June 4, 1989.

104. WP to Paul Horgan, March 28, 1989.

105. For a modified version of this interview, see *More Conversations*, pp. 216–25.

106. Interviews: Lynne B. Cheney, John McGrath, and members of the NEH staff.

107. Madison Smartt Bell to WP, May 10, 1989.

108. Interview: Judith LaCour. Sheila Stroup, "Graduation Time to Pause, Reflect," *The Times-Picayune*, May 25, 1989; also *Wolf Tracks*, June 1989, p. 9, for a photo of the class.

109. Medical records of the Mayo Clinic and George M. Riser, Jr., M.D.

110. WP to KLK, June 15, 1989.

111. WP to Ann Trousdale, July 3, 1989.

112. WP to John R. Hadd, Sept. 15, 1989.

113. Interview: Jonathan Potter. WP to Jonathan Potter, Nov. 16, 1989; Jonathan Potter to PS, SJ, July 28, 1991.

114. William MacCandless, O.S.B., to PS, SJ, Nov. 16, 1991.

115. Interviews: William A. Sessions and Thomas Key. William A. Sessions to WP, May 4, 1990. On Sept. 15, 1989, a contract was signed authorizing a play version of WP's novel *LR*, which stipulates that performances of the resulting play may take place only in Mississippi (Catalogue 44 of Joseph the Provider, Santa Barbara, California).

Appendix: Percy Family History

1. Unfootnoted references by WAP are to *LL*.
2. William F. Holmes, "William Alexander Percy and the Bourbon Era in the Yazoo-Mississippi Delta," *The Mississippi Quarterly*, 26 (Winter 1972–73), pp. 71–87.
3. Though WAP tended to discount the connection between the famous European branch of the Percys and his own family, there are two indications that his American ancestors thought otherwise: Charles Percy called his residence Northumberland House, which WP refers to in the foreword to *L*, and Col. William Alexander Percy's books, a number of which can be found in the library of the home of LP-G, have bookplates that bear the English Percy coat of arms, including the phrase *Espérance en Dieu*. No genealogist has established definitively a direct link between Henry, First Lord Percy of Alnwick, Hugh Algernon Percy, Tenth Duke of Northumberland (whose titles include Earl of Northumberland, Earl Percy, Baron Percy, and Baron of Alnwick), and the American Percys (see Israel Shenker, "Treasure and Tradition at Alnwick Castle," *Smithsonian* 15 [August 1984], pp. 72–82). Several valuable references to the history of the Percy family in the British Isles include *The Percy Chartulary*, compiled apparently in the time of Henry, Fourth Lord Percy of Alnwick, upon his creation as Earl of Northumberland (the last historical reference in this chartulary is the Charter of Creation given on the coronation day of Richard II, July 16, 1377); the privately printed *Thirty-one Generations: A Thousand Years of Percys and Pierces, 972–1969*, compiled by Barnard Ledward Colby (New London, Conn., 1969); *A History of the House of Percy: From the Earliest Times Down to the Present Century*, by Gerald Brenan, edited by W. A. Lindsay (London: Freemantle & Company, 1902); and *Annals of the House of Percy: From the Conquest to the Opening of the Nineteenth Century*, by Edward Barrington DeFlonblangue (London: R. Clay & Sons, 1887). For relevant information about the Percy genealogy, see *The House of Percy*, pp. 340–54, and *The Percy Family of Mississippi and Louisiana: 1776–1943*, compiled by John Hereford Percy (Baton Rouge: J. E. Ortlieb Prig Company, 1943). Periodically, the extended Phinizy family meets for a reunion and a group effort is made at such reunions to update the family genealogy. I am grateful to have been a guest of BPS at one of these reunions.
4. Interview of LP-G by John Griffin Jones, MDAH.
5. Mrs. Dunbar Rowland, "Mississippi's Colonial Population and Land Grants," *Publications of the Mississippi Historical Society*, 1 (1916), p. 418.
6. For additional information about grants made to the Percy family, see Frances Ingmire and Carolyn Ericson, *First Settlers of the Mississippi Territory* (St. Louis: Ingmire Publications, 1982), pp. 19, 51, 55, 68, 106.
7. *The Percy Family of Mississippi and Louisiana: 1776–1943*, pp. 48–49.
8. Part One of *The House of Percy* and "Wealth in the Natchez Region: Inventories of the Estate of Charles Percy, 1794 and 1804," edited by William B. Hamilton and William D. McCain, *The Journal of Mississippi History*, 10 (October 1948), pp. 290–316. Also Douglas Lewis, "John James Audubon (1785–1851): Annotated Chronology of Activity in the Deep South, 1819–1837," *The Southern Quarterly*, 29 (Summer 1991), pp. 63–82; Alice Ford, *John James Audubon: A Biography* (New York: Abbeville Press, 1988), es-

pecially pp. 140–42, and Shirley Streshinsky, *Audubon: Life and Art in the American Wilderness* (New York: Villard Books, 1993), pp. 144–46.

9. Stanley Clisby Arthur, *The Story of the West Florida Rebellion* (Baton Rouge: Claitor's Publishing Division [Louisiana Classic Reprint Series], 1975).

10. *Louisiana: A History*, edited by Bennett W. Wall (Arlington Heights, Ill.: Forum Press, 1984), pp. 100–1.

11. Stanley Clisby Arthur's account in *The Percy Family of Mississippi and Louisiana: 1776–1943*, pp. 40–41.

12. *The House of Percy*, p. 27.

13. For date of death, see "Wealth in the Natchez Region: Inventories of the Estate of Charles Percy, 1794 and 1804," p. 290.

14. See also "Wealth in the Natchez Region: Inventories of the Estate of Charles Percy, 1794 and 1804," pp. 294–95.

15. *The Percy Family of Mississippi and Louisiana: 1776–1943*, p. 50.

16. On Feb. 16, 1795, in Natchez, Mississippi, Robert did acknowledge that he inherited at least $2,000 from his father's estate (*The Percy Family of Mississippi and Louisiana: 1776–1943*, p. 6).

17. "Wealth in the Natchez Region: Inventories of the Estate of Charles Percy, 1794 and 1804," p. 297.

18. William Echols to LP, Jan. 5, 1926.

19. Dorothy Love Turk, *Leland, Mississippi: From Hellhole to Beauty Spot* (Leland, Miss.: Leland Historical Society, 1986), pp. 4–5. In addition, as Turk notes, William Henry Lee and his wife, Eleanor Ware Lee, the granddaughter of Charles Percy (through his daughter Sarah Percy Ellis), owned Dilthey Plantation between Leland and Arcola.

20. Her name is found in the Last Will and Testament of Dr. John Walker Percy.

21. *GD-D*, Feb. 13, 1894.

22. *GD-D*, June 27, 1882; also Bertram Wyatt-Brown, "Walker, Will, and Honor Dying: The Percys and Literary Creativity," in *Looking South: Chapters in the Story of an American Region*, edited by Winfred B. Moore, Jr., and Joseph F. Tripp (Westport, Conn.: Greenwood Press, 1989), p. 235. Source concerning this suicide: LP-G.

23. See BPS, "William Alexander Percy: His Philosophy of Life as Reflected in His Poetry" (M.A. thesis, University of Georgia, 1957), p. 3; also *The Greenville* (Mississippi) *Times*, Jan. 21, 1888.

24. *Leland Mississippi: From Hellhole to Beauty Spot*, p. 9.

25. As would be expected, Nannie Percy inherited her husband's estate. Source: WAP's Last Will and Testament. Also BD, Jan. 20, 21, 1888.

26. *GD-D*, June 28, 1882; Dec. 26, 1878. Henry Ball disliked Downs Pace and called him a "desperate reprobate" (BD, June 27, 1898). WP depicted Downs Pace as such in a draft of *The Moviegoer*.

27. Interview: LP-G.

28. William Armstrong Percy married Mrs. Lottie Galloway Morris, who died in 1901. Three years later, he married Caroline Yarborough; together they had three children: William Armstrong Percy, Jr. (born 1906), Lady (born 1907), and Walker (born 1909). William Armstrong practiced law in Memphis. William Armstrong Percy, Jr., married Anne Dent. Lady, who maintained contact with the Percys in Greenville, married Charles James McKinney (1891–1918) of Knoxville, Tennessee, and had three children: William, Charles, and Mary. Walker, who migrated to the West Coast for studies and whose activities were carefully tracked by LP, married Norma Williams in 1941. William Armstrong Percy died in Memphis on May 23, 1912; Rev. W. N. Claybrook, the

rector of St. Mary's-in-the-Highlands Episcopal Church in Birmingham, officiated at the funeral in that city. On Feb. 3, 1917, Caroline Percy, William Armstrong Percy's widow, petitioned the Chancery Court of Washington County, Mississippi, to have LP become the guardians of her three children: William, age eleven; Lady, age nine; and Walker, age seven. The estate of each of these children was estimated to be $10,000. SMH.

29. BD, Aug. 4, 1887, refers to "Capt." Bourges. It is clear from the many references in this diary that Henry Ball was a good friend of the Percys and Bourgeses, once even attending, as he notes on Feb. 26, 1887, a devotional service at the Catholic church ("14 wearying Stations of the Cross and abominable music") with Mrs. Bourges and her two daughters, Lelia and Rita.
30. BD, Feb. 20, May 22, 1888; Oct. 28, 1894; Jan. 2, 1903.
31. BD, Oct. 28, 1884.
32. LP and his brother-in-law, Charles McKinney, went on one such bear hunt together. BD, Jan. 27, 1892.
33. For a study of Trail Lake in the mid-1930s, see Raymond McClinton, "A Social-Economic Analysis of a Mississippi Delta Plantation" (M.A. thesis, UNC, 1938).
34. See Evans C. Johnson, *Oscar W. Underwood: A Political Biography* (Baton Rouge: LSU Press, 1980), p. 104, for a reference to a hunt that took place during Roosevelt's second term.
35. Bertram Wyatt-Brown, "LeRoy Percy and Sunnyside: Planter Mentality and Italian Peonage in the Mississippi Delta," *Arkansas Historical Quarterly*, Spring 1991, p. 60. I am indebted to this article and to the others in this issue, all devoted to Sunnyside.
36. *The Percys of Mississippi*, pp. 41 ff.
37. *The Jackson* (Mississippi) *Weekly Clarion-Ledger*, Jan. 13, 1919. Also *A History of Mississippi*, edited by Richard Aubrey McLemore, Vol. 2 (Hattiesburg: University and College Press of Mississippi, 1973), pp. 49–53, and Albert D. Kirwan, *Revolt of the Rednecks: Mississippi Politics: 1876–1925* (Knoxville: University Press of Kentucky, 1951), pp. 191–225.
38. William F. Holmes, *The White Chief: James Kimble Vardaman* (Baton Rouge: LSU Press, 1970), pp. 201–15. For LP's participation in an effort to oppose Vardaman, see the report of the Mississippi House of Representatives entitled *Inquiry into the Charge of Bribery in the Recent Senatorial Contest* (Jackson, Miss., 1910).
39. *Leland Mississippi: From Hellhole to Beauty Spot*, p. 39.
40. RDDDA.
41. From *The Birmingham Iron Age*, March 22, 1886.
42. "History of Benners, Burr, Stokely and McKamy of Birmingham, Ala.," *The Alabama Lawyer*, 5 (January 1944), pp. 98–101.
43. LL, pp. 270–84.
44. From the marriage license of WP-B and Mary Pratt DeBardeleben.
45. *The Percy Family of Mississippi and Louisiana: 1776–1943*, pp. 67–68.
46. See George M. Cruikshank, *A History of Birmingham and Its Environs* (Chicago: Lewis Publishing Company, 1920), and "History of Benners, Burr, Stokely and McKamy of Birmingham, Ala.," for information about WP-B's legal career.
47. *The Birmingham News*, Feb. 9, 1917.
48. SMH.
49. Information on a real estate contract, archives of PS, SJ.
50. For a helpful insider's account of the coal, iron, and steel industry in Birmingham, see Robert J. Norrell, *James Bowron: The Autobiography of a New South Industrialist*

(Chapel Hill: UNC, 1991), especially pp. 154, 186–87, 204, and Carl Harris, *Political Power in Birmingham, 1871–1921* (Knoxville: University of Tennessee Press, 1977).

51. Ethel Armes, *The Story of Coal and Iron in Alabama* (Birmingham: Chamber of Commerce, 1910), p. 465.

52. Edward L. Ayers, *The Promise of the New South: Life After Reconstruction* (New York: Oxford University Press, 1992), pp. 110–11.

53. *BA-H*, Feb. 9, 1917.

54. Marjorie Longenecker White, *The Birmingham District: An Industrial History and Guide* (Birmingham: Birmingham Historical Society, 1981), p. 111.

55. The architect's rendition of this house can be found in the Linn-Henley Research Library in Birmingham.

56. SMH.

57. From a Resolution of the Bar of Jefferson County, Alabama.

58. See the biographical sketch of Borden Burr in *The Alabama Lawyer*, 13 (October 1952), p. 418.

59. WP-B enjoyed playing golf, and the names of some of his out-of-town guests are listed in the records of the Birmingham Country Club.

60. In 1915, a group of businessmen from Birmingham led by WP-B could not find a prominent citizen they wanted to serve on the commission to give the city the leadership they felt was essential. *Political Power in Birmingham, 1871–1921*, pp. 81, 87. WP-B, "Birmingham, Under the Commission Plan," *American Academy of Political and Social Science: Commission Government in American Cities* (1911), pp. 259–64.

61. *The Percys of Mississippi*, p. 121; also "William Alexander Percy: His Philosophy of Life as Reflected in His Poetry," p. 39. For an account of WAP's first short teaching career at the University of the South, see a lecture given at the Sewanee Writers' Conference on July 17, 1991, by Monroe K. Spears; for his second stint, see the address by Frederick Hard before the Friends of the Howard-Tilton Memorial Library of Tulane University, 1944, entitled "William Alexander Percy." Also James Glass to WAP, June 15, 1920.

62. "William Alexander Percy: His Philosophy of Life as Reflected in His Poetry," p. 42.

BIBLIOGRAPHY

Works by Walker Percy

NOVELS

The Moviegoer (New York: Alfred A. Knopf, 1961)
The Last Gentleman (New York: FSG, 1966) *(LG)*
Love in the Ruins (New York: FSG, 1971) *(LR)*
Lancelot (New York: FSG, 1977) *(L)*
The Second Coming (New York: FSG, 1980) *(SC)*
The Thanatos Syndrome (New York: FSG, 1987)

NONFICTION AND LETTERS

The Message in the Bottle (New York: FSG, 1975) *(MB)*
Lost in the Cosmos (New York: FSG, 1983)
Signposts in a Strange Land, edited by Patrick H. Samway, S.J. (New York: FSG, 1991) *(SSL)*
A Thief of Peirce: The Letters of Kenneth Laine Ketner and Walker Percy, edited by Patrick H. Samway, S.J. (Jackson: University Press of Mississippi, 1995)
The Correspondence of Shelby Foote and Walker Percy, edited by Jay Tolson (New York: W. W. Norton & Company, 1996)

Selected Bibliography

William Rodney Allen. *Walker Percy: A Southern Wayfarer.* Jackson: University Press of Mississippi, 1986.
Lewis Baker. *The Percys of Mississippi: Politics and Literature in the New South.* Baton Rouge: LSU Press, 1985.
Harold Bloom, ed. *Walker Percy.* New York: Chelsea House Publishers, 1986.
Robert H. Brinkmeyer, Jr. *Three Catholic Writers of the Modern South: Allen Tate, Caroline Gordon, Walker Percy.* Jackson: University Press of Mississippi, 1985.

Panthea Reid Broughton, ed. *The Art of Walker Percy: Stratagems for Being.* Baton Rouge: LSU Press, 1979.

William C. Carter, ed. *Conversations with Shelby Foote.* Jackson: University Press of Mississippi, 1989.

Gary M. Ciuba. *Walker Percy: Books of Revelations.* Athens: University of Georgia Press, 1991.

Robert Coles, M.D. *Walker Percy: An American Search.* Boston: Little, Brown & Company, 1978.

J. Donald Crowley, and Sue Mitchell Crowley, eds. *Critical Essays on Walker Percy.* Boston: G. K. Hall & Company, 1989.

Edward J. Dupuy. *Autobiography in Walker Percy: Repetition, Recovery, and Redemption.* Baton Rouge: LSU Press, 1996.

Daniela Fortezza. *Verso Omega: Walker Percy e il mistero infinito.* Rome: Bulzoni Editore, 1990.

Ann Mace Futrell. *The Signs of Christianity in the Works of Walker Percy.* San Francisco: International Scholars Publication, 1994.

Jan Nordby Gretlund, and Karl-Heinz Westarp, eds. *Walker Percy: Novelist and Philosopher.* Jackson: University Press of Mississippi, 1991.

John Edward Hardy. *The Fiction of Walker Percy.* Urbana: University of Illinois Press, 1987.

Peter S. Hawkins. *The Language of Grace: Flannery O'Connor, Walker Percy, and Iris Murdoch.* Cambridge, Mass.: Cowley Publications, 1983.

Linda Whitney Hobson. *Understanding Walker Percy.* Columbia: University of South Carolina Press, 1988.

———. *Walker Percy: A Comprehensive Descriptive Bibliography.* New Orleans: Faust Publishing Company, 1988.

Mary Deems Howland. *The Gift of the Other: Gabriel Marcel's Concept of Intersubjectivity in Walker Percy's Novels.* Pittsburgh: Duquesne University Press, 1990.

Lewis A. Lawson. *Following Walker Percy: Essays on Walker Percy's Work.* Troy, N.Y.: Whitston, 1988.

———. *Still Following Percy.* Jackson: University Press of Mississippi, 1995.

——— and Elzbieta H. Olesky, eds. *Walker Percy's Feminine Characters.* Troy, N.Y.: Whitston, 1994.

——— and Victor A. Kramer, eds. *Conversations with Walker Percy.* Jackson: University Press of Mississippi, 1985. *(Conversations)*

——— and Victor A. Kramer, eds. *More Conversations with Walker Percy.* Jackson: University Press of Mississippi, 1993. *(More Conversations)*

Martin Luschei. *The Sovereign Wayfarer: Walker Percy's Diagnosis of the Malaise.* Baton Rouge: LSU Press, 1972.

Elzbieta H. Olesky. *Plight in Common: Hawthorne and Percy.* New York: Peter Lang, 1993.

William Alexander Percy. *Lanterns on the Levee: Recollections of a Planter's Son.* New York: Alfred A. Knopf, 1941. *(LL)*

Patricia Poteat. *Walker Percy and the Old Modern Age.* Baton Rouge: LSU Press, 1985.

Bernadette Prochaska, F.S.P.A. *The Myth of the Fall and Walker Percy's "The Last Gentleman."* New York: Peter Lang, 1992.

Kieran Quinlan. *Walker Percy: The Last Catholic Novelist.* Baton Rouge: LSU Press, 1996.

Ted R. Spivey. *The Writer as Shaman: The Pilgrimages of Conrad Aiken and Walker Percy.* Macon, Ga.: Mercer University Press, 1986.

L. Jerome Taylor. *In Search of Self: Life, Death, and Walker Percy.* Cambridge, Mass.: Cowley Publications, 1986.

Jac Tharpe. *Walker Percy.* Boston: Twayne Publishers, 1983.

————, ed. *Walker Percy: Art and Ethics.* Jackson: University Press of Mississippi, 1980.

Jay Tolson. *Pilgrim in the Ruins: A Life of Walker Percy.* New York: Simon & Schuster, 1992.

Bertram Wyatt-Brown. *The House of Percy: Honor, Melancholy, and Imagination in a Southern Family.* New York: Oxford University Press, 1994.

————. *The Literary Percys: Family History, Gender and the Southern Imagination.* Athens: University of Georgia Press, 1994.

I would like to acknowledge using the following resources: Alfred A. Knopf Collection (including letters of Elizabeth Otis and Stanley Kauffmann), Harry Ransom Humanities Research Center at the University of Texas at Austin; American Academy and the National Institute of Arts and Letters (AA/NIAL), New York City; Ball Diary (some of the spelling and punctuation in this diary has been regularized) in the William Alexander Percy Library, Greenville, Mississippi, and the Southern Historical Collection at UNC; Berg Collection (Berg), New York Public Library, New York City; Brainard Cheney Collection, Jean and Alexander Heard Library, Vanderbilt University, Nashville, Kentucky; Caroline Gordon and Allen Tate Collections, Firestone Library, Princeton University (PU), Princeton, New Jersey; Cleanth Brooks Collection, Beinecke Rare Book and Manuscript Library, Yale University, New Haven, Connecticut; College of Physicians and Surgeons (P & S), Columbia University, New York City; Dorothy Day Collection, Memorial Main Library, Marquette University (MU), Milwaukee, Wisconsin; Elizabeth Spencer Collection, National Library of Canada in Ottawa; Farrar, Straus & Giroux (FSG), New York City; *Forum*, University of Houston in Texas; Greenville High School Library in Mississippi; Gaylord Hospital (GH), Wallingford, Connecticut; Jason Berry Collection, Amstid Collection, Tulane University, New Orleans, Louisiana; Jean Stafford Collections, Norlin Library (Norlin), University of Boulder, Colorado, and the Alderman Library, University of Virginia in Charlottesville (UVA); John Kennedy Toole Collection, Tulane University; Joseph H. Fichter, S.J., Collection, Loyola University, New Orleans, Louisiana; Henley-Linn Research Library, Birmingham, Alabama; Historic New Orleans in Louisiana; Mayo Clinic, Rochester, Minnesota; National Endowment for the Humanities (NEH), Washington, D.C.; Olin Library, Washington University, St. Louis, Missouri; Pattee Library, Penn State University, University Park, Pennsylvania; Registrar's Office and Alumni Office, UNC; Robert W. Woodruff Library, Emory University, Atlanta, Georgia; St. Joseph Seminary College, St. Benedict, Louisiana; *Shenandoah*, Washington and Lee University, Lexington, Virginia; *The Georgia Review*, University of Georgia at Athens; *The Southern Review*, LSU, Baton Rouge, Louisiana; Thomas Merton Collection, Thomas Merton Studies Center, Bellarmine College, Louisville, Kentucky; Walker Percy Collection and Shelby Foote Collection, Southern Historical Collection, Wilson Library, UNC (SHCUNC: references to the Percy-Foote letters have not been cited unless a reference is out of chronological order; some spelling and punctuation in these letters has been regularized); William Alexander Percy Collection, Mississippi Department of Archives and History in Jackson (MDAH); William Corrington Collection, Samuel Peters Library, Centenary College, Shreveport, Louisiana.

INDEX

NOTE: WORKS CITED ARE BY WALKER PERCY
UNLESS OTHERWISE IDENTIFIED